SENTENCING AND SOCIETY

Sentencing and Society

International Perspectives

Edited by

CYRUS TATA and NEIL HUTTON
Centre for Sentencing Research, University of Strathclyde

ASHGATE

Published by
Ashgate Publishing Limited
Gower House
Croft Road
Aldershot
Hampshire GU11 3HR
England

Ashgate Publishing Company
Suite 420
101 Cherry Street
Burlington, VT 05401-4405
USA

Ashgate website: http://www.ashgate.com

British Library Cataloguing in Publication Data
Sentencing and society : international perspectives
    1.Sentences (Criminal procedure) 2.Sentences (Criminal
    procedure) - Government policy
    I.Tata, Cyrus II.Hutton, Neil, 1953-
    345'.0772

Library of Congress Control Number: 2002102833

ISBN 0 7546 2183 9

Reprinted 2004

Printed in Great Britain by Biddles Limited, King's Lynn.

Contents

INTRODUCTION

PART I: THE INTERNATIONAL MOVEMENT TOWARDS
          TRANSPARENCY AND 'TRUTH IN SENTENCING'

List of Figures

List of Tables

List of Contributors

Andrew Ashworth is Vinerian Professor of English Law in the University of Oxford. From 1989 to 1992 he was chairman of the Council of Europe's Select Committee on Sentencing, and in 1999 was invited to conduct a survey of sentencing trends in Council of Europe countries, of which this essay is a product. He is the author of *Sentencing and Criminal Justice* (3rd edn, 2000, Butterworths), and contributed the chapter on sentencing to the *Oxford Handbook of Criminology*. In 1999 he was appointed as a member of the new Sentencing Advisory Panel for England and Wales. He also engages in research and writing on European human rights law, pre-trial justice, and criminal law and evidence.

Mary E. Campbell is Deputy Director General of Strategic Policy in the Department of the Solicitor General Canada. She is a lawyer by profession, with a Masters in Law from McGill University in Montreal. She has worked in criminal justice for her entire career, with particular expertise in legislative policy and reform. Ms Campbell played a lead role in the 1992 reform of Canada's correctional law framework (the Corrections and Conditional Release Act), and has been instrumental in reforms to all of Canada's federal correctional legislation and related statutes in the past 15 years. She also teaches and writes in sentencing, corrections, conditional release, and criminal law reform.

B. Keith Crew, PhD is Associate Professor of Sociology and Criminology and Head of the Department of Sociology, Anthropology and Criminology at the University of Northern Iowa. His interests are critical criminology, corrections, drugs and violence. He has worked with Gene Lutz on a series of studies of substance abuse treatment and prevention needs assessments, corrections policy issues.

Hazel Croall is Senior Lecturer and Head of Division of Sociology at the University of Strathclyde. She is the author of books and articles on crime and society and white collar crime, most recently *Understanding White Collar Crime* (2001, Open University Press). Her main research interests lie in the area of white collar and corporate crime involving its conceptualisation, its status within criminology, aspects of victimisation and regulation and sanctioning (the latter with J. Ross).

Malcolm Davies is Director of the Criminal Justice Unit of Civitas, and Professor in the Ealing School of Law at TVU. He has worked for the Office of the Attorney General in California and has been a visiting scholar in the law schools at Berkeley, UC Davis and the University of Helsinki. Publications include: *Punishing Criminals: Developing Community-Based Intermediate Sanctions* (1993); *An Introduction to the Criminal Justice System in England and Wales* (with Croall and Tyrer, 2nd edn 1998); and *Penological Esperanto and Sentencing Parochialism: a Comparative Study of the search for Non-Prison Punishments* (with Tyrer and Takala 1996).

Julia Davis is a Lecturer in Law at the University of Tasmania in Australia. Her teaching interests include sentencing law, legal history, torts and legal theory. She is currently writing a PhD on the topic 'The Problem of Harm and its Relevance to Sentence'.

Gavin Dingwall is Lecturer in Law at the University of Wales, Aberystwyth. A graduate of the University of Warwick and the University of Wales, he joined the teaching staff at Aberystwyth in 1992. His research is concerned primarily with theoretical questions about criminal law and procedure, penal policy and penology. He is author, with Christopher Harding, of *Diversion in the Criminal Process* (1998 Sweet & Maxwell), and co-edited *Crime and Conflict in the Countryside* (1999, University of Wales Press), with Susan R. Moody.

Kristine Fahrney, BA was formerly a Research Associate at the Center for Social and Behavioral Research at the University of Northern Iowa, where she completed her BA. She earned the Masters of Social Research degree at the University of Stirling, Scotland. Currently, she works as a survey manager at Research Triangle Institute, and is pursuing doctoral work at North Carolina State University.

Arie Freiberg is Professor of Criminology and Head of Department of Criminology in the University of Melbourne, Australia. His research interests lie in sentencing, confiscation of proceeds of crime and, most recently, drug courts and other problem-oriented courts. He is the author (with Richard Fox) of *Sentencing: State and Federal Law in Victoria* (1999 Oxford University Press), and *Sentencing Reform and Penal Change* (1999, The Federation Press), with Stuart Ross.

Judith Greene is a criminal justice policy analyst, currently serving as a research consultant for both the RAND Corporation and Human Rights Watch. She was a 1999 recipient of a Soros Justice Fellowship, and has also served as Senior Fellow at the Institute on Criminal Justice of the University of Minnesota Law School. From 1985 to 1993 she was Director of Court Programs at the Vera Institute of Justice. Ms Greene's professional interests encompass sentencing and correctional policy; prison privatisation; community policing; and alternatives to incarceration.

Christopher Harding is Professor of Law at the University of Wales, Aberystwyth. He teaches and carries out research in the fields of international European law, and crime and penal questions. Recent publications include *Diversion in the Criminal Process* (1998, Sweet & Maxwell), with Gavin Dingwall, and a number of papers on the European and international dimension of crime and criminal justice. He is currently preparing a book which deals with the legal control of business cartels, to be published in 2002.

Ralph Henham is Professor of Criminal Justice at Nottingham Law School, Nottingham Trent University. He is an Editorial Board member of *The International Journal of the Sociology of Law, The Howard Journal of Criminal Justice* and *The Nottingham Law Journal*. His research and teaching interests lie within criminology, criminal justice, legal theory and sentencing. His publications include *Sentencing Principles and Magistrates' Sentencing Behaviour* (1990), *Criminal Justice and Sentencing Policy* (1996) and *Sentence Discounts and the Criminal Process* (2001) in addition to numerous articles on theoretical, comparative and policy-related aspects of sentencing.

Mike Hough is Professor of Social Policy at South Bank University, where he set up the Criminal Policy Research Unit in 1994. It is now the largest criminological research centre of its kind in Britain, with a staff of around 30, carrying out policy research for central government and other funders. He has extensive experience in quantitative research methods, especially large-scale sample surveys such as the British Crime Survey and the Policing for London Survey. He has published widely on attitudes to punishment.

Barbara Hudson BSc, MA, PhD teaches in the Lancashire Law School, University of Central Lancashire. She teaches and researches within the fields of criminology, penology and sociology of law, with particular interests in the impact of penal strategies on the marginalised and disadvantaged.

Publications include *Justice Through Punishment: A Critique of the 'Justice Model' of Corrections* (1987, Macmillan); *Penal Policy and Social Justice* (1993, Macmillan); *Racism and Criminology*, edited, with Dee Cook (1993, Sage); *Understanding Justice: An Introduction to Ideas, Perspectives and Controversies in Modern Penal Theory* (1996, Open University Press) and *Race, Crime and Justice*, edited (1996, Dartmouth). She has also published many articles and chapters on subjects related to the general theme of 'justice and difference' and is currently completing a new book, *Justice in the Risk Society* (Sage Publications), concerned with conflicts between logics of 'risk control' and 'doing justice' in penal strategies and the problem of how to do 'justice' to 'difference'. The book draws on recent developments in social and legal philosophy as well as on developments in criminological theory and criminal justice practice, such as discursive ethics, and restorative justice.

Neil Hutton is a Professor in the Law School at Strathclyde University. He is co-Director of the Centre for Sentencing Research. His research and scholarship for the last 10 years has focused on sentencing and he has authored many articles and reports in this field. He is a member of the team which is developing a Sentencing Information System for the High Court of Justiciary in Scotland. He is currently working on a monograph on the sociology of sentencing.

Gene M. Lutz is Professor of Sociology and Director of the Centre for Social and Behavioural Research at the University of Northern Iowa. He has directed approximately 200 basic and public service research projects for local, state, and national public agencies. Topics of greatest concentration are public health issues (especially substance abuse prevention, prevalence and dependency, and other behavioural health risks), corrections (institutional, community, and victimisation), education (higher education and work relationships), public input to strategic planning and public opinion in a variety of areas.

Grazia Mannozzi is Professor of Criminal Law at the University of Pavia, Italy. In her research activity, she has mainly focused on the sentencing system. Her main publication on this subject is: *Razionalità e 'giustizia' nella commisurazione della pena*, Padua (1996). She is also interested in Restorative Justice, on which she has published a series of articles. She has also collaborated in drafting the proposed *Recommendations to the United Nations for the Tenth UN Congress on the Prevention of Crime and Treatment of Offender* (Vienna 2000). Since May 2000, she has been charged by the Italian

'Consiglio Superiore della Magistratura' with the criminal justice training for Italian judges and prosecutors.

Candace McCoy is Associate Professor of Criminal Justice at Rutgers University, Newark, New Jersey, USA. She has published widely on topics relating to plea bargaining and sentencing and is currently working on a book about the impact of litigation against the police. She holds a law degree from the University of Cincinnati and is a member of the Ohio bar, and earned the PhD in jurisprudence and social policy from the University of California, Berkeley. At Rutgers, Dr McCoy teaches graduate seminars in sentencing, law and society, and prosecution and the courts and undergraduate courses in criminal justice ethics and courts. She was awarded the Board of Trustees Research Award for Scholarly Excellence in 1998 from Rutgers.

Patrick J. McManimon Jr is Assistant Professor of Sociology at William Paterson University, Wayne, New Jersey. He is a graduate of Bradley University, BA in Sociology and Religious Studies, and earned an MA and PhD from Rutgers University's School of Criminal Justice, Newark, New Jersey. His research foci include prison violence and management, sentencing's effects on prison behaviour, and criminal justice organisations. He is currently completing a project concerning New Jersey's No Early Release Act with Candace McCoy and is working with another colleague on a project examining policing in the twenty-first century.

Fergus McNeill has been a Lecturer in Social Work at the University of Glasgow since September 1998. Prior to this he worked for five years as a criminal justice social worker in the East End of Glasgow. His publications and research to date reflect this professional background and include work on the relationships between social work reports and sentencing, on probation workers' perspectives on the definition, delivery and development of effective probation, on the relationships between criminology and probation practice, and on contemporary probation ideologies and practices.

Neil Morgan is Director of Studies at the Crime Research Centre at the University of Western Australia and a member of the Parole Board and of the Mentally Impaired Defendants' Review Board of Western Australia. Prior to this, he was a Lecturer/Senior Lecturer in the Law Schools of the University of Western Australia, the National University of Singapore and Essex University (UK). His main research interests are criminal law and sentencing and he has published widely in these areas. His recent publications have focused on sentencing guidelines and guidance, the administration of corrections in the Asian and Pacific region and 'risk assessment' in the criminal justice system. He has also been involved in a range of law reform activities, including official reviews of restraining orders, parole and remission, prisoner disciplinary proceedings and community based sentences.

Brian J. Ostrom, PhD is a Principal Research Consultant with the National Center for State Courts in Williamsburg, Virginia. Dr Ostrom has extensive training and experience in performance evaluation and using a wide range of quantitative and qualitative analysis techniques to understand and overcome problems in the courts. While at the NCSC he has been the principal investigator for numerous national-scope research projects within the areas of civil justice, felony sentencing and the development of structured sentencing systems, the interaction between and among the state courts and other components of the criminal justice system, and the methodology of judicial workload assessment. In addition, Dr Ostrom brings extensive knowledge of state court operations through serving as the director of the Court Statistics Project. Dr Ostrom received his PhD in economics from the University of Washington. He received the NCSC Distinguished Service Award in 1997. In addition, Dr Ostrom teaches in the economics department at the College of William and Mary and is a faculty member for the Institute for Court Management.

Charles W. Ostrom Jr is Professor of Political Science at Michigan State University, where he studies presidential approval and criminal sentencing in state courts. His current research includes the development of a comprehensive model of sentencing decision-making and an investigation of court culture and its impact on court performance. He earned his PhD in political science at Indiana University.

Doris Marie Provine is a lawyer and political scientist (JD, PhD Cornell University) who specialises in institutional analyses of courts and related legal institutions. She received her undergraduate degree at the University of Chicago. Provine's books include *Case Selection on the US Supreme Court* and *Judging Credentials: Non-lawyer Judges and the Politics of Professionalism*. She has also written on comparative legal themes, including the politics of law in France and gender issues in European human rights litigation. Current work focuses on the racial dimensions of the US war on drugs. She directs the School of Justice Studies at Arizona State University.

Julian V. Roberts is Professor of Criminology at the University of Ottawa. His research interests include public opinion; sentencing; and sentencing policy. He recently edited *Making Sense of Sentencing* (University of Toronto Press) and *Criminal Justice in Canada*. In 1997 he co-authored *Public Opinion, Crime and Criminal Justice* (Westview Press). Since 1992 Roberts has served as Editor of the *Canadian Journal of Criminology*.

Jenifer Ross is Senior Lecturer in the Law School at the University of Strathclyde. She teaches, researches and writes on both criminal law and employment law, and has a particular interest in corporate criminal liability which forms a bridge between these two major areas. She is interested in corporate and individual responsibility and (with H. Croall) regulation and sanctioning. Her other major research interest is in anti-discrimination law and regulation, in particular in relation to race and ethnicity.

David Tait received his PhD from the LSE in social administration, and now teaches criminology and research methods at the University of Canberra in Australia. Interests include the social context of sentencing, court rituals, and the construction of official statistics. Current research projects include a comparative study of court performances and architecture, with Antoine Garapon and Katherine Taylor; and an analysis of different legal regimes for authorising forcible treatment for young women with anorexia, with Terry Carney and Dominique Saunders. His recent study of local courts in NSW used a natural experimental approach to estimate the impact of different sentences on re-offending.

Jukka-Pekka Takala is a sociologist and a researcher at Finland's National Research Institute of Legal Policy in Helsinki. His research includes works on alcoholism treatment and involuntary psychiatric hospitalisation as well as evaluations of community service orders and victim-offender mediation. His publications in English include *Cure, Care, or Control: Alcoholism Treatment in Sixteen Countries* (1992, SUNY Press), a volume co-edited with Harald Klingemann and Geoffrey Hunt, and an earlier collaboration with Malcolm Davies and Jane Tyrer on a book on noncustodial sentences *(Penological Esperanto and Sentencing Parochialism: A Comparative Study of the Search for Non-Prison Punishments*, Dartmouth 1996). *Evolution and the Moral Emotions: Appreciating Edward Westermarck* is a forthcoming collection of articles he edited with Arthur Wolf.

Cyrus Tata is the co-Director of the Centre for Sentencing Research at Strathclyde University. He is also Senior Lecturer in Law at Strathclyde University where he teaches legal theory, the sociology of law, law justice and society, penology and criminal process. He has conducted and published several funded empirical research studies of sentencing and criminal justice, including: a study of individual sentencing patterns; a comparative study of the performance of criminal legal aid in three European jurisdictions; the research, development and evaluation of a Sentencing Information System for High Court of Justiciary of Scotland; and the three year evaluation of the performance of the pilot Public Defence Solicitor Office. He has published numerous refereed articles and book chapters and author-edited volumes on sentencing, judicial decision support systems, and criminal legal aid.

Michael Tonry is Director of the Institute of Criminology, University of Cambridge and Sonosky Professor of Law and Public Policy at the University of Minnesota. He is author or editor of a number of books, including *Sentencing and Sanctions in Western Countries*, with Richard Frase (Oxford University Press 2001), *The Handbook of Crime and Punishment* (Oxford University Press 1998), *Ethnicity, Crime, and Immigration – Comparative and Cross-National Perspectives* (University of Chicago Press 1997), *Sentencing Matters* (Oxford University Press 1996) and *Malign Neglect: Race, Crime, and Punishment in America* (Oxford University Press 1995). He is editor of *Crime and Justice – A Review of Research*, published since 1979 by the University of Chicago Press, and the book series *Studies in Crime and Public Policy*, established in 1992 by Oxford University Press.

Hilde Tubex is Lecturer and Researcher at the Vrije Universiteit van Brussel (Free University of Brussels). In 1999 she gained her doctorate in criminology, submitting a thesis on long term imprisonment. Her principal fields of interest lie in penology and especially the problems presented by prisoners serving long sentences, sexual offenders, conditional release, the concept of 'dangerousness', and dangerous prisoners in detention. She has published on these themes in both Belgian and international periodicals, in Dutch, French and English. Dr Tubex has also been appointed as a scientific expert by the Council of Europe, where she is active in the Conditional Release and Long Term Imprisonment work-groups.

Jane Tyrer is a barrister and Chair of the Field of Law at Buckinghamshire Chilterns University College where she specialises in the teaching of criminal law and procedure. Her academic interest in sentencing is supported by 20 years' practical experience as a lay magistrate at Buckinghamshire. Publications include, *Penological Esperanto and Sentencing Parochialism* (1996) with M. Davies and J.-P. Takala, *Criminal Justice: an Introduction to the Criminal Justice System in England and Wales* (2nd edn 1998) with M. Davies and H. Croall, and *Criminological Litigation* (2000) with D. Lawton.

Dirk van Zyl Smit holds a joint appointment as Professor of Comparative and International Penal Law in the University of Nottingham and Professor of Criminology in the Faculty of Law, University of Cape Town. His books include *Prison Labour: Salvation or Slavery? International Perspectives* (1999), *Imprisonment Today and Tomorrow – International Perspectives on Prisoners' Rights and Prison Conditions* (2nd edn 2001), both edited together with Frieder Dünkel, and *South African Prison Law and Practice* (1992). He is co-editor of *Punishment and Society*. In South Africa, Professor van Zyl Smit has been actively involved in law reform and has advised on the drafting of the Correctional Services Act 1998. In 1999 and 2000 he was project leader of the committee of the South African Law Commission on a new sentencing framework. He has also advised the governments of Malawi and Uganda on new prison legislation.

Andrew von Hirsch is Honorary Professor of Penal Theory and Penal Law at the University of Cambridge, and a member of the Institute of Criminology at that university. He is also Adjunct Professor of Penology at the Law Faculty of Uppsala University, Sweden and holds an honorary doctorate of laws from that institution. He has published widely (in English, Swedish and German), on criminal sanctioning theory and practice. Titles include: *Doing Justice* (Hill and Wang 1976); *Past or Future Crimes* (Manchester University Press 1986); *Censure and Sanctions* (Oxford University Press 1993); *The Question of Parole* (Ballinger 1979); *The Sentencing Commission and its Guidelines* (Northeastern University Press 1987); *Principled Sentencing* (co-edited with Andrew Ashworth) (2nd edn Hart Publishing 1998). Professor von Hirsch is Director of the recently established Centre for Penal Theory and Penal Ethics at the Institute of Criminology. The Centre's first published volume, *Ethical and Social Perspectives on Situational Crime Prevention* (A. von Hirsch, D. Garland and A. Wakefield (eds), Hart Publishing) appeared in December 2000. Further volumes in preparation will cover restorative justice, and human rights issues in substantive criminal law and sentencing.

Kate Warner is a Professor of Law at the University of Tasmania where she teaches Criminal Law, Criminology and Sentencing. Currently she is Chair of the Degree Board for Law. She was the first woman Dean of the Faculty of Law (1992–94) and the first woman to be Head of Department in the Law School (1994–97). She was a member of the Parole Board for 10 years and is currently a member of the Board of Legal Education and the Council of Law Reporting. As a member of or consultant to many Law Reform Committees she has contributed law reform discussion papers and reports on a number of criminal justice issues including rape law reform, child witnesses and sentencing. Her current research interests include guns laws, sexual offences and sentencing.

Liling Yue is an Associate Professor at the China University of Political Science and Law. She is also a member of the Board of Directors at the Centre for Criminal Law and Justice there, where she takes care of international research projects. She has been teaching criminal procedure, evidence law and comparative criminal justice. Her publications in English and German have introduced the reform of criminal justice in China.

Sentencing and Society:
International Conference 1999

Organised and hosted by
The Centre for Sentencing Research, University of Strathclyde

List of Delegates

Jennifer Airs, Home Office, England and Wales
Andrew Ashworth, University of Oxford, England
Estella Baker, University of Leicester, England
Tim Bakken, Central Connecticut State University, USA
Ian Broom, University of Ottawa, Ontario, Canada
G.K. Buchanan, Aberdeen Sheriff Court, Scotland
Mary Campbell, Solicitor General's Office, Canada
Niall Campbell, Scottish Office Home Department, Scotland
V.J. Canavan, Hamilton Sheriff Court, Scotland
Jack Cowan, Supreme Court, BC, Canada
B. Keith Crew, University of Northern Iowa, USA
Hazel Croall, University of Strathclyde, Scotland
Michael Crossan, HM Prisons Inspectorate, Scotland
Joe Curran, Scottish Executive, Scotland
Julia Davis, University of Tasmania, Australia
Nora Demleitner, St Mary's University, Texas, USA
Lisa Dickson, University of Kent, England
Gavin Dingwall, University of Wales, Wales
Mark Drumbl, Columbia University, New York, USA
Peter Duff, University of Aberdeen, Scotland
Stephanie Eaton, Lincoln University, England
Ian Edwards, Cardiff University, England
Robin Elliott, Home Office, England and Wales
Kristine Fahrney, Stirling University, Scotland
Katrina Flynn, University of Strathclyde, Scotland
Richard Fox, Monash University, Victoria, Australia
Anne Franken, Attorney-General The Hague, Netherlands
Arie Freiberg, University of Melbourne, Australia

Kjetil Gjoen, Judge, Alesund, Norway
Judith Greene, National Institute for Justice, USA
Marie Griffin, Arizona State University, USA
Jennifer Hamilton, University of Strathclyde, Scotland
Christopher Harding, University of Wales, Wales
Ralph Henham, Nottingham, Trent University, England
John Hepburn, Arizona State University, USA
Mike Hough, South Bank University, England
Anthea Hucklesby, University of Leicester, England
Barbara Hudson, University of Northumbria, England
Neil Hutton, University of Strathclyde, Scotland
Mark Johnson, Inns of Court, Queensland Australia
Robert Kahn, Johns Hopkins University, Maryland, USA
Ruth Kannai, Bar Ilan University, Israel
Andreas Kapardis, Nicosia, Cyprus, Greece
Hugh Kerr, Statistics and Research, Northern Ireland Office, Northern
　Ireland
Michael Kilchling, Institute for Foreign and International Criminal Law,
　Germany
Carol La Prairie, Principal Researcher, Ontario, Canada
Jill Lewis, Social Work Department, Dundee, Scotland
Truls Lie, Assistant Chief Judge, Oslo, Norway
Sarah Lowrie, University of Wales, Wales
Gene Lutz, University of Northern Iowa, USA
Ann Lyon, De Montfort University, England
Robin MacEwen, Home Department, Scotland
Diane Machin, Scottish Executive, Scotland
Grazia Mannozzi, University of Pavia, Italy
Fiona McAleenan, Department of Public Prosecutions, Belfast, Northern
　Ireland
Candace McCoy, Rutgers University, New Jersey, USA
Claire McDiarmid, University of Strathclyde, Scotland
John McDonald, Transformative Justice, New South Wales, Australia
Patrick McManimon, Rutgers University, New Jersey, USA
Fergus McNeill, Glasgow University, Scotland
Sylvia Mendes, State University of New York, USA
Robert Metzger, Chief Judge, British Columbia, Canada,
Akira Miyano, University of Meiji-Gakuin, Tokyo, Japan
David Moore, Transformative Justice, New South Wales, Australia

Neil Morgan, University of Western Australia, Australia
Mary Munro, Kilmacolm, Scotland
Jan Nicholson, University of Strathclyde, Scotland
Therese O'Donnell, University of Strathclyde, Scotland
Tom O'Malley, National University of Ireland, Gallway, Ireland
Brian Ostrom, US National Center for State Courts, Virginia, USA
Charles Ostrom Jr, Michigan State University, Michigan, USA
Desmond Perry, Belfast Magistrates Court, Northern Ireland
Rainer Pfaff, South African Law Commission, Pretoria, South Africa
Franciska Pouw, Public Prosecution Service, The Hague, Netherlands
Doris Marie Provine, National Science Foundation, Virginia, USA
An Raes, Vrije Universiteit van Brussel, Belgium
Julian Roberts, University of Ottawa, Ontario, Canada
Paul Robertshaw, Cardiff University, Wales
Donald Ross, Judicial Studies Committee, Scotland
Jenifer Ross, University of Strathclyde, Scotland
Sue Ross, Director of Social Work, Scotland
Stein Schjolberg, Chief Judge, Moss Byrett, Norway
E. Dennis Schmidt, Associate Chief Judge, Vancouver, BC, Canada
Martin Schonteich, Institute for Security Studies, Pretoria, South Africa
Gerrit Schurer, Managing Director 'Giant Soft', The Hague, Netherlands
J.P. Scott, Dundee Sheriff Court, Scotland
R.J.D. Scott, Edinburgh Sheriff Court, Scotland
Adrian Shanks, Ashgate Publishing, England
Donna Spears, Sydney University, New South Wales, Australia
J. Spy, Paisley Sheriff Court, Scotland
Dato Steenhuis, Prosecutor General, The Hague, The Netherlands
Francis Sullivan, Stoughton, Massachusetts, USA
David Tait, University of Melbourne, Victoria, Australia
Jukka-Pekka Takala, Legal Policy National Research Institute, Finland
Cyrus Tata, University of Strathclyde, Scotland
Katherine Fischer Taylor, University of Chicago, USA
Carlie Trueman, Judge, Provincial Court of British Columbia, Canada
Hilde Tubex, Vrije Universiteit van Brussel, Belgium
Jane Tyrer, Thames Valley University, London, England
Reinier Van Loon, Prosecution Service, The Hague, The Netherlands
Willie Van Vuuren, South African Law Commission, South Africa
Wiebe van Zwol, Ministry of Justice, The Hague, The Netherlands
Dirk van Zyl Smit, University of Cape South Africa, South Africa

Andrew von Hirsch, University of Cambridge, England
Mark Wallace, Full Fathom Fifty Ltd, Glasgow, Scotland
Kate Warner, University of Tasmania, Tasmania, Australia
John Waterhouse, Scottish Office Inspectorate of Social Work, Scotland
Patricia White, National Science Foundation, Arlington, Virginia, USA
Hans Willemse, Ministry of Justice, The Hague, The Netherlands
Glen Williams, Justice, Supreme Court of Queensland, Australia
Michael Willis, Northern Ireland Office of Statistics and Research,
  Northern Ireland
Karen Yeung, University of Oxford, England
Liling Yue, Beijing University, Beijing, China

Preface and Acknowledgements

This volume grew out of a three day international conference on 'Sentencing and Society' held in Glasgow in June 1999. As the reader may be aware, there had been a number of international conferences on sentencing before that date (for example, the 1993 Colston Colloquium in Bristol; the 1998 Minneapolis Meeting). However, the 1999 international conference was the first major international conference held on the basis of open invitation. Our aim, in that international conference, was to develop not only well-established areas and approaches to sentencing practice and reform, but also to encourage connections with other (most notably sociological) approaches to the study of sentencing.

The papers in this volume represent fewer than one third of the total number of papers presented at the 1999 international conference and, almost without exception, have been substantially revised for publication here. Authors were encouraged to develop further and highlight connections with sociological approaches and implications. The work in this volume is not therefore intended as a basic introduction to the literature on sentencing, but rather seeks to build on the reader's existing knowledge.

Without the imagination, hard work, and dedication of many individuals this volume could not have been realised. Our greatest debt is, of course, to each of the contributors to this volume. We hope that you (the reader) will find in this volume not only some of the latest work in the study of sentencing and society, but also work which challenges some basic assumptions about sentencing scholarship, policy, practice, and reform. If it succeeds at all in that way then it is all to the credit of our contributors.

We also wish to thank staff at Ashgate publishing (most notably: John Irwin, Valerie Saunders, Adrian Shanks, Suzanne Johnson, Jan Lloyd, Ruth Peters, Rosalind Ebdon, Anne Newell and Anne Keirby) and Pat FitzGerald. Last, but by no means least, we would like to record our appreciation of the work done by Jan Nicholson of the Centre for Sentencing Research. Her meticulous work as our editorial assistant was executed with a remarkable combination of dedication and equanimity.

Centre for Sentencing Research
University of Strathclyde, Glasgow

Foreword

Michael Tonry

Sentencing and Society is an important step in the development of two strands of contemporary scholarly interest in sentencing. The first, which I only mention here, because the editors develop it more fully in their introduction and reflections, is the emergence of a fledgling sociology of sentencing which is focusing deeper and sharper attention on under-examined subjects. These include appreciation of expressed 'public knowledge and opinion' as socially contingent, use of judicial discretion as a social (not only legal or normative) process, measurement of punishment within and between jurisdictions, and elaboration of sociological theories of justice.

The second is the construction of a comparative, cross-national, and international literature on sentencing, sanctions, and penal policy. For shorthand, from here on I use the phrase 'penal policy' to refer to that related set of subjects. Penal policy has been on the political and law reform agendas of most Western countries for the past quarter century, and little has happened to suggest that that interest is likely soon to lessen.

In our shrinking world, policy makers, practitioners, and scholars do, and should, look across national and jurisdictional boundaries to see what is happening elsewhere, why, and with what effect. This is easier said than done. There is little genuinely cross-national research, and if that term is understood to mean major empirical projects using common measures and instruments in two or more countries, there is none. There is relatively little published work in which researchers systematically compare practices and processes in different countries. And, at least in English, there are relatively few works on penal policy in non-English-speaking countries. Thus, unfortunately, people looking for lessons from elsewhere soon learn that their principal resources must be personal visits, anecdotes, war stories, and hearsay.

The reasons why people should be interested internationally in penal policy are straightforward. Modern Western countries have more in common than ever before. Under the pressures of mass communications, a global economy, ubiquitous multinationals, and the emergence of English as a world language, differences will continue to diminish. Shared commitment to democratic values and human rights ideals, and their reinforcement by international conventions and courts, create other reasons to look outwards.

Penal policies result from an amalgam of instrumental, expressive, and politically expedient considerations. These vary with time and place. Some of the time, policy makers' interests are parochial and political, and at those times evidence has little relevance to their decisions. Much of the time, however, policy makers, and their critics and opponents, want to learn about experience elsewhere. There is much evidence that they do so.

Here are a few examples. Electronic monitoring of offenders in the community began in two US states in 1983, spread to seven in 1986, and was in use in all 50 in 1990. After that it was adopted in Australia and New Zealand, then in Sweden, Holland, and England, and is now in use or under consideration in much of Europe. Day fines started in Scandinavia, were adopted in Germany, Austria, and some other countries, were tried and soon abandoned in the United States and England, and were rejected outright when proposed in Holland. American populist laws and rhetoric like 'Three Strikes' and 'truth-in-sentencing', and purposely punitive programs like boot camps and mandatory minimum sentence laws, have been adopted in a few countries, considered in a few others, and given no serious consideration in most.

Another way to illustrate cross-national influences and interest is to look at a single country's borrowings. England, for example, imported community service orders from the United States in the 1970s and electronic monitoring, boot camps, and three-strikes laws in the 1990s. It authorised use of day (called 'unit') fines, based on German and Swedish models, in the 1990s. Prosecutorial diversion programs patterned on German conditional dismissals and Dutch transactions have several times been considered, but not accepted. The Home Office Sentencing Review Panel, chaired by John Halliday, closely examined sanctioning and sentencing policies in the United States, Holland, Sweden, Finland, and Germany before formulating the recommendations set out in its 2001 report.

Besides these policy-based reasons to be interested internationally in penal policy, there are intellectual and normative enquiries that can best be explored with comparative evidence. Officials in Finland, for example, after realising that its crime rates resembled those of other Scandinavian countries but its incarceration rates were 150 per cent higher, famously decided that that was indefensible and that they should do something about it. Use of imprisonment fell steadily over 30 years, by 60 per cent overall, and by the late 1990s Finnish crime and imprisonment rates compared with those elsewhere in Scandinavia. No other country has so radically altered its practices as a result of cross-national comparisons, but scholars and policy advocates in many countries find international comparisons useful.

Similarly, efforts to understand and explain penal policy changes and patterns in a single country can only be enriched by resort to international comparisons. Recent writing in England and America, for example, variously attributes prison population increases and enactment of punitive legislation to post-modernist angst and the emergence of what Anthony Bottoms of University of Cambridge characterised as 'populist punitivism'. The difficulty is that those developments affected all Western countries, but only a comparative few experienced steeply rising prison populations or frequent enactment of punitive symbolic legislation. Hans-Jörg Albrecht of Germany's Max-Planck-Institut für internationales und ausländisches Strafrecht refers to this as the 'and elsewhere' problem. English and American scholars tend, he suggests, to write of penal policy 'in the United States, England, and elsewhere', without realising that things elsewhere are often rather different.

So there are plenty of reasons why people should be, and are, interested in comparative, cross-national, and international studies of penal policy. Books like *Sentencing and Society* are beginning to build a literature that looks across national boundaries. As yet, the literature is sparse but, beginning with Chris Clarkson and Rod Morgan's 1995 *The Politics of Sentencing Reform*, based on papers presented at a 1993 conference in Bristol England, it is a-building. The editors of this volume explain its provenance and comment on its contents, so I will only say that it is a worthy successor to the path-setting Clarkson and Morgan book and constitutes a giant step forward. Some of its articles represent empirical efforts to make cross-national comparisons of penal practices and policies. Some concern jurisdictions like Belgium, Canada, Italy, and Western Australia that are not often written about in English outside their own borders. Some are examinations of timeless normative issues with whose provisional resolutions every country must wrestle. Nearly all are important additions to the comparative, cross-national, and international literature on penal policy.

INTRODUCTION

So What does 'and Society' Mean?[1]

Cyrus Tata[2]

How can we make sense of sentencing? This question has long puzzled not only scholars but also policy-makers. For, if sentencing practice is to be described (let alone 'improved'), we necessarily have to interpret and explain it.

For well over a generation, sentencing scholarship has generally recognised as inadequate the sole study of legality to answer basic questions about sentencing practice and policy.[3] Instead, a 'legal-philosophical' approach has tended to be seen as the primary mode of explanation. The main concern of a legal-philosophical approach is to explain the legal practice of sentencing and propose reform in terms of normative philosophical justifications for punishment. Almost invariably, sentencing is thus explained in terms of a list of moral philosophical justifications for punishment (e.g. denunciation, retribution, rehabilitation, deterrence etc., or some variant thereof). This normative framework answers effectively the questions: 'why punish?' and 'how ought the state to justify punishment?'. However, important as it is, such an approach tends to marginalise other fundamental questions such as: the nature of routine practice; historical changes; the origin and operation of substantive inequality; functions of and relationships between actors in the sentencing process; and the roles of culture, public attitudes and public knowledge. A legal-philosophical approach is indispensable to the study of sentencing, but it should not be seen as the only or main mode of explanation.

Although sentencing scholarship has been dominated by a 'legal-philosophical' framework, there has been clear appreciation that sentencing law and philosophies of punishment are not developed and operated in a social vacuum. Like other areas of legal scholarship, there has long been a clear recognition of the need to concede that a 'legal-philosophical' mode of explanation needs to be supplemented by an awareness of sentencing 'in context'. Typically, 'in context' tends to be understood as the political-institutional development of policy and legislation (e.g. the debates surrounding the passage of legislation), with perhaps a nod in the direction of 'culture' and vague reference to 'society'. Notwithstanding the value of an awareness of the legislative development of policy, the study of sentencing 'in context' can only ever be a way of supplementing the main 'legal-philosophical' framework.

Thus, a 'legal-philosophical in-context approach' can only therefore permit as caveats and qualifications questions which are not answered by legal and philosophical enquiry. 'Context' simply refers to a surround or environment of the assumed central phenomenon (i.e. legality and normative penal philosophy), rather than an appreciation of sentencing as fundamentally socially produced and socially practised, which the sociology of sentencing places at its heart.

This chapter aims to outline and illustrate some of the fundamental questions, which a 'legal-philosophical in context approach' necessarily struggles to answer. In so doing, it seeks to advance the case for a greater awareness of the sociology of sentencing, and the kinds of insights and new agendas for research and policy it brings.[4] Thus, this chapter does not attempt to provide a straightforward accurate summary of each of the chapters in this collection. Instead, the main purpose is to set out a 'map' to help the reader to navigate his or her way through the volume and so explain how, taken together, the chapters may represent some of the key questions which the sociology of sentencing is uniquely able to ask and answer. So it is hoped that the reader will gain a strong sense not only of an emerging sociology of sentencing and a sense of the flow and direction of the volume, but also a good idea of the major themes, arguments and evidence (if not full and complete summary), of each chapter. First I will outline four basic questions, which the sociology of sentencing is uniquely positioned to answer, and the insights which are developed in this volume.

The Sociology of Sentencing: Questions and Insights

1   Understanding and Countering 'Populist Punitveness'

A central concern of the chapters in this volume is to understand and find ways of limiting the 'punitive turn' fanned by 'populist punitiveness' (Bottoms 1995) in western societies with its staggering increases in the use of incarceration. A 'legal-philosophical in context' approach has tended to portray 'populist punitiveness' as ultimately irrational. The portrayal goes something like this: politicians have been trying to outdo each other with cheap slogans and easy fixes and so have cynically exploited fears and prejudices of a gullible public and excitable media. The only way out of this spiral of populism is said to be sincere and honest political leadership. While all this is true, it does not provide either an adequate explanation of how, when and why 'populist punitiveness' occurs, nor, therefore any credible remedy. Several of the writers in this volume[5] argue for shrewder media/information management. Yet without clear understanding of public opinion and the study of media news values this cannot become a reality. The research reported and discussed by Part II of this volume documents a much deeper knowledge of public and victim punitiveness than pollsters provide. It provides the 'honest politician' with the most in-depth evidence yet to show that while there is deep and disturbing public cynicism about criminal justice, public attitudes are, in fact, are far less punitive than is routinely portrayed and understood by the electoral common sense of politicians.

Why do opinion polls and academic studies of public attitudes to punishment each find an apparently contrasting picture of public punitiveness? It is not only because academic studies are fuller, more comprehensive and tackle previously neglected areas (e.g. public attitudes as a function of public knowledge). The main reason lies in the distinction between asking general normative abstract questions of principle and investigating attitudes about specific instances and cases. Pollsters typically ask abstract questions such as: 'Do you think sentencing should be: tougher/about the same as it is/more lenient?'. The chapters in Part Two of this volume demonstrate that asking respondents more grounded and specific questions reveals a far less punitive picture than asking normative questions of abstract principle. Public and victim attitudes to punishment are also far more nuanced when asked to discuss specific vignettes or their own experiences. As McCoy and McManimon put it in their chapter on victim satisfaction: "... abstract public punitiveness may be high, but when placed in the context of particular people and actual experiences of crime and the people who commit it, punitiveness appears to be a considerably more complex phenomenon". Thus not only can we say that these studies are more in-depth than opinion poll snapshots, but that they produce contrasting implications. While pollsters' work may be superficial and the results easily misinterpreted they are not wrong, even though they contrast sharply with the findings of qualitatively far richer academic studies. Public opinion and public attitudes to sentencing therefore need to be understood as socially contingent. In other words, expressed public opinion and attitudes to punishment depend upon and are produced by the nature of enquiry. The degree of social abstraction or social contextualisation of the questions and information presented appears to produce sharply varying differences in expressed penal attitudes and preferences. This raises the question of whether it is feasible to think of public opinion and attitudes as singular and unmediated, a question on which Julia Davis' discussion of crime seriousness touches. Unlike the properties of a physical thing, Davis explains, 'seriousness' cannot be located and measured in social abstraction. When we try to measure seriousness we are measuring our response to crime, not a property of the crime in itself.

Rather than simply calling for greater integrity from politicians and greater responsibility from the media, recognition of the mediated and contingent production of public and victim attitudes allows the scholar and policy-maker to work out a strategy to counter public punitiveness. It means not only the presentation of fuller, more detailed information from contextualised studies, but also a media management strategy to pursue its effective dissemination, by applying 'news values'. It also means finding ways of countering the portrayal of the offender in socially abstract terms and the recognition that, whether we like it or not, s/he is one of us.

A second and distinctive strategy which the sociology of sentencing offers to the attempt to counter 'populist punitiveness' is advanced by David Tait's chapter. It lies in the neglected importance of dramatic performance of the ritual of sentencing to popular comprehension of its morality. The trial ritual performance can allow the: explanation of behaviour; public demonstration of remorse; clear indication by the offender of respect for the victim; opportunities for victims and offenders to speak; and the verbal chastisement of the offender which can provide the foundation for forgiveness. Tait suggests that the trend towards ever-increasing juridification of the trial system may in fact be stoking public vengeance, while a more flexible system can mix displays of authority, symbolic violence and mercy. The public performance of ritual symbolic violence combined with the performance of mercy may reduce the public clamour for revenge, "since symbolic revenge in a powerful and dramatic form has already been achieved". The easily neglected importance of ritual, performance, and process is also highlighted by McCoy and McManimon in their work on victim satisfaction.

The need to take more seriously the dramatic performance of the ritual of sentencing both as a source of study in itself and as a strategy to alleviate 'populist punitiveness' offers one key element in the comprehension of the decision process. How can a sociological approach help us to understand the use of sentencing discretion?

2   *The Sociology of Sentencing Rules and Discretion*

A 'legal-philosophical approach' to sentencing rules and discretion tends to concentrate on the legality of sentencing and its normative philosophical justifications. More difficult questions with which that approach has wrestled include: why there may be low levels of compliance with legality; and how, in daily practice, to regulate and govern the use of discretion. Legal-philosophical writing has generally seen legal rules and legal discretion as opposites. According to this approach, legal rules are seen to ensure predictability, consistency, order, equality but tend to be inflexible and insensitive. Discretion is seen as having the opposite properties: flexible, but easily allows inconsistency, inequality, disorder. A major problem for legal scholarship has been how to order discretion without creating mechanical inflexibility to the uniqueness of individual cases. How to create a satisfactory balance between the two? While there is an internal abstract logic to this legal-philosophical paradigm of rules and discretion, its weaknesses become apparent from the empirical study of the routine daily use of rules and discretion.

Sociologically, it is difficult to sustain a clear interpretive distinction between legal 'rules' and its residual legal 'discretion'. Close empirical study of the routine interpretation and use of legal rules and legal discretion suggests that 'rules' always permit discretion and discretion is in fact far more (socially) rule-bound than would otherwise be supposed. Both 'rules' and 'discretion' are used by actors in the sentencing process as resources for negotiation which are governed by social-organisational and ideological frameworks.

A legal-philosophical approach to the use of discretion tends also to take an individualistic view of the use of discretion. It tends to assume that the discretion posited by abstract legality is determined by essentially independent. However, organisational analysis tells us that rules and discretion are in fact shaped together by work-group processes and perceived ideological considerations. In this vein, chapters in this volume by van Zyl Smit, by Tata, and by Provine present a puzzle. In different ways, each of these three chapters wonders how judges manage selectively to ignore and deny themselves the discretion which they have explicitly been given and claim to cherish. Judicial perceptions of the dominant general view may help to explain how judges come genuinely to believe that they have no discretion even though an abstract legal analysis patently shows that they do. Without organisational and ideological frameworks, such judicial selection would be barely explicable.[6]

As well as compliance, rules and discretion, and selective judicial self-denial of legal discretion, a sociological approach also allows us to comprehend the social-historical creation of ideological frameworks, and current trends. Work in the sociology of punishment can be especially helpful in this way, as for example demonstrated by connections with sentencing literature made in the chapters by Tubex and McNeill. An historical understanding of sentencing and its current and future trends and judicial understandings of the dominant expectations of them necessitate a fuller appreciation of micro and macro dynamics of power. It is only with much closer examination of power that prescriptions to realise greater substantive legal equality can be realised.

3   *Power and Social Inequity: Realising Equality?*[7]

A key concern of sentencing scholarship has been apparent disparities and inequalities in sentencing: both in sentencing processes and in their inequitable impact on particular populations. The chapters in Part V of this volume highlight not only a deep concern with social inequity, but *how* these inequities arise. In helping to explain the production of inequity we are then better equipped to begin to raise relevant questions which may help us to pursue effective remedies.

First, inequity arises because of the use and abuse of liberal-legality's preoccupation with *legal* equality. At first blush this may sound paradoxical and indeed that is part of the problem. The way in which liberal legality understands equality privileges a technical and formal notion of equality: universal procedures built on equality as synonymous with sameness. Yet liberalism also permits and encourages social diversity and social inequality. The increasing imposition of universal legal processes and values may, in fact, only reproduce and deepen social and substantive legal inequality. Chapters in this volume (Provine on the spiralling racial inequality produced by formally 'equal' mandatory sentencing; Croall and Ross on sentencing corporate offenders; Warner's deconstruction of law's implicit understanding of sexuality; and the debate between Hutton and Hudson's debate about substantively equal treatment) each explain how liberal-legal equality not only produces substantive legal inequality but deepens social inequity as well. There is developing debate (illustrated by that between Hutton and Hudson in this volume), about whether our system of law is capable of producing substantive equality before itself (or whether we need to look elsewhere), and if so how.

Secondly, inequity arises not only because of the content of legality and its protection of social inequality, but also because officials may decide not to exercise discretion to limit substantive legal injustice. Escaping the rules-discretion dichotomy (discussed above), allows us to appreciate that no matter how 'mandatory' law may appear on its face, in practice there can always be creative ways to comply (McBarnet and Whelan 1997) with the letter of the law, if not in its spirit, so ameliorating its more pernicious effects. Yet, as chapters by Provine, van Zyl Smit and Tata each confirm, time and again judges at least appear to defer to what they may perceive to be the dominant ideology. Perhaps because of their formal individual independence judges may in fact be far more vulnerable to the vagaries of reported public and political opinion than legal-philosophical sentencing scholarship has imagined. Research which undermines assumed knowledge (such as that in Part II of this volume) may well help to fortify strategies of resistance by judges who feel genuinely troubled by the substantive injustice of the decision which they would otherwise feel 'compelled' to make.

The sociology of sentencing can focus our attention on this kind of resistance to penal populism because it offers a distinctive insight into 'judicial independence'. According to the 'legal-philosophical in-context' view, individual independence can easily become a problem because it so easily permits individual judges to pursue disparate personal penal philosophies. Yet the sociology of sentencing suggests that judges do not normally work as isolated individuals but in a variety of ways necessarily form part of 'court workgroups' (Eisenstein and Jacob 1991) with mutual understandings, expectations and subtle negotiation. With only a formal individualistic notion of 'independence' for self-legitimation, judges are also ideologically vulnerable to what they may perceive to be hegemonic expectations of their decision-making. So ironically, in part because of the fetishism for formal individual independence, judges tend to be remarkably weak in resisting what they may genuinely believe to be unjust yet populist and/or hegemonic demands (e.g. Cover 1975). True, judges can be highly effective in resisting law they do not like, but only when they feel they will not have to confront what they perceive to be the dominant view. In other words, judicial resistance (in its various forms) appears to be a function of deference to the perceived dominant view, rather than a result of an independently considered evaluation of policy. Far from being a bulwark against penal populism, judges may rail against it but defer to it. In that sense they play their part in 'populist punitiveness' and their ineffectual public protests against it (while nonetheless failing to use their discretion), are in fact grist to the mill of penal populism. Although formally 'independent', judges are socially and politically vulnerable precisely because of the cult of an individualistic brand of independence.

If judges will not resist penal populism, what can be done? Joining in the complaints about the injustice and incoherence of penal populism may be cathartic, but a more fruitful strategy is to question the assumed character of public opinion and attitudes on which penal populism claims its support. This is where the skilful application of the kind of in-depth research (which focuses on social specifics rather than abstract normative principles), reported in Part II of this volume may be very useful. It provides judges (as well as other actors in the penal and policy process), with arguments and evidence for resisting penal populism without necessarily having to feel they are confronting what they perceive as 'the dominant view'. It can allow judges and others to feel able to resist penal populism without feeling that they are resisting the public will.

4   *'Comparative' Approaches – Beyond a Jurisdiction-Centred Method*

As the chapters in this volume together demonstrate, concern about penal populism and its consequences for sentencing has become a common theme throughout the western world. One way of understanding penal populism's emergence is through a 'comparative' approach, in which comparison is made between different jurisdictions around the world. This is producing a rich literature,[8] the effect of which places not only sentencing developments in one's own jurisdiction in perspective, but also allows us to raise our eyes above the parochialism of our taken for granted sentencing assumptions and practices. In this way, it allows countries to learn from each other, and in his cogent Foreword to this book, Michael Tonry outlines some recent examples of inter-jurisdiction learning and adaptation. All of this is extremely valuable. I would like, nonetheless, to invite the reader to consider the case for a more fundamentally sociological approach to 'comparative' research.

'Comparative research' has, in sentencing scholarship, been seen as synonymous with inter-jurisdictional comparison. While comparison between legal jurisdictions is important and valuable, it focuses above-all on jurisdiction, and therefore legality, as the primary categories of study. Typically, inter-jurisdictional projects tend to frustrate their authors as soon as they look for answers to questions which legality alone cannot provide and the need for 'context' has to be underlined. Yet, an 'in-context' approach can do little more than append caveats and qualifications to the primary focus: the legality of sentencing in different jurisdictions. The challenges of comparing case trajectories, seriousness, penalty etc. are not fundamentally challenges of comparing one jurisdiction with another. Rather, these same issues present the same challenges, in principle, *within* one single jurisdiction. *Within* each jurisdiction, recording practices, the functions of and relationships between personnel, understanding of seriousness and case similarity, definitions of 'a case', culture, population variations, etc. are, in principle (and often in fact) as complex and variable *as between* jurisdictions (Tata 1999).

In a jurisdiction-centred approach social categories (such as culture and population characteristics) are assumed to begin and end with jurisdictional borders. Social norms, relationships, practices, and cultures can only be noted as caveats rather than integral to the main analysis. Placing jurisdiction and thus legality at the centre of analysis obscures a fuller explanation of social practices. It is not that we cannot or should not develop global perspectives in social and legal research, but that the methodological challenges of 'comparison' are not mainly produced by the legality of jurisdiction. Comparison is, in principle and often in fact, just as troublesome in intra- as inter-jurisdictional research. Thus, unless focused exclusively on a description of legal formality, to label inter-jurisdictional as 'comparative' (in contrast to intra-jurisdictional research), is misleading and erroneously highlights legality as the main stumbling block in the struggle to compare populations, attitudes, beliefs, social practices, etc.

A Map of the Chapters

Thus far, I have attempted to outline just four areas to which the sociology of sentencing provides a distinctive approach both to sentencing scholarship and sentencing policy. While this analysis is far from exhaustive, it draws on chapters in this volume. What follows here is an attempt to provide the reader with a 'map' of the chapters and how they connect together. In so doing, it is hoped that the reader will gain a fairly strong sense of each chapter and its sociological connections, though I do not try to provide a complete and accurate summary.

The International Movement towards 'Transparency' in Sentencing (Part I)

The United States has rates of incarceration[9] of between four to 12 times those of other western countries. Such differences were not always so marked. It was not until the mid-1970s that the US prison population began to soar (Tonry 2001). Neither these staggering longitudinal increases, nor, the striking contrasts with imprisonment rates of other countries can be mainly explained by changes in recorded crime, or, increases in rates of conviction. "Imprisonment patterns are not immune to changes in crime patterns, *but they are at least as much and often more the consequence of* conscious policy made by public officials" (Tonry 2001, emphasis added). So, if we are to understand the enormous rise in the rate of imprisonment then we need to understand the social and political dynamics which shape those decisions. **Judith Greene**'s chapter submits a thorough analysis of the political-institutional roots of the US's enormous rise in incarceration, whose influence continues to reverberate in the policy considerations of other countries, as the reader will see in the chapters which follow Greene's.

How did the movement to transparency in sentencing (culminating in 'truth in sentencing'),[10] become politically so irresistible? The answer lies in how two approaches, which were normally opposed to each other, coalesced around the same virtues. On the one hand, the protean virtues of certainty, clarity, and consistency appealed to those concerned with excessively unfettered judicial discretion and inter-judge and racial disparities. On the other hand, the same virtues appealed to a more punitive crime-control strategy which mobilised the victims' rights movement; suspicious reaction to 'rights consciousness' in the wake of the Warren Supreme Court's protection and expansion of rights and critiques of welfare and collectivism. One illustration of this history is how the Sentencing Commission Guidelines pioneered by Minnesota were carefully crafted to reflect the level of correctional resources the state of Minnesota had at its disposal. However, when other states introduced guidelines they did so disinterested in their impact on the prison population.[11]

The rise in imprisonment levels also created its own logic and momentum. For example, between April 1979 and April 1980 18 states passed mandatory sentencing laws, which further contributed to the soaring prison population. In an attempt to deal with serious overcrowding some state legislatures authorised reductions in previously imposed state sentences triggered when overcrowding reached 'emergency levels'. This, in turn, led to an increased disparity between the pronounced sentence and time served which would come to play a major role in spurring calls for 'truth in sentencing'. A second illustration of the self-perpetuation of an insatiable search for evermore punitive sentencing laws is the role of interest groups, such as the powerful National Rifle Association (NRA). Aware of President Clinton's intention to introduce gun control, the NRA supported mandatory life imprisonment for a third felony offence,[12] as a way of heading-off the political pressure for gun control. As an NRA spokesman succinctly put it: "If we lock up the criminals, maybe there'll be less pressure on abandoning the Second Amendment".[13]

While we have not seen the full-blown US 'coca-colonisation'[14] of sentencing in other countries, US reforms have inspired politicians in other countries. While the US appears to be the most poignant exemplar, throughout the western world the trajectory has clearly been towards greater 'transparency' in sentencing, and suspicion of the breadth of judicial discretion, sometimes in the name of clarity, consistency and certainty, and sometimes in the name of 'getting tough'. The chapters on South Africa, Western Australia, Canada,

Italy and China in their different ways illustrate this broad trajectory.

For the first time outside the US, a grid-style approach to sentencing has become more than a threat but a real possibility. In his chapter, **Neil Morgan** demonstrates that although Australia in the 1990s saw small pockets of mandatory sentencing emerge, it was not until 1998 that a Bill was passed in Western Australia to develop a sentencing 'matrix'. The matrix Bill proposed three increasing levels of control over judicial discretion. The sad reality is that the rationale for this US-style grid-based sentencing cannot even lay any claim to a noble original motive. In the US, the very initial impetus for grid-based sentencing began in Minnesota in the 1970s as an instrument of principle. The critique then was with the vagaries of indeterminate sentencing in favour of 'desert' as the guiding principle and to develop effective appellate review. True, these early principles may have been hijacked by the 'law and order' bandwagon, or (as Greene's chapter shows), by the protean virtues of certainty, clarity and consistency which could easily be used as rallying calls for both liberal and conservative causes. Importantly, however, Australia has long had a relatively comprehensive system of appellate review and 'desert' has been a more central principle than the US of the 1970s. Therefore, "[i]n Western Australia it is hard to avoid the conclusion that the matrix is being driven, from the outset, by law and order politics".

Ill-thought-out and likely to intensify existing and produce new inequalities, the matrix proposals will relocate power to the prosecution (through the increased importance of plea-bargaining). As well-documented as this effect in the US has been and specifically highlighted by Morgan and others, the Western Australian government chose to dismiss the evidence from the US as 'irrelevant'. The lack of details on such basic issues as criminal record or multiple convictions creates a "… dangerous precedent by assuming that so much could be entrusted to regulations … In formal structural terms, power has been shifted from the courts to Parliament. In reality, power has shifted to the Executive". Such a shift may open the door to constitutional challenge. However, a more effective challenge might arise from the way in which judges themselves choose to interpret, apply, and adapt the legislation and regulations to individual cases. **Dirk van Zyl Smit**'s chapter takes up the question of how judges in South Africa have responded to aggressive attempts to reduce their discretion.

Dirk van Zyl Smit methodically traces the history, origins, and interpretation of South Africa's 1997 Criminal Law Amendment Act. In one sense it constitutes part of one of the recurring narratives of this volume. 'Populist punitiveness' has combined with concerns about disparity which appear to have restricted the legal scope of judicial discretion, most poignantly through the imposition of mandatory sentencing laws.

However, van Zyl Smit reveals that these sentences are not necessarily 'mandatory', unless judges choose to interpret them as such. The legislation allows for departures on a case-by-case basis, which simply need to be justified in terms of "substantial and compelling circumstances". "Substantial and compelling circumstances" would appear to have taken much of the sting out of the legislation. However, early signs are that South African judges appear to be doing two contradictory things. In the first case to deal with "substantial and compelling circumstances", Judge Stegmann complained bitterly that the legislation offended his conscience and would result in arbitrary punishment. Yet, his interpretation of the departure was remarkably narrow: erroneously defining "substantial circumstances" as "exceptional circumstances". In effect, Judge Stegmann annulled the permissive scope of discretion which parliament gave to judges by conjuring up a far more restrictive notion of the scope of judicial discretion than parliament had enacted or even intended! Although not every judgement on "substantial and compelling circumstances" has been so excessively self-restricting, judicial self-denial of its own cherished discretion is paradoxical. On the one hand, South African judges speak of the affront to their conscience and the dangers of restricting judicial discretion and yet on the other hand, they seem to deny themselves any opportunity to use the wide discretion which is available.

This paradox is redolent of that exposed by Robert Cover's historical work on the US's Fugitive Slave Act (Cover 1975). In a similar vein, chapters by Tata and by Provine as well as Provine (1998), focus attention on a selective judicial denial of discretion to resist the full force of populist sentencing movements. However, van Zyl Smit's story is more than a story about the paradox of the use of discretion by an embattled judiciary. Unlike, the parallels in other English-speaking jurisdictions, it is also a story played out against the backdrop of an entirely new (post-apartheid) regime. The new regime is struggling to assert itself in the face of heightened anxiety about crime. Suspicious about the commitment of the judiciary to the new regime, the same judiciary is recalled as having used 'judicial independence' as a smokescreen to avoid testifying before the Truth and Reconciliation Commission.

That not all jurisdictions have tried to imitate a US-style version of 'transparency' is also evidenced by the evolution of sentencing in Italy. In some important respects, the story of Italian sentencing contrasts markedly with that of the English-speaking world. Rather than following the movement towards a determinate/retributive model of sentencing, **Grazia Mannozzi** explains that it has instead moved towards a more rehabilitative and indeterminate model. Surveying recent trends in Italian sentencing policy and practice, Mannozzi identifies an underlying and growing tension between the operation of the rules of judicial sentencing (in the form of the Italian Criminal Code), and those governing the roles of prosecution and defence in sentencing (in the form of the Code of Criminal Procedure). The Italian Criminal Code facilitates a judge-centred unitary model of sentencing supplemented by Narrative Guidelines. The failure of the Code and the judiciary to express openly and coherently the rationales of punishment which should guide discretion has, she explains, permitted excessive discretion and "hidden forms of sentencing disparity". This unitary judge-centred model of sentencing established by the Criminal Code (CC) is now in crisis.

The crisis can be explained by the introduction of new intermediate sanctions, and especially by the introduction of the new Code of Criminal Procedure (CCP). The CCP allows sentencing to be established by negotiation between the parties and has thus transferred discretion from the judge to the trial adversaries (defence and prosecution). Given the Italian principle of mandatory prosecution, this development is better described as 'sentence bargaining' than 'plea-bargaining'. However, Mannozzi identifies several concerns which are similar to those associated with plea-bargaining in the English-speaking world. These concerns include: the practical shift of discretion away from judicial-control to the prosecution and defence; the increased disconnection between the formally supposed and real ranges of sentencing; and the more apparent use of efficiency/utility values (rather than those of legality). Mannozzi's recommendations include the need for clarity of normative rationales for punishment; explicit scaling of punishments; and, greater regulation of prosecution sentence bargaining.

Mannozzi's chapter on the shift away from the 'unitary' or judge-centred model of sentencing serves to emphasise the relative lack of attention by English-speaking scholars to the non-English-speaking world. Yet, it also underlines some common concerns about, for example, the substitution of judicial discretion by prosecutorial discretion and the need for greater clarity and penal coherence. In her chapter on the legislation and practice of sentencing in the largest (in population terms) country in the world, **Liling Yue** describes the 1997 revised Code of Criminal Law and the main penalties available. Custodial sentencing has to be understood, she implies, against the backcloth of the relatively widespread use of the Death Penalty. "Most academics and practitioners think the movement towards the abolition of the death penalty cannot be reversed." Narrowing the range of offences which can attract the death penalty will lead to its eventual abolition. Indeed Liling Yue concludes that in general for most sentences, "[t]he range of punishments is too large ... judges still retain very wide discretion. In practice, inconsistency is a serious problem" which the Supreme Court is seeking to remedy through 'guideline judgements'. In view of these developments also in China might it be meaningful to describe as 'worldwide' the trend towards clarity and determinacy in sentencing?

While the US has offered one particular model for this trend towards 'clarity', there are clearly others. Given, therefore, the immediate proximity of the lessons learned from the United States' "extreme reliance on incarceration" as the main solution to criminality and social problems, Canada's relatively high use of incarceration is puzzling. From the perspective of a senior public servant with many years experience in legislative reform,

Mary Campbell traces Canada's recent sentencing and corrections history. The paramount lesson, Campbell suggests, which governments too easily ignore is that policy must begin from the recognition of the intimate and inescapable practical interconnection between sentencing and corrections. Regrettably, Canada, once more, has been experiencing a 'traffic in quick fixes' which pretends that sentencing and corrections can be dealt with in isolation from each other. For example:

> [m]andatory sentencing rules ... are often promoted as a 'proportionate' response to crime, but are predicated on a complete disregard for the individual, his or risk of recidivism or rehabilitative potential, or what happens to him or her post-sentencing.

Specific pressures (i.e. popular media constructions of crime and punishment; single issue-drivers championed by poorly-informed Private Members' Bills; a politicised and dispirited civil service in which an interest in research is seen as suspect), have once again led to a dangerous divorce of sentencing policy from its corrections consequences. The "neon-lights of American-style reform" can only be resisted if sentencing and corrections are recognised as part of a "seamless process". Importantly, Campbell avoids the easy call of the disappointed policy-maker for "more information and more research". More research-based information is not enough. We need to be more strategic about how to communicate the information to the general public, "both in terms of *who* communicates that information and *how*".

The implication of Campbell's call for a much more strategic and unsentimental approach to communicating the findings of research for policy-formation, implies that we also need to know much more about that nebulous, yet taken-for-granted term, 'public opinion'. It is perhaps axiomatic that those who routinely trade on addressing the 'general public' (journalists, politicians, to a lesser extent, judges), tend to feel confident that they know what 'the public thinks' about sentencing. Indeed, politicians, popular commentators, judges and indeed many scholars tend to regard as obvious that 'the public' and victims of crime demand greater punitiveness. Earlier chapters by Greene, Morgan, Campbell, van Zyl Smit each discusses 'get tough' bandwagon, in which politicians and others point to public punitiveness (often citing public opinion polls) as their justification. Yet, what do we really know and not know about public opinion, public attitudes and public knowledge about sentencing?

The Truth about Public Punitiveness: What do we Know and What do we Need to Know? (Part II)

The in-depth research by **Michael Hough** and **Julian Roberts** into public opinion, attitudes, and knowledge reveals a very different story from that normally told. Their chapter summarises findings from a module of the major household British Crime Survey (BSC) which investigated public attitudes and knowledge of the sentencing process and sentencing patterns. In only two respects do the findings of this survey broadly concur with those habitually reported by opinion pollsters. First, levels of confidence in judges is very low: only 20 per cent of respondents rated judges as doing a good job (the worst evaluation of the six criminal justice professional groups). Secondly, people felt that the courts were far too lenient. All of this is grist to the 'get tough' political mill. However, very few opinion polls investigate public knowledge and fewer still have explored in any way public opinion as a function of public knowledge.

The BSC found that:

> few people had an accurate idea of imprisonment rates for [specific] offences. Public perceptions of imprisonment rates ... were systematically biased to a view that courts are treating offenders with more leniency than is in fact the case ... The belief appears to be correlated with misperceptions about sentencing practice.

In terms of sentencing preferences, when respondents were given short vignettes of actual cases (rather than asked in the abstract), their responses markedly contrasted with the highly punitive picture which opinion polls (reliant on simple abstract questions), might suggest. Indeed, the BSC findings challenge the easy notion that the public given a chance to sentence would be more punitive than the courts. "It would be wrong to characterise the British public as being, on balance, highly punitive, or as being consistently more punitive than sentencers." Indeed, there is some evidence to suggest the public may, in some respects, be more lenient than the courts. However, the further development of such comparisons between public preferences and court practices necessitates connecting public sentencing preference data about case vignettes to correspondingly high-quality in depth data about normal sentencing patterns of the courts, though the latter would have to be developed.[15]

Potentially these results are damaging to the populist political common sense. "The lesson would appear to be clear: correcting public misperceptions about sentencing ... will promote public confidence [in the administration of justice]." Hough and Roberts recommend as a priority providing the media with digestible sentencing statistics. There seem to be (at least) three important questions which flow from this recommendation. First, who should take a lead in this provision? Hough and Roberts recommend federal/central government. Yet, should the judiciaries themselves be encouraged also (perhaps through the judicial education bodies) to take more seriously the problem of popular systematic misperception (if only as a means of preserving their cherished independence from the executive branch of government)? Secondly, how 'newsworthy' will the provision of aggregate information be? Hough and Roberts themselves accept that "there is no guarantee that the data will be provided to the reader or listener". Linking this work with knowledge of 'news values' (such as individual 'human interest' stories, conflict, 'newness' etc.) must surely form part of a central strategy of countering 'get tough' with 'get media smart' (Tata 2000). A third question is whether the drive towards 'populist punitiveness' is simply or largely explained by public ignorance and misinformation. Hough and Roberts concede that public dissatisfaction will not simply be eliminated by a communications strategy. Might there be more fundamental societal explanations which drive public dissatisfaction? This question is addressed in the chapter by **Keith Crew**, **Gene Lutz** and **Kristine Fahrney**.

In their chapter 'Crisis and Contradictions in a State Sentencing Structure', Crew, Lutz and Fahrney report findings from their recent Iowa Adult Crime Victimisation Survey (IACVS). Like the BSC findings of Hough and Roberts, Crew, Lutz and Fahrney conclude that:

[t]he data reported here suggest that public opinion, when framed by realistic depictions of typical cases and informed by knowledge of actual sentencing practices and the use of intermediate sanctions, may be supportive of less punitive policies.

Indeed, similar to the "multi-track approach" which the BSC respondents supported, IACVS appeared to support a "multi-faceted, multi-goal approach to criminal sentencing, in which rehabilitation of the offender plays a significant role". When respondents reported that they had been a victim of crime they were asked to choose their appropriate sentence for their perpetrator. Again in common with the BSC, when Iowans are asked for their sentencing preferences in specific terms their responses are far less punitive than when asked in abstract principled terms.

Crew, Lutz and Fahrney suggest that Scheingold (1984) offers an important cultural explanation of the support of evermore punitive 'crime control' measures. Rather than as a reflection of crime and victimisation rates, the fear of crime and punitive attitudes reflect basic and easily manipulated values which allow easy politicisation. Most Americans share a set of beliefs and images of crime and punishment. This 'myth of crime and punishment' grows from deeply held beliefs in "individual responsibility and a cultural fascination with vigilantism and its promise of swift justice". The 'myth of crime and punishment' coexists with competing myths (such as 'the myth of redemption', and 'the myth of rights'), but the 'myth of crime and punishment' provides particularly reassuring answers in stressful times. It "allows us to project our anxieties and reaffirm community in troubled and confusing times". At its heart is a simple morality play representing a conflict between good and evil in which the image of the criminal is that of 'the other'. "Criminals are somehow fundamentally different from the rest of us and therefore not deserving of ... rights and protections." Crew, Lutz and Fahrney suggest that the absence of two conditions set out by Schiengold may diminish public punitiveness: the social abstraction of the offender as distinct from the rest of us (as 'other'); and secondly, the routine typification of crime as horror. In this way, replacement populist narratives can develop to compete with the myth of crime and punishment and its 'populist punitiveness' (Bottoms 1995).

As Hough and Roberts, and Crew, Lutz and Fahrney reveal, 'public opinion' is neither monolithic, highly punitive, nor as fixed as we have previously supposed. Be that as it may, **Candace McCoy** and **Patrick McManimon** observe that sentencing laws are increasingly said to be passed in 'the name of' a high-profile victim of crime (the most powerful example being 'Megan's Law' passed 'in the name of' the late Megan Kanka; readers may also recall the calls in the UK during 2000 for a 'Sarah's Law' which would supposedly be passed 'in the name of' the late Sarah Payne). Labouring under the name of victims, punitiveness and clarity are said to be paramount desires of victims. The 1997 No Early Release Act (NERA) passed in the US state of New Jersey mandatorily requires that the offender serves 85 per cent of the term pronounced if convicted of an offence defined as a crime of violence.

Through a victim survey, McCoy and McManimon set out to discover whether NERA increased victim satisfaction. They found that, "[n]either the length nor the certainty of the sentence, nor crime types are associated with victim satisfaction". Instead, a broader assessment of the way that the criminal justice professionals handled the case seems to be far more important to victims. At first glance, it might seem strange that McCoy and McManimon found that victims do not appear to be more satisfied with greater puntiveness, and instead seem to be so concerned with the conduct of the judge, and other professionals. Yet, it is possible that the victim's experience of the handling of the case is more important than the sentencing outcome, a point which is redolent of the research of Conley and O'Barr (e.g. 1990; 1998) as well as Tait's chapter in this volume, in emphasising the personal sense of power of the parties through the court process, rather than simple outcome. The assumption that victims would report greater satisfaction after NERA than victims before NERA is unsupported by the data. "[A]bstract public punitiveness may be high, but when placed in the context of particular people and actual experiences of crime and the people who commit it, punitiveness appears to be a considerably more complex phenomenon."

Measuring Punishment: Conceptual and Practical Problems and their Resolution (Part III)

Implicit in the chapters comprising the sections on the reality of trends towards 'transparency' in sentencing, and 'populist punitiveness' is the idea of comparison: over time, between jurisdictions, and between different social and professional populations. 'Comparative research' is normally understood by legal scholars as the effort to compare one jurisdiction with another. Yet, the attempt to compare sentencing practice between different jurisdictions is fraught with difficulty. The differences not only in sentencing law but in its practical operation between different jurisdictions make the common basis for comparison daunting. Europe, **Andrew Ashworth** explains, is the only continent in the world to make a concerted attempt to develop common standards for sentencing. The European Convention on Human Rights (ECHR), the European Union, and the Council of Europe comprise three distinct institutional sources of influence on European countries. Against this background, Ashworth sets out to answer the question: over the last decade, to what extent is the attempt to develop common European sentencing standards being realised in actual sentencing trends?

In perhaps the most comprehensive answer to this question yet, Ashworth finds that although there has been limited progress, there are some clearly emerging common trends. These emerging trends include, most notably: an increase in 'diversion' from prosecution through the courts (particularly in respect of young people); the bifurcation of sentencing practice and penal policy (on the one hand greater leniency in theft and possession of soft illicit drugs, such as cannabis) and on the other hand, a more punitive approach to supplying drugs, sexual offences, and racist crimes. Regrettable, in Ashworth's view, is the limited influence of the Council of Europe's attempt to develop a broader common approach to substantive sentencing and penal policy. Considering the paucity of and judicial resistance to in-depth empirical research on the sentencing decision process within European countries, it is perhaps hardly surprising that European-wide policy is barely being realised. It seems that for the time being the more procedural influence of the ECHR will have a more conspicuous impact.

One key question underlying discussions of possible convergence in sentencing trends across different jurisdictions is whether (and if so, how), cross-jurisdictional analysis of sentencing punitiveness is possible. **Arie Freiberg**'s chapter demonstrates not only that such comparison is possible, but that its achievement also offers real practical and intellectual rewards. The methodological challenges are enormous, yet, in principle, surmountable. His chapter candidly provides a careful overview of the key questions and possible ways of resolving them. The most frequently cited inter-jurisdictional measure of sentence severity is the 'league table' of the imprisoned population per 100,000 of the general population. Although the league table approach measures the proportion of the general population incarcerated, as a measure of severity it is flawed. "[I]mprisonment rates are not, in truth, sentencing data." Such league tables, Freiberg observes, ignore crucial variables, including: levels of and perceived seriousness of crime; differences in case processing by the criminal justice agencies of different countries; lump together juvenile with adult prison populations; as well as remand with sentenced prison populations.

Working to develop a more valid method of inter-jurisdictional comparison of sentence severity, Freiberg reports the challenges and findings of his more in-depth exploratory investigation into just one single offence type: burglary. In his survey of a small number of common law jurisdictions, Freiberg controls for mode of trial/sentence (i.e. 'higher' or 'lower courts'). He also attends to the incidence and lengths of custodial sentencing, including estimates of actual time served in the different jurisdictions. In this way, a more careful and sophisticated understanding of comparative severity is developed. Further work may develop an index which combines the effects of sentence jurisdiction (lower or higher courts), choice of sanction and the intensity of the sanction (separate from crime rates and legality). The creation of a standard unit of penal currency is the ultimate goal. That goal will continue to elude us unless such an index includes not only statistics on the behavioural practices of justice agencies but also data on attitudes to punishment and crime seriousness of the kind discussed in Part II of this volume on the truth about public and victim punitiveness.

One of the facets of inter-jurisdictional work which eludes comparisons of sentence severity is differences in the character of the sentencing decision process itself. **Malcolm Davies, Jukka-Pekka Takala**, and **Jane Tyrer** report investigation in Finland, England and Wales into the composition of offence seriousness; the identification of a custody/non-custody threshold; penal-philosophical motivations for decisions; and confidence in community sentencing.

Like Freiberg, they concentrated on one offence: burglary. It was especially difficult to capture the implications of inter-jurisdictional differences in: burglary definitions; notions of frequency and seriousness of burglary; diversion; pleading and sentence discounting; remand time and backdating; penal philosophies etc. "[C]omparative sentencing research was a bit like skiing up hill." It is "not impossible, but its possibility depends on the appreciation of the cultural context of the policies, procedures and practice of sentencing".

While both the chapters by Freiberg and Davies et al. emphasise the need for an appreciation of both material practices and the interpretive frameworks through which sentencers and others operate, to what extent is this a problem unique to inter-jurisdictional research? 'Comparative' research is normally seen as singularly synonymous with comparisons *between* jurisdictions (e.g. Frase 2001). Yet, the problems with which Freiberg and Davies et al. grapple are not fundamentally problems of jurisdiction (i.e. legality). Rather, they are fundamental problems of making *any* comparison at all.

In 'A New Look at Sentence Severity' **Brian Ostrom** and **Charles Ostrom** are concerned with identifying an index for the valid comparison of custodial penal severity not between jurisdictions but *within a single* jurisdiction. They begin with an observation which must have puzzled most researchers of custodial sentencing. Actual custodial sentence lengths are not consistent with a continuous scale of sentence severity.[16] For example, in the US state of Michigan 90 per cent of all custodial sentence lengths passed by judges were comprised of just 20 custodial sentencing lengths. Consider the intervals between these preferred (or favourite) lengths: 6, 12, 16, 18, 20, 24, 30, 32, 36, 40, 48, 60, 72, 84, 96, 120, 180, 240, 300. This phenomenon has been recognised for some time. Writing in the 1890s Francis Galton worried about the implications for penal proportionality. "[R]uns of figures like these testify to some powerful cause of disturbance which interferes with the orderly distribution of punishment in conformity with penal deserts." However, the endeavour of Ostrom and Ostrom is not to try to smooth out the prominent spikes of custodial allocation but rather to understand the underlying thinking so as then to develop an index which can be used to compare sentence severity.

Meticulous as their work is, the Ostroms' chapter is not an exercise in statistical pedantry. The erroneous supposition that sentence time (months) operates on a smooth ratio or even interval scale presents profound implications for research and policy.

> Statistical models – and analysis – are mis-specified if they use actual months of incarceration as the dependent variable. [Researchers and policy-makers] cannot interpret the coefficient estimates reliably if the metric underlying the dependent variable [months] changes over the span of the variable.

To resolve this problem, the Ostroms develop in their chapter the 'sentencing unit' (or 'senunit' for short), to reflect underlying judicial index. The senunit accepts: judicial 'choice simplification'; that the more prominent sentences are recalled more readily by judges; and psychological discounting (i.e. judges assume that penal severity experienced by the offender declines over time). The 'senunit' provides a 20-point value scale of custodial time. For example, 1–6 months is senunit value one; 7–12 is value two (intervals of 6 months); from 37 months the intervals increase to 12 months per unit, etc. Using the senunit as a tool for statistical analysis of judicial penal severity offers a more sensitive analysis of intended judicial penal severity. For example, applying the senunit to data on robbery sentencing reveals a 'trial tax' (the US inverse of guilty plea discounting) of one senunit; likewise, it uncovers specific racial effects. The implications of this (especially at the longer lengths of sentencing) are potentially enormous – as much as 5–10 years extra.

The Ostroms' chapter invites the reader to scrutinise carefully the validity of using months as a dependent variable of custodial sentencing. It is about the punishment applied by judges who necessarily make assumptions about how much penal severity offenders will experience. Yet, it is not intended as an attempt to examine the reality of custodial penal severity experienced by the offender. It is this offender experience of punishment upon which **Gavin Dingwall** and **Christopher Harding** focus. In a penal system, such as that of England and Wales, which is officially committed to 'desert' as the fundamental penal rationale, the experience of custodial punishment (and thus its severity) in different institutions has been largely ignored by scholars and especially by the Court of Criminal Appeal.

Generally, the Appeal Court of England and Wales recognises the severity of custodial punishment as measured simply by its duration (i.e. quantitatively) rather than qualitatively (i.e. the nature of different custodial regimes). On the one hand, the Court of Appeal has occasionally shown an interest in cases where there may be exceptional vulnerability or severe consequences in the event of incarceration. On the other hand, it has pretended that the varying penal experience of different regimes is a matter of no interest. Dingwall and Harding argue that if proportionality of punishment is to be realised then the punitiveness of a custodial sentence should not be measured purely in terms of its length. Indeed the (sometimes marked), variations between institutions suggest the exercise of arbitrary punishment: "is it sensible to disregard variations in the subsequent experience of imprisonment as simply good or bad fortune?". Secondly, in effect, executive agencies punish. It is interesting to observe that the same questions about the proper location of punishment (executive or judicial); and associated values (such as transparency, reviewability, 'truth in sentencing' etc.) were developed by the now vast literature on the constitutionality of executive release (especially parole). These same questions are now starting to be exposed and developed presciently by Dingwall and Harding (and others) working in the hitherto backwater of penal regime severity. The development of 'desert' theory revolutionised penology and has therefore also been the subject of careful scrutiny and critique. **Julia Davis** asks whether "the new desert is a mere slogan … [offering] no more than general guidance … [or can it produce] precise … proportionate sentences …?". In other words, can von Hirsch's model deliver "the precision it promises, or is it simply another of the ubiquitous metaphors that bedevil nearly all theoretical punishment debates?". To answer this question about measurement, Davis applies measurement theory. Measurement is more than simply pinning numbers onto things. First (like law) measurement identifies things and distinguishes them from each other. Secondly (unlike law), measurement has a more uniquely scientific purpose: to apply mathematical processes to those numbers assigned to things. Central to Davis' critique of von Hirsch's 'desert' model is that, although von Hirsch denies that his model seeks a narrow mathematical sense of proportionality, "… it is undeniable that both the substance of the model and the terminology used to describe its practical application suggest this …".

Using measurement theory, Davis evaluates three grounds on which von Hirsch's model has been attacked. First, the important distinction between cardinal and ordinal proportionality confuses more than it reveals. The (ultimately unclear) adaptation to which von Hirsch has put these terms

> can sabotage the debate by destroying the shared meaning of the words … It may be better to abandon [these cardinal and ordinal terms] and accept that desert is neither determining nor limiting, but is to provide comparative though not absolute guidance …

A second vein of criticism of von Hirsch's 'desert' model is that it is impossible to measure 'desert'. Countering this criticism von Hirsch focuses not on what people perceive to be seriousness but 'real' seriousness. Davis argues that in fact 'real' seriousness is a fiction: unlike the properties of physical thing, 'seriousness' cannot be located and measured in social abstraction. "… [T]here is no such thing as 'real' seriousness, but only 'perceived' seriousness." Seriousness is an inescapable social creation. When we try to measure seriousness we are measuring our response to crime, not a property of the crime in itself. A third line of criticism has been the 'incommensurability argument': there is no unique, non-arbitrary way to transpose a measure of crime-seriousness to a measure of punishment. A way to avoid this problem is to recognise that 'the seriousness of crimes' and 'punishment' are not separate distinct things "… linked by a mathematical process. Rather they represent the same thing expressed two ways: our response to offenders and their crimes". Instead of using a scientific style, it would be better, Davis argues, to accept that law and physical science (with its mathematical imperatives) are two distinct enterprises. Science aims to discover the regularity that exists, whereas law aims to impose a chosen order on the world.

The two short chapters which follow present a lively debate between Andrew von Hirsch and Julia Davis. In his reply to Julia Davis' critique, **Andrew von Hirsch** accepts that his use of the terms 'ordinal' and 'cardinal' are not used "in the standard scientific way" and does not purport to do so. The point of making the distinction between 'ordinal' and 'cardinal' proportionality has been to draw attention to the relative internal scaling of a punishment scale ('ordinal') and the overall dimensions of the scale itself ('cardinal'). As for the accusation that he has misleadingly adapted the term from standard scientific measurement use, von Hirsch protests: "I am entitled to adopt a term and put it to different use". He notes that physicists, for example, refer to the 'spin' of an electron. "They simply borrow words and redefine them." In her rejoinder **Julia Davis** explains that there is no problem with redefining ordinary words for a technical purpose. "[B]ut von Hirsch has done something quite different. He has taken two established technical terms, already used in the punishment debates, and changed their meanings. This is not helpful."

Aside from the debate as to whether redefinition of 'ordinal' and 'cardinal' produces clarity or confusion, there is apparent agreement between von Hirsch and Davis in that crime seriousness cannot be measured "objectively". Von Hirsch insists that he has never suggested that it could. Referring to his work to advance the construction of "a living standard" (von Hirsch and Jareborg 1993), the 'harmfulness' of conduct should be assessed (largely normatively) by that standard, while the culpability (the other central dimension of seriousness) is an entirely normative matter. Importantly, von Hirsch appears to concur with Davis by implying that 'normative' does not mean a fixed, asocial, universal or immutable standard.

His reply to Davis leads von Hirsch to recall his earlier debate with Norval Morris (1982). He candidly concedes: "I overstated my response [to Morris] in saying that desert is *determining* when it comes to comparative ordering" [emphasis added]. The reason is that 'ordinal' proportionality has three sub-requirements: parity, rank-ordering, and spacing of penalties. For Davis, however, these three sub-requirements simply amount to a restatement of the proposition that crimes should be allocated to places on a penalty scale according to perceived seriousness. It fails to provide much guidance in 'the real challenge' to identify categories of relevant similarities and differences between crimes and impose limits on the state.

Reason-Giving and Approaches to Explaining Sentencing (Part IV)

The important debate between von Hirsch and Davis is about the prescriptions for a more reasoned system of measurement and rationale for punishment. Yet there is also the more prosaic but still fundamental question of whether sentencers actually follow legislative and Appeal Court direction. For example, do sentencers comply with the legislative and Court of Appeal requirements in terms of guilty plea discounting? In England and Wales, section 48 of the Criminal Justice and Public Order Act 1984 officially obliges sentencers to take into account the timeliness and circumstances of a guilty plea and if a discount is made by the sentencer that this should be stated in open court.

Ralph Henham reports his investigation into Crown Court compliance with section 48 and guidance by the Court of Appeal. As well as demonstrating the ambiguity of the drafting of section 48, Henham found judicial compliance was surprisingly low.

> It is surprising … to note that 50.4 per cent of judges regarded the stage when the plea was entered as either 'not particularly important' or 'not important at all' with the latter category … larger than the judges regarding this factor as 'very important' …

Indeed, "a substantial minority did not comply with section 48 even in the narrow sense of referring to the plea and the fact that credit would be given for it".

Recommending a rewording of section 48, Henham is concerned to ensure that the sentencer is "forced to articulate the rationale for the sentence discount from a wider range of potentially relevant factors …". Although Henham notes the difficulty which sentencers face in being required to "… attribute substantial effects to discrete variables …", the low level of compliance is nonetheless seen as disappointing and suggestive of a lack of transparency and openness in the giving of reasons for the decision process. Section 48

> should have provided greater transparency, … improving our understanding of how the judiciary deal with [whether guilty pleas produce discounting, and the judicial explanation for the discount]. However, … it appears a substantial minority of judges are failing not only to provide an explanation of the discount, they are not stating it at all.

Why is there such a lack of openness in the decision-making process? Henham's concern that sentencers should be "forced" to articulate the reason for their decisions is part of a tradition of liberal-legal scholars who find the sentencing decision process opaque and unnecessarily mystificatory. Yet, attempts to force sentencers to provide any kind of meaningful explanation for their decision, especially on the basis of penal-philosophical rationales, have not, so far, been successful. **Cyrus Tata** asks why this has been the case.

Observing that the predominant preoccupation of sentencing scholarship has been to 'structure' sentencing discretion, Tata suggests that the daily use of discretion is in fact much more ordered and rule-bound than both policy and scholarly literature has tended to suppose. It only appears to be chaotic when viewed through a legal-philosophical lens. He argues for a way of interpreting the decision process which is neither rule-less nor represents cases analytically in terms of supposedly discrete individual 'factors' and personal philosophies, but rather recognises the constructed, typified, and holistic representation of cases. Judicial defensiveness only slightly explains the reluctance of judges to provide open, transparent and coherent accounts of the decision process. It may instead be that as scholars we need to take a hard look at the basic assumed explanatory categories of sentencing: a series of notional but sociologically unhelpful dichotomies ('offence plus offender'; 'aggravating versus mitigating factors'; 'penal philosophical principle versus incoherent judgement' etc.). In particular, the supposition of a need for a balance between the opposing forces of 'rules' and 'discretion' are called into question.

Although in the abstract we can identify legal 'rules' and legal 'discretion', in routine interpretive practice rules and discretion are indistinguishable from each other. Rather 'rules' are inherently open, malleable and discretionary; while 'discretion' is inherently patterned, regular, and in that sense, rule-governed. From this understanding, 'discretion' and 'rules' should not be counter-posed as discrete opposites.

> [S]entencing research might focus rather more on regularities in speech and behaviour, the construction of sentencing customs and folk knowledge, and the normalised construction of cases.

In so doing, research is more likely to reveal a sociological appreciation of the decision process, which is more comprehensible and coherent than by presuming legality and penal philosophy to be the natural starting point of enquiry and then adding in extra-legal 'factors'. Adapting Richard Ericson's work on the mass media as an integral part of the criminal justice system, Tata proposes an understanding of judicial sentencing accountability as socially (rather than mainly legally and/or legal-philosophically), produced. Judicial sentencing accounts are "necessarily mediated, constructed and reconstructed according to the audience and requirements of the ability to account for the decision".

Tata's chapter is intended, in part, to encourage the exploration of the daily social environment of sentencing (in which practically indistinguishable notions of rules and discretion are used as a resource). How is that daily environment constructed and negotiated? How can we interpret the dialogue and tacit negotiation between professionals engaged in setting the sentencing decision agenda? **Fergus McNeill** examines scholarly and policy thinking to date about the influence on sentencing of court Social Enquiry Reports (SERs). He outlines why "to describe the purpose of social enquiry as 'assisting sentencing' is somewhat vacuous". SERs do not transmit simple information about individuals. Rather they "reflect and embody penal-professional discourses ... [promoting specific] visions of justice". But how are the SERs themselves constructed: what are the influences upon the writing of reports?

Reviewing legislative, policy and penological frameworks in Great Britain, McNeill proposes that "... social workers (and, to some extent probation officers) stand in a different criminological tradition [to other court professionals] which stresses social and economic disadvantage". Warning against managerialist thinking about 'quality', 'effectiveness', and 'consistency' of SERs which sees the sentencer as consumer and the report writer as assistant, McNeill asks that if the SER should assist sentencing then what kind of sentencing should it assist? It is this question which 'quality' audits of 'effectiveness' fail to address. Indeed, the 'influence' of the report writer on sentencing should not be to make the task of punishment easier, but to make it more difficult: to "generate ... unease, to provoke ... bad conscience, to make punishment more morally difficult for the sentencer".

McNeill's chapter focuses on the sociological construction of SERs against a background of changing legislation and penal discourses. In 'Dangerousness and Risk', **Hilde Tubex** presents a way of explaining changes in officially pronounced sentencing discourses, objectives and techniques. Tubex traces the changes in penal legislation in Belgium, and to a lesser extent in the Netherlands and Great Britain. 'Dangerousness' is not, Tubex shows, a new concept in sentencing. Belgium and the Netherlands were important pioneers in the development of modern penology. Yet, their role is rarely described in English-speaking publications. Explaining the origins and influence of Belgian Social Defence Theory developed by Adolphe Prins in the early twentieth century, she delineates the metamorphosis of the concepts of 'dangerousness' and 'risk'. Prins saw an elaborated notion of 'dangerousness' as a means of protection from the insecurities of industrial society (personified in vagrants, beggars, the mentally diseased and habitual offenders). Through the introduction of responsibility without fault it became possible to protect against the dangerous, even if they were deemed not to be responsible for their actions.

Tubex explains the rise of 'modern penology' (with its emphasis on the individual offender, re-socialisation supported by scientific knowledge offender), and its replacement by 'new penology'. Unlike 'modern penology', 'new penology' is disinterested in the causes of criminality and the individual.

Rather there is an emphasis on the management of 'risk' (as identified by statistical and actuarial techniques). "We no longer combat criminality, we just try to live with it." This is a 'fatalistic' vision in which incarceration is not seen as redemptive or reformative but simply 'warehousing'. Contrasting with the approach of 'social defence theory', the estimation of dangerousness in the 'new penology' is not directed against the individual, "the foremost aim is to identify certain *groups* according to the risk which they represent, and to attempt to *control* that risk" [emphasis added]. Such 'risk' groups now include drug and sexual offenders, as well as illegal immigrants.

Many of the chapters in this volume capture the deep concern among scholars and practitioners about the 'punitive turn' in criminal justice throughout the Western world. The insatiable demand for ever-increasing puntiveness is easily dismissed as basically "madness", **David Tait** observes. Yet there may be a way of appreciating the evermore strident calls for vengeance and so perhaps diminish their literal punitive impact.

For Tait, much of the focus of sentencing scholarship and policy has been preoccupied with judicial reasoning and justification for sentencing decisions (see e.g. the critical review of the literature by Tata in this volume). Yet, we may be missing something crucial. Proposing that we need to take far more seriously the dramatic performance of sentencing ritual, Tait reminds us that ritual literally enlivens law. Developing Antoine Garapon's work on the quasi-religious ritual of the trial hearing, Tait outlines three vignettes of sentencing/trial hearings. Dramatic and symbolic ritual need not be seen as a mystificatory practice by professionals to exclude lay people. Illustrated by his explanation of the vignettes, Tait shows that the trial ritual performance can allow: the explanation of behaviour; public demonstration of remorse; clear indication by the offender of respect for the victim; opportunities for victims and offenders to speak; and the verbal chastisement of the offender which can provide the foundation for forgiveness. It is ironic that an evermore juridical trial system, which is designed to seek rationality, may actually be stoking public vengeance, while a more flexible system can mix displays of authority, symbolic violence and mercy. The public performance of ritual symbolic violence combined with mercy may reduce the public clamour for revenge, "since symbolic revenge in a powerful and dramatic form has already been achieved".

In advancing the case for a more serious appreciation of the role of ritual, Tait acknowledges that there may be many different types, styles and effects of ritual. Indeed, following focus led by Garfinkel on the metaphor of trials as "degradation rituals" and the revelation by Goffman of the tricks and stratagems of legal professionals, "ritual was given a bad name as a superfluous and obsolete set of practices designed to confuse and mystify ordinary people". It is this need to focus on gross inequality of power and substantive legal inequality against the background of social inequity which is tackled by Part V, 'Doing Justice: Power, Equality and Equity'.

Doing Justice: Power, Equality and Equity (Part V)

A recurring challenge of Part V is how to advance equity and genuine substantive equality in the sentencing process through legality. In her compelling history of the US 'War on Drugs', **Doris Marie Provine** raises questions not only about systematic racial injustice in a system preoccupied with rhetoric of legal equality, but how sentencing reforms intended to limit the scope of discretion in favour of a standardised approach have only resulted in a massive escalation of racial disparities and discrimination. Further, how is it possible that the appellate courts have managed to deny African Americans the reality of the constitutional guarantee of 'equal protection' before the law?

Black Americans, who account for only 12 per cent of the US population, now constitute 53 per cent of new admissions to prison and their rate of incarceration is 8.2 times higher than for white Americans. Lest this be dismissed as simply a waning legacy of historical disadvantage, these are in fact historic highs. In 1999 about one in every 12 black males in his late 20s was serving a sentence. Easily the most important cause of this explosive rise in black imprisonment (which far outstrips the increases for other races), has been the specific targeting for draconian punishment those specific drug-type offences of which African Americans are most likely to be convicted. Provine explains how the implementation of the anti-drug initiative has been highly selective. Most acute of all are the racially disparate effects when we consider 'crack' (the drug of choice, it seems, of poor African-Americans in the inner cities) as opposed to powder cocaine offences (the chic drug of choice of the rich and famous). Nearly everyone prosecuted for crack offences is African-American. Penalties for 'crack' cocaine offences were made vastly greater than for all other prohibited drug types, including powder cocaine (crack's pharmacological twin). The sentencing disparities between the two forms of cocaine are enormous. The fact that cocaine can easily be turned into crack is ignored. Federal law punishes the sale of one single gram of crack as harshly as possession and sale of 100 grams of powder cocaine. Simple possession of 1 to 5 grams of crack mandates five years imprisonment. Yet, there has been no lack of official awareness of the racial impact of the policy. The question

Provine prompts us to consider is: why and how has there has been such
political support and judicial disinterest for this flagrantly unequal treatment?

At once both puzzling and disappointing has been "[t]he role the appellate
courts have played in deflecting equal-protection challenges to federal drug
sentencing rules". Constitutional standards clearly give judges the authority
to overturn racially discriminatory practices. Despite being able to show that
the huge differentials in punishments prescribed for similar drugs offences
had an enormous racially unequal impact and occasionally winning at trial
level, challengers "consistently lost on appeal for lack of evidence that
Congress *intended* to discriminate" [emphasis added]. In effect, the appellate
courts have been saying: "if we can't see that someone consciously meant to
discriminate then we cannot see any discrimination". The appellate courts
have construed an extraordinarily narrow interpretation of its self-imposed
intent requirement. 'Treatment' seems not to be recognised by the courts as
racially unequal unless there is evidence of conscious and deliberate
discriminatory intent. It is, I would suggest, an asocial view of discrimination,
which seems only to recognise individuals who express overt racist sentiments.
In this way, racial discrimination is in effect reduced only to those limited
instances where an individual can be shown to be consciously and actively
racist, and so ignores behaviour or practices of individuals and institutions
which promote, support, or actively protects unequal treatment. This asocial
model of unequal treatment by an intentionally discriminating individual
dismisses from scrutiny social processes, procedures and effects. Yet, racism
"can be unconscious and inadvertent". While this might make its commission
less culpable than conscious and active racism, the key point to note (which
has been completely ignored by the appellate courts), is that 'intention' is
immaterial to the unequal impact on its recipients. To put it another way,
simply because a culprit cannot be identified cannot negate the fact of harm.

While the appellate courts have crafted a limited, asocial model and oft-
practically impossible test for racially unequal treatment, Congress has
generally paid little interest or scorned the very suggestion, rejecting the
Sentencing Commission's recommendation of parity between the two drugs
for similar offences. Limited to a 1960s notion, the concept of racism used by
appellate courts, Congress and some in the Sentencing Commission is, Provine
concludes, "seriously deficient". "The political system seems to lack, not just
the will to engage in a serious debate about racial justice, but the necessary
vocabulary ... of the way racism works in law."

Law's conceptions of equality, discrimination, and intent is further
developed by **Kate Warner**. Criticism has long been levelled against the courts

worldwide for sentencing rape too leniently. However, in her chapter Kate Warner takes up the challenge of how the courts should approach supposedly 'atypical' cases, i.e. those which fall outside of the 'real' rape paradigm. Beginning with an examination of maximum penalties and appellate guidance, Warner develops an application of von Hirsch and Jareborg's (1991) 'living standard' analysis of the harm of rape. Although the application of its specific instruments for the measurement of 'harm' are questionable (it treats acquaintance rape as sex and not violence), she finds this kind of principled analysis is useful in grounding an approach to sentencing rape.

Examining the approach of the appellate courts in England and Wales and Australia, Warner proposes principles to approach cases outside the 'real rape' paradigm. In so doing, she exposes and critiques a mythology of sex and sexuality in which rape is confused with sex rather than violence, and normal sex is something that the sexually assertive male does to the compliant victimised female, rather than as active choice and mutual enjoyment. Contrary to the dominant approach of the courts, Warner argues that the existence of prior intimate relationship (as opposed to 'stranger rape'), should not be seen as mitigating, but recognised as aggravating the seriousness of the case because it involves a breach of trust. The victim's forgiveness and attitude should not be given mitigatory weight.

> It is wrong to equate forgiveness with less emotional harm ... withdrawal of charges or continuation of the relationship ... may be motivated by fear ... Courts should apply the general principle that victims' attitudes and wishes cannot influence the sentence.

The view that: a deteriorating relationship; the victim's previous sexual experience; or, 'imprudent behaviour' should mitigate the seriousness of rape is premised on the flawed notion that normal sex is something that the naturally sexually insatiable man inflicts on the naturally submissive woman.

> Prior sexual history should not be a relevant factor ... To generalise that there will [for example] be less psychological harm if the victim is a prostitute confuses sex with rape and fosters stereotyping based on the moral worth of the victim ... [I]t encourages the view that some people are more rapeable than others.

Warner closes her arguments by stating that while sentencing cases outside the 'real rape' paradigm has been too lenient and these 'mitigatory' factors should be rejected, it "does not mean that an overall rise in sentence severity is advocated". Rather, we need to review the relative seriousness of different kinds of rape as the first stage in the broader review of overall offence seriousness.

Warner does not advocate an overall increase in incarceration. Rather her concern is with the relative 'worth' of offences. Earlier we saw how Provine emphasises that applying the same formal law may be neither equal nor equitable. Apparent legal equality by treating all persons the same way may in fact mask the grossest injustice and substantive inequalities. In their chapter on sentencing the corporate offender, **Hazel Croall** and **Jenifer Ross** explain why the sentences received by corporate offenders have tended to be seen as an example of injustice of the criminal justice system: 'not really crime'.

Corporations (whether firms, companies or public authorities), are understood by law as artificial persons: incapable of doing or thinking and thus being responsible for anything themselves. Where a crime involves proof of *mens rea* it is necessary to prove that the company itself had the necessary mental element. To do this, the UK courts have used the 'controlling mind' approach whereby the prosecution must prove that the crime was committed by a controlling mind: those senior officers with whom the company itself can be identified. The fundamental weakness of the 'controlling mind' approach is that it seeks to apply to a corporation the same legal framework, which it applies to an individual. "The major issue becomes the need to identify someone of sufficient seniority who is guilty of the offence and with whom the corporation can be identified": a theory, which in practice, is only suitable to the small company which is owned and controlled by a very small number of people.

Croall and Ross advance the need to develop a wider range of sanctions for corporations, which recognise the uniqueness of the corporate form. In particular, Croall and Ross consider the use of corporate probation and more especially corporate community service, which has, hitherto, been "relatively undeveloped". Not only does corporate community service offer symbolic appeal, it also provides rehabilitative and deterrent aspects. Some orders require companies to release employees to work in the community (for example, executives in car companies who have deliberately produced unsafe cars to do work in Emergency Rooms).

The need to accommodate the distinctive features of the corporate offender into the sentencing framework is in some respects paralleled by the need to accommodate the restricted choice of people profoundly socially and economically disadvantaged. It is this latter challenge which is taken up by **Barbara Hudson** and developed in the debate between her and **Neil Hutton**. Hudson has been developing a theory of sentencing which can "accommodate differences in economic situation of offenders by the application of principled criteria for economic hardship, rather than on the basis of individual representations for particularly sympathetic cases". Neil Hutton develops a broadly sympathetic analysis, but one which is nonetheless sharply critical of the technique which Hudson has proposed. His central argument is that Hudson's "social theory" of culpability confuses the sociological meaning and functions of law with politics.

For Hutton, the liberal conception of law necessarily has two faces. One face presents universal equality, formality, neutrality, objectivity. The second face (not presented openly by liberal law), is that this first face of law promotes the values of liberal society such as individual freedom and so protects unequal social division. "Law is able to conceal its ... partisan commitments behind formal procedures which promise to deliver equal justice to all." This is the necessary and inescapable fiction of liberal law and is what makes it both distinctive and creates "community in a world of difference ... Law rhetorically promises to provide justice and this serves as one source of unity in a divided society". Hudson's proposals would, for Hutton, threaten what liberal law distinctively achieves. The reason is: "Hudson wants to allocate responsibility at the level of the group rather than the individual" which is incompatible with the liberal paradigm of law. The problem with preassigning individual culpability according to membership of more or less culpable groups (thus entailing the loss of individual responsibility), would be an arbitrary exercise in which law would be revealed as politics. It would lose liberal law's distinctive ability to create community and social solidarity. Perhaps everything is political in reality, but law "allows us to forget this momentarily and to pretend that the world is not simply the struggle for power, but that human societies have more lofty aspirations". For Hutton, then, the cunning trick of law's fiction can be seen positively. "The great strength of law is that it covers its traces."

In her reply to Hutton, Barbara Hudson clarifies and develops her theory. She explains that she would not propose that all members of a social group be exempt liability from state punishment in advance. Rather, she underlines that law "should be cognizant of the social circumstances in which crimes occur". On this point Hutton and Hudson seem to agree, but not on whether law ought or is capable of developing a more *systematic method to ensure* that such cognisance systematically occurs in every single case and has a more profound impact.

Developing the idea of a 'hardship defence' (which is bound to be problematic for 'desert' theory), Hudson tackles an empirical disagreement with Hutton. He noted that "sentencers can, and do, already take account of 'nuanced notions of culpability' and 'treat freedom of choice as a matter of degree'" through the use of their substantive discretion. Observing developments from the 1980s in England and Wales, Hudson states that there has been a "general shift to downgrade substantive justice concerns". Moreover, the rationale for leniency in cases of hardship (which could work analogously to the defence of physical coercion), would be quite different from that practised currently by sentencers (such as it remains). Without the hardship defence, leniency comes at a heavy price: its recipients being seen as less than full rational responsible agents. Rather "indigent offenders should be seen as *acting rationally within a restricted range of choices*" [emphasis added].

In one sense, Hudson is concerned to try encourage 'desert' theory to be more sociologically informed by counterbalancing the measurement of harm with a more socially-grounded understanding of offender culpability. It may be, as Hudson suggests, that sentencing practice is triggered first and foremost by estimation of harm committed and revised only slightly by an estimation of the extent of choice. The reader will recall from discussion of Provine's chapter that harm/impact was of no concern to appellate courts reviewing equal treatment challenges. What mattered to the courts was the expressed intention/choice of Congress. It is this need to understand how and why concepts such as choice, harm, equality and intention are determined by the courts which necessitates a fuller understanding of social and political power.

As well as such questions about power, this Introduction has attempted to invite the reader to consider how the sociology of sentencing is uniquely equipped to answer certain questions which have inevitably tended to frustrate or be marginalised by a 'legal-philosophical in-context approach'. We have seen how, for example, a 'legal-philosophical in-context' approach is necessarily frustrated by and ultimately dismissive of 'populist punitiveness'. The sociology of sentencing can explain the mediated character of 'public opinion' as well the origins and development of and strategies to counter populist punitiveness. This volume also permits a new understanding of the use of judicial discretion, which has long puzzled and disappointed sentencing scholarship. It allows us also to consider afresh the character and vulnerability of a formal individualistic notion of 'judicial independence'. All of this is played out against perceptions of dominance and popular will; and the constructions of notions of legal equality in sentencing and social inequity.

This Introduction has also sought to sketch a map of the different contributions to this volume and highlight their sociological interconnections. Yet by no means does this chapter claim to be a comprehensive representation of all possible sociological approaches to sentencing. Rather, I have tried to develop and advance the case for the sociology of sentencing by directly drawing upon the chapters in this volume and their interconnections. I would invite the reader to contemplate the further implications of this volume, which are explained by Neil Hutton's 'Reflections'.

It is as presumptuous, of course, to talk about *the* sociology of sentencing as it is to talk of, say, *the* philosophy of law. Within that broad endeavour there are various approaches. I hope that this volume contributes both to the further development of that endeavour and to its nascent diversity.

Notes

1   I am grateful to the following people for their very valuable comments on and suggests for revision to an earlier draft of this Introduction: Neil Hutton, Julian Roberts, Julia Davis, David Tait, Lorraine Sweeney, Jan Nicholson, Grazia Mannozzi. I am also grateful to Jan Nicholson for her diligent formatting of this chapter.
2   Co-Director of the Centre for Sentencing Research and Senior Lecturer in Law, University of Strathclyde, Scotland, UK. E-mail: cyrus.tata@strath.ac.uk.
3   See for example, Green 1961, Hood 1962, Hogarth 1971.
4   There is a burgeoning and important literature on the sociology of punishment (see for example, D. Garland, 1990). While this literature forms a very important backcloth to the sociology of sentencing and is discussed in this chapter and throughout the volume, the sociology of sentencing is a different (but not isolated) enterprise from the sociology of punishment. Sentencing is about the *allocation of* punishment.
5   For example, chapters by Campbell, Hough and Roberts, Crew et al., McCoy and McManimon, and Hutton's 'Reflections'.
6   A point which I try to flesh out below in the discussion about the sociology of judicial independence.
7   Although related, by 'equity' I mean substantive social justice and fairness; as distinct from the narrower meaning of 'equality'.
8   For example, most recently Tonry and Frase (2001).
9   Measured by prison population per 100,000 of the national population.
10 The proposition that the custodial sentence pronounced should be 'truthful' to the sentence time served in custody.
11 On the interconnection between sentencing and 'corrections' see the chapter in this volume by Campbell.
12 The so-called 'Three Strikes and You're Out'.
13 Namely, "the right to bear arms". Seelye, *The New York Times*, 13 April 1994, quoted by Greene.
14 Arie Freiberg (1995), also quoted by Morgan's chapter in this volume.
15 Sadly, high-quality in-depth sentencing data is not available in most countries because police-derived administrative data about sentencing tends to be superficial and therefore barely connects with the kind of more detailed vignettes of the BSC. One project which

has collected relatively in-depth data specifically about sentencing (e.g. case seriousness etc.) is the Sentencing Information System for the senior judiciary of Scotland (Tata et al. 1998; Hutton et al. 1996). The judiciary there has the opportunity to disseminate this high quality information to counter misinformation and assist public education, thereby also protecting themselves against specious criticism. At the time of writing no decision had been taken.

16   Thus, building on the earlier work of Fitzmaurice and Pease (1986), chapter 7.

References

Bottoms, A. (1995), 'The Philosophy and Politics of Punishment and Sentencing', in C. Clarkson and R. Morgan (eds) (1995), *The Politics of Sentencing Reform*, Oxford: Oxford University Press.

Conley, J. and O'Barr (1990), *Rules Versus Relationships*, Chicago: University of Chicago Press.

Conley, J. and O'Barr (1998), *Just Words: Law, language and power*, Chicago: University of Chicago Press.

Cover, R. (1975), *Justice Accused: Antislavery and the judicial process*, Harvard: Yale University Press.

Eisenstein, J. and Jacob, H. (1991), *Felony Justice: An organizational analysis of the criminal courts*, Lanham: Little Brown.

Frase, R. (2001), 'Comparative Perspectives on Sentencing Policy and Research', in M. Tonry and R. Frase (eds), *Sentencing and Sanctions in Western Countries*, Oxford: Oxford University Press, pp. 259–92.

Freiberg, A. (1995), 'Sentencing Reform in Victoria: A Case Study', in C. Clarkson and R. Morgan (eds) (1995), *The Politics of Sentencing Reform*, Oxford: Clarendon Press, pp. 169–98.

Garland, D. (1990), *Sentencing and Modern Society: A study in social theory*, Oxford: Clarendon Press.

Green, E. (1961), *Judicial Attitudes in Sentencing: A study of the factors underlying the sentencing practice of the criminal court of Philadelphia*, London: St Martin's Press.

Hogarth, J. (1971), *Sentencing as a Human Process*, Toronto: University of Toronto Press.

Hood, R. (1962), *Sentencing in the Magistrates Courts: A study in variations in policy*, London: Stevens.

McBarnet, D. and Whelan, C. (1997), 'Creative Compliance and the Defeat of Legal Control', in K. Hawkins (ed.), *The Human Face of Law*, Oxford: Clarendon Press.

Morris, N. (1982), *Madness and the Criminal Law*, Chicago: University of Chicago Press.

Provine, D.M. (1998), 'Too Many Black Men: the Sentencing Judge's Dilemma', *Law & Social Inquiry*, Vol. 23, No. 4, pp. 823–56.

Scheingold, S. (1984), *The Politics of Law And Order*, New York: Longman.

Tata, C. (1999), 'Comparing Legal Aid Spending: the Promise and Perils of a Jurisdiction-Centred Approach', in F. Regan et al. (eds), *The Transformation of Legal Aid: Comparative and historical studies*, Oxford: Oxford University Press.

Tata, C. (2000), 'Spinning Judges? Judicial Education, Public Education, Propaganda and Truth', paper presented to the 2000 *Annual Meeting of the Law & Society Association*.

Tata, C., Hutton, N., Wilson, J. Paterson, A. and Hughson, I. (1998), *Sentencing Information System for the High Court of Justiciary in Scotland: Report of the first phase of implementation, evaluation, and enhancement*, Centre for Sentencing Research.

Tonry, M. (2001), 'Punishment Policies and Patterns in Western Countries', in M. Tonry and R. Frase (eds), *Sentencing and Sanctions in Western Countries*, Oxford: Oxford University Press.

Von Hirsch, A. and Jareborg, N. (1991), 'Gauging Criminal Harm: A Living Standard Analysis', *Oxford Journal of Legal Studies*, Vol. 11, p. 1.

PART I
THE INTERNATIONAL
MOVEMENT TOWARDS
TRANSPARENCY AND 'TRUTH
IN SENTENCING'

Chapter One

Getting Tough on Crime: the History and Political Context of Sentencing Reform Developments Leading to the Passage of the 1994 Crime Act

Judith Greene

Introduction

The concept of 'truth in sentencing' is embedded in the Violent Crime Control and Law Enforcement Act of 1994 through provisions for Violent Offender Incarceration and Truth-in-Sentencing incentive grants (under Title II, Subtitle A) that provide funds for expansion of state prison bed capacity. The roots of this concept may be traced back in time to two fairly distinct streams of American criminal justice reform which were born more than two decades ago.

As a key concept in the effort to improve US sentencing policies by providing clarity, consistency, and certainty in the duration of prison terms set by judges and served by offenders, the notion of 'truth in sentencing' can be said to have sprung from the determinate sentencing reforms begun in the early 1970s. As a punitive crime-control strategy, the foundation of 'truth in sentencing' was primarily built within the victims' rights movement which began to emerge across the nation during the same time period.

Sentencing and correctional patterns have greatly shifted since the 1960s. Legislative sentencing reforms enacted in many states in the 1970s brought new restrictions on parole release (abolishing parole outright in a few states) and set the stage for various mechanisms which were introduced over the next two decades to guide, limit, or prevent the free exercise of judicial discretion. Before these reforms, if a judge chose to reject the probation option in a particular case, he or she set a prison term (or minimum and maximum terms with a broad indeterminate range) within the durational maxima set in penal law. But the actual release of a prisoner was governed by an executive-branch parole board.

A liberalisation of laws and of attitudes toward punishment of offenders during the 1960s had led to a decline in the numbers of those imprisoned – reaching a low of 188,000 in 1969 – and this trend continued until 1973 (Gettinger 1976). But by the mid-1960s crime rates began to rise. UCR data on violent crimes reported to the police per 100,000 US inhabitants rose from 200.2 in 1965 to 363.5 in 1970; by 1975 the violent crime rate had reached 487.8 per 100,000 (BJS 1997). While crime policy experts debated about the causes of the rising crime rate, as well as about what needed to be done to address it, the general climate of social ferment in the 1960s led many Americans to a high level of anxiety about these trends.

The victims' rights movement was seeded in the fertile ground of a growing conviction among many conservative Americans that a long series of US Supreme Court decisions in the 1950s and 1960s which had safeguarded and expanded the rights of the accused was proof that the criminal justice system had become dominated by the defence bar, and by a handful of liberal interest groups.

At the same time, a new degree of 'rights consciousness' had risen in the wake of the civil rights movement and spawned a new effort to win social and economic equality for women. This mindset, when merged with concerns about crime, became a potent force. The women's movement moved briskly to challenge the treatment of rape victims by police and in the courts, as well as to combat the sex role stereotypes which too often resulted in 'blaming the victim' for the crime. In the beginning, victims' movement voices were 'frequently feminine and their tones were more of anger than of fear', according the Shirley Abrahamson, the Chief Justice of the Wisconsin Supreme Court, who had chronicled the rise of this reform effort (Abrahamson 1985, p. 524). This base of incensed feminists was augmented by advocates for the elderly, whose heightened sense of vulnerability and fear of street crime led many to near immobility. And, as Abrahamson pointed out, these constituencies formed a base for a 'rights' movement that could more fully engage middle-class Americans – as contrasted with poor minorities and their sympathisers.

The 1970s: from Rehabilitation to Crime Control

At the start of the 1970s prison population levels were low, penal philosophy was still dominated by the rehabilitationist regime, and sentencing policy was, accordingly, wed to indeterminacy. By 1971 most mandatory sentencing provisions then contained in federal law were repealed. The common criticisms which had been cast against these measures by social science researchers and practitioners alike focused on the lack of evidence of deterrent effect or of cost-effectiveness, and concerns about injustices too often resulting as they were applied in individual cases (Tonry 1996). The Attica prison riot in 1971 had thrown a harsh spotlight on the American prison system, and this led many to question basic assumptions about the fundamental purposes of incarceration, and the role of the prison in society.

In 1974 things began to shift rapidly within the crime control establishment. The FBI announced a spike in reported crime during the first quarter of that year, and then Attorney General William Saxbe began to speak out sharply against lenient judges, against the growing prison reform movement, and against the concept of rehabilitation (Serrill 1975). Robert Martinson, a sociologist at New York's City College, had completed his survey of data from hundreds of prisoner rehabilitation programmes operated over two decades and had written an article which appeared in the spring 1974 edition of the *Public Interest*, reporting that with few exceptions he found no post-programme effect on the recidivism of participants.

Martinson's pronouncements clearly fell on eager ears. His report was embraced by groups as disparate as the International Association of Chiefs of Police and the American Friends Service Committee (Serrill 1975, p. 3). Various constituencies then calling for sentencing reforms all tended to rely on his findings (quickly enshrined in the catch-phrase 'Nothing Works') and a confluence of their disparate interests set the concept of determinate sentencing in motion across the nation.

From the liberal side, many veterans of the civil rights movement (some of whom had become engaged in the push for prisoners' rights from both sides of the bars) were primarily concerned with racial and class disparity, and had already denounced the system of indeterminate sentencing and parole release as biased and oppressive (AFSC 1971). Many critics were dismayed by evidence of indefensible and severe disparity – and outright abuse of discretion. Concern for procedural fairness had already led a prominent federal judge to call for development of sentencing standards and appellate review of sentencing decisions (Frankel 1972). Others were primarily motivated by the belief that most criminals were in fact simply 'societal victims' of an inequitable distribution of wealth and opportunity, and did not deserve the severity of punishment meted out under the existing vague and arbitrary regime.

Harvard's conservative crime-control advocate, James Q. Wilson, counselled liberals to turn from their concerns about the "root causes of crime" – since rehabilitation did not "work" in any case. He urged that deterrence be tried instead. In *Thinking About Crime*, Wilson advocated definite terms of incarceration for *most* offenders (Wilson 1975).

David Fogel, a former corrections commissioner in Minnesota who was then heading up the Illinois Law Enforcement Commission, proposed simply eliminating parole boards – along with parole supervision – and making sentences "short, flat, and uniform". Like Wilson, Fogel called for a system of flat-time sentences, but insisted these be imposed only after a finding by a judge that a defendant presented a threat of "clear and present danger". Even then, a prison sentence would be mitigated by liberal good-time allowances (Fogel 1975).

While his proposal was vulnerable to criticism from those who rejected the notion that dangerousness could be predicted, or that judges should be entrusted to do this, or that the resulting sentencing decisions would be just or uniform – it appears that at least some aspects of Fogel's proposals were embraced in Maine. In June of 1975 the state became the first to abolish indeterminate sentences and parole release in favour of relatively short flat terms.

By the following year the reform pot was boiling over. Prison abolitionists on the left – Jessica Mitford, Jerry Miller, and groups like the National Council on Crime and Delinquency and the American Civil Liberties Union – were demanding a moratorium on new prison construction, and diversion of tens of thousands of offenders into community corrections programmes.

Arguing the lack of any coherent philosophical or moral justification for the existing system, Andrew von Hirsch published *Doing Justice*, laying out a rationale for a more principled system grounded in the theory which came to be known as 'Just Deserts'. He advocated dispensing with both indeterminate sentences and discretionary parole release, and replacing them with a presumptive sentencing structure that could shape and constrain judicial practice to ensure fair and proportional punishment based on the severity of offences and the culpability of offenders. Such a system would use fines and community-based sanctions for most offenders, reserving imprisonment only for those convicted of serious crimes, who therefore deserved the most severe punishment (von Hirsch 1976).

While these debates raged on, prison population levels jumped skyward, leading to severe levels of overcrowding in many prisons across the country (Gettinger 1976). A quarter of a million prisoners were held in state and federal institutions at the beginning of 1976, with every state but California reporting increases in 1975. High unemployment, soaring crime rates, and improved law enforcement methods spawned by increased federal funding through the LEAA were probably all contributing to the problem, but the cresting of the 'baby boom' into the high-crime age cohort (17–29) was held to be the primary cause by most experts – who anticipated that the prison population crisis would extend to 1985, when it would receive the predictable demographic relief.

But tougher attitudes toward the treatment of criminals were also being cited by some experts as exacerbating the problem. In Harvard criminologist Lloyd Ohlin's opinion, "What we're seeing is a massive counterattack [against community corrections programs]" (Gettinger 1976, p. 9). Many state parole boards were tightening their discretion, especially in Southern states which were also experiencing the most severe overcrowding. The overcrowding problem sparked a boom in prison construction which has continued to the present day – though many critics were already predicting that correctional systems were not likely to be able to build their way out of the problem.

It was this same year that the California legislature enacted a far-reaching determinate sentencing law. Repudiating the state's famed rehabilitationist penal philosophy by declaring that the purpose of prison was to punish offenders, legislators abolished parole release and replaced indeterminate ranges with a schedule of presumptive prison terms. Sentence enhancements were included for cases involving weapons or serious injuries, or where the offender had a prior record of violent crime.

Judges would remain free in most cases to suspend any prison sentence and impose probation. Those convicted of first degree murder and kidnapping for ransom cases would receive life sentences, but would still be subject to a parole system. For those sent to prison, a 'good-time' provision could cut up to four months off the sentence for each eight month period served.

The determinate sentence bill had won very broad support, from the California Peace Officers Association to the San Francisco-based Prisoners Union. Virtually no one defended the old indeterminate system. But at both ends of the political spectrum there were some who were opposed the bill because the they were not satisfied with the length of the scheduled prison terms: Los Angeles Police Chief Ed Davis declared them too short, while NCCD and the AFSC complained they were too long – especially for women offenders, who were spending less time in prison than men under the old system (Serrill 1976).

In the wake of California's turn to determinate sentencing many other state legislatures began work on reforms of their own. A primary attraction of determinate sentencing for many legislators was that to the extent that sentence lengths would be closely regulated, future correctional resource needs could be accurately predicted. And where the 'rules of the game' (presumptions, enhancements, and good-time discounts) could be understood by both prisoners and the public at large, all would then know 'the truth' about the sentences that were imposed and how much time would be served by prisoners.

It was around this time that experiments with voluntary sentencing 'guidelines' were first taken up in various jurisdictions (e.g. Denver, Newark, Chicago). These sentencing schemes were 'descriptive', designed by judicial initiative for the most part, to reflect their current sentencing practices. Voluntary guidelines were later embraced in many states – e.g. Maryland, Florida, Michigan, Utah, Delaware, and Wisconsin (Frase 1995) – but evaluations have since demonstrated that they had little effect on actual sentencing practices. This is not a surprising finding since – for example – the Wisconsin system was expressly designed so that the guidelines would be adjusted when necessary to match judicial shifts in sentencing practices (Greene 1996).

By the beginning of 1977 the US prison population reached 283,000. To cope, prison administrators had begun to use converted hospitals, trailers, warehouses, and tents to house the overflow of prisoners while new facilities were under construction. Deteriorating facility conditions fuelled by over-crowding were increasingly giving rise to lawsuits (Wilson 1977).

In California the year began with a drum beat sounded by conservatives for changes to the new sentencing law. Amending legislation had been expected before the law was to take effect to clear up some technical snarls – but the 'clean-up' bills soon became vehicles for law enforcement groups to press for tougher sentences, and sure enough, the 'base terms' were promptly raised (Gettinger 1979).

This brought one aspect of the policy debate about presumptive sentencing to the fore: the issue of who might best set these presumptions. California's experience showed that legislators might have great difficulty codifying presumptive prison terms which were shorter than the long sentences which were often loudly announced, though completely fictional, under the indeterminate system. Given the increasing degree of heat and light generated by criminal justice matters in the highly political legislative arena, the notion of an appointed (and at least partially insulated) sentencing commission emerged as the preferred option for states contemplating development of new sentencing systems.

Minnesota had begun its move toward sentencing reform with a determinate sentencing bill based on Fogel's 'justice model' which passed the legislature but was vetoed by the Governor in 1975. In 1977 a sentencing commission was proposed, and a bill establishing one passed in the House. Around the same time, the Minnesota parole board embraced the concept of guidelines and began experimental use of a draft set. Abolition of parole in a few states, along with the debates about it in others, spurred parole board members and staff to begin creating administrative rules for the discharge of their release function.

While determinate sentencing and sentencing guidelines were being hotly debated in some states, many states were simply passing mandatory sentence laws. And in Illinois a sentencing reform bill passed in 1978 contained elements of both. Governor James R. Thompson took hold of a Fogel-inspired bill then under consideration and gave it a very conservative spin by proposing a new 'Class X' for some felonies – e.g. armed violence, rape, and major narcotics offences. Class X offenders would receive much harsher prison terms, as would those with prior convictions. Probation was denied for Class X convicts, for whom the mandatory minimum sentence would be at least six years.

Mandatory sentencing policies had been largely discredited as the 1970s began, yet between 1975 and 1985 every state passed at least one mandatory sentencing law (Tonry 1996). Most of these provisions affected those convicted for serious violent crimes, drug and weapons offences, or offenders with prior felony records. New York state had passed stiff mandatory drug laws in 1973, along with the 'second felony offender law', which denied probation to all but first felony offenders – and if the first offence was a violent felony, a mandatory sentence was still required. The California legislature began to add mandatory minimums to its presumptive sentencing scheme as soon as they set it in place.

The relentless push for mandatory sentences which began in the late 1970s was evidence that the victims' movement was coming into its own. In 1975 a Victims Committee was created within the American Bar Association's Criminal Justice Section. That same year Frank Carrington, then the executive director of Americans for Effective Law Enforcement, published *The Victims*, a book which decried the treatment of crime victims in American jurisprudence. AELE had been founded in 1966 by Northwestern University law professors Fred E. Inbau and James R. Thompson (later the Governor of Illinois, and sponsor of the 'Class X' legislation), along with former Illinois Governor Richard B. Ogilvie, and O.W. Wilson – then Superintendent of Police in Chicago.

According to Carrington, the AELE was formed to support law enforcement, and to provide an effective counter-voice to the American Civil Liberties Union on behalf of the law-abiding citizen. It carried this effort forward by filing *amicus* briefs to defend the legal authority of the police in cases before the US Supreme Court, as well as by serving as a clearinghouse for lawyers and police departments involved in defending police officers in civil suits filed against them. Under Carrington's leadership the AELE was taking up legal representation for victims of crime (Carrington 1975).

In *The Victims*, Carrington outlined his thesis that the 'permissive' Warren Court and the prisoners' rights movement had weakened law enforcement and *caused* the increase in crime begun in the 1960s. He called for a new "victim consciousness" which would reorient the criminal justice system toward the rights of crime victims. A victim-oriented approach would eschew leniency and provide for mandatory minimum fixed prison sentences in all but minor offences (Carrington 1975).

The leadership ranks in the many grassroots victims' rights advocacy groups which sprang up during this period were filled by crime victim/ survivors, and by the bereaved relatives of deceased crime victims such as Robert and Charlotte Hullinger of Parents of Murdered Children, and Candy Lightner of Mothers Against Drunk Driving, who found a measure of relief from their personal grief through activism.

By 1979 prison growth had slowed somewhat, but the litigation efforts spurred by overcrowding had brought 17 states under some form of court order to find relief. Many prisoners remained backed-up in local jails after conviction, held there waiting for space to open up for them in state facilities. Some parole boards had begun to move prisoners out of confinement more briskly; pre-release arrangements had already moved many of these back to their communities ahead of their actual parole dates.

The 1980s: Politicisation of Sentencing Policy and the Maturing of the Victims' Rights Movement

While crime control had clearly emerged as a political issue during the 1970s, during the 1980s the national political discourse focused increasingly on a perceived need to 'get tough' on crime. Between April 1979 and April 1980, 18 states passed mandatory minimum sentencing laws – principally for repeat offenders, or for offences involving guns (Krajick 1981).

Prison populations soared again in the 1980s, causing an even more severe crisis of overcrowding by the end of the decade. Many correctional systems were forced to increase 'back-end' overcrowding relief measures. Population caps and emergency release provisions become common, some mandated by federal court action; some enacted by state legislatures. In some states these produced dramatic reductions in the proportion of time actually served of the sentence terms imposed by judges.

By 1981, in order to ease overcrowding in their prisons, state legislators in Michigan and Iowa had authorised reductions in previously imposed state prison sentences when overcrowding reached 'emergency' proportions. Early releases would be triggered whenever a predetermined prison population capacity level was exceeded for a predetermined period of time. Michigan's law contained a 90-day roll-back provision which would serve to make hundreds of prisoners parole-eligible sooner. Michigan-style emergency release mechanisms were highly controversial, but they would be replicated in many states and would come to play a major role in spurring calls for 'truth in sentencing' because they served to further broaden the gap between the length of the prison terms imposed by judges and the actual time served in prison by offenders.

By 1982 crime rates were falling but the nation's prison population growth rate was reaching astonishing proportions. The FBI index crime rate had began to decline in the early 1980s. This trend continued until 1984, when it had fallen to 5,031.3 per 100,000 Americans – from the historic high in 1980 of 5,950 (BJS Sourcebook 1997). But the increase in prisoners in 1982 had set a new record which was, "Fantastic, enormous, terrifying", according to Norval Morris (Gettinger 1983, p. 6).

Several states were showing increases in the number of offenders incarcerated for drunk driving – much of which was probably spurred by the efforts of MADD and other victims' rights advocacy groups. Parole rates were declining in some states, though in others parole release was seen an important tool for population control. Longer sentences were certainly a factor, and average time served had gone up in many states. The state of Michigan stood in sharp relief against this trend. The "emergency relief law" created by the legislature the previous year had been triggered, and the state's prison population fell by 2.8 per cent (Gettinger 1983, p. 8). California passed a new "incentive good time" law which allowed prisoners who took up a work assignment or enrolled in a school programme to cut their determinate sentences by half. Illinois discovered "meritorious good time". More states legislated population caps, while newspapers in Iowa began to publish a "countdown" of the days before that state's emergency law might force a release of prisoners to the streets (Gettinger 1983, p. 11).

The experience throughout the 1980s with sentencing guidelines was mixed. Minnesota's guidelines commission completed its drafting work and the country's first set of sentencing guidelines took effect in May of 1980. The Minnesota guidelines were carefully crafted to reflect the level of correctional resources the state already had at its disposal. A prison population impact model was used by the drafters to assure that the overall population level would remain stable. Under the 'Just Deserts' philosophy chosen by the commission, serious violent offenders would serve the longest prison terms, while most property offenders who were imprisoned under the indeterminate system would now receive probation, and be retained within the state's community corrections system. By the end of 1980 the state had experienced a seven per cent drop in its prison population – both due to the effect of the new guidelines, and because the parole board had adopted these same standards for its release decisions in pre-guidelines cases.

The sentencing guidelines idea spread during the 1980s through developments in several states, and by its introduction, through federal legislation in 1984, into the federal court system. Pennsylvania adopted guidelines in 1982 which differed in several ways from those in Minnesota. The legislature did not intend them to take tight control of prison population levels. The presumptive sentence ranges in Pennsylvania's guidelines were relatively broad, and parole release was retained with the guidelines governing the setting of a *minimum* sentence. Washington state's guidelines, introduced in 1984, were more tuned to capacity issues than Pennsylvania's, and also introduced upper limits on probation-revocation sanctions.

The federal sentencing guidelines were another matter. Termed by University of Minnesota Law Professor Michael Tonry as "the most controversial and disliked sentencing reform initiative in US history", the sentencing structure introduced in 1987 was far more complex, and technically cumbersome, than any created at the state level (Tonry 1996, p. 72). The federal commission had constructed 43 levels of crime seriousness, compared to ten in Minnesota.

The federal guidelines embodied a harsh sentencing philosophy that sought to substantially extend the use of imprisonment (von Hirsch and Greene 1993). This represented a radical departure from the sentencing patterns of federal judges before the reform. The federal guidelines were met with stiff resistance by many judges, who twisted and turned to find ways to avoid compliance.

The widely publicised 'crack crisis' in the mid-1980s produced another proliferation of mandatory minimum sentencing laws, despite continued scepticism among most social science researchers. Florida enacted seven new mandatory sentencing laws between 1988 and 1990 (Austin 1991). Arrests and prosecutions for drug offences shot up during this period. From 1986 to

1991 the number of adults sentenced to prison for drug offences more than tripled (BJS 1992).

In the 1980s the effort to win victims' rights obtained a powerful boost when – in California – it was married to a vigorously conservative social movement which had seized upon the initiative process to reform broad portions of the state's constitutional and statutory laws. The passage of Proposition 13 to revamp the state's property-tax structure in 1978 had demonstrated how an explosive political movement could be built around an emotionally potent issue, and – given both money and savvy political organising skills – could push its interests right past reluctant legislators.

Throughout the 1970s a broad national political support base of politicians and criminal justice professionals had been built to advocate for victims' rights. This network of organisations and individuals was spearheaded by California's pro-prosecution politicians and activists: Ronald Reagan, George Deukmejian, Pete Wilson, Edwin Meese III, S.I. Hayakawa, Lois Haight Harrington, and H.L. Richardson. By the early 1980s, this group had enlisted Paul Gann, the sponsor (with Howard Jarvis) of the successful 'Prop 13' tax-reform campaign. In 1981 Gann warned California legislators that if several pending victims' rights bills were not passed, their objectives would be achieved directly through the ballot box. In August of that year the Citizen's Committee to Stop Crime, chaired by Gann, kicked off its initiative campaign for Proposition 8 (Kelso and Bass 1992, p. 863).

Termed a 'Victim's Bill of Rights', Proposition 8 was passed by California voters in June 1982 with a vote of 54 per cent to 46 per cent (Corrections Magazine 1982). This measure provided curbs on plea-bargaining, it set tougher bail procedures; and it increased sentencing enhancements for prior felony convictions.

Recruited by Edwin L. Meese to chair a campaign issues committee on victims, Frank Carrington had become a prominent advisor to the Reagan campaign on criminal justice issues.

In 1983 the Heritage Foundation published a book-length 'Critical Issues' policy paper, *Crime and Justice: A Conservative Strategy*. The author was Frank Carrington, who was then serving as executive director of the Virginia-based Victims' Assistance Legal Organisation (VALOR), and as chair of the Victims' Committee of the American Bar Association.

The Heritage Foundation had been founded in 1973 by Paul Weyrich of the Free Congress Foundation with seed money from brewery owner Joseph Coors (PFAW 1996). In 1981 Heritage published *Mandate for Leadership*, a policy guidebook intended to serve as a blueprint for the new Reagan administration. Since that time it has maintained a position as the leading conservative think tank in America. The current list of resident scholars at Heritage includes many former Reagan/Bush officials, including two with impeccably conservative credentials on criminal justice issues: former Attorney General Edwin Meese, and former Education Secretary and 'Drug Tsar' William Bennett. Heritage 'Issues Briefs' and 'State Backgrounder' papers on criminal justice matters have continued to be highly influential in shaping federal crime-control legislation.

In his introduction to the 1983 Heritage publication, *Crime and Justice,* Carrington complained that "conservatives seem to cede the issue of crime to the left – to the American Civil Liberties Union, the National Lawyers Guild, and various other organisations whose stated purposes are to neutralize law enforcement and legitimate intelligence gathering" (Carrington 1983, p. xii). Pointing to indications in opinion polls that the fear of crime had risen to the top of the public's list of domestic concerns, he argued that liberal philosophy about crime and justice lacked any real base of popular support.

The conservative agenda for criminal justice reform proposed by Carrington for the Heritage Foundation covered a familiar broad list of substantive issues including bail reform; the exclusionary rule; *habeas corpus*; capital punishment; the insanity defence; and prisoners' rights. His Heritage issues paper called for increasing sentences for drug trafficking, for lowering the age limit for charging juveniles as adults, and for increasing penalties for juveniles convicted of violent crimes.

In 1984, Morgan O. Reynolds – currently teaching economics at Texas A & M University and serving as director of the criminal justice department at the National Center for Policy Analysis, a public policy think tank located in Texas which pushes for privatisation of the criminal justice system, from prosecution to prisons – authored an article on criminal justice policy which would later reappear in a book circulated to members of Congress during the 1994 crime bill debates. 'How to Reduce Crime' was first published in *The Freeman*, a magazine published by the Foundation for Economic Education in Irvington-on-Hudson, New York. The FEE had been founded in 1946 by Leonard Read to publish books and tracts on libertarian philosophy and economics then associated with the Austrian economic theorists Friedrich A. von Hayek and Ludwig von Mises (Diamond 1995, p. 27).

In his *Freeman* article Reynolds argued that the problem of crime was rooted in "socialistic" welfare-state policies, and that its solution would elude policy-makers until they turned away from collectivism and "centralised coercion", and moved toward economic and social policies determined by the dynamics of the free market (Reynolds 1996, p. 202).

By the 1988 presidential campaign sentencing and correctional policies had become hair-trigger political issues. The Republican candidate George Bush campaigned hard on an anti-crime, pro-victim platform. Early in the campaign orchestrated by Lee Atwater and Roger Ailes, an article which was published in the *Reader's Digest* helped to spark a fire-storm which would grow to consume the Democratic candidate, Michael Dukakis. (Anderson 1995). The article, 'Getting Away With Murder', was written by a freelance writer, Robert James Bidinotto (1988) (now a staff writer at the *Reader's Digest*) who had been publishing articles in *The Freeman* since 1968. Bidinotto's article detailed the now-famous 'Willie Horton' story of violent crimes committed while Horton was AWOL from a Massachusetts prison furlough leave. The publicity surrounding the Willie Horton anecdote and its inclusion in a controversial TV ad campaign proved to be critical in moving the Bush campaign to victory in November (Carrington 1989, FN 24).

The Early 1990s: Structured Sentencing, Ballot Initiatives and the Crime Bill

Despite the problems associated with the federal system of sentencing guidelines, the basic guidelines concept continued to gain ground at the state level during the 1990s. Many state-level sentencing commissions have expressly repudiated the federal model and moved ahead with their own reforms (Tonry 1996, p. 73). In North Carolina the sentencing commission at work in the early 1990s rejected the term 'guidelines' choosing instead, 'structured sentencing' to describe their system. The basic grid structure they chose – with nine offence categories – indicates that they were relying for inspiration on the more successful experience with guidelines in Minnesota, rather than on the federal guidelines structure.

North Carolina commission staff worked with a statistical impact model to carefully design a system of sentence presumptions which would produce prison population levels to fit within the number of prison beds the state legislature was able to finance. The legislature funded a new state/local partnership grant programme to complement the guidelines provision that lower-level nonviolent property and drug offenders would be sentenced to community sanctions and treatment, and they provided funding to beef-up probation services for these offenders.

Introduction of the new sentencing structure in North Carolina had replaced most of the state's rigid mandatory minimums with presumptive sentences which would emphasise the crime-control advantages which can be won by placing drug offenders in treatment programmes – a strategy with benefits now solidly documented by researchers from the RAND Corporation (Caulkins et al. 1997).

But with few exceptions, the 'Drug War' sentencing policies of the 1980s continued unabated into the 1990s. As mandatory minimum drug laws settled into place across the nation their impact on prison populations was great. Imprisonment of drug offenders increased by 510 per cent over the decade from 1983–93. In the 1990s critics of the 'War on Drugs' increasingly pointed to apparent racial disparities. African American women had especially felt the brunt of mandatory drug laws. From 1986 to 1991 their numbers imprisoned for drug crimes increased 828 per cent – double the increase among African American men and triple the increase among white females (Mauer and Huling 1995).

Near the end of the Bush administration Attorney General William Barr waged a strong campaign for further toughening America's penal policies. In March 1992 he convened a large meeting of state-level criminal justice officials in Washington, DC. He told them that most states had fallen behind federal efforts to fight crime during the 1980s, and he urged them to step up their efforts to reduce violent crime by identifying and incarcerating chronic and violent offenders.

In his 1992 presidential campaign Bill Clinton proved to have well-learned the lessons of the 1988 Dukakis campaign. He consistently 'talked tough' on crime issues, and prominently displayed his role (as Governor of Arkansas) as a vigorous, highly visible enforcer of the death penalty.

At the start of the Clinton administration in 1993 (and in the face of Clinton's strong expressions of support for gun control) the National Rifle Association announced it would launch a national campaign to get tough on criminals (Balz 1993). This was seen by many as a ploy to divert support away from Democratic gun control initiatives. NRA CrimeStrike – a division of the National Rifle Association which had been founded in 1991 to 'focus on the failures of America's criminal justice system' was then headed by Steve Twist, a close associate of Bob Corbin, the former Arizona Attorney General who had served as President of the NRA.

According to its internet advertisements, NRA CrimeStrike has worked to pass 'truth in sentencing' laws in Arizona, Mississippi, and Virginia; and 'Three Strikes and You're Out' laws in Washington, California, Delaware,

Georgia, North Carolina, Vermont, and Pennsylvania. The group has also worked to pass legislation requiring that violent juvenile offenders 'serve adult time' in eight states, and pushed for 'Victims' Bill of Rights' proposals in 13 states (NRA 1996).

Backed by NRA CrimeStrike, the nation's first 'Three Strikes and You're Out' law was enacted by ballot initiative in Washington state in 1993, sending a shock-wave reverberating through legislatures in 21 states and the US Congress over the next two years. Simply put, 'Three Strikes and You're Out' laws require mandatory life imprisonment on a third felony conviction. But 'Three Strikes' has meant different things in different states. Understanding the political value of show-casing support for the concept (while at the same time restraining its potential for stoking up the prison population) many legislators carved their bill language to minimise eligibility for a Three Strikes sentence to a very small pool of violent offenders – while preserving their right to say they had voted for it.

In California, however, the Three Strikes language was very broad – with any of 500 felonies counting as a possible third strike to trigger a 25-to-life sentence – plus it included a doubling of the prison term for a second strike. This has resulted in a very large eligibility pool of offenders subject to its stringency, and thousands sentenced under it scope. The RAND Corporation conducted a study of California's Three Strikes law in 1994 and estimated the long term costs to be huge – many times over the original state estimates – doubling the corrections share of the state budget over eight years and stripping resources from other vital state services like education (Greenwood, et al. 1994). Finally, in 1996, the California Supreme Court hobbled the law by finding it to be an unconstitutional limit on judicial discretion.

A Heritage Foundation 'State Backgrounder' paper issued in June 1993 entitled, 'How States Can Fight Violent Crime: Two Dozen Steps to a Safer America'. The Backgrounder was authored by Mary Kate Cary (1993), a former Deputy Director of the Office of Policy and Communications at the US Department of Justice, and speech writer for President George Bush – who has since served as Deputy Director of Communications for the Republican National Committee and Political Editor of its magazine, *Rising Tide*. Cary charged that the Clinton Administration was "backing away from tougher law enforcement".

Charging that violent offenders were serving only 37 per cent of their imposed prison terms, Cary called for 'truth in sentencing' with sharp restrictions limiting parole or 'good time' release to the federal guidelines standard requiring 85 per cent of the sentence to be served. She advocated mandatory minimum sentences for gun offenders, armed career criminals, and repeat violent offenders. Cary urged the states to invest in building and operating more prisons or risk collapse of the criminal justice system: "The choice is clear: More prisons or more crime".

In December 1993 another Heritage 'State Backgrounder' was published addressing crime-control issues. 'Truth in Sentencing: Why States Should Make Violent Criminals Do Their Time', was written by James Wootton, founder and president of the Safe Streets Alliance, and author of the 'truth in sentencing' provision – the 'Chapman amendment' contained in the 1994 federal crime bill (Bidinotto 1996, p. xiii). During the Reagan administration Wootton had served as the Deputy Administrator of the Office of Juvenile Justice and Delinquency Prevention. In 'Truth in Sentencing', Wootton cited the murders of Polly Klaas and James Jordan (father of basketball star Michael Jordan) and blamed "lenient early-release" practices for causing 'a fearful epidemic of violent crime' (Wootton 1993, p. 3). He supported curbs on release of prisoners before they served 85 per cent of their sentences. He referred to studies by Edward Zedlewski and others to make the argument that incarceration saves money by preventing crimes, and he credited California's massive prison building programme during the 1980s with slashing the state's crime rate.

Wootton argued that 'truth in sentencing' would deter crime, citing crime reduction estimates by Morgan O. Reynolds, and quoting Reynold's claim that 'When punishments rise, crime falls' (Reynolds 1990). Brushing aside objections that had been raised by critics of 'truth in sentencing', Wootton urged state legislators and governors to provide the financial resources that would be required to implement it.

At the beginning of 1994 another national organisation (one bearing as its primary objective to influence *state-level* policies) weighed into the crime control debates with the heavy clout of William Barr. Like Heritage, the American Legislative Exchange Council was founded in 1973 by – among others – Paul Weyrich (PFAW 1996). Its mission is to educate state-level office holders about free markets, free enterprise, limited government, and individual liberty. By 1993 ALEC had come to serve as a clearinghouse of information for 2,500 conservative 'pro-free enterprise' state legislators, providing them with a steady stream of policy recommendations and bringing them together with private sector executives of major corporations for conferences and seminars.

ALEC strives to educate its members on the issues while promoting its agenda through model legislation. The organisation maintains a standing task force on criminal justice. Its '10 Point Agenda to Fight Crime' includes recommendations for ending pretrial 'own-recognisance' release (ROR); for mandatory minimum sentences for serious offences (including 'Three Strikes, You're Out'); imposing the 85 per cent 'truth in sentencing' rule for all prison sentences imposed by state court judges; treating juveniles as adults for serious criminal conduct; and using "all available strategies, such as prison privatization, electronic home detention, boot camps for juveniles, and video remote arraignment, to maximize resources".

In late January 1994, a group of state-level law enforcement and corrections officials spoke out against 'Three Strikes and You're Out' and other mandatory sentencing provisions then contained in the pending federal crime bills which they believed would adversely affect state prison population levels. The group included Joseph D. Lehman (currently the Secretary of Corrections in Washington state) who was then serving as Pennsylvania's Corrections Commissioner (Eaton, *Los Angeles Times*, 25 January 1994). Within days, in a press conference led by William Barr, ALEC released preliminary data on crime in Pennsylvania from a national 'Report Card on Crime and Punishment' (then in preparation) and urged that the state adopt 'Three Strikes' and other mandatory prison sentencing provisions, along with a 'truth in sentencing' requirement that prisoners serve 85 per cent of their terms (ALEC, 28 January 1994; Bell, *Patriot News*, 2 February 1994). The '10-Point Agenda' appeared again later that year when ALEC published the full Report Card document with a foreword by William Barr.

In the Spring of 1994 as the House of Representatives prepared to debate the crime bill, NRA CrimeStrike targeted Representative Charles E. Schumer, chair of the House subcommittee on crime, a chief sponsor of the bill as well as of several gun control measures. On 12 April the group ran a full-page ad in *USA Today* which labelled him 'The Criminal's Best Friend in Congress'. The ad denounced Schumer for seeking to divert money from prison construction to crime prevention programmes. A spokesman for the NRA said that money for more prisons would reduce crime, and keep pressure off gun owners. "If we lock up the criminals, maybe there'll be less pressure on abandoning the Second Amendment" (Seelye, *The New York Times*, 13 April 1994).

In May 1994 Paul McNulty authored another Heritage Foundation paper, 'Rhetoric vs. Reality: A Closer Look at the Congressional Crime Bill', which signalled the position Heritage and other conservative organisations would take on the Clinton administration's crime bill as it moved toward final passage in August. Detailing major differences between the Senate version of the crime bill (s. 1488 and s. 1607) and the then-recently-passed House version (HR 4092), McNulty warned that the actual content of the anti-crime measures proposed in Congress at that time had diverged from the members' tough rhetoric (McNulty 1994).

Citing a report released the month before by Morgan O. Reynold's group, the National Center for Policy Analysis, McNulty argued that because 98 per cent of all convictions for violent crime were handled at the state court level, the death penalty provisions (which pertained only to federal crimes) would not be utilised. He sharply criticised the 'Racial Justice Act', a provision to protect against racial bias in administration of the death penalty which had strong support from the Congressional Black Caucus. This measure had been incorporated in HR 4092, but was later dropped by the conference committee. McNulty also denounced the House Bill's provision for $8 million in funding for prevention programmes. "Removing violent criminals from the streets is crime prevention, as relevant statistics prove" (McNulty 1994).

McNulty called for restraining federal judges from putting "violent criminals back on the streets" by curbing their power to impose prison and jail population caps. He praised "the one truly useful proposal" – billions of new dollars for new state prisons. He urged making this money available as an incentive for state sentencing reforms to make the bill's 'truth in sentencing' provisions real. "States must stop revolving door justice by increasing the amount of time served by violent criminals from the current 38 per cent to something closer to 100 percent" (McNulty 1994).

During the debates on the 1994 federal crime bill, NRA CrimeStrike circulated a set of charts, tables, and advocacy points to lawmakers which the staff entitled 'The Case for Building More Prisons'. According to the cover sheet, the packet of materials had been prepared for a group of gun lobbyists calling themselves the 'Criminals Cause Crime Coalition' in consultation with Michael K. Block, a former member the United States Sentencing Commission who teaches economics at the University of Arizona, and who had been active – with Steve Twist – in pushing for 'truth in sentencing' in the Arizona sentencing reform legislation passed in 1993. The thrust of the arguments contained in the packet was that the Congress should provide grants to states to finance building of 250,000 new prison beds by the year 2000 for incarceration of serious violent and repeat offenders (NRAa).

Although some of the features of NRA CrimeStrike's 1993 'get-tough' criminal justice reform agenda were ultimately included in the 1994 federal crime bill, (and CrimeStrike publications claim credit for "nearly tripling" the funds allocated for state prison construction in the bill), ultimately the

NRA ended up bitterly opposed because the bill also contained a 10-year ban on 19 assault weapons (Seelye, *The New York Times*, 4 August 1994).

In 1994 another publication was distributed widely on the hill. Robert J. Bidinotto (the staff writer for the *Reader's Digest* whose 1988 article had helped to make Willie Horton the poster-boy for the Bush presidential campaign) published the first edition of *Criminal Justice? The Legal System Versus Individual Responsibility*. Bidinotto's book contained reprints of previously published essays of his own from *The Freeman*, and pulled together in a single volume reprints of articles and essays by John DiIulio, Morgan O. Reynolds, James Wootton, and Mary Kate Cary which supported the concept of 'truth in sentencing' and called for longer terms of imprisonment for violent offenders. The book also contained a reprint of a 1992 Department of Justice Office of Policy Development paper, 'The Case for More Incarceration'. Though in 1994 Bidinotto's book was available only through mail-order from its publisher (the Foundation for Economic Education), it was bought and circulated by law enforcement and crime victims' groups, and, according to its author, was distributed to every member of the US House of Representatives, and to "key senators" (Bidinotto 1996, p. xix).

During the 1994 congressional debates the National Center for Policy Analysis issued a set of policy briefs opposing various aspects of the bills facing consideration by the conference committee. NCPA analysts argued that the measures were a mere pretence of 'getting tough', and that the federal death penalty and 'Three Strikes and You're Out' provisions were largely symbolic because the vast bulk of violent offenders were sentenced by state-court judges. NCPA analysts charged that the crime bill would create more federal crimes (e.g. gun violations) without adding capacity to prosecute them; and that it would "fund more social workers than police officers" (NCPA, August 1994).

In June of 1994, with the crime bill still pending in conference committee, the Heritage Foundation released an 'Issues Bulletin' authored by William J. Bennett. In this paper, entitled 'It's Time to Throw the Switch on the Federal Crime Bill', Bennett applauded the bill's 'truth in sentencing' provisions but he went on to complain that the bill was packed with "sixties-style social programs" for crime prevention and too many features which would federalise violent street crime and hamper state and local authorities with intrusive federal rules and regulations. He proposed, instead, a simple income-tax rebate plan to finance more prison capacity (Bennett 1994).

By August the crime bill had become stalled between NRA opposition to its assault weapons ban and Black Caucus members' anger over removal of the Racial Justice Act (the measure to prohibit imposition of the death penalty in a racially discriminatory manner). A majority of Republicans opposed the crime bill because of its funding for prevention programmes (Phillips and Benedetto, *USA Today*, 8 August 1994). Ultimately $3.3 billion was trimmed from the bill and it finally won approval in late August. Yet even after its passage, Republican leaders continued to decry the "wasteful spending" it contained.

For many years a powerful, highly-organised network of rightward leaning policy groups (Heritage, ALEC, NCPA, and the NRA) had worked to promote a broad programme of deeply conservative criminal justice reforms. Yet they pulled back from supporting their own most politically potent ideas – 'truth in sentencing', 'Three Strikes', and financial incentives to spur yet another large round of large-scale increases in prison capacity – once the Clinton administration got on board and had managed to yoke these notions to more traditionally liberal measures like gun control and crime prevention programmes. Nonetheless, in the end, many of their key policy positions had come to be soundly embraced by the Democratic leadership in Congress, and much of their slogan-driven crime-control programme had prevailed, once again, over the substantive criticisms and more rational reforms offered by the nation's most knowledgeable sentencing and corrections policy experts.

References

Abrahamson, S.S. (1985), 'Redefining Roles: The Victims' Rights Movement', *Utah Law Review*, 3, pp. 517–67.
American Friends Service Committee (1971), *Struggle for Justice*, New York: Hill and Wang.
American Legislative Exchange Council (1974), 'Every Ten Minutes a Pennsylvanian Falls Victim to a Violent Crime', *ALEC News Release*, Washington, DC: ALEC, 28 January.
American Legislative Exchange Council (1994), 'Report Card on Crime and Punishment: ALEC's 10 Point Agenda to Fight Crime', Washington, DC: ALEC.
Anderson, D.C. (1995), *Crime and the Politics of Hysteria: How the Willie Horton story changed American justice*, New York: Random House.
Anderson, J. (1991), *The Consequences of Escalating the Use of Imprisonment: The case study of Florida*, San Francisco: National Council on Crime and Delinquency.
Balz, D. (1993), 'Gun Control Foes Targeting Criminals', *The Washington Post*, Section A, p. 11, 5 November.
Bell, A. (1994), 'Lock 'em Up, Group Says In Its Preliminary Report', *Patriot-News*, 2 February.
Bennett, W.J. (1994), 'It's Time To Throw The Switch On The Federal Crime Bill', *Issues Bulletin*, No. 164, Washington, DC: The Heritage Foundation.
Bidinotto, R. J. (1988), 'Getting Away with Murder', *Reader's Digest*, July.

Bidinotto, R.J. (1996), *Criminal Justice? The Legal System Versus Individual Responsibility*, Irvington-on-Hudson, NY: The Foundation for Economic Education.

Bureau of Justice Statistics (1992), *Drugs, Crime, and the Justice System: A national report*, Washington, DC: US Government Printing Office.

Bureau of Justice Statistics (1997), *Sourcebook of Criminal Justice Statistics 1996*, Washington, DC: US Government Printing Office.

Carrington, F. (1975), *The Victims*, New Rochelle, NY: Arlington House.

Carrington, F. (1983), *Crime and Justice: A conservative strategy*, Washington, DC: The Heritage Foundation.

Carrington, F. and Nicholson, G. (1989), 'Victims' Rights: An idea whose time has come – five years later: The maturing of an idea', *Pepperdine Law Review*, 17:1: pp. 1–19.

Cary, M.K. (1993), 'How States Can Fight Violent Crime: Two dozen steps to a safer America', *State Backgrounder Series*, Washington, DC: The Heritage Foundation.

Caulkins, J.P., Peter Rydell, C., Schwabe, W.L. and Chiesa, J. (1997), *Mandatory Minimum Drug Sentences: Throwing away the key or the taxpayer's money?*, Santa Monica: RAND.

Corrections Magazine (1982), 'Californians Vote for Get Tough Measures', *Corrections Magazine*, 8(4): p. 4.

Diamond, S. (1995), *Roads to Dominion: Right-wing movements and political power in the United States*, New York: The Guilford Press.

Eaton, W.J. (1994), 'Despite Support, Critics of Crime Bill Abound', *The Los Angeles Times*, 25 January.

Fogel, D. (1975), *We Are The Living Proof: The justice model for corrections*, Cincinnati, OH: W.H. Anderson Publishing Company.

Frankel, M. (1972), *Criminal Sentences: Law without order*, New York: Hill and Wang.

Frase, R. (1995), 'Sentencing Guidelines in Minnesota and Other American States: A progress report', in C.M.V. Clarkson and R. Morgan (eds), *The Politics of Sentencing Reform*, Oxford: Clarendon Press.

Gettinger, S. (1976), 'U.S. Prisons Population Hits All-time High', *Corrections Magazine*, 2(3), pp. 9–20.

Gettinger, S. (1979), 'Tinkering with Determinate Sentencing', *Corrections Magazine*, 5(3), pp. 54–5.

Gettinger, S. (1983), 'The Prison Population Boom: Still no end in sight', *Corrections Magazine*, 9(3): pp. 6–11, 47–9.

Greene, J. (1996), 'Wisconsin Guidelines Killed, Oregon's Weakened', *Overcrowded Times*, 7(1), 1, pp. 14–20.

Greenwood, P., Rydell, C.P., Abrahamse, A.F., Caulkins, J.P., Chiesa, J., Model, K.E. and Klein, S.P. (1994), *Three Strikes and You're Out: Estimated benefits and costs of California's new mandatory-sentencing law*, Santa Monica, CA: RAND.

Kelso, C. and Bass, B.A. (1994), 'The Victims' Bill of Rights: Where did it come from and how much did it do?', *Pacific Law Journal*, 23, pp. 843–79.

Krajick, K. (1981), 'Annual Prison Population Survey: The Boom Resumes', *Corrections Magazine,* 7(2), pp. 16–20.

Mauer, M. and Huling, T. (1995), *Young Black Americans and the Criminal Justice System: Five Years Later*, Washington, DC: The Sentencing Project.

McNulty, P.J. (1993), 'What's Wrong with the Brooks and Biden Crime Bills', *Issues Bulletin*, No. 184, Washington, DC: The Heritage Foundation.

McNulty, P.J. (1994), 'Rhetoric vs. Reality: A closer look at the Congressional Crime Bill', *Issues Bulletin*, No. 189, Washington, DC: The Heritage Foundation.

National Center for Policy Analysis (1994), 'The Crime Bill: Much ado about nothing', *NCPA Brief Analysis*, No. 106, Dallas, TX: NCPA, April.

National Center for Policy Analysis (1994), 'The Crime Bill That Deserves to Stay Dead', *NCPA Brief Analysis*, No. 12, Dallas, TX: NCPA, 15 August.

NRA CrimeStrike (1996), 'Correcting the Failures of America's Criminal Justice System', Fairfax, VA: National Rifle Association Institute for Legislative Action.

NRA CrimeStrike (n.d.), 'The Case for Building More Prisons', Fairfax, VA: National Rifle Association (cited in text as NRAa).

People For the American Way (1996), 'Buying a Movement: Right-wing foundations and American politics', Washington, DC: PFAW.

Phillips, L. and Benedetto, R. (1994), 'Clinton, Police Press Crime Plan', *USA Today*, 9 August.

Reynolds, M.O. (1990), 'Why does Crime Pay?', *NCPA Backgrounder*, No. 110. Dallas, TX: National Center for Policy Analysis.

Reynolds, M.O. (1996), 'How to Reduce Crime', in R.J. Bidinotto (ed.), *Criminal Justice? The Legal System Versus Individual Responsibility*, Irvington-on-Hudson, NY: The Foundation for Economic Education.

Seelye, K.Q. (1994), 'Gun Organization Is Aiming for New Prisons, But Some Say Foes in Congress Are the Target', *The New York Times*, 13 April.

Seelye, K.Q. (1994), 'Unusual Alliance in House Unites to Stall the Crime Bill', *The New York Times*, 4 August

Serrill, M.S. (1975), 'Is Rehabilitation Dead?', *Corrections Magazine*, 1(5), pp. 3–12: 21–32.

Serrill, M.S. (1976), 'California Turns to Fixed Sentences', *Corrections Magazine*, 2(6), pp. 55–6.

Tonry, M. (1996), *Sentencing Matters*, New York: Oxford University Press.

Von Hirsch, A. (1976), *Doing Justice*, New York: Hill and Wang.

Von Hirsch, A. and Greene, J. (1993), 'When Should Sentencing Reformers Support Creation of Sentencing Guidelines?', *Wake Forest Law Review*, 28(2), pp. 329–43.

Wilson, J.Q. (1975), *Thinking About Crime*, New York: Basic Books.

Wilson, R. (1977), 'U.S. Prison Population Sets Another Record', *Corrections Magazine*, 3(1), pp. 3–8: 12–22.

Wootton, J. (1993), 'Truth in Sentencing: Why states should make violent criminals do their time', *State Backgrounder Series*, Washington, DC: The Heritage Foundation.

Chapter Two

A Sentencing Matrix for Western Australia: Accountability and Transparency or Smoke and Mirrors?

Neil Morgan

Introduction

In recent years, Australia has witnessed vigorous media, political and professional debate about sentencing. The central themes are familiar through much of the world: perceived leniency and inconsistency on the part of judges; questions of judicial accountability; an alleged lack of transparency in the system; and criticism of an apparent lack of responsiveness to public concern. In response to these concerns, the Western Australian parliament has enacted legislation which paves the way for far tighter control of judicial discretion and the development of a 'sentencing matrix'. This is the first time that a grid-style approach to sentencing has been a real possibility outside the United States and, as such, is of international as well as national significance. The first part of this paper outlines the factors behind the proposal and the process by which it has been developed. The second part discusses the model itself and the third section analyses the model in terms of its avowed benefits. It concludes that the proposed matrix will not achieve its avowed aims of greater accountability and transparency and is likely to lead to injustice, discrimination and dangerous levels of political control over sentencing.[1]

During 1999 and 2000, the matrix was regarded as a high priority by the Liberal/National Party government. In February 2001, the Labour Party was unexpectedly elected to office and does not assign the same priority to the matrix. However, there is no indication that the new government anticipates repealing the enabling legislation and the issues which gave rise to the proposal are alive and well.

The Backdrop

Australia's Sentencing Traditions

Under Australia's federal system of government, sentencing laws vary between the different States and Territories. However, the common tradition has been to entrust sentencing to the exercise of judicial discretion, within broad legislative parameters. Although there have been isolated examples of mandatory and minimum penalties, legislation has generally prescribed just a maximum penalty. This basic model survived thorough scrutiny in several official reviews in the late 1980s and early 1990s (Victorian Sentencing Committee 1988; Australian Law Reform Commission 1987 and 1988; New South Wales Law Reform Commission 1996a and b) and was embodied in major legislative reforms (Freiberg 1995; Morgan 1996). Over the same period, the courts were developing an increasingly sophisticated – and more distinctly Australian – jurisprudence of sentencing. Although legislation in some States did address general principles of sentencing, judicial discretion remained sacrosanct. Mandatory sentences and US-style sentencing grids appeared alien to Australian traditions, trends and philosophies (Zdenkowski 2000a and b).

However, in the late 1990s, pockets emerged of what Freiberg (2000) has termed the 'coca-colonisation' of sentencing. In late 1996, Western Australia introduced mandatory minimum penalties for 'third strike' home burglars (Yeats 1997; Morgan 1999b and 2000a). In early 1997, the Northern Territory introduced mandatory minima for a range of property offences (Johnson and Zdenkowski 2000). Then, in late 1998, a Bill was presented in the Western Australian parliament for the development of a sentencing 'matrix'.

Legislative History of the Matrix

The Bill anticipated that the matrix would be developed in a piecemeal fashion. The new scheme would only apply to selected offences and would involve three levels of intervention. Level one ('reporting offences') would see the judiciary reporting to the Executive, in a prescribed format, on their sentencing decisions. Level two ('regulated offences') would involve a regime of 'indicative sentences' set by regulations; the judge would be able to impose a different sentence but would be required to explain, in a sentencing report, the reasons for any deviation. In level three ('controlled offences'), judges would have virtually no scope to depart from the prescribed sentence.

The Bill was assured of an easy passage through the government-dominated Lower House (the Legislative Assembly) but a small number of Independents held the balance of power in the Upper House (the Legislative Council). The Bill also attracted strong criticism, most notably in an unprecedented Report to Parliament by the Chief Justice (Malcolm 1998). It was therefore referred to the Standing Committee on Legislation of the Legislative Council in May 1999. The Committee reported in October 2000 (Legislation Committee 2000) and split along party lines.[2] The majority (all government members) supported the Bill, subject to a number of amendments. The minority recommended that the Bill should be rejected. When the Bill returned to the whole House, the government managed to secure the support of one of the Independents for levels one and two, but not for level three.

The result is that legislation now exists for the development of levels one and two. Level three has been rejected for the time being, but may be reintroduced at a future date, using stages one and two as a base (Foss 2000a; Prince 2000).

Why a Matrix?

The Western Australian matrix was originally inspired by the sentencing grids which operate in parts of the United States (Foss 1999). However, the underlying conditions and reasons are very different. The US grids originally developed as a result of "widespread dissatisfaction with … the traditional system of indeterminate sentencing" and a lack of effective appellate review (Frase 1995; Frankel 1973). They sought to shift sentencing away from rehabilitation and incapacitation, and towards a system based on desert. The situation in Australia is quite different. First, desert has long been the central principle, at least in the "limiting retributivist" sense (Hart 1968; Morris 1974, 1998) that the seriousness of the offence sets an upper limit to the permissible sentence (*Veen* 1988; *Baumer* 1988; *Chester* 1988). Secondly, there is a reasonably comprehensive system of appellate review by way of both prosecution and defence appeals.

Although the US grids began life in Minnesota as instruments of principle (Parent 1988; Frase 1995), they soon proved vulnerable to political pressure (von Hirsch 1995; Doob 1995). In Western Australia, it is hard to avoid the conclusion that the matrix is being driven, from the outset, by law and order politics. One key facet of this is the assertion that judges are "too soft". The matrix proposal was first announced in mid-1998, in the aftermath of a public rally to protest against violence against elderly people, especially in their homes. Since then, the government has consistently railed against the fact that the median length of sentences is well below the statutory maximum. These are easy but rather cheap and overstated jibes. First, it is hard to find concrete examples of judicial leniency in cases of violence against the elderly and, secondly, the statutory maxima are inconsistent and often set at unrealistic levels (Hammond and Malcolm 1999; Morgan 1999c).[3]

However, the debates have not involved simply a form of 'populist punitiveness' (Bottoms 1995). Four more subtle criticisms have emerged. In simple terms, they are as follows:

- *accountability*: the current system, based on (unelected) judges exercising broad discretionary powers, is not sufficiently accountable;
- *consistency*: current practices are inconsistent;
- *transparency*: the current system is inaccessible (except to lawyers) and is not open to scrutiny;
- *responsiveness*: judges are somewhat out of touch and are not sufficiently responsive to public concerns.

These criticisms have been discussed in detail elsewhere (Morgan 1999a) and the arguments will not be repeated here. For present purposes, it is sufficient to note that although the criticisms are usually overstated, their objective validity may no longer be the real issue. As the Chief Justice of New South Wales has noted (Spigelman 1999), they do exercise a hold on public opinion and this seems to have affected the perceived legitimacy of the justice system. In this essay, the crucial question is whether the matrix legislation does actually address these four criteria. In order to answer this question, it is necessary first to explore the requirements of each level of the matrix.

The Model

The original Bill proposed three levels to the matrix – reporting, regulated and controlled offences. These have generally been called the three 'stages' and the government indicated that, ordinarily, the matrix with respect to any designated offence would be developed stage by stage. However, the legislation does not require this, and the government would not rule out the option of going directly to the second or third 'stage' (Legislation Committee 2000). For this reason, it is more accurate to speak of 'levels' rather than 'stages' of control.

Level One: Reporting Offences

The statutory scheme In level one, the courts will be required to "prepare and deliver" a sentencing report in a format prescribed by regulations. The sentencing report must set out each factor that was taken into account and "indicate the degree to which" each of these factors affected the sentence. These sentencing reports will then be collated and evaluated by the Ministry of Justice and will be used in working out the indicative sentence for level two.

Impact on traditional reasoning Until the regulations are promulgated, it remains unclear what exactly is involved in "indicating the degree" to which particular factors affected the sentence. Judges already give a general indication of such matters in their sentencing remarks. However, there is no uniformity in this, and some judges are more specific than others (Cock 1999). These differences reflect different philosophical positions with respect to the preferred process of reasoning. Some judges ascribe to the view (which is entrenched in Victoria) that sentencing involves a process of "intuitive (or instinctive) synthesis" and that it is "profitless to attempt to allot to all the various considerations their proper part in the assessment of particular punishments" (*Williscroft* 1975, p. 300; see also *Young* 1990; *Punch* 1993; *Verschuren* 1996). Other judges prefer a 'tiered approach'. Generally, this involves the identification of a 'starting point', based on the objective circumstances of the case, followed by an indication of the relevant mitigating factors and, in broad terms, the significance of those factors.

It would seem clear that instinctive synthesis cannot survive in level one and, in itself, this is probably no bad thing (Morgan 1994; Freiberg 1995; Von Hirsch 1995). The next section suggests that level one is also likely to require a far more specific weighting of factors than the tiered approach.

Information systems and the reporting process New South Wales developed a Sentencing Information System more than a decade ago. So far, no other Australian jurisdiction has an equivalent system. However, on the initiative of the Chief Justice, work started in Western Australia on a Judicial Sentencing Information System (JSIS) even before the matrix was conceptualised (Nunis et al. 2000). JSIS has not yet been implemented – not least because the judges have been anxious first to ensure that there is an effective, consistent and practical method of entering the relevant information – but it remains a matter of priority (Nunis et al. 2000).

During debates, the Attorney General stated that JSIS will provide the information system for level one (Foss, 2000b). However, there are two major issues with this. First, JSIS was never designed with the matrix in mind. Like the Scottish and New South Wales systems, it essentially seeks to identify sentence outcomes, factual information about the offence and the offender, and, at most, a list of the factors that were considered (Tata and Hutton 1997). It was not developed with the intention of weighting such factors for the purpose of sentencing reports. It remains to be seen whether, and how, this can be achieved (and, if so, whether the model can be adapted for use in other jurisdictions). The second problem relates to access to the system. JSIS was promoted by the judiciary and was conceptualised as an information system for sentencers. However, the Attorney General's preferred option was for the information gathered through sentencing reports to be publicly available on the internet. For obvious reasons, this remains a very sensitive issue (Nunis et al. 2000).

Level Two: 'Regulated Offences'

The statutory scheme In level two, the courts must adopt a three-stage approach:

- apply a 'sentencing method', as prescribed by regulations, to arrive at an "indication of the appropriate sentence" (called the 'indicative sentence');
- impose the 'actual sentence';
- compile a 'sentencing report', in the prescribed form. As in level one, the sentencing report must indicate the degree to which each factor affected the sentence. In addition, it must explain, in the manner prescribed by regulations, any variation between the actual sentence and the indicative sentence.

Prescribed 'sentencing method' The legislation provides few details with respect to the 'sentencing method'. It simply states that the indicative sentence is to be "determined in accordance with a prescribed formula or in such other manner as may be prescribed". However, there are some implied limitations. As Table 2.1 shows, the original Bill stated that level three regulations could specify which factors were to be considered and which were to be ignored, and also the weight to be attached to the various factors. By implication, any formula which is developed for level two should not go this far. This does not, of course, explain what can be included in level two regulations, and no

Table 2.1 Stages two and three compared

Stage Two: regulated offences	Stage Three: controlled offences
The court must first apply a prescribed sentencing method in order to arrive at an *indication* of the appropriate sentence (the '*indicative sentence*').	The court must first apply a prescribed sentencing method in order to arrive at *the* appropriate sentence (the '*relevant sentence*').
The indicative or relevant sentence (collectively termed the 'recommended' sentence) can take a number of forms, including: • a single option (e.g. a fine of $5,000); • a range within an option (e.g. a fine of $2,000–$5,000); • a combination of options (e.g. a fine of $2,000–$5,000 and/or 12–24 months' community supervision).	
The prescribed method involves applying a 'prescribed formula' or such other method as may be prescribed.	The prescribed formula or other method can: • require certain factors to be ignored or taken into account; and • state the degree to which such factors are to be taken into account.
The court must then impose the 'actual sentence'.	The court must then impose the actual sentence: • it can only depart from the relevant sentence if that sentence is 'so unreasonable as to be unjust'; and • the relevant sentence is not 'so unreasonable' if it was determined by application of the prescribed method.
The court must furnish a sentencing report which: • sets out the recommended sentence • explains the degree to which various factors affected the actual sentence • explains, in the prescribed manner, any difference between the recommended sentence and the actual sentence.	
In prosecution appeals, it is for the prosecution to establish that the sentence was 'manifestly inadequate'.	In prosecution appeals, it is for the defendant to 'show cause' why the relevant sentence (i.e. a more severe penalty) should not be imposed.
In defence appeals, it is for the defendant to establish that the sentence was 'manifestly excessive'.	In defence appeals, it is for the prosecution to 'show cause' why the relevant sentence (i.e. a less severe penalty) should not be imposed.

examples have been provided. The Legislation Committee (2000) could do no more than adopt this author's lamentably vague conclusion (Morgan 1999a) that "it seems to involve a substantial degree of numerical calculation".

Form of the indicative sentence Although the courts will be able to depart from the indicative sentence, they must explain any such departures. The number and extent of departures will obviously depend on how broadly or how narrowly the indicative sentence is confined. The original Bill contained a table (though this was removed in the final legislation) which suggested that indicative sentences will take one of three forms: a fixed penalty (e.g. a fine of $5,000); a range within a particular penalty (e.g. a fine of $5,000 to $10,000); or a range of different penalties (e.g. a fine of $2,000 to $5,000 and/or 12–24 months under community supervision). It is to be hoped that ranges are generally prescribed in preference to fixed penalties; otherwise, departures will become the norm rather than the exception. This has the potential to bring the justice system into disrepute and to encourage a large number of appeals.

Explaining departures The courts will have the power to depart from the indicative sentence but will be required to explain such departures. It should also be noted that regulations may prescribe the manner in which any departures are to be explained. Again, it remains to be seen how much such regulations will constrain judicial discretion.

Appeals In level two, the prosecution and the defence will be able to appeal on the same grounds as at present. Generally, the issue will be whether the sentence was manifestly excessive (defence appeals) or manifestly inadequate (prosecution appeals). However, there will be two differences. First, there will be a clearer benchmark – in the form of the indicative sentence – by which excessiveness or inadequacy is to be assessed. Secondly, the sentencing report will give a clearer indication of the weight attached to the various factors. Consequently, sentencing appeals may become more specific in their focus.

Descriptive or prescriptive? During debates on the Bill, it emerged that the government anticipated that indicative sentences in level two would "reflect the average of sentences imposed by the courts" (Foss 2000c); in other words, they would be descriptive of current practices. It was suggested that if changes were to be made to sentencing levels, this would be done through level three (controlled offences). However, it was not clear at the outset that this was the intention of level two (Foss 1999), and the enabling legislation does not limit future regulations to a descriptive role. It seems plausible to suggest that, with the loss of level three, governments may well seek to adjust the level of indicative sentences in level two. On its face, the legislation certainly permits this.

Level Three: Controlled Offences

Although level three has been rejected for the time being, it remains on the cards for the longer term. Level three also remains important in order to understand the scope of level two (see above). It would have been significantly tighter in four ways, as shown by Table 2.1:

- the prescribed sentencing method would have produced *the* appropriate sentence (called the 'relevant' sentence) rather than just an *indication* of the appropriate sentence;
- the sentencing method would have been more restrictive of judicial discretion;
- there would have been virtually no room for departure from the relevant sentence. Departure would only have been permitted if the relevant sentence would have been 'so unreasonable as to be unjust'; and, in a real tightening of the screw, the sentence could not be considered 'so unreasonable' if it was determined by application of the prescribed sentencing method;
- the normal rules governing appeals were discarded. In the event that the judge departed from the relevant sentence, and there was an appeal, it would not be for the appellant to demonstrate error but for the respondent to 'show cause' why the relevant sentence should not be substituted.[4]

Overview of the Model

Levels one and two of the matrix legislation will bring about considerable changes in court practices. Even without level three, the legislation heralds a significant shift in the balance of sentencing authority between the courts, parliament and the Executive (see below). Further, leaving aside the issues surrounding level three, the extent of the changes remains unclear. First, we still do not have a clear picture of exactly what will be encompassed by sentencing reports and indicative sentences. Secondly, and crucially, it is not clear whether level two will be limited to a descriptive role (as the government has now suggested) or whether it will be used to set out different levels for indicative sentences (as the legislation permits). Given the loss of level three, the later option becomes more likely. Bearing these uncertainties in mind, I will now attempt to evaluate the matrix according to the criteria of accountability, transparency, consistency and responsiveness.

Accountability and Transparency in Legislative Development

The hallmark of the development of sentencing guidelines and grids in the United States has been the establishment of sentencing commissions. For example, the Minnesota Sentencing Guidelines Commission was established following a significant period of consultation and political debate (Parent 1988). The Commission was well-funded and independent and included senior representatives of the judiciary, executive bodies, legal professionals and lay people. The Commission's first task was to draw up the guidelines. Subsequently, it has monitored and evaluated their impact.

In Western Australia, the enabling legislation was drafted in some speed. In what must have been a deliberate fovernment decision, key stakeholders, including the judiciary, the Director of Public Prosecutions, defence lawyers and the Parole Board were excluded from the process; nor was there any input from Aboriginal organisations despite the already excessive rate of Aboriginal imprisonment. In a Report to Parliament, the Chief Justice complained of the 'clear breach of long-standing conventions' to consult with the heads of affected courts and noted that his written requests for discussion had been unanswered (Malcolm 1998). The Attorney General's response was forthright and uncompromising (Foss 1998):

> The public and Parliament will always be on one side and the judges and the
> legal profession will always be on the other. No amount of talking, I think, will
> ever resolve that.

Some important issues arise from this. First, the divisive language raises some intriguing questions about the ministerial responsibility of Attorney General. It is certainly hard to reconcile with the views of a former Attorney General and Chief Justice of South Australia (King 2000, p. 169):

> [T]he Attorney General, as law minister has ... a special responsibility for the
> rule of law and the integrity of the legal system which transcends, and may at
> times conflict with, political exigencies ... It is the special role of the Attorney
> General to be the voice within the government, and to the public, which

articulates and insists upon observance of, the enduring principles of legal justice and upon respect for the judicial and other institutions through which they are applied.

Secondly, the secretive approach to developing the legislation and the lack of detail run counter to protestations that this is essentially an exercise in transparency. Thirdly, as Tonry (1995a, p. 275) noted, a lack of transparency and consultation almost invariably spells failure: "Among ambitious innovations, more fail than succeed, and the explanations often can be found in the care and thoroughness of planning and implementation". Specifically, he cautioned that the goals of sentencing reform had generally only been achieved when those reforms had the support, however grudging, of those involved in their implementation – a conclusion readily supported by Australian experience (Freiberg 1995; Morgan 1996). However, flawed processes do not inexorably lead to flawed outcomes; the next sections therefore analyse the actual model in terms of its purported objectives.

Transparency, Accountability and Regulations

The Scope of the Regulations

Level three would have involved a truly breathtaking shift in sentencing power away from the courts and into the realm of regulations, with tight prescriptions for both the sentencing method and the relevant sentence. Even in levels one and two, the cumulative effect is very significant in that regulations will prescribe:

- which offences are reporting or regulated offences;
- how sentencing reports are to be written and delivered;
- the sentencing method in level two;
- the indicative sentence in level two;
- the method to be used in explaining departures from the indicative sentence.

Further, whilst the scheme will initially apply only to the adult higher courts, it can be extended by future regulations to the lower courts and to the Children's Court.

The Process of Making Regulations

Advocates of the matrix contend that the use of regulations will render the system more transparent (in that it will be more accessible) and more accountable (in that sentencing will be more carefully monitored and controlled by the elected parliament). In order to evaluate such claims, it is important to examine the regulation – making process.

Regulations generally come into force when they are published in the *Government Gazette*. They must then be presented to parliament within six sitting days and parliament may disallow those regulations. There is a Parliamentary Standing Committee on Delegated Legislation, but it is essentially a general watchdog; it does not generally scrutinise or discuss the substance of regulations. In practice, it is very rare for regulations to be disallowed. Thus, whilst parliament does control subsidiary legislation in a formal, structural sense, there is no process of scrutiny and no need for specific approval. In practice, regulations are essentially the preserve of the Executive rather than parliament.

It was precisely these concerns that led to a proposal that a different procedure should apply to level three. Instead of the process of 'disallowance', the Matrix Bill provided that level three regulations would need the specific prior approval of both Houses of Parliament – a new and apparently untested procedure. It would have involved less parliamentary scrutiny than a debate on primary legislation – and no process for amendments to be proposed and debated – but would have involved more control than traditional regulations (Legislation Committee 2000). The Legislation Committee concluded that this process would suffice for level three and that the normal disallowance procedures would suffice for levels one and two. However, the following sections argue that this conclusion is unconvincing.

Delegation and Lack of Clarity

In an earlier article, I criticised the Bill as an example of 'skeleton legislation' – in other words, as involving an excessive delegation of power to subordinate legislation (Morgan 1999a). The Legislation Committee treated this criticism seriously but focused mainly on level three. The majority concluded that the procedural requirements for level three would meet such criticisms. However, because the Committee focused on level three, it gave virtually no specific attention to level two (one and a half pages out of a total of 155 pages) and seems to have underestimated its scope and difficulties. Put bluntly, the guts of level two do not lie in the legislative framework but in the power of the Executive to prescribe a sentencing method and a matrix of indicative sentences. These issues appear far too complex and important to be left to a simple disallowance procedure, especially when there is no independent development and monitoring body akin to the US Sentencing Commissions.

This is not simply a matter of procedure, but is about transparency and public and professional understanding of the proposal. When level three was lost, the government savaged its critics, stating that "they have failed to understand the most fundamental points". Despite acknowledging that the matrix was inspired by the US grids (especially that in Oregon) the government also criticised those who had drawn any parallels with the US experience (Foss 2000a and c). However, no detailed information has been provided, even by way of examples, of what an Australian (as opposed to an American) matrix might look like. Nor have we been given any indication of how basic matters such as criminal record or multiplicity of offences are to be addressed (Morgan 1999a). The problem of lack of detail is exacerbated by the dissonance between the scope of the legislation and government explanations about its intent – notably, whether level two may be more than merely descriptive of existing practices.

Delegation and Quality of Drafting

The extent of delegation also raises concerns with respect to the quality of drafting. Even primary legislation on sentencing has been dogged by drafting problems. For example, the original Matrix Bill contained a table which purported to demonstrate when an actual sentence would be considered to be more or less severe then a sentence prescribed by regulations. The table was so confusing when it came to combinations of sentences that it was removed from the Act following detailed debate (Morgan 1999a; Legislation Committee 2000). The laws with respect to remission and parole were also recently amended; again, it was only following academic scrutiny, and consequential representations by the judiciary that fundamental flaws were identified (Morgan 2000b). This does not augur well for regulations, especially given the lack of a clear process of consultation, review and scrutiny.

Delegation and the Rules of Law Reform

Extensive delegation can effectively alter the rules of law reform in that matters previously requiring legislative change can be effected through regulations

(Morgan 1999a). The Legislation Committee (2000, p. 16) acknowledged this: "The Bill does provide for the Executive to promulgate regulations establishing sentencing principles and policies which issues [sic] are traditionally dealt with in primary legislation". However, they concluded that the approval process which was proposed for level three would meet these objections. This seems to gloss over the fact that level two already contemplates the construction of a 'sentencing method' and that this will be subject only to the disallowance procedure. More generally, it is disturbing to see an endorsement of the view that matters traditionally involving primary legislation could, in future, be dispatched to regulations with a new and untested process of approval. By way of example, Western Australia's Criminal Code often adopts the sensible technique of defining a generic offence (e.g. burglary, assault or sexual assault) and then specifying aggravated offences carrying higher maximum penalties (e.g. home burglary, aggravated burglary, assaulting a public officer and aggravated sexual assault). These definitions and the circumstances of aggravation are currently determined by legislation and the full parliamentary process. If level three was to be introduced, all these matters could simply be dealt with in regulations.

Summary

Accountability and transparency are very important criteria for evaluating models of sentencing. They are also matters of substance, not of formal structures. The original Bill created a dangerous precedent by assuming that so much could be entrusted to regulations – even if level three would have involved a process of approval. In levels one and two, there will be little or no parliamentary scrutiny of regulations and there is no independent sentencing commission. In formal structural terms, power has shifted from the courts to the parliament. In reality, power has shifted to the Executive.

In terms of transparency, there is a curious paradox in this (Malcolm 1998). Sentencing decisions and judicial reasoning on sentencing are subject to regular – some would say almost unrelenting – scrutiny in all forms of the media. Regulations which manage to surmount the hurdle of disallowance procedures scarcely rate a mention.

Transparency, Accountability and Consistency: the Redistribution of Discretion

One of the assumptions of the matrix proposal (as with proposals for mandatory sentences) is that decisions will become more certain, predictable and accountable if judicial discretion is more narrowly constrained. However, sentencing decisions are only one part of the criminal process and limitations on sentencing discretion inevitably have a knock-on effect on other parts of that process.

Pre-trial decisions are particularly important to the construction of criminal cases (Ashworth 1998). In some cases, police or prosecuting authorities may decide not to prosecute or to pursue diversionary schemes. In those cases which do proceed to trial, the choice of charge can often determine what issues are at stake. For example, the same set of facts can give rise to a charge of either assault occasioning bodily harm or unlawful wounding. In Western Australia, provocation and consent would provide a defence to an assault charge, but neither applies to a charge of wounding. Commentators agree that, by providing more fixed outcomes, sentencing grids make these pre-trial decisions even more crucial than they are already to the outcome of the case (Hogg 1999; Zdenkowski 1999; Alschuler 1978; Tonry 1993; Knapp 1991). Since Australia's sentencing tradition has been one of judicial discretion, most of the concrete examples of the redistribution of discretion have, until recently, come from the United States. An extraordinary example was provided by Knapp (1991) who found that in Arizona, one quarter of all felonies ended up as inchoate offences rather than completed crimes. This was not because felons in Arizona were particularly inept or weak-willed, or that the police were especially effective; it was because inchoate offences did not attract the grid regime and charges were routinely bargained down.

The Western Australian government took strong exception to observations that the matrix would similarly "give enormous power to pre-trial decisions" (Morgan 1999c, adopted in the Minority Report of the Legislation Committee 2000). According to the government (Foss 2000c, p. 2256):

> This might be true in the American system but not in the Australian system ... It is a fair criticism of the American system but it is irrelevant. The pre-trial decisions will make no difference whatsoever, and the method of pre-trial charges will not change. The system will be exactly the same: the facts as they emerge will determine the ultimate penalty.

The government was equally dismissive of concern that pre-trial decisions are taken behind closed doors and are therefore less open and accountable than decisions taken in court: "that is the American matrix, not ours" (Foss 2000c).

It is true that American and Australian procedures differ. In particular, Australia does not have a formalised plea-bargaining system. Nevertheless, informal pre-trial negotiations are commonplace, and are often linked to questions of plea. Furthermore, in the Australian context, plea and charge bargaining are less open and less controlled than in the US. For example, it is not uncommon for those charged with complex corporate offences to plead guilty to some charges in return for others being dropped. Similarly, some defendants will plead guilty to a lesser offence than that with which they have been charged. If further evidence of this phenomenon was needed, it has emerged in recent Australian experience with respect to mandatory sentences. There is mounting evidence from both Western Australia and the Northern Territory that mandatory sentences are avoided or negotiated by way of decisions about dropping charges, using diversionary schemes, and by charge and plea negotiations (Johnson and Zdenkowski 1999; Goldflam and Hunyor 1999; Morgan 2000a). The message is clear; pre-trial procedures do make a great difference; and although these procedures will not formally change on the introduction of a sentencing matrix, the reduction of judicial discretion will increase their importance to the ultimate outcome.

These are all matters which involve discretionary decisions which are essentially unreviewable and which lie outside the control of the courts. The redistribution of discretion will therefore result in the criminal process as a whole becoming less rather than more transparent and accountable. It will also serve to undermine 'just deserts' and consistency in that the ultimate sentence may come to depend less on the objective circumstances of the case and more on the negotiating skills of the defendant (or lawyer) and the readiness of prosecutors to enter negotiations.

Consistency and the Piecemeal Development of the Matrix

Discriminatory Impact

On the face of it, the matrix proposal is not discriminatory. Indeed, it appears to have the advantage that it offers less scope for individual prejudices to affect a sentence. However, local and international experience suggests that mandatory sentences and sentencing grids do tend to be discriminatory in impact; in other words, they disproportionately affect certain groups – usually the young, the disadvantaged and minorities. There are numerous examples of this, both from Australia and the United States. In Western Australia, for example, Aboriginal children are grossly over-represented in the Children's Court, constituting around one third of such offenders (Aboriginal Justice Council 1999). In itself, this is a major cause of concern. However, the figures with respect to the three-strikes burglary laws are even worse; here, Aboriginal children constitute a staggering 75–80 per cent of offenders. Put another way, the one third of Children's Court offenders who are Aboriginal provide three-quarters of the 'Three Strikes' cases. Only one quarter of the three strikes cases come from the two-thirds who are non-Aboriginal.

The official explanation for these figures is that "more Aboriginal people are being charged with these offences and brought before the courts" (Government of Western Australia 2000). Staggering in its simplicity, this truism misses the point. Whilst discriminatory impact may not be 'intentional', it is not 'accidental'. In fact, it is the result of two types of deliberate choice (Morgan 2000a). The first, and crucial choice is that of offence selection. It would be equally true to say that very few Aboriginal people are charged with fraud, corporate crime or serious drug trafficking; the point is that mandatory sentences have not targeted these offences but have targeted those in which young, minority and lower socioeconomic groups are over-represented. As Provine's article in this volume demonstrates, this has striking parallels with the USA where offences involving 'crack' cocaine (in which Afro Americans are over-represented) have attracted far tougher penalties than those for powder cocaine (the drug of choice in the higher echelons of society) (see also Tonry 1995b). The second set of choices concerns the processing of cases. As we have seen, the redistribution of discretion increases the significance of pre-trial decisions; the overwhelming evidence is that in Australia, for a variety of reasons, Aboriginal children are less likely to access diversionary programmes. They are therefore more likely to acquire three strikes and less likely to avoid the mandatory sentencing requirements (Blagg 1997; Aboriginal Justice Council 1999).

The matrix is likely to exacerbate these problems. It is not based on a grid which will operate across the board but will only apply to selected offences. In the United States, the introduction of sentencing grids at least forced a consideration of issues of 'ordinal proportionality'; in other words, they required different types of offences to be ranked against one another in terms of their seriousness. Under the matrix legislation, it is almost inevitable that the offences which will be selected are those which have attracted particular media attention such as robbery, burglary, and certain types of motor vehicle offences and assault. These are the examples which have been used by the government during debates, and they are all offences in which lower socioeconomic groups, and especially indigenous young people, tend to be highly represented. There has been no suggestion that fraud and white-collar crime will be selected. Further, if stage three does come in, it is likely that the 'relevant' sentences for controlled offences will spiral upwards as a result of government action. The danger is that the system will increasingly lose a sense of ordinal proportionality.

Consistency and Different Types of Offence

The piecemeal approach of the Western Australian matrix raises further problems in terms of consistency, in that different sentencing principles will apply to different offences. For example, level three would permit regulations to prescribe that certain factors are, or are not relevant and even the weight to be attached to such factors. This could mean, for example, that regulations would require remorse or loss of status to be given little weight in the case of certain prescribed offences (e.g. burglary); but that these factors would continue to play an important role in non prescribed areas (e.g. fraud). This would promote inconsistency rather than consistency and would further subvert notions of relative proportionality.

Multiple offences create further problems. It is possible that an offender who faces a number of charges will fall to be sentenced under different regimes; in other words, there will be no consistency in the principles and procedural requirements which are applicable even to that one person. For example, a person may be sentenced for one offence to which traditional sentencing principles apply; for another which is a reporting offence and for a third which is a regulated offence. The introduction of level three would see the options expand to four. Although it is unlikely that all four would apply to one offender, it is entirely feasible that two or three will arise.

Summary: Consistency and Doing Justice to Difference

Policy-makers may be attracted to a gradualist approach to matrix development. It is certainly easier than attempting to produce a sentencing grid which covers the whole range of offences. It also allows an immediate response to areas of public concern. However, it is a strategy which will promote inconsistency rather than consistency in that different offenders will be subject to different sentencing regimes. It is also likely, by dint of decisions about offence selection and the processing of cases, to lead to discriminatory impact.

Further, consistency in sentencing is not just about treating like cases alike; it is about ensuring the capacity to do justice to differences between different offenders and different offences (Hudson 1998; Malcolm 1998). This will present some problems in level two, even though judges will be able to depart from the indicative sentence. If level three was introduced the problems would be acute.

Legal Challenges and the Position of the Courts

Judicial Interpretation, Application and Adaptation

History shows that inflexible sentencing regimes generate avoidance techniques on the part of participants in the legal system. This was true during the infamous 'Bloody Code' of the eighteenth century, when juries would regularly commit 'pious perjury' and either acquit guilty people or convict them of lesser, non capital offences (Hay 1975; Thompson 1975). It has also proved to be the case more recently both in America (Tonry 1992) and in Australia (Johnson and Zdenkowski 2000). The same is very likely to be true with the matrix, though the extent to which it occurs will depend on the degree of flexibility in the system. There are three main techniques by which Australian courts have mediated the severity of mandatory sentencing regimes:

- *interpretation*: within the confines of the rules of statutory interpretation, the laws are construed in such a way as to strictly limit their application. For example, the Children's Court of Western Australia managed to find a noncustodial alternative to immediate detention (the conditional release order) for third strike juvenile burglars (Yeats 1997; Saylor 1997);
- *application*: in considering whether the laws apply to individual offenders, the courts have required strict proof of all legal requirements. If, for example, the sentencing method in level two or level three was to place a weighting on a person's prior record (as in the US grids), this would need to be strictly proved by the prosecution;
- *adaptation*: Australian courts have sometimes adapted their practices to reduce injustice. For example, the Children's Court of Western Australia

began to 'backdate' mandatory sentences to take effect from the time a person was remanded in custody, even though they had no statutory authority to do so (Morgan 2000a).

The Ultra Vires *Doctrine*

The use of regulations means that criminal law practitioners and criminal courts will need to turn their attention to administrative law and to scrutinise regulations in all levels of the matrix in order to ensure that they are not ultra vires; in other words, that they do actually fall within the scope of the delegated power.

Constitutional Challenges

The matrix scheme is likely to be subject to constitutional challenge. The arguments are extremely complex (Morgan 1999a; Flynn 1999) but some basic points may be made. First, mandatory sentences are not unconstitutional (*Palling* v *Corfield* 1970; *Sillery* 1981); under the doctrine of parliamentary supremacy, parliament clearly has the authority to set mandatory penalties or mandatory minima for specific offences by legislation. The government's position has been that if mandatory sentences are not unconstitutional, there can be no problem with the matrix, which would permit a greater degree of flexibility.

However, the matrix involves a very different structure; it is based upon general regulations made by the Executive rather than specific legislation. It also involves the previously unknown notion that the courts must report to the Executive. In other words, the constitutional issue appears to be not so much the relationship between the courts and parliament but the relationship between the courts and the Executive. In Australian constitutional law, this gives rise to some intriguing questions. It is now clear that the laws could not be successfully challenged simply on the basis of a general 'separation of powers' argument (*Re S (A Child)* 1995; *Kable* 1996). However, the High Court has recently developed a more limited doctrine based on 'incompatibility of functions' (*Kable* 1996); in other words, courts cannot be required to perform functions which are incompatible with the integrity, independence and impartiality of a court exercising the judicial power of the Commonwealth. Since state courts have jurisdiction in a number of areas of Commonwealth law, it follows that there are limits on the extent to which state courts can be required to perform nonjudicial functions. The precise ramifications of this decision remain unclear (Johnston and Hardcastle 1998) but the Chief Justice (Malcolm 1998) has already suggested of the matrix that:

> The various reporting requirements represent an attempt by Parliament to impose upon judges executive or administrative functions incompatible with judicial independence.

An alternative way of viewing the scheme is that it involves the Executive impinging on judicial independence by 'taking over' sentencing. Either way, it can be argued that the matrix scheme involves a systematic attack on the structure and independence of the courts; and that this is so fundamental that it undermines the integrity of the courts and their ability to act – or to appear to act – independently of the Executive (Morgan 2000a).

However, in assessing the prospects for a successful constitutional challenge, it would be foolish to forget the old adage that the price of success can sometimes be failure. Those of us who are critics of the matrix have been successful in the sense that level three has been dropped; but if it had been retained, there was a greater prospect of the whole scheme being ruled unconstitutional.

Conclusion

As the first serious move towards a sentencing grid outside the United States, Western Australia's proposed matrix deserves very careful consideration. At first sight, it appears to offer greater transparency and accountability. The gradualist approach may also have some attraction in that it allows areas of particular concern to be reviewed without the complexity of a grid which traverses the whole range of offences. However, the apparent attractions are outweighed by some major deficiencies and problems. In terms of its development, the matrix has failed abjectly to meet any basic test of transparency. In terms of responsiveness, it certainly allows governments to react to perceived public concern but, in so doing, it creates dangerous levels of political control. The scheme will also exacerbate the problems faced by indigenous people.

It is easy to recite the mantras of accountability, transparency and consistency but these are matters of substance not of formal structural arrangements or simplistic catch phrases. The combined effect of using regulations, the redistribution of discretion and the potential for a range of legal challenges is to undermine rather than to promote such objectives. It is hard to avoid the conclusion that law-and-order politics has jumped well ahead of itself with the matrix. Overall, the scheme appears to involve more smoke and mirrors than genuine accountability and transparency.

Notes

1   This paper focuses on the evolution of debates on the matrix during 1999 and 2000. For a more detailed analysis of earlier debates and the background to the legislation, see Morgan 1999a.
2   The Report of the Committee and the formal evidence it received can be accessed through the website of the Parliament of Western Australia (http://www.parliament.wa.gov.au). The site provides a particularly useful resource on the themes raised in this essay, including evidence from the Chief Justice and other senior judges, the Director of Public Prosecutions and those responsible for the development of a Sentencing Information System.
3   Many of the current statutory maxima are set so high that they do not properly reflect the relative seriousness of different offences. For example, the maximum for home burglary (the main example used by the government) was increased to 18 years in 1996. This is higher than the maximum for sexual assault/rape and grievous bodily harm, and only two years less than the maximum for manslaughter. Further, the imposition of an 18 year sentence would see the offender spending more time in prison than some of those who are sentenced to life imprisonment for murder.
4   Although the majority of the Legislation Committee (2000) supported the introduction of level three, they did accept arguments (Morgan 1999a) criticising use of the phrase 'to show cause' in the context of criminal appeals.

References

Aboriginal Justice Council of Western Australia (1999), *Our Mob Our Justice: Keeping the vision alive*, Perth: Aboriginal Affairs Department.

Alschuler, A.W. (1978) 'Sentencing Reform and Prosecutorial Power', *University of Pennsylvania Law Review*, Vol. 126, p. 550.

Ashworth, A. (1998), *The Criminal Process: An evaluative study*, 2nd edn, Oxford: Oxford University Press.

Australia Law Reform Commission (1987), *Sentencing: Penalties*, Discussion Paper 30, Canberra.

Australian Law Reform Commission (1988), *Sentencing*, Report No. 44, Canberra.

Blagg, H. (1997), 'A Just Measure of Shame? Aboriginal Youth and Conferencing in Australia', *British Journal of Criminology*, Vol. 37, p. 481.

Bottoms, A.E. (1995), 'The Philosophy and Politics of Punishment and Sentencing', in C.M.V. Clarkson and R. Morgan (eds), *The Politics of Sentencing Reform*, Oxford: Clarendon Press.

Cock, R. (Director of Public Prosecutions for Western Australia) (1999), Evidence to the Legislative Council Standing Committee on Legislation (Legislation Committee 2000), Perth, 8 September.

Doob, A. (1995), 'The US Sentencing Commission Guidelines: If you don't know where you are going, you might not get there', in C.M.V. Clarkson and R. Morgan (eds), *The Politics of Sentencing Reform*, Oxford: Clarendon Press, pp. 199–250.

Flynn, M. (1999), 'Fixing a Sentence: Are There Any Constitutional Limits?', *University of New South Wales Law Journal*, Vol. 22, pp. 280–85.

Foss, P. (1998), Attorney General's ministerial media statement, 26 November.

Foss, P. (1999), Evidence to the Legislative Council Standing Committee on Legislation (Legislation Committee 2000), 28 July.

Foss, P. (2000a), 'Attorney General Slams Labor Stance on Sentencing Matrix Bill', media release, Perth, 18 October.

Foss, P. (2000b), Evidence to the Legislative Council Standing Committee on Legislation (Legislation Committee 2000), 13 September.

Foss, P. (2000c), Parliamentary debates on the Sentencing Matrix Bill, Parliament of Western Australia, Legislative Council, *Hansard*, 7 November.

Frankel, M. (1973), *Criminal Sentences: Law Without Order*, New York: Hill and Wang.

Frase, R.S. (1995) 'Sentencing Guidelines in Minnesota and Other American States: A Progress Report', in C.M.V. Clarkson and R. Morgan (eds), *The Politics of Sentencing Reform*, Oxford: Clarendon Press, pp. 169–98.

Freiberg, A. (1995), 'Sentencing Reform in Victoria: A Case Study', in C.M.V. Clarkson and R. Morgan (eds), *The Politics of Sentencing Reform*, Oxford: Clarendon Press, pp. 51–94.

Freiberg, A. (2000), 'Three Strikes and You're Out – It's not Cricket: Colonisation and resistance in Australian sentencing', in M. Tonry and R. Frase (eds), *Punishment and Penal Systems in Western Countries*, Oxford: Oxford University Press.

Goldflam, R. and Hunyor, J. (1999), 'Mandatory Sentencing and the Concentration of Powers', *Alternative Law Journal*, Vol. 24 (5), p. 211.

Government of Western Australia (2000), Submission to the Senate Legal and Constitutional References Committee, *Inquiry into the Human Rights (Mandatory Sentencing of Juvenile Offenders) Bill 1999*, Submissions 96 and 96(A), Parliament of Australia, Canberra, March.

Hammond, K.J. and Malcolm, D.K. (Chief Judge of the District Court and Chief Justice of Western Australia) (1999), Evidence to the Legislative Council Standing Committee on Legislation (Legislation Committee 2000), Perth, 9 June.

Hart, H.L.A. (1968), *Punishment and Responsibility: Essays in the philosophy of law*, Oxford: Clarendon Press.

Hay, D. (1975), 'Property, Authority and the Criminal Law', in D. Hay, P. Linebaugh and E.P. Thompson (eds), *Albion's Fatal Tree: Crime and society in eighteenth century England*, London: Allen and Lane.

Hogg, R. (1999), 'Mandatory Sentencing Legislation and the Symbolic Politics of Law and Order', *University of New South Wales Law Review*, Vol. 22, pp. 262–6.

Hudson, B. (1998), 'Mitigation for Socially Deprived Offenders', in A. von Hirsch and A. Ashworth (eds), *Principled Sentencing: Readings on theory and policy*, 2nd edn, Oxford: Hart Publishing.

Johnson, D. and Zdenkowski, G. (2000), *Mandatory Injustice: Compulsory imprisonment in the Northern Territory*, Australian Centre for Independent Journalism, Sydney.

Johnston, P. and Hardcastle, R. (1998), 'State Courts: The limits of *Kable*', *Sydney Law Review*, Vol. 20, p. 214.

King, L. (2000), 'The Attorney General, Politics and the Judiciary', *University of Western Australia Law Review*, Vol. 29, pp. 155–79.

Knapp, K. (1991), 'Arizona: Unprincipled sentencing, mandatory minima and prison overcrowding', *Overcrowded Times*, Vol. 2, p. 10.

Legislation Committee (2000), *Report of the Standing Committee on Legislation in Relation to the Sentencing Matrix Bill 1999*, Report No. 53, Perth: The Parliament of Western Australia.

Malcolm, D.K. (1998), *Sentencing Legislation Amendment and Repeal Bill 1998 and Sentence Administration Bill 1998: A Report to the Parliament of Western Australia*, Perth.

Morgan, N. (1994), 'Sentences of Imprisonment – Instinctive Synthesis or Two Tiered Approach', *Criminal Law Journal*, Vol. 18, pp. 53–5.

Morgan, N. (1996), 'Non-Custodial Sentencing under Western Australia's New Sentencing Laws: Business as usual or a new Utopia?', *University of Western Australia Law Review*, Vol. 26, pp. 364–88.

Morgan, N. (1999a), 'Accountability, Transparency and Justice: Do we need a sentencing matrix?', *University of Western Australia Law Review*, Vol. 28, pp. 259–92.

Morgan, N. (1999b), 'Capturing Crim's or Capturing Votes? The Aims and Effects of Mandatories', *University of New South Wales Law Journal*, Vol. 22, pp. 267–79.

Morgan, N. (1999c), Evidence to the Legislative Council Standing Committee on Legislation (Legislation Committee 2000), Perth, 20 October.

Morgan, N. (2000a), 'Mandatory Sentences in Australia: Where have we been and where are we going?', *Criminal Law Journal*, Vol. 24, pp. 164–83.

Morgan, N. (2000b), 'Now You See It, Now You Don't: Truth and justice under new sentencing laws', *University of Western Australia Law Review*, Vol. 29, pp. 251–86.

Morris, N. (1974), *The Future of Imprisonment*, Chicago University Press, Chicago.

Morris, N. (1998), 'Desert as a Limiting Principle', in A. von Hirsch and A. Ashworth (eds), *Principled Sentencing: Readings on Theory and Policy*, Hart Publishing, Oxford, pp. 180–84.

New South Wales Law Reform Commission (1996a), *Sentencing*, Discussion Paper 33, Sydney.

New South Wales Law Reform Commission (1996b), *Sentencing*, Report No. 79, Sydney.

Nunis, G., Whyte, P. and Hutton, C. (2000), Evidence to the Legislation (Legislation Committee 2000), Perth, 3 May.

Parent, D.G. (1988), *Structuring Criminal Sentences: The evolution of Minnesota's sentencing guidelines*, Stoneham, MA: Butterworths.

Prince, K. (2000), Parliamentary debates on the Sentencing Matrix Bill, Parliament of Western Australia, Legislative Assembly, *Hansard*, 15 November.

Saylor, D. (1997), 'Three Strikes by the Burglar', *Indigenous Law Bulletin*, Vol. 4(2), p. 14.

Spigelman, J. (1999), 'Sentencing Guideline Judgments', *Current Issues in Criminal Justice*, Vol. 11, pp. 5–16.

Tata, C. and Hutton, N. (1997), 'Scottish High Court Develops Sentencing Information System', *Overcrowded Times*, Vol. 8, p. 1.

Thompson, E.P. (1975), *Whigs and Hunters: The origin of the Black Act*, London: Allen Lane.

Tonry, M. (1992), 'Mandatory Penalties', in M. Tonry (ed.), *Crime and Justice: A review of research*, Vol. 16, Chicago: University of Chicago Press.

Tonry, M. (1993), 'Sentencing Commissions and their Guidelines', in M. Tonry (ed.), *Crime and Justice: A Review of Research*, Vol. 17, Chicago: University of Chicago Press, p. 137.

Tonry, M. (1995a), 'Sentencing Reform Across Boundaries', in C.M.V. Clarkson and R. Morgan (eds), *The Politics of Sentencing Reform*, Oxford: Clarendon Press.

Tonry, M (1995b), *Malign Neglect*, Oxford: Oxford University Press.

Victorian Sentencing Committee (1988), *Sentencing: Report of the Victorian Sentencing Committee*, Melbourne, Victoria: Attorney General's Department.

Von Hirsch, A. (1995), 'Proportionality and Parsimony in American Sentencing Guidelines: The Minnesota and Oregon standards', in C.M.V. Clarkson and R. Morgan (eds), *The Politics of Sentencing Reform*, Oxford: Clarendon Press, pp. 149–68.

Yeats, M. (1997), 'Three Strikes and Restorative Justice in Australia', *Criminal Law Reform*, Vol. 8, pp. 369–85.

Zdenkowski, G. (1999), 'Mandatory Imprisonment of Property Offenders in the Northern Territory', *University of New South Wales Law Journal*, Vol. 22, pp. 302–14.

Zdenkowski, G. (2000a), 'Limiting Sentencing Discretion: Has There Been a Paradigm Shift?', *Current Issues in Criminal Justice*, Vol. 12, pp. 58–78.

Zdenkowski, G. (2000b), 'Sentencing Trends: Past, present and prospective', in D. Chappell and P. Wilson (eds), *Crime and the Criminal Justice System in Australia: 2000 and Beyond*, Sydney: Butterworths, pp. 161–201.

Cases

Baumer (1988) 166 Commonwealth Law Reports, 51.

Chester (1988) 165 Commonwealth Law reports, 611.

Kable (1996) 189 Commonwealth Law Reports, 51.

Palling v Corfield (1970) 123 Commonwealth Law Reports, 52.

Punch (1993) 9 Western Australian Reports, 486.

Re S (A Child) (1995) 12 Western Australian Reports, 392.

Sillery (1981) 180 Commonwealth Law Reports, 353.

Veen (No. 2) (1988) 164 Commonwealth Law Reports, 465.

Verschuren (1996) 17 Western Australian Reports, 467.

Williscroft (1975) Victorian Reports, 292.

Young, Dickenson and West (1990) 45 Australian Criminal Reports, 147.

Chapter Three

Mandatory Sentences: a Conundrum for the new South Africa?

Dirk van Zyl Smit

Introduction

In late 1997, less than four years after South Africa became a democracy with a Constitution that guarantees the independence of the judiciary and includes a justiciable Bill of Rights, the first South African parliament ever elected on universal suffrage unanimously passed legislation introducing minimum sentences for specified offences. On the face of it, this legislation severely restricts the capacity of the courts to impose the sentences they deem appropriate for a greater range of serious common law offences than ever before in South African history.

The legislation tucked away in sections 51 and 52 of the neutral sounding 1997 Criminal Law Amendment Act raises a number of interesting questions. How could such legislation be passed in a country where conventional legal wisdom had long been that unfettered sentencing discretion was a hallmark of an independent judiciary? What harm was this legislation designed to address? What is the precise legal ambit of these two sections? What impact are they likely to have on sentencing practice in South Africa? Perhaps most importantly, given the ostensibly problematic nature of the legislation and the fact that, unless further steps are taken, it will only remain in operation until 30 April 2000, what form will a future sentencing system take in South Africa?

Not all these questions can be answered in this chapter. Empirical research on the impact of the Act is in progress and the South African Law Commission, which has the task of developing a comprehensive new approach to sentencing, is still considering various options. Nevertheless, an analysis of the context in which the Act emerged, of the process leading to its enactment and of the interpretation of the Act by the courts can fruitfully be undertaken. It will go some way towards providing an indication of the direction in which a future South African sentencing system is likely to develop.

The Context

Judicial Primacy in Sentencing

One aspect of the sentencing context in South Africa has already been mentioned: the perception that the judicial function must include the exercise of a wide if not unfettered sentencing discretion. Such a perception, particularly among judges themselves, is of course hardly unique to South Africa. The introduction of mandatory sentences was resisted publicly and strenuously by the judiciary in the federal system in the United States of America, where the federal sentencing guidelines effectively mandated such sentences (Doob 1995), and, more recently, by the judiciary in England, where mandatory life sentences for certain classes of recidivists were required by the 1997 Crime (Sentencing) Act (Dunbar and Langdon 1998).

In South Africa, as elsewhere, the arguments in favour of judicial sentencing discretion are a mixture of the constitutional and the pragmatic. Simply stated, the constitutional argument is that the division of powers requires the judiciary alone to decide on the sentences of convicted criminals and the pragmatic argument is that judges are uniquely positioned to impose appropriate sentences.

The latter argument was fully developed in the mid-1970s by the Commission of Inquiry into the Penal System chaired by Mr Justice Viljoen. In the extensive section of its report that dealt with shortcomings of "mandatory and minimum sentences" and its reasons for rejecting them, the Viljoen Commission focused exclusively on instances where such sentences were imposed for 'ordinary' (that is 'non-political') crime (Viljoen Commission 1976, para. 5.1.4). It emphasised the sophistication of the judicial sentencing process, which it described in some detail, and its ability to develop principles that accommodated the various purposes of sentencing. It recognised that "[t]he Legislature may feel that the proscription of a particularly virile social evil calls for severe punitive and exemplary sentences" (ibid., para. 5.1.4.1.2) but objected to such sentences including a mandatory sentence of five years imprisonment for dealing in even small quantities of drugs. It thus opposed legislation that had been pioneered by Dr Connie Mulder, a highly influential politician of the day who had campaigned for deterrent sentences to stamp out the use of drugs. The Commission objected to this approach and asserted that sentences set with deterrence as the only objective might result in outcomes, "which were, from a retributive point of view, outrageously unreasonable" (ibid., para. 5.1.4.1.7). The necessity of allowing for what modern penal theorists call 'limiting retributivism' (Morris 1974; Frase 1997) was seen by the Commission as a powerful argument for the retention of judicial discretion in sentencing. The clear opposition of the Commission to mandatory minimum sentences was stated in relatively mild terms. The Commission argued for the introduction of a permanent penal reform committee that would attempt to guide the sentencing process by making information on sentencing and its effects available to the legislature and the judiciary, and which would enable the sentencing system to be developed by legislation or persuasive authority. However, this intervention should stop short of mandatory sentences.

Even a mild form of intervention was too much for the more conservative elements of the judiciary. In *S v Holder* (1979) Chief Justice Rumpff dismissed in angry judicial tones the judgment of Acting Judge of Appeal Viljoen in *S v Scheepers* (1977) in which the chairman of the Commission had tried in his judicial capacity to develop some of his ideas for a structured sentencing discretion, albeit one that stopped well short of mandatory injunctions to sentencers. Chief Justice Rumpff emphasised the discretion of sentencing courts and the circumspection that appellate courts should show when developing guidelines. He went on to assert in categorical terms that the economic burden that prison sentences placed on the state could not be allowed to influence the determination of an appropriate punishment (*S v Holder* 1979, p. 77A).

This firm pronouncement on judicial independence in the sentencing sphere emerged in the context of dealing with 'ordinary crime' but it found a strong echo in the more political sphere, for one of the 'social evils' that from the 1960s onwards the government sought to criminalise particularly harshly was any form of political resistance to its authority. In criticising legislation creating mandatory sentences for such offences, opposition political groupings, both inside and outside parliament, emphasised not only that judicial officers were in a unique position to select the appropriate sentence but also that they were constitutionally required to do so (Hansard 1983: cols 4066–71). This was a telling criticism as the government placed considerable emphasis on the formal independence of the judiciary (Department of Foreign Affairs 1968). It was forced to admit that it did not and could not trust the judiciary to impose sentence, but it tried to limit this admission of lack of confidence to a small class of 'political' cases.

The proposition that the judiciary should not be restricted in their decisions on sentence was one on which conservative and liberal judges could easily unite. 'Conservatives', as we have seen, felt very strongly about the principle of absolute discretion in sentencing; while 'liberals', who might otherwise have been prepared to allow at least the structuring of judicial sentencing discretion, could be expected to feel very strongly about government attempts to enforce its power through the clumsy tool of the mandatory sentence. The leading cases on mandatory sentencing in political cases confirm this alliance and at the same time provide the most powerful judicial dicta against mandatory sentences (*S v Mpetha* 1985, 710E). This line of cases culminated in the matter of *S v Toms; S v Bruce* (1990) which turned on whether an apparently mandatory sentence was appropriate for two white men who had refused to do military service (Abel 1995). In this instance Chief Justice Corbett could pronounce confidently and in general terms that carried the full approval of an otherwise divided court, on the theoretical and practical defences of judicial discretion in sentencing:

> [T]he imposition of a mandatory minimum prison sentence has always been regarded as an undesirable intrusion by the Legislature upon the jurisdiction of the courts to determine the punishment to be meted out to persons convicted of statutory offences and as a kind of enactment that is calculated in certain instances to produce grave injustice (*S v Toms; S v Bruce* 1990, pp. 822C–D).

Politico-legal Changes

The decision in *Toms* and *Bruce* was handed down less than two months after the watershed address of President F.W. de Klerk in which the unbanning of the liberation movements and other changes were announced. These were to lead to the adoption of a constitution with a justiciable Bill of Rights and of course to full democracy in South Africa in 1994. Specifically mentioned in de Klerk's speech of 2 February 1990 was an undertaking to reconsider the place of the death penalty in South African law (*Cape Times*, 3 February 1990). This undertaking was fulfilled as shortly afterwards the law relating to the death penalty was amended to reduce the number of crimes for which the sentence of death could be passed and to remove the requirement of a mandatory death sentence for murder where no extenuating circumstances could be found (Criminal Law Amendment Act 1990). These developments may have been expected to signal the end of all mandatory minimum sentences in South Africa. Not only were the specific laws that purported to impose such minima being repealed, but also the Constitution itself arguably provided some safeguards against the enactment of similar laws stipulating minimum sentences in the future.

Certainly the Constitution, both in its interim version (The Constitution of the Republic of South Africa 1993) and in the 'final' form (The Constitution of the Republic of South Africa 1996), protected equality before the law and outlawed punishments that were contrary to human dignity in general or that were cruel, inhuman or degrading. In these wider principles sentencing scholars in South Africa found support for a constitutional principle that sentences should be proportionate to seriousness of the offence committed (Van Zyl Smit 1996). In the death penalty case, *S v Makwanyane and Another* (1995, p. 433) the newly-established Constitutional Court recognised proportionality in sentencing as having a constitutional base. From there it was a logical step to develop an argument that mandatory minimum sentences would be unconstitutional if they produced grossly disproportionate results. The force of this argument was strengthened by a decision in neighbouring Namibia that applied Canadian case law in a typical Southern African context and held that a mandatory sentence for stock theft was unconstitutional as it provided an outcome that was 'shocking' in the circumstances (*S v De Vries* 1996, p. 1677A).

Crime and the Renewed Rise of Popular Punitiveness

The transition to majority rule in South Africa and the period immediately thereafter were times in which there was probably some overall increase in crime rates in South Africa and certainly a dramatic increase in perceptions that crime was a major national problem. Much has been written on the causes for the change in crime patterns and the even more dramatic change in perceptions (Nedcor Project 1996; Van Zyl Smit 1999). It is certainly true that the new government did not immediately see crime as the major issue on which it would be challenged. President Mandela did not mention crime in his inaugural address as the first president of a democratic South Africa. Even when the new government began to consider how to deal with crime, sentencing did not feature prominently. The National Crime Prevention Strategy,[1] which was touted as a comprehensive state response to crime, made only minor references to punishments and said nothing about how sentences should be determined. Nor was the abolition of the death penalty and of corporal punishment the product of direct government action. Both were abolished by the Constitutional Court, which interpreted the abstract principles of the Constitution as outlawing them (*S v Makwanyane and Another* 1995 (death penalty); *S v Williams and others* 1995 (corporal punishment)). The necessary consequential changes to legislation to make arrangements for those who had been sentenced to death but not executed as a result of the death penalty decision, as well as the tidying up of the statute book to remove references to these penalties from the statute book, only came before parliament two and a half years after the decisions of the Constitutional Court.

If the government did not immediately respond to the rising crime wave by considering changes to sentencing policy, its opponents soon realised that sentencing presented them with an issue that would allow them to claim the moral high ground, much as a moral entrepreneur such as the aspirant national leader, Dr Connie Mulder, had tried to do in the 1970s, by introducing mandatory minimum sentences in the drug sphere. As the issue of crime grew in public significance, the opponents of government, both within and outside parliament, articulated demands for more punitiveness. The claim that the government was not doing enough to deal with crime was one on which all opponents of the government could unite. These included an extraordinary range of critics, from the Moslem-fundamentalist PAGAD[2] movement to Business Against Crime outside parliament – and within parliament from the right-wing Afrikaner Freedom Front to the former liberation movement, the Pan African Congress of Azania and the middle-of-the-road, liberal Democratic Party, which as the opposition in the earlier white parliament had vigorously opposed mandatory minimum sentences.

In crime control rhetoric sentencing was regarded as of particular significance and within sentencing the call for the reinstatement of the death penalty seemed to present itself as an issue of particular salience. On this matter however, the government stood firm and dismissed the calls of its opponents for the constitutional amendment that such reinstatement would require. This stance made it all the more vulnerable to calls from its more 'reasonable' critics to make sentencing more certain and more severe without returning to the death penalty. Particularly important in this regard was a private member's Bill introduced as early as 1995 by the Democratic Party MP, Mr Douglas Gibson, which sought to add to the list of authorised punishments a sentence of life without parole in addition to the 'mere' life sentence for which provision was already made (Criminal Procedure Amendment Bill 1995). Although the private member's Bill did not become law, it received 'in principle' support from the government, indicating that the government acknowledged that legislative changes were needed to ensure that accused persons spent longer in prison than had hitherto been the case.

Legislative changes in two related areas gave indications of the same thinking. In 1995 and again in 1997 the government brought forward amendments to the bail legislation, both designed to ensure that accused persons were not granted bail too easily (Criminal Procedure Amendment Act 1995; Criminal Procedure Second Amendment Act 1997). And in 1997 the law relating to parole was changed, extending significantly the period that a prisoner would have to serve before being considered for parole (Parole and Correctional Services Amendment Act 1997). A significant feature of the 1997 bail legislation in particular was the extent to which it restricted the power of the courts to release accused persons facing certain serious charges by forbidding bail in such cases unless 'exceptional circumstances' were present. Notwithstanding arguments that such legislation would undermine the power of the judiciary to exercise its discretion freely in an area in which it should properly be able to do so, and that the legislation might be placing restrictions on the right to bail that might be unconstitutional, the government persisted and the 1997 Criminal Procedure Second Amendment Act duly became law. These amendments were clear indications that, although popular punitiveness in respect of the death penalty was still being resisted, the government was not averse to introducing harsh measures that would reduce judicial discretion in other areas.

The Embattled Judiciary

At first glance the politico-legal changes of the 1990s appear greatly to have strengthened the power and the independence of the judiciary. A Constitutional Court with final jurisdiction on constitutional matters was added to the hierarchy of courts but the existing judges continued in office at all levels of the judicial system. Future appointments to the bench were to be made only on the recommendation of the Judicial Services Committee established by the Constitution rather than directly by the Minister of Justice. Formally, the sovereignty of parliament was replaced by the sovereignty of the Constitution, thus ostensibly giving the courts more, rather than less, power. The transition from the old to the new was symbolised by the swearing in of the newly-elected President Mandela by Chief Justice Corbett, who continued to hold his old office as chief justice in the new constitutional order.

In reality the transition was not so smooth: although the judiciary remained in place new appointments were made explicitly to change its previously virtually all white and male composition. Criticism of the judiciary as a whole, which previously had largely been confined to academic lawyers, increasingly became a staple of political debate as judges were told to adjust to the realities of the new South Africa (Asmal, Asmal and Roberts 1996). Particularly controversial was the unsuccessful attempt by the Truth and Reconciliation Commission to persuade judges to testify before it on the role of the judiciary under Apartheid. In refusing to do this, the judges relied on the doctrine of judicial independence and thus not only made this doctrine itself more controversial but increased the suspicion on the part of the government that it was being used as a smokescreen by those judges opposed to the new order (Dyzenhaus 1998).

This testiness in the relationship between the government and the judiciary was reflected in the area of sentencing as well. More conservative judges used the removal of their power to impose the death penalty as an occasion for intemperate criticism of the way in which sentences were being administered.[3] Correctional officials were summonsed to explain the process of parole release for lifers in particular. When their explanations were deemed unsatisfactory the officials were excoriated from the Bench and very long fixed-term sentences were imposed as a deliberate gesture of lack of confidence in the development of a sensible release policy. 'Killer gets 2410 years' was the headline in *Cape Argus* of 10 December 1997. These actions were criticised by the politicians who claimed, perhaps not without justification, that these judges were playing populist politics by appealing to the punitive gallery – a claim that did not improve relations.

The tensions also had a direct effect on sentencing. Although there was no statutory upper limit on the length of sentences that courts with the requisite sentencing jurisdiction could impose, there had been a convention in South African sentencing law that they would not impose fixed terms of more than 25 years (*S v Masala* 1968). Beyond this point only life sentences, or previously the death penalty, were regarded as appropriate. After the abolition of the death penalty, however, the Supreme Court of Appeal removed this constraint (*S v Mhlakaza and another* 1997) and a minority of judges began imposing Texan style sentences for much longer determinate terms and thus challenged this delicate convention.[4]

Finally, the issue of sentencing disparities emerged in a way that further embattled the judiciary. In particular, sentences imposed by white judicial officers on white accused were freely compared in the media to those imposed on black accused and thinly veiled accusations of racial bias were made. 'Sadist Grins at Light Fine' read a caption in the 7 November 1997 issue of the *Mail and Guardian* and more recently the *Cape Times* of 27 March 1999 led with 'Zwame Judge labelled a racist dinosaur'.

The Legislative Process

By early 1997 the context for the introduction of new sentencing legislation was therefore very different from anything that had existed previously.

Although it appeared that judicial primacy in sentencing was established by a long line of scholarship and precedent supported by the new constitutional order, the doctrine had become vulnerable to changed social conditions. Most prominent amongst these were a significant increase in rates of reported crime and an even more dramatic rise in popular punitiveness. At the same time the judiciary itself was increasingly embattled and isolated politically.

From the beginning of 1997 onwards the government began to give indications that it was thinking of introducing mandatory minimum sentences for certain categories of serious crime. An early public indication of this emerged in a general address that Mr A.M. Omar, the Minister of Justice, made to the Justice Portfolio Committee of the National Assembly on 18 February 1997. "If we have to introduce minimum sentencing, we will do it to tide us over our transition period", Omar was quoted as saying (*Cape Argus*, 18 February 1997, p. 6). He continued that he was confident that the crime situation would return to normal within a few years. When this happened, he explained, the legislation on minimum sentences for priority crimes would fall away.

When Omar spoke, work on such legislation had already started in the Ministry of Justice. On 9 June 1997 the Criminal Law Amendment Bill (B46–97) was formally tabled in parliament. The Chair of the Parliamentary Portfolio Committee on Justice, Mr J. de Lange MP, issued a press statement[5] in which he explained that the Bill dealt with matters relating to the abolition of the death penalty and with the introduction of minimum sentences. The statement listed both the offences for which minimum sentences had to be imposed and the specific sentences laid down for them, but it was silent on the fact that there was any provision for courts to depart from these minima. The press statement called for comment on the Bill.

The Bill provided for minimum sentences to be imposed by regional magistrates' and high courts for certain serious offences. Those in part I of schedule 2 should be punished with imprisonment of at least 15, 20 or 25 years for a first, a second, or a third or subsequent offence respectively (cl 52(1)(a)). For the offences listed in part II of schedule 2 the minimum periods were 10, 15 and 20 years respectively (cl 52(1)(b)). This list of offences in the schedule was relatively selective. It included, for example only specific types of murder and rape. The courts could, of course, impose heavier sentences than the prescribed minima (cl 52(1)).[6]

A noteworthy innovation in the draft legislation was the provision for a court to impose lighter sentences than the prescribed minima if in its opinion there were 'circumstances' that would justify such lighter sentences (cl 52(3)).

All that the court had to do was to record what these 'circumstances' were and it would then have the discretion to impose lighter sentences. This clause was of great significance, for the effect was that the draft Bill was not setting up a system that would create truly mandatory sentences. A simple finding of undefined 'circumstances' would in practice re-establish the discretion of the sentencing court.

The B46–97 version of the Bill was made available for public comment. Most comments focused on the two clauses and the schedule that dealt with mandatory sentences and in particular on the principle involved. A subcommittee of judges of the Supreme Court of Appeal, in a letter under the signature of Chief Justice Mohamed, expressed the established view of the judiciary:

> We are strongly opposed in principle to minimum sentence as envisaged in cl 52. We believe that all sentencing should in all cases be left to the discretion of the presiding judicial officer with due regard to the circumstances of each particular case. The Attorney General has the right to appeal against an inadequate sentence ... This, in our view, provides a sufficient safeguard. We note that provision is made for a lighter sentence if circumstances as envisaged in cl 52 are present, and that cl 52 is intended to be of limited duration (see cl 53). This to some extent takes the 'sting' out of the proposed sentences (Committee Papers 1997, GG16).

The opposition to mandatory sentences was reiterated by other judges,[7] and by the Association of Law Societies (GG32) and the General Council of the Bar (GG19), the established organisations representing attorneys (solicitors) and advocates (barristers) respectively. Opposition was also expressed by the sentencing committee of the South African Law Commission (GG49), which was just beginning its own work on a more comprehensive reform of sentencing law. The same view was adopted by the National Association of Democratic Lawyers (NADEL), the radical lawyers' organisation historically closely associated with the liberation movements (GG28), and by the Human Rights Committee (GG20), which has a similar tradition. Many of these opponents of the proposed legislation commented too that departure from the prescribed sentences when 'circumstances' justifying this step were present, would lead to uncertainty and to extended appeals. Although these comments were made as part of a wider critique of the Bill, they were open to the opposite interpretation, that the impact of the Bill could be increased by limiting the circumstances under which departure from the prescribed sentences would be allowed.

There was of course also support for the principle of the Bill. It came mainly from magistrates[8] and prosecutors,[9] but they too commented from the perspective that the impact would be blunted by a liberal interpretation of 'circumstances' justifying departure or that courts could reduce the impact of the legislation by suspending the sentences they were mandated to impose.

Finally there were special interest lobbyists. Most prominent of these were those concerned with the rights of juveniles and they lobbied strenuously to have juveniles excluded from the ambit of the legislation.[10] Conversely, there was pressure from the National Council of Women of South Africa to provide for the inclusion of "heavy mandatory sentences … on all perpetrators of rape" (GG12).

The legislation as it finally emerged from the Parliamentary Portfolio Committee on Justice, which is the body largely responsible for detailed changes to draft legislation, responds in various ways to these diverse inputs. In respect of juveniles the criticisms were accepted and the Bill was modified accordingly.

In all other material respects requests for liberalisation were ignored and the final Act is harsher than the draft Bill. The changes include the introduction of a subsection that prescribes that mandatory minimum sentences cannot be suspended (s. 51(5)), the extension of the list of offences for which minimum sentences could be imposed and the addition of a mandatory life sentence for the most serious crimes (s. 51(1)).

Perhaps the most important change relates to the conditions that have to be met before a court can depart from the prescribed minima. Whereas in the draft Bill it was envisaged that the courts could depart if they found that there were "circumstances" justifying this step, this is now qualified by requiring "substantial and compelling circumstances" before a departure will be allowed. The legislative history of the words "substantial and compelling", which are not terms of art in South African law, is somewhat obscure. It appears that the Parliamentary Portfolio Committee on Justice wished to restrict the powers of the court to depart more drastically than the draft Bill allowed and that it toyed with the qualifiers "exceptional" and "substantial and compelling". In the end it chose the latter, which it may have derived from the submission of the Human Rights Committee (GG20), which referred to the use of the words "substantial and compelling circumstances", which are grounds for departure in the Minnesota Sentencing Guidelines. If this was the case it would be ironic, as the submission of the Human Rights Committee was very critical of directly legislated mandatory sentences and suggested that a guidelines-based approach such as that in Minnesota be considered as an alternative.[11]

In its amended form the mandatory minimum sentencing legislation was unanimously adopted by parliament (*Hansard* 1997, col. 6119). One may speculate that parliament would not have been as enthusiastic about the legislation had the legislative process been slightly different. The fact that it formed part of the complex Bill that formally removed the death penalty from the statute book must have played a part. This could have been particularly important in the acceptance of mandatory life sentences, which were perceived as a substitute for the death penalty although they would apply far more widely than the death penalty had. However, the liberal Democratic Party, which one may have expected to lead the opposition to these harsh mandatory sentences for first offences, had itself introduced a bill providing for a harsher form of life imprisonment and may have found it difficult to oppose the life sentences now being required.

Secondly, the late introduction of the words "substantial and compelling" meant that they were not considered by the judiciary or by other critics of the legislation. The wide grounds for departure which a mere finding of 'circumstances' would have allowed, may have introduced a degree of complacency as the judges may have thought that the 'sting' had been removed from the legislation. This is mere speculation. It is at least as likely that no judicial protest would have succeeded and that the fear of being seen to be soft on crime would have led to the enthusiastic adoption of the legislation, no matter how it was presented. In the debate in the National Assembly not much attention was paid to detail. The Minister of Justice emphasised that departures from the prescribed minima were allowed and that the legislation was a temporary measure (*Hansard* 1997, col. 6118). This seems to have been enough to remove any doubts that may have existed in the minds of parliamentarians.

Interpreting the New Act

Once the new Act had finally come into force the interesting question was whether the judiciary would attempt to limit the impact of the Act by interpreting it strictly. Initially it appeared as if the fact that departures from the prescribed minima were allowed if "substantial and compelling circumstances" existed, gave the judges some room to manoeuvre. This is also a question of considerable practical and constitutional significance. There can be no constitutional objection to the legislature indicating to the courts that it would like them to impose severe punishments for serious offences.

On the other hand, as we have seen, mandatory sentence requirements that could reasonably result in sentences that would be grossly disproportionate could well be held to be unconstitutional in South African law. The question is whether allowing departures in "substantial and compelling circumstances" will ensure that grossly disproportionate sentences are not imposed. In this regard much will depend on how the courts interpret the words "substantial and compelling circumstances".

Thus far the response of most South African judges has been relatively timid. In *S v Mofokeng* (1999) the first judgment to deal directly with the words "substantial and compelling circumstances", Judge Stegmann complained that his conscience and sense of justice were challenged by the new legislation. Inspired by the report of the Truth and Reconciliation Commission that encouraged judges to speak out against unjust laws, he expressed his "sense of affront at the inappropriate procedure devised by Parliament for the infliction on offenders, through the instrumentality of the courts, of arbitrary punishments of its own devising" (1999, p. 527b). In spite of this protest, however, Judge Stegmann did not consider the impact of the constitutional requirement of proportionality on what should be regarded as "substantial and compelling circumstances". His interpretation of the words was in fact extremely narrow. Judge Stegmann held that

> for 'substantial and compelling circumstances' to be found, the facts of the particular case must present some circumstance that is so exceptional in nature, and that so obviously exposes the injustice of the statutorily prescribed sentence in the particular case, that it can rightly be described as 'compelling' the conclusion that the imposition of a lesser sentence than that prescribed by Parliament is justified (1999, p. 523c).

Notwithstanding the rejection in the legislative process of "exceptional" as a qualifier of "circumstances", it seems that in this exposition Judge Stegmann confused circumstances that are "exceptional" with those that are "substantial and compelling". This is apparent also from his pronouncement that "'substantial and compelling" circumstances must be factors of an unusual and exceptional kind that Parliament cannot be supposed to have had in contemplation when prescribing standard penalties for certain crimes committed in circumstances described in Schedule 2 [of the Act]" (1999, p. 524d).

In substance Judge Stegmann's interpretation does not differ from that advanced in the Natal Division by Judge Squires, a former member of the Smith government in Rhodesia who is now a South African High Court judge. Judge Squires was not critical of the legislation at all and in *S v Madondo*

(1999) sought simply to ascertain in the traditional manner what parliament might have meant by "substantial and compelling" in the context of its apparent desire to require heavy, deterrent sentences. Judge Squires too set a very high standard for departure. He focused not so much on the type of circumstance that would be "substantial and compelling" but commented that only if the prescribed sentence was so inappropriate that no reasonable court would have imposed it, would there necessarily be a compelling reason not to do so. The result in both the *Mofokeng* case and the *Madondo* case was that the court found no "substantial and compelling circumstances" and imposed mandatory sentences of life imprisonment.

There have been attempts at giving a much wider interpretation to "substantial and compelling circumstances". In *S v Cimani* (1999) Jones J declined to give a comprehensive definition of the words. Nevertheless, he expanded on them by holding that:

> In every case, however, the nature of the circumstances must convince a reasonable mind that a lesser sentence is a proper sentence and that it is justified when regard is had to (a) the aggravating and mitigating features attendant upon the commission of what is already classified by the lawgiver as amongst the most serious of offences, and (b) the interests of society weighed against the interests of the offender (1999, p. 3).

This qualification is in fact so broad that it allows a sentencing court a virtually free hand to consider all the factors it would normally regard as relevant to sentence and to impose the sentence of its choice. The decision of Judge Jones appears to have been overlooked by the media.

Less fortunate was Judge Davis in the Cape Division. In *S v Jansen* (1999), a case involving the rape of a child, Judge Davis carefully interpreted the words "substantial and compelling" in the light of their Minnesotan provenance and the constitutional rule against inflexible mandatory sentences. His conclusion, that the words allowed the court a limited but significant power to depart from the mandatory minima, was a sophisticated attempt to find an appropriate *via media*. Instead of the mandatory life sentence, he imposed a sentence of 18 years imprisonment, a heavy sentence by the standards that applied prior to the enactment of the new law. Judge Davis' sentence was subject to a storm of public criticism (*Cape Times*, 23 June 1999; *Cape Times*, 30 June 1999). Women's organisations joined editorial writers and the media in general in criticising the judge for stressing in an inappropriate way aspects of the crime that made it relatively less heinous in order to "give rapists a chance". To some extent this criticism is understandable, for in order to bring the sentence within the ambit of the "substantial and compelling circumstances" the judgment does play down aspects of the crime. However, this would not have been necessary had the statutory requirement not compelled such a strategy.

What the indignant public reaction reflects is how the legislation has placed the judiciary at a disadvantage. Prior to the legislation a sentence of 18 years imprisonment in a case like this, accompanied by some stern words from the bench, would have drawn widespread public approval. To impose the same sentence now judges have to explain why the crime is relatively not so serious. In so doing they run the risk of being perceived as being soft on crime, a perception which the political proponents of mandatory sentences can use to further their argument that such prescribed sentences are necessary because judges are too lenient and out of touch.[12]

The Future

The fact that the current mandatory sentencing provisions may be constitutional, if appropriately interpreted, does not mean that they are the most desirable means of structuring sentencing discretion. The current provisions are supposed to be temporary. If their life is not extended, it does not follow automatically, however, that nothing will be put in their place when they expire. The forces that led to their enactment are still prominent in South African society. Controlling crime remains a high national priority as reflected in the prominence given to it in the speech by President Mbeki on accepting office on 16 June 1999 (*Cape Times*, 17 June 1999). Moreover, increasing attention is being paid to other factors, such as a concern to limit sentencing disparities and the ability of the State to enforce the sentences imposed by the courts. Although most judges would like to see the mandatory sentencing provisions scrapped completely, their influence has declined, if anything, since the passage of the 1997 Criminal Law Amendment Act. If parliament is to move away from the current mandatory sentencing provisions, it is more likely that it will be persuaded by an approach that examines the shortcomings of the current provisions and proposes a more subtle but also more comprehensive sentencing framework, which would meet the clearly defined systemic objectives while leaving judges with some discretion to avoid the unjustly disproportionate sentences that blunt mandatory minima may generate.

In this context the role of the South African Law Commission is likely to be crucial. To some extent its proposals for sentencing reform are going to be influenced by the empirical work that is currently being conducted on its behalf on the impact of the new mandatory sentencing provisions on sentencing practice. Whatever the findings of this investigation, some hard choices will have to be made about how to accommodate the desire for clear sentencing guidelines, whether imposed directly by parliament, or developed by some form of sentencing commission, or by the courts, or by a combination of these three. Such guidelines will have to deal with the limited capacity of the penal system to carry out the sentences of the courts as well as the judicial demands for sentencing discretion. The possibility that something new will emerge is strong, as the unfettered judicial discretion of the past is unlikely to be reinstated fully.

Postscript

In December 2000 the South African law Commission recommended an entirely new sentencing framework to replace both the temporary mandatory sentence legislation described in this chapter and the previous *laissez faire* regime. The government has not yet responded to these new proposals. In March and April 2001 both the Supreme Court of Appeal and the Constitutional Court upheld the constitutionality of the current legislation. In May 2001 a proclamation in the *Government Gazette* extended the operation of the 'temporary' legislation for a further year. These developments cannot be analysed here. It is enough to note that, while they do not necessarily mean that the temporary will become permanent, the social forces described in this paper continue to operate. The conundrum surrounding mandatory sentences in South Africa is far from being resolved.

Acknowledgements

This paper is a revised version of a paper read at the Sentencing and Society Conference, Glasgow 24–26 July 1999. It is reprinted by permission of Sage Publications Ltd from *Punishment and Society* (2000), 2(2), pp. 197–212, © SAGE Publications. I am thankful to Paula Proudlock of the Human Rights Committee for assisting me by collecting the material on mandatory sentences that was placed before parliament, to Paul Louw of the Office of the Director General of Public Prosecutions in Pretoria for providing me with access to copies of unreported judgments and to Ricky Röntsch for her research assistance. Although I was the project leader of the committee on sentencing of the South African Law Commission, this paper reflects my views and not those of the Law Commission.

Notes

1 The *National Crime Prevention Strategy* (1996) is embodied in a document produced by the interdepartmental strategy team of the Departments of Correctional Services, Intelligence, Justice, Safety and Security and Welfare.

2 Literally, People Against Gangsterism and Drugs. For a discussion of the rise and impact of PAGAD, see Le Roux 1997; Nina 1996.

3 See, for example, the comments of Judge Els in 'Four killers sentenced to two life terms', *The Star*, 8 December 1998.

4 See *S v Mashodi en 'n ander* (1999) where an effective sentence of 60 years imprisonment was set aside on appeal; *S v Maeseko* (1998) where an appellate court had to intervene to reduce a sentence of 50 years as this might have meant in practice that the offender would serve a longer term than someone sentenced to life imprisonment.

5 Interestingly enough the very title of the press release drew a connection between the abolition of the death penalty and the introduction of minimum sentences. 'New Bill Deletes all References to the Death Sentence but Imposes Minimum Sentences for Serious Offences', Press statement by Johnny de Lange, Chairperson of the Portfolio Committee on Justice. The substance of this statement was reported in *Business Day*, 10 June 1997.

6 The regional courts were limited to five years or more than the prescribed minima. Nevertheless, the secondary effect was to increase significantly the sentencing jurisdiction of the regional magistrates' courts.

7 See the comment by Judge Friedman, Judge President of the Cape (GG 21) and that of Judge Pickard, Judge President of Ciskei (GG 2); but cf. the submission by Judge Lichtenburg, Judge President of the traditionally more conservative Free State, who gave qualified acceptance to the Bill because of the provision for departure from the prescribed mandatory minimum sentences (GG 6).

8 Historically magistrates in South Africa have been civil servants with less independence than judges, who are appointed from private practice. The new government is attempting to change this. On the views of the magistrates, see the comment by Mr J.H. Bekker, the acting regional court president, Pretoria, that: 'although we are not generally in favour of compulsory minimum sentences there is an understanding of the Government's determination to fight crime (in particular serious crime) effectively' (GG 3). Mr Bekker's primary concern though, was to argue for an increase of the sentencing jurisdiction of the regional magistrates' courts. See also Regional Magistrate H. Wolmarans (GG 5), who adopts a similar view and the Association of Regional Magistrates of South Africa who made increased jurisdiction the basis of their submission.

9 Support for the principle of the legislation came from Mr M.T. van der Merwe SC, Attorney General of the Free State (FF 12) and from Mr W. Clark, senior public prosecutor in Verulam (GG 4), Mr J. Slabbert (GG18) and Ms R. Berg (GG 25) of the Office of the Attorney General of the Cape. Qualified support was given by Mr J.A. Swanepoel, the Director of the Office of Serious Economic Offences (GG 8). However, it was opposed by Mr L.J.

Roberts, the Attorney General of the Eastern Cape and Mr C.D.H.O. Nel, the Attorney-General of Transkei.

10 See the submission for Ms Ann Skelton of Lawyers for Human Rights and Ms Julia Sloth-Nielsen of the Community Law Centre at the University of the Western Cape (GG 31).

11 For a discussion of the interpretation of the Minnesota Sentencing Guidelines in South Africa, see van Zyl Smit 1999a.

12 For a further example, see the comment by Ms Bronwyn Pithey, the legal adviser of Rape Crisis, that a sentence of 10 years imposed on a recidivist rapist was 'horrific' and that it 'sends such a clear message that rape is not taken seriously by the judiciary' (*Sunday Times*, 29 August 1999, p. 1).

References

Abel, R.L. (1995), *Politics by Other Means: Law in the struggle against Apartheid, 1980–1994*, New York: Routledge.

Asmal, K., Asmal, L. and Roberts, R.S. (1996), *Reconciliation through Truth: A reckoning of Apartheid's criminal governance*, Cape Town: David Philips.

Business Day (1997), 'New Bill to Expunge Statutory References to the Death Penalty', 10 June.

Cape Argus (1997a), 'Killer gets 2410 Years', 10 December.

Cape Argus (1997b), 'Minimum Sentencing only a Temporary Step, Says Omar', 18 February.

Cape Times (1990), 'The State President's Speech', 3 February.

Cape Times (1999a), 'Rapists Given Chances, Victims Battle', 30 June.

Cape Times (1999b), 'Give Rapists a Chance Too – Judge', 23 June.

Cape Times (1999c), 'Assuming the Mantle of Power: President Mbeki's vision', 17 June.

Cape Times (1999d), 'Zwame Judge labelled a racist dinosaur', 27 March.

Committee Papers (1997), *Submission to the Portfolio Committee on Justice*, Cape Town: Government Printers (the references to 'GG' and 'FF' are to the reference numbers given by the secretariat of the Portfolio Committee on Justice to the submission it received).

GG 2   Judge Pickard, Judge President of Ciskei.
GG 3   Mr J.H. Bekker, Acting regional court president, Pretoria.
GG 4   Mr W. Clark, Senior public prosecutor, Verulam.
GG 5   H. Wolmarans, Regional Magistrate.
GG 6   Judge Lichtenburg, Judge President, Free State.
GG 8   Mr J.A. Swanepoel, Director of the Office of Serious Economic Offences.
GG 12   National Council of Women of South Africa.
GG 16   Chief Justice Mohamed, Supreme Court of Appeal.
GG 18   Mr J. Slabbert, Office of the Attorney General of the Cape.
GG 19   General Council of the Bar.
GG 20   Human Rights Committee.
GG 21   Judge Friedman, Judge President of the Cape.
GG 25   Ms R. Berg, Office of the Attorney General of the Cape.
GG 28   The National Association of Democratic Lawyers.
GG 31   Ms A. Skelton of Lawyers for Human Rights and Ms J. Sloth-Nielsen of the Community Law Centre, University of the Western Cape.
GG 32   Association of Law Societies.

GG 49   South African Law Commission.

FF 12   Mr M.T. van der Merwe, Attorney General of the Free State.

Department of Foreign Affairs (1968), *South Africa and the Rule of Law*, Pretoria: Government Printers.

Departments of Correctional Services, Intelligence, Justice, Safety and Security and Welfare (1996), *National Crime Prevention Strategy*, Pretoria: Government Printers.

Doob, A.N. (1995), 'The United States Commission Sentencing Guidelines: If you don't know where you are going, you might not get there', in C. Clarkson and R. Morgan (eds), *The Politics of Sentencing Reform*, Oxford: Oxford University Press.

Dunbar, I. and Langdon, A. (1998), *Tough Justice*, London: Blackstone.

Dyzenhaus, D. (1998), *Judging the Judges, Judging Ourselves*, Oxford: Hart.

Frase, R. (1997), 'Sentencing Principles on Theory and Practice', *Crime and Justice*, Vol. 22, p. 363.

Hansard (1983), Debates of the National Parliamentary Assembly, Vol. 71, 28 March 1983, col. 4066–71, Cape Town: Government Printers.

Hansard (1997), Debates of the National Parliamentary Assembly, Vol. 22 , 6 November 1997, col. 6118–19, Cape Town: Government Printers.

Le Roux, C.J.B. (1997), 'People Against Gangsterism and Drugs (PAGAD)', *Journal for Contemporary History*, Vol. 22, p. 51.

Mail and Guardian (1997), 'Sadist Grins at Light Fine', 7 November.

Morris, N. (1974), *The Future of Imprisonment*, London: University Chicago Press.

Nedcor Project (1996), *The Nedcor Project on Crime, Violence and Investment: Executive Summary of the Main Report*, Johannesburg: Nedcor.

Nina, D. (1996), 'Popular Justice or Vigilantism?', *Crime and Conflict*, Vol. 7, p. 1.

The Star (1998), 'Four Killers Sentenced to Two Life Terms', 8 December.

Sunday Times (1999), 'Outrage over Judge's Findings in Rape Case', 29 August.

Van Zyl Smit, D. (1996), 'Sentencing and Punishment', in M. Chaskalson et al. (eds), *Constitutional Law of South Africa*, Cape Town: Juta.

Van Zyl Smit, D. (1999a), 'Criminological Ideas and the South African Transition', *British Journal of Criminology*, Vol. 39, p. 198.

Van Zyl Smit, D. (1999b), 'Mandatory Minimum Sentences and Departures from them in Substantial and Compelling Circumstances', *South African Journal on Human Rights*, Vol. 15, p. 270.

Viljoen Commission (1976), *Report of the Commission of Inquiry into the Penal System of the Republic of South Africa*, RP 78, Pretoria: Government Printers.

Cases

S v Cimani, unreported judgment CC 11/99 delivered in the Eastern Cape Division of the High Court on 28 April 1999.

S v De Vries, 1996 (12) BCLR 1666 (Nm).

S v Holder, 1979 (2) SA 70 (A).

S v Jansen, 1999 (2) SA 368 (C).

S v Madondo, unreported judgement CC 22/99 delivered in the Natal Division of the High Court on 30 March 1999.

S v Maeseko, 1998 (1) SACR 451 (T).
S v Makwanyane and Another, 1995 (3) SA 391 (CC).
S v Masala, 1968 (3) SA 212 (A).
S v Mashodi en 'n ander, 1999 (1) SACR 282 (O).
S v Mhlakaza and another, 1997 (1) SACR 515 (T).
S v Mofokeng, 1999 (1) SACR 502 (T).
S v Mpetha, 1985 (3) SA 702 (A).
S v Scheepers, 1977 (2) SA 155 (A).
S v Toms; S v Bruce, 1990 (2) SA 802 (A).
S v Williams and others, 1995 (3) SA 332 (CC).

Statutes

Criminal Law Amendment Act 105 of 1997.
Criminal Law Amendment Act 107 of 1990.
Criminal Procedure Amendment Bill 1995.
Criminal Procedure Amendment Act 75 of 1995.
Criminal Procedure Second Amendment Act 85 of 1997.
Parole and Correctional Services Amendment Act 87 of 1997.
The Constitution of the Republic of South Africa, Act 200 of 1993.
The Constitution of the Republic of South Africa, Act 108 of 1996.

Chapter Four

Are Guided Sentencing and Sentence Bargaining Incompatible? Perspectives of Reform in the Italian Legal System

Grazia Mannozzi

The 'Unitary' Model of Sentencing Delineated in the Criminal Code

The evolution of sentencing in Italy has followed, in some instances, a rather different course to that of other European and non-European legal systems. In other, non-Italian systems, progress has been from a model of *indeterminate sentencing* based on rehabilitation, to a *determinate* paradigm based on the principle of *proportion*.

On the contrary, the Italian system, traditionally tied to a determinate/ retributive model, has evolved towards a rehabilitative approach.

It may be helpful at this stage to provide an overview of the structure of Italian sentencing. This will help the reader to understand the significance of the relationship between the sentencing rules enacted by the criminal code and the sentencing rules enacted by the code of criminal procedure: in other words, between sentencing and sentence bargaining.

The Italian Criminal Code (CC)[1] establishes, with Articles 132 and 133,[2] a 'unitary', *monophase* sentencing model, where the judge giving the verdict also sets the punishment. The model also features '*guided*' *discretion* because it is based on a law which acts similarly to the 'narrative guidelines' adopted by Sweden (von Hirsch and Ashworth 1998, pp. 229, 240). The sentence can be appealed, both on the basis of merit and the form and amount of punishment, before a Judge of Appeal and can successively be brought before the Court of Cassation, for reasons of unlawfulness.

In particular, Art. 132 CC establishes the *discretionary power of the judge*, which must be exercised within the legal sentence ranges, and imposes the *obligation to* justify the sentence with reference to the reconstruction of the offence and the *type* and *quantity* of the punishment.

Art. 133 CC lays down the *criteria* that must guide the judge in the application of his/her discretionary powers.

The two fundamental guiding criteria are:

a) the seriousness of the crime, which is be derived from a series of *objective* and *subjective* indices (i.e. *actus reus*, *mens rea*, gravity of the damage caused, etc.);
b) the *capacity to commit crimes of the offender*, derived from a series of secondary factors implying the formulation of a predictive judgement regarding the future behaviour of the offender.

Despite its innovative character, which in its time was in the legal avant-garde, Art. 133 of our code has not provided a practical solution to the problem of grading punishment because it affords a very wide range of criteria – termed 'factual criteria' since they are related to the facts[3] – that the judge should take into consideration in order to establish the punishment. Since Art. 133 allows so many factors to be taken into account, no real policy about how to assess the relative seriousness of a case emerges. Moreover, no indications were given by the legislator regarding the aims of criminal punishment. The absence of this parameter has meant that, in practice, the discretionary powers of the judge have remained wholly without guidance.

It should be pointed out that the transparent exercise of judicial discretion has been made arduous by the fact that the Italian Criminal Code sets very severe grades of mandatory punishment, which derive from the particular cultural context (Mussolini's Fascist government) in which the Penal Code was made law, in far-off 1930. The establishment of extremely severe mandatory minimums has meant that in more recent times judges have generally applied the minimum sentence, thus foregoing, in practice, their discretionary power. This widespread lowering of sentencing rates to their minimum by judges (made feasible by the adroit use of mitigating circumstances), has ended up by making the provision for the justification for the sentence superfluous. This is because each time the sentence is close to the mandatory minimum, the judge avoids enunciating the reasons that led him to apply the punishment in question.

Jurisprudence at the highest level (that is, the Court of Cassation) has exhibited very little interest in the substantive aspects of sentencing, particularly regarding the problem of the rationale behind punishment. The doctrinal debate on this issue, both nationally and internationally, has only had a slight impact on this Court's rulings. This debate might have otherwise helped to provide an orientation for judges in the lower courts by encouraging self-regulation.

Rulings in favour of *retribution* are rare and dated; indeed, in some cases, punishment had even been spoken of as a "salve for the soul". On the subject of general prevention, jurisprudence is uncertain and contradictory. *General prevention* is at times included, at others explicitly excluded from the hierarchy of objectives of punishment. Much more numerous are the rulings in favour of *rehabilitation*, also due to the explicit mention of this ideal in the Italian Constitution.[4]

In practice, the lack of indications in the Code regarding the aims of punishment and the reluctance of judges adequately to justify the sentence when it is meted out (the most common formula is 'the punishment fits the crime' or 'the punishment is appropriate for the crime committed') have led to lack of control over the exercise of discretionary powers and more or less hidden forms of sentencing disparity.

Not even the explicit Constitutional provision for the "rehabilitation of the offender" (Art. 27, 3rd section) seems to have been able to definitively orient the criteria of sentencing as set by Art. 133 of the Criminal code. Moreover, the Constitutional Court has generally exhibited the tendency to emphasise the so-called "polyfunctional theory of punishment" (Vassalli 1961, p. 297), according to which any one of the following aims: *retribution*, *rehabilitation* and even *deterrence*, may be considered by the judge in establishing the type of punishment (imprisonment, fine, or 'semi-detention', etc.) and, above all, the length of imprisonment, according to the characteristics of each single case (see Corte Costituzionale, Judgement No. 107/1980).

The 'polyfunctional theory' – interpreted as the mere juxtaposition of retribution, rehabilitation and deterrence – however, cannot reconcile the opposing arguments associated with either of the traditional purposes of punishment. Moreover, it leads to the risk that a whole variety of features that should properly belong to each single traditional rationale will be lumped together in justification for an individual sentence, with the further effects of leaving the way open for disparate approaches to sentencing and, moreover, of strengthening the system of surveillance and repression.

The Crisis of the Unitary Model of Sentencing

The 'unitary' model of sentencing, based on Articles 132 and 133 of the Criminal Code and on a complex system of aggravating or mitigating circumstances (see Articles 61–70 and, in particular, Art. 62 *bis*,[5] of Criminal Code), has entered into a 'crisis' for two reasons.

a) *The first factor* that broke up the 'unitary model' of sentencing was the introduction of two different categories of measures to avoid incarceration of offenders: *alternative measures* (*misure alternative*) which represent a non custodial or a semi-custodial way of serving punishment[6] and *substitutive sanctions* (*sanzioni sostitutive*) which are noncustodial or semi-custodial penalties alternative to *short periods of imprisonment* (up to one year).[7] These both can be considered as 'intermediate sanctions', since they "fall between prison and probation in their severity and intrusiveness" (Tonry 1996, p. 100).

When an offender is sentenced to a term of *imprisonment* by the Sentencing Judge, the sanction inflicted can be modified qualitatively and quantitatively (even by a different judge).

Firstly, the same sentencing judge can directly suspend any term of imprisonment of up to two years, according to Art. 162 of the Criminal Code. Beginning in 1981, the sentencing judge can, within certain limits, also substitute those terms of imprisonment of up to one year with the above mentioned substitutive sanctions, which include: *semidetenzione* (semi-detention), *libertà controllata* and *pena pecuniaria* (fine).

Secondly, the sentence inflicted might be modified by a different judge – called 'Magistrato di sorveglianza' (Supervisory Judge) – who has the power to apply an *alternative measure* or to impose the *house arrest*, which is today beginning to be considered as a fully fledged *alternative* both to imprisonment and to other measures, and not simply as an alternative modality of serving imprisonment (Paliero 1998, p. 815).

The length of imprisonment, as laid down by the trial judge, can also be modified, during execution, by the 'Giudice dell'esecuzione' (Enforcement Judge).[8] Any offender who has served a certain portion of his/her sentence may be granted a conditional release (Art. 176 CC).

b) *The second factor* leading to a crisis of the unitary model of sentencing is the introduction, following a reform of the criminal trial,[9] of the so-called *differentiated* criminal proceedings: *sentence bargaining* (provided by Art. 444 of Code of Criminal Procedure [CCP]), and *summary trial* (provided by Art. 442 CCP).

The 'summary trial' is an institution of general character that can be applied to the majority of crimes. If the defendant asks for a summary trial during the preliminary hearing, the punishment in the case of the accused being found guilty is reduced by exactly one third (i.e. a sentence to six years of imprisonment is reduced to four as a reward for having chosen a summary trial).

In contrast, 'sentence bargaining' (which the Italian Code of Criminal Procedure defines as 'applicazione della pena su richiesta' (application of the sentence on request)) is not an institution of general character. In the first place, the Italian legal system is based on the principle of *mandatory prosecution*, meaning that only *sentence bargaining* is possible and *not charge bargaining*. In the second place, the parties can agree on the sentence only if, after having taken into consideration all the circumstances and any reductions for having chosen this alternative procedure, it comes to less than two years of imprisonment. One should also be aware of the fact that any reduction in punishment for having chosen the sentence bargaining procedure does not amount to exactly one third but is *up* to one third, although the reduction is usually applied in its largest extension.

However, it should be pointed out that in the Italian legal system the role of the prosecutor is less important than in the United States. With our sentence bargaining system, the prosecutor has nothing to gain (or almost), given that the reduction in punishment is not given 'in exchange' for a *plea of guilty*. This is because the sentence which concludes the trial, while still meting out a punishment, paradoxically, does not constitute an equivalent to an admission of guilt by the offender. Nor can the reduction of punishment be accorded in exchange for collaboration by the accused in handing over other offenders to justice (Grevi 1988, p. 304). The only advantage for the prosecutor is in *shortening the trial* and *simplifying the gathering of evidence*.

The fact that sentence bargaining is used mainly to enhance efficiency and the organisational problems of the judicial system and not for prevention or retribution, brings in elements which contrast with the key principles of sentencing as laid down in the Criminal Code.

The Effects of the 'Fragmentation' of the Unitary Model of Sentencing

Judge Marvin Frankel, in his work *Criminal Sentences: Law Without Order*, wrote:

> In the great majority of federal criminal cases ... a defendant who comes up for

sentencing has no way of knowing or reliably predicting whether he will walk out of the courtroom on probation, or be locked up for a term of years that may consume the rest of his life, or something in between (Frankel 1973).

The problems afflicting Italian sentencing are perhaps less serious, but it is certain that piecemeal reforms limited to a number of sectors of the criminal justice system have had a series of negative effects on sentencing and on the sanctions system in general.

These 'negative' or 'undesirable' effects following reforms which have affected the sentencing system can be summarised as follows:

The Labyrinth Effect

The first problem to emerge, chronologically speaking, could be defined as the 'labyrinth effect'.

The prison sentence, whose prerequisites of *swiftness* and *certainty*[10] have been weakened by trials which are still too long, has also become precarious, because it can become lost in a *labyrinth* of 'alternatives', which may be imposed either by the Sentencing Judge, or the Enforcement Judge.

The sentence becomes only an abstract, theoretical punishment, in relation to which the punishment to be served is at the most only a fraction of the original, often limited and subject to a whole host of variants.

The Widening of Penalty Ranges

The labyrinth effect is further aggravated by the progressive widening of penalty ranges due to the introduction of sentence bargaining. This has brought our system closer to the paradigm of *indeterminate* sentencing: in particular, close to those legal systems in which the legislator establishes the maximum penalty only (see, for example, in Europe, the French legal system where judges have wide discretion).

Two Practical Examples

The Crime of Robbery (Art. 628 CC)

For the crime of robbery, the virtual sentence range, as set down in the Criminal Code, prescribes a sentence varying from *three* to *10* years.

Let us now move into the *real* punishment frame. That is, the one emerging from a coordinate reading of *substantive* norms regarding sentencing (i.e. the aggravating and the mitigating factors) as well as *procedural* rules regarding sentence bargaining and the summary trial.

Minimum Punishment

- In the presence of more than one mitigating circumstance, the term of imprisonment may only amount to *nine months*;
- in cases of sentence bargaining or summary trial there is a further reduction by (up to) one third: the term may drop to *six months*;
- at this point, one of the following six alternatives might be chosen instead of imprisonment. One of the following three alternatives may be selected by the Sentencing Judge directly:

  a) suspended sentence (Art. 162 CC), or;
  b) *semidetenzione* (semi-detention) (Art. 53 and 55 Act No. 689/1981) or;
  c) *libertà controllata* (Art. 53 and 56 Act No. 689/1981).

Where the sentencing judge intends to impose imprisonment, the Supervisory Judge might autonomously impose one of the following three alternatives:

  a) house arrest (Art. 47 *ter* Act No. 354/1975), or;
  b) *affidamento in prova* (Art. 47 Act No. 354/1975), or;
  c) *semilibertà* (Art. 48 Act No. 354/1975).

Maximum Punishment

- In the case of more than one aggravating circumstance, a term of imprisonment of up to *24 years* may be imposed.

To sum up, the term of imprisonment set for the crime of corruption may vary from the suspended sentence (available for punishments involving less than two years of imprisonment), which in practice means *no punishment*, to 24 years of incarceration. The maximum punishment is so out of proportion with the objective seriousness of the crime, that it will never be imposed by judges. We should infer from this that punishments that are too severe (i.e. punishments not proportionate to the seriousness of the offence) are 'symbolic' punishments, with a low rate of effectiveness.[11]

The Crime of Murder (Art. 575 CC)

The crime of murder is punished by a sentence of no less than *21 years*.

Minimum Punishment

- In the presence of more than one mitigating circumstance, the term of imprisonment may be theoretically reduced to 5 years and 6 months;
- by applying a further reduction for the 'alternative' trial procedure (in this case only a summary trial and not sentence bargaining is permitted, with a reduction of exactly one third), we could come to 3 years 6 months imprisonment;
- there are three alternatives at this point:

  a) after 1 year and 6 months imprisonment the Supervisory Judge may impose the 'house arrest';
  b) after 6 months imprisonment the Supervisory Judge may impose the *affidamento in prova*; (Probation under surveillance of social services);
  c) finally, after 2 years and 2 months imprisonment, the Supervisory Judge, if unable to impose the *affidamento in prova*, may impose the *semilibertà*.

Maximum Punishment

- There is a variety of aggravating circumstances for murder in the Criminal Code. In this case (i.e. for premeditation, or for having murdered one's parents or children) the offender may be sentenced to life imprisonment.

Thus, likewise for murder, starting from a 'virtual' punishment comprising anything from *21 years* to life, there is a 'real' punishment that may range from *3 years* and *6 months* imprisonment to a *life sentence*.

Discrepancy with the Objectives of Punishment

The substantive impact of the laws regarding special procedures in the Code of Criminal Procedure (CCP) means that sentencing, in the context of sentence bargaining and the summary trial, shows markedly 'autonomous' characteristics. This in particular regards the concentration of the judge's former discretionary powers in the hands of the 'trial adversaries' (prosecutor and defendant). Hence a paradigm of sentencing has emerged which is 'parallel' to that laid down in the Criminal Code. This new paradigm has endosystematic aims (i.e. internal to the system) and creates serious problems of compatibility with the rationale of punishment which should normally guide the judge in the sentencing process.

Some have argued for sentence bargaining by referring to the aims of punishment in terms of the need for *general prevention*, since the diminished severity of the punishment would be balanced by its *swiftness* and *certainty*.

In this way, the institution of sentence bargaining would find its place at a substantive level in a theory of end-oriented sentencing. Holding the trial in the shortest possible time to decrease the case load in criminal justice and reducing punishments to reward collaboration by defendants, would inevitably lead to sentences which *no longer correspond to the* seriousness *of the crime as* originally *evaluated by the legislator* in the Criminal Code, *nor meet the need for rehabilitation*. Hence, such measures fail to satisfy both the requisite of *proportion* and the aim of *rehabilitation*.

In regard to *proportion*: the crime is no less serious because repression is swifter. In regard to *rehabilitation*: foregoing the defendant's guarantees provided by an adversary trial gives no indication as to his/her suitability as a candidate for rehabilitation (Padovani 1992, p. 932). At this point, the paradox emerges of a punishment which has been *reduced* to meet the objective of *general prevention*, justified solely on the basis of the willingness of the defendant to forgo the guarantees of the adversary trial.

Reasonable doubts persist, moreover, as to whether *swiftness* and *certainty* of punishment – now assured only by sentence bargaining and the summary trial (but without being associated with the parameter of the *adequate severity* of the sentence), can effectively play a deterrent role. This is because swiftness of punishment is counterbalanced by a scarce visibility of the punishment meted out: the summary trial and sentence bargaining prevalently occur during the preliminary hearing, which is not open to the public. Thus the *most certain* and *swift* punishments are also the *least visible*.

Unwarranted Sentencing Disparity from a Trial Source

The Italian system has experienced forms of disparity due particularly to the lack of a hierarchy organising the aims of punishment. This has given legitimacy to *different* punishments for cases with the same characteristics (at least *objective* ones).

To this historical (and chronic) problem of sentencing, other problems have been added connected to a new source of disparity: that occurring during the trial.

Two cases involving the same crime, with the same objective and subjective characteristics, may be punished very differently. The sentencing range according to the type of trial starts from a suspended sentence, implying an immediate exit from the penal/prison system, to the application of imprisonment which, although softened by the imposition of intermediate sanctions, obviously involves significantly greater suffering.

The problem becomes of even greater urgency when one realises that sentence bargaining and the summary trial are becoming the most common trial type to be followed (see Appendix B, Table 4.1 for Magistrates' Courts and Table 4.2 for Criminal Courts).

This phenomenon of disparity in sentencing, already unacceptable from the substantive point of view, risks weakening the 'internalisation' by society of the value judgements expressed by the legislator, thus frustrating the principle of general prevention which is the mainstay of the doctrine justifying the application of differentiated trial procedures.

Prescriptions for Reform

In brief, the prescriptions for reform aimed at solving the main problems of Italian sentencing can be summarised as follows.

Contrasting the 'Labyrinth' Effect by Limiting the Alternatives to Imprisonment

Here crime policy calls for restricting the variety of 'alternative measures' and 'substitutive sanctions' mentioned above which are available to judges.

Against the creative proliferation of models and types of penalties and intermediate sanctions, this approach proposes a different strategy: limiting punishment to simple alternatives of tried and monitored usefulness (Paliero 1992, p. 556). For example, intensive probation, community service, or fine (to be applied according to the German *Tagessatzsystem*, which is a day-fine system).[12]

Counteracting Widening of Sentence Range by a Clearer Legislative
Specification of Penalties Options

Rather than opposing the anachronistic sentence range of the authoritarian
1930 Criminal Code by surreptitiously reducing the minimum terms of
imprisonment through use of mitigating factors or procedural rules regarding
the so-called 'differentiate criminal proceedings' (summary trial and sentence
bargaining), the solution would lie in formally fixing new punishment options
for each crime. This means that the reform of sentencing process should be
supported by a general reform of punishment options (imprisonment,
intermediate sanctions, fine) and of penalty range. In other words, a scale of
penalties should be devised in the form of a pyramid: the tip would be the
straightforward option of imprisonment, bordered below by the need for
general prevention; the base of the pyramid should be constituted by fines,
while intensive probation, house arrest and an appropriate model of
community service would take up intermediate positions.

   The choice of precepts to associate with these levels of punishment would
take place later, following a cost/benefits analysis of the real capacity of the
state to apply each category of punishment (this proposal was made by Paliero
1992, p. 560).

Counteracting Unwarranted Substantive Disparity by Fixing a Hierarchy
of the Aims of Punishment

A theory of punishment, especially if the system of punishment is considered
an independent variable of a more thorough reform of the criminal justice
system, requires conceptual clarity and consistency. To this end, the Italian
legislature should abandon its deep seated indifference towards establishing
rationale for punishment. The vital issue in any reform of sentencing is the
definition of the goals of punishment, which must logically take place before
any choice is made by the legislator regarding types of penalties or the
'regulation' of penalty range.

   In the North American reform of sentencing, for example, just desert was
chosen as the founding principle for the coherent development of the
articulations of the sentencing system (von Hirsch 1976; von Hirsch, Knapp
and Tonry 1987; Tonry 1996; von Hirsch and Ashworth 1998). The final
objectives of this criminal policy, however, were not limited to the simple
reaffirmation of the principle of proportion.

   What then could be the rationale to give to punishment?

In seeking a response to this question, one must consider that the latest development of the modern theory of punishment was, at least in Europe, the syncretistic-dialectical model devised by Roxin in the mid-1960s (Volk 1993). In other words, for each phase of punishment – threat, infliction, enforcement – there are *dominant* criminal policy aims and *recessive* ones, having the function of *limiting* the other aims:

- the threat of punishment phase is generally guided by considerations of general prevention;
- the sentencing phase, in contrast, is guided by the principle of special prevention (and, particularly, by rehabilitation), but within the bounds of punishment proportionate to the liability of the offender;
- the enforcement phase, should strive towards the 'rehabilitation' of the offender, wherever possible and on a voluntary basis only.

Thus, the tendency should be towards a *complex* sentencing system, similar to the above mentioned Roxinian paradigm, but which also takes into account new variables, such as the *capacity* of the system *for sanction implementation*, the impact on the offender of the single models of punishment, and the results of the cost/benefit analysis applied to the sentencing system.

In this model, sentencing should essentially depend on the *type of penalties*.

a) *Imprisonment* This, above all, must be prescribed according to the principle of 'necessity', given that it is the most expensive option and that such costs are certainly not compensated by a high level of efficacy in terms (final objective) of a reduction in recidivism. Prison sentences should be imposed only in those cases where there is a high seriousness of crime, and where the perpetrators are generally unresponsive to any form of rehabilitation.

Under these conditions, sentencing cannot but follow a 'secular' retributive model: in practice, the principle of proportionality between crime and punishment. 'Costly' punishments, as prison sentences normally are, have a very low level of effective rehabilitation, and should be graded according to the guarantee of 'just deserts' (von Hirsch 1976).

b) *Intermediate sanctions* If the rehabilitative ideal appears to be inconsistent, at least in Italy, with the present features of imprisonment (with serious problems like overcrowding), this does not imply that rehabilitation should be abandoned altogether. In fact, rehabilitation should play an extremely constructive role in the evolution of the system, especially with regard to the choice of *intermediate sanctions*.

Earmarked for rehabilitation should be those noncustodial penalties, which must also be evaluated according to their efficacy. In other words, the fulfilment of rehabilitative aims should be the task of punishment forms, such as fines and community service,[13] which have shown in practice to be characterised by a satisfactory cost/benefit ratio.

It would also be positive if the application of such 'substitutive' models – to use a term which still reflects a prison centred view of the sanction system – were no longer a prerogative of the discretion of the sentencing judge, and be previously and directly defined by the legislator as pertaining to crimes of average and low gravity.

c) *Suspended sentence* Suspended sentence in Italy has been progressively impoverished of any content, because, since 1990, in association with the main sentence (detention for a period of up to two years) the so-called pene accessorie (additional sanctions) – such as prohibition from taking public office, prohibition from undertaking certain occupations or trades, prohibition from participating in tenders for public contracts, loss or suspension of parenting rights, etc.[14] – are suspended too.

Instead of the suspended sentence, it would be better to adopt the outright 'waiving of punishment', as in the *l'Absehen von Strafe* which has been given widespread application in the German legal system,[15] but which operates in Italy only within the ambit of the juvenile justice system.[16]

The conflict in this case is between the principle of expediency *principio di opportunità* which justifies the non-response of the state to events which are intrinsically deserving of punishment (Volk 1993, p. 35), and the need for general prevention, which would justify the application of a symbolic punishment, but which is not damaging from the point of view of 'rehabilitation'. Nevertheless, this punishment may still be 'useful' in ensuring 'social stability'.

Counteracting Unwarranted Sentencing Disparity with a Trial Source by 'Bargaining Regulation'

Sentencing in the Italian legal system is no longer based on a single paradigm. The impact of summary proceedings and sentence bargaining on sentencing criteria has been significant: in all cases where a sentence is not given at the end of an adversary trial, the judge is mostly deprived of his/her discretionary powers regarding the degree of punishment. Instead of issuing from an evaluation of the criteria contained in Art. 133 CC, the degree of punishment, as we have seen, is established by negotiation between the parties.[17] It is thus vital that procedural rules regarding 'non-adversary proceedings' should be made consistent with 'substantive' rules on sentencing laid down by the Criminal Code.

In the Italian criminal justice system, subject to the principle of mandatory prosecution, the powers of the prosecutor are limited and circumscribed. 'Sentence bargaining', in practice, must always begin with the initiative of the defendant.[18] On the basis of calculations regarding the crime he/she is accused of and which cannot be subjected to negotiation, and with the assistance of a lawyer[19] the defendant thus proposes what 'his/her' punishment is to be. The prosecutor has only the *power of veto*, because his/her approval is mandatory in the application of this institution.

Thus the prosecutor is able to offer a 'reduced' punishment to the defendant, which can be defined according to general rules (a reduction up to one third of the primary sentence). However, the prosecutor can also can be a source of disparity of treatment simply by denying or giving (discretionally!) his/her approval of the choice of procedure.

So, the reduction of punishment 'requested' on the basis of Art. 444 CCP by the defendant, which the judge is obliged to apply to the sentence *in practice* (i.e. to the punishment which derives from his/her evaluation of the circumstances of the case) ultimately depends on the judgement of the prosecutor which cannot be challenged.[20]

A further step forward in the process of regulating sentence bargaining could then be the introduction of guidelines 'orienting' the discretion of the prosecutor in agreeing to the request for the application of punishment according to sentence bargaining. This would ensure a more uniform application of trial institutions characterised by 'rewards' and above all preventing the power of the prosecutor to veto the summary trial or sentence bargaining being used as an "instrument of pressure on the defendants or to reward collaboration by some of them".[21]

As Alan Dershowitz has rightly stated: "there can be no understanding of any sentencing system without proper appreciation of the role played by bargaining" (Dershowitz 1976, p. 81). And if any 'unity' is at all possible in sentencing, at least in terms of its rationale, this must surely pass through a consolidation of procedural rules regarding sentencing but within the ambit of 'substantive' rules (Monaco and Paliero 1994, p. 454).

Notes

1   The Italian Criminal Code was enacted in 1930.
2   See Appendix A.
3   In the Italian criminal doctrine, the term 'fact' indicates all the elements that describe a specific crime.
4   Article 27 of the Italian Constitution states: "Le pene non possono essere contrarie al senso di umanità e devono tendere alla rieducazione del condannato".
5   *Bis* means literally 'twice'. In the legal field, when one or more new articles have to be added this Latin word is used to distinguish the new article from the others.
6   The 'alternative sanctions', introduced by Act No. 354/1975, include a measure similar to the 'Probation order' (termed 'affidamento in prova al servizio sociale'), a semi-custodial measure that imposes on the offender to stay in prison during the night, but allows him to work or to study outside during the day (*semilibertà*), and a measure similar to the early release (*liberazione anticipata*).
7   By Act No. 689/1981 three 'substitutive sanctions' were introduced: *semidetenzione*, which is a semi-custodial penalty that allows the prisoners to work outside; *libertà controllata*, which is a measure similar to intensive supervision, obliging the offender not to leave the municipality of residence unless authorised, to report to a police station once a day; moreover, the offender cannot carry weapons and his/her passport is withdrawn; *pena pecuniaria* (fine), which involves the payment of a sum of money which is proportionate to the seriousness of the crime and the income and assets of the offender.
8   In Italy a judge always oversees the application of a sentence. This judge is the prosecutor working at the Judicial Office which has issued the sentence to be enforced. The Prosecutor independently enforces the sentence when there is no dispute over its application. In case such a dispute should arise, the Prosecutor or the offender appeal to the so-called 'Enforcement' Judge, who is the judge that had previously issued the sentence. If there is a conflict between more than one sentence to be implemented at the same time, the Prosecutor or the offender must appeal to the judge that has issued the last definite sentence.
9   A new Code of Criminal Procedure was enacted in 1989.
10 These prerequisites had already been enunciated in the mid-eighteenth century by Beccaria, *Dei delitti e delle pene* (1st edn 1764), Turin 1965, § XIX. See, in part, §§ 63 and 6: "Quanto la pena sarà più pronta e più vicina al delitto commesso ella sarà tanto più giusta e tanto più utile" ('The Quicker the Sentence and the Closer to the Crime the More Just and Useful Will it be').
11 On the concept of the 'effectiveness' of the sentence, that is on the possibility that a threatened punishment be applied in reality see Paliero 1990, p. 430. See also Giunta et al. 1998.
12 The day-fine sentencing system appears to have substantial advantages compared to the 'overall sum' system. This is principally because it allows greater equality of treatment given that the number of day-fines depend on the objective seriousness of the offence, while the sum to be paid each day depends on the actual income of the offender. In the second place, the day-fine system allows for easier 'conversion' of the fine into another type of punishment, if the offender is insolvent. On the German system see Horn, last edition.
13 On the potential of community service as an alternative par excellence to detention, see Fassone 1984, pp. 231 ff.
14 See Arts. 28–37 CC.

15 The German Criminal Code provides for two institutions which both involve forgoing the execution of the sentence. The first – set down in § 59 StGB – is the warning with reservation of punishment. When the fine to be imposed does not go over 180 daily rates, the judge, after having fixed the entity of punishment, can warn the offender and make the execution of the punishment conditional on the offender going through a trial period (which may vary from one to three years). The second, is the institution of waiving punishment (Absehen von Strafe), set down in § 60 according to which "the judge can waive punishment when the consequences of the event which affect the offender are so serious as to render the application of such punishment clearly mistaken" (§ 60 StGB). The foundation of such an institution is to not to evaluate punishment according to just desert, but rather in the lack of need for punishment (because the offender has already received a sort of poena naturalis). On the institution of waiving of punishment, the latest work is Fornasari, *I principi del diritto penale tedesco*, Padova 1993, pp. 523 ff and cited bibl.

16 Law No. 448 of the 22 September 1988, setting out provisions for the criminal procedure for minors, lays down, in Art. 28, an analogous institution to the German one of warning with reservation of punishment. This is called the institution of suspension of trial with probation, on the basis of which the judge can suspend the trial for up to three years, 'when he/she believes the personality of the minor must be evaluated'. The minor who passes this test after being placed under the care of Juvenile Services for observation, treatment and support, will have the crime deleted.

17 The effects of 'sentence bargaining' on sentencing criteria is analysed by Dolcini 1990, pp. 797 ff. (in part, p. 805).

18 One may discern, in some judgement proceedings, a sort of invitation to the accused, to make use of 'bargaining' Art. 555 letter (e) CCP obliges, for example, the writ of summons to contain the notice that "if the prerequisites exist, the accused can ask for … a summary trial or the application of the punishment according to Art. 444". The same notice is provided for in Art. 460, letter (e) CCP, which regulates the prerequisites for the writ of judgement and in Art. 456, second subsection CCP, which regulates the writ of immediate judgement. Finally, in the summary trial according to Art. 451 fifth subsection CCP, the Chief Judge advises the accused of the right to a summary trial or the application of the sentence according to Art. 444 CCP.

19 The defending lawyer does not have the same power to make a request to apply the sentence or to object to or change the agreement between his/her client and the prosecutor, because his/her role "is limited to supporting the private party and assisting it during negotiations at the end of which the request is drafted". See Conso-Grevi 1994, p. 755.

20 See Illuminati, 'I procedimenti a conclusione anticipata e speciali nel nuovo codice di procedura penale', in *Politica del diritto* 1990, p. 263.

21 Illuminati, op. cit., p. 264. The author proposes, in particular, that each Public Prosecutor's Office bring out specific directives regulating the discretionary power of the Prosecutor at least regarding consent to 'summary' procedures which may be asked of the defendant.

References

Abbreviations of Italian reviews:

Arch. pen. = *Archivio penale*
Enc. dir. = *Enciclopedia del diritto*
Giust. pen. = *La giustizia penale*
Ind. pen. = *L'indice penale*
LP = *Legislazione penale*
Rass. it. crim. = *Rassegna italiana di criminologia*
Riv. it. dir. proc. pen. = *Rivista italiana di diritto e procedura penale*

Amodio, E. (1977), 'Motivazione della sentenza', *Enc. dir.*, Vol. XXVII, Milano: Giuffrè.
Bricola, F. (1965), *La discrezionalità nel diritto penale. Nozioni e aspetti costituzionali*, Milano: Giuffrè.
Cattaneo, M.A. (1989), 'Sulla filosofia penale di Kant e di Hegel', in L. Eusebi (ed.), *La funzione della pena: il commiato da Kant e da Hegel*, Milano: Giuffrè.
Conso, G. and Grevi, V. (1994), *Commentario al nuovo codice di procedura penale*, Padova: Cedam.
De Vero, G. (1983), *Circostanze del reato e commisurazione della pena*, Milano: Giuffrè.
Delogu, T. (1976), 'Potere discrezionale del giudice e certezza del diritto', *Riv. it. dir. proc. pen.*, p. 369.
Dershowitz, A. (1976), Background Paper, in *Fair and Certain Punishment: Report of the Twentieth Century Found Task Force on Criminal Sentencing*, New York.
Dolcini, E. (1974), 'Note sui profili costituzionali della commisurazione della pena', *Riv. it. dir. proc. pen.*, p. 338.
Dolcini, E. (1975), 'La disciplina della commisurazione della pena: spunti per una riforma', *Riv. it. dir. proc. pen.*, p. 34.
Dolcini, E. (1979), *La commisurazione della pena*, Padova: Cedam.
Dolcini, E. (1979), 'La "rieducazione del condannato" fra mito e realtà', *Riv. it. dir. proc. pen.*, p. 469.
Dolcini, E. (1990), 'L'art. 133 al vaglio del movimento internazionale di riforma del diritto penale', *Riv. it. dir. proc. pen.*, p. 398.
Dolcini, E. (1990), 'Razionalità nella commisurazione della pena: un obiettivo ancora attuale?', *Riv. it. dir. proc. pen.*, p. 797.
Dolcini, E. (1991), 'La commisurazione della pena tra teoria e prassi', *Riv. it. dir. proc. pen.*, p. 55.
Dolcini, E. and Paliero, C.E. (1989), *Il carcere ha alternative?*, Milano: Giuffrè.
Eusebi, L. (1985), 'La "nuova" retribuzione', in G. Marinucci and E. Dolcini (eds), *Diritto penale in trasformazione*, Milano: Giuffrè, p. 93.
Eusebi. L. (ed.) (1989), *La funzione della pena: il commiato da Kant e da Hegel*, Milano: Giuffrè.
Eusebi, L. (1990), *La pena 'in crisi'*, Brescia: Morcelliana.
Eusebi, L. (1993), 'Tra crisi dell'esecuzione penale e prospettive di riforma del sistema sanzionatorio: il ruolo del servizio sociale', *Riv. it. dir. proc. pen.*, p. 493.
Fassone. E. (1984), 'L'attuale funzione della pena', in M. de Acutis and G. Palombarni (eds), *Funzioni e limiti del diritto penale*, Padova: Cedam, p. 225.

Frankel, M.E. (1972), *Criminal Sentences: Law Without Order*, New York: Hill and Wang.

Gallo, E. (1989), 'Sistema sanzionatorio e nuovo processo', *Giust. pen.*, p. 641.

Gambini Musso, R. (1985), *Il 'sentence bargaining' tra common law e civil law*, Milano: Giuffrè.

Giunta, F., Orlandi, R., Pittaro, P. and Presutti, A. (1998), *L'effettività della sanzione penale*, IPSOA.

Grevi, V. (1988), 'Riflessioni e suggestioni in margine all'esperienza nordamericana del sentence bargaining', in E. Amodio and M.C. Bassiouni (eds), *Il processo penale negli Stati Uniti d'America*, Milano: Giuffrè, p. 299.

Horn, E. (1996), *Systematischer Leitzatz – Kommentar zum Sanktionenrecht*, Berlin (subsection 40).

Larizza, S. (1984), 'La modificazione e applicazione della pena', in *Codice penale, parte generale*, Torino: UTET.

Mannozzi, G. (1990), 'Fini della pena e commisurazione finalisticamente orientata: un dibattito inesauribile? Rileggendo "Doing justice" di Andrew von Hirsch', *Riv. it. dir. proc. pen.*, p. 1088.

Mannozzi, G. (1996), *Razionalità e 'giustizia' nella sentencing della pena. Il Just Desert Model e il nuovo sentencing nordamericano*, Padova: Cedam.

Marinucci, G. (1974), 'Politica criminale e riforma del diritto penale', *Jus*, p. 463.

Marinucci, G. and Dolcini, E. (1985), *Diritto penale in trasformazione*, Milano: Giuffrè.

Marinucci, G. and Dolcini, E. (1992), 'Note sul metodo della codificazione penale', *Riv. it. dir. proc. pen.*, p. 385.

Militello, V. (1982), *Prevenzione generale e commisurazione della pena*, Milano: Giuffrè.

Moccia, S. (1992), *Il diritto penale tra essere e valore. Funzione della pena e sistematica teleologica*, Napoli: Edizioni Scientifiche Italiane.

Monaco, L. (1984), *Prospettive dell'idea dello 'scopo' nella teoria della pena*, Napoli: Jovene.

Monaco, L. and Paliero, C.E. (1994), 'Variazioni in tema di "crisi della sanzione": la diaspora del sistema commisurativo', *Riv. it. dir. proc. pen.*, p. 421.

Morselli, E. (1988), 'La prevenzione generale integratrice nella moderna prospettiva retribuzionistica', *Riv. it. dir. proc. pen.*, p. 48.

Morselli, E. (1991), 'La funzione della pena alla luce della moderna criminologia', *Ind. pen.*, p. 505.

Mosconi, G. and Pavarini, M., *Flessibilità della pena in fase esecutiva e potere discrezionale. Sentencing penitenziario: 1986–1990*, Sintesi del rapporto finale della Ricerca promossa dal CRS – Centro Studi e iniziative per la riforma della stato (publicazione fuori commercio – no longer available).

Padovani, T. (1989), 'Il nuovo codice di procedura penale e la riforma del codice penale', *Riv. it. dir. proc. pen.*, p. 916.

Padovani, T. (1992), 'La disintegrazione attuale del sistema sanzionatorio e le prospettive di riforma: il problema della comminatoria edittale', *Riv. it. dir. proc. pen.*, p. 419.

Pagliaro, A. (1979), 'La riforma delle sanzioni penali tra teoria e prassi', *Riv. it. dir. proc. pen.*, p. 1189.

Pagliaro, A. (1981a), 'Commisurazione della pena e prevenzione generale', *Riv. it. dir. proc. pen.*, p. 25.

Pagliaro, A. (1981b), 'Correlazioni tra il livello delle sanzioni penali, la struttura del processo e gli atteggiamenti della prassi', *Ind. pen.*, p. 219.

Pagliaro, A. (1982), 'Doppio ambito edittale delle sanzioni e commisurazione della pena nell'ottica della prevenzione generale', in G. Vassalli (ed.), *Problemi generali di diritto penale*, Milano: Giuffrè.

Pagliaro, A. (1990), 'Riflessi del nuovo processo sul diritto penale sostanziale', *Riv. it. dir. proc. pen.*, p. 36.

Palazzo F.C. (1986), 'Analisi empiriche ed indicazioni di riforma in materia di sanzioni sostitutive ex officio', *Riv. it. dir. proc. pen.*, p. 681.

Palazzo F.C. (1988), 'Qualche riflessione su sentence bargaining e semplificazione del rito', in Amodio, E. and Basiouni, M.C. (eds), *Il processo penale negli Stati Uniti d'America*, Milano: Giuffrè.

Paliero, C.E. (1990), 'Il principio di effettività del diritto penale', *Riv. it. dir. proc. pen.*, p. 430.

Paliero, C.E. (1992), 'Metodologie de lege ferenda: per una riforma non improbabile del sistema sanzionatorio', *Riv. it. dir. proc. pen.*, p. 510.

Paliero, C.E. (1994), 'La riforma del sistema sanzionatorio: percorsi di metodologia comparata', *rch. pen.*, p. 95.

Paliero, C.E. (1998), 'Commento all'art. 4 della L. 165 del 1998', *LP*, p. 815.

Romano M. (ed.) (n.d.), *Commentario sistematico al codice penale*, Vol. I, Milano: Giuffrè.

Romano, M. and Grasso, G. (eds) (1990), *Commentario sistematico del codice penale*, Vol. II, Milano: Giuffrè.

Stile, A. (1991), 'La commisurazione della pena nel contesto attuale del sistema sanzionatorio. Aspetti problematici', in *Evoluzione e riforma del diritto e della procedura penale. 1945–1990, Studi in onore di G.Vassalli*, Vol. I, Milano: Giuffrè.

Tonry, M. (1996), *Sentencing Matters*, Oxford: Oxford University Press.

Vassalli, G. (1961), Funzioni e insufficienze della pena', *Riv. it. dir. proc. pen.*, p. 297.

Vassalli, G. (ed.) (1982), *Problemi generali di diritto penale*, Milano: Giuffrè.

Volk, K. (1993), *Introduzione al diritto penale tedesco*, Padova.

Von Hirsch, A. (1986 [1976]), *Doing Justice. The Choice of Punishment*, New York: Hill and Wang.

Von Hirsch, A. and Ashworth, A. (1998), *Principled Sentencing*, 2nd edn, Boston: Northeastern University Press.

Von Hirsch, A., Knapp, K. and Tonry, M. (1987), *The Sentencing Commission and its Guidelines*, Boston: Northeastern University Press.

Appendix A

Selection of Articles from the Italian Criminal Code and Code of Criminal Procedure Related to the Sentencing System

CRIMINAL CODE:

132. Discretionary power of the judge in applying the sentence – Within the limits set by law, the judge must apply the sentence discretionally; he/she must indicate the reasons that justify the use of such discretionary power.

In increasing or reducing the sentence, the limits set for each type of sentence must not be exceeded excepting where otherwise specified by law.

133. Gravity of the crime: evaluation for fixing the sentence – In the exercise of his/her discretionary power indicated in the preceding article, the judge must take into consideration the gravity of the crime, deduced from:
1) the nature, the type, the means, the object, the times, the place and each and every other modality of conduct;
2) the gravity of damage or danger caused the victim of the crime;
3) the intensity of the intention and the degree of negligence.

The judge must also take into consideration the future capacity to commit crimes of the offender, deriving from:
1) the reasons for committing the crime and the character of the offender;
2) previous criminal record and generally the behaviour and life of the offender, before the fact;
3) the conduct of the offender during or successive to the crime;
4) the lifestyle of the offender, his/her family and social environment.

CODE OF CRIMINAL PROCEDURE:

438. Premises for summary trial – 1. The defendant can request that the trial be defined in the preliminary hearing (…).
(…) *Omissis*
(…) *Omissis*

440. Measures taken by the judge – 1. On request, the judge can issue an order to instate a summary trial if he/she considers that the trial can be defined with the evidence already in his/her possession.
(…) *Omissis*

(…) Omissis

442. Decision – After having ended the discussion, the judge proceeds to judgement according to articles 529 and following (546, 651, 652).
(…) Omissis
If the defendant is convicted, the sentence which must be set by the judge having taken into consideration all the circumstances of the case, must be reduced by one third (…).

444. Application of the sentence on request – Both the offender and the prosecutor can ask the judge for an intermediate sentence, according to the type and degree indicated, or for a fine, both reduced by one third, or for a term of imprisonment having taken into consideration all the circumstances, which, after being reduced by one third, consists in not more than two years of imprisonment or detention, either singly or with a fine.

If there is agreement by the party which has not made the request, and an acquittal has not been given according to article 129, the judge, on the basis of the evidence, if he/she believes that the legal classification of the crime and the application or the comparison of the circumstances presented by the two parties to be correct, can apply the sentence indicated, after stating in its terms that it derives from a request from both parties. If there is a plaintiff, the judge cannot make a decision regarding the civil action; the terms indicated in article 75 subsection 3 are not applied.

The party in making the application, can render its application dependent on the concession of a suspended sentence. In this case the judge, if he/she believes that a suspended sentence cannot be conceded, can reject the application.

Appendix B

Statistical Data on the Distribution of Convictions and on Sentence Bargaining Rates

Table 4.1   Distribution of convictions (also expressed in percentages) by the type of proceeding from 1991 to 1997 (first six months)

Pretura – (Magistrates' Courts)

Years	Total Convictions (100%)	Convictions by Adversary Trial	Sentence Bargaining[1]	Summary Trial[2]	Summary Trial (Fines)[3]	Bargaining Justice + Summary Trials
1991	226,970	47,482 (20.9%)	50,754 (22.3%)	3,501 (1.5%)	125,233 (55.1%)	179,488 (79.0%)
1992	319,776	70,715 (22.1%)	66,675 (20.8%)	4,250 (1.3%)	178,136 (55.7%)	249,061 (77.8%)
1993	361,184	95,444 (26.4%)	89,649 (24.8%)	4,379 (1.2%)	171,712 (47.5%)	265,740 (73.5%)
1994	385,082	107,828 (28.0%)	96,984 (25.1%)	4,573 (1.1%)	175,697 (45.6%)	277,254 (71.9%)
1995	351,644	90,565 (25.7%)	89,298 (25.3%)	3,376 (0.9%)	168,405 (47.8%)	261,079 (74.2%)
1996	378,337	127,868 (33.7%)	110,008 (29.0%)	2,431 (0.6%)	138,030 (36.4%)	250,469 (66.2%)
1997 (half year)	190,903	63,346 (33.1%)	54,863 (28.7%)	1,566 (0.8%)	71,128 (37.2%)	127,557 (66.8%)

Notes

1   Judge: Magistrate (during the preliminary hearing) or Trial Judge (during the first hearing of trial).
2   Judge: Magistrate (during the preliminary hearing only).
3   Judge: Magistrate (on the prosecutor's proposal and without the defendant's opposition).

Source: Italian Ministry of Justice.

Table 4.2   Distribution of convictions (also expressed in percentages) by the type of proceeding, from 1991 to 1997 (first six months)

Tribunale – (Criminal Court [Three-Judge Panel])

Years	Total Convictions (100%)	Convictions by Adversary Trial	Sentence Bargaining[1]	Summary Trial[2]	Summary Trial (Fines)[3]
1991	55,127	15,260 (27.7%)	27,973 (50.7%)	5,794 (10.5%)	6,100 (11.0%)
1992	55,832	18,265 (32.8%)	25,688 (46.0%)	7,388 (13.2%)	4,491 (8.0%)
1993	58,800	18,649 (31.8%)	26,145 (44.4%)	6,814 (11.5%)	5,151 (8.7%)
1994	69,842	22,189 (31.8%)	33,647 (48.1%)	7,121 (10.1%)	6,885 (9.8%)
1995	62,828	19,601 (31.2%)	31,033 (49.3%)	5,976 (9.5%)	6,218 (9.8%)
1996	75,615	26,074 (34.5%)	33,912 (44.8%)	6,533 (8.6%)	9,096 (12.0%)
1997 (half year)	40,765	13,723 (33.7%)	18,216 (44.6%)	3,987 (9.7%)	4,839 (11.8%)

Notes

1   Judge: **Magistrate** (during preliminary hearing) or **Criminal Court** (during first hearing of trial).
2   Judge: **Magistrate** (during preliminary hearing only).
3   Judge: **Magistrate** (on the prosecutor's proposal and without the defendant's opposition).

Source: Italian Ministry of Justice.

Chapter Five

Legislation and Practice of Sentencing in China

Liling Yue

China has a civil law tradition. All the principles of sentencing, the range of punishments and the procedures of sentencing are provided by criminal law and criminal procedure law. The first Code of Criminal Law was enacted in 1979. It was revised in 1997. Under this new code, there are two chapters related to the sentencing system: Chapter 3 of the code provides the types of punishments and Chapter 4 the principles of sentencing. This chapter outlines the main types of punishments in China and an account of some of the debates about punishment currently taking place in China.

Penalties of Depriving or Limiting Freedom of Offenders

In Chinese criminal law, there are four kinds of penalties which could be used to deprive or limit offenders' freedom. Those are life imprisonment, fixed-term imprisonment, criminal detention and public surveillance.

Life Imprisonment

In the criminal law, there are 413 offences in total. Among them, 97 offences carry the penalty of life imprisonment. Generally there are two conditions: for offences for which the death penalty could be imposed, life imprisonment could be taken as one option. This is in order to reduce the application of the death penalty. Another condition is, for some offences, life imprisonment is provided as the maximum punishment. There is debate going on currently in China. People who oppose life imprisonment think that, firstly, life imprisonment deprives offenders of their freedom for their whole life and isolates them from society. In comparison with the death penalty, they suffer permanently, so it is as cruel as the death penalty. Secondly, if rehabilitation or correction served as one of the main goals of punishment, life imprisonment obviously has made the criminals lose their confidence to go back into society and the purpose of punishment could not be served. Thirdly, it seems unfair because if life imprisonment takes the rest of life as the term, obviously the duration could be very different.[1] Finally, it is an uneconomical punishment. A larger population of prisoners serving life sentences would significantly increase state prison budgets. People who favour life imprisonment put forward different arguments. Firstly, life imprisonment has an essential distinction from the death penalty. The right to life is the fundamental right, the right of freedom is based on the right to life, so it is hard to say that life imprisonment is more cruel than the death penalty. Life imprisonment retains the life of offenders. Thus, in miscarriage of justice cases, it could protect the lives of the innocent. China retains the death penalty. The imposition of life imprisonment could hopefully reduce the application of the death penalty. Secondly, life imprisonment in China is different from some other countries where the prisoner could never get parole. Under the Chinese criminal law, after prisoners serve a certain period of time, provided they would not re-offend and have a record of good behaviour, they would get commutation of punishment or parole. That means that prisoners have some hope of future release. Although there is debate on life imprisonment in general, however, the leading opinion on life imprisonment is that it should be improved first. Academics hold the opinion that the range of offences where life imprisonment may be imposed is too large. As mentioned above, almost one fourth of offences carry the penalty of life imprisonment. It is really necessary to limit the range to only the most serious crimes, defined not only in terms of the offences themselves, but also in terms of the seriousness of the case as a whole.

Fixed-term Imprisonment

Fixed-term imprisonment in China is between six months and 15 years. The cumulative punishment should not be over 20 years imprisonment. This sentence is widely used in practice. As fixed-term can be imposed for almost every offence, the range of fixed-term sentencing is very wide. From the provisions of law, fixed-term imprisonment can be divided into three levels. The longest term is over 10 years imprisonment. It is generally imposed for serious offences which also have serious consequences. It is designed as one of the options, and the minimum punishment, where the death penalty can be imposed. The second level is from three years up to 10 years. The lowest level is under three years; in practice, it is taken as the maximum punishment for petty crimes.

Fixed-term imprisonment is the most frequently used punishment in practice, since there are few alternatives to imprisonment. The wide range of sentence length has given judges too much discretionary and power, therefore problems of inconsistency in sentencing have emerged. Some experts on sentencing have suggested that the range of fixed imprisonment terms should be shortened.

Criminal Detention

Criminal detention in China imposes short restrictions (one to six months) on the liberty of those criminals who have committed minor offences. The criminal law provides that one day in pre-trial detention is the equivalent of one day's imprisonment or whatever the sentences which deprive the freedom. For long and complicated cases, the term of pre-trial detention may equal or exceed the term of this sentence. The punishment would be meaningless under this situation. One way to overcome those problems is to try to make the criminal process more efficient. Another way is to use the suspended sentence as the alternative.

Public Surveillance

Public surveillance is a noncustodial punishment. In criminal law there are 107 offences where this punishment may be imposed. The term of the sentence may be from three months, up to two years. The criminals who get this punishment can still continue his/her study or work, but under the surveillance of local police or the organisation of local society.

In practice, this sentence cannot be enforced efficiently. Neither the local police nor the local organisations have efficient measures to control the convicted person. Issues such as establishing an institution like the probation service or introducing a system of electronic monitoring, are currently under discussion in China.

Capital Punishment

Unofficial statistics produced by some international organisations suggest that China uses the death penalty and execution more than any other jurisdiction. In the criminal law (revised in 1997), there remain 69 offences for which the death penalty may be imposed. Although there is a policy to reserve the death penalty only for the most serious crimes and the Criminal Procedure Law provides a special procedure to review death penalty cases, the death penalty in practice can still be used widely in comparison with other countries which still retain this sanction.

Debate on the reservation or abolition of the death penalty has been initiated in China. The majority opinion holds that the death penalty should be abolished in the future but that it is impractical to do it now.[2] Some young scholars hold the opinion that there are still some economic, political and cultural elements which hinder movements towards abolition. These are as follows: firstly, the Chinese material life is still at a lower level, cultural sensibility concerning the value of life is also relatively undeveloped. Secondly, the belief in retribution, 'one life to one life' is still very strong and accepted by the majority of citizens. Finally, people believe that the death penalty is an effective deterrent and should be one of the means of protecting public security. China is facing serious crime problems, therefore, it is not reasonable to abolish the death penalty currently.[3]

Most academics and practitioners think the movement towards the abolition of the death penalty cannot be reversed. The following steps should be considered: 1) strictly restrict the application of death penalty; 2) through several criminal law reforms, the offences which carry the death penalty should be reduced significantly; 3) eventually abolish the death penalty for all offences, including murder and military offences.[4]

Property Punishments

Chinese criminal law provides two kinds of property punishments, one is the fine and the other is confiscation of property.

The Fine

The fine is a commonly used penalty for economic crimes. Among 413 offences in criminal law, there are around 190 offences for which the fine may be imposed. The amount of fine depends on the various offences and conditions. There are several measures to decide the amount of fine: 1) multiple fine – for example, for tax offences, the fine could be between one and five times the amount of evaded tax; 2) proportional fine – it is calculated as a percentage of income illegally gained; 3) fixed amount fine – this is normally for economic crimes. Generally, it will be between one and 10 times the amount gained by the offence; 4) flexible amount fine – the amount of fine may be decided by judges according to the circumstances of the case. This applies to crimes such theft or fraud. There is currently debate over its use though the fine is commonly used in practice. People who favour the sanction think that it avoids the disadvantage of short term imprisonment. Criminals can continue their study or work, and will not be affected by other prisoners. For some offenders, the fine may be an effective deterrent. For offences committed by corporations, the fine is a punishment which could not be substituted by imprisonment. Obviously the fine also reduces the state budget for prisons. Other commentators point to disadvantages of the fine: it is unfair punishment. They hold that, life and freedom are the same for every body, but people have different levels of income and wealth, therefore the fine is fundamentally an unfair punishment. However, the day fine system has been discussed in China. Critics also argue that some criminals who pay their fines do not suffer much from the punishment. In some countries, criminals who fail to pay fines have to go to prison. In China this is seen as unequal treatment by law. In China the most difficult practical problem is in enforcing the payment of fines.

Conclusion

The reform of Chinese criminal law which occurred in 1997 has not had much impact on sentencing policies. Some positive trends are a reduction in the death penalty, and greater use of the fine. However, in general, Chinese punishments still appear to be harsh in comparison with European countries.

The range of punishments available to sentencers is considered too large. For certain offences, the optional sentences could be from three years imprisonment to the death penalty. China has a continental law tradition which requires judges to pass sentences according to the law. However, judges still retain very wide discretion. In practice, inconsistency is a serious problem. For the purpose of overcoming this problem, the Supreme Court has made some guideline judgements intended to place some limits on judicial discretion.

In China, the conviction rate remains very high and most offenders receive custodial sentences. Official criminal justice statistics are very difficult to obtain in China. One recent report indicated that in Si Chuan and Gui Zhou (1998, p. 1125), prisons were 20 per cent over capacity.[5] There is a lack of alternatives to imprisonment and this has become one of the most pressing issues for penal reform in China.

Notes

1   Su Hui Yu (ed.) (2000), 'Monographs on Crime and Punishment', *Law Publisher*, August.
2   Hu, Yun Teng (1999), 'Reserving or Abolishing – Theoretical Study of Death Penalty in Comparative Perspectives', *China Prosecution Press*, December, Beijing, p. 239.
3   Chen, Xin Liang (1992), *The Philosophy of Criminal Law*, The Publishing House of China University of Political Science and Law, p. 373.
4   Jia Yu, 'The Racial Thinking and Practical Choice of Abolishing the Death Penalty', *Case Study*, p. 18.
5   *Law Yearbook of China* (1998), p. 1125.

Chapter Six

Sentencing Reform in Canada:
Who Cares About Corrections?

Mary E. Campbell

Introduction

The history of sentencing reform in Canada is chequered – it has ranged from benign neglect to an integrated approach to sentencing and corrections[1] to a compartmentalised approach. With a relatively high incarceration rate of 123 per 100,000, reliance on imprisonment has been resistant to significant reform in this country. This is, at a minimum, perplexing given that Canada enjoys a generally peaceful and prosperous quality of life, and given the immediate proximity of the lessons learned from the United States' extreme reliance on incarceration as a solution to social problems. It can be argued that one of the reasons for Canada's failure to move fundamentally away from reliance on imprisonment has been its failure to consistently consider sentencing and corrections as part of a seamless, integrated criminal justice continuum.

This chapter will, from the perspective of a public servant with many years experience in legislative reform, trace some of this history and make a case for 'caring about corrections' in sentencing reform, despite the growing pressure of adopting piecemeal, 'quick fix' reform at different pressure points in the system. Some unique aspects of the current law reform climate in Canada will be examined, and options for future directions suggested.

Canadian Sentencing and Corrections Reform

The new Dominion of Canada was quick to legislate in respect of its federal corrections system, creating the first *Penitentiary Act* in 1868,[2] a year after the country was born. The Act was a very pragmatic piece of legislation, addressing solely operational matters and taking it as self-evident that the purpose of the correctional system was simply to confine prisoners for the duration of the sentence. It was not until 1892 that the criminal law was consolidated in the country's first *Criminal Code*,[3] and it was equally parsimonious in sentencing guidance: sentencing was simply left to "the discretion of the court" (s. 932). Although both sentencing and corrections were under the federal Department of Justice, in law, policy and operation they were relatively isolated one from the other.

There things stood for nearly 100 years, when the landscape of criminal law in Canada began to change dramatically. Two events from 1982 were particularly instrumental in promoting real change. First, the enactment of the *Canadian Charter of Rights and Freedoms*[4] established specific markers of fairness in criminal and correctional law, sparking a fundamental re-examination of the existing statutes, often through extensive litigation by accused persons and inmates. Second, the federal government published a blueprint for reform of criminal and correctional law, in a document entitled 'Criminal Law in Canadian Society' (Government of Canada 1982). 'CLICS' began a process of profound law reform for the next decade. One of its most important features was its emphasis on the criminal justice system as exactly that, a system. Sentencing was not viewed as separate and distinct from corrections but rather one stage of what should be an integrated process with consistent goals and principles.

Some of the first detailed proposals for reform in this time period occurred with the report of the Canadian Sentencing Commission in 1987. While it was, as its name indicates, primarily concerned with sentencing, it also took a holistic view of the system, and 20 of its 93 recommendations were directed specifically at corrections while another dozen or so recommendations addressed improving the relationship between courts and correctional authorities.

Parliament itself also undertook a review of sentencing and corrections during this period, and issued its report in 1988 (Standing Committee on Justice and Solicitor General). A remarkable document for its time, it also strongly emphasised an integrated approach to state response to criminal behaviour. A federal election later that year derailed any possibility of legislative reform, but the momentum was regained shortly thereafter, with the government's three-part green paper of 1990, entitled 'Directions for Reform' (Government of Canada 1990). Under the heading 'The need for greater integration among components', the government made plain its vision:

> Because the criminal law and each of its agencies are the product of piecemeal, incremental change, lack of integration among the various components –

sentencing, sentence administration and release systems – has become a significant problem. The police, prosecuting attorneys, judges and corrections officials have their own priorities and practices and operate in too much isolation from each other. While the important principle of balance is served by the separate operation of these components, the equally important principle of integration must not be lost through excessive fragmentation ... The different perspectives of the components must be blended for mutual support, not aggravated for mutual frustration. We must harmonize both attitudes and mechanisms so that the sentencing, release and correctional components work smoothly together (p. 7).

The Green Paper set out three statements of purpose and principles, one for sentencing, one for corrections and one for conditional release. All had as their purpose to contribute to the maintenance of a just, peaceful and safe society, and the principles to guide the achievement of that goal were similar, with emphasis on imprisonment as a last resort, restraint in the application of any restrictive measure, and fair process.

The actual drafting of the amendment bills was split up, and the corrections and conditional release amendments were enacted in 1992, while the sentencing reforms did not come into force until 1996. Notwithstanding this difference in time, and indeed that one government passed the corrections reforms while another government was in power when the sentencing reforms were passed, the two packages still demonstrated their concurrent and integrated genesis.

This is particularly evident in the statement of purpose and principles of sentencing in the Criminal Code. The statement of purpose in section 718, for example, contains the usual uncritical, unranked shopping list of deterrence, denunciation etc., but the reference to incapacitation is modified by the phrase "where necessary". These two small words are significant in that they make it clear that incapacitation is not some kind of universal good, but must only be used where it can be demonstrably justified as conducive to some goal. Restraint in the use of incapacitation measures is also emphasised in the statements of sentencing principles in sections 718.1 and 718.2. In fact, three of the six sentencing principles directly address the use of incarceration and other incapacitation responses: that the totality of consecutive sentences must not be unduly long or harsh, that the least restrictive measure must be used in all circumstances, and that imprisonment must be the sanction of last resort, particularly in the case of Aboriginal offenders. Parliament's emphasis on noncustodial alternatives was given further emphasis through the creation of the conditional sentence in section 742.1, which allows certain sentences of imprisonment to be served entirely in the community.

These provisions are mirrored in the *Corrections and Conditional Release Act*, the new 1992 legislation governing the federal penitentiary system.[5] The statement of purpose in section 3 reflects the mandate to carry out the custodial sentence in a safe and humane manner, but also indicates that the other part of the system's mandate is to facilitate the safe and timely return of offenders to the community. This rehabilitative orientation is also reflected in the principles in section 4, which includes the requirement to use the least restrictive measures consistent with the safety of the public, offenders, and penitentiary staff.

Other statutory provisions from the two reforms which emphasise the holistic approach adopted by parliament include a requirement that judges give reasons for their sentences, that they forward those reasons to penitentiary authorities when penitentiary-length sentences are ordered, and that corrections officials must obtain those reasons as well as other pertinent trial and sentencing documents and must take that information into account in any correctional and conditional release decisions.[6]

Having said this, obviously there are still many gaps in practice. Judges still express concern about particular cases where the early release of offenders is interpreted as undermining the intention of the sentencing court,[7] and correctional authorities express great unhappiness about being sent offenders who present no risk of future danger and for whom no useful purpose is served by keeping them behind bars. While these implementation issues must continue to be addressed, the goals remain laudable and indeed achievable. While the reasons are diverse, it is worth noting that Canada's year 2000 incarceration rate of 123 per 100,000 is down from 133 per 100,000 in 1995 (Solicitor General Canada 2000).

Current Situation

Since the genesis of these sentencing and corrections reforms in the 1980s, the world has not stood still. Notwithstanding the decline in the incarceration rate, the Canadian public and political climate shows signs of significant retreat from the progressive tenor that marked the reforms. Let us turn briefly to the current environment, and some examples of law reform stemming from that climate.

Environment

It would be presumptuous to suggest that the current public or political climate is radically more *difficult* for positive, coherent reform of criminal laws than in previous decades, but there are four areas where the current climate is *different* than in the past, and these points are having a significant impact on law reform.

a) Public knowledge and attitudes First, public knowledge and attitudes. It is my perception that although public knowledge about crime and offenders remains fairly limited, attitudes have hardened. While it is true that public opinion research clearly shows public acceptance for more creative and community-based alternatives for low-risk offenders (Hann 1998), the public's definition of 'low-risk' is often quite circumscribed. Demands to 'do something' about offenders who commit crimes of violence are often based on assumptions such as: all violent offenders are predators, they are identifiably different from the majority of our families, friends, and acquaintances, they are incurable and therefore unmanageable, and if we just lock them up for extended periods of time and then put their name and address on a registry our country will be a safer place. The popular mantra of 'zero tolerance' has come to be tied with inflexible, harsh responses rather than the stimulus to balanced, proactive, effective measures to reduce the incidence of offending.

b) Politics The second shift in recent years has been on the political front, although the attitudes just referred to have been blended between the public and political sectors. What I am referring to under this second point is the more purely political in two ways. First, and this applies to many areas not just social policy in general or criminal law policy in particular, is the general drift to the centre or indeed centre right by all political parties. Whether one thinks of political parties or individual politicians, it is very difficult to come up with a long list these days of those who stand firmly and publicly on the small-l liberal side of the ledger.

The other political point of note is the recent and very public fractionating *within* parties. Naturally, any particular party has always had a certain spectrum of views within it, but in Canada this has become markedly acute within the past few years.[8] Ten years ago it was relatively easy to pick a criminal justice issue and identify fairly precisely where a party stood. It is much more difficult to do that today. Instead, one must be much more attentive to the particular individuals involved. The effect in Canada of Private Members' Bills on parliament is one current and striking result of this.[9] When the Canadian parliament dissolved for the most recent election call on 22 October 2000, there were 15 unpassed government bills on the Order Paper of the House of

Commons, of which three dealt with criminal law reform matters. At the same time there were 300 Private Members' Bills, of which seventy dealt with criminal law reform matters. It is clear from their sheer volume that the latter Bills have now become a vehicle for effecting radical change in criminal justice, even while they continue to follow a process that reflects little research or analysis and allows little consultation or connection to a more comprehensive, coherent reform agenda.

c) Single issue drivers This leads to a third environmental point, which I call the 'single issue driver'. Single serious crimes have always galvanised the media and the public. But in this age of scores of television channels devoted to 'the news' and of the immediacy of the internet, we are bombarded with tragic crimes whose occurrence is far more rare than the multiplicity of news reports would suggest. In concert with a hardening of the public attitude, the conservative political drift and the fractionating of traditional party cohesion, single issues can drive a reform agenda like never before. With simply 100 signatures from fellow Members of Parliament, an individual Canadian MP can now table a bill in the House of Commons on any isolated issue and have a fair chance of seeing it pass, be it good, bad or indifferent. This is a far cry from the government legislative process, which requires thorough policy and research development, consultation, Constitutional, Charter, gender and financial analysis, and linkage to an integrated reform agenda. This is not a 'turf' issue, the bureaucratic establishment defending its power, but rather simply a question of using the more thorough and open process to ensure balanced, responsive and effective law reform. Single issue, ad hoc deal-making is the antithesis of such reform.

d) Public service The fourth environmental point of note is the change within the Canadian public service and the perception of it from outside. Having viewed it from the inside for 16 years, it is a bureaucracy that is significantly dispirited and tired.[10] It is highly questionable whether it is attracting the best and the brightest as it once did.

Certainly in many sectors it has shifted from hiring subject-matter experts to hiring generalists. This approach first appeared at senior levels – a good manager can manage anything – but is now more pervasive: a good policy analyst can analyse anything, so it matters little whether the subject matter is national parks, fishing quotas, or parole supervision. This trend has at least two unfortunate consequences. First, the substantive decisions being made often reflect expediency rather than what makes sense in the long term for criminal justice and corrections. This reflects in particular the generalist's lack of interest in and commitment to the subject matter: if you know that you will never have to face the long term consequences of your advice or decisions because you will have moved on to an unrelated area, then the short term quick fix is obviously the more attractive. The second and related consequence is that, in the absence of having subject matter expertise to offer, many public servants move closer to the political end of the spectrum to demonstrate their 'value added' in that quarter. While no public servant can completely ignore the broader political dimensions of any issue, there is a significant danger when the predominant discourse in public service research or policy development becomes 'how will this play for the government?'.

Similarly, the further that policy advisors retreat from a knowledge-based approach, the more that ideology as opposed to research will guide advice. This is always a dangerous drift for public servants. It is tempting, because each public servant has (one hopes) a well-developed framework of values and beliefs – but as public servants, promoting personal ideology or second-guessing political ideology must be quite secondary to providing expert advice based on knowledge and research. Political ideology is an obvious part of decision-making in a democracy, but it should be exercised by those who are held accountable on that basis, i.e. politicians.

It is perhaps not surprising, against this shifting backdrop, that the public service is increasingly viewed with suspicion, as being advocates rather than experts. It has become increasingly difficult for public servants to provide suggestions for progressive, empirically-based law reform without being perceived as advancing a left-wing agenda. In large part, this may be the result of the increasing vacuum of this point of view on the political stage. Or it may indeed be the result of some public servants increasingly playing on the political field rather than restricting themselves to their more proper role of providing substantive expertise. Whatever the cause, one of the most unfortunate results has been an increase in political-style attacks on public servants. Such public efforts to politicise public servants leave the targeted bureaucracy in an untenable position: public servants are constrained by traditional rules from responding publicly, even while the critics are now playing by non-traditional rules in launching their attacks. In concert with the elimination of job tenure in the public sector (which had allowed the public servant a margin of safety when working on unpopular issues or when the research or advice took a different direction from where the government wanted to go), there is now a great deal of pressure on the public servant to avoid being perceived as a 'troublemaker'.

Results of the Environment

As political, public, and public service dynamics have fragmented and polarised, one major consequence has been that sentencing and corrections reforms are on the cusp of becoming again quite isolated from each other. This is particularly evident in some of the sentencing reforms debated since 1996. With the exception of one which would decriminalise the possession of marijuana, virtually all of the Private Members' Bills noted above were aimed at reducing discretion and applying more rigid sentencing and corrections regimes, ostensibly with the aim of making Canada a safer place. To be sure, this reflects a certain superficial unity of ideology, i.e. a very punitive one, but each Bill has been drafted with a very specific focus and no apparent regard for its impact on other parts of the criminal justice system. When one looks at the statements made by sponsors at tabling, the MPs are often careful to note that a particular crime has been the impetus for the reform at issue.

Two types of proposed amendments stand out in particular: mandatory consecutive sentences, and mandatory minimum penalties.

a) Mandatory consecutive sentences The call for mandatory consecutive sentences derives much of its strength from the American political response to crime, where offenders can be sentenced to such penalties as four life terms, or 300 years of imprisonment. The absurdity of such sentencing regimes is often clothed in the respectability of 'holding offenders accountable' and the related rhetoric of satisfying victims. In reality it appears to be nothing more or less than sheer punishment for the sake of punishment.

Canada already has legislative provisions for the imposition of consecutive or concurrent terms, in the Criminal Code since 1892. Where an offender is convicted of multiple offences at the same time, or is convicted of an offence while under sentence for a previous offence, the court may order that the custodial sentences be served consecutively.[11] All the normal sentencing purposes and principles apply in making this determination, and in particular all consecutive sentences are subject to the totality principle, which states that the "combined sentence should not be unduly long or harsh".[12] Appellate courts have fleshed out the consecutive/concurrent sentencing regime over the years, and it has attracted little controversy (although sentence administrators struggle with trying to get judges to be more explicit on their warrants of committal as to what is consecutive or concurrent to what!).

Nonetheless, due to the efforts of a handful of members of the Canadian parliament, concurrent sentences have attracted a great deal of attention in the past two years. The leading Private Member's Bill in the last session, known as C–247, was premised on the notion that longer incarceration across the board will act as a more effective deterrent to would-be offenders and restore a sense of accountability in the criminal justice system for victims. Unfortunately there is nothing in the research literature which would support this fundamental premise. It is clear that longer incarceration per se has no empirical deterrent effective and has in fact been associated with an increase in recidivism among incarcerated offenders.[13] While victims certainly look for accountability in the system, that does not equate simply to harsher penalties – it includes better access to meaningful services, compensation, and someone to respond to their concerns when they feel frustrated by action or inaction by the players in the system.

The Bill was a short two clauses, addressing sex offences in one clause, and murder in the other. In particular, the second clause of the Bill imposed American-style sentences for murder offences with more than one victim, or repeat murder offences separated in time. The automatic penalty for murder in Canada is a life sentence, with parole ineligibility periods between 10 and 25 years. There is no provision in Canada for consecutive life terms or consecutive parole ineligibility periods, although 'the clock' starts running anew if a subsequent murder conviction is imposed. This system is premised on avoiding crushing all hope of reform while at the same time allowing for lifetime incarceration where necessary. Although homicide rates in Canada are at a 30-year low (Statistics Canada 2000), C–247's supporters point to the alleged ineffectiveness of the current system. The Bill proposed a regime of mandatory consecutive parole ineligibility periods of up to 50 years for murder offences, or longer if the offender is also subject to other non-life sentences.

The Bill was an egregious example of ad hoc and ineffective responses to very real problems of crime and victimisation. The Bill was first tabled in a slightly different form in 1996, and when parliament dissolved in 2000 it was before it for the third time. During this period, the government took a wide range of positive steps to deal with sex offending and murder offences, but this Bill appears frozen in time. It was not apparently developed with any regard for sentencing or recidivism research, nor has it been the subject of consultation with subject matter experts, or victim service providers, to name a few. In the name of 'accountability', the Bill treated all offenders as though they are the worst offenders.

The entire effect of the Bill was simply to ensure that a very limited category of offenders spend a longer period of time behind bars, regardless of individual circumstances or future risk. It is unclear as to how this will improve public safety, or satisfy victims. Having said that, the Bill passed through the House of Commons and in fact had received approval in principle through a vote at second reading in the Senate at the dissolution of parliament. It is certain to be re-tabled for a fourth time when the new parliament reconvenes in 2001.

Challenging the rhetoric of the Bill is not easy, especially when to do so results in allegations of being 'soft on crime' or a supporter of 'sexual predators' and 'killers'.

b) Mandatory minimum penalties One might respond to this by dismissing the Bill as an anomaly that has been propelled largely through the efforts of a few members of parliament. Unfortunately it is not an isolated event. Notwithstanding powerful evidence that similar rigid sentencing rules have achieved nothing in the United States other than massive prison overcrowding and hardening of pervasive racial discrimination, the law and order agenda is embraced by many in Canada as the answer to perceived problems. The other example of this is the perceived attractiveness of more mandatory minimum penalties.

Since the Supreme Court of Canada struck down the mandatory minimum prison sentence of seven years for drug importation,[14] Canada has exercised some restraint in creating new mandatory minimums. The Criminal Code now largely restricts their use to murder, firearms offences and repeat impaired driving. Even at that limited use, the mandatory minimum life sentence for murder is now before the Supreme Court of Canada.

This has not stopped some from calling for the increased use of such provisions. The current target for a number of provincial Attorneys General is 'home invasion'. Some are now calling for the creation of a new offence of home invasion with a mandatory minimum sentence of four years. This is a particularly bizarre suggestion for several reasons – the actual incidence of these crimes appears to be on the decline in Canada (Statistics Canada 1997),[15] there are already a wide range of charges that can be laid in such circumstances, some of which carry the possibility of life imprisonment,[16] and actual sentences being imposed are already quite severe, well above the four year mark in serious cases (Crosbie 1999).

Again, this type of law reform is nothing more than punitive, 'quick-fix' posturing. Apart from its bankruptcy of sentencing principles, it will have only the effect of filling our prisons with individuals for lengthy periods of time, in many cases well beyond the point where the person could be safely returned to the community.

Indeed, this type of reform completely divorces the sentencing process from 'good corrections'. Mandatory sentencing rules, whether mandatory consecutive sentences or mandatory minimums, are often promoted as a 'proportionate' response to crime, but are predicated on a complete disregard for the individual, his or her risk of recidivism or rehabilitative potential, or for what happens to him or her post-sentencing.

c) Corrections and Conditional Release Act Review At the same time that we are experiencing this pressure for more inflexible sentencing reforms, a subcommittee of parliament has completed its fundamental review of the 1992 legislation regulating the penitentiary system (Standing Committee on Justice and Human Rights 2000). This review encompassed a range of matters relating to the conditions of confinement, as well as the conditional release regime. One of the best things the parliamentary subcommittee did was to travel to a range of penitentiaries across the country. For some members of parliament, this was the first time they had actually been behind the bars that they favour so much. The 'law and order' members of the subcommittee openly acknowledged that their attitudes moderated as a result of seeing the less than luxurious conditions of our penitentiaries, as well as actually talking with inmates and staff.

The result was 53 mixed recommendations for legislative and program amendments: the restricted mandate of the subcommittee prevented a more coherent analysis of the inter-relationship between sentencing and corrections. On the two key areas of debate among subcommittee members, conditions of confinement and conditional release, it seems clear that recommendations to 'tighten up' in both areas reflected frustrations with sentencing as much or more than with corrections. Corrections officials emphasised the rehabilitative and reintegrative goals of humane conditions and effective conditional release programs, but were criticised for not being punitive enough on both fronts. The government's subtle rejection (Government of Canada 2000) of the more hard-line recommendations may be seen as an effort to refrain from sacrificing a sensible corrections regime to address sentencing concerns which were only obliquely on the table.

d) Supreme Court of Canada – Gladue and Wells judgements[17] The fourth and last issue of current sentencing and corrections reform of note is a pair of recent and related judgements from the Supreme Court of Canada. In *R v Gladue*, a young Aboriginal woman pleaded guilty to manslaughter in the stabbing to death of her partner and was sentenced to three years imprisonment.

The primary issue was the appropriate interpretation to be given to the statutory sentencing principle referred to above that incarceration is to be used as the last resort, particularly in the case of Aboriginal offenders.

The Supreme Court's judgement is a sweeping indictment of the use of incarceration in Canada in general, and particularly powerful language is used to decry the treatment of Aboriginal Canadians at the hands of our criminal justice system. The Court makes a number of important points. The first is the Court's clear statement that sentencing judges have an obligation to remedy the problem of Aboriginal over-incarceration *whatever* its multifaceted causes:

> It is clear that sentencing innovation by itself cannot remove the causes of aboriginal offending and the greater problem of aboriginal alienation from the criminal justice system ... There are many aspects of this sad situation which cannot be addressed in these reasons. What can and must be addressed, though, is the limited role that sentencing judges will play in remedying injustice against aboriginal peoples in Canada. Sentencing judges ... determine most directly whether an aboriginal offender will go to jail, or whether other sentencing options may be employed which will play perhaps a stronger role in restoring a sense of balance to the offender, victim, and community, and in preventing future crime (p. 723).

Second, the Court makes it clear that they are not proposing a separate justice system for Aboriginal offenders. Rather, their judgment is directed at ensuring that the system is tailored to meet the unique circumstances of each offender, including Aboriginal offenders. This approach clearly speaks to the deficiencies of the more rigid approaches promoted by the other law reform efforts noted above, and gives some hope that should they ever become law the Supreme Court will dispatch them in fairly quick order.

Finally, the Court explicitly emphasises that a more restorative justice approach should not be viewed as a more *lenient* approach. When we reach for 'tough' sanctions, imprisonment should not be the only response. As the Court notes, accepting accountability for one's actions in a profound way, engaging in treatment, repaying the community "may in some circumstances impose a greater burden on the offender than a custodial sentence" (p. 726).

Having said this, the tone and the results in the Court's judgement a year later in *R v Wells* and five companion conditional sentence cases[18] give rise to some concern that the Court has retreated from its embrace of restoring rather than punishing. Two factors may account for this: there was a change in the membership on the Court, and there was a significant debate in the press and Parliament about alleged over-activism of the Court. While this bears further exploration beyond the confines of this chapter, the combination of these factors could account for more conservative and categorical sentencing rulings in these cases, as well as less inclination to explore offender-specific factors and broader systemic or social policy implications of sentencing.

Where Next?

Where, then, do we go next? The *Gladue* judgement, although it addresses Aboriginal sentencing in particular, offers Canadians a powerful blueprint for renewing our pursuit of the integrated sentencing reforms of a decade ago. There are three immediate challenges.

First and foremost, the environmental pressures noted above need to be shaped by a balanced debate, and the neon lights of American-style reform need to be resisted. This will require concerted action on a number of fronts, including good research and an informed public. Above all, it requires political and public service leadership, and a willingness to champion approaches that do not traffic on quick fixes. In particular, this means looking at sentencing and corrections as part of a seamless process, and avoiding the adoption of sentencing reforms that do not reflect social realities, the circumstances of the individual offender, or what we know about risk and recidivism. I am reminded of the comment of a provincial premier who instituted boot camps for young offenders several years ago, notwithstanding the dismal evaluation results of such programs in the US. "We had to do something", he said, "and this was all there was." We need to put as many resources as possible into good research and effective treatment programs, so that we can offer decision-makers positive choices, or at least make it more difficult for them to ignore empirically-based options in favour of quick fixes.

Moreover, criminal justice professionals need to provide information about research and program efficacy in a continuous and accessible manner. It is no good if there is a wealth of information that no one outside of the research community knows about. Research experts and practitioners in the field need to bombard policy advisors with information about what works. That information needs to be provided *continuously*, as it is very difficult to get thoughtful and complex ideas through in times of crisis – it is pointless to try to tell the public that parole is a good program when a parolee has just committed a terrible crime, and it is equally pointless to try to talk with politicians about positive treatment options for sex offenders in the middle of a community crisis. We need to be more strategic about how to communicate

Sentencing and Society

information to the broader public, both in terms of *who* communicates that information and *how*. When the premier announces that boot camps were the only alternative for young offenders, we need the op-ed piece the next day outlining what we know about effective responses to juvenile crime. When a member of parliament announces that it is a good thing to pile on custodial sentences for offenders, we need the pubic debate that analyses the results of such an approach and suggests more constructive alternatives.

The second challenge for Canada is to aggressively address its treatment of Aboriginal people, in effective and comprehensive ways. The Aboriginal incarceration rate is $8^{1}/_{2}$ times that of the non-Aboriginal rate, and indeed were it not for Canada's sad treatment of its Aboriginal people the country's incarceration rate would be on a par with the most progressive of western European countries (Solicitor General Canada 1998).[19] This is a multifaceted, systemic problem, and will require a combined, coordinated effort of sentencing and corrections practices in concert with other social policy measures. Isolated, ad hoc legislative or policy reforms will continue to play out with particularly disastrous results for Aboriginal peoples, with each part of the system disclaiming responsibility for the net result.

Finally, Canada must continue to invest in sound alternatives to incarceration. Sentencing judges can only work with what they are given, and cannot be expected to devise new alternatives of their own in a vacuum. In addition, judges need better information about the realities of incarceration and the possibilities of better alternatives. While judges must remain independent of improper influence in individual decision-making, they must take responsibility for the implications of their sentencing decisions and their role as one partner in an interconnected criminal justice system.

Only if these challenges are met can we avoid the polarisation of sentencing and corrections, and the failure of the criminal justice system as a whole to respond meaningfully to criminal behaviour.

Notes

1   'Corrections' is used as an omnibus term to refer to all matters relating to the administration of sentences of imprisonment, including conditional release.
2   S.C. 1868, c. 75.
3   55–56 Vic., c. 29.
4   Part I of the Constitution Act, 1982, being Schedule B to the Canada Act 1982 (UK), 1982, c. 11.
5   S.C. 1992, c. 20.

6   See sections 726.2 and 743.2 Criminal Code, R.S.C. 1985, Ch. C–46; 4 and 23 Corrections and Conditional Release Act.
7   See, for example, *R v Oliver* (1997), 147 Nfld. & P.E.I.R. 210 (Nfld. C.A.).
8   See, for example, 'Revolt among the Liberals', *The Ottawa Citizen*, 23 October 2000, in which backbench government Members of Parliament publicly proclaimed that they want to have the freedom of 'unrestricted free agents' rather than following party discipline.
9   Ministers of Cabinet are the sponsors of government legislation. At the same time, any member of parliament or Senator, whether on the government or the opposition side, may table bills on any matter of concern to them. Historically, such bills have been of limited scope and have rarely been passed by parliament.
10 See mixed results of a recent employee survey in Government of Canada 1999.
11 Section 718.3(4).
12 Section 718.2(c).
13 See, for example, Gendreau 1999.
14 *R v Smith* [1987] 1 S.C.R. 1045.
15 Statistics Canada 1997, verbal update 1998. Home invasion rates declined 17 per cent between 1993 and 1997. Residential break-ins in general have also been declining, down 10.1 per cent in 1999, the third consecutive year of decline (Statistics Canada 2000).
16 E.g. break and enter of a dwelling house – life; robbery – life.
17 *R v Gladue*, [1999] 1 S.C.R. 688; *R. v Wells*, [2000] 1 S.C.R. 207.
18 *R v Proulx* [2000] 1 S.C.R. 61; *R v Bunn* [2000] 1 S.C.R. 183; *R v RNS* [2000] 1 S.C.R. 149; *R v RAR* [2000] 1 S.C.R. 163; *R v LFW* [2000] 1 S.C.R. 132.
19 The non-Aboriginal incarceration in 1998 was 58 per 100,000, while the Aboriginal rate was 417 per 100,000. In some provinces the Aboriginal rate was well over 1,200 per 100,000.

References

Canadian Sentencing Commission (1987), *Sentencing Reform: A Canadian approach*, Ottawa: Minister of Supply and Services Canada.
Crosbie, Kim (1999), discussion paper: 'Creating a New Offence of "Home Invasion"', Ottawa: Solicitor General Canada.
Gendreau, P., Goggin, C. and Cullen, F.T. (1999), *The Effects of Prison Sentences on Recidivism*, Ottawa: Solicitor General Canada.
Government of Canada (1982), *The Criminal Law in Canadian Society*, Ottawa: Government of Canada.
Government of Canada (1990), *Directions for Reform – A Framework for Sentencing, Corrections and Conditional Release*, Ottawa: Minister of Supply and Services Canada.
Government of Canada (1999), *Public Service Survey Results for the Public Service Commission of Canada*, Ottawa: Public Service Commission.
Government of Canada (2000), *Response to the Report of the Sub-committee on Corrections and Conditional Release Act of the Standing Committee on Justice and Human Rights: A Work in Progress: The Corrections and Conditional Release Act*, Ottawa: Solicitor General Canada.
Hann, R. and Associates Limited (1998), *Report of a National Survey on Organized Crime and Corrections in Canada*, Ottawa: Solicitor General Canada.

Solicitor General Canada (1998), *Working Document*, Ottawa: A. Harris.

Solicitor General Canada (2000), *Corrections Population Report, Fourth Edition*, Ottawa.

Standing Committee on Justice and Human Rights – Sub-committee on the Corrections and Conditional Release Act (2000), *A Work in Progress: The Corrections and Conditional Release Act*, Ottawa: Government of Canada.

Standing Committee on Justice and Solicitor General (1998), *Taking Responsibility*, Report of the Standing Committee on Justice and Solicitor General on its Review of Sentencing, Conditional Release and Related Aspects of Corrections. Ottawa: Government of Canada.

Statistics Canada (1997), *The Daily*, 30 July 1997 – Crime Statistics 1996, Ottawa: Statistics Canada.

Statistics Canada (2000), *The Daily*, 18 October 2000 – Homicide Statistics 1999, Ottawa: Statistics Canada.

PART II
THE TRUTH ABOUT PUBLIC AND VICTIM PUNITIVENESS: WHAT DO WE KNOW AND WHAT DO WE NEED TO KNOW?

Chapter Seven

Public Knowledge and Public Opinion of Sentencing

Mike Hough and Julian V. Roberts

> In deciding to what extent effect should be given to the manifestations of public opinion, I think one must try to ascertain to what extent that public opinion is well informed ... (Attorney-General in the House of Commons, cited by Silvey 1961).

The need to sustain public confidence in the administration of justice means that public opinion plays an important, albeit indirect role in sentencing policy and practice. This has probably always been the case. For example, writing of the evolution of criminal law policy in the eighteenth century, Radzinowicz noted that the parliament of the day was "not indifferent to the pressure of public opinion" (1948, p. 38). Politicians, too, have frequently referred to the need to reflect or incorporate the views of the public in the evolution of sentencing policy. For example, the former Prime Minister Margaret Thatcher spoke of "the very real anxiety of ordinary people that too many sentences do not fit the crime" (cited in *The Economist* 1985; see Ashworth and Hough 1996 for a fuller discussion).

On the basis of the historical record of public opinion research, two general observations can be made about public attitudes towards the sentencing process. First, judges tend to receive more negative evaluations than any other criminal justice professional; surveys have repeatedly shown a widespread lack of confidence in the judiciary. Thus in the 1992 British Crime Survey, three quarters of the public felt that sentencers were out of touch (Hough 1998). Second, for decades now polls have revealed that members of the public feel that sentences are too lenient. In 1981, almost two-thirds of the British public were of the opinion that sentence lengths were too short (cited in Walker and Hough 1988). Responses to similar questions on representative surveys 15 years later reveal that the perception of leniency is even more widespread. In 1996, 92 per cent of respondents favoured "tougher sentences for criminals, especially persistent criminals" (*Daily Mail*, 1 April 1996). These findings have emerged consistently over a sustained period of British history.

Poll results with respect to the perception of leniency have led pollsters and politicians to assume that the courts and the public are at odds over the treatment of offenders. Taken at face value, these findings suggest a clear policy recommendation – that public support for and confidence in the sentencing process would be promoted by adopting a harsher sentencing policy. And indeed, sentencing policies of the mid-1990s pursued this line. The 1993 Criminal Justice Act amended the 1991 Criminal Justice Act to restore the courts' discretion to sentence recidivist offenders severely. The 1996 Crime (Sentences) Act provided for mandatory minimum sentences for repeat burglars and drug dealers, and mandatory life sentences for those who were convicted of a serious violent or sexual offence for the second time. One of the justifications for these swingeing recidivist premiums proposed by the former Home Secretary in 1995 was that they would promote public confidence in the sentencing process (see Henham 1997).

The legislative changes in themselves had less of an impact on the sentencing climate than did the cumulative effect of the surrounding political debate (cf. Ashworth and Hough 1996). In the five years from the end of 1992, the prison population increased by over 50 per cent – with very little change in the overall volume of business passing through the courts. The increase was largely due to an increased tendency to imprison offenders, and for longer terms. In fact, only a very small part of the increase can be directly attributed to the new legislation.

The United Kingdom is not unique in the shift to a harsher sentencing climate. Americans' desire to punish repeat offenders more harshly was the driving force behind the highly punitive recidivist sentencing premiums in the US, of which the 'Three Strikes' policy is but the most severe and visible (see Roberts 1996). When asked their opinion, 90 per cent of Americans pronounced themselves in favour of the imposition of a life term on someone convicted of a violent felony for a third time (see Lacayo 1994). In Canada, public opinion has played a role in the passage of a number of punitive legislative amendments which increased the severity of penalties for young offenders, imposed mandatory minimum penalties for offences involving firearms, and which tightened considerably the parole arrangements for inmates serving life terms for murder (see Roberts and Cole 1999).

There are three main types of explanation for the findings of successive polls and surveys. The first is that there is indeed a gulf between the sentences that people would like to see and those that are actually meted out. To the extent that this is true, the possible political responses are either to adjust current practice by increasing sentencing severity or to explain to the public the rationality of current sentencing policy. The second explanation assumes that people are ill-informed or misinformed about current sentencing practice. If this is true, then the problem is one of communication, and the only sensible political response is to improve public knowledge and understanding. The final explanation is that apparent public dissatisfaction is a methodological artefact of surveys and polls. If this is so, the correct political response is to disregard what is essentially unreliable evidence.

The limitations of the survey method in accurately reflecting opinion about sentencing has been well established by North American research (e.g. Brillon, Louis-Guerin and Lamarche 1984; Doob and Roberts 1988; Sprott 1996; Roberts and Stalans 1997). This body of work supports the following conclusions:

- people answering a general question on a poll respond punitively in part because they have the worst kinds of cases and offenders in mind;
- when responding to questions about sentence severity on polls, people recall atypical sentences, which usually means lenient dispositions reported in the media;
- when asked about the appropriateness of prison for specific cases, people fail to consider the wide range of alternative punishments available to the courts.

One final observation about the voluminous international literature regarding public opinion is the following. Almost all the research has examined public attitudes towards criminal justice issues. Very few polls have investigated public knowledge of issues such as sentencing and parole; fewer still have explored public opinion as a function of public knowledge. Some qualitative research (Hough 1996) has uncovered systematic ignorance of current sentencing patterns, and suggested that this may be helping to fuel public dissatisfaction with the courts.

That qualitative research was the point of departure for the present quantitative investigation. This chapter summarises findings from a module of the British Crime Survey[1] which addressed public attitudes towards, and knowledge of, the sentencing process and sentencing patterns. The analyses we report are based upon a survey of the British public; however, throughout the discussion we relate these analyses to results from surveys conducted in other countries.

Evaluations of the Judiciary and of Sentencing Practice

The 1996 BCS confirms the widespread public dissatisfaction with court practices and the judiciary found in previous studies. Respondents were asked 'how good a job [each of several criminal justice professionals] are doing'. Only 20 per cent of respondents rated judges as doing a good job; 49 per cent thought that they were doing a fair job and 32 per cent responded that they were doing a poor or very poor job. Judges received the worst evaluations of six criminal justice professions, far behind the group that received the most positive evaluations (the police, rated by 64 per cent of the public as doing a good job). A similarly low percentage of the sample (18 per cent) believed that judges were 'in touch with what ordinary people think'; almost half respondents thought that judges were 'very out of touch'. Almost four out of five respondents (79 per cent) thought that sentences were too lenient to some degree; slightly over half the sample (51 per cent) endorsed the view that sentences were much too lenient. This result is consistent with recent surveys that have repeatedly posed the same question in Canada, America and other common law countries (e.g. Flanagan and Longmire 1996; Roberts and Stalans 1997). Thus the dissatisfaction with sentencing practice first documented many years ago (and sustained repeatedly in subsequent surveys) continues.

Public Knowledge

Sentencing Options

It has been argued in other jurisdictions that public support for the use of imprisonment is strong because people fail to consider other possible punishments available to the court. Are they even aware of the alternative, community-based sanctions available to British sentencers? We assumed that people would be aware of prison as a sentencing option, but asked respondents to list as many other sentences as they could. The results indicated limited public awareness of many noncustodial sentencing options. Over two-thirds (69 per cent) of respondents identified community service; prison apart, this was the most widely-known sentencing option. Over half (58 per cent) identified a fine. Surprisingly perhaps, only about a third (35 per cent) of the sample identified probation. Even smaller percentages of respondents were aware of the other alternatives: compensation (16 per cent); conditional discharge (8 per cent); and electronic tagging (7 per cent). One option which is now virtually unused – the suspended sentence – was however mentioned by 30 per cent of respondents.[2] It is clear then, that although large percentages of the public are aware of some community penalties (such as community service), others such as probation are not at all salient in people's minds when they think about sentencing. As we shall demonstrate later in this chapter, this lack of awareness of the sentencing options available has important consequences for polls that explore public sentencing preferences in specific cases.

The Use of Imprisonment for Specific Offences

Several questions tested public knowledge of sentencing patterns for three familiar crimes: rape, mugging and residential burglary. For each of these offences, respondents were asked to estimate the percentage of adult convictions which result in a term of imprisonment. In our analysis of these data, we have classified respondents into various categories, reflecting their degree of accuracy in estimating the imprisonment rate for these specific crimes. We regarded as accurate those respondents whose estimates were within 10 percentage points of the correct value. The respondents whose estimates were roughly 10 to 30 percentage points too low were classified as 'a bit too low' and those who were still more inaccurate were classified as 'much too low'. When respondents fell on the boundary line, we conservatively classified them as 'a bit low' rather than 'much too low'. Table 7.1 summarises the findings from this analysis.

Large majorities of respondents provided estimates of current imprisonment rates which were too low for all three crimes. For rape, 97 per cent of adult males convicted in 1995 were sent to prison (data supplied by Home Office). Respondents' median estimate, however, was 50 per cent. Eighteen per cent of respondents could be classified as accurate; they estimated the incarceration rate to lie between 85 per cent and 100 per cent. Twenty-six per cent were 'a bit low' (estimating between 60 per cent and 84 per cent). The remaining 57 per cent made estimates which were 'much too low'.

Since there is no legal offence of mugging, on the survey it was defined as 'theft in the street by means of force or the threat of force'. The Home Office cannot provide sentencing statistics for this subgroup of robberies. However, such offences probably make up the bulk of convictions, with robberies in banks, shops and other businesses being far less frequent. Almost all (92 per cent) of adult male offenders convicted in 1995 of any form of robbery were imprisoned. Accordingly, we have conservatively estimated that

Table 7.1　Summary of public estimates of imprisonment rates

	Rape	Mugging	Burglary
Overestimate Rape: not applicable Mugging: 80–100% Burglary: 70–100%	–	5%	8%
Accurate Rape: 85–100% Mugging: 60–79% Burglary: 50–69%	18%	12%	22%
Small underestimate Rape: 60–85% Mugging: 45–59% Burglary: 31–49%	26%	20%	15%
Large underestimate Rape: 0–59% Mugging: 0–44% Burglary: 0–30%	57%	62%	55%
Total	100%	100%	100%

Question: Out of every 100 men aged 21 or over who are convicted of rape (mugging/house burglary), how many do you think are sent to prison?

the percentage of convicted adult muggers who receive custodial sentences is in the region of 60–80 per cent. Using this as a yardstick, 12 per cent of respondents can be considered accurate, while 5 per cent overestimated the imprisonment rate, providing estimates between 80 per cent and 100 per cent. Once again, however, the vast majority of the sample (fully 75 per cent) of respondents underestimated the severity of sentencing.[3] Twenty per cent made a small underestimate – between 45 per cent and 59 per cent, and 62 per cent provided larger underestimates. The median estimate of the percentage of adult muggers sent to prison was 35 per cent.

For residential burglary, the court data are clear: 61 per cent of convicted adult male house-burglars were imprisoned in 1995. Twenty-two per cent of responses were classified as 'correct', namely those falling between 50 and 69 per cent. A further 8 per cent provided an overestimate. Once again, the majority of the sample underestimated the severity of the system; 15 per cent were 'a bit low' (31–50 per cent) and the remaining 55 per cent made grosser underestimates. The median estimate was 30 per cent.

To summarise, few people had an accurate idea of the imprisonment rates for these offences. Public perceptions of the imprisonment rates for all three crimes were systematically biased towards a view that the courts are treating offenders with more leniency than is in fact the case. This finding is consistent with results from surveys in other countries which have found that the public underestimate the severity of the sentencing and parole systems (see Roberts and Stalans 1997 for a review).

The belief in leniency appears to be correlated with misperceptions about sentencing practice. For all three crime types, the lower the estimated use of imprisonment, the greater the belief that sentencers were too lenient. For example, people who believed that sentences were too lenient generated a lower average estimate of the percentage of rapists incarcerated than did people who believed that sentences were about right. These results imply that people who are dissatisfied with the severity of sentences are also those who are particularly inaccurate.

Multivariate Analysis

We carried out a logistic regression analysis to determine which aspects of public misperception were most closely associated with a belief that sentences were far too soft. Six variables were identified as statistically significant predictors, and are listed below, in order of predictive power:[4]

1) changes in national crime rate (those saying 'a lot more crime' were most likely to think sentences far too soft);
2) changes in use of imprisonment (those saying prison use 'the same/down' were most likely to say sentences far too soft);
3) estimated number of convicted muggers who were sent to prison (under-estimators were most likely to say sentences were far too soft);
4) the proportion of recorded crime involving violence (over-estimators were most likely to say sentences were far too soft);
5) estimated number of convicted burglars who were sent to prison (under-estimators were most likely to say sentences were far too soft);
6) estimates of the clearance rate of crimes (under-estimators were most likely to say sentences were far too soft).

This analysis provides strong evidence that people's dissatisfaction with perceived sentencing patterns stems at least in part from misperceptions about crime and justice.

Who Underestimates Sentence Severity?

The probability that misperceptions about crime and justice are fuelling public dissatisfaction makes it important to know which demographic groups are especially misinformed about sentencing. We carried out a stepwise logistic regression to identify the variables which best predicted 'under-estimators'. We defined this group as all those who made large underestimates of the use of imprisonment for all three offence categories. According to this definition, exactly a third of the sample were under-estimators. Poor educational attainment was the best predictor, followed by respondent gender (being female), reading tabloid newspapers, being over 50 and finally, being an owner occupier of the residence. The fact that gender is a predictor reflects the fact that women are more likely than men to underestimate rape sentences; that owner-occupation is a predictor reflects the fact that owners underestimate the severity of sentences for burglary.[5]

Sentencing Preferences in a Specific Case

As noted earlier, if people are asked a general question about the severity of sanctions, most – but not all – will respond by considering the punishment of a specific offender, usually a violent recidivist. A less ambiguous approach to measuring public punitiveness would involve providing a description of a specific offender. This approach was followed in the 1996 BCS. Respondents were given a summary of an actual case[6] and were asked to select a sentence (or sentences, as multiple choices were permitted). The details of the case were presented on a show-card as follows:

> A man aged 23 pleaded guilty to the burglary of a cottage belonging to an elderly man whilst he was out during the day. The offender, who had previous convictions for burglary, took a video worth £150 and a television which he left damaged near the scene of the crime.

The offender had been given a three-year term of imprisonment in the Crown Court, which was subsequently reduced on appeal to two years. The three-year sentence was obviously atypical. In the absence of strong mitigating circumstances, magistrates would probably pass a custodial sentence of three to six months, or commit the offender to the Crown Court for sentence. Crown Court judges would typically pass sentences ranging from six months to two years.

In asking what sentence respondents would like to see for the offender, we introduced an experimental manipulation. Specifically, we tested the hypothesis that there would be less support for imprisonment as a sanction if the question made respondents aware of the other sentencing alternatives available to the court. The reasoning was that the top-of-the-head reaction of most people is to think first and foremost about imprisonment. Therefore, half the sample were randomly assigned to select a sentence from a 'menu' of sentencing alternatives.[7] The other half of the sample were simply asked (unprompted) to say what sentence they would like to see.

Table 7.2 presents the results from this question. There are two important results. First, only a bare majority (54 per cent) of those who sentenced in full knowledge of the sentencing options favoured the imposition of a term of imprisonment. Whilst we cannot specify a precise figure, we are confident that a much larger proportion of actual judges would have opted for a prison sentence in similar cases. Secondly, the experimental hypothesis was confirmed: respondents who had to choose a sentence without the benefit of a 'menu' of sentencing options were more likely to favour imprisonment. Just over two-thirds of the 'non-menu' sub-sample chose a term of custody, whereas only half of the other group endorsed imprisonment as a sanction. This is a highly statistically significant difference (p <.001). Respondents provided with a list of options were more likely to favour imposition of a suspended sentence, probation and community service.[8] Support for compensation was also higher when respondents were aware that it was an option: almost half (44 per cent) of the 'menu' group chose compensation, compared with 22 per cent of the 'non-menu' group. Table 7.2 compares the respondents' sentencing choices, with and without the menu of options.

Of the respondents with the sentencing options, a fifth favoured a fine, and around a third favoured community penalties other than a fine. On balance, these responses are more lenient than the Court of Appeal judgement (two years) and no harsher than the Magistrates Association guidelines which suggest that the 'entry point' sentence for a domestic burglary of this sort is a short prison sentence.

It is also noteworthy that in the series of questions asking for estimates of the proportion of convicted adult offenders who are and ought to be imprisoned, respondents on average said that 80 per cent of burglars should go to prison. By implication, this typical example of burglary was, in the eyes of the public, at the less serious end of the seriousness spectrum. This underscores the dangers of guiding sentencing policy on the basis of survey findings which use a general question, such as 'Are sentences too harsh, too lenient or about right?'. If the public overestimates the seriousness of the average burglary, as appears to be the case here, those responsible for sentencing policy can derive little of value from the finding that on average, people think that 80 per cent of burglars should be locked up.

Table 7.2   Sentencing preferences as a function of awareness of options

Per cent respondents *choosing sentencing options*	Sentencing options provided to respondent %	No sentencing options provided %
Imprisonment	54	67
Suspended Sentence	18	8
Fine	21	19
Probation	9	5
Community service	26	20
Tagging	11	4
Compensation	44	22
Discharge	1	1

Note: columns exceed 100 per cent due to multiple selections by respondents.

Sentence Length

The median term of imprisonment favoured by respondents was 12 months. This result will also surprise those who believe that the British public are highly punitive. After all, there were several important aggravating factors present. The case involved a vulnerable victim, loss of property, and most important of all, the offender had several previous convictions for the same offence. Research has shown that like the courts, members of the public become far more punitive when the offender being sentenced has several related previous convictions (see Roberts 1997 for a review). On the basis of these findings it is hard to argue that the public are consistently more severe than the courts. It is clearly impossible to argue that the public want tougher sentences, on balance, than those in a significant Court of Appeal guideline judgement on burglary. And, of those members of the public who did choose imprisonment, only a quarter favoured a term of custody which exceeded the Court of Appeal sentence.

Perceptions of the Role of Sentencing in Crime Control

The perception of leniency in sentencing goes beyond dissatisfaction with sentencing patterns. It also appears to be related to public beliefs regarding crime causality. Respondents were asked whether there was more, less, or about the same amount of recorded crime as two years ago. Those who thought that there had been an increase were asked whether lenient sentencing had played a role, and those who thought that recorded crime had fallen were asked whether tough sentencing had played a part. Respondents were provided with four response options: a) [lenient or tough sentencing had been] the most important cause; b) a major cause; c) only a minor cause; d) not a cause of this change.

Fully three-quarters of the sample thought that recorded crime had risen over the past two years. More importantly, respondents saw a direct link between lenient sentencing and the rising crime rate. One quarter of respondents thought that lenient sentencing patterns were the most important cause, and almost half (48 per cent) saw it as a major cause of rising crime. Most respondents appear to be mistaken in two directions: the volume of recorded crime actually declined over the period in question[9] (Povey, Prime and Taylor 1997), and sentencing patterns are significantly harsher than most people believe (see above).[10] These trends also support the interpretation that the public regard judges as playing an important role in crime control. People tend to think that varying the severity of penalties will have an impact on crime rates; more lenient sentences will lead to higher crime rates, and harsher penalties to a fall in crime. As with the other findings reported in this chapter, there are international parallels. A recent poll in America found that when respondents were asked to explain increases in crime rates, almost half the sample identified the courts as the cause of the problem (Maguire and Pastore 1995). In Canada, over three-quarters of the polled public agreed with the statement that "There is a great deal of crime because sentences are not severe enough" (Brillon et al. 1984).

Of course, these data do not permit us to discern whether there is a causal relationship present, or the direction of causality. Do people infer that sentences are lenient because they see and read about so much crime, or do they infer that crime must be up because sentences are lenient? It probably makes little difference; what counts is that the two perceptions, (rising crime; lenient sentencing), are linked in the public mind. The lesson we might draw is that correcting public misperceptions about the rising crime rate will probably dampen enthusiasm for harsher sentencing.

It would be an oversimplification, however, to state that the British public see tougher sentencing as the only, or even the most important solution to the problem of crime. Respondents were asked to identify the single most effective strategy for preventing crime. The hierarchy of responses that emerged can be seen in Table 7.3. The response that attracted the largest percentage of respondents (36 per cent) was 'increase discipline in the family'. This was followed by 'reduce levels of unemployment' (25 per cent). Making sentences tougher was the third place option, attracting only one-fifth of respondents. Clearly then, although most people believe lenient sentencing is a major cause of increasing crime rates, they do not see the most effective solution to crime within the criminal justice process. The British public, like their counterparts in North America[11] believe that there are many causes to crime, and that harsher sentencing can play only a limited role. This is an important finding as it demonstrates that the British public is not oriented exclusively towards punishment as the exclusive panacea for rising crime rates.

Table 7.3   Views about the most effective way of preventing crime

Which is the most effective in preventing crime?

1 Increase discipline in the home	36%
2 Reduce levels of unemployment	25%
3 Make sentences tougher	20%
4 Increase the number of police officers	9%
5 Increase discipline in schools	8%
6 Increase the use of community-based sentences such as fines, community service	2%
	100%

Developments Since 1996

The analysis presented here was of the 1996 British Crime Survey. Since then, two further sweeps of the British Crime Survey have been carried out, and one further report on attitudes to punishment has been published (Mattinson and Mirrlees-Black 2000). This very largely confirms the analysis which we mounted on the 1996 data. There were further reductions in crime between 1996 and 1998. The proportion of people who were aware of this increased, but 59 per cent still thought crime was rising. People continued to overestimate the extent to which crime was violent, and continued to underestimate courts' use of imprisonment. Ratings of judges showed an improvement, though 80 per cent of people still regarded them as out of touch. Eight out of 10 still thought sentences too soft. As in 1996, sentenced 'passed' by respondents in a specific case continued to be more lenient, on balance, than actual practice. The 1998 survey asked a new series of questions about the youth justice system in England and Wales, and this revealed widespread disenchantment. Most people thought the youth justice system performed poorly.

Conclusions

Several themes emerge from this analysis of British attitudes toward sentencing and related criminal justice issues. First, there is a widespread perception that sentencers are far too lenient. This is clearly related to evaluations of the judiciary, and to a lesser extent, magistrates. While the perception persists that sentences are too lenient, criticism of sentencers will continue. Judges received the most negative evaluations of all criminal justice professionals in this survey. The lesson would appear clear: correcting public misperception about sentencing trends in this country will promote public confidence in judges and magistrates. And, since the judiciary occupy such a critical place in the criminal justice system, increasing confidence in the courts may well also promote confidence in the administration of justice. Since the perception of leniency has been around for at least two decades now, it should constitute a priority in terms of public legal education.

It would be wrong to characterise the British public as being, on balance, highly punitive, or as being consistently more punitive than sentencers. Obviously there were respondents who expressed extremely punitive views, but there were rather more whose views were consistent with, or even more lenient than, current sentencing practice. The modal set of attitudes towards crime control could be called a multi-track approach. Most people do not look exclusively to the courts to prevent crime. Crime prevention is seen as a problem for society at large; it is not primarily a criminal justice issue. Politicians may advocate tougher sentencing in order to 'do something about the crime problem', but many members of the public believe that reducing the crime rate is more a question of changing the family and school environment, and providing more employment opportunities. This is not to say that the public see no role for sentencing in preventing crime; responses to the BCS indicate that lenient sentencing is seen as being a cause of crime, but it is not the only or even the primary remedy.

While the public respond to polls by endorsing the view that sentences are too lenient, this result must be seen in light of the findings that emerge from the British Crime Survey. When asked about sentencing in general, the public think of the worst kinds of offenders (recidivists) and the worst crimes of violence, although these represent only a small minority of the total offender population. When presented with a concrete description of an actual case, the public tend to be less punitive. As well, when given adequate information about the range of legal punishments available, the public are less likely to endorse the use of imprisonment. In other words, the more detail that people are given about any given crime and the available penalties, the more that their sentencing preferences converge with actual sentencing decisions. This result has emerged from a research in other countries (e.g. Doble and Klein 1989; English, Crouch and Pullen 1989).

The most probable reason for this degree of misinformation is that people do not receive balanced information about sentencing practices in the news media, but rather a steady stream of stories about sentencing malpractices, cases in which a judge imposes what appears to be a very lenient sentence for a serious crime of violence. Quantitative analysis of press coverage does not actually suggest that newspapers are more likely to cover stories about court cases if the sentence is a light one; however when lenient sentences are passed, the attention given to it, and the editorial comment on it, tends to be strident. In such cases the news media rarely make any attempts to explain the judicial reasoning underlying the decision, or to place the sentence imposed in some statistical context. In order to reconcile the public and the courts, a rational approach must involve informing people about the nature of sentencing practices.

Improving the Level of Public Knowledge about Crime and Punishment

In our view, the main responsibility for informing people about court practices must lie with central and federal government rather than with local courts, although the latter obviously have a role to play. The anonymity of large cities means that local communication networks are ineffective in communicating information about who gets punished, in what manner and for what kinds of crimes. The most pressing need is for information systems which can successfully summarise overall sentencing patterns whilst managing to communicate what the 'going rate' is for specific sorts of crime.

Demands for harsher sentencing do not spring from a systematic study of sentencing patterns in trial courts. Members of the public do not argue that the 90th percentile custodial sentence imposed in cases of burglary is too low. They read about a sentence in a specific case which seems, in light of the summary of facts provided by the media, to be too lenient, and then generalise from this to the conclusion that we need to do something about sentencing. The conclusion leads us to suggest that there must be a way of calming public anxiety about specific sentencing decisions.

Providing a Context for Public Evaluation of Sentences

The public needs to have some frame of comparison, within which to consider whether a particular sentence is appropriate. One important framework is the average penalty imposed, or the range of sentence lengths for a particular offence. All too often the public spontaneously make (and are encouraged by the news media to make) comparisons between the sentence handed down and the theoretical maximum penalty, which is very seldom, if ever imposed. This simply feeds the desire for raising the tariff, or instituting a mandatory penalty. Providing the news media with comprehensible, up-to-date sentencing statistics is therefore a priority. There is no guarantee that the data will be provided to the reader or listener in some form when a sentencing story appears, but at least the news media will not have the excuse that these data are either unavailable or only available in an indigestible format. A necessary step then, is to ensure that systematic sentencing statistics are available. At the present such data do not exist; only the US and the United Kingdom have systematic, annual and national statistics on sentencing patterns.

Of course some people will still be dissatisfied with sentencing patterns, and knowing that a particular sentence is consistent with other sentences imposed for the same offence will lead them to argue for harsher sentences generally. But that is a broader debate about what is and is not an appropriate range of sentence for a particular offence. It is not an uninformed rant based on a selective newspaper article.

There is also a need to convey to the public much clearer information about crime trends. At the time of writing, recorded crime was falling in the United States, Canada, England and many other industrialised countries. In some countries this pattern has been established for a decade or so. Despite this, the majority view remains that crime rates are rising. In Canada for example, the annual crime statistics were released in July 2000 showing a significant decline for all categories of crime over the previous year (Tremblay 2000). Shortly after these data were released, a national survey of the public found that approximately two-thirds of the public nevertheless believed that crime was increasing (Ekos Research 2000). This misperception would be understandable if the decline in crime rates was very recent. However, as noted, the decline from 1998–99 was the eighth consecutive annual decrease!

The same divorce between public opinion and reality exists with respect to punishment trends. As noted earlier in this chapter, the vast majority of the public in all western nations see their justice system as being excessively lenient to offenders; imprisonment rates are always too low, and parole rates too high, although no-one ever has an accurate idea of how many people are imprisoned, for how long, or how many of these prisoners are eventually granted parole. It is clear that ways have to be developed of presenting crime and justice statistics in a manner which both emphasises their limitations and communicates the realities underlying the statistics.

Targeting Audiences

Whatever institutional arrangements there are for providing information about the penal process, it will always be essential to identify and target key subgroups of the population. To use the jargon of market research, audiences need to be properly segmented, and messages appropriately constructed to address different audiences. Whilst some progress can be made in reaching the general public, it is almost certainly more efficient to reach separate subgroups directly. Key groups are likely to include:

- victims;
- offenders;
- young people;
- parents with adolescent children;
- people from minority ethnic groups.

Victims, offenders and people between the ages of 12 and 25 comprise three overlapping groups forming the principal set of 'customers' of the criminal process. Leaving aside the scope to reach people of this age through schools, colleges and universities, each contact with the courts provides an opportunity (usually ignored) to shape participants' expectations about the criminal justice system, and to provide information about its true function and performance.

Styles of Communication

Once key audiences have been identified, they need to be provided with information in a way which is tailored to their specific needs and receptivity. It is hardly an exaggeration to say that the courts systems in industrialised countries collectively represent a public relations disaster. As noted, the majority of the public lack confidence in the key decision-makers within these systems, namely judges. In the absence of any accurate knowledge of the severity of typical sentences, they think that the judicial product – punishment – is totally inadequate. Any commercial organisation facing such a crisis would not hesitate to contract the skills of communication experts. The crisis in public confidence in the courts and the parole system will not be resolved by communications alone, but such an initiative will have a positive influence.

Central and federal government is not the only sector with a patchy record in getting across messages about criminal justice. Groups campaigning for liberal criminal justice reform and criminologists who share their agenda appear to have had little impact in terms of informing the public about the realities of crime and justice. In their defence, one could perhaps argue that without their efforts we would now be faced with even more poorly-informed public, and even more punitive sentencing policies. A harsher assessment is that, with a few exceptions, academics have followed rather than led public debate on penal issues.

Using new Technology

Until recently, the mass media – newspapers, television and radio – enjoyed a near-monopoly on access to the general public. Messages of any complexity had to be presented via the media, and those who wished to reach the public inevitably had to surrender some control over the process. The IT revolution has changed all this. Approximately one North American adult in four now has internet access; the figure for Britain is one in ten. The proportion with Net access will obviously grow rapidly within the next few years. There will be inevitable limits to the extent to which people seek out information about crime and punishment, but it is worth extending these limits as far as possible. Interactive websites constitute an ideal medium for rendering complex, detailed information about crime and punishment in an accessible way and for providing it in a way that is at the convenience of the consumer. In addition, the sheer volume of information that can be made accessible in a website makes the Net an ideal vehicle for communicating the results of research.

Public dissatisfaction with the sentencing process will obviously not be eliminated simply by implementing a strategy such as that which we have suggested here, but it could be significantly attenuated. Until (and unless) this happens, polls will continue to suggest a public who appear to clamour for harsher penalties, all the while being largely unaware of the actual practices of the courts. At the same time, public disenchantment with judges (and by extension, the criminal justice system), will persist at unacceptable levels.

Notes

Material from the British Crime Survey has been made available to the authors by courtesy of the Home Office. The authors would also like to thank the Home Office for funding the research which gave rise to this chapter. An earlier version of it appeared in *Punishment and Society*, Vol. 1, No. 1. pp. 11–26 and is reprinted here by permission of Sage Publications Ltd © *Punishment and Society* 1999. Further information can be found in Hough and Roberts (1998). The authors would also like to acknowledge the help and advice of Pat Mayhew and Catriona Mirrlees-Black throughout the project.

1   The 1996 core sample covered a nationally representative sample of 16,348 households in England and Wales. The response rate was 82.5 per cent for the core, higher than in the previous four years by five percentage points. One adult (defined as 16 or older) in each household was interviewed. Computer assisted personal interviewing (CAPI) procedures were used. The results reported in this chapter are derived from a 50 per cent sub-sample of 8,365 respondents. Full details of the survey's methodology are to be found in a technical report (Hales and Stratford 1997), and are also summarised in Mirrlees-Black et al. (1996).

2   This sentence now accounts for only one per cent of the total. Qualitative work also suggests that it continues to loom large in public consciousness (see Hough 1996).

3   Similar findings emerge from surveys conducted in other jurisdictions. For example, when a sample of Canadians was asked to estimate the imprisonment rate for robbery, fully three-quarters of the sample estimated this statistic to be under 60 per cent, when in reality it was over 90 per cent (Canadian Sentencing Commission 1987; see also Indermaur 1987, for Australian data).

4   Predictiveness was taken here from the order in which variables were selected for inclusion in the regression equation according to a forward stepwise procedure.

5   The analysis was carried out using weighted data. Similar findings emerged for the unweighted data-set, except that the order of entry of the last two variables was reversed.

6   The case was selected from reports of Court of Appeal cases included in reference material prepared by the Judicial Studies Board.

7   The alternatives were: imprisonment; suspended prison sentence; fine; probation; community service order; electronic tagging; compensation; conditional discharge.

8   This finding – that people are less supportive of imprisonment when the alternatives are made salient to them – has also emerged from research in the US (see, for example, Doble and Klein 1989).

9   The British Crime Survey suggested a small increase of 2 per cent per year over the same period (Mirrlees-Black et al. 1996).

10 Once again there are international parallels. Recent research in Canada has found that the public believe that youth crime is rising at an alarming rate, and also that the principal cause of this wave of youth crime is lenient sentencing in youth courts.

11 When a sample of Canadians was asked this question, with the same list of response options, the results were comparable: only 27 per cent chose 'making sentences harsher' as the most effective way of preventing crime (see Roberts and Grossman 1991).

References

Ashworth, A. and Hough, M. (1996), 'Sentencing and the Climate of Opinion', *Criminal Law Review*, pp. 776–87.

Brillon, Y., Louis-Guerin, C. and Lamarche, M.-C. (1984), *Attitudes of the Canadian Public Toward Crime Policies*, Ottawa: Ministry of the Solicitor General.

Canadian Sentencing Commission (1987), *Sentencing Reform: A Canadian approach*, Ottawa: Supply and Services Canada.

Doble, J. and Klein, J. (1989), *Punishing Criminals: The public's view*, New York: Edna McConnell Clark Foundation.

Doob, A. and Roberts, J.V. (1988), 'Public Punitiveness and Public Knowledge of the Facts: Some Canadian surveys', in N. Walker and M. Hough (eds), *Public Attitudes to Sentencing. Surveys from Five Countries*, Aldershot: Gower.

Economist, The (1985), 20 July, p. 51.

Ekos Research (2000), *Canadian Attitudes to Crime*, Ottawa: Ekos Research Group.

English, K., Crouch, J. and Pullen, S. (1989), *Attitudes toward Crime: A survey of Colorado Citizens and Criminal Justice Officials*, Denver: Colorado Department of Public Safety.

Flanagan, T. and Longmire, D. (eds) (1996), *Americans View Crime and Justice. A National Public Opinion Survey*, Thousand Oaks: Sage.

Hales, J. and Stratford, N. (1997), *1996 British Crime Survey Technical Report*, London: Social and Community Planning Research.

Henham, R. (1997), 'Anglo-American Approaches to Cumulative Sentencing and the Implications for UK Sentencing Policy', *The Howard Journal of Criminal Justice*, Vol. 36, pp. 263–83.

Home Office (1995), *Criminal Statistics for England and Wales*, Supplementary Tables, Vol. 2, London: Her Majesty's Stationery Office.

Hough, M. (1996), 'People Talking About Punishment', *The Howard Journal of Criminal Justice*, Vol. 35, pp. 191–214.

Hough, M. (1998), *Attitudes to Punishment: findings from the 1992 British Crime Survey*, Social Science Research Paper No. 7, London: South Bank University.

Hough, M. and Mayhew, P. (1985) *Taking Account of Crime: Findings from the second British Crime Survey*, Home Office Research Study No. 85, London: Her Majesty's Stationery Office.

Hough, M. and Roberts, J. (1998), *Attitudes to Punishment: Findings from the British Crime Survey*, Home Office Research Study 179, London: Home Office.

Indermaur, D. (1987), 'Public Perception of Sentencing in Perth, Western Australia', *Australian and New Zealand Journal of Criminology*, Vol. 20, pp. 163–83.

Jowell, R., Curtice, J., Brook, L. and Ahrend, D. (1994), *British Social Attitudes: 11th Report*, Aldershot: Dartmouth.

Lacayo, R. (1994), 'Anatomy of an Acquittal', *Time*, May, pp. 30–32.

Lord Bingham (1997), *The Sentence of the Court*, Police Foundation Lecture, July, London: Police Foundation.

Maguire, K. and Pastore, A. (eds) (1995), *Sourcebook of Criminal Justice Statistics*, US Department of Justice, Bureau of Justice Statistics.

Mattinson, J. and Mirrlees-Black, C. (2000), *Attitudes to Crime and Criminal Justice: findings from the 1998 British Crime Survey*, Home Office Research Study 200, London: Home Office.

Mirrlees-Black, C., Mayhew, P. and Percy, A. (1996), 'The British Crime Survey', *Home Office Statistical Bulletin*, Issue 19, 1996.

Povey, D., Prime, J. and Taylor, P. (1997), *Notifiable Offences. England and Wales, 1996*, Home Office Statistical Bulletin No. 3, March.

Radzinowicz, L. (1948), *A History of the English Criminal Law and its Administration from 1750*, Vol. 1, London: Stevens and Sons Ltd.

Roberts, J.V. (1996), 'Public Opinion, Criminal Record, and the Sentencing Process', *American Behavioural Scientist*, Vol. 39, pp. 488–99.

Roberts, J.V. (1997), 'The Role of Criminal Record in the Sentencing Process', in M. Tonry (ed.), *Crime and Justice. A Review of Research*, Vol. 22, Chicago: University of Chicago Press.

Roberts, J.V. and Cole, D. (1999), 'Sentencing and Parole Arrangements for Murder in Canada', in J.V. Roberts and D. Cole (eds), *Making Sense of Sentencing*, Toronto: University of Toronto Press.

Roberts, J.V. and Grossman, M.G. (1991), 'Crime Prevention and Public Opinion', *Canadian Journal of Criminology*, Vol. 32, pp. 75–90.

Roberts, J.V. and Stalans, L. (1997), *Public Opinion, Crime and Criminal Justice*, Colorado: Westview Press.

Silvey, J. (1961), 'The Criminal Law and Public Opinion', *Criminal Law Review*, Vol. 25, pp. 349–58.

Sprott, J. (1996), 'Understanding Public Views of Youth Crime and the Youth Justice System', *Canadian Journal of Criminology*, Vol. 38, pp. 271–90.

Tremblay, S. (2000), 'Crime Statistics in Canada 1998', *Juristat*, Vol. 19, No. 9.

Walker, N. and Hough, M. (1988) (eds), *Public Attitudes To Sentencing. Surveys from Five Countries*, Aldershot: Gower.

Chapter Eight

Crisis and Contradictions in a State Sentencing Structure

B. Keith Crew, Gene M. Lutz and Kristine Fahrney

Introduction

For decades, at least since the 1960s, the notion that the justice system is 'too soft' on crime has been a common theme in public opinion and political discourse in the United States. Despite evidence to the contrary, large portions of the public, and most politicians, believe that increasingly punitive measures such as lengthy mandatory prison sentences, will reduce crime (Irwin and Austin 1994; Scheingold 1984). The United States thus went on an 'imprisonment binge', more than doubling the size of the imprisoned population between 1980 and 1992, and surpassing South Africa as the nation with the highest incarceration rate in the world (Irwin and Austin 1994). Although it may be partially true that the increasingly punitive public attitudes and public policies began as a response to the rising crime rates of the 1960s, the punitive response has continued even though crime rates have levelled off and even declined. These contradictions – the beliefs that the US criminal justice system is too lenient in the face of increasingly punitive measures, and that tougher sanctions are necessary to stop 'rising' crime rates – are precipitating a fiscal crisis at the state and local levels, as increasing resources are spent on building and operating prisons. They may also precipitate a crisis in legitimation, as increasingly punitive sanctions inevitably generate cases where justice and fairness are called into question.

The state of Iowa provides an interesting natural laboratory to examine the relationship between crime, public opinion, political discourse, and criminal justice policy. As a largely rural state with no large pockets of urban poverty, Iowa has not been hit as hard by the crime problem as have more populous states. Nevertheless, the state's prison population growth reflects the national trend, roughly doubling from 1980 to 1992. The Department of Corrections, the state agency that administers the prison system, projects continued growth in the prison population through 2008, far surpassing current or projected capacity. Such growth must eventually precipitate a crisis in policy, as the state reaches a point where it simply cannot afford to build and maintain enough prison space to house all those sentenced to incarceration. Other states have already felt the impact of similar crises. In this essay, we shall argue that what we call the 'punitive response', the almost automatic assumption that the way to deal with any criminal problem is to increase penalties, is shaped by certain political and cultural contexts, and by the typical discursive practices that frame the issue in ways that make escalating punishment virtually inevitable.

To be more specific, media and political constructions about crime are typically centred on either abstractions about crime or criminals in general, or they are responses to concrete but atypical cases. A good example of the latter is the debate in the US Congress over a loophole in the gun control law that took place in the wake of the shooting spree at Columbine High School in Littleton, Colorado. The President pushed Congress to require background checks of persons buying guns at trade shows. Background checks are required of persons purchasing guns at stores, so it seemed inconsistent to say the least that a person barred from purchasing a gun at a store could make a same-day purchase at a gun show. Conservative opponents of this measure proposed, as an alternative, increasing the penalties for gun-related criminal offences. Realistically, neither measure could have prevented the Littleton massacre: background checks would not have stopped the two perpetrators from buying guns, or, as was the case, getting a friend to buy the weapons. It is doubtful that mandatory minimum sentences for using a gun in a crime would have deterred the Littleton shooters either, since apparently they were not deterred by Colorado's death penalty. Nevertheless, the legislative response was all too typical of the process we describe: a particularly appalling crime dominates the news media; politicians feel compelled to offer a response; the response inevitably takes the form of calling for increasing the severity of legal sanctions.

Sentencing policy in the United States has not only been driven by the goal of 'getting tough' on criminals. Concerns about fairness have also been raised. A contradiction has arisen, however, due to the construction of fairness as consistency. The overriding direction of sentencing policy has been to guarantee fairness by removing discretion from judges, either by imposing mandatory sentences for particular categories of crime, or imposing guidelines for sentencing. While such policies increase consistency by limiting the range of sentencing options available, they may actually produce other types of unfairness. Generally, sentencing guidelines reduce to a linear model, where the sentence severity is determined primarily by the 'seriousness' of the offence category and the extent of the defendant's prior criminal record. Thus like cases are treated alike, the fundamental requirement of fairness is consistency. However, 'likeness' is defined by a limited set of facts about any specific case. Justice is reduced to a mathematically determined response to a somewhat arbitrary abstraction.

The role of public opinion in shaping the justice response follows a parallel course. Public opinion, especially when measured in opinion polls, is usually framed in abstracted, objectified terms. When a respondent to an opinion poll is asked, for example, whether courts should be tougher on criminals, it is likely that s/he frames a response on the basis of media images of particularly scandalous cases. It is unlikely that s/he is aware that the US already has the toughest penalties in the world. He/she is also unlikely to be thinking of a 'criminal' as the fellow living next door; more likely the word conjures up stereotyped images of the deviant, dangerous stranger.

It is clear that the continued escalation of sentence lengths cannot continue indefinitely without creating a crisis. Yet it is not clear how the cycle of public opinion and escalation of the punitive response can be short circuited before the crisis is realised. Two possible sources of 'replacement discourses' (Henry and Milovanovic 1996) are explored in this essay: newsmaking cases that present alternative images of the criminal as dangerous 'other', and survey data that address public opinion on concrete cases rather than general abstractions about the crime problem.

Prelude to the Crisis

Crime rates in the United States, as measured by the FBI's Uniform Crime Reports, began rising in the early 1960s. Although numerous criticisms can be made of the UCR, and reporting practices have evolved over time, it is generally agreed that the UCR documented a real increase in crime that began about 1963, peaked in the 1980s, and has declined steadily in the last six years. However, Victimization data from the National Crime Surveys (NCS) show a consistent decline in crime beginning in the early 1970s (Lanier and Henry 1998). Although neither UCR data nor NCS data are taken to accurately measure the amount of crime, criminologists tend to agree that the overall trend since the 1980s has been a decline or leveling off of most types of crime (see, e.g., Inciardi, 2000; Lanier and Henry 1998; Miller 1996; Tonry 1995).

As a small, mostly rural state, Iowa has experienced consistently lower crime rates than the nation as a whole, or even the surrounding Midwestern states. UCR data for the years 1987 to 1996 show Iowa's total index crime rates to be lower than the nation and the Midwest each year. The gap between the state and the national crime rates has widened recently, with Iowa's rate about 72 per cent of the nation's in 1996.

Arrest data from 1978 to 1997 also show a consistent pattern. Taking into account an artificial peak caused by redefinition of crimes in 1991, the arrest data suggest a fairly steady rate of crime. Moreover, the level of juvenile crime appears to have remained fairly constant throughout this period. Therefore, the perception of an increasingly serious crime problem is not supported by the official data; nor can such a perception be validly attributed to an increase in juvenile crime.

In contrast to the picture of a steady and even declining crime rate are the prison population data. Again, Iowa reflects national trends on a smaller scale. Prison populations have increased dramatically since the 1970s. Figure 8.1 shows the actual and projected prison population for Iowa, from data produced by the state's criminal justice planning agency. Given that no new prisons or cell-houses are scheduled to be open by 2008, the data show the projected population being nearly double the capacity by that time.

Up to a point, the citizens of Iowa have been supportive of building new prisons, and willing to fund new construction with taxes. Data from the Iowa Poll (sponsored by and reported in the *Des Moines Register*, the statewide newspaper) for 1978 through 1994 show increasing support for new prisons, with nearly 70 per cent indicating that support in 1994. However, support for new taxes to pay for new prisons peaked in 1988. In 1994, only 55 per cent of those polled indicated they would support new taxes to fund more prisons. Clearly, a number of factors influence the public's willingness to be further taxed. Given the enormous expense of building and operating new prisons, the data in Figure 8.1 point to a coming crisis, especially since the need to build new prisons is becoming critical precisely as public support for funding them is beginning to decline. Clearly, something must give, as policies begin to contradict resource allocations.

Public opinion surveys suggest that the public's fear of crime also rose beginning in the mid 1960s, when the first such survey data are available. 'Fear of crime' is crudely measured in these surveys, often as a single question inquiring whether there is any place within a mile of his/her residence where the respondent is afraid to walk alone at night. Nevertheless, the findings from several different surveys and polls appear to tell a consistent story, that the public's fear of crime began rising during the mid-1960s, and leveled off in the mid-1970s (Scheingold 1984, p. 39; Skogan and Maxfield 1981). By

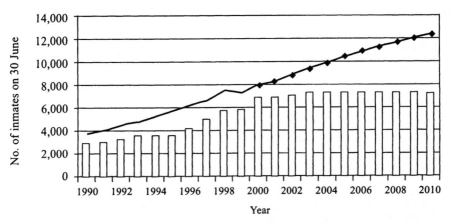

Figure 8.1   Prison capacity and total inmates: actual and forecast

the late 1960s, crime was consistently named in public opinion surveys as one of the most important social problems confronting the nation (Flanagan 1997). Gallup polls show that the per cent of Americans who named 'crime or violence' in response to the question 'what is the most important problem facing America today?' was actually fairly low from 1982 to 1992, never over 6 per cent. For most of those years, more people thought 'drugs and drug abuse' was the most serious problem, along with economic issues such as inflation, unemployment, and poverty. In 1992, however, the number identifying crime as the most important problem jumped to 9 per cent. It then jumped even more dramatically, peaking at 52 per cent in August of 1994, then leveling off to around 20 per cent by April of 1998. Harris polls asked the question in a somewhat different manner, inviting respondents to identify the two most important issues for the government to address. Paralleling the Gallup results, crime was the number one issue in 1994 (37 per cent), but dropped to third place, behind taxes and education, by 1998 (see Maguire and Pastore 1997, for the NORC, Harris and Gallup polls cited here).

Regardless of how the public ranks the importance of crime relative to other issues, crime is clearly of concern to the public. In a culture where complaints about taxes are the norm, it is jarring to realise the level of support for increased spending on the criminal justice system. Since 1982, NORC surveys show that about two thirds of the American public believe we are spending 'too little' to halt crime. Interestingly, the wording of this question in the NORC surveys contains a bias that illustrates the reification of the crime problem. The question asked if we are spending too much, about the right amount, or too little, on 'halting the rising crime rate', even though the crime rates actually dropped and leveled off during these years (1982–96) (Maguire and Pastore 1997).

Since the increasing crime rates appeared during the era of the Warren Court, with its record of restricting police powers, the courts were easy targets for political rhetoric aimed at discrediting liberal policies in general. That the courts, led by the Supreme Court, were 'too soft on crime' became almost a cliché in American political discourse. Chief Justice Earl Warren, the architect of many of these decisions, was a Republican appointed by Eisenhower, and a former prosecutor. Nevertheless, the common reading of his decisions is that of a liberal biased against the police and too sympathetic to the criminal element.

In the 1960s and 1970s, the concern that the system was too lenient was directed at the practice of indeterminate sentences, which were tied to the therapeutic/rehabilitative model of penal practice that emerged in the post-World War II era. The public, spurred on by politicians, began to demand a 'return' to a more punitive-oriented justice system. Anecdotal accounts of violent offenders being released with a metaphorical 'slap on the wrist' became a staple of popular accounts of judicial practice, along with stories of criminals escaping justice on 'technicalities' (meaning violations of constitutional rights) and dangerous perpetrators escaping justice by pleading insanity. This latter myth persisted in spite of the fact that insanity pleas are entered in less than one per cent of criminal cases, are only successful about 25 per cent of the time, and often resulted in terms of incarceration in psychiatric hospitals longer than the prison term that would have been served (see, e.g. Inciardi 1987; Kittrie 1977).

In the 1970s, the movement for tougher sentences meshed in some ways with unlikely allies: prisoners and their advocates calling for an end to the practice of indeterminate sentences (Fogel 1979). Those following the crime control model called for an end to indeterminate sentences because they saw them as too lenient; those following the 'just deserts' position saw them as allowing too much variation, and also questioned the efficacy and equity of the 'therapeutic state'.

From 1980 to 1992, the prison population in the US doubled, from 329,821 to 883,593. This far outstripped growth in the general population: the incarceration rate (number of prisoners per 100,000 population) grew from 138 to 329 in this same period (Irwin and Austin 1994).

In Iowa, prison populations had actually declined from 1962 to 1972. Beginning in 1973, however, the state experienced yearly increases in prison population, a trend that has continued up to the present. Since 1989, the actual prison population has exceeded prison capacity by an increasing margin. In 1997, prison population was at 158 per cent of capacity. This overpopulation was reduced to 130 per cent in 1998 as the result of the opening of new prisons (Prell 1998). The prison population nearly doubled from 1982 to 1992, even though the state of Iowa actually lost population during the 1980s. State projections indicate the population will rise, outstripping capacity. Indeed, the projections indicate the population will double capacity by the year 2008. The cost of doubling the prison capacity of the state in time to meet this demand is prohibitive both financially and politically.

Public Opinion and Criminal Justice Policy

Public opinion about crime policy has remained remarkably stable on certain issues over the last 25 years. About 75 per cent of respondents to polls typically support requiring police permits for handguns, capital punishment for convicted murderers, and more severe sentencing of offenders (Flanagan 1997). However, Flanagan also notes that Americans' opinions about criminal justice policies tend to be pragmatic and multidimensional. Public opinion simultaneously favours lengthy prison sentences, particularly for the most serious offences, but also supports rehabilitation and education programs; the public is not ignorant of the fact that most prisoners eventually return to society.

Flanagan notes that crime policy has consistently followed public opinion. It is not clear, however, that the direction of causation has been one-way, i.e. politicians simply enacting new policies in response to public opinion. Scheingold and others have pointed out that crime is simply too tempting an issue for politicians to use in elections. A particularly infamous example of this is the notorious Willie Horton ads used by the Republican Party during the 1988 presidential race to paint Governor Dukakis as dangerously soft on crime. Nobody is for crime; it is always easy to call for 'tougher' measures and accuse one's opponents of not being tough enough.

In *The Politics of Law and Order*, Stuart Scheingold (1984) proposes a cultural explanation for the public support for more punitive crime control measures. Scheingold suggests that the public's fear of crime is not closely tied to actual changes in crime rates, or exposure to risk of victimization. Rather, the fear of crime and the punitive attitudes that accompany such fear reflect 'basic values' that are easily invoked and manipulated by politicians and depicted as reality in the mass media. Scheingold argues that there is "an enduring sensitivity to crime that makes for relatively easy politicization".

Scheingold proposes that most Americans share a consistently held set of beliefs about and images of the nature of crime and punishment. This "myth of crime and punishment" grows out of deeply held beliefs in individual responsibility and a cultural fascination with the tradition of vigilantism and its promise of swift justice. Although the myth of crime and punishment coexists with competing myths, such as the myth of rights and the myth of redemption, the myth of crime and punishment dominates because of the affinity of its simplistic nature to political and mass media needs, and because it provides reassuring answers to the problems of stressful times. Thus, Scheingold presents a Durkheimian argument: the myth is reinforced, because it allows us to project our anxieties and reaffirm community in troubled and confusing times.

The myth of crime and punishment, according to Scheingold, is at its heart a 'simple morality play that dramatizes the conflict between good and evil: because of bad people, this is a dangerous world', and the appropriate response to these bad people is punishment. In this myth, the image of the criminal is that of the 'other'. Criminals are somehow fundamentally different from the rest of us, and therefore not deserving of the rights and protections supposedly accorded the average citizen. This belief is sustained by the constant and intense attention given to the most horrific (and therefore atypical) crimes. Hough and Roberts (1999) have illustrated this process empirically in their analyses of British public opinion regarding sentencing.

Other authors have commented on the attention given to atypical crimes and criminals, and the effects of that attention on public attitudes. For example, Surette (1994) notes the media's reproduction of what he refers to as the "icon" of the predator criminal. Surette links the popularity of the predator criminal icon to the media's reliance on two other fundamental myths of American culture: a nostalgic image of simpler times past, and a belief in technological solutions to problems. Surette sees the icon of predator crime functioning as a "metaphor for a world gone berserk". Like Scheingold, he sees this iconography as feeding a cultural response that is increasingly punitive, even in the face of evidence that the punitive response is not resulting in increased security.

Scheingold's argument suggests a converse position. If the general public attitude supportive of increasingly punitive measures depends, to a significant extent, on the abstraction of the criminal as other, and the typification of the most horrific crimes, then it should diminish when these two conditions are not met or are contradicted. To the extent that criminals are viewed as recognizable members of the community ('there but for fortune go I ...'), and the criminal acts portrayed are more mundane, the kinds of things respondents might imagine themselves doing in certain circumstances, an alternative discourse about the nature of crime and punishment becomes possible.

This possibility is dramatically illustrated by the media and public's responses to a seemingly ordinary criminal case in Iowa that received attention in the national media. Jeff Berryhill was a 21-year-old college student who got into a drunken argument with his girlfriend. She went to another man's apartment. Berryhill followed her there, kicked open the door, and resumed the argument. She sat on the other fellow's lap, at which point Berryhill threw a single punch to the other fellow's face, causing injury requiring stitches. Normally, such an offence would result in a sentence of probation, perhaps with the requirement that the defendant enrol in 'anger management' counselling. But the problem for Berryhill was that bit about kicking in the door of his victim's apartment. Technically, that was an unlawful entrance that could be charged as burglary. And since the assault occurred subsequent to that unlawful entry, it could be charged as first degree burglary, which is exactly what the prosecuting attorney proceeded to do. Under Iowa law, first degree burglary carries a mandatory 25 year prison term. As a 'forcible felony', probation is not an option. Under such a sentence, parole can be granted, but usually only after at least four years of the sentence have been served. Therefore even though he served only 22 months of the 'mandatory' sentence, Berryhill received a sentence well beyond that which would have been imposed had he been charged with an assault.

The case received attention in the national media, carried by such papers as the *Los Angeles Times*, and was the subject of an episode of the nationally broadcast television show *20–20* (ABC News). A similar case, which received somewhat less attention nationally, is that of Troy Jones. Jones shoplifted $52.56 worth of merchandise from a department store. As he was making his getaway from the store, he scuffled with a security guard, causing her slight injury. The altercation with the security guard resulted in the case being prosecuted as a robbery, with a possible sentence of fifteen years, rather than as shoplifting, which would have carried a maximum sentence of thirty days in jail.

The Jeff Berryhill case illustrates the following points about the contradictions in public opinion and public policy.

1) The general desire is for increasing levels of violence, threat of violence, and injury, to result in increasing levels of punishment. Mandatory laws that define a category of criminal actions simply as 'violent' negate this commonsense equity.

2) The public's support for 'get tough' laws in general, including mandatory sentences, is based on an abstraction of the criminal as 'other'. People are outraged when the law is 'unfairly' applied to someone who is known and in otherwise good standing as a neighbour, student, employee, family member, etc.

3) The mandatory sentencing laws place discretion in the hands of the prosecutor, rather than the judge. While prosecutors have been known to reduce charges below that which the facts support, or even refuse to prosecute entirely, 'in the interests of justice', it is more common for the prosecutorial mindset to support 'throwing the book at' a defendant, and there is very little to balance the zeal of an aggressive prosecutor.

4) The prosecutor in the case adopts a point of view that puts the events in this case in the context of domestic assaults ("we don't just laugh off lovers' spats anymore ..." he is quoted as saying, *Des Moines Register*, 18 September 1998) ... however, it is common in domestic assaults involving partners not living together, for a 'burglary' like the one in this case to occur, and it is rare for such cases to be prosecuted as burglaries.

5) The way the prosecutor frames the case illustrates precisely the danger of mandatory minimums. From his point of view, anything less than the maximum penalty would be too soft. Those protesting the penalty, including Berryhill himself, are virtually unanimous in saying that he deserves punishment, even jail time; they are objecting to the *amount* of prison time given. But the prosecutor responds as if the only alternative is to let him go completely unpunished.

The trend toward increasingly severe sentencing has been driven in part by the perception that the rehabilitative ideal was an abject failure. Since the uncritical acceptance of the mantra that 'nothing works' to rehabilitate criminals (Martinson et al. 1974) began to dominate the politics of punishment, emphasis has shifted to making sure that criminals at least get their 'just deserts'. Recent work by Cullen and associates (Cullen and Gilbert 1982; Cullen, Cullen, and Wozniak 1988; Cullen et al. 1990) however, suggests that the public still exhibits a fairly strong level of support for the concept of rehabilitation. In addition, the public may be far less punitive than the politically and media-constructed common sense would lead one to believe. Hough and Roberts (1999), in their study of British attitudes toward sentencing, found this to be the case, arguing that public clamour for 'tougher' sentences is based in part on ignorance of actual sanctions. Findings from a recent survey conducted in Iowa tend to support this notion.

Public Attitudes Toward Sentencing: Findings from a Recent Survey

In 1997, the Iowa Adult Crime Victimization Survey (hereinafter IAVCS) was conducted by the Center for Social and Behavioral Research at the University of Northern Iowa. The purpose of the survey was to supplement the incident-based crime figures that comprise the Uniform Crime Reports, in order to create a comprehensive picture of the amount and distribution of crime in Iowa. Iowa is so small in population that, even given the large samples used in the National Crime Victimization Surveys conducted by the federal government, so few Iowans are sampled as to make generalisations about the extent of victimization in Iowa from this source problematic. For the IACVS, a random digit dialling procedure was used to sample Iowans aged 18 and older. Within each household contacted, the adult with the most recent birthday was selected to be interviewed. A final sample of n=2036 completed interviews was obtained, representing a response rate of 62.3 per cent of households contacted. In addition to questions about the respondents' criminal victimization during the preceding 12 months, respondents were asked a series of questions about the use of criminal sanctions. It is these questions that are of most interest for the present study.

When respondents reported that they had been a victim of a crime, they were asked for their choice of appropriate sanctions for their perpetrator. A total of 135 respondents reported that they had been the victims of an assault. Most reported assaults that did not involve the use of a weapon (79.3 per cent), and resulted in minor injuries such as bruises, cuts or scratches (61.8 per cent). More than half did not report the crime to police; the most common reason given for non-reporting was that the respondent considered it a 'private matter'. This reflects the fact that in most cases the offender was known to the victim. All of these characteristics are typical of assaults as described in other crime sources.

Table 8.1 presents the victims' views on what they think should have been done to their assailants. Respondents were allowed to select more than one response. The majority of victims indicated that their assailant should receive some sort of treatment or rehabilitation, while only 15.9 per cent wanted their assailant to go to prison. Respondents were somewhat more likely to support less lengthy confinements, such as boot camp, work release, or a jail term.

The low support for prison for these actual assaults perhaps sheds light on the public response to the Berryhill case. The fact that Berryhill was technically convicted of first degree burglary is probably irrelevant to the public, especially in view of the fact that when similar 'appropriate sentencing' questions were

Table 8.1   Sentence for assault endorsed by assault victims

Sentence	Per cent*
High intensity sentences	
Prison term (more than one year)	15.9
Boot camp	22.8
Jail term (less than one year)	25.7
Medium intensity sentences	
Work release	20.2
Halfway house	17.5
Intensive probation	21.1
House arrest	14.0
Electronic monitoring	18.4
Low intensity	
Regular probation	33.3
Pay fine to state or local government	33.3
Pay restitution to victim	33.3
Community service	37.7
Treatment/rehabilitation programme	56.1
No punishment needed	27.9
Other	14.0

n=135

*   Multiple responses possible; percentages do not sum to 100.

posed to burglary victims in this survey, an even smaller proportion, 7.1 per cent, endorsed prison sentences. It may be that these victims' 'leniency' is driven by the fact that most of them knew their assailants. We feel that is precisely the point, since it is characteristic of assaults in general that victims usually have a prior relationship with perpetrators. Another set of questions about appropriate sentencing, asked of all 2036 respondents in the survey, removes the effect of personal victimization by asking about appropriate sentences for the perpetrator of a hypothetical crime.

Each respondent was read two hypothetical crime scenarios, one involving a theft and the other an armed robbery (with victim injured). Two elements of the scenarios were randomly varied: the age of the offender (14, 16, or 25 years old), and whether or not the offender had a prior felony record. The age of the offender was a primary interest at the time of the study, because one of the salient issues in the current 'get tough' on crime political debate was a proposal to make it easier, or even mandatory, to waive certain juvenile offenders to adult court. In the case of the armed robbery scenarios, this would mean a mandatory prison sentence of either 25 years for first degree robbery, or 10 years for second degree. Either first or second degree robbery fall under the '85 per cent rule' enacted in 1996. The theft scenarios described a crime that would most likely be classified as an 'aggravated misdemeanour', which could result in a jail term of up to one year, or a prison term of two years, or a term of probation.

Table 8.2 displays the percentage of respondents favouring a prison sentence, for each age and prior record category for each offender. In only two cells do a majority of respondents favour sentencing the hypothetical criminal to prison: 55.7 per cent favoured prison for a 16-year-old criminal with a prior record, and 72.4 per cent favoured prison for the 25-year-old with prior record. For the theft (nonviolent) scenarios, the per cent favouring prison approaches half (44.7 per cent) for the 25-year-old with prior record. Otherwise, only small percentages favour the prison option. Clearly, age, violence, and prior record are important influences on the public's endorsement of imprisonment as an appropriate punishment. Further, it appears that there is actually little public support for routinely applying imprisonment to juvenile offenders, even for violent crimes.

Table 8.2   Per cent of respondents selecting prison as an appropriate sentence by age of offender and type of offence (n=2,036)

Age of offender, prior record and type of offence	Robbery	Theft
14-year-old with no prior record	21.9	5.6
14-year-old with prior record	47.1	21.8
16-year-old with no prior record	28.0	10.5
16-year-old with prior record	55.7	28.5
25-year-old with no prior record	29.9	12.9
25-year-old with prior record	72.4	44.7

As with the victim recommendations for assault described earlier, however, the reluctance to send criminals to prison does not mean the public desires that no punishment be given these offenders. Given a menu of options, there is fairly strong support for a range of intermediate sanctions, several of which include an element of short term incarceration, such as boot camps or work release programs. Tables 8.3 and 8.4 display the per cent endorsing each item in a list of alternative sentences for the hypothetical robbers, controlling for prior record and age, respectively. Respondents could choose more than one alternative.

Table 8.3 displays the sentencing options endorsed for the robbery perpetrator, controlling for prior record. Whether or not the offender was described as having a prior record made a significant difference in the per cent of respondents endorsing several options. Most dramatically affected is the choice of prison: over half recommended prison for the offender with the prior record, but only just over a quarter recommended prison for the offender with no prior record. The disclosure of the prior record increased the number recommending electronic monitoring and intensive probation, and decreased the number recommending regular probation and work release. Regardless of what other punishment option they select, an overwhelming majority of respondents thought that criminals should pay victim restitution, perform some type of community service, and receive some sort of treatment rehabilitation.

Table 8.3   Per cent of respondents endorsing sentences for robbery by prior record (n=2,036)

Sentence	Prior record	No prior record
High intensity		
Prison term (more than 1 year)*	59.7	26.8
Boot camp	57.1	52.8
Jail term	56.7	53.7
Medium intensity		
Work release*	42.5	51.6
Halfway house	33.8	29.8
Intensive probation*	67.7	58.6
House arrest	36.5	40.8
Electronic monitoring*	51.4	45.1
Low intensity		
Regular probation*	54.7	75.2
Pay fine to state or local government	77.0	77.0
Pay restitution to victim	97.0	97.0
Community service*	80.9	88.9
Treatment/rehabilitation*	88.0	81.3

*   Difference is statistically significant at p<.05.

Table 8.4 displays the per cent selecting each sentencing alternative for the hypothetical robber, controlling for age. Age affects the per cent selecting six of the alternatives: prison, boot camp, house arrest, electronic monitoring, community service, and treatment/rehabilitation. More select prison as appropriate for the 25-year-old compared to the juveniles, while boot camp, house arrest, and electronic monitoring are more likely to be seen as appropriate for the juveniles. Although the per cent selecting community service and treatment/rehabilitation declines as the age of the offender increases, the overwhelming majority, more than 80 per cent, favour these sanctions for offenders in all three age categories.

Table 8.4   Per cent of respondents selecting sentences appropriate for robbery by age of offender (n=2,036)

Sentence	Age of offender		
	14	16	25
High intensity			
Prison term (more than one year)*	34.2	40.0	51.9
Boot camp*	65.6	59.9	41.0
Jail term (less than one year)	54.7	54.7	56.0
Medium intensity			
Work release	44.3	48.2	48.8
Halfway house	32.6	34.0	29.1
Intensive probation	65.5	62.0	61.6
House arrest*	47.3	39.9	30.2
Electronic monitoring*	52.6	43.9	47.9
Low intensity			
Regular probation	69.0	64.9	62.7
Pay fine to state or local government*	75.2	74.9	81.4
Pay restitution to victim	96.3	97.3	97.2
Community Service*	87.5	85.5	82.5
Treatment/rehabilitation*	88.7	83.6	81.6

*   Difference is significant at p<.05.

The findings are similar for the nonviolent theft scenarios, with the exception that far fewer respondents endorse prison as an appropriate sanction. Tables 8.5 and 8.6 display the per cent of respondents who selected each sentencing alternative for the theft scenarios, controlling for prior record and age, respectively. Again, almost all of the respondents felt that community service, treatment/rehabilitation, and victim restitution should be part of the punishment response. Prior record affected the response to 11 of the 13 sentencing alternatives. Prior record increased the number endorsing fines, intensive probation, prison, jail, house arrest, halfway house, electronic monitoring, and treatment/rehabilitation. It decreased the per cent endorsing community service, and regular probation.

Table 8.5   Per cent of respondents endorsing sentences for theft by prior record (n=2,036)

Sentence	Prior record	No prior record
High intensity		
Prison term (more than 1 year)*	31.9	9.9
Boot camp*	59.1	43.7
Jail term*	60.5	45.7
Medium intensity		
Work release	52.2	55.7
Halfway house*	36.7	24.4
Intensive probation*	73.1	42.9
House arrest*	46.7	40.4
Electronic monitoring*	52.1	37.0
Low intensity		
Regular probation*	59.7	78.5
Pay fine to state or local government*	81.4	76.1
Pay restitution to victim	97.6	97.8
Community service*	88.8	92.3
Treatment/rehabilitation*	87.1	77.6

*   Difference is statistically significant at p<.05.

These survey results suggest rather strongly that the public, at least in Iowa, supports a multi-faceted, multi-goal approach to criminal sentencing, in which rehabilitation of the offender plays a significant role. Given that, in their survey of British respondents, Hough and Roberts (1999, p. 15) found remarkable public ignorance about community-based sentences, it is noteworthy that Iowans seem reluctant to send young, particularly non-violent and first-time offenders, to prison. The endorsement of a variety of intermediate sanctions such as electronic monitoring, work release, and intensive probation suggest that the public is ready for a sentencing policy other than the continual upgrading of mandatory sentences or other policies that increase the likelihood and the length of prison terms.

Table 8.6 Per cent of respondents selecting sentences appropriate for theft by age of offender (n=2,036)

Sentence	Age of offender		
	14	16	25
High intensity			
Prison term (more than one year)*	14.5	19.1	29.6
Boot camp*	59.6	59.0	37.8
Jail term (less than one year)*	48.5	48.9	62.0
Medium intensity			
Work release*	45.6	55.1	60.5
Halfway house	33.2	29.6	29.7
Intensive probation	59.7	56.6	59.5
House arrest*	51.8	44.2	35.6
Electronic monitoring	45.4	44.2	44.9
Low intensity			
Regular probation	68.7	68.8	68.9
Pay fine to state or local government*	77.4	76.8	82.2
Pay restitution to victim	96.7	98.1	98.2
Community Service	90.2	91.1	90.0
Treatment/rehabilitation	81.0	81.8	84.6

* Difference is significant at p<.05.

Discussion

Public opinion and political discourse about crime policy are typically framed in such a way that increasing penalties appears as the most rational or desirable response. What Scheingold (1984) refers to as the 'myth of crime and punishment' drives much discourse and policy about crime. Public opinion is often presented, under this myth, as 'demanding' that the criminal justice system get tougher on criminals. But this 'demand' depends on certain abstractions, and an almost wilful ignorance of how 'tough' we already are.

The effect of abstraction can be illustrated by comparing the results of the victimization/public opinion survey reported here with other sources of public opinion. National opinion polls for years have asked, in slightly varying forms, whether judges, courts, etc. should increase the severity of their response to offenders. For example, a 1994 Iowa poll showed that 63 per cent favoured 'trying more youngsters in adult court' as a 'very effective' solution to juvenile crime. When asked about this issue in a more specific fashion, as was done in the Iowa Victimization Survey, however, it is clear that on the whole, Iowans are reluctant to send 14- and 16-year-old offenders to prison, even for a violent crime.

In the case of Iowa, the trend away from rehabilitation and toward punishment has set the stage for a fiscal disaster. This is because the piecemeal legislative responses to the crime problem have largely taken the form of mandatory minimum sentences tacked onto a sentencing structure already characterised by long sentences. The original intent of Iowa's lengthy sentences was rehabilitative, with the bulk of discretion placed in the hands of a parole board. It was never intended that the majority of prisoners actually serve anywhere near the maximum term. The myth of crime and punishment and the rhetoric of truth in sentencing imply that anything less than the full sentence is somehow a miscarriage of justice, regardless of the amount and severity of the sentence actually served. That is, as long as the rhetoric is about the abstraction of the 'criminal' as the dangerous, unpredictable other. It seems likely that the outrage generated by the Berryhill case is largely a function of the fact that he is recognised by many as 'one of us'. We know people like him, perhaps we even see a bit of ourselves in him, and hence 25 years seems like too much punishment, even though it apparently is what the law requires in this case. It is not surprising that our victims of assault recommend sentences far below what they might endorse for criminals in general who commit similar crimes; McCoy and McManimon report elsewhere in this volume that victim satisfaction with the justice system is not affected by severity of sanction imposed.

From 1978 until 1990, the per cent of Iowans supporting the building of new prisons rose steadily. This support was closely paralleled by a rise in the per cent saying they would favour increased taxes to fund new prison construction. From 1990 to 1994, the per cent favouring new prisons continued to rise, but the per cent willing to pay for it with new taxes steadily declined. The current sentencing policy is demonstrably out of synch with existing resources and the public's willingness to be taxed further to provide new resources. This crisis will inevitably force the state to rethink its sentencing policy, a reality acknowledged by the creation in 1996 of a legislative commission tasked with proposing sentencing reform. The data reported here suggest that public opinion, when framed by realistic depictions of typical cases and informed by knowledge of actual sentencing practices and the use of intermediate sanctions, may be supportive of less punitive policies. Scheingold (1999) challenges the assumption that punitive policies are imposed on politicians 'from below'; the data presented here also challenge that assumption.

References

Cullen, F., Cullen, J. and Wozniak, J. (1988), 'Is Rehabilitation Dead? The Myth of the Punitive Public', *Journal of Criminal Justice*, Vol. 16, pp. 303–17.

Cullen, F. and Gilbert, K. (1982), *Reaffirming Rehabilitation*, Cincinnati: Anderson.

Cullen, F., Skovron, S., Scott, J. and Burton, V. (1990), 'Public Support for Correctional Treatment: The tenacity of rehabilitative ideology', *Criminal Justice and Behavior*, Vol. 17 (1), pp. 6–18.

Flanagan, T. (1997), 'Public Attitudes Toward Crime and Criminal Justice Related Topics', in K. Maguire and A. Pastore (eds), *Sourcebook of Criminal Justice Statistics*, Washington, DC: US Government Printing Office.

Fogel, D. (1979), *We Are the Living Proof*, Cincinnati: Anderson.

Henry, S. and Milovanovic, D. (1996), *Constitutive Criminology*, London: Sage.

Hough, M. and Roberts, J. (1999), 'Sentencing Trends in Britain: Public knowledge and public opinion', *Punishment and Society*, Vol. 1(1), pp. 11–26.

Inciardi, J. (1987), *Criminal Justice*, New York: Harcourt, Brace, Jovanovich.

Inciardi, J. (2000), *Elements of Criminal Justice*, New York: Harcourt Brace.

Irwin, J. and Austin, J. (1994), *It's About Time: America's imprisonment binge*, Belmont, CA: Wadsworth.

Kaminer, W. (1995), *It's All the Rage: Crime and Culture*, Reading, MA: Addison Wesley.

Kittrie, N. (1977), *The Right to be Different*, Harmondsworth: Penguin.

Lanier, M. and Stuart, H. (1998), *Essential Criminology*, Westview, Boulder, CO.

Lutz, G., Fahrney, K., Crew, K. and Moriarty, M. (1998), 'The 1997 Iowa Adult Crime Victimization Survey', Cedar Falls: Center for Social and Behavioral Science, University of Northern Iowa.

Maguire, K. and Pastore, A. (1997), *Sourcebook of Criminal Justice Statistics*, Washington, DC: US Government Printing Office.

Miller, J. (1996), *Search and Destroy: African American Males in the Criminal Justice System*, Cambridge: Cambridge University Press.

Newman, G. (1983), *Just and Painful*, New York: Macmillan.

Prell, L. and Roeder, L. (1998), 'Iowa Prison Population Forecast', Des Moines: Iowa Division of Criminal and Juvenile Justice Planning.

Scheingold, S. (1984), *The Politics of Law and Order*, New York: Longman.

Scheingold, S. (1999), 'Book Review: Politics, Punishment, and Populism', *Punishment and Society*, Vol. 1(1), pp. 115–17.

Skogan, W. and Maxfield, M. (1981), *Coping with Crime: Individual and neighborhood Responses*, Beverly Hills, CA: Sage.

Surette, R. (1994), 'Predator Criminals as Media Icons', in G. Barak (ed.), *Media, Process, and the Social Construction of Crime*, New York: Garland, pp. 131–58.

Tonry, M. (1995), *Benign Neglect: Race, Crime, and Punishment in America*, New York: Oxford University Press.

Von Hirsch, A. (1976), *Doing Justice*, New York: Hill and Wang.

Chapter Nine

Harsher is not Necessarily Better: Victim Satisfaction with Sentences Imposed under a 'Truth in Sentencing' Law

Candace McCoy and Patrick J. McManimon Jr

What do victims want? Surely every victim wishes that the crime had never happened at all; realistically, most at least wish to 'be made whole again'. Restitution is the most common demand from victims of the widest variety of crimes, perhaps because it is the most commonly available option and one that reduces the victimisation to the lowest common denominator: money. For victims of violent crime, moreover, the psychological aspect becomes particularly important, because 'becoming whole again' means that the victim has confronted and overcome deep pain, both physical and emotional. Surely the criminal justice system should do nothing to prevent this healing, but whether courts can affirmatively help victims by tailoring offenders' sentences to what the victims need or want is unproven.

Overcoming the pain of victimisation is a very personal journey for each victim. It is expressed in the language of medicine and psychology more often than in monetary terms. But these discourses do not necessarily include the language of revenge. Certainly they *can* and often do, especially insofar as it may be therapeutic for many victims to see their assailants punished. But this healing process is very different for different people, contingent on their personalities, experiences, attitudes toward punishment and relationships to the offenders, and certainly on the characteristics of the crimes themselves (Hagan 1983; Borg 1998. Accounts in popular news abound: random examples: *New York Times* 1999).

Yet legislation passed in the name of 'victims' rights' is uniformly intended to make prison sentences longer, assuming that victims' primary wish is retribution – an assumption that often fits political agendas of law-and-order activists more than it addresses the complex circumstances of actual crime victims (Smith 1988; McCoy 1993; Elias 1983). Any reader of daily newspapers in the United States can recite a list of sentencing laws that have been passed in the name of victims; indeed, it seems that any sentencing law destined for passage in a state legislature will have a victim's name attached to it.[1]

One relatively new type of victim-oriented legislation assumes that victims will be more satisfied with the sentences given their assailants if they can be assured that the offender will be imprisoned for exactly the amount of time the judge announces. Advocates of 'truth in sentencing' laws claim that the victim's certain knowledge that the offender will not be quickly released and find the victim again, and the simple courtesy of being told exactly what the system will and will not do, will increase victim satisfaction with sentences. Even more strongly, they claim that, since the laws will nearly abolish parole and most certainly make sentences significantly harsher, victims will be more satisfied with sentencing outcomes because victims want offenders to be treated more harshly.

Yet previous evaluation of victims' assistance programs that aimed to involve the victim more fully in court hearings has found that victim satisfaction under these programs does not necessarily increase much (Goldstein 1982; Sebba 1982). Moreover, the link between satisfaction and high punitiveness is by no means proven, and thus the assumption that severe 'victims' rights' sentencing laws will better satisfy victims' wishes is unproven. In general, the attitudes of crime victims are no more punitive than those of the general public (Boers and Sessar 1990). Previous research has demonstrated that victims' feelings about punishment are considerably more nuanced and complex than political rhetoric would portray. For instance, felony victims in Erez's studies (Erez 1989, 1990) participated in sentencing hearings, but they rarely requested the court to impose the maximum sentence. Only about one third requested incarceration, and only about one third of the victims viewed harsher sentences as important to them. However, research by the same author and her colleague separated the punitiveness issue from the question of victim satisfaction and found that victim satisfaction was highly correlated with satisfaction in the actual sentence imposed, whatever it was, but not its degree of severity (Erez and Tontodonato 1992, p. 407). Interestingly, their research found that victims of crimes against persons were more satisfied with sentencing outcome than were victims of property offences. Satisfaction with the operation of various criminal justice agencies was highly correlated with satisfaction with the sentence, and victims who were unhappy with the disposition and who believed the sentence was too lenient were dissatisfied regardless of the quality of service they received by the various criminal justice agents (Erez and Tontodonato 1992, p. 412). In interviews with 100 felony victims, Kelly also found that victims regarded their experiences in the court process (i.e. how well they were informed of the progress of the case and whether they felt that they themselves were treated like criminals) to be more important than the severity of the sentencing (Kelly 1984).

There is some support in the literature about victims and punishment indicating that victims wish for retributive sentences depending on their own personal characteristics and their relationships to the offenders (Hall 1991). For instance, Borg (1998) analysed 135 cases of people who knew a person who had been the victim of a homicide in the past year. This included family members and friends of homicide victims, with a heavy representation from the South. She found that people who knew a homicide victim were more likely to support capital punishment than those who did not, although punitiveness diminished the closer the relationship between the victim and the respondent was. That is, acquaintances of homicide victims were more likely to support capital punishment than were close friends and family members of homicide victims, a surprising finding that Borg hypothesises might be explained by the fact that "family members who have lost an intimate are more likely to know the offender compared to vicarious victims who have lost an acquaintance" (ibid., p. 552). Furthermore, support for capital punishment varied depending on the race and religious orientation of the 'vicarious' victims. "The odds of support for the death penalty are between three and four times greater among white respondents than among blacks", Borg found (ibid., pp. 547–8), and members of evangelical churches were significantly less likely to support capital punishment than fundamentalists were.

Considering that this research cuts against the notion that victims of serious crimes are uniformly pleased if offenders are given harsh punishments, we would expect that victims would not necessarily be unified in support of legislation making sentencing more severe. But activists and legislators who speak for victims demand harsher sentencing. No previous research has directly tested whether a reform intended to make sentencing more severe and its imposition more comprehensible has actually increased victims' satisfaction with the punishment their assailants receive. This is a study of victim satisfaction conducted with a before/after methodology, testing the effect of a law that its proponents said they passed in order to increase victim satisfaction with sentencing by making it harsher.

History and Background of the No Early Release Act

The genesis of New Jersey's 'No Early Release Act' (NERA) is traceable to sentencing reform developments spanning the last three decades. At NERA's heart is the concept of 'truth in sentencing', a term that had been used repeatedly in policy statements and debates before the US Congress when the federal Sentencing Reform Act of 1987 was being considered. The main thrust of the argument was that an indeterminate sentence was a fraud because, although the sentencing court would announce a severe prison sentence, in fact the offender would become eligible for parole and often would be granted parole after serving only a third of the prison term imposed. The Sentencing Reform Act of 1987 enacted the federal Sentencing Guidelines, which were very controversial. Almost forgotten in the wrangling over their implementation was the fact that the Act also effectively abolished parole in the federal system by requiring that all offenders would serve 85 per cent of their sentences before becoming eligible for parole.[2]

More recently, truth in sentencing has been embedded in the Violent Crime Control and Law Enforcement Act of 1994 (Omnibus Crime Bill) through provisions for Violent Offender Incarceration and Truth in Sentencing incentive grants (Title II, Subtitle A). Through this legislation, the federal government provides incentives to states to pass their own Truth in Sentencing acts and require their own state prisoners to serve 85 per cent of their sentences before becoming eligible for parole. A powerful incentive is that the federal government will provide federal funds for expansion of state prison bed capacity, probably through new prison construction, to any state that passes the requisite legislation. New Jersey passed its version of the Act in 1997.

Quite clearly, 'truth in sentencing' is regarded by its proponents as another in a series of 'get tough' laws designed to keep felons in prison for as long as possible (National Rifle Association 1991; Carrington 1983). But its advocates in the states, at least in New Jersey, have added into the equation a claim that such legislation is necessary to serve the needs of victims of crime. Many well-organised victims' rights organisations around the nation make this claim. In New Jersey, these groups include organisations that work with the family of Megan Kanka (the young girl murdered by paroled sex offender Jesse Timendequas, thus sparking the community notification statutes known as 'Megan's Laws'), and the Friends of Amanda Foundation, named for a young girl murdered by her neighbour. State politicians called for passage of the 'Truth in Sentencing/85% No Early Release Act' referring to these cases in their arguments, indicating that the legislation should be passed because this is what victims demanded.

New Jersey's 'No Early Release Act' (NERA) was introduced in the state Senate as Senate Bill 855 on 26 February 1996. Its lone sponsor was Senate Majority Leader John O. Bennett. NERA required "that any inmate sentenced for a crime of the first or second degree involving violence shall not be eligible for parole until the inmate has served not less than 85 per cent of the court-ordered term of incarceration". Victims groups quickly embraced the SB–855 as a victim's rights law. On 2 April 1996 Senator Bennett called a press conference to tout the merits of his proposed legislation. At that press conference, Karen Wengert and her father, Bill Thomas, the mother and grandfather of Amanda Wengert (the young girl who had been murdered by a neighbour) attended and stated their support for passage of the legislation, as did various law enforcement groups. As the founders of the Friends of Amanda Foundation, a group dedicated to protecting children from becoming victims of crime, they were and remain a strong voice in the victims' advocacy community in New Jersey. Citizens of Senator Bennett's district, they are well known and influential members of that community. The Chair of the Senate's Law and Public Safety Committee, Senator Lou Kosco, announced at the press conference that he had scheduled a public hearing on the proposed legislation on 24 April 1996, and Senator Bennett was appointed as a special, voting member of the committee for this legislation. Two years after passage of the federal Omnibus Crime Act, the move toward 'truth in sentencing' had begun in New Jersey.

The public hearing on Senate Bill 855 was conducted on 24 April 1996. This hearing was held during Crime Victims' Rights Week, intentionally signalling the merger between 'get tough on crime' policies and victim's rights advocates in New Jersey. The list of witnesses at the public hearing demonstrated the strength of this alliance. Witnesses included the sponsors of the legislation in both houses of the legislature, a former Attorney General who is an outspoken and respected advocate of 'get tough on crime legislation', representatives of the New Jersey Chiefs-of-Police Association and the Fraternal Order of Police, a clinical psychologist from the Adult Treatment and Diagnostic Center (New Jersey's Sex-Offender Prison), several victims/ survivors of murder victims, a representative from the Prosecutors' Association, and several private citizens. Letters of support were also on record from a variety of law enforcement organisations and victims' rights groups both national and state-based (records from public hearing, 24 April 1996).

The testimony during the public hearing illustrates the strong influence of victims' rights advocates and the victims' movement on the political process in New Jersey and their political power with members of the legislature. Both sponsors, Allan and Bennett, as well as the Chair of the Law and Public Safety Committee, Kosco, repeatedly recounted their associations with victims of crime and said that the true purpose of the legislation was to alleviate the pain and suffering of victims of violent crime. Kosco stated in his opening remarks; "I hope that this measure will assist in comforting the many victims and their families whose lives have been destroyed by violent crime" (transcript of Public Hearing, 24 April 1996, pp. 1–2).

Assemblywoman Allan stated; "I am proud to support the rights of crime victims ... This bill goes beyond 'truth in sentencing'" (p. 3). "'In this bill we can say to crime victims, you're not alone. We stand with you. We stand against excuses'" (p. 4). Senator Bennett in his testimony stated that "[t]he bill known as SB855 tells the victims of violent crimes that their loss is our loss, that their pain in our pain, that we will remember the violation of human life, and we hold their attacker accountable". Both sponsors noted that this hearing was conducted as part of National Crime Victims Rights Week. However, Senator Bennett also made reference to the fact that if New Jersey was to receive any of the prison construction funds available from the Federal Government, this legislation had to be passed.

The public hearing closed on a note clearly equating 'truth in sentencing' with get-tough policies and also 'populist punitiveness', as it has been labelled in literature on the politics of sentencing reform (Bottoms 1995, p. 39). Chairman Kosco made the following statement:

> This is just part of a plan, of a long range plan that began three years ago. We are putting this plan together ... We started it ... with the Three Strikes legislation ... [and] the Bootcamp ... to address the problem we are having with our juveniles ... We are spending the money ... The plan is a 'get tough on crime' plan now to include 'truth in sentencing' legislation (pp. 50–51).

The senators each stated in their closing remarks that this was a clear message from the citizens of New Jersey.

The second reading of the bill in the Senate Law and Public Safety Committee occurred 11 months later. There is no written record of the reason for the length of time between the readings, but the Office of Legislative Services staff advised that the legislation had been delayed to consider recommendations from a governor-appointed Commission that had been studying parole reform for some time before the No Early Release Act was introduced. As it emerged from this legislative 'reading', the Act had two additional sponsors, Senator Kosco (Chair of the Senate Law and Public Safety Committee), and Senator Scott, a member of the committee, both of whom faced tightly contested electoral races in the fall and would benefit from being able to say they sponsored pro-victim legislation.

The third and final revision of the bill's text closely resembled the legislation as it was finally enacted. The language clearly stated that crimes of violence were the only appropriate targets of this law. But the category was defined to include simple assaults, and any type of sexual assault, which might be regarded as felonies at the lower end of 'seriousness' depending on the facts of the particular cases. Specifically, the bill required judges to sentence offenders to terms of imprisonment under the existing New Jersey sentencing guidelines, with the mandatory requirement that the offender would serve 85 per cent of the term if convicted of a target offence defined as a crime of violence. Interestingly, a search of newspapers throughout the state during this period did not produce any coverage of the legislation, and the victims' organisations were silent as well. The Act was signed into law in July 1997.

Research Questions

Based on this legislative history, we can safely state that the No Early Release Act was intended to achieve many goals. From the sentencing language, it is clear that the law requires judges to sentence serious offenders to prison terms from which there is no parole release until 85 per cent of the sentences have been served, although there is no language in the Act that specifically addresses the discretionary decisions of prosecutors as they charge and litigate these cases. From the corrections side, it is clear that the parole board is forbidden from releasing these offenders until they have served sentences significantly longer than would have been contemplated prior to passage of the Act, a policy that could have a significant impact on the numbers of offenders required to be housed in New Jersey prisons and also the inmate disciplinary system operating within those prisons. From the history of the Act's passage (both in New Jersey and in the federal system, where these laws are labelled 'truth in sentencing') and from the literature on the purposes of 'get tough' sentencing and how it is expected to help victims, it is clear that the legislation was intended to assure victims that their assailants would be incarcerated for long periods of time and that they would not be released, thus satisfying victims' demands and increasing the approval of the sentencing outcomes in their cases.

Did this in fact occur? To find out, we studied the period before and after passage of New Jersey's No Early Release Act and formulated the following two research questions:

1) Do victims of violent crimes report higher satisfaction with sentences imposed when the punishment is harsher?
2) What factors are significantly associated with victims' high satisfaction with sentencing?

Data and Methodology

New Jersey's structure for assisting victims includes an Office of Victims' and Witnesses' Advocacy housed and administered in each county prosecutor's office. A series of interviews with each of the victim/witness advocacy directors for three target counties and the Assistant Director of the State Victim-Witness Advocacy Office helped ascertain their functions and how they receive feedback from the crime victims they serve. Some counties regularly mail questionnaires to victims after their cases are concluded, asking client/victims to tell them about the quality of their experiences with the justice system. We asked for and received permission to add a few questions to the existing questionnaires. In other counties that did not regularly ask for feedback, we arranged to distribute questionnaires similar to those used elsewhere.

We asked the state Victim-Witness Advocacy staff to consult with us in selecting counties for observation and in distributing the questionnaire. The selection of counties to be surveyed was done in conjunction with the statewide office for two reasons. First, the statewide office had established relationships with all county offices. Working through this agency provided credibility for the research, assuring the counties' offices that the research would be conducted professionally and confidentially. Because the climate surrounding victims' issues is extremely sensitive among the victims' services providers, the statewide office's assistance was valuable in paving the way for positive initial interactions between researchers and the county victims' services directors. Second, the statewide office was aware of each office's strengths and the political climate throughout the state. We requested that the questionnaire be given to a group of counties reflecting New Jersey's widely varied population density levels and resident ethnic populations so as to ascertain whether urbanisation or ethnicity made any difference in victims' satisfaction with sentencing.

The statewide victims-witness office selected three counties that were already giving surveys to each of their clients/victims at the end of each case, and these became our study sites. They included one urban, one suburban, and one rural county. The counties selected for study were already using a mostly-uniform instrument to elicit feedback from crime victims. In each of the three counties, at the end of sentencing in each case the victim is given a survey asking about his or her experiences and feelings regarding the case. Each victim received the survey in a packet whose cover page is the most important document at issue here: the judge's sentencing order. The sentence the judge imposed is written out, and, if the victim attends the sentencing hearing, he or she also hears it announced in open court. Prior to enactment of the No Early Release Act, the document would state the sentence and also the date that the offender would become eligible to be considered for parole. After passage of the No Early Release Act, the document states the sentence and also the fact that the offender is required to serve a mandatory sentence of 85 per cent of the term imposed before becoming eligible for parole, also with the date that would be. (Obviously, the time until release from prison would be considerably less in the pre-NERA group.) Included with the judge's order was the survey, which asked victims many questions about their levels of satisfaction with various agencies of the justice system that handled the case (i.e. police, prosecutors, judge, victims/witnesses office). The survey also gathered data about personal characteristics of the victims, such as age, race, and sex, and also offence-related data, such as type of crime committed. We added questions about whether a weapon had been used and a five-point ordinal scale rating of the victims' overall satisfaction with the sentence imposed on the offender

Given that this survey was an accepted and normal part of existing victim/ witness court procedure and that it is distributed to every victim of a felony, we had expected a fairly robust response rate, but we were disappointed. Only about 1 per cent of these surveys were returned to the Victims'/Witnesses' Advocacy Offices, a rate that has apparently never been any higher since the surveys were first instituted. We met with managers in all three counties and determined that the response rate was so low partly because, in each county, the survey is distributed without a postage-paid envelope for return. We helped the offices to redesign their distribution so as to make it more attractive to return the surveys, and the response rate increased to about 5 per cent. This was still exceedingly low, and we further determined that virtually no surveys were being returned from victims in the urban county. Further investigation led us to the conclusion that the heavily Hispanic population in that county were not returning the surveys, and indeed never had, because they are in English.

Thus, the sample that returned the survey is drawn almost exclusively from two counties, one suburban and one rural. The respondents were almost 85 per cent Caucasian, although the suburban county has a populous African-American community, which accounts for most of the 15 per cent of the sample labelled 'non-white'. Certainly, this is scarcely a random sample of crime victims across the state. On the other hand, for purposes of testing our research questions it is very appropriate. Suburbanites are presumably the types of victims the sponsors of the No Early Release Act had in mind when they announced their support for the bill, because the victims' advocacy groups that had lobbied for the legislation were composed almost exclusively of white people from suburban counties (Mercer County, Monmouth County) and the sponsor of the bill was from suburban Monmouth County. As Smith (1988) has noted, the ethnic and class characteristics of people who participate actively in victims' rights activism are very different from those of the larger group of victims generally. Insofar as the victims' advocacy groups that supported the No Early Release Act regarded it as a 'tough on crime' bill, and their ethnic and geographic characteristics roughly match those of the respondents on this survey, the survey respondents would be expected to be more sensitive to the punitive aspects of sentencing and express their satisfaction with it more strongly than would crime victims from other ethnicities and geographic areas. This population, in turns out, is perfect for testing the question of whether the No Early Release Act achieved its goal of improving victims' satisfaction with sentencing by making it harsher.

The study's timeframe was long enough to complete a 'before' and 'after' study. The 'No Early Release Act' was enacted in July 1997 and initial data collection began in April 1998. Because of the time between indictment and disposition in serious felony cases in New Jersey, it was possible to gather 'before' data for the study. Most felons sentenced in April 1998 and for several months thereafter had committed their crimes before the NERA took effect. We gathered questionnaires from victims of those crimes and continued in the same way when the courts finally began sentencing felons who had committed their crimes under the new law. Also, responses from victims of crimes both covered (violent felonies) and not covered (less serious felonies) were gathered.

Thus, we had data from four groups of victims: victims of serious felons sentenced *before* the Act, victims of serious felons sentenced *after* the Act, and victims of *non*-serious felonies sentenced before the Act and after the Act. We included victims of non-serious felonies that would not have been included under this legislation at any time so as to test whether victim satisfaction with sentences imposed depends significantly on the seriousness of the crime and not on the sentence.

The data include 118 cases, 48 of them sentenced before the No Early Release Act was passed and 70 of them sentenced after. Eighty-five per cent of the respondents were white and 15 per cent were non-white. The ages of the victim respondents were nearly normally distributed, with a bit of over-representation from the range of 45–64 years old. There were 118 victims/respondents. The types of crime they experienced were:

nonviolent felony B – 44;
assault B – 33;
sexual assault B – 13;
robbery B – 10;
homicide, relative of the victim – 18.

To test the first research question, we asked respondents how satisfied they were with the sentence imposed. We asked them to rank their satisfaction level on an ordinal scare from 'not at all satisfied' to 'very satisfied'. Because of the small size of our sample, we constructed the dependent variable 'satisfaction with sentence' expressed binomially, as 'satisfied yes' versus 'satisfied no'. We then applied a chi-square test of significance to test whether there was a statistically significant difference in satisfaction between the two groups (not satisfied/satisfied) depending on the independent variable 'sentenced before the No Early Release Act applied versus sentenced under the No Early Release Act'.

To test the second research question, we used a series of correlations on the dependent variable, sentence satisfaction, correlating it one-at-a-time with the other variables in the data such as victims' characteristics, characteristics of the crime, and satisfaction with various agencies of the justice system. Because our sample is small, these tests are the only appropriate possibilities.

Analysis

We first tested whether there was any statistically significant difference in levels of satisfaction with sentencing before and after the Act among all felony victims. Table 9.1 shows the distribution of these cases in terms of satisfaction levels expressed, among the two 'before' and 'after' groups. The number of victims satisfied with the sentences are almost identical before and after passage of the law. However, strangely, of those respondents giving the lowest ranking ('*not* satisfied' with the sentence announced by the court) the number is higher *after* passage of the Act. The number of cases is too small to make any strong conclusions from this.

Table 9.1   Victims' satisfaction with sentences imposed: before versus after the 'No Early Release Act'

	Before NERA	After NERA	
Not satisfied with sentence	14	30	Row total: 44
Satisfied with sentence	34	40	Row total: 74
Column total	48	70	n: 118

Applying chi square tests, the value of Pearson's R was 2.28, with a significance level of .131, which does not approach statistical significance. Perhaps the most unusual finding, however, is not seen in the tests of significance, but simply in the direction of the data's values. Although approximately the same number of people was satisfied with the sentence imposed both before and after application of the No Early Release Act, the number *not* satisfied doubled from 14 to 30. We cannot make too much of this, since the number of respondents returning their questionnaires after the Act took effect was higher and thus the pool of available subjects who were possibly dissatisfied had expanded along with the overall response rate. Note, too, that for this test we grouped the victims into two groups: whether the crime had been committed while the Act was in effect or not. Thus, these two groups included victims of both serious and non-serious felonies. We discuss separately, below, the question of whether satisfaction with sentences imposed was related to whether the crime was serious or non-serious.

In sum, it is clear that *there was no trend toward greater satisfaction with sentences imposed when the sentences became longer.* In fact, by chance the opposite was true, and thus these statistical tests were actually applied to data running in the direction opposite of what had been expected. Legislators who pass laws requiring harsher sentencing because they believe that victims will feel better about these punishments are apparently operating under a mistaken notion of what victims feel and want.

But not all these respondents were victims of crimes that had been covered by the NERA or would have been had it been in effect. Perhaps there is a difference in satisfaction with sentencing depending on how serious the crime was. We analysed only the two groups of victims of serious felonies actually covered specifically by the Act B that is, offences specifically listed in the Act. There were 74 such cases: 35 from before the No Early Release Act was passed, and 39 from after. We applied the same statistical tests to see whether sentencing satisfaction had significantly increased when victims knew the offenders would serve 85 per cent of their sentences before being eligible for parole. There was no significant association (using Pearson's test, significance is .119). Furthermore, the direction of the data was the same as in the overall population of felony cases: almost twice as many people were dissatisfied with the sentence *after* the Act passed (10 dissatisfied before NERA, 18 after). Since the two groups before/after were about the same size, it seems that the observed direction of the data is confirmed: not only did sentencing satisfaction fail to improve under the New Early Release Act, but for some reason victims were more likely to be dissatisfied when their assailants were sentenced under the Act. We do not attribute this drop in victim satisfaction to anything related to the law; rather, it seems to indicate that the truth in sentencing law is simply irrelevant to what victims think about the punishment offenders receive, and that something else is affecting victims' feelings about sentencing.

Thus, *we conclude that victims of serious felony crimes are generally not more satisfied with sentencing when parole is curtailed.* This conclusion is drawn from a self-selected sample of victims who were mostly white suburbanites, and it might change if respondents were ethnically diverse and/ or from urban areas. However, other research (Borg 1998) indicates that the findings would only become stronger because victims who are ethnic minorities are generally less inclined to support severe sentencing than are white suburbanites.

Satisfaction with sentencing, therefore, apparently flows from factors other than its punitiveness. We used the other variables in the database to see if any correlated significantly with victims' high levels of sentencing satisfaction. We had three types of variables: descriptions of the victims themselves (age, race, gender); descriptions of the crime (nonviolent felony, violent felony covered by NERA by charge of conviction; use of gun in the crime/no gun); and victims' reported satisfaction with the work of justice professionals in their cases (police, prosecutor, judge, victim-witness advocate). Two separate analyses were conducted on these variables, the first using the entire database of all victims (n=118) and the second using solely victims of violent crimes as defined in the No Early Release Act (n=74). (Incidentally, 18 of these were family members of homicide victims, the same type of 'vicarious victim' studied by Borg (1998).) Results were:

Table 9.2   **Correlations between victim satisfaction with sentencing and variables related to victim characteristics, offence type, and justice professionals' performance**

	All felonies (114)	Violent felonies (74)
	Chi square significance	*Chi square significance*
Victim's gender	.419	.585
Victim's race	.720	.667
Victim's age	.031*	.119
Felony violent or not	.872	N/A
Gun used or not	.679	.666
Felony type (i.e. homicide, assault, rape, or robbery)	.634	.472
Police work on case	.001*	.011*
Prosecutor's work	.000*	.000*
Judge's work	.000*	.000*
Victim advocate work	.041*	.135

*   Significant at p<.05.

In the group of victims of all felonies, only one of the variables on characteristics of the victims themselves were significantly correlated with high satisfaction with sentencing outcomes. That variable was age: people aged 30–65 years old were more likely to be satisfied with the sentence imposed than were people aged 13–29 or over 65 years old (significance of .03, where p<.05 deemed significant). African-Americans tended to be more dissatisfied with sentences imposed than did whites (7 not satisfied/6 satisfied, compared to whites with 37 not satisfied/64 satisfied) but the difference was not statistically significant. None of these variables were significant in the group of only violent felonies covered by NERA, suggesting that the type or seriousness of the offence might have some influence on victims' satisfaction with sentencing regardless of other factors. This led to consideration of variables describing the offence.

There was no statistically significant relation between victim satisfaction with sentencing and whether the crime was violent as defined under the NERA, versus a less serious felony. Nor was there any significant association between victim sentencing satisfaction and whether a gun had been used in committing the crime, in the category of violent felonies. Similarly, the type of violent felony for which the offender was convicted had no significant association with sentencing satisfaction, although some interesting trends appeared in the data. Specifically, the ratio of robbery victims satisfied with the sentence imposed versus those not satisfied was 4:1, while victims of assault and sexual assault were generally satisfied/not satisfied by a ratio of 3:2. Finally, relatives of homicide victims were least likely to be satisfied; the 18 'vicarious victims' split evenly 9–9 over satisfied/not satisfied.

The picture changes drastically when analysis moves to variables related to the justice system itself. In both groups of all felony cases and only violent felonies covered by NERA, all variables (with the exception of one) relating to satisfaction with justice professionals (police, prosecutors, judges, victim-witness staff) were significantly related to whether the victim was satisfied with the sentence imposed. Put another way, victims who were satisfied with the performance of police in their cases (or prosecutors, or judges, or victim-witness assistants) were also satisfied with the sentences, while those who were dissatisfied with the justice system were also dissatisfied with the sentences imposed. Statistical tests of the significance of these associations were 'off the charts' ranging from .0000 for both prosecutors and judges, to .0015 for police, to .041 for victims' assistants in the 'all felonies' category. In the category of only violent felonies covered by NERA, the same results appeared, except that satisfaction with the Office of Victims and Witnesses was *not* significantly related to satisfaction with sentencing. To elaborate, a look at the data that produced these very strong results demonstrates why the correlations were so significant. Respondents had been asked to rate the work of justice professionals in their cases on an ordinal scale from poor to excellent. They tended to give answers at the extremes of the scale, and these were sharply divergent according to whether victims were satisfied or dissatisfied with the sentence imposed. Respondents who were satisfied with the sentences imposed were likely to rank the justice professionals' work as either good or excellent, while those who were not satisfied tended to rate the work on the absolute lowest end of the scale. For instance, here is a chart of the data concerning victims' rating of the judges' performance in their cases. (Note that most of these cases ended in guilty pleas, so the only occasion the victim is likely to have had contact with the judge would have been if the victim was in court when the defendant pleaded guilty, when the victim sent the judge a 'victim's impact statement', if any, and/or at the sentencing hearing and imposition of sentence if the victim chose to attend.)

Table 9.3   Satisfaction with the sentencing judge, by victim satisfaction with the sentence

	Poor	Fair	Good	Excellent
Not satisfied	26	6	4	4
Satisfied	4	16	26	24

Row total: 40 not satisfied, 70 satisfied.
Column total, level of satisfaction: 30 poor, 22 fair, 30 good, 28 excellent.

Chi-Square, Pearson value 46.36463, DF 3, significance .00000.

Answering the second research question 'What factors are significantly associated with victims' high satisfaction with sentencing?' we conclude that *neither the length nor certainty of the sentence, nor personal characteristics of the victim, nor crime types are associated with victims' satisfaction with sentences imposed. The factor that is significantly associated with high victim satisfaction with sentencing is whether justice professionals performed their jobs well, in the victim's opinion.*

This is *not* to say that a victim's high regard for the work done by justice professionals like police, prosecutors, judges, and victims' assistance staff *caused* his or her high satisfaction with the sentence imposed. The causation more probably runs in the other direction B i.e. *when victims are satisfied with the sentence imposed, they tend to ascribe good job ratings to the professionals who handled the cases.* But why they are satisfied or not is still unexplained, because factors not included in this analysis might be more important to a victim's opinion about whether 'justice was done' than those included here. It would be a mistake to conclude that there is necessarily any causative dynamic here. The classic statement in social science, 'correlation is not causation', applies. All that can reliably be said is that victims' satisfaction with sentencing is dependent on many factors, but that 'truth in sentencing' does not make a difference; instead; factors related to how well the victim believes the justice system worked are related in unexplained ways to that satisfaction.

One important deviation from the typical response from victims about their ratings of the justice system and sentencing satisfaction, however, emerged from this survey. In violent felony cases, victims who were satisfied with the sentences imposed on their assailants were *not* significantly likely also to be satisfied with the help provided by the victims' assistance personnel. Victims may regard their quasi-personal relationship with victims' assistance providers as different from the professional relationship they have with other justice workers. Put another way, victims' satisfaction with sentencing was significantly correlated with all justice system professionals' performance except for that of the victim-witness office in violent felony cases. In that one category, victims who were satisfied with sentences were often nevertheless dissatisfied with how the victim-witness advocates handled their cases.

We have no data to interpret this finding carefully. However, if our experience in administering the survey among the various New Jersey victims-witness offices is any indication, these offices are extremely overburdened and perhaps fuzzy as to their organisational mission. (Recall that there were very few surveys returned, for instance, in one county that had in fact never received much feedback, because the office persisted in sending out a survey in a language few of the respondents could read. This victims-witness office had never addressed the issue, although it continued to give a feedback sheet to every client served.) The question of how well victims-witness support offices are able to do their work is emerging as a concern in research on victims (Beatty et al. 1999; Moriarty and Jerin 1998). This study adds to it by noting that our preliminary data indicate that victims of felony crime regard the work of the victims-witness office as different from that of other justice professionals, and that future research should probe this perception.

In sum, this research demonstrates that victims are not happier when parole is virtually abolished and they are notified of the exact sentences the offenders will serve. Furthermore, victims do have concerns about how well the victim-witness advocates help them through the court process. There is some question whether anything anybody could do would help them emotionally, at least in the violent felony cases, but this is an important question for future evaluation research. Moreover, returning to the issue at hand, it is important to point out that the victims' advocates and their allies in the legislature might have done better in addressing the needs of crime victims had they not passed 'get tough' legislation but instead concentrated on improving the operation of existing victims-witness offices throughout the state.

Conclusion

Assuming that victims want harsher sentencing is a politically-constructed outlook that is not necessarily in tune with the personal experiences of the wide spectrum of actual crime victims. Popular punitiveness in the abstract changes when placed in the context of real experience. If we had asked the people who answered our survey to tell us in general about their attitudes toward crime and punishment prior to their experiences of being victimised at the hands of criminals, they might have called for harsher sentencing and abolition of parole. But in the end the severity of sentencing was not the most important consideration for people who have actually been victims of crime, with the exception of a very few victims who become politically mobilised after suffering victimisation. In other words, in the abstract public punitiveness may be high, but when placed in the context of particular people with actual experiences of crime and the offenders who commit it, punitiveness appears to be a considerably more complex phenomenon. Real victims do not jump immediately to demand harsh sentencing when an actual offender sits before them in court. They are concerned that the court must treat the case carefully, and this has more to do with how they regard the sentence than the severity of the sentence itself does. Often the offender is someone they know or the offence is something they can 'deal with' through compensation other than seeing the offender sent to prison for a very long time.

Returning to the example that sparked this inquiry, in the state of New Jersey politicians passed 'truth in sentencing' legislation with the support of particular victims who had horrific individual experiences and great dissatisfaction with the law applicable to their cases. But these victims experiences are not typical of the broad range of other victims' experiences, characteristics, or satisfaction with sentences imposed. It is thus not surprising that passage of legislation which makes sentencing harsher does not affect these victims' satisfaction with the sentences imposed on the offenders who wronged them, because their personal motivations and experiences of victimisation are different from those of the politicians and the victims' rights advocates who are involved in the political arena.

If any strong conclusion can be drawn from this study of victim satisfaction with sentencing, it is that victims regard the justice system itself as an important part of how favourably they regard sentences imposed. There is a significant correlation between sentencing satisfaction and perceptions of how well the justice system handled the case. But the direction of any causation in this correlation is still ambiguous. A victim pleased with a sentence will also be pleased with the justice system, while a victim dissatisfied with the sentence will also be dissatisfied with the system. Or perhaps a victim who is satisfied with the justice system's response to the case will in turn be satisfied with the sentencing outcome, whatever it may be.

The more fundamental conclusion this analysis suggests is that victims of felonious crimes respond to their victimisations, and process them as part of their life experiences, mostly unconnected to anything legislators do. Abstract laws supposedly passed to help victims cannot address the complexity of their actual experiences and relationships with the real people involved in the crimes. Truth in sentencing legislation is surely successful in making sentencing harsher, but the idea that its purpose is to help victims is probably a political rationalisation for the legislature's true goal of making punishment more severe.

Notes

This research was supported by a grant from the National Institute of Justice, US Department of Justice, number 98–CE–VX–0007. Opinions are those of the authors and not the National Institute of Justice.

1   Megan Kanka and Polly Klaas, for example, are names associated with state laws passed after these children died in highly publicised crimes. Community notification of the presence of a paroled sex offender (Megan's Law) and Three Strikes legislation passed in California (a response to Klaas's murder at the hands of a recidivist) in turn became models for other jurisdictions. These are only two of the most well known among many such state laws. The parents of these children have been ardent political activists. The Kanka family continues to work to support public announcement of the names and addresses of paroled offenders, including the most recent such law in New Jersey, a ballot initiative requiring ex-offenders' names and addresses be posted on the internet (it was passed overwhelmingly in November 2000). Mr Klaas, by contrast, has publicly stated that he believes the Three Strikes law passed in his daughter's name has turned out to be too harsh in practice.

2   Thus, the sentence when served would roughly match the same amount of time typically served previously, before the Act passed. This has not been so in any of the states that have recently followed the federal example in passing truth in sentencing legislation, to our knowledge.

References

Beatty, D., Howley, S.S. and Kilpatrick, D.G. (1996), *Statutory and Constitutional Protection of Victims Rights: Implementation and impact on crime victims*, Washington, DC: National Victim Center.

Borg, M.J. (1998), 'Vicarious Homicide Victimization and Support for Capital Punishment: A test of Black's Theory of Law', *Criminology*, Vol. 36, No. 3, August.

Bottoms, A. (1995), 'The Philosophy and Politics of Punishment and Sentencing', in C.M.V. Clarkson and R. Morgan (eds), *The Politics of Sentencing Reform*, New York: Oxford University Press.

Carrington, F. (1983), *Crime and Justice: A Conservative Strategy*, Washington, DC: Heritage Foundation.

Elias, R. (1983), *Victims of the System: Crime victims and compensation in American politics and criminal justice*, New Brunswick, NJ: Transaction Books.

Erez, E. (1990), 'Victim Participation in Sentencing: Rhetoric and reality', *Journal of Criminal Justice*, Vol. 18, pp. 19–31.

Erez, E. and Tontodonado, P. (1992), 'Victim Participation in Sentencing and Satisfaction with Justice', *Justice Quarterly*, Vol. 9, No. 3.

Goldstein, A.S. (1982), 'Defining the Role of Victim in Criminal Prosecution', *Mississippi Law Journal*, Vol. 52.

Hagan, J. (1983), *Victims Before the Law: The organizational domination of criminal law*, Toronto: Butterworth.

Hall, D.J. (1991), 'Victims' Voices in Criminal Court: The need for restraint', *American Criminal Law Review*, Vol. 28, No. 2.

Hallett, M. (1994), 'The Push for Truth in Sentencing: Evaluating competing stakeholder constructions in the case for contextual constructionism in evaluation research', *Evaluation and Program Planning*, Vol. 17, No. 2.

Kelly, D. (1984), 'Symposium: Victims' perceptions of criminal justice', *Peppardine Law Review*, Vol. 11, No. 1.

McCoy, C. (1993), *Politics and Plea Bargaining: Victims' rights in California*, Philadelphia: University of Pennsylvania Press.

Moriarty, L.J. and Jerin, R.A. (eds) (1998), *Current Issues in Victimology Research*, Part III, Durham, NC: Carolina Academic Press.

National Rifle Association (1992), 'Combating Violent Crime: 24 recommendations to strengthen criminal justice'.

New Jersey Legislature (1996), Public Hearing on Senate Bill 855, 24 April, Trenton, NJ: Office of Legislative Services.

New York Times, articles from http://nytimes.com archives: Pam Belluck, 'In Nebraska, Amendment for Equal Rights Keeps Condemned Killer Alive', 20 February 1999; Andrew Jacobs, 'Subway Victim Says He Harbors No Anger', 3 June 1999, p. B3.

Sebba, L. (1982), 'The Victim's Role in the Penal Process', *American Journal of Comparative Law*, Vol. 30.

Smith, B.L. (1988), 'Victims and Victims' Rights Activists: Attitudes toward criminal justice officials and victim-related issues', *Criminal Justice Review*, Vol. 13, No. 1.

PART III
MEASURING PUNISHMENT –
CONCEPTUAL AND
PRACTICAL PROBLEMS AND
RESOLUTIONS

Chapter Ten

European Sentencing Traditions: Accepting Divergence or Aiming for Convergence?

Andrew Ashworth[1]

1 Introduction

As the chapters in the other parts of this book demonstrate, the problems of sentencing are worldwide, and the explanations for different approaches in different countries are often tied to social and political factors as much as to purely legal traditions. English-speaking sentencing scholars and policy-makers have tended to look towards other English-speaking jurisdictions for comparisons and for 'new ideas'. However, Europe appears to be the only region of the world to make concerted attempts to develop common standards for sentencing, and this chapter outlines the endeavours that have been made and the extent to which they have been reflected in actual sentencing trends in Europe in the last decade of the century.

One source of influence has been the Council of Europe, an organisation formed in the aftermath of the Second World War to promote cultural, environmental and legal cooperation among member states. One of its earliest and most enduring achievements was the European Convention on Human Rights, which has exercised considerable influence over legal developments in member states. Other aspects of the Council's work are discussed in section 2 of this chapter, and the Council is acquiring a higher profile in regional affairs as several Central and Eastern European states have become members, swelling the numbers to over 40.

Another source of influence has been the European Union. This, as is well known, is a more powerful economic and political union of a smaller group of European nations. Criminal policy has tended to be somewhat on the periphery of its concerns but, as we shall see in section 2 of this chapter, there is evidence of a greater interest in criminal justice in recent years.

The plan of the chapter is that section 2 will discuss some of the major sources of influence over sentencing in Europe; section 3 will consider the movement towards diversion in various European jurisdictions; section 4 will discuss trends in court sentencing in European countries; and in section 5 some general themes will be described and examined. The chapter adopts an inclusive definition of 'sentencing', and for that reason there is discussion of various schemes for disposing of cases without bringing them to court, and also of the seizure and confiscation of offenders' assets. A fuller survey might also encompass regulatory penalties, administrative sanctions, plea-bargaining, parole and release systems, and so forth; but many of those issues are discussed in other chapters, and this chapter will focus on diversion and on court sentencing without implying that they are the only or most significant issues in sentencing.

2   European Sources of Influence

This section deals with three related sources of influence on sentencing policies in Europe. They will be discussed separately, but it is evident that the European Convention on Human Rights informs the policies of the Council of Europe and also, particularly in recent years, those of the European Union. Some international initiatives on criminal justice are also common to the Council of Europe and the European Union, as we will see.

The European Convention on Human Rights

A cursory glance at the provisions of the European Convention might suggest that it has little to say about sentencing. The only provision which refers directly to sentencing is Article 7, prohibiting the imposition of a heavier penalty on an offender than was applicable at the time of the commission of the offence. However, other Articles have been applied to sentencing issues: for example, Article 3 on 'inhuman and degrading punishment', and the requirements of proportionality where a person is sentenced for an offence which is accepted as a justifiable interference with one of the rights declared in Articles 8, 9, 10 or 11. The recent jurisprudence of the European Court of Human Rights points to one particular area of concern – the use of sentences of life imprisonment, in relation to Articles 5 and 6.

The European Court of Human Rights has accepted that the mandatory sentence of life imprisonment for murder by an adult complies with the

Convention, even though the decision to release is in the hands of a politician rather than an 'independent and impartial tribunal' as required by Article 6: *Wynne v United Kingdom* (1994) 19 EHRR 353. However, the Court has now held that where the murder was committed by a person under the age of 18, the purpose of the sentence is not merely punitive but also preventive, and that therefore the offender must have the right to periodic review of the need for continued detention and that decision must be in the hands of an 'independent and impartial tribunal': *Hussain v United Kingdom* (1996) 22 EHRR 1, *T and V v United Kingdom* (2000) 30 EHRR 121. Most of the Court's decisions on life sentences concern the United Kingdom because this is the country that uses life imprisonment most frequently. It is expected that there will soon be a challenge to the 'automatic' life sentence which British courts are required to impose on offenders convicted of a second serious sexual or violent offence, a challenge which is likely to be mounted under Article 3 ('inhuman punishment' because totally out of proportion to the offence(s)) as well as under Articles 5 and 6. There are also those who believe that the Court will have to reconsider its ruling in Wynne (above), and to take from the Home Secretary the power to decide on the effective length of time served by adult murderers.

Beyond the specific issue of life imprisonment, a fuller survey would show that the Convention may have an impact on disproportionate sentences imposed on persons whose rights under Article 8, 9, 10 or 11 are justifiably curtailed; on sentences which discriminate against certain types of offender; on the need for consent to community sanctions; on recommendations for deportation; on orders for costs; and on other matters (see Emmerson and Ashworth 2001, ch. 16). However, it remains true that the Convention has not yet had a major impact on sentencing policies in Europe, and is unlikely to do so. But its standards of fair procedure clearly apply to the sentencing process, and there are also some points (under Articles 3, 8, 9, 10 and 11) at which notions of proportionality may be invoked.

The Council of Europe

The Council of Europe has been active in sentencing matters for many years. It has produced a string of recommendations which have a bearing on different aspects of sentencing. For example, in the 1980s there was Recommendation R(85) 11 on the position of the victim in the framework of criminal law and procedure, and Recommendation R(87) 18 on the simplification of criminal justice; in the 1990s there was Recommendation R(92) 16 on European rules on community sanctions and measures, and Recommendation R(95) 12 on the management of criminal justice, among others.

In relation to sentencing in general, however, the Council has proceeded more cautiously. The Council of Europe's Committee on Crime Problems delivered a report on 'Sentencing' in 1974, arguing *inter alia* for closer contact between sentencers and others involved in the administration of justice, for a gradual relaxation of the severity of penal sanctions, for more research into the sentencing process, and for the development of a "scientific and rational sentencing policy" (Council of Europe 1974). Although the reference to reducing the use of imprisonment was a substantive policy of the Council of Europe, the remainder of the recommendations show a preference for avoiding issues of substance and conceding the ground to the judiciary and to the separate legal traditions of member states.

It seems that there was support at Strasbourg for 'improving' and 'reforming' sentencing, but that so many particular issues within sentencing were regarded as 'off limits' that the Council decided to target the rule-of-law ideal of consistency. The Council decided to devote its 8th Criminological Colloquium, in 1987, to 'Disparities in Sentencing: Causes and Solutions'. Among the topics discussed were the concept of disparity, statistical methods for identifying it, and techniques for reducing it (Council of Europe 1987). As a result of that colloquium, the Council agreed to establish a Select Committee of Experts on Sentencing. Its report, accepted by the Council of Ministers in 1992 as Recommendation R(92) 17, signals the importance of declaring the rationale(s) in a sentencing system, of setting out a coherent penalty structure which offers guidance on the exercise of discretion in the sentencing system, and of pursuing the principle of restraint in the use of custody.

Two observations may be made on this report. First, its contents illustrate the tensions among member states about recommendations for sentencing reform. The Committee insisted that it could not discuss consistency without dealing with certain substantive topics – not just reducing the use of custody and enhancing the use of community sanctions, which were established Council of Europe policies, but also the aims of sentencing, the approach to previous convictions, matters of aggravation and mitigation, and several other contentious issues. The result was a formalistic compromise, so that the Committee's recommendations as approved by the Committee of Ministers appear only as an appendix to the Recommendation itself, which is a rather bland statement about greater consistency which clearly preserves the liberty of member states to pursue their own legal traditions. The second observation is that there seems to be relatively little discussion of the Council of Europe's sentencing report. It is almost never referred to by officials in the United Kingdom, and it seems that it has exerted relatively little influence in most established member states, although it was referred to in recent reform processes in Greece and in Slovenia, for example, and it has been discussed with officials in new member states from Greater Europe. In the early 1990s there were some in Strasbourg who hoped that the Committee would produce a blueprint from a pan-European approach to sentencing policy, whereas there were others resolutely opposed to any suggestion of interference in the criminal justice policies of member states. It seems that what has triumphed, in the end, is apathy.

The European Union

It is now a major project of the European Union to develop it into an 'Area of Freedom, Security and Justice'. This movement originated in the Amsterdam treaty, and three illustrations of its progress may be given. First, the summit of the European Council (held at Tampere in October 1999) concluded that member states should move towards adoption of the principle of mutual recognition of judicial decisions and judgments, and the approximation of legislation. Secondly, there are moves to incorporate into the structure of the EU the Schengen *acquis*, which includes provisions for cross-border surveillance. And thirdly, the European Union is developing its interest in human rights: the EU Charter of Fundamental Rights was agreed at the meeting of the European Council at Nice in December 2000. The Charter is more extensive than the European Convention on Human Rights since it includes several social rights. Chapter VI, on Justice, goes beyond the ECHR in some respects.

3 Diversion from the Courts

The last decade has seen continuing emphasis on the diversion of certain cases from prosecution, so that they are disposed of outside the court process. Some of the new policies may be connected to the increasing attention to victim concerns, through mediation or other forms of restorative justice, whereas others may have their origins in attempts to resocialise the offender (or, at least, not to 'de-socialise' the offender by subjecting him or her to the formal criminal process, unless the case is a serious one), and still others may reflect the economic savings to be made from non-prosecution in times of fiscal constraints in many countries: see generally Council of Europe Recommendation R(87) 18 on The Simplification of Criminal Justice. Thus the Netherlands continued to use prosecutors' transactions widely in the 1990s, with the result that the great increase in reported crimes has been reflected in only a small increase in the number of cases sentenced by the courts (Tak 1997, 2001). Similarly in England and Wales the procedure of cautioning offenders was used increasingly in the 1990s, while the numbers sentenced in the courts fell significantly – a fall that cannot be attributed entirely to the slight fall in the level of recorded crime in the later 1990s (Ashworth 2000). In Germany a law of 1993 increased the powers of prosecutors to discontinue cases where the offender's guilt does not necessitate a penalty, a development that was in direct response to the economic pressures on the criminal justice system following the reunification (Albrecht 1997). The new power is in addition to section 153a of the Code of Criminal Procedure, which since 1975 has permitted the diversion of offenders on payment of a sum of money (Weigend 1997). A similar development took place in Slovenia, with the enactment of the new Law on Criminal Procedure in 1994. This provides (in Articles 162–63) that the state prosecutor may under special circumstances discontinue the prosecution of a minor offence, in which the penalty would be less than one year's imprisonment; this procedure is being used increasingly. In the context of diversion the growth of victim-offender mediation as a response to crime should also be mentioned. For many years there have been some small mediation schemes in several member states, and it is apparent that these initiatives increased during the 1990s. For example, in Finland there are voluntary mediation schemes in the three largest cities, and the number of offenders participating in mediation is only a little smaller than the number sent to prison in any one year. Mediation remains outside the criminal justice system, but in practice its results are taken into account in decisions on non-prosecution (Lappi-Seppala 2001). In Belgium the number of offenders participating in mediation has risen to around one-half of the numbers sentenced to imprisonment, and the number of mediations in 1997 rose over 20 per cent on the 1996 figure, although there appear to be different perceptions of mediation between French-speaking and Dutch-speaking citizens (Snacken 1997). In Norway the position has been formalised by a law on conflict resolution commissions in 1991. New legislation in Germany requires a court to take account, when sentencing, of any compensation and of victim-offender reconciliation. In Austria, victim-offender mediation has been central to the resolution of juvenile cases since 1989, and it is now gaining acceptance as a response to adult offences too.

In the UK the new English law on juvenile justice, introduced by the Crime and Disorder Act 1998, is designed to include elements of 'restorative justice', although some commentators have doubted whether the 'conferencing' envisaged by the government would really be committed to the ideals of restorative justice (Morris and Gelsthorpe 2000; Ball 2000). All the above developments in different countries have an effect on the flow of cases into the sentencing system, and raise various questions about fairness between offenders committing similar offences. Many of the innovations can be viewed as part of a trend that has its modern roots in the writings Hulsman (1981), Braithwaite (1989) and other proponents of restorative justice. Much of the rhetoric is about 'community' justice, but in times when much of the public debate is punitive (see Hough and Roberts, in this volume) it is important to recognise the dangers. A form of community justice was also practised in several of the Central and Eastern European states that were formerly in the communist *bloc*, and in some forms this was distinctly non-restorative and tended towards severity (Bard 1986, pp. 6–7; Krapac 1995).

Diversion from the criminal courts remains the foremost policy in dealing with young offenders in almost all member states. In most countries there is no possibility of a young offender appearing in a criminal court until the age of 14, although there are some well-known exceptions to this (such as Ireland, where the minimum age is 7, and England and Wales, where it is 10), and there are some states in which it is possible to prosecute children under 14 for grave offences (such as the Czech Republic and Slovakia, where there is a lower age-limit of 12 for certain serious offences: Selih 1996). However, where a young offender is convicted in a court, there are manifest differences among member states in their willingness to use the sanction of imprisonment. A small survey of Central and Eastern European states by Selih (1996) showed that the Czech Republic and Hungary used imprisonment for juveniles at the relatively high rate of 12–13 per cent of those convicted at court, whereas Poland's rate was 2 per cent and Slovenia used custody hardly at all. However, all of these statistics must be viewed in the light of the legal and political heritage of those states: some of them started from a relatively punitive baseline, and the trend in the 1990s was towards greater emphasis on the resocialisation of young offenders and the introduction of a greater range of educational and community-based measures for juveniles. Another part of the context in states such as Poland and Russia is the considerable rise in recorded crime by juveniles, particularly in the early 1990s (Eser and Huber 1994, pp. 1099, 1204). When one turns to Western European states, the direction of movement is less clear because the baselines are often different.

Thus in England and Wales around 85 per cent of offenders aged 10–14 are cautioned and not prosecuted; but in the 14–18 age-group only around 55 per cent are cautioned and, of those convicted in court, the proportion sentenced to custody increased from 9 to 14 per cent in the 1990s. The latter figure, like the others mentioned earlier, must be considered in the light of the widespread diversion of young offenders from court. But in the late 1990s there were more young offenders receiving custodial sentences in England and Wales than there were in the early 1990s, which marks a contrast with states such as France, Belgium, Netherlands and Germany (Tubex and Snacken 1995). The UK parliament's approach to England and Wales in the Crime and Disorder Act 1998 and the Youth Justice and Criminal Evidence Act 1999, is to regulate more tightly the diversion of young offenders from court and to provide for more severe penalties for many young offenders who go to court, notably persistent offenders.

4 Court Sentencing

We turn now to the general sentencing system for all ages, and begin by considering rates of custodial sentencing for different types of offence.[2] One apparent trend in the 1990s in many Western European states is an increasingly lenient response to theft. In France the proportion of convicted prisoners serving sentences for theft has continued its steep decline, from 37 per cent in 1985 to 16 per cent in 1998 (Kensey and Tournier 1998). A similar but less spectacular decline is evident in Finland, where the percentage use of custody for theft went down from 44 per cent in 1980 to 36 per cent in 1991, and over the same period the average length of sentences declined from 3.4 months to two months (Tornudd 1997). Further reductions took place in the mid-1990s, so that by 1997 the vast majority of persons convicted of theft were fined or given a suspended sentence. The maximum sentence for theft in Slovenia was reduced from five to three years in 1994. In England and Wales the Criminal Justice Act 1991 reduced the maximum sentence for theft from 10 to seven years, but this signal to the courts was not followed by a reduction in the use of custody: between 1992 and 1997 the proportionate use of immediate prison for theft and handling stolen goods rose from 7 to 14 per cent, an increase that probably reflects the growing emphasis on recidivism in English sentencing practice as part of the general hardening of English penal policy. To this extent England and Wales may be out of line with many other member states, where theft appears to have been re-evaluated as a less serious offence.

For example, in Switzerland average custodial sentences for theft were over 16 per cent shorter in 1992 compared with 1984 (Killias, Kuhn and Ronez 1997). In Norway a law of 1990 introduced fines as an alternative to imprisonment for property offences. However, the above remarks relate only to Western European states, and it seems that in several Central and Eastern European states the punishment for theft is more severe, with a relatively high proportionate use of imprisonment for theft offences.

The transition between these mostly lenient sentencing practices and the more repressive sentencing policies is provided by sentencing for drug offences. Despite the Europe-wide rhetoric about the 'war against drugs', it remains true that many member states regard the possession of a small amount of a soft drug as requiring nothing more than a small penalty. The effective decriminalisation of soft drugs for personal use in the Netherlands is well known, if not always well understood; less well-known is the Polish law that regards the possession of drugs as lawful, thereby effectively preventing the police from intercepting consignments within Poland (Hebenton and Spencer 1998). In Belgium there are new alternative measures for drug offenders, such as mediation and community service orders. In the UK the sentence for possessing a soft drug for personal use would usually be a fine, and not a prison sentence. Several states have introduced treatment orders for drug abusers, including England and Wales and Denmark (Kyvsgaard 1998, p. 9).

However, all these approaches change when the person to be sentenced has been convicted of supplying drugs to others, importing drugs, or otherwise trafficking in drugs (see Traskman 1995). The European Community directive on Prevention of the Use of the Financial System for the Purpose of Money-Laundering (91/308/EEC), which followed the 1988 UN Convention against Illicit Traffic in Narcotic Drugs and Psychotropic Substances, is but one example of the effects of the global movement towards harsher sentences for drug traffickers. Perhaps the clearest example of the effect of this global movement may be found in the Netherlands, a state which until the late 1980s had one of the lowest incarceration rates in Europe. But prison capacity has been more than doubled during the 1990s, and one factor in this was the enormous increase in the number of drug offences, although the average length of sentence for drug crimes fell slightly between 1985 and 1995 (Tak 2001). The general European trend has been towards more severe sanctions (Tubex and Snacken 1995). In Belgium, research at the Brussels court revealed that the number of drug offenders had risen by some 350 per cent between 1986 and 1996 (de Pauw 1998). One phenomenon reported in many member states is that the prison population contains a higher proportion of offenders with long sentences in the 1990s than in the 1980s, and the more severe sentencing of drug offenders has been offered as the main reason for this both in France (in relation to sentences longer than five years: Kensey and Tournier 1998) and in Germany (Weigend 1997). Even in Switzerland, where the overall stability of the prison population masks changes in its composition, the largest increases (comparing 1991–92 with 1984–85) were in drug trafficking generally (up 38 per cent) and serious forms of drug trafficking (up 65 per cent: Killias, Kuhn and Ronez 1997). In Italy there have been increases in the statutory penalties for drug trafficking, and the new criminal code in France introduced similar increases. Concerns about drug trafficking have been high on the agenda of Western European states that have offered 'expert advice' to the new Central and Eastern European countries, and it is recognised that some of the growth of organised crime in these states derives from the drug trade. Nonetheless, at least one of those countries (Poland) declined to ratify the European Convention on money-laundering, largely because a prohibition would have adverse effects on the economy (Hebenton and Spencer 1998), although various measures have been taken in Poland to combat organised crime (Eser and Huber 1997, p. 577).

There is also evidence that sentences for sexual offences have become more severe in some states during the 1990s. The average length of sentence served by sex offenders doubled in the Netherlands between 1985 and 1995 (Tak 2001), putting them higher than drug offences in terms of average sentence. A similar trend is evident in France, where the number of rape convictions increased by some 50 per cent between 1984 and 1992, and the proportion of prison sentences for rape which were for 10 years or longer doubled from 17 to 35 per cent (Kensey and Tournier 1998, p. 13). The result is that offenders serving sentences for rape or other sexual offences constituted 18.3 per cent of the prison population in metropolitan France in 1995, compared with only 7.9 per cent in 1985. In England and Wales the pattern is less clear: average sentence lengths for sexual offences increased from 34.5 months in 1987 to 39.7 months in 1997, but the number of convictions declined slightly. In Belgium there were at least six new laws and royal decrees on sexual crimes between 1989 and 1995, most of them prescribing higher penalties, and there was also legislation on sex offences in Sweden which introduced higher penalties (Eser and Huber 1997, p. 621). In some countries, such as Norway, particular attention has been focused on sexual offences against children (Eser and Huber 1997, p. 484). Even in the relatively stable sentencing system of Switzerland, average sentences for rape increased in length by some 24 per cent between 1989 and 1992 (Killias, Kuhn and Ronez 1997, p. 207). Increased sentence levels for crimes of violence are also reported from some countries: in the Netherlands average sentence lengths increased by some 60 per cent between 1985 and 1995 (Tak 2001).

Racially motivated crimes have become a growing preoccupation of some sentencing systems. In Spain a law of 1995 extended the provision on aggravation of sentence for racist, discriminatory or anti-Semitic motives to all forms of crime (de la Cuesta and Varona 1996, p. 230). The Swedish Criminal Code was amended in 1994 so as to provide for aggravation for racial motivation (Ch. 29, section 2.7); new laws against racist propaganda and racial discrimination were enacted in Switzerland (Eser and Huber 1997, pp. 672, 683); and provisions for the aggravation of racially motivated offences were introduced into the laws of England, Wales and Scotland by the Crime and Disorder Act 1998. 'Hate crimes' became a particular source of concern in post-reunification Germany, and, because many of the perpetrators were young, this also turned attention towards policies on youth crime (Albrecht 1997, p. 187).

Difficulties of racial integration in some member states have also manifested themselves in other ways, giving rise to the suggestion that sentencing practices may operate unfairly against members of certain racial groups. A sophisticated study of race and sentencing in England and Wales identified significant differences in the sentence levels for white defendants and those from an Afro-Caribbean background, but concluded that 80 per cent of the difference was attributable to the greater seriousness of the offences of which Afro-Caribbean defendants were convicted, 13 per cent to the fact that fewer Afro-Caribbeans pleaded guilty and received the sentence discount for doing so, and only 7 per cent was not explained by objective factors (Hood 1992, pp. 124–30). Such detailed studies have not been carried out in most member states, but there are statistics suggesting that the proportion of non-nationals among people convicted of serious offences, most especially drug offences, is rather high in many countries. Thus sentencing statistics from France show that, for the most serious types of offence in 1991, the imprisonment rate for French nationals was 17 per cent but for foreign defendants 44 per cent (Kensey and Tournier 1998, p. 15). A detailed study of the sentencing of drug offenders in a Brussels court shows only a slight disparity between white Belgians and Moroccans in terms of average length of prison sentence but a distinct disparity in decisions to implement such sentences immediately (33 per cent for Belgians, 48 per cent for Moroccans) rather than to suspend or use probation: de Pauw 1998. That author explains the disparity by reference to the prevalence of certain negative evaluations of the attitude and social ties of Moroccan offenders which incline judges towards custody and away from resocialisation.

Perhaps related to 'hate crimes' and to apparently discriminatory sentencing are the various increases in penalties for offences connected with illegal immigration. Thus in Sweden the penalties for trafficking in illegal immigrants were increased in the mid-1990s, as were the penalties attached to the immigration laws in Germany. In turn, German concerns about illegal immigration have led to a more repressive attitude towards immigrants in Poland (Hebenton and Spencer 1998, p. 38). Generally speaking, the effects of opening the frontiers between Western and Eastern European states and of the wars in the Balkan region have led to considerable migration, and correspondingly to various fears among native populations, to which legislators have found it prudent to respond (see e.g. Eser and Huber 1994, p. 1016, on Austria).

5 Divergence or Convergence?

What is clear from this brief survey is that there is no evidence of a single sentencing movement across Europe in recent years. In terms of trends towards more severe or more lenient sentence levels, there is no clear pattern either: some states have increased the use of prison sentences (e.g. Sweden, Netherlands, Spain, Portugal, England and Wales), whereas others have not pursued more repressive policies (e.g. Germany, France, Denmark, Finland, and Czechoslovakia until secession in 1992). Moreover, references to increases and decreases can only be interpreted in the context of the different baselines: for example, although the Netherlands has shown great proportionate increases in its use of custodial sentences, its prison rate remains below that of many other member states.

However, it is possible to identify certain pressures towards severe sentences for some types of crime – for example, European initiatives against drug trafficking and money laundering; the widespread re-evaluation of the seriousness of the crime of rape; the greater reporting of child abuse in recent years, with many more cases coming to court; the growing concern about terrorism; and various initiatives, e.g. by the European Union, against racism. Moreover, in some Central and Eastern European states there have been other pressures in the same direction, arising from the spread of organised crime (e.g. Eser and Huber 1994, p. 1099 on Poland and p. 1204 on Russia). It is in the countries of the former eastern bloc that the social context of sentencing is seen at its most vivid: Russia and several other such jurisdictions have historically had relatively high rates of prison use and, even if it were desired to move away from those practices, it would be difficult to do so abruptly, and especially difficult at a time when there is a high degree of social dislocation together with the growth of criminal organisations.

In many countries, however, pressures towards severity have not always led to overall increases in sentence length because of what is called 'la politique de dualisation' (in English, bifurcation or twin-track sentencing). Thus in several states there has been a simultaneous pressure towards diversion of certain types of offender – particularly young offenders, and also those who commit minor thefts. Policies of diversion usually operate at the stage of prosecution, but they sometimes occur in court sentencing and in policies of release from custody. As mentioned above, there are many possible reasons for pursuing policies of diversion, ranging from strong beliefs in resocialisation or restorative justice, through to simple economic judgements about the least controversial method of controlling the costs of criminal justice. Some states have sought to resolve the tension by one or more amnesties, e.g. France and Hungary. The pressure towards diversion is felt in most countries, whereas it appears that the pressures towards severity are felt much more strongly in some member states than in others – perhaps because of legal tradition, social stability, the power and inclinations of those who run popular newspapers and television, and the emergence of crime and sentencing as political (rather than merely 'legal') issues (for discussion, see Victor 1995; Morgan 1998).

Positive responses to the Council of Europe's recommendations on sentencing are difficult to discern in the evidence set out in sections 3 and 4 above. Those recommendations also indicated the importance of an orderly hierarchy of sentencing principles, with proportionality safeguarded. Such laws were already in place in Finland (Tornudd 1997, p. 190; Lappi-Seppala 2001) and in Sweden (Jareborg 1995). The Criminal Justice Act 1991 in England and Wales also conformed to this model, although subsequent events during the 1990s show that the courts distanced themselves from the statutory framework and the Court of Appeal handed down judgments inconsistent with it (Ashworth 2000, ch. 3). In effect the English position is now similar to that in Scotland, where "the clash [between the ideologies of welfare and punishment] makes a major contribution to the continuing lack of a coherent philosophy underlying sentencing" (Duff and Hutton 1999, p. 6). The Home Office has initiated a 'Review of the Sentencing Framework' which seems likely to move away from the priority given to proportionality by the 1991 Act, probably in favour of greater emphasis on deterrence and incapacitation, and it will be interesting to see whether any reference is made to the Council of Europe's recommendations when the report of this review is published.

One continuing feature of sentencing as a social practice is the paucity of empirical research on the decision-making processes of sentencers. As long ago as 1974 the Council of Europe report on Sentencing recognised the importance of detailed research into the motivations and practices of judges in the sentencing process (Council of Europe 1974, p. 13), but there remains considerable judicial resistance to this in most member states, and there are still very few studies of sentencers which involve interviews and close observation (cf. Flood-Page and Mackie 1998, which includes interviews with magistrates but not judges; and the Scottish research reported by Hutton 1999, p. 175).

One striking innovation, based on numerical sentencing research, is the development of the Scottish High Court Sentencing Information System. This incorporates a computerised database of all High Court sentences passed since 1993, subdivided and categorised so that a judge who consults the SIS can specify the key facts of a particular case and will then be informed of sentences passed in materially similar cases by other judges (Hutton 1999, pp. 177–9). The SIS was used by half of the judges in the Scottish High Court in 1998, and will soon be extended to all judges. The system is for information only, but it has the potential to supply guidance which may assist in the development of consistent sentencing practices within the jurisdiction.

Reference to the Scottish move towards greater internal consistency serves to point up the absence of any significant drive towards greater consistency among European jurisdictions. Insofar as there is agreement, it is in the sphere of diversion from court, considered in section 3 above, where many countries have initiatives among similar lines, particularly in respect of young offenders. Beyond that, however, the Council of Europe's 1992 recommendations seem to have had little effect, even within jurisdictions, and so the idea of a European convergence in sentencing policies seems to be a long way from taking root. One reason why the omens seem unfavourable is that there is a stark conflict of policies which has not been confronted in official statements. On the one hand, the Council of Europe has consistently made declarations, endorsed by the Committee of Ministers, in favour of the lowering of penal severity, reductions in the use of imprisonment, the promotion of community sanctions, the diversion of minor offenders, etc. On the other hand, there has been growing concern in the Council and in many member states about forms of wrongdoing which have been either ignored or undervalued in the past – for example, rape, sexual harassment, child abuse, racially motivated crimes, corporate crimes, and so on. These are justifiable concerns; and yet the consequence of taking them seriously is that more repressive measures (in procedure, law and sentencing) are usually regarded as the appropriate response. This should not necessarily result in greater overall severity, because part of a systematic re-evaluation of criminal wrongs may be to reduce the seriousness with which certain other crimes are viewed, notably some offences of theft. Although we have noted that in some states there has been a trend towards treating theft less seriously during the 1990s, there remain several states, many of them in Central and Eastern Europe, in which the proportion of the prison population serving sentences for types of theft other than robbery is 35 per cent or higher.

This may, however, be nothing more than a further demonstration of the close connections between criminal justice systems and social problems, and of the political subservience of sentencing laws in many, even most, member states. Thus the substance of sentencing laws is likely to remain a matter for politics and legal traditions within each state, and the best that can be done at European level, perhaps with the assistance of a developing jurisprudence of the European Court of Human Rights, is to insist on procedural fairness and the avoidance of disproportionately severe sanctions. Beyond that, scholars and those working for the Council of Europe might turn their attention towards reversing the tide of repression evident in much contemporary penal politics. The importance of public safety can be accepted, but it does not necessarily indicate greater penal severity: the Cambridge study of deterrence shows the fallacies of that connection (von Hirsch, Bottoms et al. 1999). There is a need for a replacement discourse in public affairs, one that does not rest on the connection between higher sentences and lower crime, or higher sentences and greater safety. Advocates of restorative justice believe that theirs is the replacement discourse (e.g. Braithwaite 1999), but others doubt that this is the right direction and argue that we should recognise the limited effects of post-offence dispositions (i.e. 'sentencing') on social behaviour, and should pursue a wider social approach to criminal policy (von Hirsch and Ashworth 1998, ch. 8).

Notes

1 The bulk of the comparative research reported in sections 3 and 4 of this chapter was conducted as part of a survey of recent trends for the Council of Europe. A fuller version has now been published, in a different form, by Council of Europe (2000). I am grateful to Estella Baker for her comments on the draft, and to Council of Europe Publishing for permitting publication of material in sections 3 and 4.

2   Limiting the survey to rates of custodial sentencing yields an inevitably crude picture of trends, and the possibility that prosecution policies and other factors might have influenced the trends was not investigated in this small survey. However, analysis of other influences on criminal justice in Europe may be found in the various chapters in Council of Europe (2000).

References

Albrecht, H.-J. (1997), 'Sentencing and Punishment in Germany', in M. Tonry and K. Hatlestad (eds), *Sentencing Reform in Overcrowded Times: A comparative perspective*, New York: Oxford University Press.

Ashworth, A. (2000a), 'The Decline of English Sentencing, and Other Stories', in R. Frase and M. Tonry (eds), *Punishment and Penal Systems in Western Countries*, New York: Oxford University Press.

Ashworth, A. (2000b), *Sentencing and Criminal Justice*, 3rd edn, London: Butterworths.

Ball, C. (2000), 'A Significant Move towards Restorative Justice, or a Recipe for Unintended Consequences?', *Criminal Law Review*, pp. 211–22.

Bard, K. (1986), 'Some General Traits of the Criminal justice Systems of the Socialist Countries, with special reference to Hungary', *Papers on Crime Policy*, Helsinki: HEUNI.

Braithwaite, J. (1989), *Crime, Shame and Reintegration*, Cambridge: Cambridge University Press.

Council of Europe (1974), *Sentencing*, Strasbourg: Council of Europe.

Council of Europe (1987), *The Simplification of Criminal Justice*, Recommendation (87) 18, Strasbourg: Council of Europe.

Council of Europe (1992), *Consistency in Sentencing*, Recommendation (92) 17, Strasbourg: Council of Europe.

Council of Europe (2000), *Crime Policy in Europe*, Strasbourg: Council of Europe.

De la Cuesta, J.L. and Varona, G. (1996), 'An Approach to the New Spanish Penal Code of 1995', *European Journal of Crime, Criminal Law and Criminal Justice*, Vol. 3, pp. 226–35.

Duff, P. and Hutton, N. (eds) (1999), *Criminal Justice in Scotland*, Aldershot: Dartmouth.

Emmerson, B., and Ashworth, A. (2001), *Human Rights in Criminal Proceedings*, London: Sweet and Maxwell.

Eser, A. and Huber, B. (eds) (1994), *Strafsentwicklung in Europa, 4.1 and 4.2*t, Freiburg: Max-Planck-Institut fur auslandisches und internationales Strafrecht.

Eser, A. and Huber, B. (eds) (1997), *Strafsentwicklung in Europa, 5.1 and 5.2*, Freiburg: Max-Planck-Institut fur auslandisches und internationales Strafrecht.

Flood-Page, C., and Mackie, A. (1998), *Sentencing Practice: An examination of decisions in magistrates' courts and the Crown Court in the mid-1990s*, Home Office Research Study 180, London: Home Office.

Frase, R. and Tonry, M. (eds) (2000), *Punishment and Penal Systems in Western Countries*, New York: Oxford University Press.

Hamai, K. (1999), 'Prison Population in Japan stable for 30 Years', *Overcrowded Times*, Vol. 10, No. 1, p. 1.

Hebenton, B. and Spencer, J. (1998), 'Law Enforcement in Societies in Transition', *European Journal of Crime, Criminal Law and Criminal Justice*, Vol. 1, pp. 29–37.

Hood, R. (1992), *Race and Sentencing*, Oxford: Oxford University Press.

Hood, R. (1996), *The Death Penalty: A world-wide perspective*, 2nd revised edn, Oxford: Oxford University Press.

Hulsman, L. (1981), 'Penal Reform in the Netherlands', *Howard Journal*, Vol. XX, pp. 150–60.

Hutton, N. (1999), 'Sentencing in Scotland', in P. Duff and N. Hutton (eds), *Criminal Justice in Scotland*, Aldershot: Dartmouth.

Jareborg, N. (1995), 'The Swedish Sentencing Reform', in C. Clarkson and R. Morgan (eds), *The Politics of Sentencing Reform*, Oxford: Oxford University Press.

Kensey, A. and Tournier, P. (1998), 'French Prison Numbers Stable Since 1988, but Populations Changing', *Overcrowded Times*, Vol. 9, p. 4.

Killias, M., Kuhn, A. and Ronez, S. (1997), 'Sentencing in Switzerland', in M. Tonry and K. Hatlestad (eds), *Sentencing Reform in Overcrowded Times: A comparative perspective*, New York: Oxford University Press.

Krapac, D. (1995), 'The Position of the Victim in Criminal Justice: A restrained central and Eastern European perspective on victim-offender mediation', *European Journal of Crime, Criminal Law and Criminal Justice*, Vol. 3, pp. 230–39.

Kyvsgaard, B. (1998), 'Penal Sanctions and the Use of Imprisonment in Denmark', *Overcrowded Times*, Vol. 9, No. 6, p. 1.

Lappi-Seppala, T. (2000), 'The Decline of the Repressive Ideal: Criminal Policy and Penal Practices in Finland', in R. Frase and M. Tonry (eds), *Punishment and Penal Systems in Western Countries*, New York: Oxford University Press.

Larsson, P. (1999), 'Norway Prison Use up Slightly', *Overcrowded Times*, Vol. 10, No. 1, p. 1.

Morgan, R. (1998), 'Imprisonment in England and Wales: Flood Tide, but on the Turn?', *Overcrowded Times*, Vol. 9, No. 6, p. 1.

Morris, A. and Gelsthorpe, L. (2000), 'Something Old, Something Borrowed, Something Blue, but Something New? A Comment on the Prospects for Restorative Justice under the Crime and Disorder Act 1998', *Criminal Law Review*, pp. 18–30.

de Pauw, W. (1998), 'Sentencing of Drug Offences: Focus on ethnic minorities', unpublished paper for American Society of Criminology conference: author at wdepauw@vub.ac.be.

Pieth, M. (1998), 'The Prevention of Money Laundering: A comparative analysis', *European Journal of Crime, Criminal Law and Criminal Justice*, Vol. 2, pp. 159–67.

Selih, A. (1996), 'Juvenile Criminal Law and Change: Trends in some East- and Central-European countries', *European Journal of Crime, Criminal Law and Criminal Justice*, Vol. 2, pp. 173–81.

Snacken, S. (1997), 'Surpopulation des Prisons et Sanctions Alternatives', in P. Mary (ed), *Travail d'Interet General et Mediation Penale: Socialisation du Penal ou Penalisation du Social?*, Brussels: Bruylant.

Snare, A. (ed.) (1995), *Beware of Punishment*, Scandinavian Studies in Criminology, Vol. 14, Oslo: Pax Forlag.

Tak, P.J.P. (1997), 'Sentencing and Punishment in the Netherlands', in M. Tonry and K. Hatlestad (eds), *Sentencing Reform in Overcrowded Times: A comparative perspective*, New York: Oxford University Press.

Tak, P.J.P. (2000), 'Changes in Sentencing in the Netherlands, 1970–1995', in R. Frase and M. Tonry (eds), *Punishment and Penal Systems in Western Countries*, New York: Oxford University Press.

Tonry, M. and Hatlestad, K. (eds) (1997), *Sentencing Reform in Overcrowded Times: A comparative perspective*, New York: Oxford University Press.

Tornudd, P. (1997), 'Sentencing and Punishment in Finland', in M. Tonry and K. Hatlestad (eds), *Sentencing Reform in Overcrowded Times: A comparative perspective*, New York: Oxford University Press.

Traskman, P.-O. (1995), 'The Dragon's Egg: Drugs-related crime control', in Snare, A. (ed.), *Beware of Punishment*, Scandinavian Studies in Criminology, Vol. 14, Oslo: Pax Forlag.

Tubex, H. and Snacken, S. (1995), 'L'Evolution des Longues Peines: Apercu international et analyse des causes', *Deviance et Societe*, Vol. 19, No. 2, pp. 103–20.

Victor, D. (1995), 'Politics and the Penal System – a Drama in Progress', in Snare, A. (ed.), *Beware of Punishment*, Scandinavian Studies in Criminology, Vol. 14, Oslo: Pax Forlag.

Von Hirsch, A. and Ashworth, A. (eds) (1998), *Principled Sentencing: Readings in theory and policy*, Oxford: Hart Publishing.

Von Hirsch, A., Bottoms, A.E., Burney, E. and Wikstrom, P.-O. (1999), *Criminal Deterrence: An analysis of recent research*, Oxford: Hart Publishing.

Wasik, M., and von Hirsch, A. (1997), 'Civil Disqualifications attending Conviction: a Suggested Conceptual Framework', *Cambridge Law Journal*, pp. 599–623.

Weigend, T. (1997), 'Germany Reduces Use of Prison Sentences', in M. Tonry and K. Hatlestad (eds), *Sentencing Reform in Overcrowded Times: A comparative perspective*, New York: Oxford University Press.

Chapter Eleven

What's It Worth? A Cross-Jurisdictional Comparison of Sentence Severity

Arie Freiberg

Introduction

Do nations, or states or provinces within nations, differ in the severity of their sentencing policies and practices? This apparently simple question has proved to be surprisingly difficult to answer. Although there is much speculation and a great deal of estimation, cross-jurisdictional comparisons of sentence severity have been few and their findings relatively narrow and inconclusive. To some degree, this is not surprising, as international criminal justice data are rarely completely comparable and there are even significant variations between jurisdictions within federalised nations. The effort of obtaining and standardising the data is rarely thought worthwhile: most countries tend to be juricentric and their criminal justice systems solipsistic.

With a number of notable exceptions (Lynch 1988; Farrington and Langan 1992; Farrington, Langan and Wilkstrom 1994; Lynch 1993; Forst and Lynch 1997), comparative sentencing observations and studies have, to date, tended to focus upon variations in imprisonment rates possibly because these data tend to be widely collected and published. Yet imprisonment rates are not, in truth, sentencing data. Sentencing can be described as the dispositional process followed by a criminal court which is consequent upon a finding of guilt or the recording of a conviction (Fox and Freiberg 1999, p. 73). The dispositions available to a court include not only custodial orders, but also fines, community orders, conditional and unconditional releases and many combinations and variations of these orders. Imprisonment rates, therefore, represent information about only one of the possible sentencing outcomes of the courts, which reflect, however, the decisions of other subordinate sentencing authorities such as parole boards, release on licence authorities and prison managements in jurisdictions where remissions still exist.

'League' tables of imprisonment rates are commonly produced (Kuhn 1998; Walmsley 1999). These tend to show that the United States and Russia are amongst the highest imprisoning nations in the world whilst Japan and some Scandinavian countries are among the lowest. From this it is sometimes deduced that the United States is one of the most punitive nations on earth and Japan one of the least. To the extent that the number of people in prison at any one time can be regarded as an index of 'punitiveness' then this deduction may have some validity, but there significant problems in using imprisonment rates, or prison populations as indices of penal severity (Lynch 1988, p. 182; Young and Brown 1993, pp. 8ff.). In many jurisdictions, a sentence of imprisonment is an infrequently used sanction, so that using prison populations, or even prison sentence lengths, provides a very narrow view of *sentence* severity. But even if one accepted the iconic status of the sentence of imprisonment as an index of severity, commentators have differed as to whether its severity should be measured in terms of its incidence (the number of admissions to prison) or its severity (the length of sentence) (Lynch 1988; Tak 1998, p. 1). The degree of deprivation, that is, whether an offender is kept in maximum or minimum security institution, may also be relevant in determining severity (Lynch 1988).

However, there are a number of other, more serious objections to the use of imprisonment as a measure of penal severity generally, or sentence severity in particular. In summary, these objections are that the imprisonment rate measure:

- does not take into account the amount of crime in the jurisdiction. By using the total population, or adult population, rather than the population at risk, that is, the offenders, it does not provide a truly comparable measure of sentence severity;
- does not take into account differences in the severity of crimes across jurisdictions (Lynch 1988, p. 183);
- does not take into account differences between jurisdictions in the range of activity which is criminalised (Lynch 1988, p. 181);
- by including remand populations, which vary widely between jurisdictions, does not give an accurate picture of *sentence* severity;
- does not take into account differences in the structure of adult and juvenile correctional systems;
- in some jurisdictions, excludes some forms of custody, such as jail sentences of under one year, from the calculations;
- by using *stock*, rather than *flow* data, tends to highlight the length of sentences (intensity) rather than their incidence or use (breadth); stock studies tend to overestimate the propensity to incarcerate in those countries

with higher rates of serious crime (Lynch 1988, p. 184);
- may be influenced by factors external to the issue of penal severity, such as prison capacity (Tak 1998; Young and Brown 1993).

Imprisonment rates then may be reflective of the sentencing process, but they do not capture its range and complexity. The purpose of this chapter is a limited one: it is to examine some of the methodological problems involved in measuring sentence severity by indices other than the imprisonment rate. It will then attempt to compare some sentencing practices across a small number of jurisdictions using the offence of burglary as the basis of comparison.

Why Compare?

Comparative research can be justified simply on the basis of its curiosity value alone. However, comparative research also has a utilitarian value. Increasingly, comparisons, or benchmarking processes, are used to assess the performance of individuals, organisations or whole systems (Forst and Lynch 1997, p. 99). Thus the relationship between sentencing practices and crime rates may provide an insight into the relative effectiveness of different sanctions or the level of use of such sanctions (Farrington and Langan 1992). Comparisons might enable one to determine whether equivalent levels of criminal or social control can be achieved by less costly or more 'humane' means, however one defines them (Frase 1990, p. 648).

On a broader level, comparative research may allow cross-cultural generalisations about social behaviour (Bierne 1983, p. 372). Comparative sentencing data can reveal a great deal about the nature and function of punishment in a society and possibly provide an insight into that society's economic, social and psychological structures (Young and Brown 1993, p. 2). Crime and punishment, it has been suggested, cannot be understood separately from their cultural context and it has been argued that cultural factors, rather than crime rates, hold the key to understanding changes in sanctioning patterns in general, and imprisonment rates in particular (Young and Brown 1993; Zimring and Hawkins 1991).

Severity

'Severity' in sentencing is a complex concept. On both an individual and socio/cultural level, it is a relative concept. Sanctions vary in their nature and duration, they may be voluntary or involuntarily assumed and may be imposed for different purposes. They are phenomenologically complex. What is severe to a sentencer may not be perceived as such by the offender being sentenced. What the public perceives as severe may not accord with the intentions of the criminal justice system. What may be thought of as a deprivation in one country, may not be so in another, or the values attributed to that loss, whether it be of life, freedom or movement, of goods or money, of reputation or other values may differ (Freiberg 1987). As Bierne observes (1983, p. 377):

> ... the severity of punishment in a given culture must initially be understood in its own cultural milieu, within its own system of meaning. It is not an objective category: punishment must be seen as subjectively and culturally problematic.

Acknowledging these difficulties does not mean that comparisons of sentencing practices are impossible – only that the results must be interpreted carefully. Some of the problems of cultural relativity can be mitigated by choosing indices which are not too culturally dissimilar.

Sentencing Burglars

The approach adopted in this study is to focus upon one offence, in this case burglary, and to attempt to determine whether it is possible to compare sentencing patterns for that offence. Though this study examines court outcomes, it is recognised that the sentencing decision of the court is only one of many decision steps involved from the commission of the crime to the completion of sentence (Forst and Lynch 1997, p. 100).[1] Data collection took place by way of questionnaire distributed to key experts in selected jurisdictions[2] and by collecting publicly available data which was readily accessible in Australia.

Choice of Offence

Previous cross-national studies of levels of crime and punishment have found that jurisdictions vary not only in the amount of crime, but in the mix of crime (Forst and Lynch 1997, p. 100). Studies show that differences in the nature and seriousness of offending account for some of the variations in incarceration (Young and Brown 1993). Large scale comparisons of crime rates and imprisonment rates tend to mask these differences[3] and to produce misleading results because of the lack of standardisation of offence mix and crime seriousness. Lynch found that when comparable offences were used, the differences between countries diminished, but did not disappear altogether (Lynch 1988:196). He therefore recommended that cross-national comparisons of sentencing practices specify the offences for which the comparisons apply.

In order to obviate this problem, it was decided to undertake an offence specific comparison of sentencing practices. The offence of burglary, or breaking and entering, was selected because it is one of the most frequently committed offences (and therefore would have a not insignificant effect upon imprisonment rates), it is an offence of medium seriousness, and thus allows of a considerable degree of sentencing discretion and variation and, in many jurisdictions it is triable in both higher and lower courts. Finally, burglary has been the subject of a number of cross-national studies which could serve to confirm or contradict my findings (Farrington and Langan 1992; Langan and Farrington 1998; Lynch 1993; Forst and Lynch 1997).

The choice of burglary as the comparator offence is open to criticism. Burglary is a protean offence. It is particularly problematic because of major differences between jurisdictions in offence definitions. Burglary may differ in its nature, definition and recording patterns depending upon the nature of the premises entered (e.g. dwellings, commercial premises or other), whether or not the premises were occupied, the degree of entry, whether or not the offender carried or used arms, was in company or alone, used or threatened force, the requisite ulterior offence and the mental element. Further, burglary may include not only the breaking and entry, but the offence committed in consequence of the burglary. In relation to the theft of goods, for example, there are questions whether charging practices include theft, possession of stolen goods as well as breaking and entering (Frase 1990, p. 660).

In the practice of sentencing, the relative prevalence of some of these factors may skew the sentencing patterns of the jurisdiction. For example Langan and Farrington (1998, p. 46), noted that in the United States, 68 per cent of murders involved the use of firearms, compared with 7 per cent of murders in England. Similarly, 41 per cent of US robberies involved firearms, compared with 5 per cent in England. It might be possible to speculate that, on average, United States burglaries might involve more force or violence, or the threat of it, than in other jurisdictions, thus explaining differences in sentence severity.

However, other 'mid-range' offences produce similar problems of breadth and comparability. Thus robbery can be divided into robbery, aggravated robbery or specially aggravated robbery; assaults can be divided into common assault, grievous bodily harm, bodily harm and so on, while sexual assaults have even more permutations: indecent assault, sexual intercourse without consent, aggravated sexual assault, incest etc. There is no perfect comparative offence.

Comparison Jurisdictions

The exploratory nature of this survey required it to be restricted to a relatively small number of common law jurisdictions in order to determine whether there are significant differences within superficially like jurisdictions. Discussions with colleagues in civil law jurisdictions indicated that the differences in the systems of processing of offenders through the criminal justice system were likely to be so great as to defeat the purpose of the exercise. The jurisdictions for which relatively reliable data were obtained were:

- Australia: Victoria (1997–98),[4] Western Australia (1998),[5] New South Wales (1996),[6] Tasmania (1996–97) and South Australia (1997);
- New Zealand (1997);
- England and Wales (1996);[7]
- Scotland (1997);[8]
- Canada (1993–94);
- United States: Minnesota (1995).[9]

The information obtained related to a number of key sentencing factors, namely: 1) the statutory maximum penalty, including statutory circumstances of aggravation; 2) offence classification and mode of trial; 3) sentencing options available to the courts and 4) sentencing outcomes. The results of the survey are summarised in Tables 11.1–11.3.

Statutory Maximum Penalties and Variations

The statutory maximum penalty serves important symbolic and practical functions. First, and for current purposes, it can provide a simple measure of penal value as indicated by the legislature. This itself, may be a useful and revealing index of severity. Secondly, in some jurisdictions, by classifying each crime as indictable or summary and by specifying a maximum (or in some cases a mandatory) sentence for each specific offence, the legislature provides both the public and sentencers with a guide to the seriousness with which the community should view the offence. It is supposed to be both a reflection of the level of communal abhorrence and a directive to sentencers on how to weigh the gravity of this kind of offending. It provides the yardstick against which all cases falling within that class of proscribed conduct are measured.

Table 11.1 Sentencing structures and jurisdiction of courts

Jurisdiction	Statutory Maximum	Aggravation Summarily	Triable	% Higher Courts
Victoria	10	25	Yes	3%
Western Aust.	14	18–20	Yes	–
NSW	14	20–25/1yr min.	Yes	–
Tasmania	21		Yes	–
South Aust.	Life		Yes	8%
NZ	10	14	Yes	0%
England	14/10	Life/3yr min.	Yes	36%
Scotland	At large			12%[10]
Canada	Life/14			
Minnesota				
1st degree	20	6 month min.	No	100%
2nd degree	10		No	100%
3rd degree	5		No	100%
4th degree	1		No	100%

Finally, in some jurisdictions, statutory distinctions are made between various forms of offending and types of offenders. Thus a burglary which is classified as a 'home invasion' (i.e. when there is someone in the house at the time of entry) may carry a higher maximum penalty. Other forms of aggravated burglaries may involve use of weapons, committing the offence in company and so on. In relation to offenders, those with one, two or more prior convictions may be subject to enhanced maximum penalties or to mandatory or minimum sentences. These will affect sentencing practices.

Table 11.1 indicates a wide range of statutory maximum penalties ranging from one year for a burglary in the fourth degree in Minnesota to life in Scotland. Tasmania's maximum of 21 years is a generic maximum for all indictable offences. A 14 year maximum was not uncommon, stemming from the nineteenth-century English maximum penalty structure.

Almost all jurisdictions surveyed had a variety of maximum penalties reflecting the different circumstances of the offence. Victoria's maximum was increased by 250 per cent (10 years to 25 years) if the burglary was aggravated by the possession of firearms or the presence within the building of a person. The nature of the building was important in Western Australia (14 > 18 years); England (10 > 14 years) and Canada (14 years > life). In England a third offence could require a 3 year mandatory minimum sentence and in Western Australia, a 12 month minimum. Minnesota law requires a mandatory six months' minimum sentence if the person is convicted of committing burglary of an occupied building.

Case Processing, Offence Classification and Mode of Trial

The imposition of a sentence by a court is the culmination of a series of earlier decisions by victims, police and prosecutors. Sentence outcomes cannot be understood in isolation from these earlier decisions and their consequences upon the number and seriousness of offences which ultimately come before the courts must be considered (Frase 1990, p. 661). As Forst and Lynch observe (1997, p. 101):

> Failure to include multiple decision points in cross-national comparisons will, in any case, prevent our understanding more specifically why cross-national differences do occur.

'Punitiveness' can be represented at a systemic level as being the total incidence of sanctions upon those eligible to receive them (e.g. Farrington and Langan 1992). All systems screen cases from the time of reporting to the time of trial. This includes police and prosecution discretion, both formal and informal. It may include measures to deal with juveniles and the mentally ill or intellectually disabled.

In some jurisdictions, particularly some European systems, prosecutors have substantial power to divert cases, so that the cases that eventually reach the court may be more severe than those where little screening or diversion occurs. In common law systems, plea-bargaining occurs in various forms and to greater or lesser degrees. Plea-bargaining leading to charge reduction may give a misleading indication of sentence severity. A growing feature of some criminal justice systems is the use of diversionary conferences, in which minor, and in some cases not so minor, offences are diverted from courts to family group conferences or other mediation or reparation programmes. It is difficult to determine empirically how many cases are 'processed' or diverted from the court system prior to trial.

One measurable form of case processing which may be important in gauging sentencing severity is the distribution of matters between the higher and lower courts. Jurisdictions differ in their classification of offences and the mode of trial. Distinctions may be made between felonies, misdemeanours and infractions, summary and indictable offences or solemn and summary offences. Court structures will also differ. Jurisdictions may have one, two, three or more levels or types of court which may deal with an offence. Some courts may have dual jurisdictions. They will vary in their sentencing powers.

Victoria, for example, has three levels of court: the Supreme Court, the County (intermediate) Court and the Magistrates' Court. Burglaries are triable both on indictment and summarily with different maxima applicable for each individual offence and, in the Magistrates' Court, for aggregate sentences. Almost all Anglo-Australian jurisdictions provide for some form of summary trial, although some forms of aggravated burglary were ineligible for this form of trial. Minnesota, on the other hand, does not have provision for any summary or non-jury trials, although fourth degree burglaries are triable by a six person rather than a twelve person jury. The sentencing powers of the court do not differ depending on the size of the jury.

For those jurisdictions for which information was available, jurisdictional maxima[11] in the summary courts ranged from six months (England) to five years (Victoria, New Zealand). There are differences in maxima for single and multiple offences. Lower courts adopt a different mix of sanctions and their intensity is likely to be less, reflecting, in part, the less serious nature of the offences coming before them. Because jurisdictions differ in the way they allocate cases between courts, it can be argued that these decisions are a crucial component in determining how 'punitive' a criminal justice system is. Punitiveness, in this context, includes both the incidence and intensity of all sanctions, not just imprisonment.

Jurisdictions will vary between themselves and across time in the way that courts deal with particular offences. The trend in common law jurisdictions over recent years has to allow for offences previously dealt with in the higher courts to be dealt with by lower courts, at the election of the prosecution or the defendant, sometimes requiring the consent of the court. This will have an effect on the general severity of sentences imposed.[12]

Table 11.1 also indicates that there are significant differences between jurisdictions as to the mix of cases heard in the courts. In Minnesota, all burglary cases are tried before a judge and jury. In comparison, South Australia and Victoria try between 97 per cent and 98 per cent of all burglary cases in courts of summary jurisdiction. It is reported that in New Zealand 100 per cent of cases are heard in the lower courts. In England, some 64 per cent of all cases (45 per cent of all offenders) are tried in the magistrates' courts rather than the Crown Court. In Scotland, the High Court hears less than 1 per cent of cases, but the Sheriff Court in Solemn Jurisdiction hears nearly 12 per cent of cases.

Sentencing Outcomes

This section seeks to explore the sentencing outcomes of those cases that eventually reach court and in which a finding of guilt has been reached or conviction has been recorded. It separates, where relevant, outcomes for higher and lower courts. In Australia, for example, most statistical series distinguish between the higher courts (Supreme Court and intermediate court), and the lower courts or Magistrates' Courts.

Comparing sentences across jurisdictions in terms of their relative severity is a problematic exercise (Freiberg and Fox 1986; Wasik and von Hirsch 1988; Schiff 1997). As well as cultural differences between jurisdictions as to the relative severity of penal measures, there are also disagreements within jurisdictions, between legislators, sentencers and the sentenced. Overlaps between sanctions also complicate any simple model (i.e. a $10,000 fine may be regarded as being more severe than a five day sentence of imprisonment) although, in the abstract, a sentence of imprisonment would probably be regarded as the more severe sanction. Particularly problematic is the extraordinarily wide range of measures which fall within the 'intermediate sanction' rubric.

For the purposes of this broad exercise, and to take into account the vast array of sanctions and sanctioning nomenclature, a broad, relatively simple, a priori, classification of sanctions was adopted:

- *imprisonment*: including all forms of imprisonment such as intermittent custody and the like, but excluding suspended sentences;
- *community supervision or work*: including all forms of probation, intensive supervision, community work or conditional order, brokered programs for offenders; outpatient treatment and day reporting centres where some form of supervision is involved;
- *fine or financial penalty*: including restitution or compensation sanctions if they are considered as part of the sentence rather than an ancillary sanction;
- *conditional or unconditional unsupervised release*: including all forms of court ordered dismissals, discharges or adjournments, conditional or

otherwise, where no formal supervision is required. Excluded from this category are dismissals or discharges on the merits (i.e. prior to a finding of guilt or conviction).

Higher Courts

Table 11.2 shows the sentencing patterns of those courts and reveals that there are wide variations in the proportion of cases in which persons found guilty or convicted of burglary received a sentence of imprisonment. This indicator seeks to identify one aspect of sentence severity, namely the *incidence* or breadth of imprisonment.

Table 11.2   Higher courts sentencing patterns: burglary

Jurisdiction	Imp.	Susp. Sent.	Community Order	Fine	Dismissals etc.
Victoria	58%	33%	6%	0%	3%
West Aust.	67%	10%	28%	2%	0%
NSW	~70%	~15%	~8%	1%	0%
Tas	92%	–	–	–	–
Sth Aust.	75%	25%	0%	0%	0%
Eng. and Wales	77%	1%	21%	0%	1%
Scotland	88%	NA	11%	<1%	0%
Minnesota	94%	–	–	–	–

In Victoria, 92 per cent of the 3 per cent of cases which were sentenced in the higher courts received a custodial sentence, although 34 per cent of those sentences were suspended, leaving in effect, 58 per cent of offenders who received an executed sentence of imprisonment. In Western Australia, 67 per cent of offences in the higher courts received a custodial sentence and a further 10 per cent were suspended. 1998 data for offence outcomes showed variation in proportions imprisoned for aggravated burglary (49 per cent), home burglary (74 per cent) and other burglary (73 per cent). The New South Wales higher courts imprisoned around 70 per cent of burglars, with a further 10–15 per cent receiving suspended sentences.

In South Australia, of the 8 per cent of cases heard in the higher courts, approximately 74 per cent received a sentence of imprisonment, with a further 25 per cent receiving a suspended sentence. In England and Wales of the 36 per cent of cases heard in the Crown Court 77 per cent received a custodial sentence (65 per cent non-dwelling; 81 per cent dwelling)[13] while in Scotland, of the 12 per cent of cases heard in the Sheriff Court, Solemn Jurisdiction, 88 per cent received a custodial sentence. In Minnesota, all cases were heard in higher courts, of which 94 per cent received a sentence of executed custody (31 per cent prison, 63 per cent local jail).

The matter of the intensity of punishment can be partly gauged by the length of the prison sentence imposed, although it is important for this purpose to distinguish between the imposed, or nominal sentence, and the actual time served in custody. In relation to the former, the median sentence is statistically probably the best indicator of the 'tariff' or going rate for the offence, although some data series may only provide averages. The median excludes outlying cases which may skew the mean figure, if total numbers are small.

In relation to the differences between nominal and actual sentences, it is important to note that in many jurisdictions there are significant differences between the sentence imposed by the court and the length of time the offender spends in custody (Jones and Austin 1993, p. 1). Time served in custody is a truer measure of punitiveness or severity than the nominal sentences announced by the courts. There are three major areas of difficulty in arriving at the actual time served as a measure of severity:

- *pre-trial custody*: in many jurisdictions offenders may spend long periods in custody before trial, in some cases, in facilities different to those in which they will spend time as convicted prisoners. The law will differ as to whether and how that time is taken into account in sentencing. Some systems will require the court to impose the appropriate sentence, but to announce that the period of pre-trial custody will be credited to the time to be served. Others may impose shorter nominal sentences after having taken into account the time already served. In this second case, sentence severity will appear to be less because of shorter nominal periods;
- *parole*: jurisdictions with parole systems allow the release of an offender prior to the expiration of the head sentence. Whether the release can be ordered by a parole board or by some statutory or administrative formula, actual time served will be less than the announced term, in the absence of parole revocation. Estimates of actual time served in parole jurisdictions may be made by examining court imposed non-parole periods, parole board release practices or the operation of the statutory formulae;
- *remissions or good time*: some jurisdictions permit earlier release for good behaviour. This may be mandatory or discretionary and may vary from

offence to offence and over periods of time. It may or may not interact with the parole rules. However, in those jurisdictions where remissions apply, it is necessary to calculate their effect on actual time served.

The differences between the sentence announced by the courts and the actual time served can be considerable. In England, for example, since 1992, all inmates are required to serve a minimum of 50 per cent of the sentence; those with sentences under four years are automatically released; those over four years are eligible for parole. In the United States, parole regulations vary between jurisdictions. Some have abolished good time; some require a minimum percentage of sentence to be served.

The results of the present survey produced the following results in relation to time imposed and time served in respect of higher court sentences:[14]

Median sentence		Estimated time served	
Victoria:		18 months	12 months
Western Aust.:		29 months	8 months
NSW:		20 months	20 months
Sth Aust.:		27 months[15]	27 months
England:		26 months	13 months
Scotland:		16 months	6.6 months
Minnesota:	(prison)	36 months	24 months
	(jail)	3 months	2 months
	(total)	5.9 months	4 months

For those jurisdictions in which information is available, Table 11.2 also shows wide variations in their use of noncustodial options. However, it is clear that lower order sanctions such as fines and dismissals are not widely used in the higher courts.

Lower Courts

Table 11.3 summarises the available data in relation to the lower courts. As is evident, jurisdictions appear to vary widely in their sentencing patterns in the lower courts. Of course, much will depend upon the jurisdictional limits of the lower courts, with courts hearing a higher proportion of the more serious cases expected to make more use of imprisonment for longer periods of time.

Imprisonment use varied from 16 per cent in Western Australia to 61 per cent in Canada, although the range of sentence lengths was more limited. In the lower courts, the disparity between sentence imposed and time served (if any) is far lower than it is in the higher courts. In the only jurisdictions for which this information was available, the differences were nil in Victoria, approximately 2 months in Scotland (6.7m > 4–5 m) and 1.5m in Canada (4.5m > 3m).

Table 11.3   Lower courts sentencing patterns: burglary

Jurisdiction	Imp.	Av. Sent.	Susp. Sent.	Comm'y Order	Fine	Dismissals etc.
Victoria	51%	6m	17%	21%	4%	6%
West Aust.	16%	N/A	–	55%	28%	–
NSW	40%	8m	–	19%	4%	3%
Tasmania	NA	7m	48%	5%	0%	5%
Sth Aust.	42%	13m	45%	5%	3%	4%
NZ	34%	5.9m	11%	57%	6%	–
Eng. and Wales	23%	3m	0%	53%	9%	14%
Scotland	39%	3.76m	0%	12%	19%	30%
Canada	61%	4.5m	–	3%	–	–

The major intermediate sanctions were the suspended sentence and community orders, although it is sometimes difficult to distinguish the two in jurisdictions where the suspended sentence is a form of community order.

Summary

Unsurprisingly, this limited survey has revealed significant variations between jurisdictions in the processing of cases, in their relative use of imprisonment and its length and in their use of a range of other sentencing measures. Median imprisonment sentence lengths in the higher courts varied widely, from 18 months in Victoria to 36 months in New South Wales and Minnesota. These figures must be approached with great caution as the data obtained refer inconsistently to sentencing of *offenders* and *offences*. Nor do the data reveal the impact of decisions relating to cumulation or concurrency.[16] Data about total effective sentences may be a better indication of sentence severity than data about individual sentences.

The disparity between jurisdictions shrank when average time served is used as a measure, but they remain considerable. For a host of technical reasons, it was not possible accurately to gauge the intensity of noncustodial sentences, although some indication has been obtained about their incidence.

Are Some Jurisdictions more Punitive than Others?

The data presented suggest that there are differences between jurisdictions in their sentencing behaviours as indicated by both the incidence and intensity of imprisonment as well as intermediate and other sanctions. By focusing upon the offence of burglary, without reference either to the number of those offences or imprisonment rates in general, a distinction is made between the severity of sentences and the number of sentences which are imposed.

Previous studies of burglary sentencing have also concluded that there are major differences between jurisdictions in terms of punitiveness.

In 1992, Langan and Farrington (1992, p. 8) carried out a comparison of changes in crime and punishment in England and America between 1981 and 1987. They examined a number of offences in relation to levels of reported and unreported crimes, attrition rates and sentencing practices. Further studies were undertaken later in the 1990s and reported in 1998 (Langan and Farrington 1998). Their study is valuable in that it takes a broad view of both the *incidence* and *severity* of penal measures. By incorporating into their analysis the likelihood of an offender being detected, prosecuted, convicted and incarcerated they have constructed a comprehensive index of punitiveness across the whole population. Punitiveness, in this aggregate context, is represented not only by the number and length of custodial sentences, but the overall number of offenders eventually subject to sanction. As Farrington and Langan concede, these data are problematic and become more so as more jurisdictions are added to the comparison. Farrington and Langan found that in 1987, burglary rates in England and the United States were not markedly dissimilar, nor were rates of custody for burglary offences. There were, however, major differences in the proportion of those sentenced to custody (35 per cent in England, 57 per cent in the USA), in imposed sentence lengths (15.1 months in England, 48 months in the USA) and actual time served (2.9 months vs 4.65 months). Nominal sentence lengths in the United States were over three times as long as in England, although time served was just over twice as long in the United States as in England.

By 1995, however, there had been dramatic changes in burglary in both countries. The rate of burglary was much higher in England than it was in the US. According to victim surveys it was 82.9/1,000 households in England vs

47.5/1,000 in the US. Police statistics also showed a higher rate of offending (23.9/1,000 population England vs 9.9 USA). American courts were more likely to sentence an offender to incarceration than in England. In relation to burglary, the relative figures were 60 per cent in the United States against 38 per cent in England.[17] However, for technical reasons, it was necessary for Langan and Farrington to combine Crown Court and Magistrates' Court sentences. From their study they also concluded that incarceration sentence lengths are longer in the US than in England. For 1994–95 the figures were for burglary were 43 months against 15 months in England.[18]

In terms of time served, Farrington and Langan estimated that prisoners served about 40–50 per cent of their sentences in both countries (Langan and Farrington 1998, p. 35). Concomitantly with the longer sentences, time served in the United States was longer: burglary 18 months against six months.[19]

A 1997 study by Forst and Lynch drawing upon an earlier study by Farrington, Langan and Wilkstrom (1994) also looked at changes in crime and punishment over time and comparing jurisdictions, in this case, the United States, England and Sweden. Forst and Lynch (1997, p. 104) concluded that during the 1980s the US had a substantially larger ratio of persons imprisoned for burglary offences (from 20 per 100,000 residents in 1980 to 47 in 1990) than England (from 18 to 16) and Sweden (five to four) and that the primary reason for the higher gross imprisonment rate was the much higher ratio of burglary prisoners to burglaries in the United States, that is, the United States was substantially more likely to incarcerate those convicted of burglary.

The data also showed that American burglars served sentences which were nearly four times as long as Swedish burglars (17.1 months vs 4.7 months). This, they concluded, could be due to greater punitiveness or possibly because American burglaries tended to be more serious than English or Swedish offences.

Other Measures

There are also other means by which sentence severity may be measured. The weaknesses of the imprisonment rate measure have been discussed but other measures also have their problems. In some jurisdictions, prescriptive material is available which may indicate the preferred level of severity in the form of guideline judgments, sentences, grids or prosecution service recommendations. Under some sentencing systems, detailed guidelines provide detailed specification of sentences depending upon the amount stolen, the offender's prior convictions and similar factors. However, there may or may not be a high degree of congruence between prescription and practice and there is considerable difficulty distinguishing between nominal and actual sentences.

Another method of determining sentencing severity is through sentencing simulations: that is, giving sentencers a case-study incorporating a number of elements of a case and comparing both outcomes and the means of reaching those outcomes (e.g. Lovegrove 1997; see also Davies and Tyrer 2001). Lovegrove (1997, pp. 171ff.) has identified a number of problem which arise from these means of determining judicial outcomes. First, because the cases are fictitious, there are no significant consequences arising out of the decision. There is no appellate court looking over the judge's shoulder. Second, the vignettes presented tend to be simpler factually than real cases with fewer factors and less redundancy and conflict. They may also ignore subtle offender characteristics and focus too much on offence characteristics. Finally, the cases themselves may be atypical, especially where they focus on single, rather than multiple offending.

Conclusion

This exploratory study has found major differences in sentencing for the offence of burglary in the small number of jurisdiction surveyed. One important feature which emerged was the importance of the level of court in which offenders are tried, which in turn affected the proportion of offenders sentenced to imprisonment and the lengths of their sentences. Another important feature which emerged was the differences between the sentence imposed and time served. What initially appeared to be large differences between jurisdictions diminished considerably. It is probably not possible to combine these indicators into one measure, though it might be useful to capture the combined effects of jurisdictional choice, sanction choice and sanction intensity in one index. What would be valuable would be to separate the rate of crime and the legal reaction to it.

This exploratory study exposes some of the methodological difficulties of estimating what a crime is 'worth' in some common law jurisdictions. The creation of a standard unit of penal currency equivalent to the international 'Big Mac' index (which measures the cost of the same hamburger in different countries and enables a measure of the relative cost of living) still eludes us. If it were possible to do so, it may provide a more accurate gauge of the nature and level of punishment in different societies. If, as Young and Brown argue, it is true that (1993, p. 41):

> ... differences between jurisdictions in imprisonment practice are likely to mirror more general differences in judicial and public attitudes, not so much toward the rationale for punishment as toward the quantum of punishment

then it will be far more important to study those attitudes than it is to study levels of crime, victimisation or clear up rates.

Notes

1   This is intended to be a static analysis and does not attempt to gauge changes within jurisdiction over time. However, it is recognised that estimates of change are as important as estimates of level (Farrington and Langan 1992).

2   My thanks are due to Andrew Ashworth (England and Wales), Tony Doob (Canada), Richard Frase (Minnesota), Neil Hutton (Scotland), Neil Morgan (WA), Ivan Potas (NSW), Julian Roberts (Canada), Kate Warner (Tasmania), Warren Young (NZ) and George Zdenkowski (NSW). Richard Fox and David Tait made many valuable comments on earlier drafts.

3   See further discussion below.

4   Data are based on 'principal offence'.

5   Data are offence based.

6   Data are offence based.

7   Data available are 'person based', not offence based; see Home Office, Criminal Statistics, England and Wales 1996.

8   Data available are 'person based', not offence based.

9   Although excellent data were available in respect of Minnesota sentences, it must be noted that this jurisdiction is probably highly unrepresentative of United States sentencing patterns as a whole. Its imprisonment rate is one of the lowest in the United States.

10 The relevant jurisdiction is taken to be the Sheriff Court in Solemn jurisdiction. The High Court hears only 0.15 of cases.

11 That is, the maximum sentence which may be imposed by the summary court, irrespective of the statutory maximum penalty for that offence set out in general legislation: see Fox and Freiberg 1999, p. 239.

12 Jurisdictions will also differ in relation to the age of offenders coming before the courts. In most jurisdictions a defendant is considered an adult from the age of 18, though in some, the age is 17 and in a very few, 16. Adult and juvenile courts will have very different sentencing powers and practices. Thus the number of offenders coming before the courts and the severity of sentences imposed may be influenced by age/jurisdictional factors.

13 Includes young offender institutions.

14 It should be recalled that jurisdictions differ as to whether the data are offence or offender based.

15 Non-parole period.

16 In some cases, multiple offences are cumulated or made fully or partly concurrent. In some jurisdictions, data is provided in relation to total effective sentences for multiple similar offences, but insufficient data were available for the current survey.

17 Similar differences were found in relation to other offences: murder: 96 per cent vs 94 per cent; rape: 82 per cent vs 95 per cent; robbery 79/67; assault 62/27; motor theft 55/30.

18 For other offences the comparisons were: murder 266 months/230 months; rape 123 months/ 77 months; robbery 89 months/40 months; assault 48 months/14 months.

19 In relation to other offences the differences were: murder $10^1/_2$ years vs $8^1/_4$ years; rape $5^1/_2$ years vs four years; robbery $3^1/_2$ years vs two years; assault two years vs six months; burglary $1^1/_2$ years vs six months.

References

Bierne, P. (1983), 'Cultural Relativism and Comparative Criminology', *Contemporary Crises*, Vol. 7, p. 371.

Davies, M., Takala, J.-P. and Tyrer, J., this volume.

Farrington, D.P. and Langan, P.A. (1992), 'Changes in Crime and Punishment in England and America in the 1980s', *Justice Quarterly*, Vol. 9(1), p. 5.

Farrington, D.P., Langan, P.A. and Wilkstrom, P.-O.H. (1994), 'Changes in Crime and Punishment in England and Sweden in the 1980s', *Studies on Crime and Crime Prevention*, Vol. 2, p. 142.

Forst, B. and Lynch, J.P. (1997), 'The Decomposition and Graphical Analysis of Crime and Sanctions Data: A cross-national application', *Journal of Quantitative Criminology*, Vol 13(2), p. 97.

Fox, R.G. and Freiberg, A. (1999), *Sentencing: State and federal law in Victoria*, 2nd edn, Melbourne: Oxford University Press.

Frase, R. (1990), 'Comparative Criminal Justice as a Guide to American Law Reform: How do the French do it, how can we find out, and why should we care?', *California Law Review*, Vol. 78, p. 545.

Freiberg, A. (1987), 'Reconceptualizing Sanctions', *Criminology*, Vol. 25, p. 223.

Freiberg, A. and Fox, R.G. (1986), 'Sentencing Structures and Sanction Hierarchies', *Criminal Law Journal*, Vol. 10, p. 216.

Jones, M. and Austin, J. (1993), *How Much Time Do Prisoners Really Do?*, Washington: NCCD Focus.

Kuhn, A. (1998), 'Incarceration Rates: The United States in an international perspective', *Criminal Justice Abstracts*, Vol. 30, p. 321.

Langan, P.A. and Farrington, D.P. (1998), *Crime and Justice in the United States and in England and Wales, 1981–96*, Washington: US Bureau of Justice Statistics.

Lovegrove, A. (1997), *The Framework of Judicial Sentencing*, Washington: Cambridge University Press.

Lynch, J.P. (1988), 'A Comparison of Prison Use in England, Canada, West Germany, and the United States: A limited test of the punitive hypothesis', *Journal of Criminal Law and Criminology*, Vol. 79, p. 180.

Lynch, J.P. (1993), 'A Cross-national Comparison of the Length of Custodial Sentences for Serious Crimes', *Justice Quarterly*, Vol. 10, p. 639.

Schiff, M.F. (1997), 'Gauging the Intensity of Criminal Sanctions: Developing the criminal punishment severity scale (CPSS)', *Criminal Justice Review*, Vol. 22, p. 175.

Tak, P.J.P. (1998), 'Prison Population Growing Faster in the Netherlands than in the US', *Overcrowded Times*, Vol. 9(3), p. 1.

Walmsley, R. (1999), *World Prison Population List*, Home Office, Development and Statistics Directorate, Research Findings No. 88, London.

Wasik, M. and von Hirsch, A. (1988), 'Punishments in the Community and the Principles of Desert', *Criminal Law Review*, p. 555.

Young, W. and Brown, M. (1993), 'Cross-national Comparisons of Imprisonment', in M. Tonry (ed.), *Crime and Justice: A review of research*, Vol. 17, Chicago: University of Chicago Press.

Zimring, F. and Hawkins, G. (1991), *The Scale of Imprisonment*, Chicago: University of Chicago Press.

Chapter Twelve

Sentencing Burglars in England and Finland: A Pilot Study

Malcolm Davies, Jukka-Pekka Takala and Jane Tyrer

Introduction

The aim of our research was to understand how judges make decisions with regard to sentencing in the very specific case of dwelling house burglary. As cross-European harmonisation is currently a hot issue in the field of criminal justice we sought to identify some of the differences in the way that judges went about the business of sentencing burglars in two European jurisdictions.

This chapter describes the methodology used in a comparative project to contrast the approach that judges adopt when sentencing for dwelling house burglary in England and Wales, and Finland. This chapter also describes the pilot study with judges in England and contrasts the differences in the way burglars are sentenced in Finland.

The study focused on the following aspects of sentencing in each jurisdiction: firstly, the factors and influences that make up the assessment of offence seriousness; secondly, whether it is possible to identify the type of case that straddles the custodial/noncustodial threshold; thirdly, clarifying the objectives that judges have in mind when sentencing for this type of offence or offender; and, finally, an evaluation of the degree of confidence that judges have in the available sentences for this offence and to identify the innovations or additional requirements that would increase their confidence in the use of community sentences.

We focused on sentencing for the offence of dwelling-house burglary because it is less ambiguous and easier to define than most offences, and thus facilitates comparisons across jurisdictions. It is also an offence which can result in either a custodial or noncustodial sentence.

Methodology

Focus groups were used to ask judges to consider six scenarios (reduced to five in the main study) describing a range of examples of offences of burglary involving adult offenders. The scenarios varied in value of property stolen, the degree of premeditation, and in the criminal background of the offender. One scenario included a heroin user. Thus the scenarios focused on the variables of offence seriousness, culpability and recidivism. In response to these scenarios each judge was asked to indicate broadly the type of sentence they would have given and the purpose of sentencing in relation to the objectives of retribution, denunciation, rehabilitation, deterrence, restitution or incapacitation. The panellists were asked if they have any proposals that would enhance their confidence in using particular sentences, especially as regards their willingness to use community sanctions.

Secondary statistical data was used to provide information about the distribution of aggregate sentencing decisions in the different jurisdictions for dwelling house burglary.

The focus group setting proves a more informal and relaxed environment which can generate greater insight than more structured methods of seeking information. The generation of unanticipated information in the respondents' own words allows the respondents an opportunity to introduce their own themes, issues and questions. The interactive and group nature of the discussions allow for clarification of ideas through probing by other panellists as well as the moderator, to provide information on the:

- extent of knowledge about a topic;
- perceived objectives of the task;
- opinions about the topic;
- degrees of sympathy or hostility towards an existing practice or a new policy;
- underlying assumptions, stereotypes and imagery used.

In this project we used stimuli material provided by six scenarios of burglars as a concrete starting point for the discussions. A list of questions and the scenarios were sent to the judges in advance with brief descriptions of the offence, the offender and the response of the victim (see below). During the discussions we asked them to clarify the factors influencing their choice of sentence, and asked what factors would enable them to consider a noncustodial sentence. We sought to identify the factors, assumptions and objectives that shape individual judge's approaches to sentencing within the framework provided by legislation, policy and guidelines.

The group discussions in England and Wales involved between three and eight judges with a moderator and a research assistant. The meeting started with the moderator asking each judge to indicate in very general terms what type of sentence they would think appropriate before going on to discuss the wider sentencing issues raised by the questions. In the final full report from the three jurisdictions the specific sentences given for each case will be set out in a comparative tabular form.

The session was moderated to encourage a free discussion of opinion and typically lasted about 90 minutes. The moderator conducted the meeting more as a prolonged discussion rather than as a meeting with a set agenda and the research assistant recorded the session and made notes on the comments. These comments were used as the basis of a written report indicating the range of views (see examples below). The written report does not indicate the individual source. The session was audio-recorded to ensure accuracy. In England and Wales the report was sent to the Resident Judge for circulation to check for accuracy and for further clarification if necessary.

In each jurisdiction a pilot group or groups was conducted. In England and Wales two pilot groups met: one with a group of magistrates and a second with Crown Court judges. An extract from the report on the pilot study conducted with Crown Court judges follows, including a summary of substantive issues raised, and a selection of responses to the scenarios and comments in relation to the questions and scenarios. The answers given by the five judges in the pilot study were not necessarily the same as the views of the 51 judges at the 11 Crown Court centres that formed the main body of the study in England and Wales (a report of the full study will be published in due course).

To illustrate the process, details of Case 1 and 2 are included below with some of the comments from the pilot study with judges in England and Wales. Case 1 was constructed to be the least serious example of burglary we presented judges with and Case 2 the most serious:

Case 1

Burglary of an unoccupied flat, during the hours of daylight, when the residents were at work. Access was gained through an open window with no damage to property. The offence was opportunistic and the items stolen were foodstuffs for the defendant's own consumption.

The offence was discovered as a result of information from an informer, and the defendant admitted guilt to the police when first interviewed and pleaded guilty in court at the first opportunity.

Offender Defendant is of previous good character and has been unemployed for over one year.

Victim Working couple who were in their mid-20s who did not realise initially that they had been victims of a burglary.

Case 2

Burglary of a house at 2 a.m. when the residents were asleep upstairs. An associate of the defendant had visited the house previously to assess the possibility of entry and the likely belongings, posing as salesman. Entry was gained by forcing the outer door. There was some damage. An untidy search was carried out by the defendant though the residents were not disturbed. Jewellery worth £1,000 and of sentimental value was taken and not recovered.

Offender The defendant had three previous convictions for burglary, the latest being for dwelling house burglary for which he was given a custodial sentence and released from prison two months prior to the commission of this offence.

Victims Retired couple who were in their late-60s. The wife was semi-invalid.

In response to Case 1 a prison sentence was possible but all the judges considered a noncustodial sentence most likely. Before arriving at a final decision they indicated that they would have sought further offender information as provided in case papers, pre-sentence report and defence counsel's mitigation statement. Case 2 was seen as the most serious by the judges. They were unanimous that prison was highly likely and one judge said: "Custody is pretty much a certainty in this case". Another judge stated:

> It has all the aggravating features … It's 2 o'clock and they [the victims] were asleep upstairs, there was damage, jewellery of sentimental value [was taken], and he's got convictions. There is some suggestion that he [the offender] might be targeting the weak. [Taking] jewellery, that is an aggravating feature, because it might have substantial victim impact, whether it actually [does or not].

With Case 2 a prison term of four years was indicated by two judges. Another commented that he would like to hear as much as he could about the offender but would expect to give a custodial sentence.

The Context of Sentencing Burglars in England and Finland

To understand the way that burglars are sentenced it is important to clarify how the context differs between the jurisdictions. We have summarised four of these contextual factors in the subheadings that follow.

Legal Definition of Dwelling House Burglary

Burglary is defined in the International Crime Victimisation Survey as "gaining access to a dwelling by the use of force to steal goods". This definition corresponds to the common sense understanding of domestic burglary in England and Wales in which the two essential elements are firstly the idea of illegal entry and secondly the intention to steal money or other property. However, one of the complexities of this research is that even within the very specific activity known as burglary the legal definitions in our two jurisdictions are not the same, in fact there is no separate offence for burglary in the Finnish Penal Code.

The statutory definition in England and Wales (Theft Act 1968, s. 9) means a person can only be a burglar if they enter a building as a trespasser (i.e. without permission or legal entitlement to be in the building). The building can either be a domestic home (dwelling house) or a commercial or public building such as a warehouse or office. In England and Wales the illegal purpose is not limited, as in common understanding, to theft but in England includes the intention to commit rape, grievous bodily harm or criminal damage. Our scenarios focused on the theft motive for burglary.

In most cases the burglar commits an illegal activity having entered a building for that purpose. However under the criminal law in England it is also possible to be defined as a burglar if a person has unlawfully entered a building without an intention of committing a crime and subsequently carries out a theft or serious assault.

A more serious offence called aggravated burglary is committed if the offence outlined above is committed by someone who is in possession of a weapon or explosives, and is punishable by life imprisonment. Our study was explicitly not concerned with aggravated burglary.

In Finland domestic burglary is not an independent crime label in the Penal Code. An individual case would be dealt with as a 'theft' or an 'aggravated theft' – or, under very extenuating circumstances, as a 'petty theft'. The relevant articles are in Chapter 28 of the Penal Code of Finland, 'Theft, embezzlement and unauthorised use' (Act No. 769 of 1990). The relevant basic article states that a person who appropriates movable property from the possession of another shall be sentenced for theft (Article 1 – Simple Theft).

Article 2 defines that a theft is aggravated if it meets two conditions. First, at least one of five alternative specific conditions must be satisfied. Second, the theft must also be deemed aggravated "when assessed as a whole". One of the five conditions relates directly to domestic burglary: "the offender breaks into an occupied residence". (The other four alternatives relate to the high value of the stolen object, the victim's exceptional loss, the victim's helplessness, and use of firearms, explosives or similar dangerous instruments.)

Petty theft is defined in the law as a theft that, "when assessed as a whole, with due consideration to the value of the appropriated property or to the other circumstances connected with the offence, is to be deemed petty".

Aggravated theft has a punishment scale of four months to four years in prison, simple theft goes from a fine to imprisonment for 18 months, and petty theft can only be punished with a fine.

Our expectation was that Finnish judges would normally consider domestic burglaries to be an 'aggravated theft'. Many judges in the Finnish pilot panels indeed took the view that the satisfaction of the criterion 'breaks into an occupied residence' already creates the presumption that the theft is aggravated. However, others placed more emphasis on the 'as a whole' criterion and, when discussing actual scenarios, they often were not quite sure whether they would label the case as 'simple theft' or 'aggravated theft'. For example, a few judges said that Case 1 might even be a petty theft – depending on the nature of further information that such a case in reality would have.

The classification of the offence as simple, aggravated, or petty theft is obviously part of the assessment of its seriousness. Pondering about this allocation also seemed to be a salient part of the judges' overall sentencing deliberation in the pilot sessions. This is why we decided to ask the judges to give a specific crime label for each of the cases presented.

Extent of Burglary

The evidence is that householders in England and Wales have a higher risk of burglary than those in Finland. The International Crime Victimisation studies shows England and Wales as having the highest rate of burglary of the 11 countries included in the 1996 study, with 6.1 completed or attempted burglaries per 100 households during 12 months, whereas Finland had the lowest victimisation rate, 1.2 per every 100 households (Mayhew and White 1997, p. 2). Differences in perception of burglary risk follow the same pattern: In England and Wales 41 per cent of the survey subjects thought burglary very or fairly likely in the coming year while in Finland only 11 per cent thought so (Mayhew and van Dijk 1997 p. 27).

In England and Wales the police recorded 473,000 dwelling house burglaries in 1999; and only 19 per cent of all recorded burglaries were cleared up by the police in 1998/9 (Home Office 2000a, p. 31).

A more reliable guide to the amount and risk of burglary is provided by the British Crime Survey. In 1999 the British Crime Survey (BCS) estimated 1,284,000 burglaries or attempted burglaries of dwellings (Kershaw et al. 2000, p. 17) and that only 32 per cent of all burglaries are reported and recorded by the police. (Home Office 2000a, p. 24). But both the recorded crime rate and the British Crime Survey show a downward decline in burglaries in recent years. The 2000 British Crime Survey shows that "Between 1997 and 1999 the total number of burglaries fell significantly, by 21 per cent" and that the 4.3 per cent of households in England and Wales experienced at least one burglary or attempted burglary in 1999 (Kershaw et al. 2000, pp. 17 and 19).

In Finland, the number of domestic burglaries recorded by the police has remained at about 10,000 a year since 1980 and was 9,763 for 1999 (NRILP 2000). The count includes completed and attempted crimes of theft (both simple, aggravated and petty) from dwellings with an unauthorised entry. Also holiday dwellings, such as summer cottages, are included, but separate spaces such as a basement storage lockers, separate warehouses, garages or saunas are excluded. Victimisation surveys give a picture that is fairly compatible with the police statistics. The 1997 National Victimisation Survey estimated there were 14,000 completed and 13,800 attempted domestic burglaries from the 2.35 million households in Finland; of these, 11,000 were reported to the police (Statistics Finland 2000). The international victimisation surveys conducted in Finland in the 1990s estimate that 0.4 to 0.6 per cent of households have been targets of a completed burglary (Aromaa and Heiskanen 2000). As for trends in domestic burglary, the police statistics show a slight decline since about 1993, but as other burglaries have increased simultaneously researchers suspect that this may be an artefact. During the 1990s, the police may have adopted a stricter definition of *domestic* burglary in its recording practice i.e. the exclusion of separate storage structures etc. might be stricter now than in the early 1990s (NRILP 2000).

Court Process

In England and Wales burglary is a triable-either-way offence, which means that either the magistrates' court or the Crown Court can deal with cases of burglary. The more serious and most adult cases are sent to the Crown Court. In 1998, 20,183 offenders were found guilty or were cautioned by the police for burglary of a dwelling (Home Office 2000a, p. 117).

Cautioning is a form of diversion used by the police for appropriate cases where the offender admits their guilt and is released without a conviction or any penalty. Other cleared cases are sent to the prosecutors: the Crown Prosecution Service. In 1998 for all types of burglary the Crown Prosecution Service started criminal proceedings against 34,400 defendants aged over 18; of these, 9,500 were committed for trial at the Crown Court (Home Office 2000a, p. 141). The rest of the cases, unless they were discontinued, were dealt with in the magistrates' court.

Most burglars admit their guilt and do not therefore have a contested trial. In 1998, of those aged over 18 sent to the Crown Court (all forms of burglary offences) having indicated an initial plea of 'not guilty', 77 per cent decided to plead guilty (Home Office 2000a, p. 135). This high proportion of guilty pleas in England and Wales is explained to a considerable extent by the inducement of a sentence discount for a guilty plea.

In Finland, most domestic burglaries would go to court but in exceptional circumstances burglary cases might not reach the court. Some cases go to mediation and may be dropped by the prosecutor if a settlement is reached. The prosecutor can also give a summary penal order, which can be at most a fine. Also, for the prosecutor to be able to consider issuing a summary penal order, the original crime must not carry a reasonable possibility of attracting a prison sentence that is longer than six months.

In Finland, there is only one court of first instance that deals with crimes. Of those crimes that are disposed of by the court, 75 per cent are decided by a group of judges consisting of both professional and lay judges, the most common composition being that of one professional judge plus three lay judges (in complicated cases, there can be an additional professional judge and an additional lay judge). A single professional judge handles the remaining 25 per cent of court decisions. Summary proceeding with a single professional judge is possible for cases carrying a maximum of 18 months imprisonment.

The single judge can only impose a fine. This means that in principle, a single judge could decide not only cases of petty theft but also of simple theft, but it must be clear from the very beginning that such a theft is at the lower end of the potential punishment scale.

Sentencing Process and Sentencing Options and Usage

In Finland the courts have available a very limited range of sentencing options when compared to England and Wales. The Finnish Penal Code lists 'general punishments' as follows: "imprisonment, community service, fine and summary penal fee" (Ch. 2, Art. 1, as amended 12 December 1996). However, 'imprisonment' can mean either unconditional or conditional imprisonment the latter of which is rather similar to the suspended sentence in England and Wales, i.e., the offender does not go to prison. A further complication is that community service is strictly considered an alternative to unconditional imprisonment. Technically, it is an unconditional prison sentence that has been commuted to community service (see Takala 1993, p. 24). By law, commuting is the general rule if the sentence is not longer than eight months and the person is deemed suitable (i.e. likely to be able to carry out the order) by the court. The court usually follows the suitability assessment prepared by the probation and after-care association. Even if the offender is found suitable, commuting to community service may be prevented, if it is 'deemed that unconditional prison sentences, earlier community service sentences or other weighty reasons constitute a bar for sentencing to community service' (Law on Community Service, Art. 3). In practice, slightly less than one half of the commutable cases are commuted (44 per cent in 1998).

In England and Wales judges and magistrates have guidelines when sentencing burglars. The statutory maximum is rarely if ever used and there is a limited degree of disparity between judges, most noticeably when different Crown Court centres are compared. Guidance to judges in England and Wales is given through the Court of Appeal decisions on sentencing appeals with special significance attached to the guideline cases (e.g. Brewster 1998 for dwelling house burglary). When dealt with in the magistrates' courts the Magistrates' Guidelines list factors and principles to apply. These guidelines indicate the offence is more serious if it was committed at night; by a group of offenders; with a professional element; if ransacking, vandalism or soiling took place; or, if the occupants were at home.

Unlike Finland there are few minimum sentences and there is no minimum for first time offenders convicted of dwelling house burglary; the maximum sentence is 14 years (Theft Act 1968) although this period is rarely if ever used. Of all the 7,484 adult burglars (for all types of burglary) received into prison in 1999, 165 had a sentence of between 5–10 years, and nine had sentences over ten years (Home Office 2000b, p. 90).

A recent change to sentencing law in England and Wales has introduced a minimum sentence for those convicted of burglary on more than two occasions. The Crime (Sentences) Act 1997 came into force in 1999 and requires a three-year mandatory minimum sentence to be imposed (except in the most exceptional circumstances) for offenders convicted of a third separate offence of dwelling house burglary.

It is an accepted principle formalised by the Criminal Justice and Public Order Act 1994 (s. 48) that a timely plea of guilt will be rewarded by a sentence discount. For all types of burglary cases sentenced at the Crown Court in 1998 the average sentence for those pleading guilty was 22.8 months and 28.5 months for those convicted following a not guilty plea (Home Office 2000a, p. 153).

Non-custodial penalties are used for burglary. In England and Wales in 1996 of the total number of offenders (17,087) sentenced in magistrates' courts and Crown Court for dwelling house burglary: 6,261 (37 per cent) received a community sentence and 9,101 (53 per cent) were given immediate custody, other sentences accounting for 1,726 (10 per cent) (Home Office, 1997). The figures for community sentences given above reflect, in part, their greater use by magistrates in the Youth Court when sentencing those aged less than 18 years of age.

The judges in our study made it clear that adults convicted in the Crown Court for dwelling house burglary could expect a prison sentence. This was confirmed by the results of a Home Office study of sentencing (Flood-Page and Mackie 1998) based on a survey of 3,000 sentencing cases in 25 magistrates' courts and 2,000 sentencing cases in 18 Crown Court centres. The results showed that in the Crown Court 72 per cent of domestic burglaries were given a prison sentence (Flood-Page 1998, p. 82).

Burglars make up 17 per cent of the sentenced prison population. On 30 June 1999 of those in prison who had been sentenced 8,780 had been convicted of burglary out of a population of 51,298 sentenced prisoners or 17 per cent of all sentenced prisoners (these figures exclude those who are held on remand in prison awaiting trial or sentence). On release from prison it is unlikely that the burglar will change their ways as 76 per cent of male prisoners convicted and imprisoned for burglary are reconvicted of an offence within two years of release (Home Office 2000b, p. 156).

Finnish court data and prison statistics have no separate figures for burglaries, domestic or otherwise. In 1998, 496 people were found guilty of aggravated theft, 4,857 of simple theft, and 28,031 of petty theft (Statistics Finland 1999). For simple theft, 24 per cent of those found guilty received an unconditional prison sentence, 10 per cent a community service order, 19 per cent a conditional (suspended) prison sentence, and 46 per cent fines. For aggravated theft, the corresponding figures were: 52 per cent unconditional prison, 11 per cent community service, 35 per cent conditional (suspended) sentence, and 0.6 per cent fines. Almost all unconditional prison sentences for simple theft and 55 per cent of those for aggravated theft were 8 months or less, which means that they were in principle commutable to community service. However, only 31 per cent of them were actually commuted. This means that thieves are less often than the average offender (44 per cent) deemed suitable for community service.

The Finnish prison population on an average day in 1999 was 2,743. When robbery is excluded, a little less than a quarter (23.4 per cent) of them were serving time for a property crime, based on the offence for which the longest sentence had been imposed (Prison Service in Finland 2000).

In this section we have described the definition of burglary, differences in the extent of burglary and the processing of burglary cases in the two jurisdictions. In the next section we include comments in response to the questions about sentencing that developed out of the specific issues of what to do with the burglar in the scenarios we described. We have limited the next section to the response of judges in the pilot in England and Wales.

The impact of the different ways of defining burglary, the different criminal justice processes and diverse sentencing options are self-evident. Less immediately obvious in their impact on such a study as this are the rates of crime, public and judicial perceptions of crime, the information available at the time of sentencing, the assumed purpose of sentencing, and the credibility and appropriateness of the different types of sentences available to the judges. The comments that follow indicate the significance of these factors to the judges who took part in the pilot study in England and Wales.

Judges' Views on Sentencing in England and Wales: Extracts taken from the Report on the Pilot Study with Judges in England and Wales[1]

(Words appearing in brackets have been added by the authors to enhance clarity.)

What Information is Needed to give a Specific Sentence?

In discussing the scenarios the judges stated that they would normally wish to see a pre-sentence report even if a prison sentence was likely. The judges commented that they looked at a variety of information about the person's background and motivation, and, given that, in the scenario in Case 1 we presented an offender aged 24 with no previous convictions, why he would have started offending at this age.

The importance of a pre-sentence report was recognised as potentially influencing in some cases whether custody was used. One judge commented:

> (If we) sentence this person without a pre-sentence report and there is a possible end (to the commission) of domestic burglaries ... custody is not necessarily inevitable.

Another judge said: "In virtually every case, I ask for a pre-sentence report even if I know I'm going to send them to prison because sometimes something crops up that is relevant as to the length".

When asked how they responded to the recommendations in pre-sentence reports from the Probation Service, a judge said: "Some (probation officers) ... I would take on trust what they said about the situation and some I wouldn't". This view, repeated by many judges, has obvious implications for judges' views about the credibility of using community sentences.

What is the Purpose of Sentencing Burglars?

Judges were asked about their sentencing objectives. The multiple goals that need to be kept in mind was commented upon by one judge:

> Depending on the facts, your objectives may change. Potentially there is a range of objectives one may have. You might have *protection of the public*, particularly for night time burglaries, which is why people would think a substantial sentence would be appropriate ... At the lower end of the scale it may be (that) something constructive could be done to help *prevent a particular offender from offending*

again. So one can't say what one's sentencing objectives are specifically until one knows more about the case.

Another judge showed reluctance to articulate sentencing objectives:

> I don't think of myself in that posh term ... that I come into court with objectives. My only objective is to pass a *just sentence* in the circumstances. I don't have high flown philosophical ideas such as denunciation.

Another commented with the approval of several others:

> I believe the primary expectation should be that if you commit a burglary you would go to prison ... I don't think in fact, speaking personally that I have a sentencing objective. I think that is a fallacy. We don't have sentencing objectives ... (other than) to pass a just sentence ... Circumstances are infinitely variable and ... people are being sentenced this very day, up and down the country, by 550 other circuit judges ... we try to achieve some sort of parity within the guidelines set down by the Court of Appeal.

However, several judges did refer to *general deterrence* as a primary objective of sentencing in burglary cases. A judge said as part of a statement articulating a general deterrent approach: "I'm in the business of reducing the number of burglaries". Another stated:

> I believe the primary purpose for this kind of offence is to set down a marker ... a framework for this particular kind of offence ... is to show that there is a risk of something unpleasant happening to you if you commit this type of offence.

One judge commented on the ineffectiveness of deterrence in that burglars do not calculate the benefits of their crime. Another judge disagreed with this and argued that a prison sentence does have a deterrent value. He said:

> If we were not sending domestic burglars to prison, I would be quite satisfied in my mind that there would be many more ... burglaries committed. Deterrence does work, you can see it in a totally different context if you look at the fact that it is generally known that if you exceed the speed limit by more than 30 miles an hour you are in danger of being disqualified ... A fear of the consequences I am certain is a motivating factor in a significant number of peoples' minds.

The word 'marker' was used by one judge, to indicate the potential deterrent for those contemplating burglary. Another judge used the word 'marker' to indicate that the purpose of sentencing is *denunciatory*. The judge said:

I'm not sure that I don't think it is a marker more for ... denunciation rather than deterrence. I'm not a great believer that deterrence really deters ... I don't think it's unduly cynical to look on most sentencing as a largely theatrical exercise. The tiny proportion of crime that leads to an arrest and actually ultimately comes to a sentence is minute. Therefore what one is doing is ... by way of sentencing, within the legal framework to do something that appears just and that means just in the eyes of the right thinking and normal people. If they think about it, burgling houses is a very cruel and horrible thing to do and custody is the nastiest thing that a court can do to reflect that view. I think that's a perfectly legitimate and proper reason for imposing sentences of imprisonment almost as a norm for domestic burglaries.

Under what Circumstances is Prison Inevitable for Burglars?

The judges were asked whether there were any circumstances that made prison inevitable when sentencing in burglary cases. One judge was clear: "Yes, night time burglary". Although another judge said: " I don't think there's such thing as inevitability in a sentence". One judge commented: "If the crime is not so serious then you are able to think of noncustodial. You might try something else that hasn't been tried in the last 10 years".

When asked about unusual cases of burglary one judge concluded that almost anything could happen: "One would be thinking of a very long sentence but is not inconceivable that there might be something that would cause you to send him for rehabilitation". A judge illustrated this with an example:

> If he had walked into a police station and they weren't even investigating (the crime and) he admits he has a drug habit and has done these dreadful things (and says) I have got myself lined up to go to a clinic and I want to get these things off my chest ... it could be the difference between 8 or 9 years and a (much lesser sentence).

In one of the cases the burglar was a heroin addict. We found in both the pilot and the wider study of judges that the sentence in this case was the least predictable with some judges regarding this as a potential case for rehabilitation. Other judges took the view that in all likelihood the offending behaviour would continue because of drug use. No judge excluded the possibility of a rehabilitative noncustodial sentence although the need to demonstrate the effectiveness of the treatment strategy was a key influence on their willingness to consider such a sentence.

What could Lead to a Greater use of Community Penalties?

The judges were asked whether there were reforms to the existing method of implementing community sentences that would allow them to make greater use of them when sentencing burglars.

One judge commented that offenders were not afraid of community penalties. Another commented about their perceptions of community penalties:

> Community service has missed the boat as being a serious sentence, in the sense of being closer to a prison sentence, because it is seen as being a rehabilitative sentence.

Another agreed and offered an explanation of this:

> Community service is conceived of as a soft option in this country ... because of the gentle and pleasant attitude of the nice probation officers and community service organisers who run it all, who faint with horror at the idea that anyone on an order should be seen by any member of the public.

There were comments about the reluctance of probation officers to bring breach proceedings for offenders who have broken the terms of their community sentence. A judge commented: "Breaches take far too long to reach us". And another said: "They should be breached at once instead of giving them endless chances". Another judge commented: "They need to be breached at once. Sometimes it can take nine months before they are back in court".

Another judge commented in response to a suggestion that weekend imprisonment could be introduced: "A good idea. Sometimes just a short time in prison will work".

Conclusion

A judge in our pilot study observed: "Sentencing is not a science" and another believed: "There is no pattern, it's all part of a general complicated issue". If sentencing is not a science it does not follow that it is a random or unpredictable activity as recognised by the judge who commented on the shifts in the tariff over time.

> From the time I have been in this business ... the fashion about what sentencing is about, what is normal, what is the right sentence, has changed and changed

and changed again. I am absolutely convinced that nobody knows what the right sentence is.

The reality is that sentencing is not a science in the sense of being able to measure on an independent scale the level of seriousness of an offence, or to calibrate the exact amount of punishment to dispense. Offences can however be ranked in terms of seriousness of offence as measured by harm done, and a list of penalties can be drawn up based on a criterion of more or less serious, i.e. ordinal proportionality. This raises issues as to the basis of judgements about achieving proportionality in sentencing terms and how, and who, is to determine in each jurisdiction:

- the seriousness of an individual offence within the general pattern of offending behaviour;
- the priority given to the multitude of objectives or purposes of sentencing (deterrence, retribution, denunciation, incapacitation, rehabilitation and restitution);
- the particular needs of, and the risk presented by, the offender;
- the incorporation of the expectations of the public in general and victims in particular;
- the definition and criteria of consistency; and
- how we identify an unjust sentence?

People differ in their rankings of seriousness and judgements about desert and the purpose of sentencing, but without some consensus the idea of a just sentence becomes difficult to demonstrate.

Sentencing is akin to other cultural activities and changes with the intellectual fashions of the time. Hence the question is raised of how best to respond to change and the relative influence of bodies in England and Wales such as parliament, the Judicial Studies Board, the Sentencing Advisory Panel and the Court of Appeal. The question of how to deal with change underlines the importance in sentencing research of understanding the criminal justice context in which sentencing operates. It is therefore necessary to analyse sentencing in the appropriate context and with methods that are sensitive to culturally derived perspectives of the key actors.

The reliance on a qualitative and ethnographic approach to comparisons in sentencing policy has brought home to us the problems of making comparisons across jurisdictions. We have come to further appreciate the crucial need to understand the domestic context of sentencing. In particular we found it important to understand the implications of differences across jurisdictions of the following details: the definitions of the offence; the common perceptions of the seriousness of the offence; ideas about the frequency of the offence; role of the victim and the public; the system differences concerning diversion and the inter-dependencies in the system that directly affect sentence, decisions such as diversion which affects the type of cases that reach court, the effect of pleading guilty or time spent in custody awaiting trial; the differences in the role and status of the judges; understanding of the goals of sentencing and how these are balanced by individual judges; the range of sentencing available and their significance; views about the implementation and effects of sentencing; and the differences in the discretion available to judges.

Trying to take all these considerations into account led us to the conclusion at one business meeting in Oslo that comparative sentencing research was a bit like skiing up hill.

Arie Freiberg's work in this book shows that he is not averse to attempting an uphill struggle in his analysis and search for a more reliable guide to measuring penal severity across jurisdictions. He has identified many of the complexities that get in the way of such a comparison and seeks to overcome the problems of cultural relativity and system difference which make life hard for the comparative scholar. Freiberg attempts (along with Farrington and Langan 1998) to provide a more sophisticated approach which involves comparing specific offences such as burglary.

The difficulties do not lead us to suggest that comparative research is impossible, but its possibility depends on an appreciation of the cultural context of the policies, procedures and practice of sentencing. Statements to the effect that country X sends more (or fewer) criminals to prison than other countries for the crime of Y must be understood within the complexities of the differing systems and cultures.

Focusing on one offence is in our opinion the way forward to allow for realistic comparisons across jurisdictions. However we have opted for a more qualitative approach to comparisons through a case study of specific scenarios. We have not therefore used the existing indices that are usually constructed for other purposes, because of the potential misperceptions and misunderstanding. The cross-jurisdictional indices of league tables are very crude measures that might confuse as much as illuminate the issue of penal severity.

We do not see our comparative case study approach as competing with the attempts to quantify and measure penal severity. Before any meaningful comparisons can be made we would argue that first a qualitative case-by-case comparison in a systematic way should be undertaken to ensure that the measures used in the league tables are comparable. To adopt a metaphor from Association Football, if we compare the German and Italian league tables could we reach any conclusions, about the relative excitement of the game as measured by the number of goals scored? We would have to ensure that both leagues are playing by the same rules, with the same size grounds and goalposts, that the referees interpret the rules in the same way, that the crowds have the same influence on the referee's decisions, and that the crowd, players and coaches in both countries were equally interested in, and committed to, a high scoring game.

Comparative sentencing research is important but it must be done firstly, in a contextual way so that the different legal-cultural meanings are understood. Secondly, comparative scholars should be familiar with the complexities of the criminal justice system they are contrasting because of the nature of the interdependencies within a criminal justice system, e.g. the effect of plea on sentence.

So far this study has confirmed our conclusion in an earlier work, *Penological Esperanto and Sentencing Parochialism* (Davies et al. 1996) in that attempts to achieve jurisdictional harmonisation across Europe (see Ashworth in this book) will not be easy even in the very limited case of sentencing dwelling house burglars. Our study has become in part a study of comparative judicial cultures and legal systems. It is also, our experience so far suggests, about contrasting cultural evaluations of the significance of burglary within a society. As the issue of censuring bad behaviour is central to the way society come to define itself it is therefore not surprising that countries with different problems and histories have different views on such matters. This is a problem for those who think harmonisation of crime policies is primarily a matter of getting governments to sign up to cross-jurisdictional policy statements.

Acknowledgements

We wish to express our thanks to the Scandinavian Research Council for Criminology, the Nuffield Foundation, London, and Thames Valley University for funding the project.

Note

1   In this section we give some of the comments made by the judges during the pilot focus group discussion in England and Wales. The comments that follow illustrate the extent of the variations in attitudes amongst the judges in one Crown Court Centre towards such key issues as the purpose of sentencing and the use of prison and community penalties when sentencing burglars.

Such variations give cause to be wary of comparative studies that are based on assumptions about the homogeneity of outlook amongst the judiciary. It also reinforces the need to take care when making cross-jurisdictional generalisations and to adopt methodologies that can encompass the complexity of the phenomena under study.

A full report of this comparative study that includes England and Wales, Finland and Norway will be published at a later date.

References

Aromaa, K. and Heiskanen, M. (2000), 'Risk of Crime in Finland: Advance results on Finland from the 2000 International Crime Victims Survey' [in Finnish], mimeograph, 22 June, Helsinki: National Research Institute of Legal Policy.

Ashworth, A., this volume.

Davies, M., Takala, J.-P. and Tyrer, J. (1996), *Penological Esperanto and Sentencing Parochialism*, Dartmouth: Aldershot.

Farrington, D. and Langan, P. (1998), *Crime and Justice in the United States and in England and Wales, 1986–96*, Washington: US Department of Justice.

Flood-Page, C. and Mackie, A. (1998), *Sentencing Practice: An examination of decisions in magistrates' courts and the Crown Court in the mid-1990s*, Home Office Research Study 180, London: Home Office.

Freiberg, A., this volume.

Home Office (1995), *National Standards for the Supervision of Offenders in the Community*, Home Office Probation Service Division, London: Home Office.

Home Office (1997), Crime and Criminal Justice Unit, special figures produced on request, 28 November 1997, Home Office, London.

Home Office (2000a), *Criminal Statistics England and Wales 1998*, London: Stationery Office.

Home Office (2000b), *Prison Statistics England and Wales 1999*, London: Stationery Office.

Kershaw, C., Budd, T., Kinshott, G., Mattinson, J., Mayhew, P. and Myhill, A. (2000), *The 2000 British Crime Survey*, Home Office Statistical Bulletin 18/00, London: Stationery Office.

Law on Community Service (Finland 1997), Finnish Statute No. 1055/1996 as amended by No. 754/1997.

Mayhew, P. and White, P. (1997), *The 1996 International Crime Victimisation Survey*, Home Office Statistical Bulletin No. 57, London: Stationery Office.

NRILP (2000), *Crime and Criminal Justice in Finland 1999*, Helsinki: National Research Institute of Legal Policy.

Prison Service in Finland (2000), 'Principal Offence of Prisoners According to their Age', available via http://www.vankeinhoito.fi/5127.htm as http://www.vankeinhoito.fi/uploads/w7wl8ji5q4.pdf. (accessed 24 October 2000]).

Statistics Finland (1999), *Yearbook of Justice Statistics 1999*, Helsinki: Statistics Finland.
Statistics Finland (2000), Preliminary Results from the 1997 National Victimisation Survey, unpublished tables, Helsinki: Statistics Finland.
Takala, J.-P. (1993), 'Finland's Experiment with Community Service: How to combine mitigation, quality experience and fairness?', *The IARCA Journal on Community Corrections*, Vol. 5, No. 5 (April), pp. 23–8.

Chapter Thirteen

A New Look at Sentence Severity

Brian J. Ostrom and Charles W. Ostrom Jr

Introduction

Measurement matters. Measuring the severity of prison sentences is fundamental to analysing and interpreting sentencing practices in US courts. The issue is finding a measure of sentence severity that fits the actual decision-making practices of judges. Since convicted offenders serve a period of incarceration usually stated in months or years, the uttered sentence offers the obvious choice. Indeed, many see the uttered sentence as the natural dependent variable for explaining the severity of prison sentences. In this article, however, we show that using months or years as a measure of sentence severity causes problems for statistical analysis, and may result in misleading and inappropriate policy conclusions.

Actual sentence length may not be consistent with a continuous 'scale of severity'. Consider the distribution of prison sentences among 9,586 offenders convicted in the State of Michigan in 1995. As can be seen in Figure 13.1, prison sentences range from one month to 480 months.[1] Michigan judges are free to assign any term of days, months, or years they wish. However, it is clear that a small number of sentences predominate: 12, 18, 20, 24, 30, 36, 48, 60, 72, 84, 96, and 120 months. These 10 terms account for over 78 per cent of sentences issued in 1995. In addition, there are prominent 'spikes' at 180, 240, 300, 360, and 480 months. The interval between the prominent sentences varies over the range, increasing in intervals of six months from 12 to 36 months, of 12 from 36 to 96 months, of 24 from 96 to 120 months, of 60 from 120 to 360 months, and by an interval of 120 months thereafter. Recognising these patterns – the small number of selected sentences as well as their irregular spacing – is of more than theoretical interest. It is fundamental to designing and evaluating sentencing policy.

How the dependent variable – sentence severity – is measured clearly affects the conclusions reached by the research and policy community concerning consistency, disparity, and proportionality in sentencing. The lack of consensus about what the data say is a reminder that there continues to be

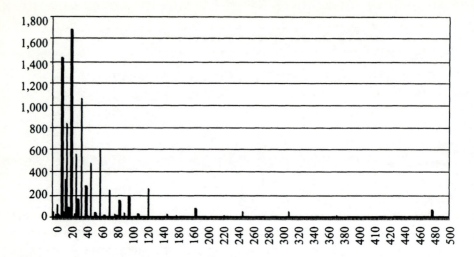

Figure 13.1   1995 prison sentences

considerable debate and experimentation in the literature about how to best measure the basic incarceration outcome. We contend that an important foundation of credible, statistically based inferences of sentencing outcomes is explicit recognition of the *sentence* decision-making process. Efforts to model felony sentencing should be based on how judges actually sentence.

We present our argument in five sections. First, we examine earlier efforts to explain and develop a rationale for the observed pattern of judges selecting from among a limited or 'preferred' set of sentencing options. In the second section, we review the strengths and weaknesses of the two major research strategies employed to measure sentence severity. In section three we develop a new measure of sentence severity – the sentencing unit – based on theoretical responses to three fundamental questions posed by observed patterns of judicial sentencing as shown in Figure 13.1:

- why do judges choose from among a limited number of sentencing options?
- what explains the prevalence of certain prominent sentences?
- what accounts for irregular spacing between prominent sentences?

In section four, we test the statistical strength of the new measure, and clarify the nature of the improved inferences about the sentencing process using an extensive set of recent sentencing data drawn from the circuit courts of Michigan. The paper concludes with a discussion of the research and policy implications of the new measure of sentencing severity.

Sentencing by the Numbers

The notion that there are 'irregularities' in sentencing is not new. Writing in the 20 June 1895 issue of *Nature*, Francis Galton (p. 174) remarked: "it would have been expected that the various terms of imprisonment awarded by judges should fall into a continuous series. This is not the case ... ". Galton's observation of the 1890s regarding the "extreme irregularity of terms of imprisonment" (p. 175) applies with equal force to sentencing practice today, 105 years later.

Assessing a diagram similar to Figure 13.1, Galton (1895, p. 175) went on to say:

> It is impossible to believe that a judicial system acts fairly, which, when it allots only 20 sentences to 6 years imprisonment, allots as many as 240 to 5 years, as few as 60 to 4 years, and as many as 360 to 3 years. Or that, while there are 20 sentences to 19 months, there should be 300 to 18 months, none to 17, 30 to 16, and 150 to 15 ... *Runs of figures like these testify to some powerful cause of disturbance which interferes with the orderly distribution of punishment in conformity with penal deserts* (emphasis added).

Galton contended that these gaps (e.g. many sentences are given for 15 and 20 years but none for 16, 17, 18, and 19) do not occur by chance, and believed we must make an effort to understand the "disturbing cause or causes that stand in the way of appropriate sentences" (Galton, 1895, p. 175).

Galton (1895, p. 176) summed his discussion of sentence 'irregularity' this way:

> I will conclude by moralizing on the large effects upon the durance of a prisoner, that flow from such irrelevant influences as the association connected with ... *the unconscious favour or disfavour felt for particular numbers*. These trifles have been now shown on fairly trustworthy evidence to determine the choice of such widely different sentences as imprisonment for 3 or 5 years, of 5 or 7 years, and of 7 or 10, for crimes whose penal deserts would otherwise be rated at 4, 6 and 8 or 9 years respectively (emphasis added).

Profound policy consequences follow from observed judicial preferences for only a limited number of sentence options. We may compromise the goal of individualised sentencing, fine-tuned to the circumstances of each offender. Questions of public safety arise if offenders receive less than their just deserts. At the same time, if "favour for particular numbers" leads to sentences that exceed penal deserts, then prisoners suffer unduly, and we may squander scarce, expensive prison space because of a 'quirk' of judicial decision-making.

Fitzmaurice and Pease (1986) explore two theoretical rationales for observed irregularities in felony sentences. First, they look at the possibility that the pattern is a matter of "just noticeable differences". Using the Weber-Fechner Law, which holds that just noticeable differences in the intensity of various responses are proportional to the intensity of the stimulus, they investigate the proposition that the differences between observed sentences are proportional. However, as an examination of the differences between prominent sentences in Figure 13.1 reveals, such proportional increases are *not* the case. The jump from 12 to 18 months represents an increase of 50 per cent, from 18 to 24 a 33 per cent increase, from 24 to 30 a 25 per cent increase, from 30 to 36 a 20 per cent increase, from 36 to 48 is 33 per cent again, and from 48 to 60 months is 25 per cent. The same holds for longer sentences: the jump from 60 to 72 is a 20 per cent increase, from 72 to 84 is 16 per cent, from 84 to 96 represents a 14 per cent increase, from 96 to 120 months is 25 per cent, and from 120 to 180 months we are back to a 50 per cent increase.

Fitzmaurice and Pease (1986, pp. 106–7) also investigate the idea of "preferred numbers".

> An alternative way of looking at the choice of length of sentence would be to take the idea of preferred numbers and assume that the choice of sentence length, expressed in numbers, had to do with some property of the numbers themselves. Indeed, if there were not a marked preference for certain sentence lengths, one would expect that all sentence lengths would be imposed and the gaps in [Figure 13.1] would not have appeared.

They then ask whether the scale of preferred numbers can be generated by some mathematical formula, echoing the work of Baird and Norma (1975). They do not successfully obtain a formulaic generator for the preferred numbers, except to note that judges appear to "operate with multiples of 3 with short sentences, with multiples of 6 in the middle range sentences, and on a scale based on 12 for long sentences" (1986, p. 108). The changing nature of the scale of preferred numbers leads Fitzmaurice and Pease to hypothesise that judges employ a sentencing scale where "no sentences are more than 25 per cent or less than 10 per cent higher than the sentence below …" (p. 112). By extension, they seem to suggest that judges use an approximate and underlying severity scale that is different from an interval/ratio scale measured in terms of months of incarceration.

While Fitzmaurice and Pease failed to uncover a mathematically derived severity scale that fully and accurately describes observed sentencing practice, they contend their analysis does have heuristic value for policy development:

> What the pattern of preferred numbers and jnds (just noticeable differences) shows is rough justice, not injustice. Judges increase sentence length apace with what they regard as culpability. They are approximate in their sentence lengths because they are approximate in the assessment of culpability: in this sense the crudity of assignation of sentence length does not seriously distort the proportionality between culpability and sentence length. Nonetheless there are important policy implications of the work for penal policy. First, the number preferences in sentencing should be taken into account in sentencing legislation. Second, the use of conventional number preferences in sentencing choice probably protects sentencers from thinking about what a sentence means in practice, and the implications of this need to be explored (p. 113).

The policy implications of "conventional number preferences" are at least threefold. First, the potential for inconsistency – or at least the appearance of inconsistency – is rampant. If, for example, the 'just' sentence for an offender is 180 months, but the judge goes down one preferred sentence level for one offender and up one preferred sentence for another offender, the difference between the two sentences could be as much as ten years, and a difference of ten years for similarly-situated offenders looks like inconsistency. Second, inconsistency can easily become disparity if judges enhance the sentences of racial minorities relative to the sentences of racial majorities. In such instances, actual disparities could be quite substantial. Third, public support for state and federal initiatives to increase sentence length for violent offenders puts considerable pressure on available prison space. If judges increase the average sentence for all violent offenders by *one sentencing unit*, the actual period of incarceration for violent offenders entering prison increases substantially more than *one year* on average.

Measuring Sentence Severity in Practice

For the research community, conceptualising sentence severity is critical to choosing a dependent variable. Most empirical sentencing research uses statistical techniques that require an interval measure of severity. However, as noted in the Introduction, it does not appear that uttered sentences constitute an interval scale.[2] Consequently, the field of sentencing research is marked by wide ranging efforts to conceptualise and measure sentence severity. These efforts lead Hagan and Bumiller (1982, p. 10) to note:

One problem in the cumulation of the results from sentencing studies is that they operationalize the dependent variable – sentence – in a variety of different ways. The only clear areas of agreement on this issue seems to be an implicit consensus that sentences can be ordered in terms of severity; the type of ordering applied, however, varies considerably from study to study.

That the extent of agreement within the research community about sentence severity is limited solely to *ordering* underscores the ongoing difficulty of finding a measure of severity that captures what judges are actually doing. We misspecify statistical models if the metric of the dependent variable is not consistent with judicial sentencing practices, and cannot reliably interpret the coefficient estimates they produce. This, in turn, affects the validity of conclusions about such perennial policy issues as consistency, disparity, and proportionality in sentencing.

What have we learned from the last 30 years of experimentation in measuring and scaling sentence severity? Hagan and Bumiller (1983, p. 11) suggest that "[i]n order to cumulate findings [from the sentencing literature], it is necessary to adopt a common standard, or a variety of standards, to be used in some meaningful way across studies". We agree, and distinguish past sentencing research according to which of two primary methods of measuring sentencing severity is used: actual sentence length, or subjectively-derived indexes.

Actual Length of Incarceration

The most widely used method measures severity in terms of the number of months (or years) of the offender's sentence (e.g. Chiricos and Waldo 1975; Kelly 1976; Clarke and Koch 1977; Lizzotte 1978; Zalman et. al. 1979; Thomson and Zingraff 1981; Miethe and Moore 1986; Crew 1991). The advantage of this measure is that it appears on the individual's record, and it is (holding aside the issues of pretrial time served, good time, and parole) the length of time the individual must serve.[3] The problem, however, is that it may not be an interval scale.

Many argue that there is more to a sentence than merely the elapsed time of incarceration. At the very least, one need also consider the length of supervised probation, fines, and/or intermediate sanctions. The split sentence (i.e. one in which the offender receives both incarceration and probation) is an important focus for criticism. It is possible to simply add the term of incarceration to the term of probation. Myers and Talarico (1987), for example, propose a transformation that weights the two and yields an overall measure of severity. It is important to note, however, that they analyse this new dependent variable separately from pur incarceration; it is not directly comparable to their measure of pure inc rceration.

Many observers also question whether the actual months of incarceration constitute an interval or ratio scale. That is, is a sentence of 60 months five times more serious – in the mind of the judge[4] – than a sentence of 12 months? Is a sentence of 120 months – in the mind of the judge – twice as serious as a sentence of 60 months? The answer, for those raising the question, is generally no. Furthermore, the lack of empirical support of regression models of sentencing severity that use months of incarceration may be a consequence of the lack of interval-ness of actual months (e.g. Blumstein et al. 1983).

Those using actual sentence length as the dependent variable employ variations seeking to create interval-ness via a mathematical transformation. Several analysts use a logarithmic transformation. For example, Wheeler, Weisburd, and Bode (1982, p. 653) use the natural log, because it "serves to pull the longest sentences closer to those of six or twelve months, better approximating the actual intervals of the decision that judges make". At least one analyst (Brantingham 1985, p. 300) takes the opposite perspective and squares the actual sentence "to accentuate the difference between short and long jail sentences". The lack of consensus over how to measure months of incarceration (e.g. actual, log, squared), and the relatively low explanatory power of models using any of these measures, has spurred development of alternative scales of sentence severity.

Latent Indexes of Sentence Severity

In response to criticisms levied against using actual sentence as the dependent variable (i.e. it ignores non-incarceration penalties and it is not an interval scale), a number of analysts argue that judges possess a *latent severity scale*, along which they compare all sentencing options. They contend all information relevant to the sentencing decision is summarised in placing the offender on this underlying scale. Because the scale is unobservable, this method assumes judges make decisions *as if* each offender were placed on such a scale.

To tap this latent severity scale, numerous indices of sentence severity have been developed that seek to: (a) include all sentencing outcomes (e.g. suspended sentences, fines, probation, and incarceration) on the same scale;

and (b) weight each of these options to introduce interval-ness to the scale. There are two widely used approaches to this type of scaling.

The first scaling technique, the Administrative Office model, initially developed by the Administrative Office of the US District Court (1967), draws on the subjective experience of the researcher. Tiffany, Avichai, and Peters (1975) (hereafter TAP) use "a slightly modified version of a scale created by the Administrative Office" to express sentence severity 'quantitatively'.[5] The TAP index, shown in the second column of Table 13.1, consists of 12 levels weighted to reflect overall severity.

Cook (1973) modified the TAP scale by multiplying the weights by four and developing combinations of punishments weighted from 0 to 100. Uhlman modified the scale further yet (1977, 1978, 1979). His measure of sanctioning severity "de-emphasizes the breaking point between prison and non-imprisonment, and instead taps subtler differences along a broader sanctioning continuum". Since Uhlman's measure consists of over 90 categories, we rely on his overview (Uhlman 1977, p. 22):

> Joining past theory and practice to the data at hand results in a detailed 93-point sentence severity scale that makes meaningful distinctions between and among degrees of deprivation of individual freedom and the varying severity of non-prison sanctions. The scale breaks down into the following general categories (in increasing order of severity): (1) suspended sentences only (scale value 1); (2) fines only (scale values 2–6); (3) suspended sentences and fines (scale values 7–11); (4) probated sentences and probated sentences with fines (scale values 12–31); and (5) active jail sentences (scale values 32–93). Since all but two of the 93 categories are used, it is evident that judges both perceive and respond to a wide variety of sentencing possibilities available to them.

Uhlman interprets the resulting scale as an interval measure of sentence severity.[6]

The second major scaling strategy, consensual scaling, uses opinion surveys to assess how citizens and/or judges perceive potential penalties, which are then used to construct a severity or seriousness scale based on public perception (e.g. Alpert and Apospori 1993; Buchner 1979; Crouch 1993; Erickson and Gibbs 1979; Petersilia and Deschenes 1995; Sebba 1978; Sebba and Nathan 1984; Spelman 1995; Tremblay 1988). Tremblay (1988) notes:

> Penal severity scales provide ... a reasonable, if only tentative, basis for calculating current exchange rates between qualitatively incommensurable penalties (probation, community work, fine, prison, etc.).

A perceptual study of penal metrics by Buchner (1979) illustrates the strategy. Beginning with a statement of purpose, "to create an interval scale measuring the comparative severity of types of criminal sentences", she notes:

> No successful attempt to place sentences on an interval scale has been made thus far. This situation is remarkable in view of the fact that no sophisticated or reliable comparisons based on severity of sentence can be made without such a tool (p. 182).

Looking for such a scale, she offers the following rationale:

> To have any validity, the ordering of severity should be rooted in either a consensus of community feeling, in the perceptions of those who sentence or in the perceptions of those who are sentenced; otherwise it is an arbitrary and therefore suspect order (p. 182).

Drawing on opinions of 58 judges from a Common Pleas Court in a large metropolitan city, Buchner compares 16 sentences (divided into three groups) using Thurstone's Case Percent Scale Score Program. The survey results provide estimates of a scale measuring the severity that judges attribute to different types and lengths of sentences.

Scales purporting to unveil latent severity, whether based on the Administrative Office approach or consensual scaling, raise three fundamental issues. First, they differ on how many sentencing options a judge considers. The TAP scale focuses on 12 sentencing options, the Uhlman scale identifies over 90 options, and the Buchner scale 16 options. Second, each scale offers a different view of the relative severity of punishments. If one accepts these indices as interval (or ratio) scales, the relative magnitude of various sentences is quite different among the alternative scales. For example, the TAP scale assigns weights of 5 and 14 to 12 and 60 months respectively, the Uhlman scale assigns weights of 44 and 78 to these outcomes, and the Buchner scale 5.5 and 26.9. Finally, these scales remain subjective, and do not offer a compelling line of theoretical argument to defend the assigned weights.

This review of techniques pursued by the research community to measure sentence severity shows basic conceptual challenges for measures based on actual months, as well as for subjective indices. Table 13.1 illustrates the disagreement by comparing months of incarceration with seven existing scales of sentence length.

Despite some similarities, these scales each tell a substantially different story about the comparative harshness of various sentences. Presented at the bottom of the table is the ratio between the scale score for 120 and 12 months, and 120 and 60 months, respectively. Clearly, there is substantial variation in the ratios, especially when looking at the relationship between 10 year and one year sentences. This disagreement underscores the need for a means to assess and choose between the possibilities. Researchers simply assume that all of the proposed measures are interval scales – they make no effort to ascertain whether the resulting scales indeed have interval properties. We need an empirical technique to assess inter-categorical distances as a means to validate pre-existing scales. In this regard, Klepper, Nagin, and Tierney (1983) suggest that n-chotomous ordered probit can be used to develop an interval scale of sentence severity given a pre-existing ordinal measure. We develop this approach more fully below.

The Sentencing Unit

In this section, we introduce the concept of the sentencing unit (hereafter *senunit*), a measure designed to overcome many of the problems associated with existing scales of sentencing severity. The development of the senunit builds on the following desiderata. First, we seek a theoretically grounded measure that reflects the sentencing options actually considered during the sentencing process. Specifically, the rationale for the measure must explain why sentencing options are restricted; why, given restricted choices, certain prominent sentences tend to dominate; and why intervals between successive prominent sentences tend to increase. Second, we seek a measure that weights categories in a manner that creates an interval scale. Third, we seek validation for the interval-ness of the resulting measure.

Theoretical Foundation

We find three compelling explanations for the observed pattern of judicial sentencing outcomes shown in Figure 13.1. First, the restricted choice set reflects the tendency of decision makers (including judges) to simplify choice situations by reducing the number of alternatives considered. Simon (1979, p. 3) observes:

> Human powers are very modest when compared with the complexities of the environments in which human beings live. If computational powers were

Table 13.1 A sample of existing sentencing severity measures

Months of incarceration	TAP	LaFree	Hagan Nagel Albonnetti	Uhlman	Miethe Moore (years)	Buchner	Logarith months
0	0	0	0	0	0	0	0
1–3	3	4	4	32	0.25	0.56	1.10
4–6	3	4	4	33	0.50	2.20	1.79
7–9	3	4	6	33	0.75	3.85	2.20
10–12	5	6	6	44	1.00	5.50	2.48
13–18	7	8	8	44	1.50	7.15	2.89
19–24	7	8	8	54	2.00	10.45	3.18
25–30	10	10	10	54	2.50	13.74	3.40
31–36	10	10	10	64	3.00	17.03	3.58
37–48	12	11	12	72	4.00	20.35	3.87
49–60	14	12	14	78	5.00	26.93	4.09
61–72	25	14	17	83	6.00	33.52	4.28
73–84	25	14	17	86	7.00	40.10	4.43
85–96	25	17	21	88	8.00	46.69	4.56
97–108	25	17	21	88	9.00	53.28	4.68
109–120	25	17	21	91	10.00	59.86	4.79
121–144	50	21	30	93	12.00	66.49	4.97
145–180	50	30	30	93	15.00	79.71	5.19
181–240	50	30	30	93	20.00	99.56	5.48
241–360	50	30	30	93	30.00	132.71	5.89
361–480	50	30	30	93	40.00	198.57	6.17
481–600	50	30	30	93	50.00	264.43	6.40
120:12	5.00:1	2.83:1	4.20:1	2.07:1	10.00:1	10.88:1	1.93:1
120:60	1.79:1	1.42:1	1.50:1	1.17:1	2.00:1	2.22:1	1.17:1

288 *Sentencing and Society*

> unlimited, a person would choose the course of action that would yield maximum
> utility under the given circumstances ... But real human beings ... cannot follow
> this procedure. Faced with complexity and uncertainty, lacking the wits to
> optimize, they must be content to satisfice – to find 'good enough' solutions to
> their problems and 'good enough' courses of action.

To simplify the selection process, human beings limit their search to alternatives that are 'good enough'. Thus, choice sets are subject to self-imposed restrictions.

The relevant cybernetic literature (e.g. Newell and Simon 1969; Simon 1979) concludes that the response set for all human activities is limited, if for no other reason than to ease the burdens of calculation. In the sentencing context, we hypothesise that *judges consider and use only a relatively small number of sentencing options*. To assess this proposition, Table 13.2 (drawn from Figure 13.1) presents the frequency distribution for the most prominent sentences.

As one can see, 20 sentences (in months) dominate judicial choices: 6, 12, 16, 18, 20, 24, 30, 32, 36, 40, 48, 60, 72, 84, 96, 120, 180, 240, and 300. These 20 sentences account for over 90 per cent of all sentences issued by Michigan judges. Either by convention, or to ease the drain on decision-making resources, Michigan judges – even in those cases where they have maximum discretion – appear to make use of a very small number of sentences.

Second, when reducing their choice set, judges rely on a small set of prominent sentences. The process of identifying elements of the reduced choice set may be an example of what Kahneman, Slovic, and Tversky (1982) refer to as the availability heuristic.[7] The availability heuristic leads to several predictable decision-making biases. In the context of sentencing decisions, judges select the most easily retrievable options. Therefore, even though judges can sentence a convicted felon to any period of incarceration up to legislatively mandated maximums, they will recall some sentences more readily than others. Those sentences that come to mind most easily will be chosen most frequently. This may account for the relative prominence of sentences of 6, 12, 18, 24, 36, 48, 60, 120, 180, 240, 300, and 480 months, and the relative absence of such sentences as 17, 23, 37, 52, and 93 months. All the former sentences are divisible by 6 or 12, and hence measurable in either half or full years.[8]

Third, judges not only reduce their choice set to a small number of prominent sentences, but the interval between the prominent sentences is inconstant. A crucial question is why the scale changes with increasing severity (see also, Fitzmaurice and Pease 1986). An examination of prison sentences in Michigan indicates that, at the low end, they cluster at six-month intervals

Table 13.2   Twenty prominent sentences from 1995

Rank	Prison sentence	Frequency	Per cent	Cumulative per cent
1	24	807	19.30	19.30
2	36	509	12.17	31.47
3	18	350	8.37	39.84
4	60	338	8.08	47.92
5	12	336	8.03	55.95
6	30	248	5.93	61.88
7	48	236	5.64	67.53
8	120	138	3.30	70.83
9	72	120	2.87	73.70
10	72	120	2.87	73.70
11	16	81	1.94	78.19
12	180	80	1.91	80.11
13	32	77	1.84	81.95
14	84	76	1.82	83.76
15	40	70	1.67	85.44
16	450	62	1.48	86.92
17	240	53	1.27	88.19
18	300	49	1.17	89.36
19	42	46	1.10	90.46
20	6	45	1.08	91.54

up to sentences of 36 months, at 12-month intervals in the middle range of 36 to 120 month sentences, and at the high end, at 60-month intervals from 121–360 months and at 120-month intervals thereafter.

Judges tend to abide by these uneven intervals, we argue, because they engage in a form of 'psychological discounting' (Abelson and Levi 1985, p. 276). We assume that offenders experience disutility for each year incarcerated, and that a primary goal of sentencing is to achieve a particular level of *total* disutility for each offender. Further, we contend that judges discount the future when evaluating possible punishments. That is, they act as if the offender's disutility declines with successive years of imprisonment. Polinsky and Shavell (1999) suggest this form of disutility is the case from the offender's perspective:

> because an offender becomes accustomed to prison life or because he ceases to care as much about those he knew from the outside. Also, the disutility associated with the first year of prison might be particularly great compared to that of later

years ... [because the] stigmatization of the prisoner (which lowers earning capacity an status) may be primarily due to being in prison at all, and it may not increase much with the number of years spent there.

Likewise, it is not too much to assume that judges, who, of course, do not serve the sentence themselves, might fail to view the distant future as vividly and forcefully as the immediate future. According to one interpretation, judges act as if the disutility per year falls with each additional year of incarceration, so that total disutility does not rise in proportion to sentence length.[9]

We can calculate the total disutility of a particular prison sentence by discounting it to the present at some positive rate. Although selecting the appropriate discount rate is not without uncertainty, we prefer a rate of 10 per cent. The US Office of Management and Budget (1988) has long specified a discount rate of 10 per cent as the reference point for comparing values at different points in time. This is in line with estimates in the area of 11 per cent Viscusi and Moore (1989) found in a study of the implied rates of interest with which workers discount the years of life at risk on the job.

If the immediate disutility of each year in prison is c and the rate of discount is r, then the present disutility of a sentence of length s is given by the discounted total:

$$d(s) = c_1 + \frac{c_2}{(1 + r)} + \frac{c_3}{(1 + r)^2} + \ldots + \frac{c_s}{(1 + r)^{s-1}}$$

This means that the true subjective valuation of the disutility of the prison sentence to the judge is not the total number of months or years imposed, but rather the present value of the sentence. Therefore, if we assume a 10 per cent discount rate, the prospect of 10 years' imprisonment is 1.62 times more onerous than five years in prison and 6.76 times more onerous than one year in prison (Table 13.3). Comparing results to those in Table 13.1, these are different ratios from those implied by existing scales, even though the differences are not substantial. The primary advantage of discounting is that it allows calculation of a scale value for every possible sentence.

Since a year in prison now is viewed more seriously than a year in prison ten years from now, it is necessary for judges to add ever-increasing blocks of time to sentences to achieve a given level of total disutility, or, in other words, sentence severity. Consequently, if judges view the disutility of prison declining over time, discounting to present value provides a rationale for expecting that the intervals between judges' uttered sentences will increase as severity increases. Calculating the present value of the prominent sentences (assuming

Table 13.3 Present value of prominent sentences (assuming 10 per cent discount rate)

Actual sentence	Present value sentence (in months)	Change in present value from previous sentence
6	5.45	–
12	10.91	5.45
18	15.86	4.96
24	20.82	4.96
30	25.33	4.51
36	29.83	4.51
48	38.03	8.20
60	45.48	7.45
72	52.25	6.77
84	58.40	6.16
96	64.01	5.60
108	69.10	5.09
120	73.73	4.63
144	81.76	8.03
180	91.26	9.51
240	102.17	10.91
300	108.94	6.77
360	113.12	4.24
480	117.36	4.20

a 10 per cent discount rate) produces a fairly consistent scale, with the difference between successive intervals being approximately six months (Table 13.3). While there are some exceptions (e.g. 48, 144, 180, and 240), it is remarkable that the prominent elements are approximately interval in nature.

It is therefore clear that rather unequal increases in sentence length can be seen as approximately equal if judges engage in some form of psychological discounting.

Operationalising Senunit

Based on our theoretical discussion, and the actual observed sentencing practices of judges, four principles guide the development of our index of sentence severity:

1) judges adopt an approach to decision-making that makes the task feasible;
2) judges simplify decision-making by reducing the size of choice sets to a relatively small number of available sentences;
3) judges focus on a set of preferred or prominent sentences;
4) when sentencing, judges employ a form of psychological discounting, hence the actual interval between successive elements in the choice set increases as severity increases.

The senunit scale results from mapping the prominent elements of the judicial choice set onto an interval scale. Based upon development to this point, Table 13.4 displays the proposed senunit value for each prison sentence between 0 and 600 months.

The ratios between 120 and 60 months, and 120 and 12 months, are 1.63 and 6.5 respectively. These ratios are almost identical to the ratios presented

Table 13.4   The sentencing unit

Actual prison sentence	Senunit value	Interval
No prison sentence	0	–
1–6 months	1	6
7–12 months	2	6
13–18 months	3	6
19–24 months	4	6
25–30 months	5	6
31–36 months	6	6
37–48 months	7	12
49–60 months	8	12
61–72 months	9	12
73–84 months	10	12
85–96 months	11	12
97–108 months	12	12
108–120 months	13	12
121–144 months	14	24
145–180 months	15	36
181–240 months	16	60
241–300 months	17	60
300–360 months	18	60
360–480 months	19	120
481–600 months	20	120

in Table 13.3 using the present value of the sentences (based upon a 10 per cent discount rate).

The sentencing unit differs from other measures of severity for four, theoretically based reasons. It makes decision-making *feasible*. It focuses attention on a *reduced* number of *prominent* options. It hypothesises that judges engage in a form of *psychological discounting* so that the just noticeable difference between successive sentences requires increasing the intervals between elements of the sentencing unit. Two questions remain. Is the sentencing unit an interval/ratio scale? Does senunit make a substantive difference to our inferences?

Is Senunit an Interval/Ratio Scale?

Like the Administrative Office-type scales, the senunit scale is at least an ordinal index. Statistical analysis of sentencing and disparity conventionally requires that the dependent variable is interval.[10] Rather than simply assert that the senunit scale is interval or ratio, we use a quantitative technique designed to estimate models with ordinal dependent variables – n-chotomous ordered probit (McKelvey and Zavoina 1975; Winship and Mare 1984; Klepper, Nagin, and Tierney 1983, and Greene 1990). Our goal is to determine whether the 'distance' between sentences on the senunit scale is constant. That is, this statistical technique makes it possible to test the interval (ratio)-ness of the senunit scale.

The test estimates 'threshold values', the distance between successive sentences on the senunit scale. As noted earlier, the senunit scale has nearly 20 ordered categories. To estimate reliable threshold values, it is imperative that one has sufficient cases in each of the categories. As a compromise, we choose to break the senunit scale into five subsets, where the 0 category contains all who are not incarcerated, and the remaining subsets contain an equal number of sentencing units (i.e. subset #1 includes senunit values 1–5, subset #2 includes senunit values 6–10, etc.).

The numbers 0 to 10 constitute an interval scale where the distance between each number is known and constant (i.e. a change of 1 unit). If senunit is an interval scale, the values separating each of the five subsets of senunit should also be constant. Let us assume a scale where μ_0 marks the point separating category 0 from category 1, μ_1 is the point separating category 1 from category 2, μ_2 is the threshold between category 2 and category 3, and μ_3 is the threshold between category 3 and category 4. If these threshold values (the μs) are an interval scale, then:

$$\mu_1 - \mu_0 = \mu_2 - \mu_1 = \mu_3 - \mu_2$$

This, in turn, suggests:[11]

$$\mu_3/\mu_1 = 3.0$$
$$\mu_3/\mu_2 = 1.5$$
$$\mu_2/\mu_1 = 2.0$$

While this test is limited to five subsets of senunit, it does provide a feasible means to determine whether the senunit scale is an interval/ratio scale.

We conducted the test using a large sample of offenders convicted and sentenced for armed robbery in the state of Michigan between 1987 and 1988.[12] We selected this particular sample because judges have unlimited discretion in sentencing for armed robbery in Michigan (armed robbery carries a statutory maximum of life or any term of years), it is a frequently committed crime, and because sentencing violent offenders has important implications for prison population and sentencing disparity.[13] We hypothesise that judges use information to differentiate one offender from another who has committed the same crime.[14] We gathered information on the following classes of factors: 1) prior criminal history; 2) relative seriousness of the offence; and 3) control variables. We believe that certain characteristics, like a more extensive prior record, or conviction for a more serious offence, will be associated with longer sentences. We also look to the effects of 'extralegal' variables like offender age, gender, and race to further our understanding of the sentencing process.

Our statistical analysis (variables and results are show in Table 13.5) examines the influence of each of the variables on the judge's sentencing decision, and is the basis for estimating the distance between successive sentences on the senunit scale. The analysis produced three sets of results relevant to the issue of sentencing severity.

The first result is whether the model as a whole is able to predict which of the five subsets of senunit each of the offenders falls into – based on factors hypothesised to affect sentencing outcomes – better than chance (i.e. always picking the most frequently occurring category. As we can see, the model correctly predicts over 56 per cent of cases, compared to a null, or chance, model of 39 per cent, an improvement of 44 per cent.[15]

The second result is a set of numbers that shows the effect of each prior record, offence, and control characteristic on sentence severity, taking into account the simultaneous effects of the other characteristics. The number that illustrates the impact of each variable in the model is called a coefficient (shown in Table 13.5). A positive coefficient indicates that the characteristic increases sentence severity, and a negative coefficient indicates it decreases sentence severity.

The statistical significance of the coefficient is indicated by its p-value, and the smaller the p-value, the greater our confidence in the inference that the characteristic makes a difference in sentencing. The characteristics having statistically significant effects generally have p-values less than .05.

Turning to the individual coefficients for prior criminal history and seriousness of offence, we find: 1) four of the prior record variables (high severity conviction, low severity conviction, juvenile conviction, and no prior record) are statistically significant in the predicted direction; and 2) all but two of the variables on offence severity (excepting offender role and multiple victims) are also statistically significant in the predicted direction.[16]

Of the 'control' variables, only two (convicted at trial and sentenced in a metropolitan court) are significant at the .05 level or better. In this regard, it is noteworthy that the race of the offender does not appear to play an independent role in the sentencing decision once we take account of other factors.[17] These results show that the model does a reasonably good job of accounting for the variation in observed sentences. This lends additional confidence to our inferences concerning cut-points between groups of sentences – μj.

The third set of results focus on the threshold values. Table 13.5 clearly indicates that intervals between the estimated μs are approximately constant, based on the following empirical-based distances: 1.40 (1.40–0.00), 1.48 (2.88–1.40), and 1.44 (4.32–2.88). Turning to the previously specified ratios between estimated thresholds, we find:

$$\mu_3/\mu_1 = 4.32/1.40 = 3.09$$
$$\mu_3/\mu_2 = 4.32/2.88 = 1.50$$
$$\mu_2/\mu_1 = 2.88/1.40 = 2.06$$

These results are extremely close to hypotheses based upon the equal interval expectation of the senunit scale. While not definitive proof, empirical results, in conjunction with theoretical argument, provide ample justification for using senunit as a ratio measure of severity of incarceration.

Table 13.5 Estimated coefficients for robbery armed model

Variable	Description	Coefficient	Standard error	p-value
X_{2i}	High severity felony conviction	0.593	0.235	0.006
X_{3I}	Low severity felony conviction	0.300	0.112	0.004
X_{4I}	Similar felony convictions	0.228	0.243	0.174
X_{5I}	Juvenile felony-type convictions	0.328	0.143	0.011
X_{6I}	Misdemeanour convictions	0.273	0.202	0.088
X_{7I}	Current relationship CJ system	0.071	0.106	0.251
X_{8I}	No prior record	-0.251	0.141	0.038
X_{9I}	Use of firearm	0.241	0.057	0.000
X_{10I}	Victim injury	0.216	0.053	0.000
X_{11I}	Victim held captive	0.727	0.126	0.000
X_{12I}	Victim exploitation	0.466	0.109	0.000
X_{13I}	Organised crime/ring	0.349	0.151	0.010
X_{14I}	Offender role	0.120	0.086	0.099
X_{15I}	Contemporaneous acts	0.849	0.141	0.000
X_{16I}	Multiple victims	0.043	0.090	0.317
X_{17I}	Convicted at trial	0.364	0.120	0.000
X_{18I}	Privately-retained attorney	-0.067	0.117	0.567
X_{19I}	Sentenced in SE Michigan	-0.657	0.097	0.000
X_{20I}	Gender	-0.283	0.209	0.176
X_{21I}	Race	0.121	0.093	0.195
X_{22I}	Marital status	0.301	0.186	0.104
X_{23I}	Dependents	-0.183	0.099	0.062
X_{24I}	Assets over \$1500	-0.272	0.153	0.074
X_{25I}	Education	0.022	0.165	0.896
X_{26I}	Current alcohol problem	-0.125	0.109	0.254
X_{27I}	Current drug problem	-0.017	0.093	0.857
X_{28I}	Age	0.088	0.049	0.071
X_{29I}	Age-squared	-0.001	0.001	0.131
Λ_1	1.402	0.085	0.000	–
Λ_2	2.878	0.094	0.000	–
Λ_3	4.325	0.117	0.000	–
-2xLLR		431.071	–	–
% correctly predicted (% null)		56% (39%)	–	–

Does Senunit Make a Difference?

The critical issue is whether the senunit scale makes a difference in drawing inferences about such policy debates as consistency, disparity, and proportionality in sentencing. As an initial test of this hypothesis, we will compare the results from using senunit as the dependent variable against those obtained using months of incarceration. Which dependent variable appears to be a better measure of how judges actually sentence? Which defendant characteristics are associated with differences in sentence length? What is the relative explanatory importance of different characteristics?

We can address these questions through a regression analysis of each of the variables in Table 13.5 for each of the two dependent variables. Regression analysis determines the degree to which variation in measures of offence severity, prior record, and other control factors account for variation in the two measures of sentence severity. The results from the two regressions are presented in Table 13.6.

Interpreting regression results involves assessing the overall strength of the model, as well as the size and significance of the individual coefficients, but in a somewhat different manner than the n-chotomous probit model discussed earlier. With regression, one key number is the proportion of variation in sentence severity explained by the variables in the model. This number, which ranges from 0 (no variation explained) to 1.0 (all the variation explained), is called the Adjusted R^2. Clearly, there are differences between the two sets of results. The model using actual months of incarceration has an R^2 of 21.6 (i.e. it accounts for 21.6 per cent of the total variance), while the model using senunit as the dependent variable has an R^2 of 37.3. The marked increase in the overall level of explained variance leads us to conclude that senunit reveals a great deal more consistency in sentencing.

Regression models also produce coefficients. In this case, a given coefficient indicates the estimated change in the dependent variable brought about by the presence or absence of a particular characteristic. For example, the presence of victim injury during an armed robbery (X10 in Table 13.6) adds about 1 senunit (i.e. a coefficient of .985 in the senunit regression) to estimated sentence length, while it adds an estimated 18 months to the sentence (a coefficient of 17.975) in the actual months regression. An asterisk indicates statistical significance.

The primary difference between the two models shown in Table 13.6 is with respect to using a firearm in committing robbery.[18] In the regression using actual months as the dependent variable, using a firearm is not significant.

Table 13.6 Estimating equation (2)

Variable	Description	Senunit Coefficient	Months of incarceration Coefficient
X1	Constant	-1.646	-73.515
X2	High severity felony conviction	2.451**	24.130**
X3	Low severity felony conviction	1.421**	14.327
X4	Similar felony convictions	0.419	15.091
X5	Juvenile felony-type convictions	6.479*	133.729*
X6	Misdemeanour convictions	1.760**	16.343
X7	Current relationship CJ system	-1.223*	-31.267**
X8	No prior record	-0.900	-18.941
X9	Use of firearm	1.203**	4.365
X10	Victim injury	0.985**	17.975**
X11	Victim held captive	2.049**	26.005*
X12	Victim exploitation	1.255**	19.842**
X13	Organised crime/ring	0.854	15.517
X14	Offender role	1.467	30.999
X15	Contemporaneous acts	2.454**	26.994**
X16	Multiple victims	0.254	5.619
X17	Convicted at trial	0.915*	1.715
X18	Privately-retained attorney	-0.603	-5.617
X19	Sentenced in SE Michigan	0.294	18.104
X20	Gender	-0.182	3.547
X21	Race	1.139**	20.475**
X22	Marital status	0.649	6.421
X23	Dependents	-0.079	-2.336
X24	Assets over $1500	0.259	-0.912
X25	Education	0.107	8.717
X26	Current alcohol problem	0.968**	14.660*
X27	Current drug problem	-0.033	-6.688
X28	Age, age-squared	0.165	3.388
X29		-0.002	-0.038
	R-squared	0.373	0.216
	SE	3.779	77.961

* $p < .05$.   ** $p < .01$ (statistical significance).

In the regression using senunit as the dependent variable, using a firearm is very significant – adding an estimated 1.2 senunits. It is difficult to believe that using a firearm in an armed robbery would not have a significant impact on judges' sentencing decisions. This finding provides additional plausibility to the results of senunit.

There are major differences regarding the substantive inferences one can draw from interpreting the coefficients in the two equations. For example, we begin by comparing the coefficients for 'high severity felony convictions'. In the senunit regression, the coefficient is 2.415, whereas in the actual months regression the coefficient is 24.130. The presence of prior high severity convictions leads judges to increase sentences by 2.5 sentencing units (i.e. 2.415) over and above the 'base sentence' implied by the values of the other variables in the model. Figure 13.2(a) is a visual representation of the impact of this variable for different base sentences. At the low end of the scale, where one senunit corresponds to 6 months, the impact is about 15 months (2.415 x 6). At the high end, when one senunit equals 10 years, the effect of high severity convictions is about 25 years (2.415 x 10).

* * *

The offender having a substantial number of other aggravating factors has his sentence enhanced substantially in actual months; it increases two and one half sentencing units. The ultimate marginal impact depends on the values of the other variables in the model.

In the actual months regression, the coefficient indicates a high severity conviction leads to a sentence increase of two years, no matter what values the other variables take on. Figure 2(b) is a visual representation of the impact in the actual months regression.

The ratios between 120 and 60 months, and 120 and 12 months, are 1.63 and 6.5 respectively. These ratios are almost identical to the ratios presented in Table 3 using the present value of the sentences (based upon a 10 per cent discount rate).

The sentencing unit differs from other measures of severity for four, theoretically based reasons. It makes decision-making *feasible*. It focuses attention on a *reduced* number of *prominent* options. It hypothesises that judges engage in a form of *psychological discounting* so that the just noticeable difference between successive sentences requires increasing the intervals between elements of the sentencing unit. Two questions remain. Is the sentencing unit an interval/ratio scale? Does senunit make a substantive difference to our inferences?

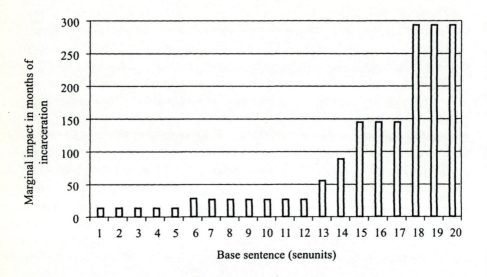

Figure 13.2(a) Marginal impact of high severity felony on senunit

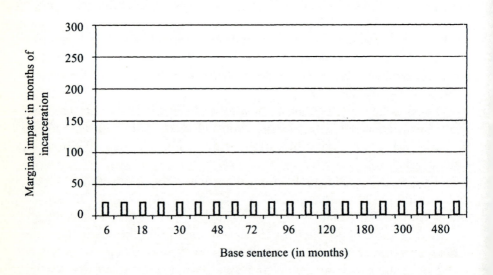

Figure 13.2(b) Marginal impact of race on months of incarceration

Turning to the question of disparity, the results of two extra-legal variables are most interesting. Consider first 'convicted at trial'. Criminal justice literature distinguishes two primary types of plea bargain. The first, the explicit plea bargain, refers to overt negotiations between the prosecutor and the defendant that result in an agreement on the terms of the bargain. The second type, the implicit plea bargain, describes an understanding on the part of the defendant that he will receive a longer sentence if convicted at trial than a similarly situated defendant who pleads guilty without trial.

This sentencing differential, based solely on the manner of disposition – one sentence if the defendant pleads guilty, another, higher sentence if the defendant is found guilty at trial – is sometimes, following Newman (1966), referred to as a 'trial tax'. The 'trial tax' does not appear using months of incarceration, but proves a significant influence using the senunit variable. Specifically, for the offender convicted at trial, it adds .915 sentencing units to the final sentence. This 'trial tax' is very substantial for offenders found guilty of serious offences – the marginal impact of conviction at trial could be five or ten years. This is evidence of a 'graduated' trial tax.

Regression results on the variable 'race' are also noteworthy. Both regression equations point to statistically significant racial disparities in sentencing. With the senunit regression the coefficient is 1.139, indicating an increase of a little over one sentencing unit for persons of colour. In the actual months regression the coefficient is 20.475, indicating an increase of 20 months in the average sentence for persons of colour. While 20 months additional incarceration due to race is an important concern for public policy, the inference from the senunit regression is even more serious. For those offenders committing relatively serious versions of serious offences, and having extensive prior records, the mere fact of race could add five to 10 years to an already long sentence. This suggests a much more pressing and pernicious policy problem.

Conclusions and Subsequent Research

Choosing a dependent variable is not a mere esoteric quibble among statisticians. Conceptualising and measuring 'the sentence' holds important implications for designing and evaluating sentencing policy. As the quality and practical significance of inferences about such perennial topics as consistency and disparity improve, the closer statistical models come to representing actual sentencing practices. This article develops and tests a new interval-level measure of sentence severity – the sentencing unit. The sentencing unit differs from the number of months of incarceration for four, theoretically driven reasons:

- it makes decision-making feasible;
- it insures the number of options considered will be relatively small;
- it restricts the small number of options to those that are prominent;
- since judges engage in psychological discounting, the just noticeable difference between successive sentences leads to increasing intervals between elements of the sentencing unit.

Six research and policy implications follow from the theoretical discussion underlying the sentencing unit.

1) Statistical models – and analysis – are misspecified if they use actual months of incarceration as the dependent variable. We cannot interpret the coefficient estimates reliably if the metric underlying the dependent variable changes over the span of the variable.
2) Inferences about consistency in sentencing,[19] as well as sentencing disparity, are also inaccurate when months of incarceration is the dependent variable, because they do not reflect the true nature of the sentencing decision.
3) Insights into proportionality in sentencing must take into account that sentencing may be proportional in intent (using an underlying scale), but appear non-proportional when measured using months of incarceration.
4) Judges issue sentences that do not account for the fact that offenders may discount time differently than judges.
5) Judges using the underlying senunit scale may increase sentences beyond requirements of penal deserts, thus increasing demand for secure prison space, and hence the costs to society.
6) The potential for discrimination is rampant. Consider, for example, offenders who should receive a sentence of 180 months. If a judge goes down one unit for one offender and up one unit for another, the difference in sentences is 10 years. If racial minorities receive enhanced sentences relative to majority offenders, the actual disparities may be quite substantial.

These implications underscore the importance of ongoing efforts to better understand the actual practice of judicial decision-making as part of any program of effective sentencing reform.

Notes

1   The data for Figure 13.1 include all 1995 Michigan felony sentences to state prison as opposed to county jail/probation. The statutory maxima for felonies range from two years to Life (or term of years).

2   Kerlinger (1973, p. 437–8) notes: "Interval scales possess the characteristics of nominal and ordinal scales, especially the rank-order characteristic. In addition, numerically equal distances on interval scales represent equal distances in the property being measured". He also observes: "the highest level of measurement is ratio measurement, and the measurement ideal of the scientist … ". A ratio scale, in addition to possessing the characteristics of nominal, ordinal, and interval scales, has an absolute or natural zero that has empirical meaning. Insofar as sentencing is concerned, it is common to say that a sentence of 12 months is one-half the severity of a sentence of 24 months.

3   A problem that frequently arises in the context of the indeterminate sentence is whether to count the minimum, maximum, or some combination (e.g. mean of the two).

4   We wish to make a distinction between the judge's view of the sentence and the offender's experience of serving the sentence. At issue at this point in the argument is what the judge thinks about sentence severity.

5   They report McCafferty developed the scale in a paper entitled 'Weighting', presented at the 96th Congress of Corrections, 30 August 1966, Baltimore, Maryland.

6   Uhlman (1977, p. 45) notes that even though "there is an inevitable degree of arbitrariness in the ranking scheme; it is appropriate to think of this scale in interval terms". He goes on: "Sentence severity as measured here is most precisely an ordinal scale. The index is, however, open to interval interpretations. With the expectation that the results will be roughly linear to the scale, we may take advantage of stronger interval statistical techniques. While some valid ordinal transformation of the scale might be possible, it is unlikely to change the results significantly".

7   Kahneman, Slovic, and Tversky (1982, p. 11) define the availability heuristic as follows: "There are situations in which people assess the frequency of a class or the probability of an event by the ease with which instances or occurrences can be brought to mind".

8   There are four anomalous sentences in the list in Table 13.2: 16, 20, 32, and 40. Each of these sentences arises from a peculiarity of Michigan sentencing. Michigan uses an indeterminate sentencing scheme in which the minimum sentence is the effective sentence. *People v Tanner* restricts the sentencing judge to minimum sentences that are less than or equal to two-thirds of the legislatively mandated statutory maximum (see Palmer and Zalman 1978). The anomalous sentences 16, 32, 40, and 42 are two-thirds of the following statutory maxima: 24, 30, 48, and 60 months. Offenders receiving these sentences were given the maximum sentence allowed. If *People v Tanner* were not in effect, it is our contention that the offenders would have been bumped to the next prominent sentence (i.e. 16–>24, 20–> 30, 32–>48, 40–> 60).

9   This view also meshes with that of many criminologists. See, for example, James Q. Wilson and Richard Herrnstein, *Crime and Human Nature*, 416–21 (1985).

10 Shively (1974, p. 71) argues that "… we should always try to raise data to a higher level of measurement, it is possible to do so. As it turns out, this is an operation which frequently is possible given a certain amount of boldness and ingenuity". After suggesting several ways to 'enrich' the level of measurement, Shively (1974, p. 76) concludes, "[o]ne mark of a

good researcher should be that he boldly seeks out all chances – not just the obvious ones, not just the safe ones – to raise the level of measurement of his work".

11 We can see the logic of these proposed relationships by substituting the numbers 0 to 3 for the threshold values μ_0 to μ_3.

12 In an earlier section of this paper, we presented sentencing data from 1995 taken from the Michigan Department of Corrections Basic Information Report Data Base. While this is an accurate and up-to-date data set, it does not contain any of the sentencing-relevant variables needed to adequately specify the model in Equation [1]. To find such a complete data set, we turn to the sentencing guidelines database maintained by the Michigan State Court Administrative Office. The most current data for which we have adequate sentencing-relevant variables is from 1987 and 1988. A comparison of the actual sentences given to the 784 convicted offenders in our 1987/88 sample show a pattern that is quite similar to that of the 1995 data displayed in Figure 13.1.

13 During 1987–88, Michigan judges were required to use a set of limited, and empirically based, sentencing guidelines while imposing sentences on felony offenders. The guidelines were implemented to determine whether it was possible to improve consistency while eliminating potentially discriminatory practices. Unlike many states, this program was developed through an advisory committee appointed by the Michigan Supreme Court. Since the legislature was not involved, the indeterminate sentencing structure was not altered. *Sentences were still imposed under the indeterminate sentencing statute.* Since they were empirically based, the guidelines were designed to emulate the judicial decision-making process as it had unfolded in the past. Consequently, the sentencing guidelines a) focus on factors relevant to the evaluation of the offence and the prior criminal history of the offender and b) recommend a range of sentences similar in severity to current sentencing practices. The goal was the elimination of the *unusual sentence*. Judges maintained their legislated discretion.

14 The presence of a sentencing guidelines system has a number of important implications for the present study. First, data were collected from the Sentencing Information Report (SIR) and the Basic Information Report (BIR), which are centrally collected for all cases sentenced in Michigan under the guidelines. Second, the factors reported on the SIR were developed by the Supreme Court Sentencing Guidelines Advisory Committee as representative of the legitimate considerations in sentencing of violent offenders. Moreover, use of the guidelines meant that each judge did look at each of these factors before handing down the sentence.

15 The overall fit of the model is statistically significant: $\chi^2 = 431.07$ with 28 degrees of freedom.

16 The set of prior criminal history variables is very significant considered as a whole ($\chi^2 = 102.19$ with 8 degrees of freedom), as is the set of offence variables ($\chi^2 = 76.06$ with 13 degrees of freedom).

17 The complete set of control variables does contribute significantly to the overall fit of the model ($\chi^2 = 76.06$ with 13 degrees of freedom).

18 Whereas there are substantial differences in goodness of fit, the differences between the significant variables are less substantial. For the model using actual months of incarceration, four of the six prior record variables are statistically significant, five of eight of the offence variables are significant, as well as three of the 13 extra-legal variables. Turning to the senunit model, we find that six of seven prior record variables, six of eight offence variables, and three of 12 extra-legal variables are statistically significant.

19 For example, Blumstein et al. (1983, p. 10) note that 'despite the number and diversity of factors investigated as determinants of sentences, two-thirds or more of the variance in sentence outcomes remains unexplained'.

References

Abelson, R.P. and Levi, A.L. (1985), 'Decision Making and Decision Theory', in G. Linzey and E. Aronson (eds), *The Handbook of Social Psychology*, Vol. I, 3rd edn, New York: Random House.

Administrative Office of the US District Court (1967), *Federal Offenders in the United States District Courts, 1964*.

Albonetti, C. (1991), 'An Integration of Theories to Explain Judicial Discretion', *Social Problems*, Vol. 38, pp. 247–66.

Alpert, G. and Apospori, E. (1993), 'Research Note: The role of differential experience with criminal justice system in changes in perceptions of severity of legal sanctions over time', *Crime and Delinquency*, Vol. 39, pp. 184–94.

Baird, J.C. and Noma, E. (1975), 'Psychological Study of Numbers', *Psychological Research*, Vol. 37, pp. 281–97.

Berk, R.A. (1983), 'An Introduction to Sample Selection Bias in Sociological Data', *American Sociological Review*, Vol. 48, pp. 386–98.

Blumstein, A., Cohen, J., Martin, S. and Tonry, M.H. (1983), *Research on Sentencing: The search for reform, Vol. II*, Washington, DC: National Academy Press.

Brantingham, P.L. (1985), 'Sentencing Disparity: An analysis of judicial consistency', *Journal of Quantitative Criminology*, Vol. 1(3), pp. 281–305.

Buchner, D. (1979), 'Scale of Sentence Severity', *Journal of Criminal Law and Criminology*, Vol. 70(2), pp. 182–7.

Chiricos, T. and Waldo, G.P. (1975), 'Socioeconomic Status and Criminal Sentencing', *American Sociological Review*, Vol. 40, pp. 753–72.

Clarke, S.H. and Koch, G.G. (1977), 'The Influence of Income and Other Factors on Whether Criminal Defendants go to Prison', *Law and Society Review*, Vol. 11, pp. 57–92.

Cook, B.B. (1973), 'Sentencing Behavior of Judges', *Cincinnati Law Review*, Vol. 42, pp. 597–633.

Crew, B.K. (1991), 'Race Differences in Felony Charging and Sentencing', *Journal of Crime and Justice*, Vol. XIV, pp. 99–122.

Crouch, B. (1993), 'Is Incarceration Really Worse?', *Justice Quarterly*, Vol. 10, pp. 67–88.

Erickson, M. and Gibbs, J. (1979), 'On the Perceived Severity of Legal Penalties', *Journal of Criminal Law and Criminology*, Vol. 70, pp. 102–16.

Fitzmaurice, C. and Pease, K. (1986), *The Psychology of Judicial Sentencing*, Manchester: Manchester University Press.

Galton, F. (1895), 'Terms of Imprisonment', *Nature*, Vol. 52, pp. 174–6.

Greene, W.H. (1990), *Econometric Analysis*, New York: Macmillan.

Hagan, J. and Bumiller, K. (1983), 'Making Sense of Sentencing', in A. Blumstein et al. (eds), *Research on Sentencing: The search for reform, Vol. II*, Washington, DC: National Academy Press.

Hagan, J. Nagel, I. and Alboneti, C. (1980), 'The Differential Sentencing of White Collar Offenders in Ten Federal District Courts', *American Sociological Review*, Vol. 45, pp. 802–20.

Kahneman, D. Slovic, P. and Tversky, A. (1982), *Judgment Under Uncertainty*, New York: Cambridge University Press.

Kelly, H.E. (1976), 'Comparison of Defense Strategy and Race as Influences in Differential Sentencing', *Criminology*, Vol. 14, pp. 241–9.

Kerlinger, F. (1992), *Foundations of Behavioral Research*, Fort Worth, TX: Harcourt Brace.

Klepper, S., Nagin, D.and Tierney, L. (1983), 'Discrimination in the Criminal Justice System', in A. Blumstein et al. (eds), *Research on Sentencing: The Search for Reform, Vol. II*, Washington, DC: National Academy Press.

LaFree, G.D. (1985), 'Adversarial and Nonadversarial Justice', *Criminology*, Vol. 23, pp. 289–312.

Lizzotte, A.J. (1978), 'Extra-Legal Factors in Chicago's Criminal Courts', *Social Problems*, Vol. 25, pp. 564–80.

McCafferty, J. (1966), 'Weighting', paper presented at the 96th Congress of Corrections, Baltimore, MD.

McDavid, J. and Stipak, B. (1981/82), 'Simultaneous Scaling of Offense Seriousness and Sentence Severity Through Canonical Correlation Analysis', *Law and Society Review*, Vol. 16, pp. 147–62.

McKelvey, R. and Zavoina, W. (1975), 'A Statistical Model for the Analysis of Ordinal Level Dependent Variables', *Journal of Mathematical Sociology*, Vol. 4, pp. 103–20.

Miethe, T.D. and Moore, C.A. (1986), 'Racial Differences in Criminal Processing', *Sociological Quarterly*, Vol. 27, pp. 217–37.

Myers, M. and Talarico, S.M. (1987), *The Social Contexts of Criminal Sentencing*, New York: Springer-Verlag.

Newell, A. and Simon, H.A. (1969), *Human Problem Solving*, Englewood Cliffs, NJ: Prentice-Hall.

Newman, D. (1966), *The Determination of Guilt or Innocence at Trial*, Boston: Little Brown.

Palmer, J. and Zalman, M. (1978), 'People v. Tanner', *New England Law Review*, Vol. 14, pp. 82–118.

Petersilia, J. and Deschenes, E.P. (1995), 'Perceptions of Punishment: Inmates and staff rank the severity of prison versus intermediate sanctions', *The Prison Journal*, Vol. 74, pp. 306–28.

Peterson, R.D. and Hagan, J. (1984), 'Changing Conceptions of Race', *American Sociological Review*, Vol. 49, pp. 56–70.

Polinsky, A.M. and Shavel, S. (1999), *Journal of Legal Studies*, Vol. 28, pp. 1–16.

Schiff, M. (1997), 'Gauging the Intensity of Criminal Sanctions: Developing the Criminal Punishment Severity Scale (CPSS)', *Criminal Justice Review*, Vol. 22, pp. 175–206.

Sebba, L. (1978), 'Some Explorations in the Scaling of Penalties', *Journal of Research in Crime and Delinquency*, Vol. xx, pp. 247–65.

Sebba, L. and Nathan, G. (1984), 'Further Explorations in the Scaling of Penalties', *British Journal of Criminology*, Vol. 23, pp. 221–49.

Shively, W.P. (1974), *The Craft of Political Research*, Englewood Cliffs, NJ: Prentice-Hall.

Simon, H.A. (1979), *Models of Thought*, New Haven: Yale University Press.

Spelman, W. (1995), 'The Severity of Intermediate Sanctions', *Journal of Research in Crime and Delinquency*, Vol. 32, pp. 107–35.

Thomson, R. and Zingraff, M.T. (1981), 'Detecting Sentencing Disparity', *American Journal of Sociology*, Vol. 86, pp. 869–80.

Tiffany, L., Avichai, Y. and Peters, G.W. (1975), 'A Statistical Analysis of Sentencing in Federal Courts', *Journal of Legal Studies*, Vol. 4, pp. 369–90.

Tremblay, P. (1988), 'On Penal Metrics', *Journal of Quantitative Criminology*, Vol. 4, pp. 225–45.

Uhlman, T.H. (1977), 'The Impact of Defendant Race in Trial-Court Sanctioning Decisions', in J.A. Gardiner (ed.), *Public Law and Public Policy*, New York: Prager.

Uhlman, T.H. (1978), 'Black Elite Decision Making: The case of trial judges', *American Journal of Political Science*, Vol. 22, pp. 884–95.

Uhlman, T.H. (1979), *Racial Justice*, Lexington, MA: Lexington Books.

US Office of Management and Budget (1988), *Regulatory Program of the United States Government. April 1, 1988–March 21, 1989*, Washington, DC: US Government Printing Office.

Viscusi, W.K. and Moore, M.J. (1989), 'Rates of Time Preference and Valuations of the Duration of Life', *Journal of Public Economics*, Vol. 38, pp. 297–317.

Von Hirsch, A. (1976), *Doing Justice*, New York: Hill and Wang.

Wheeler, S., Weisburd, D. and Bode, N. (1982), 'Sentencing the White Collar Offender: Rhetoric and reality', *American Sociological Review*, Vol. 47, pp. 641–62.

Wilson, J.Q. and Herrnstein, R. (1985), *Crime and Human Nature*, New York: Simon and Schuster.

Winship, C. and Mare, R. (1984), 'Regression Models with Ordinal Variables', *American Sociological Review*, Vol. 49, pp. 512–23.

Zalman, M., Ostrom, C.W., Peaslee, G. and Guilliams, P. (1979), *Sentencing in Michigan: Report on the Michigan Felony Sentencing Project*, Lansing: Michigan State Court Administrative Office.

Chapter Fourteen

Desert and the Punitiveness of Imprisonment

Gavin Dingwall and Christopher Harding

Introduction

This chapter does not set out either to defend or question desert as the primary justification for imprisonment (see generally the readings and bibliography in von Hirsch and Ashworth 1998) nor does it attempt to explain the political factors bound up in a retributive penal policy (Home Office 1990; Hudson 1996; James and Raine 1998). Instead, our aim is to address critically one crucial component of any retributive penal policy: the measurement and appreciation of punitiveness (that is, the amount and kind of punishment in retributive terms) in relation to one significant measure, imprisonment. Any penal system which depends, or claims to depend, upon desert as a justification for punishment ought to analyse fully the punitiveness of the measures at its disposal so that their subsequent use can be proportionate to the offending conduct and hence can be morally justified (see, on the issue of measuring sentencing severity, the chapters by Davies et al., Davis, Freiburg, and Ostrom and Ostrom in the present volume). Just as a desert model requires penologists to consider ways of measuring the penal harm associated with various forms of offending (von Hirsch and Jareborg 1991; von Hirsch 1993), so ways of assessing the punitiveness of different forms of punishment also need to be carefully considered. In practice, however, sentencers appear to have considered punitiveness in a theoretically superficial manner. As Pease has commented (1994, p. 118):

> ... There is every reason to suppose that the criminal justice process incorporates only extremely crude devices for ensuring a uniform method for converting distaste into sentence ... the simplification of punitiveness in the analyses which follow is as nothing to its simplification in the actions of sentencers supposed to be operating according to retributive principle.

Ironically, penologists in England and Wales have considered notions of 'punitiveness' with regard to other forms of punishment in the 1990s. This interest was fuelled by the Criminal Justice Act 1991 which placed desert at the forefront of sentencing decision-making. However, this work was often concerned either with exposing the Act's theoretical inconsistencies or by more prosaic problems concerning its effective implementation. Particular attention was given to the new 'Unit Fine' system which was designed to ensure that fines had a proportionate punitive effect by explicitly taking account of the offender's financial position (Criminal Justice Act 1991, s.18). This was widely seen as a theoretical improvement over the pre-Act case-law which demonstrated an apparent reluctance to increase fines for wealthy offenders (Wasik 1993) combined with the morally problematic practice of courts to use other forms of punishment with poorer offenders, largely for administrative ease (Carlen 1989). In practice, however, the scheme's attempt to equalise the punitive effect of the fine led to its downfall. The media gave considerable coverage to the alleged unfairness of offenders receiving widely differing fines depending upon their economic position which led in turn to the system being hastily abolished at a time of low popular support for the Government (Wasik 1993). It is worth noting the irony that this popular perception was based on a perceived lack of proportionality between the offence and the punishment. Yet this view failed to take account of the range of factors which need to be considered in calculating a proportionate punishment.

Penologists have also considered how one should take account of the inherent penalty of community sentences, especially as such sentences were primarily designed to serve rehabilitative purposes (Weston 1978; Rex 1998). Writing from a desert perspective, Wasik and von Hirsch (1988) have argued that the probation regime imposed both by the sentencer and by the probation service introduces a clear element of penality into the order due to the potentially onerous requirements made on the offender. According to their analysis, probation should be regarded as a middle-range penalty in a desert-based framework.

Towards the end of the 1980s, the government in England and Wales also started to emphasise the punitive nature of community sentences, albeit for more pragmatic reasons at a time when there was considerable strain on the prison system. The government believed that the way in which community sentences had previously been described as alternatives to custody had helped perpetuate a common belief amongst sentencers and the population at large that they were no more than a "soft option" (Home Office 1990). Accordingly the White Paper which preceded the 1991 Act sought to highlight the punitiveness of the various community orders and did so in terms of a scaled reduction in the individual's liberty (Home Office 1990). Brownlee provides a perceptive account of this repackaging exercise (1998, p. 19):

> In order to promote the use of non-custodial sentences for 'appropriate' offenders, the 1990 White paper challenged the assumption that custody is the only 'real' punishment. However, far from offering any radical deconstruction of traditionalist notions of punishment and of societal responses to anti-social behaviour, the White Paper chose instead to recast community-based sanctions in terms of their punitive possibilities. It acknowledged that a new approach was needed if the use of custody was to be reduced, but the 'new approach' was launched on a wave of punitiveness, consistent with the prevailing tide of law-and-order rhetoric evident in much of what the governing party of the time had been saying.

Given that the punitiveness of other forms of punishment have been analysed in a desert-based context, it may appear somewhat odd that the punitiveness of imprisonment tends to have been considered in a more limited, and, almost without exception, in a quantitative fashion. One would have thought after all that the form of punishment reserved for the most serious cases in most jurisdictions would have merited detailed consideration. The next section considers why there has been an unwillingness to consider qualitative aspects of imprisonment in a desert context.

The Failure to Consider Qualitative Variations in Imprisonment

There are reasons why a purely quantitative approach to measuring the punitiveness of imprisonment may have developed in England and Wales. Although the Criminal Justice Act 1991 provided that proportionality was the primary justification for a custodial sentence (s. 1(2)(a)), the legislation did not provide detailed guidance on how this general principle was to operate in practice. Sentencers were, therefore, meant to calculate the severity of the offending conduct and, after analysing the relative punitiveness of different forms of punishment, find a punishment that was somehow proportionate to this conduct without actually having any criteria to guide them at any stage in the process. It was envisaged (Home Office 1990) that the Court of Appeal would provide this guidance so that a consistent approach would develop. The reality is that the Court of Appeal's response has been mixed. What has tended to happen is that it has avoided giving detailed guidance on the problematic "disposition threshold" cases (Ashworth and von Hirsch 1997) but has provided more detailed guidance on sentencing particular serious offences where the use of imprisonment in itself is not in doubt but the length of sentence is (Dingwall 1997). In other words, there has been a reluctance to consider when an offence is "so serious" that only a custodial sentence can be justified (s. 1(2)(a)) but some willingness to enunciate principles to calculate the proportionate length of such a sentence (s. 2(2)(a)) *when the appropriateness of custody has already been determined.*

The latter determination, once the sentencer has calculated the gravity of the offending conduct, is purely quantitative in nature – what length of sentence would be commensurate with the seriousness of the offence? The former, however, would require a qualitative dimension. Not only would the sentencer have to consider the gravity of the offending conduct but he or she would also have to look at qualitative aspects of imprisonment, some of which will be considered later, before determining whether the offence was 'so serious' that only custody could be justified. To make such a decision the sentencer would have to consider exactly what serving a custodial sentence entails. The diverse range of qualitative aspects which impact on an individual's custodial experience makes such a calculation difficult, though this strengthens not weakens the need for appellate guidance. On the other hand, it is comparatively easy to determine the length of a custodial sentence with reference to sentences imposed for other offences, the statutory maxima and common aggravating and mitigating factors (although this is not to imply that calculating a proportionate term of imprisonment is not fraught with difficulty in itself).

This reluctance on the part of sentencers in England and Wales to consider qualitative aspects of the custodial experience has also been demonstrated in the context of cases where it has been argued that the adverse treatment of prisoners should result in a sentence reduction on appeal. For example, there are a number of authorities where the court rejected the argument that keeping the appellant in solitary confinement to protect him from violence from other inmates should result in a lesser sentence (*Kirby* [1979] 1 Cr.App.R.(S.) 214; *Kay* [1980] 2 Cr.App.R.(S.) 284; *Parker* [1996] 2 Cr.App.R.(S.) 275). The Court of Appeal has taken the view that such matters can be dealt with more appropriately in other contexts, in particular when it comes to assessing an individual's parole eligibility. At a theoretical level this is somewhat intriguing – surely solitary confinement, whatever the initial justification, represents a more punitive form of imprisonment than that originally envisaged by the sentencer and, consequently, it is necessary to reduce the length of the sentence in order to maintain proportionality between the offending conduct and the punishment imposed? The reality may be somewhat more pragmatic; the Court does recognise that qualitative factors associated with the regime directly affect the overall punitiveness of the sentence, hence their position that other forms of remedy can respond to this problem more effectively rather than an outright rejection of the underlying argument. However, this general acceptance that it may be relevant for some other body to consider qualitative factors again absolves the Court of Appeal of this responsibility and, by switching the emphasis from a judicial to an executive remedy, prevents a norm being created through legal precedent.

What is more problematic is trying to reconcile this stance with those cases where exceptional vulnerability or unusually severe consequences of imprisonment have influenced the Court of Appeal with regard to sentence (e.g. *Bibi* [1980] 2 Cr.App.R.(S.) 177; *Bernard* [1997] 1 Cr.App.R.(S.) 135), although the authorities on this are few and sometimes dated (see generally Walker 1999). This practice can legitimately be defended by desert theorists on the basis that a sentence reduction stops the abnormally vulnerable offender receiving disproportionate punishment. What is less easy to defend is the distinction that appears to have been drawn between factors which make the offender particularly vulnerable *to custody in general* and factors relating to a particular penal regime which would increase the overall penal severity of that offender's experience of imprisonment, even though both of these factors impact on the totality of the punishment imposed and both of these factors could be made available to the sentencer.

This uneasy distinction has not always existed. Historically there have been significant attempts to categorise and rank different forms of imprisonment according to ideas of relative severity of punishment. Indeed, the major experimentation with the concept of the penitentiary in the later eighteenth century and early nineteenth century and subsequent nineteenth-century regimes of imprisonment were very much based on notions of a "just measure of pain" (Ignatieff 1977). Schemes of "hard labour" (Mayhew and Binney 1862; Priestly 1985), because they had a manifest quantitative character, were finely calibrated: so many steps on the treadwheel, turns of the crank, or so much lifting and carrying of shot. The concept of "hard labour, hard fare and hard bed" (Carnarvon Committee 1863) similarly lent itself to fine grading, not only as regards amount of repetitive 'useless' labour, but also as regards such matters as diet and the award of material privileges. A fascinating mid-nineteenth century example of quantitative penal calculation is provided by Joshua Jebb's scheme in the early 1850s for converting years of transportation into years of penal servitude (Radzinowicz and Hood 1986, pp. 498–502). Later nineteenth-century schemes of imprisonment had a punitive ranking both in terms of sentence length and the content of the regime: penal servitude, imprisonment with hard labour of different classes and imprisonment without hard labour (see generally Harding et al. 1985: Ch. 8). Returning then to Pease's assertion (*supra*), we should bear in mind that the Victorian sentencer probably had a sophisticated methodology for converting 'distaste into sentence' compared to his contemporary counterpart. Penal calibration is therefore best regarded as a lost art.

Pragmatic factors may explain the more recent reluctance amongst sentencers to broaden the debate regarding the punitiveness of imprisonment but it does not account for the lack of academic consideration of this topic. Amongst penologists there appears to have been an assumption that imprisonment does not merit such theoretical investigation as its "onerousness appears measurable in large part by its duration" (von Hirsch 1993, p. 29). That is not to say that regime differentials and other qualitative aspects of imprisonment have escaped academic scrutiny (see e.g. Ashworth and Player 1998), but rather that the contexts of these enquiries were different, the primary focus usually being comparative, historical or humanitarian in nature (a comprehensive overview of recent research on imprisonment is provided by Morgan 1997). Yet it is our main contention that qualitative aspects of imprisonment also impact directly on the punitiveness of the inmate's experience and therefore need to be addressed in a system reliant on a desert model. The rest of this article will suggest how such qualitative aspects could be incorporated into the calculation of penal severity thereby strengthening the retributive foundations of the penal system.

Towards a Qualitative Measure: the Continuum of Incarceration

In taking a first step beyond a simply quantitative assessment of the penality of imprisonment, it may be helpful to place the familiar sentence of imprisonment in the context of a broader continuum of carceral activity in order to identify some of the key elements of 'quality of life' which may be lost or affected by experiencing some kind of incarceration (c.f. Walker and Padfield 1996, p. 147 who list the "pains of imprisonment"; and von Hirsch and Jareborg 1991, who use a "living standard analysis" for the purposes of measuring criminal harm). No catalogue of carceral types could ever hope to be exhaustive; there is an infinity of forms and much depends upon social and cultural context. Moreover, the boundaries between types of incarceration will inevitably be open to argument and one type may shade into another. Nonetheless, some main forms may be identified in the context of late twentieth-century penal systems:

1) *Intermittent control over freedom of movement* This could well include, of course, the restrictions on freedom of action and obligations to do or not to do certain things which occur as part of 'community sentences' such as probation and community service. It could extend to electronic monitoring ('tagging') and 'day reporting' or 'intensive supervision' (see McDevitt and Miliano 1992).

2) *'Curfew' and 'house arrest'* This comprises a noninstitutional but nonetheless significant restriction on freedom of movement. Curfew restrictions may be imposed as an element of probation or supervision (see Byrne, Lurigio and Petersilia 1992, for US practice). House arrest may be employed in particular in relation to 'political' offenders; a notorious (though, strictly speaking, not a 'penal') example is the recent confinement of Senator Pinochet to his Virginia Water residence pending extradition proceedings.

3) *Part-time imprisonment* One example is weekend imprisonment, as provided for (but rarely used) in Belgian legislation; the French Code of Criminal Procedure provides for the sanction of *'semi-liberté'* (van Kalmthout and Tak 1988; see also ACPS 1970, ch. 7).

4) Full-time imprisonment, in conditions of association with other prisoners. This could be regarded as the present norm as a sentence of imprisonment.

5) *'Shock incarceration'* This refers to the kind of tough, intensive but short-term regime sometimes used for young offenders (such as the former system of detention centres in England and Wales, contemporary American 'boot camps' (Mackenzie and Parent 1992; Nathan 1995), and the recently revived idea in Britain in the form of the 'high intensity' training centre (Thorn Cross YOI).

6) *Full-time imprisonment in solitary confinement* 'Rule 43' segregation, although not intended to be penal in itself, may be seen as a variant of this; the notorious regime of the 'control units' in the early 1970s would provide a clearer example, although there were legal arguments relating to its penal character: *Williams v Home Office* (No. 2) [1981] 2 All ER 564.

7) *Imprisonment while awaiting capital punishment ('death row confinement')* Many would no doubt be willing to rank the above types of incarceration as being progressively more punitive. Such ranking need not depend on

the length of time spent incarcerated, indeed this could be varied considerably for each of the above. Instead the ranking would largely depend upon a perception of the degree of restriction of individual freedom of action and movement. In so far as the latter is then seen as a significant criterion of punitiveness, it is based on qualitative considerations, which are essentially a matter of lifestyle opportunities or, to be more exact, the deprivation of such. This then may be a feasible basis for measuring the penality of the experience of imprisonment in qualitative rather than quantitative terms.

Censure and Penal Severity

Another qualitative aspect which may be taken into account in assessing the relative severity of different forms of imprisonment is the less tangible element of censure which is implicit in the decision to resort to that particular form of incarceration. This is most relevant in ranking different measures but would also apply to sub-categories of a particular measure (for instance, as was formerly the case with imprisonment in the English system, when there were different sentences of penal servitude and imprisonment with or without hard labour). Taking into account the symbolic or rhetorical element of censure may help to understand different perceptions of severity which actually then translate into different experiences of severity. For example, it may be asked, is one week of imprisonment more severe than three years on probation? In material terms (restriction on individual freedom), it may well be convincing to say that the probation order would be the more severe measure. Yet intuitively many would be inclined to say that imprisonment is still more severe. What is implicit in this second view is that the *sentence* of imprisonment is more severe as a measure of *formal public censure* and many offenders would doubtless experience the sentence in this way.

This line of enquiry therefore takes us even further away from quantitative assessments into a second domain of qualitative experience - not simply an alteration of lifestyle opportunities, but a psychological experience of altered status, which is achieved through a formal and publicly enunciated process of moral condemnation. Indeed, it may be argued that this latter process of disapproval is central to the whole business of punishment (Harding and Ireland 1989) and so it is not surprising that it may inform the ranking of the severity of punishments in a significant way. But, at the same time, it should be recognised that there is in some sense a circular process of reinforcement: imprisonment conveys a greater degree of moral censure than probation, but that is because it comprises tangible elements of greater severity in the first place. Thus the degree of deprivation of liberty, of material comfort and lifestyle opportunities is converted into a scale of censure, which in turn is converted back into an experience of severity. The sentencer, in attempting to convert disapproval into sentence, takes an estimate of severity and incorporates that into his ranking of penal measures.

Censure is therefore relevant to the calculation of penal severity, but largely as something which is instrumental in producing a perception of severity rather than as one of its components. It is therefore necessary for us to find more objective data for assessing the qualitative factors that impact on the punitiveness of imprisonment.

Qualitative Criteria: Other Contexts of Discussion as Sources of Data

Before attempting some kind of measurement of qualitative aspects of penal severity in the case of imprisonment, it is useful to note some alternative contexts in which this subject has been discussed in the past, since such debate and literature is likely to provide some relevant source material for the present exercise. There are three contexts of prison research which would appear to be particularly beneficial: the evaluation of rehabilitative programmes, humanitarian critique of institutional conditions and comparative evaluation.

Rehabilitative aspects of penal measures, and imprisonment in particular, have been very much concerned with *features* of regimes, institutional conditions and resources and the *impact of regime activities*, all of which may also be relevant to a retributive enquiry into the impact of penal measures on lifestyle opportunities. Therefore, any attempt to assess the punitiveness of imprisonment could usefully draw upon such data and discussion even though it was originally intended for the purposes of rehabilitative measurement.

Similarly, ethical and legal arguments in favour of humanitarian limitations on the operation of penal measures have also addressed qualitative aspects of penal measures in attempting to define the morally tolerable bounds of penality. The concepts of "cruel and unusual punishment" in the Bill of Rights 1689 and of "inhuman or degrading treatment or punishment" under Article 3 of the European Convention on Human Rights are examples of legal controls exercised over the severity of penal measures, largely by reference to qualitative aspects of penality. Thus European Convention case law, and material relating to the European Prison Rules (formerly the Council of Europe Standard Minimum Rules for the Treatment of Prisoners) and the inspections of the European Committee for the Prevention of Torture and Inhuman or

Degrading Treatment or Punishment (CPT 1990) could also provide useful source material for the purposes of assessing punitiveness.

Finally, some comparative studies have addressed the issue of the relative severity of penal systems in different jurisdictions (and often the focus in such studies is on the use of imprisonment). These studies have sometimes touched upon qualitative aspects (e.g. Downes 1988; Pease 1994) which are clearly of relevance to the current discussion. The next section considers what use can then be made of this source material.

Qualitative Variation: Objective Differences in the Experience of Imprisonment

The question of whether sentences of imprisonment may be more or less severe, not only according to their length (i.e. raw deprivation of liberty) but also in terms of their 'internal' features (such as the impact on lifestyle opportunities) assumes importance in the context of a system which formally proclaims no such internal differences but in fact embodies such differentiation with some regularity. The point is well made by Fitzmaurice and Pease (1986, p. 102):

> The principle that the same sentence should have equal impact across people is negated by the differences in prison conditions. A year's sentence served in a local prison is unarguably a worse experience than a year's stay at an open prison. Yet equality of impact according to prison regime receives scant attention, in contrast with the wider application of the principle in calculating fine amounts.

The basic question being posed here is clear enough: in terms of retributive rigour and distributive justice, ought manifest and regular differences in prison regime and conditions be taken into account by sentencers? If it were the case that such differences were either infrequent or very haphazard or unpredictable then it might be convincing to argue that little could be done in this respect. However, it is implicit in Fitzmaurice and Pease's argument that: a) there are *objective criteria* for differentiating the severity of penal experience in prison; and b) within the contemporary British system such differences *occur with sufficient regularity* as to constitute a basis for prediction which is capable of incorporation into sentencing practice. These two elements may be considered in turn.

Objective Criteria of Internal Penal Severity

Such criteria are likely to be qualitative in character and relate for the most part to what has been termed above as the denial of lifestyle opportunities. There have been some earlier attempts to construct such criteria. Von Hirsch, addressing the issue of sanction severity, suggested an examination of the extent to which punishment interferes with valued interests of the subject of the penalty – this would involve an interests analysis based on a taxonomy of living standards : "the means and capabilities that *ordinarily* assist persons in achieving a good life" (1993, p. 35). Von Hirsch, Wasik and Greene, drawing upon Sen (1987), referred to "the normative importance of the personal interests compromised by the operation of the penalty" (1992, p. 378). More specifically, von Hirsch and Jareborg (1991), considering the measurement of severity of criminal harm, list criteria comprising: a) levels of intrusion; b) interference with generic interests such as physical integrity, material support and amenity, freedom from humiliation, and privacy and autonomy (as the main kinds of legally protected interests); and c) a temporal element – over what period of time? This last set of criteria in particular might usefully be employed in constructing a measure of denial of lifestyle opportunities in that it might help to identify the way in which normal lifestyle expectations may be defeated by aspects of the prison regime and experience.

Aspects of prison regimes and conditions which readily come to mind as indices of a measure of severity of experience would include: prison population density (affecting in particular conditions of accommodation and regime opportunities for work and training); the material condition of the institution; the morale, expertise and authority of prison staff (especially how that may translate into staff-inmate relations and control of oppressive inmate culture); the psychological environment; the risks of abuse from either staff (perverse discipline) or other inmates (perverse inmate culture); and degree of isolation from family and normal community (Woolf 1991). This is not an exhaustive list and there may be overlap and inter-linkage between these aspects, but the list arguably constitutes the basis for a viable set of indices of objectively differential treatment and experience.

It is possible then to explore, tentatively, one or two examples of the way in which any of these indices of penal treatment could be combined with the von Hirsch/Jareborg criteria as a calculus of punitiveness. For instance, density of population leading to overcrowded accommodation would qualify as an interference with interests of material amenity and privacy (and perhaps freedom from humiliation). This would then be multiplied against the level of intrusion (extent of overcrowding and shared accommodation) and the length of time the condition is experienced, thus:

(shared cell as loss of amenity) x (degree of sharing) x (duration).

Or to take another example: abuse from other inmates would qualify as an interference with physical integrity and autonomy, to be multiplied against the likelihood and degree of abuse and its duration, thus:

(abuse from inmates as a violation of integrity and autonomy) x (degree) x (duration).

It would also have to be considered whether indices of penal treatment as interference with interests should each be given an equal weighting, or whether there may be an objective basis for their differential weighting. To take but one example, should the sharing of a cell have a different weighting than isolation from family and community, or should any differential be based on the factors of level of intrusion and duration? These are important questions that would need to be addressed. One would also need to consider the frequency with which these differentials occur although, as the next section argues, this would ordinarily be less problematic.

Regular Occurrence of the Differentials

The regularity with which these differential factors operate can be seen at two levels. Firstly, it depends upon the category of the institution. Largely by design and official purpose there are clear differences of regime and conditions according to whether a prison is classified as local, open, closed 'training' or 'dispersal'. There are also unintended but nonetheless regular differences in conditions associated with these categories (e.g. the persistent overcrowding in local prisons, affecting accommodation and facilities). Secondly, there is clear evidence, especially from regular inspections, of either short-term or longer-term differences as between prisons of the same category as regards conditions, regime opportunities and management problems (see also Leech and Cheney 2000). Admittedly these differences may change over time, but it is unlikely to be so quickly as to disturb a sentencer's ability to predict that being allocated to prison X may be a significantly better or worse experience than being allocated to prison Y. An example of the kind of significant differences that can be found between two institutions with the same classification is appended below. This example is in no way isolated.

In summary, it may be possible to carry out a qualitative assessment of punitiveness of imprisonment by combining the calculation of denial of or reduction in lifestyle opportunities with a test of regular occurrence of the latter within a particular institution, and so arrive at relative measures of punitive experience as between different institutions. To date this has not happened in England and Wales. We believe that this has serious theoretical and practical consequences which we address in the remaining sections.

Making Use of a Qualitative Measure of Punitiveness of Imprisonment

This discussion has a number of implications for both penal theory and penal practice. Although much of our argument has been located within the context of a retributive, desert-based model of dealing with offenders and has responded to the requirements of such a model, the discussion also raises a number of broader issues which are not limited to dilemmas of distributive justice. In particular, questions relating to humanitarian control arguments and to the definition of punishment also come to mind. Although we discuss these issues in turn, they are, to some extent at least, inter-related.

Retributive Rigour

In the context of a system which places a premium on achieving proportionality between offence seriousness and the ranking of penalties, it may be asserted that the failure to take into account objectively measurable and consistently occurring differences as regards the "internal penal experience within prisons" undermines the retributive rigour of penal policy (see also the discussion by Ashworth and Player 1998). A further aspect of this situation which disturbs the retributive rigour of the sentencing decision lies in the fact that, while the sentencer may chose the sentence of imprisonment, the allocation of the prisoner to a particular prison depends to a large extent on non-retributive and pragmatic considerations, particularly perceived security needs and the administrative and managerial requirements of the prison system. In other words, the retributive thrust of the penal system is not in practice carried through in the implementation of the penal measure. If 'subjective' retributive factors relating to the personal circumstances, position and character of the offender may sometimes be taken into consideration when presented as pleas in mitigation or as part of the decision-making concerning early release from custody (Walker 1999), it does not then seem justifiable to exclude 'objective' retributive factors relating to the penal environment from the calculus. It is not far-fetched, for example, to argue that the Category C prisoner who spends four years at Blantyre House Prison experiences 'less' punishment than the Category C prisoner who spends four years at Coldingley Prison (see Appendix). In that sense, just desert is not achieved.

There remains of course a further crucial question: is it *feasible* for sentencers to take on board such differences? Admittedly, the exercise is not without its difficulties and challenges as regards constructing a convincing measure of such factors. But, as can be seen from the discussion above, it is not impossible. It is, moreover, also possible to envisage a number of remedies which might be used to rectify disparities in penal experience. Ashworth and Player (1998), for instance, have suggested reduction of sentence length, financial compensation and review by the Prison Ombudsman of alleged breaches of the 'contracts' between the Prison Service and individual prisoners. Perhaps more problematical, however, would be the objection that such an outcome would be disastrous for the operation of the prison system. Any process of establishing a recognised hierarchy of 'good' and 'bad' institutions would damage the prison system's reputation and credibility and devastate internal morale. This political objection would no doubt prove to be a far more formidable hurdle than any intellectual difficulties.

There are perhaps both shorter and longer term implications in this argument. In the shorter term, this retributive logic may be called upon to support criticism of the present unintended but *de facto* established diversity of prison conditions and experience as unacceptable, not only in humanitarian terms but also as a matter of distributive justice and penal policy. In the longer term – if it is desired to pursue the just desert philosophy through to its logical conclusion – it may inspire an *intended and regulated* differentiation of internal prison regime experience, at least as far as what might be called its more positive aspects are concerned. Thus, for example, the more 'lenient' open prison model could be integrated as a component of the sentence rather than simply being a security consideration. In a sense (and intriguingly) that would be a return to the nineteenth-century policy in relation to the use of imprisonment. One would have to be aware, however, that such an argument could also be adopted by those who advocate more Draconian prison conditions: a 'short, sharp shock' could be 'justified' on the basis that it is as punitive as a longer sentence served in more enlightened conditions. Nonetheless, one could address this possibility by providing national minimum standards for all penal institutions.

Minimum Standards

A further reason for asserting that sentencers ought to give some thought to regime differentials and the possibility of *excessive severity* of penal experience is the risk of violating threshold norms of minimum humane treatment of prisoners. In one sense this is again an issue of 'desert': the standards are so poor in the institution, that the punishment is not a proportional response to the offending conduct. Such is the language used in some of the Prison Inspectors' Reports that it would not be fanciful to construct an argument concerning violation of provisions of the European Human Rights Convention, especially as regards the possibility of prisoners suffering inhuman or degrading punishment. Conditions of detention in prison institutions were considered by the European Commission on Human Rights in *McFeeley v UK* (No. 8317/78, 20 DR 44 (1980)). It was the Commission's view that the self-imposed cell conditions of those prisoners taking part in a 'dirty protest' campaign would, *if imputable to the state*, have amounted to inhuman treatment as condemned under Article 3 of the Convention. It was held that prison authorities should exercise their custodial powers in a humane and flexible way, reviewing the situation constantly in order to protect the health and well being of prisoners, although with due regard to the ordinary and reasonable requirements of imprisonment. It is interesting to speculate whether such responsibility could also be imputed via the sentencing decision, if the latter has been taken in reasonable knowledge that the sentence could be carried out under such conditions. The 1987 European Prison Rules could also be invoked in this context, although noncompliance with this standard does not necessarily imply a violation of Article 3.

The other potential line of argument which could be pursued as a strategy in prisoners' rights litigation relates to the possibility of unacceptable discrimination (e.g. under Article 14 of the ECHR), although in a Convention context this is more likely to be used in order to reinforce an alleged violation of a 'substantive' right, as under Article 3. The differential treatment, if manifest, could be seen as adding to the injury but the essence of such legal claims is a sense of excessive punishment, and as such is a humanitarian manifestation of disproportionate treatment.

In any event, it is clear that basic rights and minimum standards claims raise issues relating to a qualitative measure of the severity of punishment and such a measure should be taken into account in working out any remedies. As Ashworth and Player argue (1998, p. 265):

The first response would be to ensure that all steps are taken to prevent the occurrence or recurrence of substandard treatment; but that, if such treatment does occur, consideration should be given to compensating prisoners financially for the violation of basic rights or making significant reductions in sentence-length.

The Concept of Punishment

Finally, the discussion raises questions about the very definition of punishment. In a theoretical context, definitions of punishment tend to be cast in abstract terms, focusing on phenomena such as the expression of disapproval and the infliction of unpleasantness. The precise agency of punishment and its locus may not be in the forefront of such discussion; Hart (1968) famously relegates issues of agency and locus to the level of 'secondary' cases of punishment. But the more precise location of penality may be a pertinent issue for the purposes of both moral and practical judgments about punishment.

In the context of imprisonment, where does the penality reside – in the act of passing sentence, in its implementation, or in both? The famous aphorism, that the offender is sent to prison *as* punishment, not *for* punishment (originally attributed to Alexander Patteson: Ruck 1951) suggests that the essence of the punishment is located in the sentence, i.e. the formal act of deprivation of liberty. But, if so, is it sensible to disregard variations in the subsequent experience of imprisonment as simply good or bad fortune? It would seem, on the contrary (as has been implied in the argument above), that inconsistent implementation could effectively undermine the rigour of the disapproval expressed in the sentence and so detract from the essential penality of the whole process. Reflecting on the nature of the penal experience, as the sentence is worked out, therefore raises, and perhaps clarifies, definitional issues concerning the boundaries of what is involved in the process of punishment. In particular, there are important and interesting questions of agency and responsibility in relation to the imposition of penal measures that ought to be addressed both in terms of penal policy and legal procedure. To what extent can the bundle of issues being discussed here be simply determined by courts acting as sentencers, or is it necessary to involve other agencies – for instance, the Prison Service, Inspectorate and Ombudsman – in such decision-making? In a sense, executive agencies such as the Prison Service, the Home Secretary and the Parole Board have already been significantly involved in the chronologically advanced aspects of the sentencing process. What is required, therefore, is an honest recognition that for many practical purposes some 'executive' agencies do (and arguably rightly so) act as 'sentencers'. Consequently, the distinction between 'authority' and 'agent' in the penal process (Harding and Ireland 1989) may not always be as clear as it seems. What is then important, however, is that, if sentencing is to be viewed as an executive as well as a judicial activity, the former aspects of the process should be as transparent and reviewable as the more obviously public and court-based elements (Ashworth and Player 1998, p. 270).

Such discussion therefore invites a fundamental re-evaluation of what is understood by the term 'sentencing process' and in particular the allocation of decision making and consequent accountability for action taken within that process. On the one hand, calls for greater penological expertise in sentencing have to some extent already been addressed, *de facto* and in a rather unsystematic fashion, via subsequent executive agency involvement in the working out of penal measures. On the other hand, the present kind of executive input into the *eventual* shape and size of the sentence of imprisonment is unsatisfactory for the reasons explored in the above discussion – it is haphazard, of low visibility, and for the purposes of the rigour of sentencing principle needs to be fully acknowledged and taken on board at the beginning when the public sentencers make their initial choice.

Conclusion

The important point to grasp in general terms is that the punitiveness of a custodial sentence should not be measured purely in terms of its length. Recognising, and responding, to the diversity of conditions found in British penal establishments may, like other aspects of calculating offence-seriousness or the proportionate penal response, prove difficult under a desert-model, but that does not mean that the task is impossible or should be ignored. Our essential argument may appear to be theoretically compelling yet at the same time readers may feel that the political and practical reality is that qualitative factors cannot, or indeed should not, inform sentencing decisions. We do not share this view and have outlined, albeit tentatively, how such factors could be taken into account in an overall calculation of punitiveness. By addressing an area that has largely escaped the attention of penologists and of sentencers working in a system where desert is of importance, this chapter seeks to emphasise important basic questions not just about achieving proportionality but also about the very concept of punishment.

References

ACPS (1970), *Report of the Advisory Council on the Penal System: Non-custodial and semi-custodial penalties*, London: HMSO.

Ashworth, A. and Player, E. (1998), 'Sentencing, Equal Treatment, and the Impact of Sanctions', in A. Asworth and M. Wasik (eds), *Fundamentals of Sentencing Theory*, Oxford: Clarendon Press, pp. 251–72.

Ashworth, A. and von Hirsch, A. (1997), 'Recognising Elephants: The problem of the custody threshold', *Criminal Law Review*, March, pp. 187–200.

Brownlee, I. (1998), *Community Punishment: A critical introduction*, Harlow: Longman.

Byrne, J.M., Lurigio, A.J. and Petersilia, J. (eds) (1992), *Smart Sentencing: The emergence of intermediate sanctions*, Newbury Park: Sage.

Carlen, P. (1989), 'Crime, Inequality and Sentencing', in P. Carlen and D. Cook (eds), *Paying for Crime*, Milton Keynes: Open University Press, pp. 8–28.

Carnarvon Committee (1863), *Report from the Select Committee of the House of Lords on the Present State of Discipline in Gaols and Houses of Correction*, London: Parliamentary Papers.

Committee for the Prevention of Torture and Inhuman or Degrading Treatment or Punishment (CPT) (1990), *Report to the UK Government on the Visit to the UK from 29 July to 10 August 1990*, Strasbourg: Council of Europe.

Dingwall, G. (1997), 'Guideline Judgments and the Court of Appeal', *Northern Ireland Legal Quarterly*, Vol. 48, pp. 143–51.

Downes, D. (1988), *Contrasts in Tolerance: Post-War penal policy in the Netherlands and England and Wales*, Oxford: Clarendon Press.

Fitzmaurice, C. and Pease, K. (1986), *The Psychology of Judicial Sentencing*, Manchester: Manchester University Press.

Harding, C., Hines, B., Ireland, R. and Rawlings, P. (1985), *Imprisonment in England and Wales: A concise history*, London: Croom Helm.

Harding, C. and Ireland, R. (1989), *Punishment: Rhetoric, rule and practice*, London: Routledge.

Harding, C. and Koffman, L. (1985), *Sentencing and the Penal System: Text and materials*, 1st edn, London: Sweet & Maxwell.

Hart, H.L.A. (1968), *Punishment and Responsibility: Essays in the philosophy of law*, Oxford: Clarendon Press.

Home Office (1990), *Crime, Justice and Protecting the Public*, Cmnd 965, London: HMSO.

Hudson, B.A. (1996), *Understanding Justice: An introduction to ideas, perspectives and controversies in modern penal theory*, Milton Keynes: Open University Press.

Ignatieff, M. (1978), *A Just Measure of Pain: The penitentiary in the Industrial Revolution, 1750–1850*, London: Macmillan.

James, A. and Raine, J. (1998), *The New Politics of Criminal Justice*, Harlow: Longman.

Leech, M. and Cheney, D. (2000), *The Prisons Handbook 2000*, 4th edn, Winchester: Waterside Press.

MacKenzie, D.L. and Parent, D.G. (1992), 'Boot Camp Prisons for Young Offenders', in J.M. Byrne, A.J. Lurigio and J. Petersilia (eds), *Smart Sentencing: The emergence of intermediate sanctions*, Newbury Park: Sage, pp. 103–19.

Mayhew, H. and Binney, J. (1862), *The Criminal Prisons of London and Scenes of Prison Life*, London: Griffin.

McDevitt, J. and Miliano, R. (1992), 'Day Reporting Centres: An innovative concept in intermediate sanctions', in J.M. Byrne, A.J. Lurigio and J. Petersilia (eds), *Smart Sentencing: The emergence of intermediate sanctions*, Newbury Park: Sage, pp. 152–65.

Morgan, R. (1997), 'Imprisonment: Current concerns and a brief history since 1945', in M. Maguire, R. Morgan and R. Reiner (eds), *The Oxford Handbook of Criminology*, 2nd edn, Oxford: Clarendon Press, pp. 1137–94.

Nathan, S. (1995), *Boot Camps: Return of the short, sharp shock*, London: Prison Reform Trust.

Pease, K. (1994), 'Cross-national Imprisonment Rates', *British Journal of Criminology*, Vol. 34, Special Issue: *Prisons in Context*, pp. 116–30.

Priestly, P. (1985), *Victorian Prison Lives*, London: Methuen.

Radzinowicz, L. and Hood, R. (1986), *A History of English Criminal Law and its Administration from 1750: Volume 5, The Emergence of Penal Policy*, London: Stevens & Sons.

Rex, S. (1998), 'Applying Desert Principles to Community Sentences: Lessons from two criminal justice acts', *Criminal Law Review*, June, pp. 381–91.

Ruck, S.K. (ed.) (1951), *Paterson on Prisons*, London: Frederick Muller.

Sen, A. (1987), 'The Standard of Living', in G. Hawthorn (ed.), *The Standard of Living*, Cambridge: Cambridge University Press, pp. 1–38.

Van Kalmthout, A.M. and Tak, P.J.P. (1988), *Sanctions-systems in the Member-states of the Council of Europe*, Deventer: Kluwer/Gouda Quint.

Von Hirsch, A. (1993), *Censure and Sanctions*, Oxford: Clarendon Press.

Von Hirsch, A. and Ashworth, A. (eds) (1998), *Principled Sentencing: Readings on theory and practice*, 2nd edn, Oxford: Hart.

Von Hirsch, A. and Jareborg, N. (1991), 'Gauging Criminal Harm: A Living-standard analysis', *Oxford Journal of Legal Studies*, Vol. 11, pp. 1–38.

Von Hirsch, A., Wasik, M., and Greene, J. (1992), 'Scaling Community Punishments', in A. von Hirsch and A. Ashworth (eds), *Principled Sentencing*, Edinburgh: Edinburgh University Press, pp. 368–88.

Walker, N. (1999), *Aggravation, Mitigation and Mercy in English Criminal Justice*, London: Blackstone Press.

Walker, N. and Padfield, N. (1996), *Sentencing: Theory and practice*, 2nd edn, London: Butterworths.

Wasik, M. (1993), *Emmins on Sentencing*, 2nd edn, London: Blackstone Press.

Wasik, M. and von Hirsch, A. (1988), 'Non-custodial Penalties and the Principles of Desert', *Criminal Law Review*, September, pp. 555–72.

Weston, W.R. (1978), 'Probation in Penal Philosophy: Evolutionary perspectives', *Howard Journal*, Vol. 17, pp. 7–22.

Woolf, Lord (1991), *Prison Disturbances, April 1990, Report of an Enquiry by Lord Justice Woolf and Judge Stephen Tumim*, Cm 1456, London: HMSO.

Appendix

Contrasting Experiences of the Penal Experience within Two Category C Prisons (Source: Prison Inspectors' Reports*)

* *Note* This material is being used as a convenient and ready source of relevant data for purposes of the present argument. This is not to imply that it should be regarded *finally* as a sufficient or infallible source of such data. It is recognised that the reports compiled by HM Chief Inspector of Prisons may be subject, like other comparable sources, to a particular interpretative filter (see in particular the comment in the *Howard Journal of Criminal Justice* 1999, pp. 347–8 regarding the attitude towards public and private sector prisons in the Inspector's reports).

Blantyre House (Spring 1998)

A prison for long-term inmates with a CNA of 120. Praised at the previous inspection as an example of all that was best in the Prison Service and it remains so. The best testimony was a comment from a group of prisoners that drug taking was not worth the risk as detection led to immediate transfer and that a 'no smoking' policy worked because there was little stress in the prison. There were a number of instances of best practice which were noted as transposable to other prisons. Some concern about shortage of work places and staff shortages and that HQ had not responded to queries until well after individual prisoners' parole eligibility dates (a 'system' problem).

Coldingley (Summer 1996)

Has a CNA of 289. Opened in the 1960s as an 'industrial prison' and now said to be showing signs of developing into such. The prison was so dirty that inspectors went so far as to take photographs of this condition, including discarded food on walkways and outside the kitchen, damage to electrical installations and building equipment and discarded furniture, which jeopardised security. There was particular concern over fire safety. The filth was indicative of a deeper malaise, with staff not fully in control of prisoners and there were sometimes breakdowns in communications between staff, inmates and managers. The latter had spent too long on 'management restructuring' and too little time on getting the elements of a stable regime right. Long-running industrial disputes had undermined stability and there had been three acting governors within two years. In some respects the prison had deteriorated since the last adverse report in 1993.

Chapter Fifteen

The Science of Sentencing: Measurement Theory and von Hirsch's New Scales of Justice

Julia Davis[1]

Introduction

Andrew von Hirsch has been a leader in the movement towards establishing proportionality in sentencing since the revival of interest in just deserts began in the 1970s. His sentencing model, which has been developed in the public arena over a period of more than 20 years, contains detailed philosophical justifications for state punishment and is supported by specific practical proposals for constructing a sentencing system.[2] No doubt because of these three features, von Hirsch's ideas have attracted much attention and comment. Not all of it, however, is positive. This paper focuses on von Hirsch's model and its critics and uses the theory of measurement as a source of critique instead of the more usual choice of the philosophy of punishment. Measurement theory is particularly relevant to the discussion because it defines the features of the ordinal and cardinal scales of measurement that von Hirsch has used in his model, and was developed to set limits on the kinds of statements that can meaningfully be made about the numbers which each scale produces and the uses to which they can properly be put.

Part 1 summarises von Hirsch's model and introduces some of the criticism directed at it. In part 2, I outline the development of modern measurement theory and, in part 3, I apply measurement theory to von Hirsch's sentencing model to see whether any of the criticism is well founded. I conclude that while measurement theory shows that there may not be any basis for the claim that desert has two distinct roles in the construction of a scale of penalties, it also reveals that much of the criticism of von Hirsch's model misses the mark once we recognise the true nature of punishment and the meaning of our assessments of the seriousness of crimes. Finally, in part 4, I conclude by suggesting some revisions to von Hirsch's new 'scales of justice' that will strengthen the model and avoid some of the criticism it has attracted.

1   The von Hirsch Model

Von Hirsch's most recent account of criminal punishment gives desert the "central role in deciding sanctions" but permits other non-desert aims such as crime-control to operate at a secondary level (1998, pp. 169-177). Focusing on the censuring feature of punishment, von Hirsch modifies the traditional Kantian conception of retribution which requires an *equal* paying back of evil for evil and calls instead for punishments that are *proportionate* to the seriousness of the criminal conduct (1998, p. 170). This move is aimed at avoiding the criticism that retribution is cruel in its traditional requirement of 'an eye for an eye' and is consistent with von Hirsch's argument that desert allows for considerable penalty reductions provided all penalties are scaled back on a pro-rata basis (ibid.). The model aims to give to modern systems of sanctions the promise of precision, parity and certainty that the *lex talionis* supposedly brought to the task of devising just punishments. The issue is whether the notion of a just return becomes impossibly vague once it has been twice diluted: first into Kant's "equal, but not necessarily identical" version; and then into von Hirsch's "proportionate, but not necessarily equal" interpretation.

The suggestion that desert can provide precise guidance has been challenged by many commentators who argue that it can only ever amount to a rough guide, one that is reduced to relying on conventional subjective assessments and is incapable of giving any practical guidance without the support supplied by other principles (Hart 1984; Morris 1984; Galligan 1981; Lacey 1988; Scheid 1997). Mathieson (1990) and Braithwaite and Pettit (1990) object to the claims to mathematical precision implicit in the terminology used in von Hirsch's model. Lacey (1988) points to the issue of incommensurability between crimes and punishments which arises when the 'harm for harm' standard is abandoned and in fact many view the equivalence requirement as a purely conventional or symbolic one that is not grounded in any natural or inevitable relation (Ashworth 1997; Lacey 1988). So, is the new desert a mere slogan that can safely be ignored, is it a powerful symbol that offers no more than general guidance, or is it capable of producing precise, though not uniquely determined, proportionate sentences as well as certainty, humanity in punishment and equal justice?

Von Hirsch has argued that a penalty scale should feature two different aspects of proportionality: the ordinal aspect, which determines how crimes should be punished relative to each other; and the cardinal aspect, which relates to the overall magnitude of the scale.[3] The use of these terms had been pioneered by other philosophers writing about punishment before von Hirsch adapted them for use in developing his own desert-based sentencing model (Pincoffs 1966; Kleinig 1971; Bedau 1984; Scheid 1977 cited in von Hirsch 1985). They are widely used in the related fields of criminology and sociology when attempts are made to measure public attitudes to crime and punishment, as well as in the literature on the comparative assessment of utility, well-being and living standards, and in discussions of economic theory and practice (Rawls 1971; Griffin 1986; Broome 1991; Gardbaum 1998).[4] Von Hirsch, however, uses these terms in a way that no others writing in any of these fields do.

Von Hirsch's interpretation of ordinal proportionality embraces three distinct sub-requirements: parity between offenders, rank-ordering, and spacing (1993, p. 18). Beyond the requirement that defendants whose criminal conduct is equally serious should be treated equally, von Hirsch (1983, p. 213) also takes ordinal proportionality to include the

> ... requirement that the ranking of severity of penalties should reflect the seriousness-ranking of the criminal conduct. Punishments are to be ordered on a scale so that their relative severity corresponds to the comparative blame-worthiness of the conduct ... Ordinal proportionality involves the further requirement of spacing. The size of the increment from one penalty to another should reflect, in relation to the dimensions of the whole scale, the size in the step-up in seriousness from one species of criminal conduct to another.

'Cardinal' or non-relative proportionality, on the other hand, is (von Hirsch 1983, p. 214):

> ... the requirement that a reasonable proportion be maintained between the absolute levels of punishment and the seriousness of the criminal conduct. It refers not to the internal architecture of the scale, but its anchoring points and overall magnitude. Even where penalties on the scale have been ranked in order of the crimes' seriousness, the scale may infringe cardinal proportionality if its overall severity levels have been sufficiently inflated or deflated.

Von Hirsch maintains that the 'elementary' distinction between the ordinal and cardinal aspects of proportionality is crucial because it links the two different roles of desert (strong and weak) with the two different aspects of the scale.[5] He argues that the ordinal dimension or "internal architecture" can be wholly *determined* by desert with a high degree of precision (1985, p. 39; 1998, p. 173). Cardinal proportionality, by contrast, is only *limited* by considerations of desert. It is "considerably less precise" and more dependent on other moral assumptions (1990, p. 284). Consequently, the cardinal aspect of the scale can allow for the operation of other principles when actual punishment values are allocated. If, however, this critical distinction is shown to be spurious, the different roles for desert may also be lost, taking with them the structure and the central principles underpinning the model.

The model contains a practical strategy for developing a sentencing system that is striking for its continual invocation of mathematical terminology and images, interwoven with a frank acknowledgement of the need for value judgments, impressions and imagination.[6] It is necessary, von Hirsch writes, to "establish a metric" using "qualitative rules of thumb" or "formulae" which can convert values from a living standard [LS] onto an "explicit harm-scale" [H1] using a "mapping rule". We then combine any primary [ph] and secondary harms [sh] into a 'net harmfulness grade' [H2] first by using a 'formula for premiums' and then by making an 'appropriate discount' for remote harms. These discounts depend on the different 'values' given to threatened harms [th], attempted harms [ah] or risked harms [rh]. The final 'net harm rating' [H3] is then converted into a seriousness rating [S] by 'controlling' for culpability [C], using four different values corresponding to the different degrees of culpability (purposeful, knowing, reckless, negligent [C 1–4]).

The next step is to convert from the seriousness rating to the penalty scale [P1], using a chosen rate [f] bearing in mind the constraints of 'ordinal proportionality', the limits of 'cardinal proportionality' and the impact of the other relevant factors of humanity, crime control, and resource availability. This scale can be either 'deflated or inflated', made 'milder or toughened to a degree' while the 'relative proportions are held constant' by making 'pro-rata increases or decreases'. The 'slope' of the 'in-out' imprisonment threshold line may be 'tilted', made 'more or less steep', 'relative to the horizontal or vertical axes', depending on these other constraints. Finally, in each case, there must be an adjustment to the final sentence according to 'set values' for aggravating and mitigating factors [af, mf], to obtain the individual punishment for any given offender [P2]. This process involves four conversions of values: from the living standard to the harm scale; from the harm scale to the net harm value; from the net harm value to seriousness; and from seriousness to penalty. The resulting punishment of an offender is thus directly proportional to the combination of the degree that the living standard of a typical victim would be affected by the crime, the remoteness of the harm, and the culpability of the offender, plus any aggravating factors, less any mitigating factors. Using the symbols I have added to the text, the process can be reduced to two equations: P1 [standard penalty for a crime] $= f[\{H3 = (k \text{ LS x } [ah, rh, th]) + ph + sh\} \text{ x } C(1-4)]$; P2 [individual penalty] $= P1 + af - mf$.

I must point out that von Hirsch thrice denies that his model seeks a 'narrow mathematical' sense of proportionality, and stresses that he is proposing a way of thinking about criminal harm, not a mathematical formula (1984, p. 1100; 1990, pp. 283–4; 1991, p. 38). However, it is undeniable that both the substance of the model and the terminology used to describe its practical application suggest this interpretation. If we want to avoid mathematics, we need to remove this type of language from the model because talking about 'net harmfulness grades', 'converting values' using a 'mapping rule', 'maintaining relative proportions', 'pro-rata increases', 'formulae' and 'establishing a metric' robs the caveat of its force. I propose to take the model at its face value and consider whether it can be taken literally, as some critics like Crocker (1992) and Mathieson (1990) have assumed, or whether it should be taken as providing only symbolic, and not literal, guidance.

2   Measurement Theory and Law

Von Hirsch has used mathematical terms to describe the 'ordinal' and 'cardinal' aspects of his penalty scale that will measure out the punishments that each offender deserves. The point of these new 'scales of justice' is to produce the right number every time, just as the traditional legal scales were supposed to weigh each case and arrive at the right measure. Mathematics is the most precise of all human languages and by shifting from the traditional image to this mathematical imagery, von Hirsch has given his model some of the cachet and precision that we associate with measurement, and the authority, rigour and objectivity that we associate with science. There are obvious similarities between the rule-seeking pursuits of science (e.g. the equivalence of mass and energy: $e = mc^2$) and the rule making and enforcing found in law (e.g. the principle that the penalty should vary according to the seriousness of the crime: $P = fS$). The question whether his model can deliver the precision it promises, or is simply another of the ubiquitous metaphors that bedevil nearly all theoretical punishment debates, may be resolved by applying measurement theory to the substance of von Hirsch's proposals.

Measurement has been defined by the pioneer of modern measurement theory, S.S. Stevens, as "the business of pinning numbers onto things" or "the assignment of numerals to objects or events according to rule – any rule" (1959, pp. 18–19). But measurement is more than just pinning numbers onto things. Measuring, like judging, is a purposive activity. In science, there are two possible purposes for assigning numbers to conceptual constructs or things, and only the first is shared with the law. The first purpose is simply to identify the things and distinguish one from another. The second, more important scientific purpose for assigning numbers to things is to apply mathematical processes to those numbers (Frankfort-Nachmias 1996, p. 157; Roberts 1984, p. 2). The results of these processes allow us to make precise inferences about the things we have measured: we can quantify the attributes of the thing and make comparisons with other similar things; we can describe clearly how two things are related; or we can predict their future behaviour.

Science is an activity that is aimed at discovering regularity, but law aims to create order by imposing regularity. Science seeks out the underlying order existing in the world, with the purpose of understanding it and exploiting it. But law is different. The numbers imposed by law are imposed as an act of will, and the rules it constructs are aimed at bringing order into the world. Law creates order, by order. It is order that is chosen, not discovered, and it is enforced by acts of power, not by the force of nature. It is for these reasons that no amount of science can substitute for legal decision-making (Yannopoulos 1997). The validity of these rules, and the numbers they produce, lies in our agreement that they are the right rules to follow. Before they can properly be chosen as law, they must be argued for, justified by principle and be grounded in the values of the community that both constructs the law, and is constructed by that law.

Lacey argues for a pluralist conception of punishment as a social practice that pursues and respects the community's central goals and values (1988). I suggest that our sentencing practice is not only characterised by a plurality of values, but is marked out by choice, because choices must be made when values conflict. Law is chosen all the way through, and the numbers it pins on offenders, are not being "deputised" to represent an underlying state of affairs (Borgatta and Bohrnstedt 1981, p. 24) rather, they order a state of affairs into existence. Measurement theory tells us that any metric will do for scientific scales because the numbers are important only in so far as they faithfully represent the underlying observed relational system (Roberts 1984, p. 50; Broome 1991, p. 145). This means that no one set of numbers is the 'right' scale – we simply choose a set and use it. But the numbers attached to punishments have a very different meaning and function. These 'numbers' set the limit on the amount of hard treatment that state officials may impose on an offender and they cannot be chosen arbitrarily in the way that the numerals for the scales made by scientists may be chosen. Just as arbitrary acts of power are not law,[7] so sentences are something more than mere numbers. Whether they can properly be described as 'measures' is the next question to be resolved.

Simply establishing the difference between the reasons behind the legal as opposed to the scientific assignment of numbers is not enough to decide this question. It is necessary to go further because of the express connection that von Hirsch's principle of commensurate deserts makes between the degree of seriousness of the crime and the degree of severity of the punishment; in the direction it gives to proportion one to the other; and in the quantitative language used to express the relation. This leads us directly to consider the nature of the link and how it is to be made in practice. Von Hirsch's method specifies that once we have assigned seriousness values to crimes we can arrive at the proper value of punishment by applying a chosen multiplier or rate to those numbers (punishment is thus a function of seriousness, or, $P=fS$). Other theorists also invoke the "penal equation" (Norrie 1996). Nozick (1974, p. 62) proposes the formula punishment $= r$ (responsibility) x H (harm). Scheid talks of "ratio-proportional" judgments that "preserve spacing" (1997, pp. 491–6) and Crocker (1992, p. 1105) argues that "we know there *is* a value and that it is perfectly precise". He points out that (1992, p. 1104):

> To say that the severity of the penalty must be proportionate to the seriousness of the offense is to say that there is some number, whole or fractional, which is multiplied by the latter to yield the former.

Others have found the lure of numbers and formulas equally irresistible. Robinson (1987) makes extensive use of mathematical formulas in his sentencing system and von Hirsch and Jareborg (1991, p. 30) suggest that parts of Robinson's system could be appropriated for use in their model. Although von Hirsch denies that he seeks a formula, he does use specific mathematical terms to describe the linking process, and indeed, many criminologists and social scientists have taken up the controversial task of measuring and linking crimes and punishments.[8] This connection between justice and mathematics is not new. Aristotle wrote about law in mathematical terms and made explicit use of the concept of proportionality, in both its arithmetic and geometric forms, to distinguish between the nature of corrective and distributive justice.[9] The Pythagoreans before him saw justice as reciprocity and maintained not merely that things were knowable, i.e. measurable or numerable, but that things were numbers (Joachim 1951, p. 147). So, although we have established that sentences themselves are not mere numbers, we need to decide whether they can be produced by a process of measurement, i.e. a process that assigns numbers to crimes according to rules, so that the chosen multiplier applied to them can tell us the right number to use to limit the hard treatment imposed on offenders. We need to see if there is a difference between the legal and the mathematical concepts of proportionality and to consider whether some retributivists may have confused our need for precise sentences with a desire for accuracy in measurements.

Von Hirsch's model leans heavily on the difference between the 'ordinal' and 'cardinal' aspects of a scale. These terms originated in measurement theory but have been used extensively in the theoretical and philosophical debates over desert and the construction of modern penalty systems,[10] as well as in debates about utilitarianism and in the related disciplines of economic and welfare theory, criminology and sociology. The scales that bear these names were first classified and described by Stevens, a psychophysicist, who conducted research aimed at measuring the perceived loudness of sounds and other sensory stimuli. He was also interested in the extension of this work to the measurement of other social constructs like the seriousness of crimes. To counter accusations that these fields of research did not produce 'true' measurements, he entered the field of theory, and proceeded to define the different kinds of scales and the mathematical processes associated with each one.

Unlike earlier conceptions that saw measurement as arising from a numerical relationship between a standard and some property in the object being measured, Stevens' approach emphasised that the different levels of measurement correspond to properties of the numbers attached to the item being measured and the allowable tasks that those numbers can be made to perform.[11] Each scale expands on the one before it, and the allowable empirical operations associated with each scale accumulate as they increase in complexity and usefulness (Stevens 1959, p. 25). Stevens distinguished four levels of measurement ranging from the least to the most complicated: the nominal, ordinal, interval and ratio scales (see Appendix A). This scheme reveals that an ordinal scale or ordinal level of measurement denotes only ordering relations. It gives no indication of the degree to which one item on the scale varies in relation to the others, because the values reveal only relationships of 'equality', 'more than' or 'less than' between items. Thus it makes no sense to say that a sixth-placed competitor in a race ran three times as fast as the one placed second, because these numbers indicate only the relative order in which competitors cross the finish line. So, an ordinal scale of crime seriousness would indicate only the bare ordering of crimes and would not show the extent of any differences in seriousness between them.

There are two scale types that can provide what are known as 'cardinal' values. They are the interval and ratio scales. These scales contain an additive function and indicate the degree to which one item on the scale differs from another.[12] However, they can validly be constructed only if it is meaningful to add up and compare degrees of value. Thus, the interval scale gives an indication of relative spacing (today is 10 degrees hotter than yesterday) but it does not allow meaningful ratio-proportional statements to be made because its origin (zero point) and unit of measurement are arbitrary. Ratio scales, by contrast, allow the expression of ratio proportions (this stick is twice as long as that one) because they exhibit a natural zero and only their unit is arbitrarily chosen. So, if we can first establish that it is meaningful to add up crime seriousness, an interval scale of seriousness would allow us both to compare the difference in seriousness between two crimes and to add up the total value of those crimes, and, provided further that it is also meaningful to say that one crime is so many times more serious than another, it would be possible to construct a ratio scale of crime seriousness.[13]

3 Measurement Theory and von Hirsch's Model

Von Hirsch's model and the theory that underpins it have been attacked on three grounds which will be considered in turn. The first is the claim that the distinction between ordinal and cardinal proportionality is unclear and that the link which the model makes between the two kinds of proportionality and the strong and weak roles for desert is untenable. The second suggests that it is impossible to measure desert, crime seriousness, or punishments. The third criticism of the model, and indeed all retributive models, raises the issue of the incommensurability between crimes and punishments.

The Unclear Distinction Between Ordinal and Cardinal Proportionality

Critics from the first category suggest that von Hirsch's model, based on the allegedly critical, but factually unclear, distinction between ordinal and cardinal proportionality, is flawed (Morris and Tonry 1990, p. 87; Frase 1997,

p. 384). At first glance it appears odd that von Hirsch has linked the strong or determining role for desert with the weaker and more vague ordinal scale type and the weaker, limiting role for desert with the more precise cardinal scale. So, under the model, desert is strong when the scale is vague and it is weak when the scale is most precise. It is also apparent that von Hirsch uses these terms in a unique and problematical way. As noted above, an ordinal scale indicates only relative order and contains no connotation of spacing or interval. Von Hirsch has, nevertheless, imported the extra aspects of parity and spacing into his conception of ordinal proportionality and this is what makes it difficult to determine exactly what the distinction between his notions of 'ordinal' and 'cardinal' really is. No assistance in this matter can be gained by consulting von Hirsch's sources for the terms, because Kleinig (1971, 1973), Scheid (1997) and Bedau (1978) all apply them correctly and use ordinal to indicate only rank-ordering and use cardinal to indicate spacing or intervals. This means that von Hirsch's 'ordinal' aspect of a penalty scale actually extends to cover the same functions as the 'cardinal' aspects referred to by these other writers in the same field.

It also means that von Hirsch's statement that the ordinal aspect can be determined with a "high degree of precision" means something quite different, and is far more controversial, compared with the same statement made by those who properly take it to cover only rank ordering and not relative spacing. This idiosyncratic use of the terminology can serve only to cause confusion, to create false agreement and to mask underlying disagreement.[14] For example, it would allow someone, thinking that the 'ordinal' aspect of the scale referred only to rankings, to agree with von Hirsch's statement that ordinal proportionality is capable of determination with a high degree of precision. But if von Hirsch has meant by the statement that *spacing* is capable of determination with a high degree of precision, then the agreement may be only apparent rather than real.

A further difficulty is encountered when the attempt is made to move from the general theoretical propositions to the construction of a practical sanctioning system. In substance what von Hirsch has described could amount to either of two alternatives. The first alternative, depicted in Scenario 1, would require the construction of two cardinal scales, e.g. a ratio scale of seriousness and a ratio scale of punishment, that are related to one another in a proportional way, with each giving an indication of relative spacing or intervals. The second alternative, depicted in Scenario 2, would involve two steps: the first is to construct a true ordinal ranking of crimes; and the second would be to 'space out' the offences using gradations of hard treatment. This scale would use

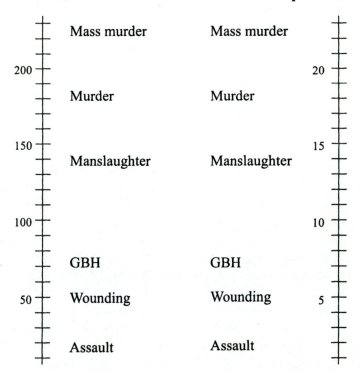

A scale of seriousness   **A punishment scale**

Figure 15.1   Scenario 1: two linked scales: both indicating order and 'spacing'

units of punishment as the interval, but would not need any separate unit of seriousness. If either of these scenarios is the one von Hirsch intended to describe, then it is difficult to give any meaning to the distinction he makes between the 'ordinal' and 'cardinal' aspects of proportionality or to find any significant difference between the role that desert could play in creating the resulting sentencing scale.

As can be seen in Scenario 1, the first interpretation reveals its derivation from the Kantian view that requires equivalence between crimes and punishments. In this scenario, once desert has locked the offences into their relative positions, a second punishment scale is produced by making pro-rata increases or decreases (i.e. multiplication by a rate determined by desert and the other relevant factors like crime control, prison availability, etc.). However, as the scenario also shows, it is only the final form of the scale that really counts: the one that attaches the penalty to each crime. But that scale, von

Hirsch says, is only limited by, and not determined by, desert. Yet once we recognise that the two scales are not of two different kinds at all, but are both cardinal scales, it seems much less clear why desert should have two different functions in each one.

Measurement theory tells us that the numbers or 'spacing' used on a seriousness scale are purely arbitrary. Any numbers will do, so long as they represent the perceived differences in seriousness between the crimes. If this scenario is the intended one, then von Hirsch has linked desert's determining role to the one arbitrary part of the scale. Furthermore, it does not matter how the seriousness scale is numbered or spaced because the numbering or, more accurately, the effective amount of hard treatment, will be changed when we apply the rate chosen by the requirements of humanity in punishment, resources, crime control, etc. At this point, desert has only a share in deciding the conversion rate, along with the other factors, and so again, it cannot be the sole determining factor in any meaningful sense. More importantly, constructing a ratio scale that maintains the relative positions or ratios of the difference in seriousness between crimes would be possible only if we can meaningfully make ratio-proportional comparisons between them (this crime is four times more serious than that one) and if we can validly add up crime values in cases of multiple offending. Neither of these propositions has been established, and in fact, common law sentencing practice indicates that they are false.

If spacing is as important as von Hirsch has suggested, then it also seems apparent from Scenario 1 that one of the scales is redundant, as both appear to be doing the same thing. We could place a third scale called 'blameworthiness' into the model, or a fourth labelled 'desert', and they would all function as proxies for one another. Significantly, no one set of numbers would provide the 'right answer', and again, only the one prescribing actual punishments would be worthy of our attention and debate because only that scale provides the numbers that have any real meaning in the world of hard treatment. I suggest that once von Hirsch introduced the idea of spacing into his 'ordinal' aspect he also introduced redundancy for the determining role for desert that he associated with that scale and lost the strong sense of precision that went with it. The only way for desert to retain the strong or determining role would be if there is a relation of equality between seriousness and punishment, i.e. if the other factors are given no effect. Of course, the mathematical concept of 'proportional' does include the concept of 'equal', just as the true cardinal includes the ordinal. However, given von Hirsch's rejection of the notion that we can provide equal punishments, his insistence on the difference between

Phase 1: ordering

Phase 2: penalty spacing

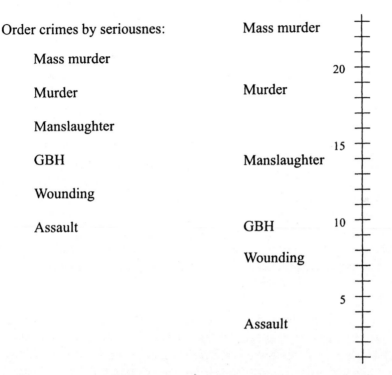

Order crimes by seriousnes:

   Mass murder

   Murder

   Manslaughter

   GBH

   Wounding

   Assault

Figure 15.2   **Scenario 2: an ordinal scale of seriousness and a 'cardinal' scale of penalties**

the two aspects of proportionality, and his repeated assertions that there are two roles for desert, it will be necessary to return to the issue of the structure of the model after we have considered the second scenario.

Scenario 2 represents a different approach: one that allows desert to have two roles, but this too is an approach that robs it of the kind of primacy claimed for it by von Hirsch. This interpretation is faithful to the true meaning of the terms ordinal and cardinal, but runs counter to von Hirsch's use of the term ordinal. Taking this view, the first step would be to rank crimes in order of seriousness, and then, having set an upper limit of punishment, the next step would be to allocate each crime a position on the scale. This approach would place desert at the centre of the model, but its role would be secondary in the sense that crime seriousness would be the sole determining factor only in the first stage, where simple rankings are to be decided. At the second stage desert would have two roles: it would be one of the other factors taken into account when setting the outer limit; and would be decisive, again in a secondary sense, only after the outer limits have been set and the positions of the crimes are being allocated.[15] This is similar to the function that Kleinig (1973, p. 51–2) and Scheid (1997, pp. 478–82) identify for desert when they point out that desert claims are notoriously vague in an absolute sense but can be given much more precision once a merit-based institution has been established which has set limits on punishments. It is also consistent with von Hirsch's own view that cardinal desert claims are much more difficult to quantify and more dependent on other moral assumptions (1990, p. 284).

Given that von Hirsch has not used the standard meaning of the terms ordinal and cardinal to describe his model, nor adopted the meaning used by others working in the same field, it is difficult to determine how to give practical substance to this 'crucial' distinction. Neither is it obvious why the one vague umbrella term 'ordinal' should contain the three distinct aspects of parity between individual offenders, rank ordering of crimes, and relative spacing of penalties on a scale. To find some clue, it is necessary to look at how von Hirsch has defined the difference between 'ordinality' and 'cardinality' in the 16 years since he first adopted the terms.[16]

Appendix B summarises the different descriptions that von Hirsch has used to amplify the meaning and scope of the three incarnations of the desert principle: a) the general principle; b) the 'ordinal' aspect; and c) the 'cardinal' aspect. Although each statement on its own is clear enough, as a whole they do not seem to add up to the package that von Hirsch claims they do. Looking carefully at the substance of the distinction, it appears that von Hirsch has described more than simply the difference between the two technical aspects of a scale. There also seems to be a shift in focus between the two different phases of the punishment process: the first stage is setting maximum penalties for crimes; and the second is the allocation of a particular penalty to an individual offender.[17] So the substance of the distinction lying at the heart of the model may be wider than the distinction that the use of the technical scaling terms ordinal and cardinal suggests because what has also been described is the amplification of the foundational principle of desert into its general application (i.e. the setting of maximum penalties), its specific application (to individual cases) and the logical consequences of its application (parity between offenders).

This second distinction is not immediately obvious because of the ambiguity of the word punishment which is used at critical points in the description. Punishment can refer either to the maximum penalty set for each crime or to the specific sentence given to an individual offender for the actual crime committed. This ambiguity allows for slippage during a debate about the role that desert plays in deciding 'punishments'. What may begin as a discussion about the importance of comparative desert in allocating individual sentences, say, to two different burglars (the controversial issue between Morris and von Hirsch) may end up as a debate over the role of desert in structuring a maximum penalty scale for crimes in general – an area where there is more agreement on desert's role. The fact that the slip has taken place is obscured by the veil of uncertainty created by the problematic use of the terms ordinal and cardinal and the ambiguity of the words penalty and punishment. It is worth noting that others, like Ashworth, who use von Hirsch's ordinal/cardinal distinction appear to restrict its use only to the structure of general penalty scales and do not include the extra aspect of parity between individual offenders in their description (Ashworth 1995).

Although this may clarify the underlying issue in the debate between von Hirsch and Morris, we are still no closer to uncovering which of the two scenarios is the better interpretation of von Hirsch's sentencing model. We have, however, established these points:

1) the terms 'ordinal' and 'cardinal' do not illuminate the problem because von Hirsch uses them in such a way that his intended meaning is contrary to the technical meaning of the terms which continue to be used in philosophical debates over punishment and in other closely related disciplines. The appropriateness of extending an established term with a specific technical meaning like 'ordinal' to cover the three distinct aspects of parity, ranking and spacing is questionable. Furthermore, this usage can sabotage debate by destroying the shared meaning of the words;

2) the substance of von Hirsch's distinction may actually be between the general and the specific applications of the desert principle: i.e. between the setting of maximum penalties and the individual sentencing phases of the criminal justice system. If this is so, we can conclude that merely pointing to the technical ordinal/cardinal distinction does not advance von Hirsch's position in the debate with Morris because he places the issue of parity under the term 'ordinal' by stipulation rather than argument;

3) the application of the concepts of measurement to the model suggests the tentative conclusion that Scenario 2 is the more appropriate interpretation, but this approach may rob desert of the two roles that von Hirsch claims it has in the construction of a penalty scale. If Scenario 2 is the better model, it may be better to abandon the terms cardinal and ordinal and accept that the role of desert is neither determining nor limiting, but is to provide

comparative though not absolute guidance in the task of devising penalties for crimes.

We Cannot Measure Desert, Crime Seriousness or Punishment

A second stream of critics argue that von Hirsch's model suffers from the same problem that plagues all retributive systems, namely, that it is simply impossible to measure desert, the seriousness of crimes, or the severity of punishments.[18] If they are correct, then Scenario 1 would appear to be ruled out. Despite these philosophical doubts and a number of methodological problems,[19] researchers have attempted to measure our capacity to assess desert and to scale the seriousness of crimes and deserved punishments. To avoid these problems, and the criticism made by van den Haag (1982, 1987), for example, that what counts is not what people *think* seriousness is, but rather what it *really* is, von Hirsch has suggested that we need more research on what the actual effects of crimes are. This raises the issue of whether there is such a thing as 'real' seriousness as opposed to perceived seriousness. Von Hirsch emphasises, however, that this empirical research would have to be supplemented by value judgements (1983, p. 215), and so appears to avoid confronting the issue of whether seriousness is a measure of a property in a crime or a measure of our response to it. While it does appear from the psychophysical research that individuals are able to make remarkably consistent estimations of such things as temperature, loudness, electrical current, etc., the issue of measuring the seriousness of crimes presents more difficulty (Stevens 1959; Duncan 1984).

There is a crucial difference between the scaling of perceptions of seriousness and the scaling of perceived temperature. In the case of concepts like temperature we have external, objective physical sources of standardisation. We can compare the expansion of mercury with different perceptions of 'hotness', or measured units of sugar in an ice-cream with perceptions of its sweetness. In the social sphere, we can check our assessments of 'anomie' against observed suicide rates, or assessments of political leanings with actual voting behaviour. But when we assess the seriousness of crimes there is no externally observable, objective source of 'real' seriousness that we can use to standardise assessments made by different people. I suggest that our assessments of seriousness are more akin to the kinds of aesthetic or moral assessments we make which are judgments or conclusions drawn about events and people, and not measurements of a property found within them. These kinds of assessments tell us more about ourselves and our values than they do about the nature of the things that evoke them. In this sense the 'seriousness' of a crime is not like the sweetness of an ice-cream or the heat of a day but is more like the 'deliciousness' of an ice-cream or the 'friendliness' of an act. This view does not deny that there are identifiable aspects to crimes, but it means that we need to focus on developing the criteria for a reasoned discussion of the relative seriousness of crimes based on community values, rather than treating seriousness as a property of a crime and attempting to measure it, and indeed, this is what von Hirsch and Jareborg have begun in their pioneering work on the living standard (1991). If there is no such thing as 'real' seriousness, but only 'perceived' seriousness, then the process of sentencing cannot be seen as the scientific discovery of the seriousness in a crime and the allocation of a number to it which is then converted into a punishment unit by applying a rate of exchange. If seriousness is not an objective attribute of a crime, then there is no 'right' number to be discovered simply by observation, recognition, or research surveys of emotional responses. This confirms the point that there is no instrument that can do our work for us or one single concept like desert that can determine a just punishment. It suggests that the search for a measured scale of seriousness is misconceived because what we are really trying to calibrate and control is not crime, but ourselves.

The measurement of punishment is a different issue because hard treatment is a physical act and it appears that some of its effects can be measured.[20] It is important therefore that the nature of our assessments of seriousness and the nature of punishment are clearly understood. Criminal punishment is the imposition by the state of hard treatment on offenders for their offences. Because of the values we hold dear like liberty and personal autonomy, we have chosen to react to crimes after they occur, rather than take extreme measures to prevent them occurring. So punishment, like our assessments of seriousness, is also a response to crime. I have already noted in the discussion of Scenario 1, that both 'seriousness' and 'deserved punishment' appear to be doing the same thing, i.e. giving effect to a response to crimes. The first, seriousness, is the intellectual or mental judgement formed in response to an offender's crime and the second, punishment, is our action taken in response to it.

This intuition finds some confirmation in the studies on crime seriousness. Parton has speculated that people find it difficult to separate cognitive notions of crime seriousness from notions of deserved punishment (1991, p. 73), and reported a scaling study in which persons instructed to judge crimes in terms of seriousness generated the same cognitive map as those instructed to judge deserved punishment (1985, cited in Parton et al. 1991, p. 74). He argued that this finding is troublesome, and indicates that perhaps both ordinary people and investigators are confused as to the nature of the seriousness of crimes, but I argue otherwise. Gescheider, Catlin and Fontana conducted studies to establish psychological scales of the seriousness of 20 crimes and the perceived severity of their associated punishments. The judged seriousness of the crimes and the judged severity of punishments were "related to the physical duration of punishment by the same non-linear function" and the researchers argued that these results suggested that "in general it seems to be true that for our sample of subjects, that the punishment matches the crime" (1982, pp. 275, 278).

I suggest that these studies may go some way towards confirming my argument made above that our assessments of the severity of crimes amount in substance to the same thing as our assessments of the proper punishments for crimes. If we are, in fact, quantifying our chosen response to crimes using punishment as the unit, then these research results are not surprising. They bear out what I have already suggested, that both represent our responses to crimes. This indicates that the sentencing process is better seen as a valuing process rather than a mathematical one, and is further evidence for preferring Scenario 2 over Scenario 1. Once seriousness and punishment are no longer seen as two 'things' produced by a measuring process and linked arithmetically by a chosen rate, we no longer need to search for the elusive 'criminal' property in an offence that can be quantified and transposed into a just measure of pain.

Adopting the second scenario would confirm that there are significant differences between the legal and the mathematical concepts of proportionality and shield the model from much of the criticism that has been levelled at it. In particular it would save the model from Mathieson's accusations that it has begged the question to be decided and falsely claimed a mathematical precision (1990), Walker's charge that it amounts to pseudo science (1971, 1978, 1997), and Braithwaite and Pettit's assertion that it is impossible to put into practice (1990). Given that psychophysical and anthropological studies show that we are calibrating beings who persistently develop and abide by systems of valuation,[21] Scenario 2 appears closer to describing the reality of the human process of sentencing. I suggest that the mathematical imagery has led us in a false direction and that the process should be reconceived to rid it of this hangover from the past that saw justice simply as retaliation. The model works better without it.

The Problem of Incommensurability

The third criticism relates to the issue of the incommensurability of crimes and punishments and the doomed search for a common element existing between them. These critics argue that even if the two could be measured, there is no unique, non-arbitrary way to transpose a measure of crime seriousness into a measure of hard treatment.[22] One way to avoid the problem of incommensurability is to argue that the relation is symbolic, not literal, and does not require there to be a common element between the two, but I suggest that re-conceiving the process as one of evaluation, rather than measurement, provides a better solution. If we are simply calibrating our responses to crimes using punishment as the unit of value, then it is not necessary to find a common element between the two things because there is only one meaningful way to rate the worth of a thing, and that is necessarily by reference to something else, something different in kind.

A similar point was made by Aristotle in his meditation on justice, and by Marx in his exposition of the nature of capital.[23] This view recognises that value is given to a thing, not found within it, and forces us to reconsider the nature of the sentencing process. The opportunity that sentencing offers us each time is the opportunity to choose what to do. What is common between crimes is the fact that we have chosen to respond to them by imposing hard treatment on those who commit them. Their significance is not that they are 'things' of a particular kind containing a common element, but that for our own reasons we have chosen them as things worthy of a particular response. This suggests that we are not comparing two different things (crimes and punishments) but comparing things of a similar nature (separate state acts of punishment). Accepting this interpretation of the sentencing process disposes of the problem of incommensurability between crimes and punishments (although admittedly it raises the deeper problem of the commensurabilty of values) and puts us in a position to consider some modifications to von Hirsch's model.

Conclusions

Applying measurement theory to von Hirsch's model reveals that his new 'scales' of justice do not yet provide enough practical guidance for the construction of a system of sanctions. I have sought to show that they return us to a conception of punishment that von Hirsch rejected when he abandoned the Kantian notion of equality in punishment and encourage an unhelpful mathematical interpretation of the legal concept of proportionality by implying that sentencing is akin to a scientific process. Critics have argued that the distinction von Hirsch makes between ordinal and cardinal proportionality is unclear and the application of measurement theory to the model supports this assessment. There are two sources of confusion: the first is von Hirsch's peculiar use of the technical terms and the link he makes between the ordinal and cardinal aspects of the scale and the determining and limiting roles of desert; the second is his inclusion of parity between offenders in his description of the 'ordinal' aspect of a penalty scale. Certainly, neither link can be accounted for merely by pointing to the 'elementary' difference between 'ordinality' and 'cardinality' (von Hirsch 1984, p. 1097). I have questioned whether it is appropriate or helpful to include the aspect of parity between individual offenders in a discussion of the construction of a crime/penalty structure, and I suggest that including this aspect in the model begs an important question that should be debated only after the primary task of allocating maximum and minimum penalties to crimes has been carried out.

In the light of these difficulties I suggest that we should reconsider the usefulness of von Hirsch's distinction between 'ordinal' and 'cardinal' proportionality,[24] and at very least restrict the use of these terms to the setting of statutory penalties and not extend the ordinal aspect to include parity. As it stands, the ambiguity of these terms can sabotage debate as participants fill the gaps with their own conceptions, thereby allowing slippage during the course of debate and creating risks of false agreement and the masking of deeper disagreements. Instead we should refocus debate more directly on the separate issues of the proper spacing of sanctions for offences, the absolute values and limits of punishment, parity between offenders (including the justification for any departures from the parity principle) and the role that our conceptions of fairness, desert and offence seriousness should play in deciding these questions.

Although measurement theory has shown that von Hirsch's new 'scales' of measurement are no better as an image of the sentencing process than the old representation of justice as a balancing scale, it has also revealed that the model can be adapted without loss of substance and with an increase in clarity if the process is reconceived as a process of evaluation rather than one of measurement and transposition. This would protect the model from the criticism that it attempts the impossible task of measuring and comparing two incommensurables: crime and punishment. In Part 3, I suggested that what we are really doing when sentencing is using our evaluative response to the crime to guide the calibration of our chosen physical action made response to the offender. I argued that we ourselves and our own values are the only source of a scale, and that the 'seriousness of crimes' and 'punishment' are not two different 'things' linked by a mathematical process. Rather they represent the same thing expressed two ways: our response to offenders and their crimes.

The first of these two responses – our assessment of seriousness – can be expressed in the adjectives of comparison and does not require any numbers or calibration beyond the descriptive words we use, nor any more technical a method of production than reasoned discourse. The arguments and evidence and the values that underpin them are what give these judgments their legal and moral force. This means that we need only one set of numbers, not two, because it is only the second response – the amount of hard treatment imposed on the offender – that requires a numerical limit to be placed upon it. We could begin with the legislative task of deciding on the outer limits for punishment using all the factors, including offence seriousness, that von Hirsch has identified. The next step would be to allocate crimes to positions on that scale using our perceptions of their seriousness as a guide. At this point seriousness would be central in deciding positions but would not solely determine absolute values. Finally we would need to consider the principles that should be applied at the second stage of deciding sentences for individual offenders. I suspect that just as the role played by desert is modified by other factors in the setting of absolute penalties, so too will its role be modified in the second stage of giving individual sentences, and that we will find that desert is always subject to adjustments required by other fundamental values.

Under this approach, desert would remain a central guiding value that limits the effect that can be given to other competing values at both stages of the criminal sentencing process, but it may never operate alone in the strong 'determining' role that von Hirsch has argued for. Accordingly, I suggest that this modified version of Scenario 2 provides the best model, but before closing the discussion I want to consider the implications of my position. If I am right in my claims about the nature of the seriousness of crimes and the nature of punishment then we can drop the mathematical imagery from the sentencing model altogether. This would affirm that the language of proportionality is the language of the law and not mathematics, and recognise that the method to be employed is not the scientific method, but the principled, practical reasoning of the common law. The application of the insights gained from measurement theory to von Hirsch's proposals has shown that sentencing is not a science, because science aims to discover order and exploit the regularity that exists in the world, whereas law aims to bring a chosen order into the world by imposing regularity upon it. Does this mean then, that sentencing is, as the judges in our courts often remind us, 'an art and not a science' and amounts to no more than relying on a feeling, an intuition, or a simple matter of preference?

I suggest that sentencing is no more an art than it is a science, because art's aims for itself are very different from those of the law. Bate (1997, pp. 307–11) building on Empson's work on the art of ambiguity, has described Shakespeare's genius as "the refusal of either/or" and this implies that art is a pursuit aimed at breaking and blurring the rules and challenging order, rather than one aimed at justifying and enforcing the rules, as law is. The purpose of this essay has been to show, by an analysis of von Hirsch's new scales of justice, that sentencing is neither an art nor a science, but something apart, because where art blurs the lines, and science discovers the lines, law must take the responsibility to choose where to draw the lines.

Notes

1   I would like to thank Kate Warner for her valuable comments on earlier drafts of this paper and the participants at the Glasgow Sentencing and Society Conference for their helpful input.
2   Von Hirsch's theory and his model have been developed over many years since 1981 and have been presented in many forms (1981, 1983, 1984, 1985, 1990, 1991, 1993, 1998). I have generally provided references to the most recent version (1998).
3   Von Hirsch has developed this approach in a number of works (1981, p. 253; 1983, p. 212; 1985, p. 3; 1990, p. 282; 1993, p. 18; 1998, p. 173).
4   One of the debates, for example, is whether utility or preference can be measured on a cardinal level as opposed merely to an ordinal one.
5   Von Hirsch (1984, pp. 1096–7; 1985, p. 39–45; 1998, p. 173–4). The distinction forms the basis of his debate with Norval Morris over the role of desert in criminal sentencing. Both Morris and Frase have suggested that the distinction is unclear (Morris 1982, pp. 199–202; Morris and Tonry 1990, p. 87; Frase 1997, p. 384).
6   This description of the process is gleaned mostly from von Hirsch and Jareborg (1991), though some references can be found throughout other works (1983, 1984, 1985, 1990, 1998). I have added the symbols to the text.
7   *Hurtado v California* 110 US 516 at 536 (1884).
8   The first landmark study was Sellin and Wolfgang (1964). See also Borg (1988), Carlson and Williams (1993), Duncan (1984), Durham (1985), Fitzmaurice and Pease (1985), Gescheider et al. (1982), Golash and Lynch (1995), Katz (1999), Miethe (1984), O'Connell and Whelan (1996), Parton et al. (1991), Pease et al. (1974), Rauma (1991), Samuel and Moulds (1986), Sebba and Nathan (1984), Tyler and Boekmann (1997), Wagner and Pease (1978), Walker, M. (1978), Walker, N. (1978).
9   See Aristotle's *Nichomachean Ethics*, Book 5, translated by David Ross (1925), and Vinogradoff (1908), Joachim (1951), von Leyden (1985), Barnes (1995) and Benson (1992).
10   See Kleinig (1973), Davis (1992), Scheid (1997), and Hoffman (1989).
11   This becomes significant later when we consider whether 'seriousness' is an inherent property of offences, or whether it is something quite different.
12   Roberts (1979, p. 51). The term cardinal is used in discussions of utility (Griffin 1986, p. 94).

13 Both these propositions are open to doubt (Fitzmaurice and Pease 1986; Pease et al. 1974; Wagner and Pease 1978).

14 Von Hirsch's unorthodox use of the term 'ordinal' has caused confusion. Hoffman (1989) is one who encountered difficulties in applying the model's linking of 'ordinal' with spacing, greater precision, and the stronger role for desert. While Hoffman's underlying argument is sound, it becomes entangled in the false distinction between ordinal and cardinal.

15 It is not clear from von Hirsch's writings whether he advocates this approach. At times he suggests that the limits should be set first, followed by the spacing of crimes according to seriousness; at others it appears that the crimes should be spaced out according to seriousness and then anchored according to the combination of other factors and desert. I would adopt the former course.

16 Over the years it has not been entirely clear whether the terms refer to a penalty scale, to proportionality itself, to punishment severity, to seriousness, to desert, or to all of these aspects. See especially (1985, ch. 4) for the variety of referents for 'ordinality' and 'cardinality'.

17 This approach to the distinction between the 'ordinal' and 'cardinal' aspects of a penalty scale has also been suggested by Gardner (1998, p. 39).

18 Mathieson (1990) and Braithwaite and Pettit (1990) direct their criticism specifically to von Hirsch's model; Hart (1984) and Lacey (1988) identify these as weaknesses of retributive theories in general.

19 See especially Parton et al. (1991), Miethe (1984), Duncan (1984), Wagner and Pease (1978), Fitmaurice and Pease (1984) and Walker, M. (1978). See also note 8, above.

20 Duncan (1984); Mathieson (1990); Ashworth and Wasik (1998, Part III). But see the chapter by Dingwall and Harding in this volume.

21 Handy (1970, pp. 93–4). See also Whitman (1995).

22 See, e.g. Hart (1984, pp. 161–2); Gross (1981, p. 273); Mathieson (1990, p. 131), Kleinig (1973, pp. 118–20).

23 See Aristotle *Nichomachean Ethics*, Book 5, translated by David Ross (1925), and Benson (1992).

24 Possibly this conclusion comes too late, as references to von Hirsch's ordinal/cardinal distinction are now common in sentencing literature: see the Editors' Introduction, Ashworth and Wasik (1998).

References

Aristotle (1925), *The Nichomachean Ethics*, trans. David Ross, Oxford: Oxford University Press.

Ashworth, A. (1995), *Sentencing and Criminal Justice*, 2nd edn, London: Butterworths.

Ashworth, A. and von Hirsch, A. (1997), 'Recognising Elephants: The problem of the custody threshold', *Criminal Law Review*, p. 187.

Ashworth, A. and von Hirsch, A. (eds) (1998), *Principled Sentencing*, 2nd edn, Oxford: Hart.

Ashworth, A. and Wasik, M. (eds) (1998), *Fundamentals of Sentencing Theory*, Oxford: Clarendon Press.

Barnes, J. (1995), *The Cambridge Companion to Aristotle*, Cambridge: Cambridge University Press.

Bate, J. (1997), *The Genius of Shakespeare*, London: Picador.

Bedau, H. A. (1978), 'Retribution and the Theory of Punishment', *Journal of Philosophy*, Vol. 75, p. 601.

Bedau, H. A. (1984), 'Classification-Based Sentencing: Some conceptual and ethical problems', *Criminal and Civil Confinement*, Vol. 10, p. 1.

Benson, P. (1992), 'The Basis of Corrective Justice and Its Relation to Distributive Justice', *Iowa Law Review*, Vol. 77, p. 515.

Bohrnstedt, G. and Borgatta, E. (eds) (1981), *Social Measurement*, Beverly Hills: Sage.

Borg, I. (1988), 'Revisiting Thurstone's and Coombs' Scales on the Seriousness of Crime', *European Journal of Social Psychology*, Vol. 18, p. 53.

Bottoms, A. (1998), 'Five Puzzles in von Hirsch's Theory of Punishment', in A. Ashworth and M. Wasik (eds), *Fundamentals of Sentencing Theory*, Oxford: Clarendon Press.

Braithwaite, J. and Pettit, P. (1990), *Not Just Deserts: A republican theory of punishment*, Oxford: Clarendon Press.

Broome, J. (1991), *Weighing Goods: Equality, Uncertainty and Time*, Oxford: Basil Blackwell.

Carlson, J.M. and Williams, T. (1993), 'Perspectives on the Seriousness of Crimes', *Social Science Research*, Vol. 22, p. 190.

Caws, P. (1959), 'Definition and Measurement in Physics', in C.W. Churchman and P. Ratoosh (eds), *Measurement: Definitions and theories*, New York: John Wiley and Sons, p. 3.

Christie, N. (1992), 'Against Just Desert', *Canadian Journal of Law and Jurisprudence*, Vol. 5, p. 5.

Churchman, C.W. (1959), 'Why Measure?', in C.W. Churchman and P. Ratoosh (eds), *Measurement: Definitions and Theories*, New York: John Wiley and Sons, p. 83.

Churchman, C.W. and Ratoosh, P. (eds) (1959), *Measurement: Definitions and Theories*, New York: John Wiley and Sons.

Crocker, L. (1992), 'The Upper Limit of Just Punishment', *Emory Law Journal*, Vol. 41, p. 1059.

Davis, M. (1992), *To Make the Punishment Fit the Crime*, Westview Press: Boulder.

Duncan, O.D. (1984), *Notes on Social Measurement: Historical and Critical*, New York: Sage.

Durham, A. (1985), 'Weighting Punishment: A commentary on Nevares-Muniz', *Journal of Criminal Law and Criminology*, Vol. 76, p. 201.

Fitzmaurice, C. and Pease, K. (1986), *The Psychology of Judicial Sentencing*, Manchester: Manchester University Press.

Frankfort-Nachmias, C. and Nachmias, D. (1996), *Research Methods in the Social Sciences*, London: Arnold.

Frase, R. S. (1997), 'Sentencing Principles in Theory and Practice', *Crime and Justice*, Vol. 22, p. 363.

Galligan, D.J. (1981a), 'Guidelines and Just Deserts: A critique of recent trends in sentencing reform', *Criminal Law Review*, p. 297.

Galligan, D.J. (1981b), 'The Return to Retribution in Penal Theory', in C. Tapper (ed), *Crime, Proof and Punishment*, London: Butterworths, p. 144.

Gardner, J. (1998), 'Crime: In proportion and in perspective', in A. Ashworth and M. Wasik (eds), *Fundamentals of Sentencing Theory*, Oxford: Clarendon Press, p. 31.

Gescheider, G.A., Catlin, E.C., and Fontana, A.M. (1982), 'Psychophysical Measurement of the Judged Seriousness of Crimes and Severity of Punishments', *Bulletin of the Psychonomic Society*, Vol. 19, p. 275.

Golash, D. and Lynch, J. P. (1995), 'Public Opinion, Crime Seriousness, and Sentencing Policy', *American Journal of Criminal Law*, Vol. 22, p. 703.

Goldman, A.H. (1979) 'The Paradox of Punishment', *Philosophy and Public Affairs*, Vol. 9, p. 42.

Griffin, J. (1986), *Well-Being: Its meaning, measurement and moral importance*, Oxford: Clarendon Press.

Gross, H. (1981) 'Proportional Punishment and Justifiable Sentences', in H. Gross and A. von Hirsch (ed.), *Sentencing*, Oxford: Oxford University Press, p. 272.

Gross, H. (1986), 'Culpability and Desert', in J. Feinberg and H. Gross (eds), *Philosophy of Law*, 3rd edn, Belmont: Wadsworth, p. 646.

Gross, H. and von Hirsch, A. (1981), *Sentencing*, Oxford: Oxford University Press.

Handy, R. (1970), *The Measurement of Values*, St Louis: Warren T. Green.

Hart, H.L.A. (1984), *Punishment and Responsibility*, Oxford: Clarendon Press.

Hoffmann, J.L. (1989), 'On the Perils of Line-Drawing: Juveniles and the death penalty', *Hastings Law Journal*, Vol. 40, p. 229.

Joachim, H.H. (1951), *The Nichomachaean Ethics: A Commentary*, Oxford: Clarendon Press.

Kinsella, N.S. (1997), 'A Libertarian Theory of Punishment and Rights', *Loyola of Los Angeles Law Review*, Vol. 30, p. 607.

Kleinig, J. (1971), 'The Concept of Desert', *American Philosophical Quarterly*, Vol. 8, p. 71.

Kleinig, J. (1973), *Punishment and Desert*, The Hague: Martinus Nijhoff.

Kleinig, J. (1978), 'Crime and the Concept of Harm', *American Philosophical Quarterly*, Vol. 15, p. 27.

Krantz, D.H., Luce, R.D., Suppes, P. and Tversky, A. (1971), *Foundations of Measurement, Volume 1*, London: Academic Press.

Lacey, N. (1988), *State Punishment: Political principles and community values*, London: Routledge.

Mathieson, T. (1990), *Prison on Trial*, London: Sage.

Miethe, T. (1984), 'Types of Consensus in Public Evaluations of Crime: An illustration of strategies for measuring "consensus"', *Journal of Criminal Law and Criminology*, Vol. 75, p. 459.

Morris, N. (1982), *Madness and the Criminal Law*, Chicago: University of Chicago Press.

Morris, N. and Tonry, M. (1990), *Between Prison and Probation: Intermediate punishments in a rational sentencing system*, New York: Oxford University Press.

Neyers, J.W. (1998), 'The Inconsistencies of Aristotle's Theory of Corrective Justice', *Canadian Journal of Law and Jurisprudence*, Vol. 11, p. 311.

Norrie, A. (1996), 'The Limits of Justice: Finding Fault in the Criminal Law', *Modern Law Review*, Vol. 59, p. 540.

Nozick, R. (1974), *Anarchy, State and Utopia*, Oxford: Basil Blackwell.

Nussbaum, M.C. (1997), 'Flawed Foundations: The philosophical critique of a particular type of economics', *University of Chicago Law Review*, Vol. 64, p. 1197.

Nussbaum, M.C. and Sen, A. (1993), *The Quality of Life*, Oxford: Oxford University Press.

O'Connell, M. and Whelan, A. (1996), 'Taking Wrongs Seriously', *British Journal of Criminology*, Vol. 36, p. 299.

Parton, D.A., Hansel, M. and Stratton, J. (1991), 'Measuring Crime Seriousness: Lessons from the National Survey of Crime Severity', *British Journal of Criminology*, Vol. 31, p. 72.

Pease, K., Ireson, J. and Thorpe, J. (1974), 'Additivity Assumptions in the Measurement of Delinquency', *British Journal of Criminology*, Vol. 14, p. 256.

Pincoffs, E. (1966), *The Rationale of Legal Punishment*, New York: Humanities Press.

Rauma, D. (1991), 'The Context of Normative Consensus: An Expansion of the Rossi/Berk Consensus Model, with an application to crime seriousness', *Social Science Research*, Vol. 20, p. 1.

Rawls, J. (1971), *A Theory of Justice*, Oxford: Oxford University Press.

Roberts, F.S. (1984), *Measurement Theory*, Cambridge: Cambridge University Press.

Robinson, P.H. (1987), 'A Sentencing System for the 21st Century', *Texas Law Review*, Vol. 66, p. 1.

Robinson, P.H. (1996), 'The Criminal-Civil Distinction and the Utility of Desert', *Boston University Law Review*, Vol. 76, p. 201.

Robinson, P.H. (1997), 'One Perspective on Sentencing Reform in the United States', *Criminal Law Forum*, Vol. 8, p. 1.

Robinson, P. H. and Darley, J. (1997), 'The Utility of Desert', *Northwestern Law Review*, Vol. 91, p. 453.

Samuel, W. and Moulds, E. (1986), 'The Effect of Crime Severity on Perceptions of Fair Punishment: A California case study', *Journal of Criminal Law and Criminology*, Vol. 77, p. 931.

Scheid, D. (1997), 'Constructing a Theory of Punishment, Desert, and the Distribution of Punishments', *Canadian Journal of Law and Jurisprudence*, Vol. 10, p. 441.

Sebba, L. and Nathan, G. (1984), 'Further Explorations in the Scaling of Penalties', *British Journal of Criminology*, Vol. 23, p. 221.

Stevens, S. S. (1959), 'Measurement, Psychophysics, and Utility' in C.W. Churchman and P. Ratoosh (eds), *Measurement: Definitions and Theories*, New York: John Wiley and Sons, p. 18.

Tonry, M. (1996), *Sentencing Matters*, Oxford: Oxford University Press.

Tyler, T. and Boekmann, R. (1997), 'The Psychology of Public Support for Punishing Rule Breakers', *Law and Society Review*, p. 237.

Van Den Haag, E. (1982), 'The Criminal Law as a Threat System', *Journal of Criminal Law and Criminology*, Vol. 73, p. 769.

Van Den Haag, E. (1987), 'Punishment: Desert and crime control', *Michigan Law Review*, Vol. 85, p. 1250.

Van Ness, D.W. (1995), 'Anchoring Just Deserts', *Criminal Law Forum*, Vol. 6, p. 507.

Vinogradoff, P. (1908), 'Aristotle on Legal Redress', *Columbia Law Review*, Vol. 8, p. 548.

Von Hirsch, A. (1981), 'Doing Justice: The principle of commensurate deserts', in H. Gross and A. von Hirsch (eds), *Sentencing*, Oxford: Oxford University Press, p. 243.

Von Hirsch, A. (1983), 'Commensurability and Crime Prevention: Evaluating formal sentencing structures and their rationale', *Journal of Criminal Law and Criminology*, Vol. 74, p. 209.

Von Hirsch, A. (1984), 'Equality, "Anisonomy" and Justice', *Michigan Law Review*, Vol. 82, p. 1093.

Von Hirsch, A. (1985), *Past or Future Crimes*, Manchester: Manchester University Press.

Von Hirsch, A. (1990), 'Proportionality in the Philosophy of Punishment', *Criminal Law Forum*, Vol. 1, p. 259.

Von Hirsch, A. (1993), *Censure and Sanctions*, Oxford: Clarendon Press.

Von Hirsch, A. (1998), 'Proportionate Sentences: A desert perspective', in A. Ashworth and A. von Hirsch (eds), *Principled Sentencing*, 2nd edn, Oxford: Hart, p. 168.

Von Hirsch, A. and Ashworth, A. (1992), 'Not Just Deserts: A response to Braithwaite and Pettit', *Oxford Journal of Legal Studies*, Vol. 12, p. 83.

Von Hirsch, A. and Jareborg, N. (1991), 'Gauging Criminal Harm: A living-standard snalysis', *Oxford Journal of Legal Studies*, Vol. 11, p. 1.

Von Leyden, W. (1985), *Aristotle on Equality and Justice*, London: Macmillan.

Wagner, H. and Pease, K. (1978), 'On Adding up Scores of Offence Seriousness', *British Journal of Criminology*, Vol. 18, p. 175.

Walker, M. (1978), 'Measuring the Seriousness of Crimes', *British Journal of Criminology*, Vol. 18, p. 348.

Walker, N. (1971), 'Psychophysics and the Recording Angel', *British Journal of Criminology*, Vol. 11, p. 191.

Walker, N. (1997), 'Harms, Probabilities and Precautions', *Oxford Journal of Legal Studies*, vol. 17, p. 611.

Warner, R. (1992), 'Incommensurability as a Jurisprudential Puzzle', *Chicago-Kent Law Review*, Vol. 68, p. 147.

Whiteley, C. (1956), 'On Retribution', *Philosophy*, Vol. 31, p. 154.

Whitman, J.Q. (1995), 'Ancient Rights and Wrongs: At the origins of law and the state: Supervision of violence, mutilation of bodies or setting of prices?', *Chicago-Kent Law Review*, Vol. 71, p. 41.

Yannopoulos, G.N. (1997), *Modelling the Legal Decision Process for Information Technology Applications in Law*, The Hague: Kluwer.

Young, A. (1993), 'Two Scales of Justice', *Criminal Law Quarterly*, p. 355.

Appendix A: Stevens' Scales: Four Levels of Measurement[1]

A Nominal Scale

Method: Determination of equality: allocate numbers to identify items. Two things are assigned the same number [or symbol] if they have the same value of the attribute.

Examples: Numbering offices; numbering crimes in a criminal code; or identifying religions in a survey by code numbers: atheist = 1, Buddhist = 2, etc.

Features: Cannot add numbers, no proportion between numbers, e.g. crime No. 6 is not twice as bad as crime No. 3. Could use letters or other symbols instead of numbers.

An Ordinal Scale

Method: Determination of greater than or less than: things are assigned numbers so that the order of the numbers reflects an order relation between the items.

Examples: Placings in a race: 1st, 2nd, 3rd, etc.; grades of wool; hardness of minerals.

Features: Preserves order relations of <, >, =, but gives no indication of how much greater than, or less than. No indication of spacing between items. Cannot add up the numbers, no proportion between numbers allocated. It makes no sense to say for example that the 6th placed competitor ran twice as fast as the one placed 3rd.

An Interval Scale (a type of cardinal scale)

Method: Determination of equality of intervals or of differences: things are assigned numbers such that the differences between the numbers reflect differences in the attribute being measured.

Examples: Temperature in degrees F; elapsed times for competitors finishing in a rally race.

Features: Preserves order and some spacing relations, but origin [zero point] and unit of measurement are arbitrary. Allows addition, and specific comparison, as it tells 'how much' one item differs from another, but cannot meaningfully say that a day of 60 degrees F is twice as hot as a day of 30 degrees F. [It is 30 degrees hotter, but not twice as hot.]

A Ratio Scale (a type of cardinal scale)

Method: Determination of the equality of ratios: things are assigned numbers such that the differences and ratios between the numbers reflect analogous properties of the attribute.

Examples: Temperature in degrees Kelvin; duration in seconds, length, density, loudness.

Features: Preserves order and ratio relations. Only the choice of unit is arbitrary, there is a natural zero. Allows addition, comparison, and ratio-type statements: e.g. can meaningfully say both that a 60 second measurement is 30 seconds longer than a 30 second measurement, and that it is twice as long as a 30 second measurement.

Note

1   Adapted from Stevens (1959).

Appendix B: Von Hirsch's Description of the Ordinal/Cardinal Distinction

The General Principle

(1983, p. 211)	The severity of the punishment should be commensurate with the seriousness of the offender's criminal conduct.
(1985, p. 31)	Sentences should be proportionate to the gravity of the offender's criminal conduct.
(1990, p. 282)	Punishment should comport with the seriousness of the crime.
(1998, p. 173)	The severity of the penalty should be proportionate to the gravity of the defendant's criminal conduct.

Reading: There are two interpretations, each with a different focus.

General:	Penalties allocated to crimes on a scale should reflect the seriousness of the crime category; and
Specific:	individual sentences given to particular offenders Should reflect the seriousness of the offender's actual criminal conduct.

The Ordinal Aspect: Desert is 'Determining'

(1983, p. 212)	a) The ranking and spacing of penalties relative to each other should reflect the comparative gravity of the criminal conduct involved.
	b) Defendants whose criminal conduct is equally blameworthy should be punished with equal severity.
(1984, pp.1096, 1101)	The ordinal aspect relates to:
	a) The question of how crimes should be punished relative to each other.
	b) The question of how defendants should be punished relative to each other.
(1985, pp. 39–40)	The question of how crimes should be punished relative to each other includes two aspects:

	a) Penalties should be graded in severity so as to reflect gradations in relative seriousness of the conduct.
	b) Defendants whose criminal conduct is equally serious should be punished equally.
(1990, p. 282) and	a) Relates to comparative ranking of punishments.
(1998, p. 173)	b) Persons convicted of crimes of comparable gravity should receive punishments of comparable severity.

Reading: The ordinal aspect could also be given two interpretations.

| General: | The general penalty for a crime on the penalty scale should reflect the seriousness of the crime category; and |
| Specific: | Individual offenders committing similar crimes should receive similar sentences [the parity aspect]. |

The Cardinal Aspect: Desert is Merely 'Limiting'

(1983, p. 214)	There should be a reasonable proportion between absolute levels of punishment and the seriousness of the criminal conduct.
(1984, p. 1096) and (1985, p. 39)	The question of what absolute levels of severity should anchor the scale.
(1990, p. 282)	Deals with the overall magnitude and anchoring points of the scale.
(1998, p. 174)	Deals with the overall dimensions and anchoring points of the penalty scale.

Reading: The cardinal aspect appears to refer only to general penalty values. Penalties on a scale should be in proportion to the seriousness of the crimes.

Conclusion

The 'cardinal' aspect appears to refer only to the construction of a penalty scale, whereas the 'ordinal' aspect could refer both to the construction of a penalty scale and the secondary phase of the sentencing process – the allocation of individual sentences to individual offenders.

Chapter Sixteen

Scaling Punishments:
A Reply to Julia Davis

Andrew von Hirsch

Julia Davis's thoughtful essay raises a number of issues, some of a rather technical nature. Since time and space do not permit a full answer, let me confine myself to making a few simple points.

Do I use the Terms 'Ordinal' and 'Cardinal' in the Standard Scientific Way?

I do not, and do not purport to do so. In formulating the distinction between 'ordinal' and 'cardinal' proportionality, I wanted to call attention to an important difference between the relative scaling of punishments within a penalty scale, and the overall dimensions of the scale itself (von Hirsch, 1985, ch. 4). I chose 'ordinal' as a convenient term for the former, (because I was speaking of the comparative ordering of punishments), and 'cardinal' as the term for the latter. It may well be that 'ordinal' has a different meaning in S.S. Stevens' quantitative measuring system, as Ms Davis asserts, but I am entitled to adopt a term and put it to different use – so long as I define that use adequately, as I believe I have done. (Indeed, this renaming process takes place all the time, even in the physical sciences. Physicists refer to the 'spin' of an electron, and to a certain subatomic particle, the quark, having or not having 'charm'. In using these terms, physicists are not misleadingly implying that the electron actually rotates like a top, or that a quark would be an engaging dinner-table companion. They are simply borrowing words, and redefining them.)

Can Matters Relating to Proportionality be Scientifically or Mathematically Determined?

Of course not. A main theme of my writing on sentencing theory has been that deciding on punishment is a normative matter, and not one of discovering relationships in the external world. But normative matters can also be addressed on a principled basis that provides a modicum of guidance – albeit, of course, not mathematical precision.

Are Assessments of Crime-seriousness the Same in Substance as Assessments of the Appropriate Penalties for the Crimes Involved?

They are not. You and I can agree on the seriousness of, say, common residential burglary; yet you still may opt for a tougher penalty for the offence than I, for a variety of reasons. Some of those reasons may relate to our having divergent penal theories: I prefer desert, whereas you favour an incapacitative approach and thus opt for lengthy prison terms to restrain burglars from re-offending. Or alternatively, you and I may both support a desert model, and both agree that burglary is an offence of intermediate blameworthiness warranting a given seriousness-rating somewhere in the middle of the seriousness-scale; yet you may favour a higher penalty for the crime, because you opt for anchoring the penalty scale as a whole at higher overall severity levels – for example, because you may place less value than I on parsimony in anchoring the scale (see von Hirsch 1993, pp. 109–11).

Can Crime-seriousness be Measured 'Objectively'?

I have never suggested it could. True, we should begin the assessment with certain empirically-based generalisations about the typical consequences of various kinds of crime. But the crucial steps of evaluating those consequences are normative. The harmfulness of the conduct, Nils Jareborg and I have suggested, should be assessed by a 'living-standard' conception: but that standard is largely a normative one concerning the role and importance of various kinds of interests for the pursuit of a good life (von Hirsch and Jareborg, 1991). The culpability involved in the conduct, the other central dimension of seriousness, is almost entirely a normative matter. The fact that normative evaluations are involved, however, does not preclude fashioning rankings for degrees of seriousness – provided one is clear that these rankings will change if the normative criteria regarding harmfulness and culpability are altered.

How much Guidance do my Principles of 'Ordinal Proportionality' give in Deciding the Comparative Severity of Punishment?

Norval Morris, it will be recalled, argued that desert was not a 'determining' but merely a 'limiting' principle (Morris 1982, ch. 5). My response was that desert provides only certain limits in setting the cardinal magnitudes and anchoring points of a penalty scale; but that it provides considerably more guidance than that in deciding on the comparative ordering of penalties within a given penalty scale (von Hirsch 1985, ch. 4). I still think this position is basically correct, but I overstated my response in saying that desert is 'determining' when it comes to comparative ordering. The reason it is not fully determining relates to the character of spacing conventions. Let me explain.

In providing this explanation, let me make a few simplifying assumptions. We are working, say, with a system of numerical guidelines. The rule maker, (a sentencing commission), is charged with developing a numerical grid of sentences, akin to that used in Minnesota or Oregon. The commission assigns seriousness-grades to categories or subcategories of crimes, using the living-standard analysis just referred to. The penalties in the grid are to be presumptive sentences: that is, quanta of penalties that are ordinarily to be invoked by sentencing courts, in the absence of aggravating and mitigating circumstances. Let us assume that the commission has already completed its task of grading crimes in seriousness, and is now deciding on the comparative severity of presumptive penalties within the grid. To separate the task of deciding comparative penalties from that of fixing the scale's anchoring points, the commission is deciding at the moment upon rankings of *comparative* sanction severity: say, severity-gradations from 1 to 20. Our question then becomes: to what extent do my 'ordinal proportionality' principles help guide the commission in deciding on such rankings?

Ordinal proportionality, as I define it, has three sub-requirements. The first of these is *parity*. This calls for crime-categories (or subcategories), having the same seriousness-ratings to receive presumptive sentences of comparable severity (von Hirsch 1993, p. 18).[1] This requirement does yield certain definite results: if crime of type A and crime of type B both have the same seriousness rating, then their presumptive penalties should be of approximately the same comparative severity. (Of course, valuations are involved even here, in deciding which crimes are of equivalent seriousness, and which presumptive penalties are of equivalent comparative severity.)

The second sub-requirement is *rank-ordering*.[2] Punishing crime category Y more than crime category X expresses more disapproval for the former conduct, which is warranted only if it is more serious. Punishments should thus be ordered on the scale of penalties so that their relative severity-rankings are consistent with the seriousness-ratings of the crimes involved. This requirement also yields certain identifiable results: if crime-category Y has a significantly higher seriousness-rating than crime-category X, it should receive (comparatively), the greater penalty.

The third sub-requirement concerns the *spacing* of penalties.[3] Suppose crimes X, Y, and Z are of ascending order of seriousness; but that Y is considerably more serious than X but only slightly less so than Z. Then, to reflect these crimes' differing comparative degrees of blameworthiness, there should be a larger space between the presumptive penalties for X and Y than those for Y and Z. This requirement, however, is considerably less precise, for it merely calls for differences among the relative severities of penalties to be sufficient to call attention to significant comparative differences in the degree of gravity of the offences involved. While Jareborg's and my proposed seriousness analysis might point, to some degree, to such degrees of difference in the seriousness of the offences involved, this will not be sufficiently precise to provide definitive answers concerning spacing. There thus may be various possible spacing conventions that might serve to give reasonable cognisance to such differences. Since there seems to be no uniquely appropriate spacing convention, there would be more than one way to arrange the spacing among penalties on the scale. It is here, then, that I made an overstatement in saying that the ordinal-proportionality requirements are 'determinative'. I should have said that they provide considerably more guidance than mere limits, but no unique set of results. We are speaking here, it should be noted, of the spacing among *relative* severity-rankings: how much larger the comparative 'gap' between the penalties for offences X and Y, than that between Y and Z. However, the absolute differences among these penalties (for example, the differences in durations of imprisonment, if prison is the sanction for these three offences), is a matter that ordinal-proportionality requirements definitely do *not* determine, for these are influenced by the anchoring points and magnitude of the penalty scale. With a given set of comparative rankings and spacings, the distances between penalties in absolute number of months will increase, the more attenuated, and hence severe, the penalty scale as a whole becomes.

So far, I have spoken of a penalty system that utilises numerical seriousness- and severity-rankings, and presumptive sentences. However, some important desert-oriented sentencing systems, such as Sweden's, rely on general statutory principles instead of specific numbers, (Jareborg 1995). Here, the application of proportionality principles would have to be more qualitative.[4] I have referred to the numerical guidelines/presumptive sentences scheme simply for purposes of illustration – to help clarify the extent to which ordinal-proportionality requirements might potentially provide guidance.

A Final Word

Debates over proportionality of sentence have had a tendency to suffer from an all-or-nothing approach: that either proportionality requirements are supposed to be capable of achieving scientific precision and a unique set of penalties, or else they can be nothing more than vague limits or rules of thumb. My purpose in having originally formulated the ordinal-cardinal distinction was to challenge this all-or-nothing assumption – to suggest that desert can provide considerable guidance for some purposes (the comparative ordering of penalties), but less so for others (the fixing of the overall magnitude and anchoring points of the scale). Current debate about penalty scaling under a desert model should also guard against assuming a similar all-or-nothing perspective, that ordinal proportionality must either yield precise rankings or else can be nothing more than vague guidance. These are not the only alternatives. Ordinal proportionality tells us quite a bit about how penalties should be ordered relative to one another, and yet they cannot be expected to yield unique ranking solutions. By assuming differing spacing conventions, my hypothetical sentencing commission could adopt alternative solutions to its problem of relative scaling that are somewhat different from one another; but the commission would still receive a considerable degree of guidance.

Notes

1 This parity requirement has one possible exception, concerning the role of prior convictions – where first offenders might receive modest discounts, compared to repeatedly-convicted offenders convicted of similar crimes. For the rationale of such a first-offender discount, see von Hirsch 1998.
2 Ibid.
3 Ibid.
4 For discussion of the relative merits of numerical guidelines vs. statutory sentencing principles, see von Hirsch, Knapp and Tonry 1987.

References

Morris, N. (1982), *Madness and the Criminal Law*, Chicago: University of Chicago Press.

Von Hirsch, A. (1986), *Past or Future Crimes*, Manchester: Manchester University Press.

Von Hirsch, A. (1993), *Censure and Sanctions*, Oxford: Clarendon Press.

Von Hirsch, A. (1998), 'Desert and Previous Convictions', in A. von Hirsch and A. Ashworth (eds), *Principled Sentencing*, 2d edn, Oxford: Hart Publishing.

Von Hirsch, A. and Jareborg, N. (1991), 'Gauging Criminal Harms: A living standard analysis', *Oxford Journal of Legal Studies*, Vol. 11, p. 1.

Von Hirsch, A., Knapp, K., and Tonry, M. (1987), *The Sentencing Commission and Its Guidelines*, Boston: Northeastern University Press.

Chapter Seventeen

Scaling Punishments:
A Response to von Hirsch

Julia Davis

1 Redefining Words

The gravity of my criticism was not simply that von Hirsch uses the terms ordinal and cardinal in a way that is contrary to the standard scientific usage, but rather that his usage differs from the way that other philosophers *writing about punishment* use the terms (as well as all those who use them in the related fields of criminology, sociology, economics, and in the literature on comparative assessment of utility, well-being and living standards). Von Hirsch's examples of legitimately redefining words like charm and spin illustrate the appropriation of *ordinary* words for use in a *technical* field, but von Hirsch himself has done something quite different. He has taken two established technical terms, already used in the punishment debates, and changed their meanings. This is not helpful.

Beyond the point about usage, I argued that, even if we accept von Hirsch's definition, his model nevertheless contains a number of flaws that prevent desert from having the sole determining role in deciding penalties. These conceptual flaws were revealed by applying the deeper insights of measurement theory to the model. I have no quarrel with von Hirsch's argument that there is a difference between the question of how crimes should be punished relative to each other and the issue of the overall levels of punishment within a sentencing system. What I sought to argue was that he had packed too much into his private definitions (e.g. the inclusion of parity between offenders under 'ordinal' proportionality) and had adopted a misleading image of the scaling process that was based on transforming values of seriousness into values of punishment. Consequently, I agree with von Hirsch that he has 'overstated' the matter when he said that desert is determining when it comes to comparative ordering. And I am happy to note that, in the text of his reply, von Hirsch has restricted the parity aspect of ordinal proportionality to cover only a comparison between crime categories.[1] However, when we look closely at the latest version of the sub-requirements of ordinal proportionality we can see that they restate, in three ways, the straightforward proposition that crimes should be allocated to places on a penalty scale on the basis of their perceived seriousness. The requirements of parity between crime categories, rank-ordering, and spacing are simply different applications of the rational principle that we should treat like cases alike and different cases differently. However, while most would agree with that principle, the real challenge is to identify the categories of relevant similarities and differences between crimes, and to set limits on the state's responses to offenders, and on these questions there is much less guidance to be found in the principle of commensurate deserts. In this area, desert, like justice, is a concept that points more towards process than to content.

2 Redundancy in the Scaling Process

I suggested that the fact that people who were asked to assess 'crime seriousness' generated the same cognitive maps as those asked to assess 'deserved punishment' indicated that we are not translating one 'thing' into another 'thing' when we use seriousness to guide the setting of penalties and that therefore we do not need to construct two separate scales of values when allocating penalties to crimes. (I agree with von Hirsch, and did not intend to suggest, that all those who agree on offence seriousness would arrive at the same values on a scale of actual penalties.) However, before the debate over penalties can have any meaning it must use an interval (or spacing convention) to express the relation between different crime and penalty pairings that itself has real meaning. I argued that the three steps of allocating values to the perceived seriousness of crimes, transforming them, first into arbitrary values of 'comparative sanction severity' (e.g. using von Hirsch's suggestion of gradations from 1–20), and then into a third scale of actual punishments, are misguided. Consequently, I suggested that we need to carry out only one process of evaluation: the spacing of crimes directly onto a penalty scale using seriousness as a guide to position and actual punishment values as the interval. I am disappointed that von Hirsch did not address this fundamental point and so while some might welcome the improvements that he has made to his model, they are, in my view, refinements to a step that is redundant.

Note

1   A slip from parity between crime categories to parity between individual offenders is easy
     to understand, because crimes as categories do not really 'deserve' anything. It is only
     when we have before us an individual offender who has been convicted of a particular
     crime and who stands to be sentenced under a particular sentencing regime that we can
     speak of desert and parity in their fullest senses.

PART IV
REASON-GIVING AND
APPROACHES TO
EXPLAINING SENTENCING

Chapter Eighteen

Sentencing Policy and Guilty Plea Discounts

Ralph Henham

Introduction

This chapter reports the results of an empirical investigation into the operation of sentence discounts in the Crown Court. It focuses, in particular, on the extent to which judges comply with section 48 of the Criminal Justice and Public Order Act 1994 and discusses (*inter alia*) the relationship between sentence discounts and the nature of the charges faced by the defendant, the strength of the prosecution case and the choice between custodial and non custodial sentences. It also examines the relative use made of sentence discounts and the nature and relevance of Court of Appeal guidance. The chapter begins by describing the socio-legal context in which sentence discounts operate and, following description of the research methodology and presentation of the results, concludes with an assessment of the implications of the research for sentencing policy and practice. More generally, the analysis is concerned with the relationship between sentencing and penal policy-making by providing an explanation of the structure of the sentence discount decision-making process and seeking to demonstrate its wider significance for sentencing policy. This focus on transparency also draws attention to themes addressed in other contributions to this collection concerned with public accountability, proportionality, victim participation and discrimination in the sentencing process.

Background

In February 1994, the then Home Secretary Michael Howard announced an amendment to the Criminal Justice and Public Order Bill which would oblige courts to take into account the timing of guilty pleas when exercising their discretion to allow sentence discounts (*The Times*, 9 February 1994, p. 8). In essence, the proposal was for a statutory system of sentence discounts for guilty pleas based on the general principle that the earlier a defendant pleads guilty the greater the reduction in the sentence. The resultant section 48 of the Criminal Justice and Public Order Act 1994, which came into force on 3 February 1995, provides as follows:

(1)   In determining what sentence to pass on an offender who has pleaded guilty to an offence in proceedings before that or another court, a court shall take into account
(a) the stage in the proceedings for the offence at which the offender indicated his intention to plead guilty, and
(b) the circumstances in which this indication was given.
(2)   If, as a result of taking into account any matter referred to in subsection (1) above, the court imposes a punishment on the offender which is less severe than the punishment it would otherwise have imposed, it shall state in open court that it has done so.[1]

The new sentence discount procedure was roundly condemned by Thomas who described it as "a clumsy and partial attempt to turn [the general principles governing discounts for pleas] into statute" (Thomas 1994, p. 12) which unnecessarily increased the criteria by which a sentence must be justified. Thomas also castigated the provision on a number of other grounds. For example, did it create an obligation to allow a discount in all cases or only where there had been an early plea? Could a court refuse to give a discount having taken the stage at which the offender indicated his intention to plead guilty into account? The provision appeared to conflict with the mandatory nature of section 2(2)(b) Criminal Justice Act 1991 which required a court to impose a longer than commensurate sentence for a violent or sexual offence to adequately protect the public from serious harm from the offender; were offenders who pleaded guilty on a limited basis or to lesser offences charged in the indictment within the provision's scope? To what extent did the provision preclude consideration of other relevant matters in determining the extent of the discount, such as the strength of the prosecution case? And, finally, was the sentencer effectively prevented from allowing a discount for a last minute plea (Thomas 1994, p. 12)?

Although the drafting of the provision is convoluted and woefully inadequate, it clearly imposes a *mandatory* requirement for the court to take into account the *stage* in the proceedings at which the offender indicated his intention to plead guilty (and the circumstances in which that indication was given). The second *mandatory* requirement is that the sentencer must state in open court that he has imposed a lesser punishment, if he has done so, as a result of taking into account any matter that he is required to take into account by virtue of subsection (1), namely, the stage in the proceedings at which the intention to plead guilty was indicated and the circumstances in which the indication was given. What the statute does *not* appear to require is that the sentencer should indicate that a sentence discount has been given simply on the basis of the guilty plea *simpliciter* (Thomas 1995, p. 7). Neither does section 48 impose an obligation on the sentencer to explain why a sentence discount has *not* been allowed, irrespective of when indication of the intended guilty plea was given.

The extent of the sentencer's duty to explain under section 48(2) does, however, require further clarification. The wording of section 48(2) read together with section 48(1) implies that the obligation of the sentencer goes beyond that of a mere statement that he has given a sentence discount. The sentencer's decision must have been reached as a result of taking the matters he is required to take into account by virtue of subsection (1) and it should, I submit, consequently be necessary for the sentencer to articulate (i.e. make an explanatory statement) that he has reached his decision to allow a sentence discount on that basis. In this respect I do not entirely agree with Wasik and Taylor's following comment on the scope of section 48(2):

> An explanatory statement must be made in open court *in every case* where the court has, in the light of the defendant's guilty plea, imposed a sentence less severe than it would otherwise have imposed (1995, p. 18).

I would suggest that the sentencer's obligation to make an explanatory statement in open court is restricted by section 48(2) to those situations where the decision to give a sentence discount has been reached as a result of taking those matters in subsection (1) into account (supported by Thomas 1995, p. 7).

The difficulty is produced by the convoluted wording of this section since, although it is mandatory to comply with section 48(1), it is impossible to know whether section 48(1) has been complied with without an explanation of the basis on which the decision to give credit for the guilty plea is made. To elaborate: where a sentencer states "I give credit for your guilty plea", or, "in your favour is the fact you have pleaded guilty", this *appears* to take into account the *fact* of the guilty plea only, without further explanation. Such a statement does not explain the basis on which the sentence discount has been calculated. It does not indicate that the plea discount resulted from taking the stage in the proceedings when it was indicated and the surrounding circumstances into account (as required by section 48(1)). Thus, in such cases, the mandatory requirement in subsection (1) should be taken *not* to have been complied with. The reason for this is that we are unable to determine what the sentencer has subjectively considered – for example, he may in reality have subjectively complied with section 48(1) and simply failed to externalise his reasoning process – but, there is surely no point in having a mandatory requirement unless it can be inferred that failure to articulate the *basis* upon which the fact of the guilty plea has received credit and produced a sentence discount amounts to a breach of section 48.

The only caveat is that the statute itself does not appear to require the sentencer to indicate that a discount has been given simply on the basis of the plea itself, yet we are unable to determine what is *actually* in the sentencer's mind when phrases such as "I give you credit for your plea of – guilty" are used. Consequently, we are unable to discriminate between circumstances where sentencers need to have complied with section 48 and those where they need not, although the probability that the fact of the plea itself will form the basis of the sentencer's decision to allow a sentence discount is likely to be small. To make any sense of the section, we should, therefore, apply the principle of *de minimis* and infer a failure to comply with section 48 in circumstances where no further explanation is given beyond a simple statement stating that credit has been given for the guilty plea. This wider interpretation has been adopted when discussing the research findings below.[2]

It is also important to note that, despite the fact that most decisions on sentence discounts relate to indictable offences tried in the Crown Court, the same principles apply to the magistrates' courts (Wasik and Turner 1993). This is specifically recognised in the Magistrates' Association Sentencing Guidelines (1997) which, whilst preserving the principle of maximum judicial discretion, emphasise the desirability of operating a system of graduated sentence discounts:

> The law requires that the court reduces the sentence for a timely guilty plea, but the provision should be used with judicial flexibility. A timely guilty plea may attract a sentencing discount of up to one third but the precise amount of discount will depend on the facts of each case and a last minute plea of guilty may attract only a nominal reduction.[3]

As Wasik and Taylor (1995, p. 18) point out, however, the imposition of the further obligations under section 48 on the magistrates' courts is somewhat unrealistic in view of the high rate of guilty pleas, but it does draw attention to important *lacunae* in Court of Appeal decisions on sentence discounts, namely, the absence of guidance on the use of sentence discounts for noncustodial sentences, and more particularly, on the circumstances in which a guilty plea might influence the choice between a custodial and noncustodial sentence.

Since section 48 clearly contains no guidance relating to the appropriateness and extent of any sentence discount in particular circumstances, sentencers have continued to rely on Court of Appeal decisions to guide them in this respect. In the leading case of *Buffrey* (1993) 14 Cr.App.R(S.) 511 at 515 Lord Taylor CJ stated that:

> as general guidance ... this court believes that something of the order of one-third would very often be an appropriate discount from the sentence which would otherwise be imposed in a contested trial.

The facts, involving a complex fraud where the defendant had pleaded guilty at a late stage just before the trial, prompted Lord Taylor to emphasise that even in such cases, a considerable discount may be appropriate to reflect the saving in time and money and the stress caused to jurors, judges and witnesses. Lord Taylor also suggested that each case had to be judged on its merits and there could be considerable variance between one case and another.[4] As Ashworth (1995, p. 137) points out, pragmatic justifications for the guilty plea discount, rather than contrition, now seem more likely to predominate, and it is usually palpable that the latter is absent where a last minute guilty plea has been entered. Recent research by McCoy and Cohen (1998) in the United States tends to confirm the view that the remorse justification for the plea discount is in fact disingenuous and used to conceal the utilitarian (or pragmatic) reality of the decision.[5] The Court of Appeal in *A* and *B* (*The Times*, 1 May 1998) has recently endorsed a pragmatic approach to the use of sentence discounts in the context of defendants who provide valuable information to the prosecuting authorities. Lord Bingham CJ laid down valuable detailed guidance to deal with those situations where the information had been given in the reasonable expectation that the assistance was reflected by the judge in an appropriate discount of the sentence. In so doing Lord Bingham stated explicitly that defendants who cooperated with the prosecuting authorities by incriminating co-defendants could expect an enhanced sentence discount, particularly where this resulted in a conviction or a guilty plea. The extent of any sentence discount given in return for assistance provided and expected in the investigation, detection, suppression and prosecution of serious crime necessarily depended on the value of the help given, which was a function of the quality and quantity of that assistance. Where, as in the instant case, the value of the information was not fully appreciated when sentence was passed, it was appropriate for the Court of Appeal to review the sentence and reduce it to reflect the true value of the assistance.

With regard to the limits of the sentence discount, the Court of Appeal, in *Sharkey and Daniels* [1994] Crim.L.R. 866 (considering *Costen*)[6] confirmed that a maximum sentence was wrong in principle, and a small discount was necessary to reflect a guilty plea, notwithstanding the fact that the maximum sentence permissible was considered appropriate. The *Costen* exceptions were again considered in *Landy* and *Hastings* [1999] Crim.L.R. 660 when the Court of Appeal again confirmed that, where the defendant had been caught red-handed and had no option to plead guilty, the sentencer was justified in allowing no discount, and if (as in *Hastings*) the maximum sentence was otherwise considered appropriate, it could be imposed.[7] In his commentary, Thomas points out that these principles were decided before the implementation of section 48(1) which appeared to contemplate taking into account so-called inevitable pleas of guilty in the expression "the circumstances in which the indication was given". Although the provision did not indicate what should be the impact of such a plea, legislative policy clearly contemplated encouraging and rewarding early indications of plea, and, in these circumstances, the Court of Appeal's decision to support pre-Act principles could prove problematic.

In *Fearon* [1996] Crim.L.R. 213 the Court of Appeal stressed that it was "highly desirable in *every* case where a defendant pleads guilty in the Crown Court for the judge invariably to say so in his sentencing remarks". This would serve the dual purpose of informing the defendant that it had been taken into account and confirming to the Court of Appeal that this factor had been considered should an appeal follow. I have already argued that where section 48 applies the sentencers obligation should only be discharged if an explanation of the basis for the sentence discount is given in open court. This clearly goes beyond stating the *fact* of the plea itself which, as Thomas (1995, p. 7) suggests, is not mandatory under section 48(2). Regrettably, the Court did not go further and suggest that in those exceptional cases where a sentence discount is *refused* this fact should also be stated by the sentencer in open court and an explanation of the basis for the decision given.

Finally, it is important to note some recent significant procedural changes relating to 'plea before venue' and pre-trial hearings[8] which may have indirectly impacted on the operation of sentence discounts. Of these only the latter has any relevant bearing on the research reported in this chapter, since the present system of mandatory Plea and Directions hearings was introduced in 1995 prior to the commencement of the empirical stage of the project.[9] The system ensures that, having taken the defendant's plea, the judge should proceed to sentence whenever possible. Recent statistical evidence appears to indicate that these hearings reduced the rate of 'cracked trials' from 26 per cent in 1993 (Zander and Henderson 1993, p. 95) to just below 19 per cent in 1997.[10] It was, therefore, anticipated that these changes would be reflected in the research findings.

Methodology

At the project's inception in 1994 it was decided to select one First Tier Crown Court Centre from each of the six circuits, i.e. Nottingham (Midland and Oxford); Leeds (North Eastern); Manchester (Northern); Norwich, later replaced by Lewes (South Eastern); Cardiff (Wales and Chester); and Winchester (Western). This number represented 6.7 per cent of the 90 Crown Court Centres (including Greater London Centres) and ensured adequate representation from each circuit (Hazell and Co. 1995).

The Judicial Statistics for 1994 showed that overall, of the 90,759 defendants dealt with by the Crown Court, 66 per cent (59,577) pleaded guilty. Averaged between the 90 Crown Court Centres this produced a figure of 662 cases. Over the six-month period chosen for data collection a 5 per cent sample of the average number of guilty pleas for each Centre chosen would have necessitated a sample size of 33 cases per Centre. It was felt that greater representation of the use of sentence discounts would be achieved by this sample design rather than attempting to create Circuit or Centre subgroups to reflect differences in guilty plea rates as between Circuits which was impractical. Furthermore, a 3 per cent sample of the overall number of guilty pleas was unrealistic since some 2,979 cases would have required detailed examination. In the event, permission was eventually sought to increase the sample size for each Centre to 50 cases, this reflecting approximately 7.6 per cent of the annual average number of guilty pleas for each Centre and 0.5 per cent of the annual number of guilty pleas for defendants dealt with in all Crown Court Centres according to the 1994 figures.[11]

Resource implications and analytical complexity suggested that a written record of the relevant decision-making process would be more reliable than verbatim notes of judicial sentencing comments obtained by a trained researcher attending selected guilty plea hearings.[12] For these reasons it was decided to select the sample of 50 cases for each Centre retrospectively to cover the period April to September 1997, permission to access relevant court records having been obtained from the Lord Chancellor's Department. Approximately two guilty plea cases per week over the six-month period[13] were identified on a random basis, and Form 5089[14] extracted from the court record was used to obtain transcripts of judicial sentencing comments direct from the court reporting firm present at sentence. Hence, the information derived from the court record together with the verbatim transcript of the judge's sentencing remarks in each case constituted the empirical input subsequently analysed. The final sample of 310 cases from the six selected Crown Court Centres where full information was available was ultimately comprised as follows; Cardiff (57), Leeds (55), Lewes (57), Manchester (29),[15] Nottingham (50) and Winchester (62).

Results

Judicial Compliance with Section 48

This section provides an analysis and assessment of the extent to which Crown Court judges can be said to comply with the provisions of section 48(1) and (2) of the Criminal Justice and Public Order Act 1994. It is apparent from Table 18.1 that a bare majority of judges (53.2 per cent) stated in open court that they had given a sentence discount in return for a guilty plea. This leaves a sizeable minority who made no such statement, which is clearly a cause for concern. Therefore, if the narrow interpretation of what constitutes compliance with section 48 is accepted, i.e. if phrases such as "I give you full credit for your guilty plea" are sufficient to satisfy the requirements of section 48(2), the evidence from this study indicates a significant judicial failure to comply with section 48. However, as previously explained, a wider interpretation of

Table 18.1 Judicial compliance with s. 48

	Frequency	Per cent
Yes	165	53.2
No	145	46.8
Total	310	100.0

what constitutes compliance with section 48 should be adopted which regards the *mere* statement of a sentence discount for a guilty plea as insufficient without further explanation that it was given as a result of the matters referred to in section 48(1) being taken into account. The results indicate that of the 165 sentencers who stated that they had given a sentence discount in return for a guilty plea, only 58 (35 per cent) went on to give some kind of explanation of the basis upon which they had reached their decision in open court. Of the 310 cases examined, 58 represents a mere 18.7 per cent who could be said to have complied with section 48 on this wider interpretation of the section. A typical example of the kind of phraseology that would satisfy this criterion of explanation, and hence constitute judicial compliance is provided by the following extract:

Case 1
I am however going to pass a lesser custodial sentence than I would otherwise have passed having regard to your pleas of guilty which you entered on the first reasonable opportunity.

Nevertheless, although Case 1 makes a clear reference to the matter referred to in section 48(1)(a) – the stage in the proceedings for the offence at which the offender indicated his intention to plead guilty – the sentencer did not explain further how this particular factor (usually in combination with others) was translated into a specific numerical discount from that which would otherwise have been the appropriate sentence level based on existing sentencing principles.

The study also examined the degree to which sentencers actually made clear in open court the extent of the sentence discount allowed following an explanation of the basis upon which it had been given. Only 28 (17.0 per cent) of the 165 sentencers recorded as notionally complying with section 48 in fact gave a complete explanation of the reasons for, and effect of, the sentence discount on the sentence. The represents a mere 9 per cent of the total of 310 cases examined. As a proportion of the overall number of defendants pleading guilty dealt with by the Crown Court in 1997, 9 per cent represented just 5,920 from 65,782 cases (HMSO 1995, p. 66) where a proper explanation might have been provided by the judge. An example of a judicial comment which can be regarded as satisfying the definition of a sufficiently complete explanation of the rationale, calculation and extent of the sentence discount is given below:

Case 2

It seems to me in all the circumstances that the normal tariff sentence for an offence of this kind, and given your background and other circumstances, would be one of twelve months; but because you have pleaded guilty at the first opportunity I am going to give you a very substantial discount and I propose to sentence you to a sentence of eight months imprisonment in regard to this offence.

In only six (4.1 per cent) of the 145 recorded cases where section 48 was not complied with did the sentencer indicate that 'no discount' had been given in return for the guilty plea, and, in only half of these cases, did the sentencer go on to provide any kind of rationale or explanation for this decision. However, it should be borne in mind that there is no statutory obligation under section 48 to articulate the fact that no sentence discount has been given for the guilty plea or explain the basis for that decision. Clearly, the 145 cases referred to contained a mixture of those cases where a sentence discount may have been given, but not articulated, and those cases where *no* sentence discount was given. Since the six 'no discount' cases were identified, the likelihood of other similar cases was negligible. It is, therefore, reasonable to conclude that the remainder of those 145 cases where there was a failure to state the fact that a sentence discount had been given were in reality cases where a sentence discount *was* allowed.

Although not relevant to specific decisions, it was considered important to obtain an indication of sentencers' general approach to the concept of the guilty plea discount in fixing sentence. Surprisingly, as many as 34.5 per cent of sentencers considered the guilty plea as either 'not particularly important' or 'not important at all' and, whilst the largest percentage (36.8 per cent) did attach 'some importance' to it, fewer (28.4 per cent) regarded it as 'very important'. However, of more direct concern was the judicial approach to those matters referred to as mandatory in section 48(1) in deciding what reduction in sentence to give for a guilty plea, i.e. (a) the stage in the proceedings for the offence at which the offender indicated his intention to plead guilty, and (b) the circumstances in which this indication was given. The results relevant to section 48(1) are shown in Table 18.2 and again, it is surprising, particularly in view of the emphasis given to the need to reflect the timing of the plea in the sentence discount, to note that 50.4 per cent of judges regarded the stage when the plea was entered as either 'not particularly important' or 'not important at all', with the latter category (35.2 per cent) larger than the judges regarding this factor as 'very important' (26.2 per cent).

As far as the circumstances surrounding the guilty plea indication are concerned (s. 48(1)(b)), the research results reveal that the majority of judges

(67.1 per cent) did take 'other circumstances' into account. For the purposes of the research the following factors were regarded as circumstances normally associated with the extent of any guilty plea discount in addition to the stage in the proceedings when the guilty plea was entered; remorse, the avoidance of the time and expense of a trial, and the fact that the victim and/or witnesses are spared the ordeal of a trial. A number of 'other factors' generally regarded as mitigating factors, and often weighed together with the guilty plea in fixing sentence, were also mentioned.[16] The results show that the significance of the variables normally associated with the guilty plea discount[17] (particularly remorse) is far outweighed in the penal equation that determines penality by mitigating (i.e. other) factors commonly taken into account.

Table 18.2   Importance attached to stage when guilty plea entered

	Frequency	Per cent
Very important	83	26.8
Some importance	71	22.9
Not particularly important	47	15.2
Not important at all	109	35.2
Total	310	100.0

Closely related to the timing of the plea and the circumstances in which the indication was given is the strength of the prosecution case and, in particular, whether the appropriate sentence reduction should be affected by the fact that the defendant was caught red-handed. The study investigated this issue by first establishing whether there was any indication of the strength of the prosecution case and secondly, if so, whether this had any effect on the sentence discount. Evidence regarding the strength of the prosecution case was present in 62.3 per cent of all cases examined, and some indication of whether the strength of the prosecution case had an effect on the sentence discount was apparent in 60.4 per cent of those cases. In fact, in only 4.2 per cent of cases could the strength of the prosecution case be said to have had a 'substantial effect' on the sentence discount. Furthermore, predominantly negative relationships were found to exist between judicial compliance with section 48 and the impact of the strength of the prosecution case on the sentence discount, and cases where the defendant was caught red-handed and the strength of the prosecution case appeared to have had a substantial effect on the sentence discount. It should also be borne in mind that the interrelationship of the timing of the plea and other significant circumstances which together might dictate the extent of any sentence discount is a complex process, and it is, therefore, not particularly surprising that it should be difficult to attribute substantial effects to discreet variables in the sentence discount decision-making process. Certainly, the research results do not provide any evidence that would lead us to question the conclusion that the extent of any sentence discount does not vary significantly according to the strength of the prosecution case.

Structural Factors and Sentence Discounts

We now turn to consider a series of structural or organisational variables in the criminal process and their relationship to the decision to allow a sentence discount in return for a guilty plea.[18] In the first instance, it was decided to investigate whether the fact the defendant pleads guilty to a lesser included offence has any effect on the sentence discount. In essence, this deals with the kind of case where the prosecution agrees to drop a more serious charge in return for a guilty plea to a lesser included offence, a typical example being where the defendant agrees to plead guilty to wounding or inflicting grievous bodily harm contrary to section 20 of the Offences Against the Person Act 1861 having been charged with the more serious offence of wounding or causing grievous bodily harm with intent contrary to section 18 of the same Act. In only one case included in the research was this factor described by the judge as having a 'substantial' effect, although specific reference was made to it in nine cases (2.9 per cent). A related situation is whether the fact the defendant indicated a willingness to plead guilty on a limited basis to the charges in the indictment has any effect on the sentence discount. This factor was mentioned as relevant to the sentence discount decision in a mere three cases (1 per cent) and its effect described as 'substantial' in one case only. Notwithstanding, it should again be borne in mind that the significance of charge bargaining in relation to sentence discounts is ultimately connected to the timing of the plea and the opportunities for those activities in the pre-trial process. Further, since the notion of the guilty plea discount in principle occurs without reference to charge bargains a limited connection to those processes is to be expected (because the defendant has, in effect, already negotiated a sentence reduction).

Similar arguments apply in the case of fact bargains (Ashworth 1998a, pp. 257–76), where the prosecution agrees to present a particular version of the facts (usually lowering the seriousness of the offence) in return for a guilty plea. In such circumstances the sentence will be effectively further reduced by the guilty plea discount. Alternatively, the prosecution's version of the facts may be challenged post-conviction through a *Newton* hearing (1982 4 Cr.App.R.(S.) 388; see Ashworth 1995, p. 300). The extent to which the process of awarding a sentence discount is influenced by the fact that the defendant has previously disputed the facts of the charge to which he eventually pleads guilty was examined in the research. This phenomenon occurred in only three (1 per cent) cases and, therefore, could not be regarded as a significant influence on sentence discounts in the research sample. However, it can again be seen as a factor closely-related to the timing of the plea in its impact, as seen in one case where the defendant eventually pleaded guilty shortly before trial when the prosecution were prepared to accept the basis of the plea as the non-commercial supply of a Class A drug. Although this consequently reduced the seriousness of the offence and, to that extent, produced a sentence discount, the lateness of the plea precluded any further sentence reduction based on the stage in the proceedings when the plea was entered.

Penal Decisions and Sentence Discounts

This section examines two important issues involving the operation of sentence discounts neither of which has received much attention in previous sentencing studies (Wasik and Taylor 1995, p. 18). The first concerns the extent to which sentence discounts are available for sentences other than custody. Flood-Page and Mackie report briefly that no significant difference in the length of a community service order or probation order by plea was found, whilst noting, significantly, that those pleading guilty and fined were fined less on average – £548 as against £835 (Flood-Page and Mackie 1998, p. 92). The present study was not designed to measure the differential impact of sentence discounts on the various custodial and noncustodial sanctions available to sentencers. It was, however, able to explore whether any significant relationships existed between sentence discounts and penal sanctions. For example, a negative relationship was observed between noncustodial sentences (excluding fines) and judicial compliance with section 48. This was particularly marked in the case of community service orders, conditional discharges, suspended sentences and probation orders of between 12 months and three years, whereas in the case of fines the relationship was positive. The rate of compliance with section 48 was 60.4 per cent for custodial sentences, whilst the rate for the most commonly used community sentences (community service orders, combination orders, probation orders) was only 38.3 per cent.

The fact that the need to comply with section 48 appears to have been ignored in so many cases involving noncustodial sentences also helps to explain the lack of any relationship between the timing of the guilty plea and the choice between a custodial and noncustodial sentence. Notwithstanding, as previously acknowledged, the stage at which the plea is entered is not the sole determinant of a sentence discount. However, it seems that remorse is not necessarily one of the other most relevant circumstances since, although a significant relationship was found to exist between remorse and whether the guilty plea influenced the choice between a custodial and noncustodial sentence, remorse was *not* found to be a relevant factor in 58.5 per cent of cases where the influence of the guilty plea was acknowledged. It would appear instead that it is the existence of 'other factors', not usually acknowledged as direct reasons for allowing a sentence discount, which, taken together with the plea, produce a reduction in the sentence. A strong relationship was evident between these 'other factors' and cases where the guilty plea *did* influence the choice between a custodial and noncustodial sentence.

Differences in Practice Between Centres

It is necessary to preface what follows by emphasising that, whilst no attempt was made to match defendants in terms of age, sex, offence, etc. for each Crown Court Centre examined, this was considered unnecessary in order to establish the internal validity of the research method since section 48 is mandatory (whenever its conditions are fulfilled) irrespective of any of these factors.[19] This is not, of course, to say that these factors could not impact on the variables which were taken into account in the sentence discount decision-making process, or the weight attached to them in each case. Notwithstanding, this study did not attempt to discover those factors which are responsible for disparities in sentence decision-making[20] across Circuits, but, rather, it was concerned to identify ways in which Crown Court Centres[21] may differ in their approach to the application of section 48 and those variables instrumental in this process.

With these considerations in mind, the research attempted to determine whether there were any significant differences in practice between Crown Court Centres in the use made of sentence discounts. As may be seen from Table 18.3, considerable differences were observed between Crown Court Centres in the extent to which judges complied with the basic requirement in section 48(2) to state in open court that a sentence discount had been given. Although many variables (including judicial training) may affect the rate of compliance, differences in compliance rates of between 38.6 per cent for Lewes and 74.5 per cent for Leeds should be a cause for concern and merit further investigation. Similarly, a significant relationship was found between Crown Court Centres and whether judges who had complied with the basic statutory requirement in section 48 went further and gave some kind of explanation of the way the discount had been arrived at in open court.[22] In this case the compliance rate for each Centre varied from 8 per cent for Nottingham to 27.4 per cent for Winchester, from an overall total of 58 (35 per cent) of all cases (165) who complied with the basic requirement in section 48 to state in open court that a sentence discount had been given.

Table 18.3 Judicial compliance with s. 48 by Crown Court Centre

Centre	Yes	No	Total	Compliance rate
Cardiff	26	31	57	45.6
Leeds	41	14	55	74.5
Lewes	22	35	57	38.6
Manchester	13	16	29	44.8
Nottingham	34	16	50	68.0
Winchester	29	33	62	46.8
Total	165	145	310	–

A number of differences were also found between Crown Court Centres in their general approach to the question of sentence reduction in return for a guilty plea. For example, centres differed in the importance attached to the guilty plea in fixing sentence, ranging from 9 per cent in Leeds regarding it as 'very important' to 48.3 per cent in Winchester. Similar results were obtained in connection with the importance attached to the stage when the guilty plea was entered though, contrary to the overall trend, the proportion remained the same for Leeds and Lewes and actually fell for Cardiff, Manchester and Winchester confirming in general terms, that the stage when the plea is entered is not necessarily the most important significant variable affecting the sentence discount decision. The importance of 'other factors'[23] in the decision to allow a sentence discount is somewhat equivocal. There appears to be little consistency in the role played by such other mitigating factors in the sentence discount decision-making process as between the Crown Court Centres examined. For example, 'other factors' were cited in 86.0 per cent of cases examined for Cardiff, 96.0 per cent for Manchester and 74.2 per cent for Winchester, but in only 15.8 per cent for Lewes and a mere 4 per cent for Nottingham. I would suggest that these differences in approach and consistency in sentence decision-making observed between Centres may be related to differences in offender and offence characteristics that were not investigated in this research. In addition, a negative relationship was found between Crown Court Centres and the strength of the prosecution case as a factor in discount decisions, it being cited on average in only 24.8 per cent of cases.

Finally, some conclusions may be drawn from the comparison of national data for 1997 and some of the research data in Table 18.4.

Table 18.4 Comparison of national and research data relating to guilty plea variables

Circuit	Centre	Guilty plea committals[a] (%)	Defendant pleads guilty at trial[b] (%)	Importance attached to stage plea entered (%)	Judicial compliance with s. 48 (%)
A[c]	Nottingham	73.4	61.7	34.0	68.0
B[d]	Leeds	79.2	67.5	9.0	74.5
C[e]	Manchester	65.9	70.5	34.5	44.8
D[f]	Lewes	62.1	64.6	21.1	38.6
E[g]	Cardiff	62.7	67.4	22.8	45.6
F[h]	Winchester	68.6	61.1	34.0	46.8

Notes

a Extracted from HMSO 1997b, Table 6.8.
b Extracted from HMSO 1997b, Table 6.7.
c Refers to the Midland and Oxford Circuit.
d Refers to the North Eastern Circuit.
e Refers to the Northern Circuit.
f Refers to the South Eastern Circuit (excluding London).
g Refers to the Wales and Chester Circuit.
h Refers to the Western Circuit.

These figures suggest little or no relationship between the stage when the plea is entered and judicial compliance with section 48. For example, Leeds had the highest compliance rate (74.5 per cent) yet recorded the lowest percentage given to the stage when the plea was entered (9 per cent). Although Lewes recorded the lowest percentage accorded to the stage (21.1 per cent), it had the lowest rate of compliance with section 48 (38.6 per cent). Further, the North Eastern circuit (Leeds) had the highest guilty plea rate (79.2 per cent) whilst the South Eastern circuit (Lewes) had the lowest (62.1 per cent). Despite this, the significance to be accorded to the stage when the plea is entered as an element in the decision-making process is confirmed by the Northern circuit where the highest rate of 'cracking' at the trial date occurred (70.5 per cent), and Manchester where the highest percentage given to the stage when the plea was entered (34.5 per cent) was recorded. These results again confirm the complexity of the sentence decision-making process.

Some differences between the Crown Court Centres examined existed in the use made of sentence discounts in relation to custodial sentences, community sentences and fines.[24] For example, Centres varied in the extent to which noncustodial sentences were passed without reference to the guilty plea entered by the defendant, and the extent to which the guilty plea (either alone or in combination with other mitigating factors) tipped the balance between a custodial and noncustodial sentence. The fact that guilty pleas were ignored for noncustodial sentences more frequently in one Centre than another may have been due to the fact that the sample for that Centre included more cases than other Centres where noncustodial sentences were appropriate. However, the important point is, as indicated earlier, that the guilty plea was ignored at all, and that there was a failure to comply with section 48.

A particularly interesting aspect of the analysis was concerned with the relationship between judicial status and a number of research variables. The distribution of status categories for each Crown Court Centre is shown in Table 18.5 and, as would be expected, the overwhelming majority (83.2 per cent) of cases were heard by Circuit judges, although percentages varied from 58.1 per cent in Winchester to 100 per cent for Nottingham. The most significant finding was the wide variation existing between the Centres examined regarding the extent to which Crown Court judges complied with the basic requirement of section 48(2), namely to state that a sentence discount had been given in return for a guilty plea. As Table 18.6 illustrates, this ranged from a 33.3 per cent compliance rate for Lewes to 76.5 per cent for Leeds – a substantial inconsistency and a cause for concern

Statistically, there was no significant relationship between judicial status and compliance with section 48, and overall, the balance was slightly in favour of compliance with section 48. However, significant relationships were found between judicial status and the importance attached to the guilty plea when fixing sentence, and judicial status and the importance attached to the *stage* when the guilty plea was entered. In relation to the latter the degree of agreement was fairly uniform as between Circuit judges and, whilst a greater percentage of Recorders may have rated this variable as 'very important' (38.1

Table 18.5   Judicial status by Crown Court Centre

Centre	High Court Judge (%)	Circuit Judge (%)	Recorder (%)	Assistant Recorder (%)	Total (%)
Cardiff	–	84.2	10.5	5.3	100.0
Leeds	–	96.4	3.6	–	100.0
Lewes	1.8	82.5	10.5	5.3	100.0
Manchester	–	82.8	17.2	–	100.0
Nottingham	–	100.0	–	–	100.0
Winchester	–	58.1	37.1	4.8	100.0
Total	3.0	83.2	13.5	2.9	100.0

Table 18.6   Judicial compliance with s. 48 by Status and Centre

Centre	Compliance with s. 48	High Court Judge (%)	Circuit Judge (%)	Recorder (%)	Assistant Recorder (%)	Total (%)
Cardiff	Yes	–	41.7	66.7	66.7	45.6
	No	–	58.3	33.3	33.3	54.4
Leeds	Yes	–	76.5	–	–	73.6
	No	–	23.5	100.0	–	26.4
Lewes	Yes	–	33.3	50.0	100.0	38.2
	No	100.0	66.7	50.0	–	61.8
Manchester	Yes	–	37.5	80.0	–	44.8
	No	–	62.5	20.0	–	55.2
Nottingham	Yes	–	69.2	–	–	69.2
	No	–	30.8	–	–	30.8
Winchester	Yes	–	44.4	52.2	33.3	46.8
	No	–	55.6	47.8	66.7	53.2

per cent as compared to 25.0 per cent of judges), a larger percentage (45.2 per cent as compared to 33.6 per cent of judges) rated it as 'not important at all'.

Court of Appeal Guidance and Sentence Discounts

This section considers the extent to which Court of Appeal guidance on the use of sentence discounts can be regarded as imprecise and inadequate. In general terms, the results do not detract from what Lord Taylor CJ stated clearly in *Buffrey* (1993) 14 Cr.App.R.(S.) 511 that, whilst a one-third discount might be appropriate as general guidance:

> It would be quite wrongful to suggest that there was any absolute rule as to what the discount should be. Each case must be assessed by the trial judge on its own facts and there will be considerable variance as between one case and another.

Nevertheless, despite its reference to the significance of the stage when the plea was entered, this ringing endorsement of the virtues of unrestricted judicial discretion provided no particular assistance to judges. Once section 48 came into force its future interpretation was left entirely to the judiciary since the provision was silent as to how an appropriate discount might be calculated and on what basis (as no practice direction was issued). Inevitably, this resulted in the application of pre-Act principles such as those relating to the exceptional circumstances when the sentence discount principle might be ignored established in *Costen* (1989) 11 Cr.App.R.(S.) 182.

Turning now to the research, as far as the level of sentence discounts is concerned, this was necessarily a function of the cases included in the analysis. The most important finding in this context is that the extent of the discount is often not articulated even when its appropriateness may not be called into question. However, there was no evidence to indicate the extent of compliance with the exceptions laid down in *Costen* and, more particularly the fifth exception that indicates that the sentence discount principle might be ignored where the defendant was caught red-handed and there was no possible defence to the charge. In any event, no significant relationship was found to exist between those cases where the defendant was caught red-handed and those where no sentence discount was given.

The research indicated that the Court of Appeal's advice in *Fearon* [1996] Crim.L.R. 213, that where the defendant pleads guilty in the Crown Court the judge should say so in every case, is often ignored and has had little impact on judicial compliance with section 48, since (as Table 18.1 shows) in this

study a substantial minority did not comply with section 48 even in the narrow sense of referring to the plea and the fact that credit would be given for it. It was also stated in *Fearon* that the defendant should be given a guilty plea discount however strong the prosecution case may be. The results indicate that although there was no significant relationship between cases where the defendant was caught red-handed and compliance with section 48, in 61.4 per cent of cases where the defendant was caught red-handed section 48 was in fact complied with. Moreover, that fact that only 17.0 per cent of the 165 cases regarded as complying with section 48 actually explained the full effect of the sentence discount on the sentence ignores what was really implicit in *Fearon* (see Thomas 1996, p. 213) i.e. that an explanation should be given in any case where the sentence is reduced as a result of the guilty plea whatever stage of the proceedings the intention to plead guilty is indicated. The conclusion must be that despite the fact the study could not substantiate whether the fifth exception in *Costen* was being consistently applied by judges, following implementation of section 48 the advice of the Court of Appeal in post-Act cases such as *Fearon* would, on the evidence of this research, appear to have been largely ignored.

Conclusions and Implications

It was assumed from the outset that in order to fully understand the operation of sentence discounts in the Crown Court the following (apparently) straightforward questions needed to be answered:

1) did the guilty plea produce a sentence discount;
2) what explanation was given for the sentence discount by the judge;
3) how was the sentence discount actually reflected in the sentence?

As explained in the opening section, numerous studies (including most recently Flood-Page and Mackie 1998, p. 90) have dealt with the third question[25] but no previous attempt has been made to monitor the operation and effectiveness of section 48 of the Criminal Justice and Public Order Act 1994 on the criminal process. In addition to its overtly crime control function of reducing the number of 'cracked trials', the section should have provided greater transparency to a process with fundamental due process and human rights implications, through improving our understanding of how the judiciary deal with the first two questions stated above in the actual sentence decision-making process.

However, as we have seen, it appears a substantial minority of judges are not only failing to provide an explanation of the basis of the discount, they are not stating it at all.

There are also two areas of particular difficulty concerning the ambit of section 48 which need to be addressed. The first is that section 48 imposes no obligation on the sentencer to state the fact of a guilty plea or explain further the implications of this for any sentence discount. The second problem is that no obligation lies on the sentencer under section 48 to declare that *no* sentence discount has been given or to explain further the basis upon which such a decision has been reached. The consequences are that in these two situations in particular, we may have no idea of the sentencer's rationale in each case, unless he or she chooses to elaborate this further. It will be recalled that for the purposes of this research, it was suggested that failure to elaborate on the reasons for allowing a sentence discount when the sentencer had taken the positive step of stating that credit would be given for a guilty plea (but going no further) should be regarded as a breach of section 48(2). These ambiguities and anomalies and the convoluted language of the section are exacerbated by what appear as logical flaws in its conception relating to the sentence decision-making process. For example, the reference in section 48(1)(b) to "the circumstances in which" the plea indication was given is specifically related to the timing of the plea in section 48(1)(a) rather than with wider concerns[26] which may together be instrumental in deciding on the extent of any sentence discount allowed. The study found that other mitigating factors were present in 51 per cent of cases where circumstances other than the timing of the plea were referred to.

One approach to dealing with the difficulties referred to is to recast the wording of the section in its entirety as follows:

48. Reduction in sentences for guilty pleas

(1) In determining what sentence to pass on an offender who has pleaded guilty to an offence in proceedings before that or another court a court shall take into account:
(a) the fact that the defendant has pleaded guilty
(b) the stage in the proceedings when the offender indicated his intention to plead guilty
(c) the extent to which the offender has shown remorse for the offence
(d) the extent to which the offender cooperated with the Police and (or) the Crown Prosecution Service before he indicated his intention to plead guilty

(e) the extent to which the guilty plea has avoided the time and expense of a trial

(f) the extent to which the victim(s) and (or) witness(es) have been spared the ordeal of a trial.

(2) If factors other than those referred to in subsection (1) above are taken into account by the court they shall be stated in open court.

(3) (a) If, as a result of taking into account any matter referred to in subsections (1) and (2) above, the court imposes a punishment which is less severe than the punishment it would otherwise have imposed, it shall state in open court that it has done so and explain its effect to the offender in ordinary language.

(b) If, having taken into account any matter referred to in subsections (1) and (2) above, the court decides not to impose a sentence which is less severe than that which it otherwise considers appropriate, it shall state this fact in open court and explain its effect to the offender in ordinary language.

It is apparent from the rewording that the objective in section 48(1) and (2) is to ensure that the sentencer is forced to articulate the rationale for the sentence discount from a wider range of potentially relevant factors than exist under the present section, including where the discount has been given simply on the basis of the plea itself. Moreover, by virtue of the recast section 48(3)(b) the sentencer would be forced to state and explain why no sentence discount had been given at all.

There are, however, other areas where more specific guidance from the Court of Appeal is required. Firstly, the position regarding offences taken into consideration ('tics') and sentence discounts remains unclear,[27] and secondly, and more importantly, it is unclear whether courts are consistently following the Court's advice in *Fearon* that a plea discount should be given irrespective of the strength of the prosecution case or continuing to apply the fifth exception in *Costen* regardless. Such guidance could, of course, follow a recommendation from the newly constituted Sentencing Advisory Panel established by section 81 of the Crime and Disorder Act 1998,[28] but any initiative to clarify the courts approach to the application of section 48 should preferably emanate from the Court of Appeal itself which must, in any event (as provided by the Crime and Disorder Act 1998 s. 80), also have regard (*inter alia*) to the need to promote consistency in sentencing and the need to promote public confidence in the criminal justice system. It was, in fact, following the Government decision *not* to implement Chapter 1 of Part II of the Crime (Sentences) Act 1997 (Henham 1997, p. 337) that the Lord Chief Justice issued a Practice Direction requiring sentencers to explain fully the effect of custodial sentences (Practice Direction 1998; Thomas 1998b, p.12) as part of a campaign to restore public confidence in sentencing.[29] I would suggest that the need for greater transparency in the operation of sentence discounts highlighted by this research could be adequately met by a similar practice direction from the Lord Chief Justice directed towards ensuring that sentencers not only make it clear that a sentence discount has been given, but that they also explain fully the reasons for it and state the precise effect of the discount on the sentence.

Nevertheless, Ashworth has convincingly argued that more fundamental reform of the system of sentence discounts is necessary principally on the basis that it openly contravenes a number of fundamental rights and freedoms enshrined in the European Convention on Human Rights;[30] namely, the presumption of innocence, the privilege against self-incrimination, the right to equality of treatment and the right to a fair and public hearing (Ashworth 1998a, p. 286). Ashworth also supports a reappraisal of the whole system of guilty pleas and suggests that either complete abolition or major changes in criminal procedure could produce a fairer system for both victims and witnesses (Ashworth 1998a, p. 292). It is certainly true, as Fenwick (1997, p. 317) points out, that victims currently have no right to participate in decisions to accept a guilty plea in return for a sentence discount or to accept a plea to a lesser charge. Hence, the victim's likely desire that the trial should proceed without the offer of a sentence discount may be ignored. Such a result may be regarded as detrimental since victims (actual and potential) clearly have an interest in seeing a true offender convicted. Further, some victims may prefer the ordeal of a court appearance to seeing the defendant receive a light sentence as a result of a sentence discount, whether graduated or not. Past support for plea discounts and the crime control ideology, with its emphasis on financial constraint, speed and finality of conviction, has been on the basis that it is broadly in the interests of victims because it spares victims the ordeal of giving evidence whilst recognising that due process rights such as the right to a fair trial and public hearing may be infringed and some innocent defendants may be induced to plead guilty. Fenwick is surely correct in suggesting that the perceptions of victims towards this process are actually more complex and that there is a case for establishing rights of consultation and participation in those decisions, at least for victims of serious offences (Fenwick 1997, p. 330).

Although cogent arguments for reform of the guilty plea system undoubtedly exist, in the short-term this research has highlighted the pressing need for increased guidance to Crown Court judges and the need for more information to be made available to defendants on the implications of the choices they make, and to victims, witnesses and the public at large, on the real consequences of the guilty plea.[31] The research has indicated that, although the strategic policy goals of sentence discounts (i.e. helping to reduce the number of 'cracked trials') are being achieved, the rationale and extent of discount decisions (via section 48) are not being articulated consistently by the courts. This failure is compounded by the fact that there appear to exist unjustifiable differences between sentence discounts for different offences, differences in regional and judicial practice and cogent reasons to support a gradual reduction in the amount of the discount itself. I submit that there is consequently an urgent need for section 48 of the Criminal Justice and Public Order Act 1994 to be amended along the lines suggested to correct its manifold weaknesses; for the Lord Chief Justice to issue a practice direction on the correct approach to the use of sentence discounts by the Crown Court; for additional judicial training to reinforce the need for consistency of approach and transparency in decision-making;[32] and for increased Court of Appeal guidance on sentence discounts (following consideration of the issue by the Sentencing Advisory Panel) to rationalise their effect as between different offences.

In retrospect, Thomas' (1994, p. 12) salutary warning as to the likely effect of section 48 has regrettably proved correct:

> The recent history of sentencing legislation is full of examples of provisions added to the statute book without adequate consideration of their practical effects, producing serious difficulties or a need for immediate amendment or both. This new clause threatens to provide another.

Notes

1   The Crime (Sentences) Act 1997, Para 17, Schedule 4 added a further subsection to the Criminal Justice and Public Order Act 1994, s. 48 as follows: "In a case of an offence the sentence for which falls to be imposed by subsection (2) of Section 3 or 4 of the Crime (Sentences) Act 1997, nothing in that subsection shall prevent the court, after taking into account any matter referred to in subsection (1) above, from imposing any sentence which is not less than 80 per cent of that specified in that subsection". Note that the subsection is only effective in so far as it concerns the Crime (Sentences) Act 1997, s. 3 (mandatory minimum sentences of seven years for third Class A drug trafficking offence) since s. 4 (mandatory minimum sentences of three years for a third domestic burglary) has not yet been implemented (see Thomas 1997, p. 7; and The Crime (Sentences) Act 1997 [1998] CLR 83, 90).

2   See, in particular, that relating to judicial compliance with s. 48 and the proposed redrafting of the provision.

3   The Magistrates Association 1997, para. 2.4, p. iii. The paragraph continues to state that discounts may be given in respect to fines, periods of community service and custody although para 2.5.4 which deals with fines, points out that the guideline fines have not been discounted for a guilty plea. It is important to note that until 1989 the Magistrates' Association Sentencing Guidelines made no mention of the possible effect of a guilty plea and my own study found that two-thirds of the 129 magistrates interviewed regarded a guilty plea as of minor or no significance in mitigation (Henham 1990, p. 133). As Sanders and Young (1994, p. 268) point out, even the 1993 version of the guidelines was muted in its enthusiasm for the discount principle.

4   In *Akbar* (*The Times*, 29 September 1993), Scott Baker J at first instance, indicated that those who pleaded guilty in trials involving enormous expense 'could expect a considerable discount in sentence'.

5   McCoy and Cohen 1998, p. 6. For an interesting analysis of current debates regarding the legitimacy of plea-bargaining, see McConville 1998, p. 562.

6   (1989) 11 Cr.App.R. (S) 182. There are five exceptions to the sentence discount principle: 1) the maximum may be imposed on an offender under 18 who pleads guilty in a case almost falling within the special powers under the Children and Young Persons Act 1933, s. 53(2). See *Godber* (1986) 8 Cr.App.R.(S.) 460; (2) where a longer sentence is thought necessary to protect the public from a dangerous offender (see *Bowler* (1993) 15 Cr.App.R. (S.) 78); 3) where the offender has been convicted on a 'specimen' count; 4) where the offender has pleaded not guilty until the last minute before changing it to guilty; 5) where the offender was caught red-handed and there was no possible defence to the charge. Exceptions 2) to 5) above were recognised by the Court of Appeal in *Costen*.

7   The reasoning is difficult to reconcile with *Carroll* (1994) 16 Cr.App.R.(S.) 488 (see further Thomas, [1995] CLR 662).

8   For a useful discussion see Redmayne 1997, p. 79 and, more generally, as regards mode of trial decision-making see, Ashworth 1998a, ch. 8.

9   Practice Direction: Plea and Directions Hearings [1995] 1 WLR 1318. The 'plea before venue' system introduced by the Criminal Procedure and Investigations Act 1996 s. 49 came into force on 1 October 1997 and, therefore, had no impact on the cases included in this research.

10 HMSO 1998, Table 6.7. The percentage of 'cracked trials' as a proportion of all cases disposed of fell from 19.5 per cent in 1996 to 18.6 per cent in 1997. The percentage of defendants pleading guilty on the trial date was 64.9 per cent in 1997. The rate varied between 59.4 per cent (London) to 70.5 per cent (Northern).

11 HMSO 1998, Table 6.8. The equivalent figures for 1997 were 95,696 defendants dealt with, with 65,782 (68.7 per cent) having pleaded guilty (see HMSO 1998, Table 6.9). Averaged between the 90 Crown Court Centres the figure was 731 cases. A sample size of 50 cases per Centre reflected approximately 6.8 per cent of the annual average number of guilty pleas for each Centre and the final sample size of 310 cases represented 0.5 per cent of the annual number of guilty pleas for defendants dealt with in all Crown Court Centres.

12 It proved difficult to identify cases in advance from the weekly criminal firm list produced by each Court.

13 In the case of two Courts, Manchester and Cardiff, a small proportion of the sample had to be drawn from cases dealt with up to December 1997.

14 This form provides the following information in respect of each person appearing for trial: name and date of birth, date of committal and from which magistrates' court, whether

committed on bail or in custody, whether legally aided, the name of the judge at trial and sentence, name of counsel and solicitors, date of the trial and the result, whether further remanded for reports, date of sentence and penalty imposed, court reporters present at each appearance.

15 In a large number of cases it proved impossible to obtain the relevant sentencing transcript since the necessary information had been incorrectly recorded on Form 5089.

16 For example: previous convictions – gaps in offending; lack of pattern; reduction in serious offences; dissimilar offences; previous good character; successfully completed previous sentences; behaviour following charge; age; health; voluntary reparation; assistance to the police.

17 Excluding the stage in the proceedings when the guilty plea was entered.

18 For detailed discussion see Ashworth 1998a, pp. 271–5. In 1997 the percentage of trials which cracked because the prosecution accepted a plea of guilty to an alternative charge was 14.7 per cent (HMSO 1998, Table 6.7).

19 Limited comparisons can be made with national data from the Home Office (Government Statistical Service 1998, No. 18). For example, as regards offence distribution, the research figures were burglary (19.0 per cent), theft (12.3 per cent) and assault occasioning actual bodily harm (7.4 per cent) whilst comparable national figures were 8.1 per cent, 39.5 per cent and 11.4 per cent (Table 18.4). Table 18.12 reveals that the percentages pleading guilty to these offences nationally were burglary (84.0 per cent), theft (69.0 per cent) and violence against the person (53.0 per cent). The high proportion of offenders pleading guilty to burglary probably accounts for the greater representation of this offence in the research sample.

20 This has proved to be a particularly difficult task: see further, Hogarth 1971 and Hood 1972.

21 It cannot be assumed that differences in practice between Centres necessarily reflect differences between Circuits.

22 It will be recalled that, according to the wider interpretation adopted in this research, failure to provide such an explanation was treated as failure to comply with section 48(2).

23 I.e. mitigating factors not directly associated with the guilty plea discounts (note 16).

24 Beyond analysis of differences in approach in the application of s. 48 described above, it was not feasible, because of small numbers, to analyse the data further in terms of different sentence decisions.

25 For example, by recording the average custodial sentence length by plea for different offences (Flood-Page and Mackie 1998, Figure 8.17, p. 91).

26 Such as, for example, providing assistance to the police, as in *A* and *B* (*The Times*, 1 May 1998).

27 Important issues of principle are involved regarding (*inter alia*) the presumption of innocence, the right to a fair and public hearing and the rights of victims.

28 The Panel is empowered to initiate such recommendations, or make recommendations if so requested by the Secretary of State.

29 See Gibb 1998 and Hough and Roberts 1997. For contextual analysis see Ashworth and Hough 1996, p. 776 and Shute 1998, p. 465.

30 The implications for sentencing law of the incorporation of the European Convention by the Human Rights Act 1998 are addressed by Ashworth 1998b, p. 141 and Cheney 1999, ch. 5.

31 As Ashworth (1998a, p. 296) points out, "the pressures to plead guilty are at present too great and the effect on innocent defendants (especially those from certain racial minorities) is unacceptable".
32 The obstacles presented by the judicial cult of individualism are discussed by Malleson 1997, p. 655.

References

Ashworth, A. (1993), 'Plea, Venue and Discontinuance', *Criminal Law Review*, p. 830.
Ashworth, A. (1994), *The Criminal Process: An evaluative study*, 1st edn, Oxford: Oxford University Press.
Ashworth, A. (1995), *Sentencing and Criminal Justice*, 2nd edn, London: Butterworths.
Ashworth, A. (1998a), *The Criminal Process: An evaluative study*, 2nd edn, Oxford: Oxford University Press.
Ashworth, A. (1998b), 'The Impact on Criminal Justice', in B. Markensis (eds), *The Impact of the Human Rights Bill on English Law*, Oxford: Clarendon Press.
Ashworth, A. and Hough, M. (1996), 'Sentencing and the Climate of Opinion', *Criminal Law Review*, 776.
Baldwin, J. (1985), *Pre-Trial Justice*, Oxford: Basil Blackwell.
Bottoms, A.E. and McClean, J.D. (1976), *Defendants in the Criminal Process*, London: Routledge.
Cheney, D. et al. (1999), *Criminal Justice and the Human Rights Act 1998*, London: Jordans.
Fenwick, H. (1997), 'Procedural Rights of Victims of Crime: Public or Private Ordering of the Criminal Justice System', *The Modern Law Review*, Vol. 60, p. 376.
Flood-Page, C. and Mackie, A. (1998), *Sentencing Practice: An examination of decisions in magistrates' courts and the Crown Court in the mid-1990s*, Home Office Research Study No. 180, London: HMSO.
Gibb, F. (1998), 'Judges Move to Restore Public Confidence in Sentencing', *The Times*, 21 January.
Government Statistical Service (1998), 'Cautions, Court Proceedings and Sentencing, England and Wales 1997', *Statistical Bulletin 18/98*.
Hazell, R. and Co. (1995), *Hazell's Guide*, Henley-on-Thames: R. Hazell and Co.
Henham, R. (1990), *Sentencing Principles and Magistrates' Sentencing Behaviour*, Avebury: Aldershot.
Henham, R. (1997), 'Sentencing Policy and the Abolition of Parole and Early Release', *International Journal of the Sociology of Law*, Vol. 25, p. 337.
Hogarth, J. (1971), *Sentencing as a Human Process*, University of Toronto Press, Toronto.
Home Office (1995), *Judicial Statistics, Annual Report 1994*, Cmnd 2891, London: HMSO.
Home Office (1997a), *Criminal Statistics, England and Wales 1996*, Cm 3764, London: HMSO.
Home Office (1997b), *Judicial Statistics, Annual Report 1996*, Cm 1736, London: HMSO.
Home Office (1998), *Judicial Statistics, Annual Report 1997*, Cm 3980, London: HMSO.
Hood, R. (1972), *Sentencing the Motoring Offender*, London: Heinemann.
Hood, R. (1992), *Race and Sentencing*, Oxford: Oxford University Press.
Hough, M. and Roberts, J. (1997), *Attitudes to Punishment: Findings from the 1996 British Crime Survey*, Home Office Research Study No. 179, London: Home Office.

McConville, M. (1998), 'Plea Bargaining: Ethics and politics', *Journal of Law and Society*, Vol. 25, p. 562.

McConville, M. and Baldwin, J. (1981), *Courts, Prosecution and Conviction*, Oxford: Clarendon Press.

McCoy, C. and Cohen, N. (1998), *Trial Penalty or True Confessions? An Analysis of 'Acceptance of Responsibility' in the Federal Courts*, paper presented at Law and Society Annual Meeting, Aspen, Colorado.

The Magistrates' Association (1997), *Sentencing Guidelines*, London: The Magistrates Association.

Malleson, K. (1997), 'Judicial Training and Performance Appraisal: The problem of judicial independence', *The Modern Law Review*, Vol. 60, p. 655.

Practice Direction: Custodial Sentences, 22 January 1998.

Practice Direction: Plea and Directions Hearings [1995] 1 WLR 1318.

Redmayne, M. (1997), 'The Criminal Procedure and Investigations Act 1996', *The Modern Law Review*, Vol. 60, p. 79.

Sanders, A. and Young, R. (1994), *Criminal Justice*, London: Butterworths.

Shute, S. (1998), 'The Place of Public Opinion in Sentencing Law', *Criminal Law Review*, p. 465.

Thomas, D. (1994), 'Viewpoint', *Sentencing News*, Vol. 2, p. 12.

Thomas, D. (1995), 'Criminal Justice and Public Order Act 1994: Implications for sentencing', *Archbold News*, Vol. 1, p. 5.

Thomas, D. (1996), *Criminal Law Review*, p. 212.

Thomas, D. (1997), 'Crime (Sentences) Act 1997', *Archbold News*, Vol. 9, p. 5.

Thomas, D. (1998a), 'The Crime (Sentences) Act 1997', *Criminal Law Review*, p. 83.

Thomas, D. (1998b), 'Honesty in Sentencing', *Sentencing News*, Vol. 1, p. 12.

Thomas, D.A. (1979), *Principles of Sentencing*, London: Heinemann.

Wasik, M. and Taylor, R. (1995), *Blackstone's Guide to the Criminal Justice and Public Order Act 1994*, London: Blackstone Press.

Wasik, M. and Turner, A. (1993), 'Sentencing Guidelines for Magistrates' Courts', *Criminal Law Review*, p. 345.

Zander, M. and Henderson, P. (1993), *Crown Court Study*, Home Office Research Study No. 19, London: HMSO.

Chapter Nineteen

Accountability for the Sentencing Decision Process – Towards a New Understanding[1]

Cyrus Tata[2]

Summary

Traditionally, legal academic writing and scholarship has tended to regard sentencing discretion as lacking sufficient structure and coherence. This lack of coherence, it has been argued, means that there is a lack of genuine openness and accountability in sentencing decision-making. According to this view, an important job of the sentencing scholar is to uncover the penal philosophies, which are said to drive individual sentencers' interpretations of case-factors. Therefore, it is said that transparency and accountability can only be achieved by explanations of sentencing in analytical and penal-philosophical terms.

This chapter suggests the need to develop a new approach to understanding the decision process, which is neither rule-less, nor, explained by the weighting of discrete individual case factors, or, combinations of discrete case factors. Arguing that accounts given by sentencers are necessarily socially produced, the chapter advances the case for a fundamental reappraisal of explanations of the structure of the sentencing decision process.

The chapter begins by describing the scholarly dissatisfaction with the coherence of sentencing discretion and the various methods intended to increase the coherence in the structure of sentencing discretion. Each of these methods has encountered serious criticisms. The second section examines the elusive search for 'coherence' in sentencing. It argues that judicial defensiveness does not provide a sufficient explanation for the apparent lack of openness in sentencing. Instead, basic assumed categories of sentencing have had an obscuring effect. These categories represent a series of dichotomies: 'the offence plus the offender'; 'aggravating versus mitigating factors', 'penal philosophy versus non-coherent judgement' and 'discretion versus rules'. In the third section the reader is invited to consider why attempts to introduce greater transparency and accountability have largely disappointed advocates of transparency, and are likely to continue to do so without a re-conceptualisation of sentencing accountability. Using this re-conceptualisation the chapter attempts to begin to open out new and under-explored questions for sentencing research and policy.

Introduction

The concept of 'accountability' is axiomatic to modern legal thinking. If decisions are to be just they should be explicable through reasoned explanation. This chapter reappraises the conventional wisdom which supposes the sentencing decision process to be incoherent or lacking structure because of penal-philosophical disagreement. One objective of this chapter is to challenge the assumed conception of 'coherence'. In doing so it attempts a more critical evaluation of the efficacy of penal-philosophical explanation and calls for greater legal transparency, and thus interpretation of accountability for the sentencing decision process.

Sentencing decision-making has often been assumed by legal scholars to be a relatively formless process with little or no coherent structure. A generation after Marvin Frankel's 1972 "law without order" polemic against the "arbitrary fiat"[3] of the discretionary power of individual judges, the suspicion of excessive and therefore order-less judicial discretion endures. For example, Miller (1989, p. 20) depicts sentencing as a mysterious and hidden process of decision-making. Jareborg (1995, p. 22) states that new sentencing legislation in Sweden replaced "… a black box …". Von Hirsch (1987, p. 4) claimed that under indeterminate sentencing in the US sentencing patterns "… emerged largely by happenstance … . There was no coherent pattern of sentences sought". In his book on the development of Minnesota's Sentencing Guidelines, entitled *Structuring Sentencing*, Parent explains that his intention is to convey

> … the message that sentencing can be rationally guided by a system of law to replace … wide-open discretion that prevailed in the past. Discretionary sentencing … conferred unguided discretion … [which] allowed anarchy among judges and produced both arbitrariness and unwarranted disparity [sic] (Parent 1988, pp. 2–3).

I will argue that the accepted wisdom of a lack of coherence in fact presupposes one particular understanding of the use of legal discretion. If sentencing is not seen to be governed by formal legal principles and official procedures it has been labelled as 'chaotic', 'incoherent' and 'unstructured'. The purpose of this chapter is to suggest different ways of making sense of sentencing discretion, which permits a rethink of transparency and accountability for the decision process. In so doing, I will suggest that using philosophically-derived justifications for punishment should not be assumed to be the only or main theoretical way to understand sentencing practice and judicial discourse about that practice.

The sentencing reform movement throughout the western world has been inspired, at least in part, by the concern among sentencing scholars that the sentencing decision process is inadequately structured and coherent. The major approaches to reform have understood the sentencing discretion through particular legal, cognitive and philosophical categories. Their dominance of these categories has obscured other useful ways of thinking which may in turn help to interpret the troubled history of sentencing reform policy. First, however, I will explain the scholarly dissatisfaction with different methods to encourage greater coherence in the sentencing decision process.

1 Dissatisfaction with Coherence of Sentencing Discretion and the Search for Reform

In historical terms sentencing in western jurisdictions has undergone a considerable programme of reform (e.g. Ashworth 1995; Tonry 1996; Tonry and Hatlestad 1997). The main thrust of this programme has been to reduce alleged disparity in sentencing (e.g. Blumstein et al. 1983; Tarling 1979; Tonry 1996; Tata and Hutton 1998) and also to ensure 'truth in sentencing'. However, given the liberal-legal conception of judicial independence, there has not been a concerted academic call to direct judges to decisions in specific cases. Indeed even the advocates of stricter numerical guidelines and of 'expert systems' have stressed that their work should not be seen as an attempt to appropriate the proper exercise of judicial discretion but rather simply as an 'aid' or way of helping judges to 'structure' the use of discretion in individual cases. Thus, none of the major methods of reforms, discussed below, consciously intends to remove the judicial power to make the sentencing decision in individual cases. Rather, they claim to 'inform' so as to 'structure' that discretionary power (Ashworth 1995; Tonry 1996; Cavadino and Dignan 1997, p. 105). The implication is that sentencing is insufficiently or inadequately 'structured': deficient in reasoned explanation by the sentencers. There have been three main methods intended to inform so as to better the structure of sentencing discretionary process: appeal court leadership, legislatively legitimised guidelines and judicial information systems. How has the academic literature evaluated these three methods' attempts to better inform the structure of sentencing?

1   Institutional Consistency: Appeal Court Judgements

Scholars of legal doctrine have been concerned to describe and explain the use of sentencing discretion by analysing Appeal Court Judgements. This has been a rich source of academic commentary and the attempt to try to extract more general even universal 'principles' about how sentencing can and should operate. Indeed, over the last 15 years or so the Court of Appeal of England and Wales may arguably have begun to try to present some kind of observable jurisprudence of sentencing involving 'Guideline' judgements intended to provide sentencers with starting points in similar cases (Thomas 1995). However, two main inter-related limitations of this method to explain and enhance the structure of sentencing discretion have been identified. These two limitations are: weak impact of Appeal Court judgements on first instance sentencing, and secondly, deficiency in principled coherence of Appeal Court behaviour.

Limitation one: weak impact of appeal court decisions on first instance sentencing Ascertaining knowledge about the influence of Appeal Court 'policy' on first instance sentencing practice is problematic. Although Appeal Court judgements are collated together with academic commentaries in sentencing texts (e.g. Nicholson 1992; Walker and Padfield 1996; Kelly 1993), or, as part of an on-going digest, these are essentially case-by-case presentations of Appeal Court sentencing rather than 'normal' sentencing practice in 'similar cases'. For example, commenting on Thomas' sagacity about the England and Wales Court of Appeal, von Hirsch (1987, p. 194) carefully observed that it is "not certain to what extent trial courts and magistrates actually follow the Court of Appeal's opinions in unappealed cases, and the extent of such compliance or non-compliance has not been systematically measured". More recently, Ashworth (1998) notes that there has been no research into the effectiveness of the England & Wales Court of Appeal Guidelines in fostering consistency of approach with Appeal Court Guidance. Although Tonry (2001, p. 24) generously concedes that "many English judges and informed observers believe that guideline judgements do influence sentencing patterns", he has to point out that "there is no credible evaluation literature" of their impact.

However, there are a number of reasons to expect that compliance is limited. First, Appeal Courts are reluctant to 'interfere' with first instance sentencing even if that original sentence is not one which the Appeal Court itself would have imposed. Writing about sentencing in Canada, Brodeur (1989, p. 28) has observed that "... unless a Court of Appeal sees reason at least to double the sentence or cut it by half, it will generally uphold the decision of the trial judge". Similarly, Doob (1990, p. 10) noted that Appeal Court judges try not to "tamper with sentences unless they are more than twice as long or less than half as long as they should be". In the South African context, Hutton (1998, p. 320) suggests that the previous reluctance of the Appeal Court to intervene in a first instance sentence, unless it was held to be "shocking or startlingly inappropriate" is unlikely to change under the new regime.

Secondly, Doob (1990, p. 10) shows that this reluctance to 'interfere' (which is meshed with individual judicial 'ownership' of sentencing), can easily provide sentencers with a false sense of security. Appeal Court permissiveness encourages first instance sentencers a false comfort in the conclusion that because very few of his/her sentences are appealed, and even fewer successfully, the sentencer is 'in line' with normal practice (e.g. Tata and Hutton 1998).

Thirdly, given their sense of distance from the Appeal Court and the unlikelihood of appeal first instance sentencers may not necessarily wish to emulate the view of the Appeal Court, if it is believed by first instance sentencers to lead to substantive injustice.

Fourthly, Guideline Judgements in England and Wales, (the jurisdiction to have pursued the technique with more vigour than any other), are very limited in scope. They remain "clustered around serious offences which tend to attract substantial prison sentences" rather than areas of everyday sentencing – notably burglary, theft etc. (Ashworth 2001, p. 74).

Limitation two: deficient in 'principled coherence' A second main limitation has been popularised by academic criminal lawyers who have advocated greater systematisation and coherence in Appeal Court decision-making (e.g. Henham 1995, 1996; 1998b; Ashworth 1995; Fox 1994). Appeal Courts in common law jurisdictions have tended to stress the limits of extrapolation of the judgement to other cases. Either it is argued that the judgement cannot be compared with other cases; or, in 'leading' or 'guideline' judgements the court has said that a tariff can be established but that it can only apply when cases share the specific combination of 'facts'. The fundamental problem with this approach is in the inherent interpretability of legal 'facts' (Ashworth et al.

1984). Thus as long as Appeal Courts hold to the fiction that because each individual case is unique (in some sense) therefore sentencing each case is a 'unique' exercise,[4] first instance sentencing will elude attempts to systematise the extrapolation of Appeal Court Guideline.

On the basis of Appeal Court (including 'Guideline') Judgements, it tends to be difficult to identify clearly any overall systematic pattern, or, attempt to structuring of sentencing overall. Academic lawyers have repeatedly called for greater overall coherence based on some kind principled reasoning (e.g. Ashworth 1995; Henham 1995, 1996; Fox 1994; Stith and Cabranes 1998). Yet, why does this incoherence of Appeal Court Judgements persist? The conventional explanation is that incoherence is due to a lack of penal philosophical consensus: different judges pursuing diverging penal philosophies. However, this hypothesis cannot, in itself, fully explain the lack of philosophical coherence in a single Appeal Court judgement, or, indeed the diverging philosophies expressed by a single judge from one case to another.

2   Legislative and Administrative 'Guidelines'

The attempt to 'structure' sentencing through the use of non-judicial legal controls (such as legislative and administrative guidelines and mandatory penalties) has failed to render the sentencing discretionary process more transparent.

Probably the single most dramatic response to perceived lack of coherent structure in sentencing has been the introduction of the numerical guidelines in the US. Whether guidelines in their various forms can and do reduce 'disparity' even on their own definitions of disparity is hotly debated. However, numerical guidelines have not in themselves provided sentencing scholarship with a more satisfactory explanation of how judges use the discretion which the guidelines have to permit. Legal discretion necessarily remains indispensable to the interpretation, and operation of numerical guidelines, and the opportunities for creative compliance are extensive. The vast literature on 'departures' from the guidelines demonstrate the inherent malleability of the supposed clarity and firm structure. Writing about guidelines and 'mandatory' sentencing, Mears (1998, p. 673) states that a major

> ... limitation of sentencing research is the relatively scant attention that has been given to ... the unintended uses and effects of ... recent sentencing reforms. That various reforms generate uses and effects unintended by legislatures is difficult to contest [sic].

Even the apparently most clearly structured of reforms (such as mandatory penalties and determinate sentencing) allow plentiful opportunities for creative uses of discretion to subvert and circumvent surreptitiously what may be regarded as the worst excesses of a substantively unjust system of guidelines (Tonry 2001, p. 21).

> [T]here is sufficient empirical evidence to suggest that internal resistance and deliberate evasion of the new pertinent rules have been prevalent in the United States. No specific type of sentencing reform has demonstrated the ability to achieve a substantial level of internal support for the reform; to establish the most effective form of statutory or administrative authority to promote compliance ... (Wicharaya 1995, p. 161).

Yet while many judges and others may protest publicly and some may find subtler ways to ensure "creative compliance" (McBarnett and Whelan 1997), other judges (or the same judges in different instances), appear to convince themselves that their 'hands are tied' and refuse to exercise the discretion available. Numerical guidelines may have coincided with a change in sentencing not through the force of legality. Rather, many judges appear to have convinced themselves (seemingly on the basis of compliance with the perceived dominant view), that in certain types of cases they have lost their discretion.

Provine (1998) suggests, there may be striking parallels with Robert Cover's (1975) study of judicial decision-making under the Fugitive Slave Act. "Time and again, the judiciary paraded its helplessness before the law; lamented harsh results yet nonetheless declined to use their legal discretion to make 'ameliorist' solutions possible" (Cover 1975, pp. 5–6).

Provine (1998) documents that on the one hand, although sentencers in the US Federal Courts are appalled by the substantive racial injustice of the aspects of the guidelines combined with mandatory penalties for crack cocaine,[5] they nonetheless generally tend to decline to use their discretion so as to subvert, or, at least ameliorate the worst racial effects (e.g. in the way that is described above by Wicharaya). Under certain circumstances judges may defer to their sense of the dominant political rhetoric even though they may say they hate to do so, and in fact, the law continues to permit far greater freedom than they claim.

Indeed, the selective admission and denial of the ever-presence of discretion (even in a supposedly highly restrictive scheme like the Federal Guidelines), is redolent of the reaction of the judiciary of England and Wales to the 1991 Criminal Justice Act. It was commonly claimed both by rank-and-file and magistrates and the Lord Chief Justice that the legislation "tied the hands" (Taylor 1993) of sentencers even though, as with the US Federal Guidelines, departures for 'exceptional circumstances' featured throughout the scheme. Indeed, creative use and interpretation of judicial discretion seems to have been highly selective (Ashworth 1998).

Neither presumptive numerical guidelines nor mandatory penalties have succeeded in illuminating or more clearly structuring the judicial discretionary decision process. Changes in the use/non-use of discretion appear to have resulted only because judges may choose to assume (erroneously) that substantive discretion has largely been eliminated.[6] At other times, judges may feel able routinely to circumvent or ameliorate the guidelines. Thus guidelines appear not to have achieved the greater clarity in judicial use of discretion which sentencing scholarship has long sought.

Controversies in achieving reform through both numerical guidelines (Tonry 1996; Alschuler 1991; Frase 1995; Miller 1995; Doob 1995; Nagel and Johnson 1994; Nagel 1990; McDonald and Carlson 1996); and in narrative guidelines (Brownlee 1994; Thomas 1995) have been very well documented and have led to interest in 'systems' of providing aggregate data about sentencing to sentencers (Tata 1998b). Although US-style numerical guidelines have influenced thinking around the globe there has been remarkably little systematic emulation of that approach to reform.[7] In recent times outside of the USA another method of pursuing structure has been pursued. Aggregate information systems have been developed to provide judges with information about what previous sentencers decided when faced with similar cases.

3   Aggregate Information Systems

The idea of providing sentencers with information on what their colleagues have done when faced with similar cases is not a new one. In 1953, Norval Morris suggested that trial judges be provided with data on sentences imposed so that judges could "see clearly where they stand in relation to their brethren" (Morris, 1953, p. 200, quoted in Frase 1997, p. 366). However, it was not until the 1980s that systems were developed (unsuccessfully) in Canada by John Hogarth in British Columbia (Hogarth 1988); and, by Tony Doob in other Canadian provinces (Doob and Park 1987; Doob 1990). More recently, there have been two jurisdictions, which have implemented an SIS, New South Wales (Potas et al. 1998) and Scotland (Hutton et al. 1996; Tata 1998), with interest from a number of other jurisdictions (see, for example, Morgan in this volume).

All systems of providing judges with information are inescapably normative: they measure disparity according to how those systems define 'disparity'. The implication is that if there is systematic information about previous practice then judges should be 'informed' by it. Some commentators have suggested that, given the relative dearth of systematic aggregate information about sentencing practice "judges ought not only to be provided with, but would positively delight in, access to detailed information [about sentencing practice] [sic]" (Zdenkowski 1986, p. 232); and others have appeared to recommend at least the serious consideration of the greater dissemination of systematic aggregate information (e.g. Hedderman and Gelsthorpe 1997; Henham 1998a, pp. 351–2; Morgan in this volume; Ashworth 1997a; Ashworth 1995, pp. 340–41). However, to argue that there is a relative dearth of available, good quality and systematic information about 'normal practice' available to sentencers is only one part of the overall question of whether there is a 'need' for such information.

According to Doob and Broduer (1995, p. 378):

> There is a natural tendency to explain away the problems of sentencing by asserting that, to a considerable extent, they are the result of a lack of knowledge. Hence it is sometimes argued that the problems of disparity could be lessened … by providing additional information to judges about court practice and the 'tariffs' that are applied by their colleagues.

Essentially, then, Doob has argued that from his experience and also, he implies from similar fate met by Hogarth's system, judges do not perceive there to be a need for aggregate information about 'normal practice'. Since judges cannot be coerced into paying attention to such information systems, then judges do not perceive a 'need' for such information. In this situation, the fact that it might seem strange that there is so little systematic data about normal sentencing practice is immaterial to the incoherence of the sentencing decision process. According to Doob and Brodeur, this lack of coherence has more to do with a lack of a coherent theory about the purposes of sentencing.

So far in this chapter we have seen that each of the three methods which attempt to inform so as to structure have encountered serious criticisms and have not illuminated the sentencing decision process. These flaws are attributed to a fundamental lack of coherence. It is to the quest for coherent explanation to which this chapter now turns.

2   The Quest to Explain the Sentencing Decision Process

Explanation through the (Normative) 'Aims' of Sentencing

To 'explain' sentencing we have to begin, it is conventionally argued, with an explicit consideration of the goals of sentencing. However, the history of attempts to require sentencers to provide penal-philosophical 'reasons' for sentence has not been a happy one.

In her study of the 1982 English Criminal Justice Act and section 1(4) which required sentencers to state the reason, (e.g. protection of the public; failure to respond to noncustodial penalties; retribution), for passing a custodial sentence on a young person, Burney (1985) found that in 60 per cent of the sample the reasons given were incomplete, invalid or not given at all.

> In a story that may be apocryphal, it [was] said that some magistrates courts [had] rubber stamps bearing the legendary 'nature and gravity of the offence' ... It is commonly observed that reasons are often expressed as terse formula ... rather than as thought out justifications specific to individual cases ... In short ... reasons tend to become bland, brief and standard (Fitzmaurice and Pease 1986, p. 36).

Although Ewart and Pennington suggest that this statement may be too emphatic, (for example 'seriousness of the offence' was by no means the only 'reason'[8] cited), their study of Crown and Magistrates Courts' reason-giving nonetheless found reason-giving to be superficial as a way of explaining the decision process. In common with an observation made by Ashworth et al. (1984), they concluded:

> [t]his study demonstrates that it was unusual for sentencers to describe how factors of the case were weighed to produce the final sentence. Sentencers confine themselves to noting what contributes to the sentence chosen, rather than describing the grounds for rejecting alternatives (Ewart and Pennington 1988, p. 597).

This may well be familiar to the reader who has tired of reading or listening to sentencers routinely opaque 'explanation' that s/he "took all of the facts into account".

Why has there been such a marked reluctance by sentencers both individually and collectively to articulate their substantive reasoning? Given the central position accorded to the role of penal philosophy by most of the sentencing discretion literature it is frustrating that judges are so unwilling to reveal the reasoning which led to the sentence imposed.[9] Disagreement between sentencers over the correct normative aims of sentencing has been the most cited cause.[10] It has normally been thought that sentencing practice tends to lack openly-stated aims, because there is no clear agreement about goals.

Indeed penal-philosophical goals are widely seen as the starting point to any theoretical understanding of sentencing behaviour. Open almost any English language introductory text on sentencing published over the last 40 years and the reader will most likely be presented with some kind of 'theory' section consisting largely of an exposition of the classic menu of penal philosophies as the starting point for explaining sentencing practice (e.g. Gottfredson 1999; Walker and Padfield 1996; Ashworth 1997c; O'Malley 2000; Boyle and Allen 1990; Henham 1996; Roberts 2000). The precise terminology may vary slightly, but it seems to be taken for granted that normative penal aims must be the starting point to any appreciation of the sentencing decision process. The credence of this assumption was empirically developed and legitimised by John Hogarth's seminal work published in 1971.

The legacy of Hogarth's *Sentencing as a Human Process* endures today as empirical justification for the view that the sentencing decision process lacks satisfactory explanation because of penal-philosophical disagreement between individual sentencers. Hogarth concluded that in their use, (implicitly or explicitly), of penal philosophy,

> [t]here was a considerable amount of internal consistency in the thinking of magistrates. Once one knew the social purpose that a magistrate attempted to achieve through sentencing, the whole of the penal philosophy unfolded from that (Hogarth 1971, p. 361).

From the outset of *Sentencing as a Human Process*, Hogarth sets out implicit normative disagreement between individual sentencers as the problem:

> In summary, the fundamental problems in sentencing arise from the fact that there is lack of agreement as to the social purposes that sentencing should serve, lack of evidence of effectiveness to achieve these objectives, and lack of uniformity in the way knowledge is used. In this situation it is not surprising that there is some uncertainty, confusion, and lack of agreement among judges in their approach to sentencing problems which, in turn, leads to disparity in sentencing practice (Hogarth 1971, p. 6).

Other sentencing scholars have also argued that until and unless there is agreement about the 'goals' of sentencing there cannot be either consistency or coherence in sentencing practice. For example, Doob and Brodeur (1995, p. 378) argue that the provision of aggregate information to help judges orientate the tariff is "… fundamentally wrong. The problems of sentencing – disparity in particular – can be seen to relate to problems of accountability". Adapting Day's and Klein's (1987) work on accountability, Doob and Brodeur argue that it is the lack of a set of shared expectations and common currency of justifications which necessarily means a lack of substantive accountability in sentencing. To rectify this lack of accountability Doob and Brodeur call for a sentencing "'theory' or a set of guiding principles on sentencing and an explanation of how a sentence followed from the guiding principles" (1995, p. 384). Although Doob and Brodeur are explicit in arguing that incoherence is a matter of accountability, they are very far from alone in calling for greater 'coherence' in sentencing practice (e.g. Ashworth 1995; Henham 1996, 1997; Wasik; Fox 1994; Hutton 1998; Jobson and Ferguson 1987).

I would like now to invite the reader to examine this proposition further so as then to develop an alternate appreciation for this supposed lack of coherence. Judicial defensiveness will be suggested to be only partial explanation for this apparent lack of coherent transparency. Rather, I will suggest that the assumed categories, (including the standard menu of legal-philosophical justifications for punishment), of sentencing scholarship themselves limit and obscure appreciation of the decision process.

Transparency, Openness and 'Reasons'

Is judicial defensiveness the main cause of a 'lack of transparent coherence'? It might be argued that the lack of agreement about a set of coherent sentencing guiding principles and how a decision should follow those guiding principles is symptomatic of a judicial refusal to accept the need for openness in discussing sentencing practice (Fox 1994; Miller 1989; Parent 1988). For example, in his chapter in this volume on European sentencing traditions, Ashworth observes:

> the paucity of empirical research on the decision-making processes of sentencers. As long ago as 1974 the Council of Europe report on Sentencing recognised the importance of detailed research into the motivations and practices of judges in the sentencing process (Council of Europe 1974, p.13), but there remains considerable judicial resistance to this in most member states, and there are still very few studies of sentencers which involve interviews and close observation.

Judges tend to be suspicious of anyone (especially academic researchers), asking questions and exposing the limitations of their practice. This is due only partly to personal vanity. It is also due to a defensiveness about the implications of such enquiry. Judiciaries throughout the western world tend to be highly suspicious of empirical scholarly enquiry, especially in sentencing. Malleson (1999, p. 198), for example, states that

> [t]o date, the judiciary has been insulated from any pressure to participate [in scholarly enquiry] since it has been legitimate for judges to refuse to co-operate in research on the grounds that it might undermine judicial independence.

Harlow found that non-cooperation is due to a "prevailing climate of hostility to critical appraisal" (Harlow 1986, cited by Malleson 1999, p. 198). Indeed, the history of empirical research into sentencing practice has been far from happy. Even where scholars have been able, after protracted and delicate negotiation, to gain access it is normally followed by judicial reaction (e.g. Ashworth et al. 1984; Hood and Cordovill 1992; Tata and Hutton 1998; Baldwin and McConville) and either complete refusal to participate, or, a forceful attempt to prevent the publication of at least part of the findings.[11] Some sentencers may seek to celebrate their individualistic independence by claiming to delight in their disparity. Broadly, the judicial approach to empirical sentencing research has been normally suspicious, even hostile.

However, although an individualistic brand of 'independence' is invoked as a way of preventing research from asking awkward questions and uncovering uncomfortable truths, there are, I would suggest, far more fundamental reasons for the apparent lack of coherent transparency. We need to think more critically about the ability of sentencers to 'explain' sentencing decisions according to the dominant categories and conception of sentencing scholarship. These categories represent a series of dichotomies: 'the offence *plus* the offender'; 'aggravating *versus* mitigating factors';[12] 'penal philosophy or non-coherent judgement'; and 'discretion *versus* rules'.

The 'offence-offender' dichotomy and penal-philosophical aims Much of the literature calling for coherence assumes that sentencers are motivated in their decision-making by a consideration of options from the classic menu of the aims of punishment. Yet, do sentencers decide sentence on the basis of even crude penal-philosophical theories or principles, or are these too abstract ever to be operationalised as determinants of everyday social practice? Let us briefly examine an essential distinction commonly assumed as a basic unit of enquiry. This taken-for-granted distinction is fundamental to desert theory: 'the offence' and 'the offender'.

Logical 'coherent' sentencing is normally assumed to either begin with, or, ought to begin with, consideration of the offence, *then* orientate a sentence which is adjusted in the light of the nature of the offender. For example, in advancing a more principled approach to the problem of determining the 'custody threshold' Ashworth and von Hirsch (1997, p. 1999) recommend: "After the seriousness of the offence has been properly assessed, the next step would be to make an appropriate adjustment for previous criminal record". While this typical division of the sentencing decision process into two basic units of analysis ('offence' and 'offender'), may be appropriate to legal and penal-philosophical discourse it is doubtful that it is a meaningful way of capturing the routine social practice of the decision process. In his research into the flow of criminal cases and the character of court organisational culture, Feeley observed that, "... for a charge to assume meaning it must be given substantive content by a description of the incident and information about the defendant's character, habits and motivation"(Feeley 1979, pp. 160–61). Sentencers must necessarily make judgements about the moral responsibility and moral character of 'the offender' if they are to understand and interpret the seriousness of 'the offence' before them. The operational abstraction of 'offence' and 'offender' from the whole case is impracticable.

One of the main tenets of desert theory is that it is unethical to punish or treat offenders on the basis of what they might be 'expected' to do (von Hirsch 1993) rather than on what they have done. Instead desert theory proposes that sentencing ought to be proportional to the seriousness of the current offence(s). Seriousness is to be judged on the basis of the harm of the offence and culpability of the offender. However, it is far from clear that the implementation of desert (or indeed other philosophical theories of punishment) is achievable in routine practice which *necessarily* produces organisational imperatives which are strongly embedded in court activities (Ulmer 1997; Mears 1998; Eisenstein and Jacob 1991). Attempts to try to implement legislation inspired by desert have run into judicial hostility and public controversy (e.g. Brownlee 1994). It is normally implied that this hostility is a problem of judicial conservatism: a deep reluctance to relinquish the power which is associated with substantive discretion (e.g. Ashworth 1998).

Yet, how in practice are sentencers expected to implement the requirement to ignore the question of expected future behaviour of an offender? In estimating seriousness of the harm and culpability of 'the offence' the sentencer necessarily judges the offender's moral character and history and practices. For example, in trying to make sense of culpability the sentencer also judges the motivation, intention, and awareness, and thus necessarily the social situation of the offender in committing the offence. The attempt to abstract these considerations from the context of the 'whole offence story' tends to assume a singular kind of offender abstracted from his/her social identity and social representation (Hudson 1995; Tata 1997; Tonry 1996; see also the Hutton/Hudson debate in this volume). Von Hirsch recognises that social deprivation, for example, may reduce culpability, but simply states that there would be considerable difficulties in producing specific criteria (von Hirsch and Roberts 1997, p. 235, fn. 14; von Hirsch 1993, pp. 106–8).

Numerical sentencing guidelines illustrate perhaps the starkest attempt to abstract 'the offence' and 'the offender' from each other. In operating numerical sentencing guideline grids the sentencer is required to divide the case into two distinct parts ('offender' and 'offence') so as to plot the sentence. Such grids are irreducibly "two-dimensional" (Tonry 1996) in their conception of sentencing as 'offence' plus 'criminal history/offender'. It is possible to produce an analytical representation of the decision process, (the most elaborate versions of which have been developed by Lovegrove 1997). Yet although it is analytically *possible* to abstract information into the categories of 'the offence' and 'the offender', it does not follow that the sum of the parts is the same as the whole case. For example, so-called 'offender' categories (such as social background, character, family, employment status etc.) necessarily confer meaning and explain 'motivation' and intention, and thus 'offence' characteristics such as harm and culpability.

Thus, we should not expect judicial articulation of the decision process (i.e. 'reasons) using these analytical terms ('offence' as distinct from 'offender') to be sophisticated, meaningful, or, coherent. Asking judges to 'explain' sentencing decisions by way of an implicit analytical model (using 'offence' as distinct from 'offender' and other supposedly discrete 'factors' or variables), effectively requires judges to 'explain' the production of judgement in artificially abstracted terms. Of course, judges employ these analytical terms in the writing of official judgements, but as scholars repeatedly demonstrate these opinions are often bland, terse and superficial. In so doing, this 'legal-analytical' 'offence/offender' dichotomy obscures the social production of the sentencing decision process as a purposive, routinely intuitive and holistic process based on a necessarily limited number of meaningful normalised (or typified) plots (e.g. Sudnow 1964; Moody and Tombs 1992), or what may be described as 'Typical Whole Case Stories' (Tata 1997). In these more interpretive sociological terms the sentencing decision process is rendered comprehensible, predictable and patterned.[13]

Penal-philosophical aims of sentencing do not explain adequately the routine practice of judgement (as opposed to abstract normative analysis). However there are further, even more fundamental reasons why sentencers have been so reluctant openly to provide 'coherent reasons' for sentencing. These lie in to how legal scholarship has tended to understand discretionary legal judgement, and secondly, in the production of judicial accounts of the exercise of that discretion. First, let us briefly consider how legal scholarship has tended to understand discretionary legal judgement, and how sentencing scholarship might "escape the legal paradigm" (Lacey 1992).

Order and disorder in sentencing: the privileged position of legality and the social-routine uses of (sentencing) discretion Much of the literature seeks to understand the sentencing decision process using legality[14] as the natural starting point of enquiry. Many enquiries explore 'extra-legal factors'. Such enquiries necessarily begin with legality as their basic starting point. This approach is redolent of Dworkin's vision of discretion is as "like the hole in a doughnut, [which] does not exist except as an area left open by a surrounding belt of restriction" (Dworkin 1977, p. 31). Operating in that gap or hole, according to this metaphor, are 'extra-legal factors'. The concern has been to 'tame' and 'confine' those 'extra-legal factors'. Yet this 'legal plus extra-legal' approach still begins with an implicit concern to distinguish 'law' from 'non-law' to analyse behaviour as either 'legal' or 'extra-legal', 'law' from 'discretion' or, in Dworkinian terms to distinguish the doughnut from the hole.

Rather than regarding official principles, sources and analytical legal reasoning as the basic starting point for an understanding of discretionary legal behaviour, we can instead look to the way in which discretionary actors are not mainly actors determined by legality but fundamentally social actors at the same time. Importantly, these two roles are exercised *simultaneously* and, in routine practice, impossible to distinguish from each other. In this conception, 'discretion' and 'rules' are not counterposed as opposites. Rather 'rules' are inherently open, malleable and discretionary while 'discretion' is inherently patterned, systematised, and rule-governed. Thus from this understanding legal principles, legal doctrine and legal rules are not necessarily the assumed starting point in describing, explaining or indeed reforming the sentencing decision process. It becomes less viable to talk of 'more' or 'less' discretion or rules; and of 'a balance' between rules and discretion. Rather, sentencing research might focus more on: regularities in speech and behaviour; the construction of sentencing customs and folk knowledge; and the normalised construction of cases. In so doing, research may be more likely to reveal a sociological portrait of the decision process, which is more comprehensible, coherent and meaningful than by presuming legality to be the natural starting point of enquiry and then adding in extra-legal 'factors'. When, as sentencing scholars, we begin to escape the 'rules "versus" discretion' mind-set, the implications for how we might appreciate judicial reason-giving, crystallise.

Thus far, I have argued that we have too easily assumed an analytical interpretation of cases mediated by individual penal philosophies, rather than as constructed and holistic. Legal rules and discretion have been supposed as opposites: a supposition which makes sense in the abstract but far less so in detailed sociological empirical enquiry. As long as we persist with a legal-analytical approach we will continue to be disappointed by the quality of judicial reasoning and thus disappointed by the apparent lack of coherent accountability and transparency. In the next section I try to develop new ways of thinking about accountability which permit new questions for research.

3   The Call for Openness

It is normally argued by sentencing scholars that the reasons for decisions are shrouded behind a veil of mystery and if sentencing is to be 'coherently structured' then that veil must be lifted. For example, Miller (1989) argues for the further development of written sentencing Opinions by federal US judges because "[w]ithout an opinion practice, sentencing in a guideline system remains hidden – just under a more modern veil" (Miller 1989, p. 21).

> ... The best way to overcome suspicions and criticisms raised by a system where the decision process was 'hidden' is to create a system that is public ... [In a system] that does not require explanation for the vast majority of cases, the ability of observers to gain confidence in the system is inherently limited (Miller 1989, p. 20).

In a similar vein, Fox (1994) welcomes the "*dissection*" of cases by judges in Victoria as "... being more informative about the manner in which they reach their decisions. Such openness can only benefit the jurisprudence and psychology of judicial sentencing" (Fox 1994, p. 510).

Thomas' Conflation of 'Reason' with 'Reason-giving'

This tradition of sentencing scholarship concerned with judicial reason-giving can be traced to the immense work of David Thomas. In his highly influential

1963 advancement of *The Case for Reasoned Decisions*, Thomas forcefully argued that the open and public giving of reasons will deliver an improved quality of reasoning in sentencing decisions.

> If a judge is under an obligation to formulate and state the reasons for his decision, it will be necessary for him to arrive at a decision for which proper reasons can be given ... The immediate effect of an obligatory statement of reasons [would remove] the danger of sentences based on an immediate emotional reaction to some feature of the offence (Thomas 1963, pp. 246–7).

On the face of it, the suggestion that requiring judges to give reasons means that decisions will be better "thought through" (Thomas, p. 247) seems obvious: make the judge think about it and s/he will come up with a more logically reasoned (as opposed to emotional) decision. This view envisages sentencing as an essentially individualistic, asocial process in which the decision-maker wrestles with sentencing as basically a problem of reasoning.[15] In Thomas' conception, reasons given are assumed simply to be the articulation of reasoning: there is very little consideration afforded to *the process of how* reasons are produced and presented. Instead it is assumed that once reasoning has been completed then reasons are divulged. It is perhaps ironic that although Thomas' work has long been critical of a mechanistic approach to sentencing reform, his conception of the provision of reasons is itself mechanistic: the judge simply conducts his reasoning and then gives his reasons. However, the view that the 'reason' for a decision given in court is a simple unmediated expression of the judge's thinking is highly questionable. If we accept that (even to some extent) sentencers, like other discretionary legal actors, not only operate in the context of a 'social world' but also that the use of this discretion is socially produced,[16] then the conflation of reason-giving with the simple exposition of 'reasoning' becomes untenable.

On the broader canvas of reason-giving, Kenneth-Culp Davis' influential *Discretionary Justice* (1969) can be located in a similar tradition to Thomas. Davis marshalled a forceful critique of legal discretion as a force for arbitrary and lawless decision-making. Discretion, in Davis' view, could not be eliminated (it was a 'necessary evil') but had to be "confined, structured and checked" (Davis 1969, p. 26). Although Thomas has not been nearly as hostile to legal discretion as Davis, both have advocated that the best way to avoid the arbitrary use of discretion is through the requirement upon officials for greater transparency in decision-making. In their focused critique of Davis' prescription, Robert Baldwin and Keith Hawkins (1984) call for a re-examination of assumptions about legal discretionary behaviour. "Such is [Davis'] approach that his argument almost boils down to a simple plea for greater openness ... [calling for] 'open standards, open findings, open reasons, open precedents [sic]'" (Baldwin and Hawkins 1984, p. 575). As attractive as this may be, Hawkins and Baldwin suggest that it is too simplistic to suppose that mandating 'openness' will enhance the quality of substantive (as opposed to procedural) justice. "What decision-makers may articulate as 'criteria' or 'principles' may amount to no more than justifications for judgements already reached on other grounds" (Baldwin and Hawkins 1984, p. 583).

Similarly, Fitzmaurice and Pease (1986, p. 45) observe that in sentencing "[I]f reasons have a place in court, it is because they are defensible, not because they are true". Thus the requirement to give reasons for a decision does not therefore mean that the decision itself is a simple revelation of the decision process, nor, does it mean that the process becomes more logically reasoned. The formal requirement of reason-giving may satisfy a formal notion of accountability which may tell the researcher little about how the decision maker arrived at the decision. So, how might research progress the understanding of accountability for the use of sentencing discretion?

The Social Production of 'Accountability'

A more interpretive sociological conception of accountability can be informed by the recognition that all decision-makers who provide explanations or accounts of their decisions do so in a way, which is dependent on the purpose(s) and audience(s) for whom it is intended. Writing about the news media as an integral part of criminal justice, Ericson (1995) argues for the need to distinguish two conceptions of 'accountability'. One (formal) view is of accountability as entailing an obligation to give an account of activities within one's ambit of responsibility. Another understanding has led to the coinage of the term,

> *account ability*: the capacity to provide a record of activities that explains them in a credible manner so that they appear to satisfy the rights and obligations of accountability. Clearly, the formal obligation to give an account does not ensure uniformity in the ability to give an account. The ability varies, for example, by what has to be accounted for; who makes the demand ...; who is the intended audience ...; and the spatial, social, cultural and communications format capacities to make an account (Ericson 1995, p. 137).

In thinking about the practice of *account ability* there is no reason to suppose that judges are a complex subdivision of the human race deserving a theory of their own (van Duyne 1987). In their everyday interactions human beings are:

> [R]eflexive, knowledgeable agents who perpetually adjust their senses of rights and obligations to organizational contingencies such as knowledge resources, ... political interests, authority structures, communication formats and occupational cultures (Ericson 1995, p. 136).

In this way (and since every account necessarily requires selection), *account ability* necessarily invokes the continual practice of revelation and secrecy.

So rather than simply seeing the giving of reasons as a means of revealing 'the real' reasons for a decision[17] and providing greater transparency the focus of enquiry is shifted to questions of negotiation, context, perceived audience expectations and so on. Judges should be expected to give a rather different style of account of sentencing practice to different audiences (for example to each other; to themselves; to academic researchers), according to the purpose and context of the account. In this way, rather than seeing the provision of sentencing 'reasons' for sentencing decisions as a simple mechanistic action we might view it as a necessarily shifting, subtle and negotiated process whose expression of reality is contingent on the social situation. Thus, reasons, which are given in open court, are defensible rather than the unmediated 'truth'. What is the nature, then, of this audience? Briefly the judgement is for public consumption, the person sentenced; court officials and 'Court Workgroups' (Provine 1998; Eisenstein and Jacob 1991). Parts of it may be quoted in the mass media; sentencers and academic lawyers give it some scrutiny. One symbolic expectation is that the judgement maintains the supposed 'law-like' features: linear logic; based in abstract moral-philosophical principles. Thus, the text of Appeal Court Judgements may tell us more about the needs of responding to expectations about the symbolic character of law as providing definition, certainty, closure. At the same time judgements remain open in character and perform a balance between two visions of justice: between, in Weberian terms, formal and substantive justice. These two visions of justice are in perennial and irresoluble tension.[18]

Thus, I would suggest that the reluctance to provide explicit and transparent reasoned judgements need not be explained by judicial defensiveness. It is highly questionable that sentencers operate (or ever could operate), according to philosophical theories of punishment and abstract analytical categories of the case or that indeed it is possible for them to identify a single narrative or reason for a sentencing decision. True, judges are normally required to provide an account for their decisions to a variety of audiences, but this is distinct from simply reporting the stream of consciousness of thinking in deciding sentence. Rather, I would suggest that these accounts are necessarily mediated, constructed and reconstructed according to the audience and requirements of the ability to account for the decision.

> Every act of publicity for accountability is also an act of selection and distortion in which some things are left out and some alternative formulations are ignored ... Communications do not stand apart from reality. There is not first reality and then second communication about it. Communications participate in the formation and change of reality. Facts arise out of communication practices ... (Ericson 1995, pp. 137–44).

In this conception, accountability is seen as necessarily a selective and negotiative phenomenon, rather than being about a straightforward revelation of a notional objective truth. Inevitably, it is not possible to explain or articulate some notionally 'complete' or singularly accurate, full and unmediated pattern of consciousness of the sentencer. Necessarily this must be a selective process mediated by the social production of account-giving.

In this light, it is problematic to expect that the sentencer (or indeed any discretionary decision-maker), ought or is able to apply a sentencing theory grounded in philosophical justifications for punishment. The account supplied by a sentencer cannot be a simple reflection of the decision process, but necessarily mediated by the particular context. Philosophically-derived principles are employed post hoc to enable a credible appearance of accountability. We might instead envisage the sentencing decision process as an intuitive one, which constructs and reconstructs 'typical whole case stories' rather than a linear, logical, analytical or formal process about 'unique' cases (Tata 1997).

In his research on sexual story-telling, Plummer (1995) concludes that story telling is about constituting and reconstituting identity of the story teller. In this sense the story tells us more about the teller than the ostensible story. If sentencers' stories about sentencing are transient, elusive and ephemeral (as academic lawyers have revealed they are), then this reflects the shifting and social situationally-specific nature of the sentencing judge's identity. Sentencing judges continually emphasise the 'balance' of sentencing between the demands of consistency and equality as against the demands of doing

justice to 'unique' individual cases.[19] These two visions of justice are in
perennial tension in Modern Law: they contradict each other and cannot be
logically reconciled. However, sentencing judges play out this tension in the
performance of account-giving.[20] Indeed, the ability to be able to literally flip
between these visions is played out in the sentencing information system for
Scottish judges (Tata et al. 1998). They value being able literally to flip between
a formal vision of justice in sentencing (graphs and tables of sentencing
patterns) and a substantive vision of justice (individual sentenced cases).

As we have seen there has been a tendency to suggest that the reluctance
to give substantive reasons or explain sentencing is due to the arbitrary,
unstructured practice of sentencing due, as Doob and Brodeur (1995) argue,
to a lack of any shared set of penal-philosophical justifications. However,
like Plummer, Ericson (1995) points to the socially constructed and necessarily
shifting nature of stories. Stories or accounts of decision-making are not a
fixed historical account of the sentencing decision, but are contextually
dependant and mediated. This helps to explain the difficulty which empirical
researchers and scholars of sentencing judgements have had in eliciting
'coherently reasoned' (i.e. in terms of normative aims of sentencing)
explanations from sentencers when asked about specific cases or issues. It
also helps to explain the difficulty experienced in jurisdictions, which have
attempted to require judges to state openly their reasons for a sentence.

Conclusions

Legal accountability is axiomatic to modern law. There has been considerable
academic dissatisfaction with the quality and openness of this accountability.
Efforts at reforming sentencing by informing sentencing discretion have
tended to disappoint scholars. Appeal Court judgements have limited impact
on first instance sentencing and the judgements themselves are found to be
deficient in principled reasoning. Seemingly more rigorous reforms like
numerical guidelines inescapably allow for discretion, while information
systems have tended to eschew philosophical principles. Thus even through
these reforms, sentencers have been deemed to have failed to 'reveal' how
they decide sentence. This can be only slightly understood by defensiveness
and the judicial self-perception, which values individualistic independence.
It is more fully explained by the taken-for-granted expectation that judges
explain their decision-making according to a legal-analytical approach;
normative penal principles; and the counter-pose of rules and discretion.

Rather, I have tried to show in this chapter that judicial explanation of the sentencing decision processes is necessarily socially produced. In so doing, I have sought to problematise the notion that the sentencing process lacks coherent structure. I have tried to make explicit the inescapably fluid and ambiguous account of the use of sentencing discretion. Rather than seeing 'coherence' as a simple one-dimensional, mechanical and exclusive property of legal rules, this chapter has argued for an understanding of the accounts of sentencing as socially produced. Narrative accounts of the decision process by the decision-maker are not simple factual presentation of the linear decision process, but necessarily socially constructed and reconstructed by situation, expectations of the audience; self-identity of the narrator (or storyteller). According to the standards of the legal-analytical view of the decision process, sentencing may appear to be order-less and chaotic, but a more sociological and interpretive approach permits a far more structured and meaningful understanding. This may for example help to explain the limited success of sentencing reforms worldwide (Tonry 1996).[21]

To expect sentencers to be able to provide the reasons for sentencing based on philosophically-derived justifications for punishment is to suppose an asocial fixed reality of story telling rather than one which is socially constructed and reconstructed. Perhaps it might be valuable, at least, to accept that the quest for defined and settled philosophical reasoning at the crux of sentencing is inherently and inevitably elusive. We might instead concentrate more attention towards the specificities of how sentencing accounts are socially produced and performed together with the process of the social preparation of cases and their implicit sentencing agendas.

Notes

1   I am grateful to Julian Roberts, Tony Doob, Travis Pratt, Ralph Henham, Fergus McNeill and David Tait for their comments on an earlier draft of this chapter and its ideas, and to Jan Nicholson for her diligent formatting of this chapter.
2   Co-director of the Centre for Sentencing Research, Senior Lecturer, Law School, University of Strathclyde, Glasgow, Scotland, UK. E-mail: cyrus.tata@strath.ac.uk.
3   Frankel 1972, p. 8.
4   Although every individual person is unique, no case is or can be completely unique. Sentencing is inescapably comparative and the claim that 'every case is unique' is incompatible with the emphasis judges place upon experience. Further, the criminal process systematises, streamlines and normalises cases into a typical number of limited plots.
5   See Tonry 1996 and 1995 and Provine, in this volume.

6   In her article, Provine (1998) asks why many judges seem to fail to resist law that they seem genuinely to despise given that the law allows them ample opportunities to resist routinely. Drawing a parallel with Robert Cover's examination of judicial non-resistance to slavery, Provine highlights the importance of Court Workgroups (see also Eisenstein and Jacob 1991).

7   Readers should consult Neil Morgan's chapter in this volume, which discusses recent developments in Western Australia.

8   In a contestable definition, Ewart and Pennington (1988, p. 587) assert: "A reason for sentence is defined as a factor which the sentencer clearly stated to be one which was taken into account in deciding sentence".

9   Of course it would be possible to attribute this unwillingness to lack of time: judges are simply too busy. Yet the movement to require judges to give reasons, especially where they 'depart' from an official norm, seems to provide powerful counter-incentive. Moreover, 'incoherent' reason-giving is routinely uncovered in documents which judges spend time crafting (e.g. Court of Appeal judgements).

10 By aims or goals in this context I am referring to the standard normative menu including desert/retribution, rehabilitation, general and/or individual deterrence, incapacitation, denunciation, etc.

11 For example, in a study of individual patterns of sentencers in three of Scotland's Sheriff Courts (Tata and Hutton 1998), at the completion of the study, the sentencers objected vehemently to publication of the research. They objected not so much to the comparison of their individual (anonymised) sentencing patterns, but to the publication of interview data reporting their *responses* to presentations of their sentencing patterns (defined according to previously agreed narrative and numerical 'scales of seriousness') compared with those of their colleagues. The publication of the suggestion that sentencers may not be able to estimate accurately their own sentencing patterns appears easily to outweigh concern that they may be disparate from their colleagues.

12 I have addressed briefly elsewhere (Tata 1997) the meaningfulness of 'aggravating and mitigating factors' and so will not repeat that material here.

13 It is vital to underline that the recognition that sentencing as a sociologically intuitive, typified and holistic process is quite different from saying that sentencing cannot be understood or is a matter of individual whim.

14 By 'legality' I mean the concern with legal doctrine enshrined in cases, statutes and legal principles.

15 Interestingly, this image of the individual producing the sentence (as opposed to social or organisational productions) fits easily with judges' cherished notion of individualistic independence discussed earlier. Notwithstanding its immense and original contribution, it may be in part because of Thomas' implicit conception of sentencing as a fundamentally individual process that his work finds such resonance among judges, and, above all others, appears as standard text on the book-shelves of English-speaking judges across the world.

16 See for example: Ulmer 1997; Mears 1998; Eisenstein and Jacob 1991; Provine 1998.

17 As supposed by Behaviourist methodology which necessarily relies on the analytical representation of the decision process discussed earlier.

18 These competing visions of justice in sentencing are manifested in two images of sentencing discretion. The response for example of the NSW and Scottish Appeal Courts to the institutionalisation of their judicial decision support systems manifests a firm and "resolute ambivalence" (Tata 2000). These Appeal Courts carefully and deliberately neither rule out nor embrace the use of such systems.

19 Although every individual person is unique no case is or can be unique. Sentencing is inescapably comparative and the claim, as exposed by Hood (1962) is incompatible with the emphasis judges place upon experience. Further, the criminal process systematises, streamlines and normalises cases into a typical number of limited plots. Yet the point here is not whether the stories judges tell about themselves are tenable or not but simply that they tell them by way of constructing the performance of sentencing.

20 In his essay in this volume David Tait empahsises the performative (rather than legal, philosophical, or cognitive) character of sentencing.

21 It might be suggested that this does not provide a prescription for sentencing reform. Indeed, this chapter is limited to trying to understand scholarly disappointment with 'the structure' of sentencing discretion. In understanding the future of reform we might consider incorporating this re-think of accountability.

References

Alschuler, A. (1991), 'The Failure of Sentencing Guidelines: A plea for less aggregation', *University of Chicago Law Review*, Vol. 58, pp. 901–51.

Ashworth, A. (1995), *Sentencing and Criminal Justice*, 2nd edn, London: Butterworths.

Ashworth, A. (1997a), 'Sentencing by Computer: What next ?', *Criminal Law Review*, March, pp. 153–4.

Ashworth, A. (1997b), 'The Value of Empirical Research in Criminal Justice', editorial, *Criminal Law Review*, August, pp. 533–4.

Ashworth, A. (1997c), 'Sentencing', in M. Maguire, R. Morgan and R. Reiner (eds), *Oxford Handbook of Criminology*, New York: Oxford University Press, pp. 1095–135.

Ashworth, A. (1998), 'The Decline of English Sentencing and Other Stories', symposium on *Sentencing Policy in Comparative Perspective*, University of Minnesota, May.

Ashworth, A. (2001), 'The Decline of English Sentencing and Other Stories', in M. Tonry and R. Frase (eds), *Sentencing and Sanctions in Western Countries*, New York: Oxford University Press.

Ashworth, A., Genders, E., Mansfield, G., Peay, J. and Player, E., (1984), 'Sentencing in the Crown Court: Report of an exploratory study', Occasional Paper No. 10, University of Oxford Centre for Criminological Research.

Ashworth, A. and Hough, M. (1996), 'Sentencing and the Climate of Public Opinion', *Criminal Law Review*, Vol. 43, pp. 776–87.

Ashworth, A. and von Hirsch, A. (1997), 'Recognising Elephants: The problem of the custody threshold', *Criminal Law Review*, pp. 187–200.

Baldwin, J. and McConville, M. (1977), *Negotiated Justice Pressures to Plead Guilty*, London: Martin Robertson.

Baldwin, R. (1996), 'Discretionary Justice and the Development of Policy', in D.J. Galligan (ed.), *Reader on Administrative Law*, New York: Oxford University Press.

Baldwin, R. and Hawkins, K. (1984), 'Discretionary Justice: Davis reconsidered', *Public Law* Winter, pp. 570–99.

Blumstein, A., Cohen, J., Martin, S. and Tonry, M. (1983) (eds), *Research on Sentencing: The search for reform*, 2 vols, National Academy Press.

Bottoms, A. (1995), 'The Philosophy and Politics of Punishment and Sentencing', in C. Clarkson and M. Morgan (eds), *The Politics of Sentencing Reform*, New York: Oxford University Press.

Boyle, C.K. and Allen, M.J. (1990), *Sentencing in Northern Ireland*, NI: SLS Publications.

Brodeur, J-P. (1989), 'Truth in Sentencing', *Behavioral Sciences and the Law*, Vol. 7, No. 1, pp. 25–49.

Brownlee, I. (1994), 'Taking the Strait-jacket Off: Persistence and distribution of punishment in England and Wales', *Legal Studies*, Vol. 14, No. 3, November.

Burney, E. (1985), 'All Things to All Men: Justifying custody under the 1982 Act', *Criminal Law Review*, Vol. 32, p. 284.

Cavadino, M. and Dignan, J. (1997), *The Penal System: An Introduction*, London: Sage.

Conley, J. and O'Barr, W. (1990), *Rules versus Relationships: The ethnography of legal discourse*, Chicago: University of Chicago Press.

Cover, R. (1975), *Justice Accused: Anitslavery and the judicial process*, New Haven: Yale University Press.

Darbyshire, P. (1997), 'An Essay on the Importance and Neglect of the Magistracy', *Criminal Law Review*, pp. 627–43.

Davis, K-C. (1969), *Discretionary Justice: A preliminary inquiry*, Louisiana: Louisiana State University Press.

Day, P. and Klein, R. (1987), *Accountability: Five public sector services*, Tavistock.

Doob, A. (1990), 'Evaluation of a Computerized Sentencing Aid', Select Committee of Experts on Sentencing, European Committee on Crime Problems, Council of Europe, Strasbourg.

Doob, A. (1995), 'The United States Sentencing Commission Guidelines: If you don't know where you are going, you might not get there', in C. Clarkson and M. Morgan (eds), *The Politics of Sentencing Reform*, New York: Oxford University Press.

Doob, A. and Brodeur, J-P. (1995), 'Achieving Accountability in Sentencing', in P. Stenning (ed.), *Accountability for Criminal Justice*, Toronto: University of Toronto Press.

Doob, A. and Park, N. (1987), 'Computerised Sentencing Information for Judges: An aid to the sentencing process', *Criminal Law Quarterly*, Vol. 30, p. 54.

Dworkin, R. (1977), *Taking Rights Seriously*, Cambridge, Mass.: Harvard University Press.

Eisenstein, J. and Jacob, H. (1991) *Felony Justice: An organizational analysis of criminal courts*, 2nd edn, Boston: Little Brown.

Ericson, R. (1995), 'The News Media and Account Ability', in P. Stenning (ed.), *Accountability for Criminal Justice*, Toronto: University of Toronto Press.

Ewart, S. and Pennington, D.C. (eds) (1987), *The Psychology of Sentencing: Approaches to consistency and disparity*, Oxford: Centre for Socio-Legal Studies.

Feeley, M. (1979), *The Process is the Punishment: Handling cases in a lower criminal court*, Russell Sage Foundation.

Fitzmaurice, C. and Pease, K. (1986), *The Psychology of Judicial Sentencing*, Manchester: Manchester University Press.

Fox, R. (1994), 'The Meaning of Proportionality in Sentencing', *Melbourne University Law Reviews*, Vol. 19, Pt. 3, pp. 489–511.

Frankel, M. (1972), *Criminal Sentences: Law Without Order*, New York: Hill & Wang.

Frase, R. (1995), 'Sentencing Guidelines in Minnesota and other American States: A progress report', in C. Clarkson and M. Morgan (eds), *The Politics of Sentencing Reform*, New York: Oxford University Press.

Frase, R. (1997), 'Sentencing Principles', in Tonry, M. (ed.) *Crime and Justice: A review of research*, Vol. 22, Chicago: University of Chicago Press.

Gottfredson, D. (1999), *Exploring Criminal Justice*, Los Angeles: Roxbury Publishing Company.

Hawkins, K. (ed.) (1997), *The Human Face of the Law: Essays in honour of Donald Harris*, Oxford: Clarendon.

Hedderman, C. and Gelsthorpe, L. (eds) (1997), *Understanding the Sentencing of Women*, Home Office Research Study 170.

Henham, R. (1995), 'Sentencing Policy and the Role of the Court of Appeal', *Howard Journal Criminal Justice*, 34, pp. 218–27.

Henham, R. (1996), *Criminal Justice and Sentencing Policy*, Aldershot: Dartmouth.

Henham, R. (1997), 'Protective Sentences: Ethics, rights and Sentencing Policy', *International Journal of the Sociology of Law*, 25(1), pp. 45–64.

Henham, R. (1998a), 'Sentencing Policy and the Abolition of Parole and Early Release', *International Journal of the Sociology of Law*, Vol. 25, pp. 337–61.

Henham, R. (1998b), 'Making Sense of the Crime (Sentences) Act 1997', *Modern Law Review*, Vol. 61, No. 2, pp. 223–35.

Hogarth, J. (1971), *Sentencing as a Human Process*, University of Toronto Press in association with the Center of Criminology, University of Toronto.

Hogarth, J. (1988), *Sentencing Database System: User's Guide*, Vancouver: University of British Columbia.

Hood, R. in collaboration with Cordovill, G. (1992), *Race and Sentencing*, Oxford: Clarendon Press.

Hood R.G. (1962), *Sentencing in Magistrates' Courts: A study in variations of policy*, London: Stevens.

Hough, M. (1996), 'People Talking about Punishment', *Howard Journal of Criminal Justice*, 35, pp. 191–214.

Hudson, B. (1995), 'Beyond Proportionate Punishment: Difficult cases and the 1991 Criminal Justice Act', *Crime, Law and Social Change*, 22, pp. 59–78.

Hutton, N. (1996), 'Sentencing, Rationality and Computer Technology', *Journal of Law and Society*, 22(4), pp. 549–70.

Hutton, N., Paterson, A., Tata, C. and Wilson, J. (1996), 'A Prototype Sentencing Information System for the High Court of Justiciary: Report of the Study of Feasibility', Edinburgh: HMSO/Scottish Office Central Research Unit.

Jareborg, N. (1995), 'Swedish Sentencing Reform', in C. Clarkson and M. Morgan (eds), *The Politics of Sentencing Reform*, New York: Oxford University Press.

Jobson, K. and Ferguson, G. (1987), 'Towards a Revised Sentencing Structure for Canada', *The Canadian Bar Review*, 66(1), pp. 1–48.

Kelly, D. (1993), *Criminal Sentences*, Edinburgh: T&T Clark.

Lacey, N. (1992), 'The Jurisprudence of Discretion: Escaping the legal paradigm', in K. Hawkins (ed.), *The Uses of Discretion*, Oxford: Clarendon Press.

Lovegrove, A. (1997), *The Framework of Judicial Sentencing: A study in legal decision-making*, Cambridge: Cambridge University Press.

Magistrates Association (1997), *Sentencing Guidelines*, April, London: Magistrates' Association.

Malleson, K. (1997), 'Judicial Training and Performance Appraisal: The problem of judicial independence', *Modern Law Review*, Vol. 60, pp. 655–67.

Malleson, K. (1999), *The New Judiciary: the Effects of Expansion and Activism*, Aldershot: Ashgate/Dartmouth.

McBarnett, D. and Whelan, C. (1997), 'Creative Compliance and the Defeat of Legal Control', in K. Hawkins (ed.), *The Human Face of Law*, Oxford: Clarendon Press, pp. 177–98.

426 *Sentencing and Society*

McDonald, D. and Carlson, K (1996), 'Does Race and Ethnicity Matter in Federal District Courts? An Evaluation of the Impact of Federal Sentencing Guidelines on Judicial Sentencing Decisions', Meetings of the Law and Society Association and Research Committee on the Sociology of Law, Glasgow.

Mears, D. (1998), 'The Sociology of Sentencing: Reconceptualizing Decisionmaking Processes and Outcomes', *Law and Society Review*, Vol. 32, pp. 667–724.

Miller, M. (1989), 'Guidelines Are Not Enough: The need for written sentencing opinions', *Behaviorial Science and the Law*, 7(1), Winter.

Miller, M. (1995), 'Rehabilitating the Federal Sentencing Guidelines', *Judicature: The Journal of the American Judicature Society*, January–February, Vol. 78, No. 4.

Moody, R. and Tombs, J. (1992), *Prosecution in the Public Interest*, Edinburgh: Scottish Academic Press.

Nagel, I. (1990), 'Structuring Sentencing Discretion: The new federal sentencing guidelines', *Journal of Criminal Law and Criminology*, 80, pp. 299–317.

Nagel, I. and Johnson, B. (1994), 'The Role of Gender in a Structured Sentencing System: Equal treatment, policy choices, and the sentencing of female offenders under the United States Sentencing Guidelines', *The Journal of Criminal Law and Criminology*, Vol. 85, No. 1, pp. 181–221.

Nelken, D. (1983), *The Limits of the Legal Process: A study of landlords and crime*, London: Academic Press.

Nicholson, C.G.B. (1981), *The Law and Practice of Sentencing in Scotland*, Edinburgh: W. Green & Son.

Nicholson, C.G.B. (1992), *Sentencing: Law and practice in Scotland*, Edinburgh: W. Green/ Sweet and Maxwell.

Parent, D. (1988), *Structuring Criminal Sentences: The evolution of Minnesota's Sentencing Guidelines*, Butterworth Legal Publishers.

Parker, H., Sumner, M. and Jarvis (1989), *Unmasking the Magistrates*, Milton Keynes: Open University Press.

Plummer, K. (1995), *Telling Sexual Stories: Power, change and social worlds*, London; New York: Routledge.

Potas, I. (1997), 'Consistency of Approach in Sentencing: A Description of the Judicial Commission's Sentencing Information System', paper delivered to the Workshop on 'Decision Support Systems' under the auspices of The International Conference on Artificial Intelligence and Law, Melbourne.

Potas, I., Ash, D., Sagi, M., Cumines, S. and Marsic, N. (1998), 'Informing the Discretion: The sentencing information system of the Judicial Commission of New South Wales', *International Journal of Law and Information Technology*, Vol. 6, No. 2, pp. 99–124.

Provine, D.M. (1998), 'Too Many Black Men: The sentencing judge's dilemma', *Law and Social Inquiry*, Vol. 23, No. 4, pp. 823–56.

Provine, D.M. (2002), 'Sentencing Policy and Racial Justice', in N. Hutton and C.Tata (eds), *Sentencing and Society: International perspectives*, Aldershot: Ashgate.

Roberts, J. (1999), 'Introduction to Sentencing and Parole', in J.V. Roberts and D. Cole (eds), *Making Sense of Sentencing*, Toronto: University of Toronto Press, pp. 3–31.

Rock, P. (1993), *The Social World of an English Crown Court: Witness and professionals in the Court Centre at Wood Green*, Oxford: Clarendon Press.

Schild, U. (1998), 'Statistical Information Systems for Sentencing: A cookbook', *International Journal Law and Information Technology*, Vol. 6, No. 2, pp. 125–43.

Schild, U. (2000), 'Statistical Information Systems: The Israeli approach', *International Review of Law, Computers and Technology* (Special Issue on Judicial Decision Support Systems), Vol. 14, No. 3, pp. 317–24.

Scottish Office Home Department League Tables.

Stith, K. and Cabranes, J. (1998), 'Fear of Judging: Sentencing guidelines in the Federal Court', Chicago: University of Chicago Press.

Sudnow, D. (1964), 'Normal Crimes: Sociological Features of the Penal Code in a Public Defender's Office', *Social Problems*, Vol. 12, pp. 255–76.

Tait, D. (1998), 'Judges and Jukeboxes', *International Journal of Law and Information Technology*, Vol. 6, No. 2.

Tarling, R. (1979), *Sentencing Practice in Magistrates Courts*, Study No. 56, Home Office Research Unit, HMSO.

Tata, C. (1997), 'Conceptions and Representations of the Sentencing Decision Process', *Journal of Law and Society*, Vol. 24, No. 3, pp. 395–420.

Tata, C. (1998a), 'The Application of Judicial Intelligence and Rules to Systems Supporting Discretionary Judicial Decision-Making', *Artificial Intelligence and Law: An international journal*, Vol. 6, Nos 2–4, pp. 199–225.

Tata, C. (1998b), '"Neutrality", "Choice", and "Ownership" in the Construction, Use, and, Adaptation of Judicial Decision Support Systems', *International Journal of Law and Information Technology*, Vol. 6, No. 2.

Tata, C. (2000), 'Resolute Ambivalence: Why judiciaries do not institutionalise their decision support systems', *International Review of Law Computers and Technology*, Vol. 14, No. 3, pp. 297–316.

Tata, C. and Hutton, N. (1998), 'What "Rules" in Sentencing?', *The International Journal of the Sociology of Law*, Vol. 26, pp. 369–94.

Tata, C., Hutton, N., Wilson, J. and Hughson, I. (1998), *A Sentencing Information System for the High Court of Justiciary of Scotland: Report of the study of the first phase of implementation and enhancement*, Centre for Sentencing Research.

Taylor, Lord Chief Justice of England (1993), 'Judges and Sentencing', *Law Society's Journal*, Vol. 38, pp. 129–31.

Thomas, D. (1963), 'Sentencing – The Case for Reasoned Decisions', *Criminal Law Review*, pp. 245–53.

Thomas, D. (1995), 'Sentencing Reform: England and Wales', in C. Clarkson and M. Morgan (eds), *The Politics of Sentencing Reform*, New York: Oxford University Press.

Tonry, M. (1995), *Malign Neglect: Race, crime and punishment in America*, New York: Oxford University Press.

Tonry, M. (1996), *Sentencing Matters*, New York: Oxford University Press.

Tonry, M. (2001), 'Punishment and Policies in Western Countries', in M. Tonry and R. Frase (eds), *Sentencing and Sanctions in Western Countries*, New York: Oxford University Press, pp. 3–29.

Tonry, M. and Hatlestad, K. (eds) (1997), *Sentencing Reform in Overcrowded Times: A comparative perspective*, New York: Oxford University Press.

Ulmer, J.T. (1997), *Social Worlds of Sentencing: Court communities under Sentencing Guidelines*, Albany: State University of New York Press.

Van Duyne, P. (1987), 'Simple Decision Making', in D.C. Pennington, and S. Lloyd-Bostock (eds), *The Psychology of Sentencing: Approaches to Consistency and Disparity*, Oxford: Centre for Socio-Legal Studies.

Von Hirsch, A. (1993), *Censure and Sanctions*, Oxford: Clarendon Press.

Von Hirsch, A., Knapp, K. and Tonry, M. (eds) (1987), *The Sentencing Commission and its Guidelines*, Boston: Northeastern University Press, pp. 47–61.

Von Hirsch, A. and Roberts, J. (1997), 'Racial Disparity in Sentencing: Reflections on the Hood Study', *The Howard Journal of Criminal Justice*, 36(4), pp. 227–36.

Walker, M. (1995), 'Criminal Justice and Offenders', in M. Walker (ed.), *Interpreting Crime Statistics*, Oxford: Clarendon Press.

Walker, N. and Padfield, N. (1996), *Sentencing: Theory, law, and practice*, London: Butterworths.

Warner, D. (1990), 'The Role of Neural Networks in Law Machine Development', *Rutgers Computers and Technology Law Journal*, 16, pp. 129–44.

Wasik, M. (ed.) (1997), *The Sentencing Process*, Brookfield, Vermont: Ashgate.

Weatherburn, D. and Lind, B. (1996), 'Sentence Disparity, Judge Shopping and Trial Court Delay', *Australian and New Zealand Journal of Criminology*, Vol. 29, No. 2, August.

Wicharaya, T. (1995), *Simple Theory, Hard Reality: The impact of sentencing reforms on courts, prisons, and crime*, New York: State University of New York Press.

Wilkins, L., Kress, J., Gottfredson, D., Calpin, J. and Gelman, A. (1978), *Structuring Guidelines: Structuring Judicial Discretion. Report on the Feasibility Study*, US Justice Department, February.

Zdenkowski, G. (1986), 'Sentencing: Problems and Responsibility', in D. Chappell and P. Wilson (eds), *Australian Criminal Justice*, Oxford: Butterworths.

Chapter Twenty

Assisting Sentencing, Promoting Justice?

Fergus McNeill

Introduction

The purpose of this chapter is to explore key themes concerning the relationships between sentencing and probation or social work reports provided to assist sentencing. The chapter draws on some of the available British and North American literature and research, as well as on professional experience of 'assisting sentencing' by providing social enquiry reports (SERs) to the Scottish courts.[1] Court reports are of interest for a variety of reasons. They represent an important and interesting point of exchange between professional groups with different responsibilities, purposes and perspectives. Implicitly, they conjoin attention to issues of social justice and criminal justice, of substantive justice and formal justice, and of rights and risks. In addition, court reports constitute an interface between public administration and criminal justice. As such, they merge concerns around bureaucratic justice in public administration with issues around discretionary justice in sentencing. These exchanges and interfaces offer rich fields of enquiry which are of profound value and importance in terms of contemporary socio-legal and penological theory.

The central argument of the chapter is that the provision of reports (as assistance for sentencers) cannot be properly understood merely as an essentially technical activity, aimed at meeting the needs of its consumers (sentencers). Rather, court reports reflect and embody penal-professional discourses and ideologies; further, they serve to substantiate and promote certain visions of justice. Therefore, the social construction of assisting sentencing merits closer examination. Hence, after outlining the context and significance of court reports prepared by social work and probation staff, the chapter explores a range of influences *upon* these reports and their authors, before considering the influence on sentencing *of* these reports, specifically addressing contemporary concerns around issues of consistency, effectiveness and quality. The conclusion reached is that further research, scholarship and professional reflection are required in order to assess not merely whether such reports in fact assist sentencing, but also if and how they promote justice.

Sentencer Decision-making and Social Enquiry

Tata (1997) has argued against conceptualising sentencer decision-making as the expression of a "legal-analytical paradigm". Rather, on the basis of an informative review of available research, he posits an alternative understanding, beginning "from the recognition that the criminal justice process constructs and reconstructs cases for the purpose of sentencing as 'typical whole case stories'" (p. 395; see also Tata's contribution to this volume). Thus, the sentencer is properly seen as a "skilled problem solver", like any other, adopting a "purposive approach", isolated and reliant primarily on documentary sources (Shapland 1987), which represent not the 'facts' of the case, but rather a series of narrative constructions of the events and the persons concerned. As Tata (1997, p. 404) puts it:

> The evidence before the sentencer cannot provide an objective factual account of human behaviour [but rather] merely 'constructed convention': pragmatic, purposive, and negotiated representation of a notional objective reality.

Tata's (1997) characterisation of the mental process of sentencer decision making as problem solving runs something like this: "I recognise this; this is one of these kinds of case; I usually deal with these cases in this manner; if there is no reason why I should not do what I usually do, then I will do what I usually do". One important implication of such a conceptualisation relates to how the appropriate function of the probation officer's or social worker's court report is to be understood. Clearly, it is one of the chronologically latest in the series of narrative constructions building towards the 'whole case story'. Yet, unlike their English, Welsh and North American colleagues, court report authors in Scotland typically work in isolation from other narratives such as police reports and witness and victim statements. The Scottish report writer therefore relies primarily on information from the offender, the criminal complaint and a list of those previous convictions libelled by the procurator fiscal. The impact of this isolation in undermining the 'professional objectivity' that report writers are instructed to pursue is a matter of considerable contemporary concern (SWSI 1996, p. 44). Indeed, recent Scottish research suggests that a chronic problem for Scottish report writers (and thus for sentencers) is "poor information on the offence which can lead to inappropriate

... recommendations ... and unrealistic reports" (Paterson and Tombs 1998, p. 27).

However, the issue of objectivity is about more than available information sources. Report writers trade in interpretations as well as 'facts', in pragmatic and purposive analysis rather than ideal and neutral description, in "negotiated representation of a notional objective reality". These are some of the parameters of their 'professional objectivity', properly understood within a complex context of professional interests, values and skills. The report writer is another professional lens through which the 'facts' are refracted in a unique way. Arguably, there may be both practical and ideological reasons why it might be considered a professional duty for the report author to present information and argument which interrupts the sentencer's problem solving search for a 'routine remedy' by challenging the too readily formed hypothesis, by questioning the too-easy assumption of typicality, by introducing the specificity of context to upset the generalisation of type. The extent to which reports written with this kind of objectivity might impact upon the sentencers' decisions depends, to some extent, on how reports are read in practice. But such questions of impact must be properly contextualised within the broader analysis of the influences upon and the influence of social enquiry that this chapter aims to build.

Court Reports in National and International Context

Social enquiry reports are intended to "assist sentencing" in criminal cases in Scotland (SWSG 2000, para. 1.2).[2] The newly revised national standards (ibid., para 1.6) state that, for the social workers who construct these reports,

> the central task is to provide advice and information about the feasibility of a community disposal or the need for supervision on release from custody by assessing the risk of re-offending, and in more serious cases, the risk of possible harm to others. This requires an investigation of offending behaviour and of the offender's circumstances, attitudes and motivation to change.

The standards delineate the range of this enquiry which should address issues of offending behaviour, finance, family relationships, education, training, employment, accommodation, lifestyle, physical and mental health, risk of self-harm and substance misuse (ibid., paras 2.8–2.21).

The Social Work Services Inspectorate (1996) reported that some 108,000 reports were completed between 1991 and 1996, at a cost of £23,500,000.

This level of investment reflects policy makers' recognition of the pivotal role that SERs play in pursuit of governmental objectives for social work services to the criminal justice system in Scotland (discussed below). Since SERs are both the key entry point to criminal justice social work services and the prime opportunity to promote the use of these services, it is easy to see why they attract this level of fiscal investment and policy attention.

The business of social work probation or corrections professionals assisting sentencers is part of the sentencing process in many jurisdictions. Literature relating to the use of pre-sentence reports (PSRs) in the English and Welsh courts will be discussed below. However, it is worth noting here that in many North American contexts, a combination of plea-bargaining and determinate sentencing reforms makes for a very different context for providing such assistance. Indeed, some American scholars have argued that the pre-sentence investigation report (PSIR) continues to exist only as a marginalised discourse and an institutionalised form of the "myth of individualized justice" (Hagan, Hewit and Alwin 1979; Walsh 1985; Rosencranz 1988). More recently, following research in California, Kingsnorth et al. (1999) have argued that PSIRs are no longer needed to conceal punitive agendas and thus to uphold the "myth of individualized justice" because punitive values are now openly acknowledged. This broader penological shift produces a "dramatic role transformation" for the probation officer – "from being an 'agent of individualisation' to being an 'agent of the state' – fully committed to contemporary norms of punishment and incapacitation, and recognized as such by all court room participants" (Kingsnorth et al. 1999, p. 271).

By contrast, in the Scottish context, court reports are written by generically trained social workers, perhaps more committed to welfare ideals (McNeill 2000a) than their counterparts in California and elsewhere. Furthermore, in the Scottish courts, judicial discretion remains highly prized. The limits of this discretion, by and large, are set only by the procedures under which cases are prosecuted (summary or solemn) and by the court (District, Sheriff or High) in which they are heard (for illuminating accounts of contrasting systems see the contributions in Part I of this volume). Sentencing guidelines, matrices and policies do not exist as such in Scotland (Hutton 1999, p. 169). High Court appeals subject the practice of sentencers to some scrutiny, but sentencers are effectively independent within their localities (see also Tata, this volume). This discretionary sentencing context set alongside the more welfare-oriented professional identity of SER authors make both the nature of their practice of social enquiry and its effectiveness in influencing sentencing matters of particular interest. However, since every report writer is at least as much the subject of a series of influences as well as source of influence, it is necessary firstly to explore some of the practical and ideological factors which construct the process of social enquiry.[3]

Influences on Social Enquiry

Penology and Policy

Part of the broader academic context of studies both of sentencing and of social enquiry is penology, a field currently preoccupied with talk of transformations (see, for example, Feeley and Simon 1994; Garland 1996, 2000). Feeley and Simon (1994, p. 173) suggest that 'old penology' is essentially about individuals; their culpability, their guilt, the diagnosis of their deviance, discovering and applying the proper treatment. They observe that "one of its central aims is to ascertain the nature of the responsibility of the accused and hold the guilty accountable". The 'new penology' in contrast focuses on groups, and is "concerned with techniques for identifying, classifying and managing groups assorted by levels of dangerousness" (see also Tubex, this volume). Because crime is seen as inevitable and because individualised interventions are viewed with scepticism as to their efficacy, the new penology seeks cost-effective methods aimed at regulating groups as part of a strategy of managing and minimising danger. Garland (1996, 2000) offers a compelling account of the emergence both of new strategies of crime control and of a new punitiveness which serves particular expressive and re-legitimating functions for the state in the face of its failure to control crime (see also Bottoms 1995; the contributions in Part III of this volume provide interesting discussions of the related issue of supposed public punitiveness).

Clearly, if such transformations are affecting criminal justice processes, a profound impact on sentencing and social enquiry would be expected. Although Kingsnorth et al.'s (1999) study, reviewed above, provides neither any longitudinal comparison of practices nor any analysis of the literature on transformations, it might be construed as providing evidence of transforming probation identities and report practices in California. In England and Wales, new standards for pre-sentence reports (PSRs) followed the Criminal Justice Act of 1991, arguably the high point of the revival in that jurisdiction of ideals of proportionality and 'just deserts'. As the Anglo-Welsh probation service was compelled to redefine itself so as to offer (proportionate) 'punishment in the community' (Worrall 1997), so PSR practice required a stronger focus on offence-analysis, crucially including judgements about 'seriousness', related to aggravating and mitigating factors, thereby informing the calculation of 'just deserts'. However, PSRs prepared in cases of violent or sexual offences were also required to address the risk to the public of serious harm (Raynor et al. 1994, pp. 53ff). In addition, information on the offender, as opposed to the offence, was to be included, though only where it was demonstrably relevant to past offending, previous experience of the justice system or to a proposed disposal. Yet despite this drive towards PSR practice serving an essentially retributive agenda, Raynor et al. (1994, p. 55) argued that:

> [there] is still scope for individualisation of sentences under the Act, despite the apparent rigidity of 'just deserts' ... Individual considerations are to operate both at the stage of judging seriousness and, where relevant, at that of choosing between community penalties ...

In the Scottish context, both the 'just deserts' and the 'punishment in the community' agendas have been far less evident.[4] Neither the advent of a New Labour government, nor a new Scottish parliament, nor a new Scottish Executive has signalled, as yet, any explicit shift in the prevailing criminal justice social work policy in Scotland originally articulated by the former Scottish Secretary Malcolm Rifkind (1989). His language was certainly the 'old' language of individual transformation: he saw 'The Way Ahead' as requiring the imprisonment only of those for whom no reasonable alternative disposal existed. This marked a critical distinction between those who pose a threat to society by committing serious and violent crimes necessitating incarceration and other offenders who would be better taught to live a 'normal and law-abiding life', while remaining in the community. Thus in Rifkind's (1989) speech, alongside the rehabilitative terms of the old penology stood the systems management language and the 'bifurcation' of the new (Bottoms 1983, 1995).

However, while ideas of proportionality and discourses of punitiveness have been less evident in Scotland, latterly public protection has become a clearer and more explicit aspect of policy discourses around community-based disposals and post-release supervision. In Scotland, a report of the Social Work Services Inspectorate (1996, p. 44) into court report practice, recommended shifting focus away from risk of custody and onto risk of re-offending and harm to others. Clearly, the first 'risk' is pertinent for those pursuing system management strategies of diversion and decarceration while the latter two 'risks' are pertinent for those pursuing public protection. Revisions to the Anglo-Welsh National Standards in 1995 introduced risk assessment to all reports, generalising the notion of public protection beyond 'dangerousness' to a more diffuse concern with 're-offending'. According to the new Scottish standards (SWSG 2000), as quoted above, risk of re-offending and risk of harm analyses are now to be centre-stage in the task of social enquiry, although these analyses remain carefully tied into issues around individual transformation (or perhaps individual 'transformability').

Despite these significant changes, the 11 policy objectives specified for social work practice in the criminal justice system in the original national standards (SWSG 1991) remain unchanged. The first two objectives (paras 12.1 and 12.2) are perhaps of critical importance, requiring the pursuit of a reduction in the incidence of custody "where it is used for want of a suitable, available, community based social work disposal"; and the promotion of the range and quality of community based social work disposals in such a manner they have "the confidence of the courts, the police and the public at large". These objectives place criminal justice social work and social enquiry, in some senses, in an invidious position. The service becomes accountable for effects on sentencing over which it may have some influence, but in respect of which it has neither power nor formal authority. The Scottish government's reluctance to impose more direct forms of sentencing reform may relate in some way to the well-documented shift towards a more regulatory state; essentially, one which prefers 'steering' to 'rowing' (Braithwaite 2000; Rose 2000). In this 'neo-liberal' context, and specifically given the political cost of getting crime and justice policies wrong, indirect methods of control seem likely to hold greater appeal. While it makes little sense to talk of social workers performing a regulatory function over sentencing on behalf of government, creating a policy which promotes attempts to influence might be seen as suggesting an albeit weak form of political governance of sentencing.

The inspection of social enquiry report practice mentioned above (SWSI 1996) noted the tensions that may arise where social workers are bound to pursue practice in line with a policy which in no way binds sentencers. Occasional controversies over the issue of social workers making 'recommendations' to the courts may find some of their roots in this anomaly. The first standards (SWSG 1991) had encouraged the making of recommendations, perhaps partly because Scottish Office-commissioned research had suggested a correlation between proactive, credible recommendations for community-based disposals and reductions in the use of custody (Creamer and Williams 1989). Nonetheless, the Inspectorate proposed change and the new standards (SWSG 2000, para. 5.6) follow their advice in precluding recommendations but permitting opinions to be expressed on the most appropriate community based disposal, if custody is not seen as necessary. Clearly if social enquiry is to play its key part in delivering the results intended by the policy, then whether described as offering 'opinions' or making 'recommendations', the business of making constructive proposals to the court must remain vitally significant. But, beyond the influence of policy, what else might shape such proposals?

Theories, Ideologies, Philosophies and Values

Whether implicitly or explicitly, every sentencer operates with some ideology, some set of values, some penal philosophy. Others have ably summarised different theoretical justifications for punishment, typically distinguishing consequentialist approaches like deterrence, rehabilitation or incapacitation, from non-consequentialist approaches, primarily retribution (Braithwaite and Pettit 1990; Duff and Garland 1994; Hudson 1996). Some have argued for 'mixed theories of punishment' combining these themes. The leading text on sentencing in Scotland delineates a wide range of relevant factors, clearly drawing on competing philosophical bases (Nicholson 1992, 9.01–9.39). This is suggestive of a mixed approach to sentencing in practice as well as in theory. Similarly, recent policy developments, discussed above, seem to employ mixed theories with elements of retribution, incapacitation, deterrence and, perhaps, even rehabilitation playing a part.

By implication, report writers must also have an implicit or explicit sentencing philosophy, or more properly, an assisting sentencing philosophy. Although there may be an historical connection between social work, probation and rehabilitative philosophies, in reality, the position is more complex; social enquiry in particular can serve any sentencing philosophy. Whatever the report writer's philosophy and intentions in writing the report, the information provided can be interpreted in other, sometimes unforeseen, ways. For example, information about social or educational disadvantage offered as evidence of a need for rehabilitative work, might assist 'just deserts' theorists with one of their more recently admitted operationalisation problems: how to accommodate social background and other offender 'variables' in the calculation of 'blameworthiness'. As Hudson (1996) puts it, "the problem of how there can be just deserts in an unjust society is critical for modern retributivists, and, at the very least, indicates that the social facts of each case should be given as much recognition as the legal facts ..." (p. 150; see Hudson and Hutton, this volume, as well as the contributions in Part IV). Despite this kind of appropriation of the report's information, however, many Scottish report authors might still agree with Garland (1989, p. 12) that "punitiveness ... is inimical to [probation] work, both in principle and in practice", preferring instead to pursue what Nellis (1995) describes as 'anti-custodialism'.

Social enquiry might also serve deterrence approaches, at least in the individual sense, in two ways. Firstly, one purpose for social enquiry might be about advising the sentencer what might and might not deter future offending in any given case (SWSG 1991, para. 91.1). Secondly, the interpersonal process of social enquiry itself, the necessary discussions with offenders, might be seen as opportunities to strengthen deterrent effects by addressing offenders' understandings of the consequences of further misconduct.

As has been noted above, more recently a strong focus on assessing risk has been apparent in pronouncements on social enquiry practice. Primarily this emerges from developing notions of effective public protection and community safety (see McNeill 2000a). However, it is important to note that, in sentencing, the same overriding concern with public protection might provide justification for a diverse range of approaches, including; exemplary sentencing for general deterrence, selective or preventive incarceration, and rehabilitation. Choosing between these approaches leads beyond philosophical questions into empirical criminological debates about 'what works' to reduce reoffending (McGuire 1995; Chapman and Hough 1998; Pease 1999). However, it is worth noting that sentencers and systems concerned only with retribution need have no regard for the consequences of sentencing practices. Hence, compelling critiques of the effectiveness of punitive responses (McGuire and Priestley 1995) are not always heeded. Nonetheless, where the provision of public protection is a common aspiration of policy makers, sentencers and social workers, the current interest in effectiveness becomes readily intelligible; one of the keys to influencing sentencing practice seems to become evidence of the effectiveness of different sanctions.

Another aspect of criminology merits some attention. Despite criminology's 'aetiological crisis' (Young 1981), it may be that report writers' views concerning the 'causes' of offending behaviour could and should have a significant impact on their social enquiry practice. Here, the relationships between rationalisation, justification, mitigation, aggravation and explanation tend to blur and obfuscate the interactions between welfare and justice professionals. Sentencers operate within a legal framework that reflects classicist understandings of choice in the criminal act and individual responsibility. It may be that social workers (and, to some extent, probation officers) stand in a different criminological tradition which stresses social and economic disadvantage as accounting, at least in part, for both criminality and criminalisation (Moore and Wood 1992, p. 79; Drakeford and Vanstone 1996; McNeill 2000b). The corollary of this is a stance which recognises society's responsibilities to the offender as well as the offender's responsibilities to society.

This kind of profession-specific or role-specific variation in preference for certain kinds of aetiological theories may underlie reported differences in perceptions of offence seriousness. Cavadino and Wiles (1994) have conducted research in England on the perceptions of different criminal justice practitioners in this area. They found remarkable inter-professional consensus on the question of ordinal ranking (that is, the seriousness of one offence vis-à-vis another) and considerable difference across the professions, though not generally within them, on the question of cardinal ranking (that is, the appropriate penalty). Predictably, social workers and probation officers came bottom of the 'cardinal' league, being less custody inclined even than defence solicitors. This need not be the consequence of minimising the seriousness of the offending, as is often supposed. Rather, it may be the operationalisation of different perspectives on personal responsibility, crime, justice and punishment. Cavadino and Wiles (1994) suggest that the perceptions of the social workers and probation officers should be seen as "both appropriate and understandable ... in fact, it could be seen as worrying if they were not [less custody inclined], for it could impair their ability to fulfil their roles within the criminal justice system" (p. 497).

In Scotland too, if social workers are to practice in line with the 'twin track' policy elucidated above, it becomes important for them to reach informed conclusions about what kinds of view courts are likely to take of individual cases. However, the report writer does not merely try to assess and respond to the court's view of seriousness; s/he seeks to influence it (Raynor 1980; 1985). The information and analysis provided by social enquiry therefore pertains *both* to the 'ordinal' ranking of offence seriousness vis-à-vis other offences and to the 'cardinal' ranking of the offence vis-à-vis the available disposals.

A fuller analysis of the grounding of such complex inter-professional differences not only in differing roles and preoccupations but also in related academic disciplines might require the consideration of sociological, abolitionist and feminist critiques of both philosophical jurisprudence and the practice of punishment (Duff and Garland 1994; Hudson 1996). Daly (1989), for example, has argued that existing systems contain 'voices' that speak broadly for justice and for care. To some extent, it may be possible to construe social enquiry as tacit recognition of the need for a 'different voice'; allowing the 'system' to recognise the problem that no two cases are alike; a problem that the very notion of a 'system' suggests must ultimately be overlooked in some senses. Hudson (1996) concludes her discussion of justice with sentiments which perhaps echo the unease that properly characterises, motivates and expresses itself in social enquiry reports:

> Punishment cannot ... be used as a synonym for justice. The weakness in the philosophical approaches, the insights of the sociological approaches, the challenges of abolitionism and of feminist jurisprudence should mean that punishment is restricted and reduced. Rather than imposing penalties with self-righteous confidence, we should always punish with a bad conscience (p. 151).

From this perspective, it might be argued that the task of the court report writer is sometimes to generate this unease, to provoke this bad conscience, to make punishing more morally difficult for the sentencer. Perhaps social enquiry should be part of the drive to promote and to realise what Braithwaite and Pettit (1990, p. 9) term the principle of parsimony in punishment; "the onus of proof must always be on the side of justifying criminal justice intrusions". If social enquiry can and should promote parsimonious justice in sentencing, then it might already be apparent why that generates a paradox such that social enquiry, despite being intended to assist sentencing, might make sentencing more rather than less difficult. Here then, in this paradox, the tension between assisting sentencing and promoting justice emerges. In the remainder of this chapter, research around issues of consistency, quality and effectiveness is reviewed and discussed to further explore this tension.

The Influence of Social Enquiry

Consistency, Sentencing and Social Enquiry

Concern around the issue of consistency arises as much in connection with social enquiry reports as it does in connection with the sentencing decisions they assist. Fitzmaurice and Pease (1986) raise the fundamental problem in addressing this issue when they note that "differences in the use of punishment are easy to find. Disparities are difficult to demonstrate" (p. 10; on related issues see also Ashworth, this volume). From the discussion above the reason for this should be obvious: disparity rests in treating like cases differently but the determination of what are 'like cases' is highly problematic. Tata and Hutton (1998) provide a brief review of the literature on consistency and disparity in sentencing alongside the findings of their recent Scottish research. Rather than imposing an external construction of similarity or difference in cases, they worked instead with sentencers to develop a narrative scale of seriousness as well as a numerical scale, combining this with the offender's criminal history (the second important variable in determining similarity and difference in cases). Their research found evidence of considerable inter-judge consistency in sentencing but also found that "of 10 sheriffs in three courts one sheriff systematically passes longer sentences than his colleagues ... [arguing that] public expectations of legal equality may be damaged by this kind of systematic disparity" (Tata and Hutton 1998, p. 351).

McNeill's (1993) small scale study compared SER recommendations and court disposals at three sheriff courts, examining 50 randomly selected cases in each court. The study found closely matching variations in both social enquiry and sentencing practice across the three courts. These variations could not be accounted for by any detectable variations in the cases. Indeed the court which seemed to be dealing with the least serious cases had the highest rate of custody and the lowest rate of recommendations for social work disposals (that is, probation and community service).

One possible explanation of these apparent disparities in SER practices posits an association between the reputations that courts accrue in terms of their sentencing and the kinds of recommendations made by social workers (McNeill 1993, pp. 36–40). This association has been described as the 'tariff-minus-one approach' or as 'second-guessing' sentencers where social workers anticipate the likely disposal and pitch their recommendation just below it in the notional sentencing 'tariff'.

In the original conference paper on which this chapter is based, I compared the pattern of my own recommendations over five years with Scottish Office statistics on national returns (McNeill 1999). Significant differences were apparent (in general, higher rates of lower tariff recommendations and lower rates of higher tariff recommendations), but firm conclusions as to whether these differences represented disparity proved elusive because the comparability of the cases could not be established. Hence, ultimately it could not be shown that the different patterns rested on my operational philosophy and on my interpretation of the nature and purpose of social enquiry. However, differences in my practice over time also emerged; the marked pattern being a steep decline and then a slight recovery in social work recommendations (for probation and/or community service). Again, these differences might reflect changes in the nature of the cases. However, they could alternatively reflect changes in my operational philosophy and practices concerning social enquiry. Thus the high initial rates of probation and community service recommendations early in my social enquiry career may relate to an understandable enthusiasm for providing the 'welfare' services for which I had been trained, as well as perhaps a lack of confidence in recommending lower tariff disposals.[5] Initially, in practice, I may have been insensitive to Harris's (1992, p. 150) plea for 'just welfare'; admitting a need that social work interventions should "be subject to a test of proportionality ... to the seriousness of the offence". My subsequent practice was, perhaps, tempered by a developing appreciation of that principle, of the broader policy context, of the implications of net-widening (McIvor 1992), and by an emerging confidence about 'risking' more parsimonious proposals.

Whether my efforts at promoting parsimony were effective in influencing sentencers might be judged, at least in part, by the decisions that they made in these cases. This question leads on to the wider contemporary debate about the effectiveness and quality of court reports.

Effectiveness

The disposal data detailed in the conference paper (McNeill 1999) suggests that just as my recommendation practice differed from the national pattern, so the disposals in those cases differed in a similar fashion from the national pattern. Crucially, as with so many attempts to alter the rate of imprisonment by influencing sentencing, my different practices were associated not with a significant reduction in the use of custody, but with a redistribution among noncustodial disposals (cf. Ashworth 1997, pp. 1125–7, for some possible explanations of this problem). This outcome is very much in line with the broader evaluation of criminal justice social work reported in Paterson and Tombs (1998, pp. 20–21).

Comparisons of patterns of recommendations and disposals can, however, be misleading, since an apparently perfect coincidence of the two patterns could be achieved even where the recommendation and the disposal never match in any individual case. Hence researchers, and increasingly practitioners and managers, have shown a keen interest in 'conversion' or 'concordance' (for example, Curran and Chambers 1982; Creamer and Williams 1989; McNeill 1993). The terms 'conversion' or 'concordance' describe the court disposing of a case in the manner proposed in the SER.

To further complicate matters, it is important to note that even where a proposal is 'converted' into a disposal, this may not represent effective SER practice (Paterson and Tombs 1998). If a report writer proposes, for example, community service, in a case that might otherwise have attracted a lesser penalty, the recommendation may indeed be 'converted'. However, rates of custody have not been reduced and might yet be increased if the order is subsequently breached. The net has been widened, the policy frustrated and the offender's future liberty jeopardised. The pursuit of the policy delineated above may therefore suggest that a more appropriate and complex concern for researchers, managers and practitioners alike should be the relationships between seriousness, risk of custody, conversion, 'up-tariffing' (where the court settles on a disposal 'higher' up the tariff than the recommendation) and 'down-tariffing' (where the court settles on a disposal 'lower' in the tariff than the recommendation).

However, the idea of the tariff is itself limited, better reflecting the abstraction of categories and classifications than the individual complexities of the events and the people of whom sentencers and report writers try to make sense. If social enquiry and sentencing are about the construction and reconstruction of 'cases', then quantitative information about recommendations, disposals and 'conversion' can only take us so far in the discussion of effectiveness. So, what qualitative information is available, for example, about 'customer' or sentencer satisfaction with court reports?

Quality

Recent research in England and Wales has been generally positive about the improving quality of pre-sentence reports (PSRs) subsequent to the changes in format and focus reported above, following the Criminal Justice Act 1991 (Gelsthorpe and Raynor 1995; Cavadino 1997). In Scotland, the Social Work Services Inspectorate's report 'Helping the Court Decide' (SWSI 1996) and Brown and Levy's (1998) recent research have also been broadly positive about developments in the quality of practice subsequent to the introduction of the national standards (SWSG 1991). However, there were some important qualifications to this positive view. Hence, the SWSI (1996) report states that:

> Whilst sentencers' comments about the overall quality of reports were positive, they identified some specific aspects of report writing which they thought could be improved. The most important of these was the need for greater detachment

and objectivity and the avoidance of any special pleading on behalf of the offender (p. 44).

This view might relate to the Inspectors' clear insistence that viewing the offender as the 'client' undermines objectivity and leads to a neglect of social work's responsibilities to the victims of crime. But perhaps most importantly, they argue tha':

> The framework of law and national standards surrounding social enquiry reports allows for significant differences of view between individual sentencers and social workers about how the general purposes of reports are translated into practice. This must reduce their efficiency and effectiveness ... Achieving ... [agreement] will require frank and focussed discussion between sentencers and service providers locally and between the representatives of Government, sentencers and service providers nationally ... (pp. 46–7).

What is missing from this prescription for a 'sense of common purpose' is the recognition, discussed above, that purpose is about more than policy and law; it is also about ethics and professional philosophies. As with many debates which appear to be about effectiveness, in fact the dialogue is not only or even primarily about operationalising policy, it is also about questioning the ideological basis of existing policy and practice. It is not only about developing the *means* of effective social enquiry within a 'technicist penology'; it is about determining the proper *ends* of social enquiry within the philosophy and sociology of punishment (Hudson 1996, p. 10, see above).

Brown and Levy's (1998) research (summarised in Paterson and Tombs 1998, p. 19ff) provides recent information which relates to some of these broader perspectives. For example, they note that criminal justice social work policy is:

> primarily based on a reformative and rehabilitative model of criminal justice ... [and that] this sets limits to the potential for social work to impact on sentencing ... [because] a range of factors was mentioned [by sentencers] as affecting choice of sentence and, importantly, social work services can impact on some, but not all, of these (Paterson and Tombs, 1998, pp. 20–21).

Brown and Levy (1998) also found that, in contrast to PSRs (Cavadino 1997), SERs continue to focus on personal background information so that, for example, social history was reported in 96 per cent of cases. Offence and offending behaviour analysis was far less prevalent, other than in terms of the offender's attitude to the offence. Thus, the 'pattern of offending' was addressed in only 22 per cent of cases. Remarkably perhaps, sentencers themselves identified welfare information as key in SERs, since they thought that family and personal background might explain the cause of the offending. Paterson and Tombs (1998, p. 27) speculate that sentencer satisfaction, in spite of the conspicuous lack of attention to offending behaviour analysis, might relate to sentencers' feeling that they already have an expertise vis-à-vis criminality, but lack information about the social and individual circumstances of the offender. If they are correct in this view, there may be implicit permission here for the 'different voice' to speak.

Consumer satisfaction studies therefore hint at the ideological complexity of assessing quality in social enquiry. If quality means 'fit for purpose', quality cannot be assessed until purpose is clearly defined. The discussion above perhaps illustrates why, in a context where the purposes of sentencing are ill defined, the purposes of social enquiry must similarly remain unclear. Therefore, the question of quality is necessarily obscured.

Quality and Effectiveness

Despite these complexities, assessing quality has been approached for practical purposes by devising evaluative tools for undertaking content analysis of court reports related to their compliance with national standards (Gelsthorpe, Raynor and Tisi 1992; Whyte et al. 1995). But even where the reports evidence quality in these relatively narrow terms, is there a positive correlation between quality and effectiveness?

Gelsthorpe and Raynor (1995) assessed the quality of a sample of Crown Court reports using a "self-coding quality appraisal instrument" which drew on official guidance and on existing quality checklists used in probation training. The researchers' ratings of the reports agreed with sentencers' ratings in 82 per cent of cases and, including cases where they differed by only one point (on a 16-point scale), the level of agreement rose to 97 per cent (p. 197). Examining the disposal outcomes of the PSRs, Gelsthorpe and Raynor (1995) argue that their findings "strongly suggest that the better reports were more successful in enabling sentencers to pass community sentences with confidence and to rely correspondingly less on imprisonment" (p. 197).

Table 20.1 Two studies relating the quality and effectiveness of pre-sentence reports

	Gelsthorpe and Raynor (1995)		Downing and Lynch (1997)	
	Below average (n=80)	*Above average (n=71)*	*Below average (n=28)*	*Above average (n=30)*
Per cent of reports recommending probation or community service	43	62	64	77
Per cent of such reports resulting in probation or community service	16	25	50	53
Per cent of all reports where there was a custodial sentence	48	39	14	17

However, Downing and Lynch (1997) have more recently questioned Gelsthorpe and Raynor's (1995) conclusions. Their study of reports, this time for a Magistrates Court, found no statistically significant association between quality, similarly measured, and effectiveness in terms of concordance, although there was some association in reports which recommended a community sentence. The findings of both of these research studies are included in Table 20.1 above.

Again, the comparison is highly problematic. Gelsthorpe and Raynor's (1995) sample was of reports written for the Crown Court dealing with more serious cases where both more focus (represented in the recommendations) and less success (represented in the disposals) in pursuing community based disposals and alternatives to custody might reasonably be expected. By contrast, Downing and Lynch's (1997) sample may relate to a court dealing with slightly less serious cases and with lower custody rates. Nonetheless, at present it would appear that the common sense association between quality and effectiveness remains open to question, perhaps serving again to underline that efforts to influence sentencing practice which fail to consider the influence of the theoretical strands discussed above, may provide a recipe for frustration.

The argument of Downing and Lynch's (1997) study is that the probation service in England and Wales, under the pervasive influence of new managerialism with its stress on quantitative targets, and of the movement towards 'administrative-punishment', is in danger of losing "its distinctive character in court and [of] becoming superfluous" (p. 186). They fear that court reports may become merely an expensive and futile exercise in 'rubber-stamping' sentencing decisions, based on the imposition of the same 'rubric of seriousness'. Their argument is thus similar to that in the North American literature concerning the 'myth of individualized justice'. To avoid this future, they propose a notion of quality which relates not to "instrumental objectives but to the expressive goods of fulfilling client needs, reducing harm to the individual and society and excellence in practice" (p. 186). They advocate greater involvement of sentencers, probation staff and offenders in evaluating both the *process of assessment* and the *content* of reports. In essence their proposals derive from a different vision of citizenship which entails a critical view of existing probation policy and posits a need for "a shift from holding the individual offender as solely a moral, cognitive actor to encouraging the community to promote the potential of all individuals" (p. 187). Thus, this analysis of practice leads inevitably back to theory.

Conclusions: Promoting Justice?

This chapter has reviewed some of the available literature and research, as well as utilising reflections on professional experience, in beginning to map out the influences upon and the influence of social enquiry reports. It is hoped that this analysis has illustrated the complexities of the report writer's task and its place in the sentencing process, making good on the claim made at the outset that this is a rich field of enquiry which can contribute to contemporary socio-legal and penological theory.

Difficulties in understanding and implementing the apparently 'simple' injunction to 'assist sentencing' have been exposed and set in wider context. Both the theoretical discussion and the empirical evidence concerning the consistency, quality and effectiveness of court reports have illustrated these difficulties. It seems that social enquiry cannot and should not be properly understood as a merely technical, policy-driven 'service' provided to sentencers. Rather it is a professional activity which inevitably raises fundamental and challenging questions of ideologies and values for both report writers and sentencers. Ultimately to describe the purpose of social enquiry as 'assisting sentencing' is somewhat vacuous. At the very least there is an adjective missing from that injunction; the issue is not only about what kind of 'assistance' inging.

social enquiry should provide, it is about what kind of sentencing it should assist. Determining the proper function of social enquiry is not primarily about working out what social workers' responsibilities are to sentencers; it is about tackling social workers' and sentencers' common obligation to work for a just society (see Hudson and Hutton, this volume). To this end, both sentencers and social workers need to make better sense of one another; to develop clearer mutual understandings of one another's concerns, perspectives, values, understandings, roles and responsibilities.

In the future study of court reports therefore, research methodologies must be developed which move beyond consumer studies of sentencer opinions, 'quality' studies of adherence to standards, and 'effectiveness' studies trying to uncover impacts on sentencing through the analysis of 'conversion' rates. None of these existing approaches offers the prospect of enhancing communication and improving practice because, in focusing on the outputs and outcomes of reports, they fail to adequately analyse the complex social processes through which the reports are both constructed and employed. Only by engaging with the rich complexity of these processes can future research and reflection explore intriguing questions concerning whether such reports assist sentencing, and, more importantly, whether they may or may not promote justice.

Acknowledgements

I am very grateful to Cyrus Tata, Neil Hutton, Robert Harris and Gwen Robinson for their comments on earlier versions of this paper.

Notes

1   Between 1993 and 1998, I worked as a criminal justice social worker in the East End of Glasgow. During that time, I retained records concerning my SER recommendations and the courts disposals in those cases. In total, I have this information for 245 cases. This represents about three-quarters of all the report requests allocated and excludes cases where reports could not be completed, pre-trial reports and reports for English courts, and cases where disposal information was not available.

2   The duty to prepare reports became a function of the local authority under Section 27 of the Social Work (Scotland) Act 1968. Under Section 201(1) of the Criminal Procedure (Scotland) Act 1995 the court has the power to "adjourn the case for the purpose of enabling inquiries to be made or of determining the most suitable method of dealing with [a] case". It is worth noting that this statute does not prescribe by whom these enquiries should be

made. Delegating the task to social workers is required neither by statute nor by legal principle; rather it is a matter of established practice, albeit practice that is now enshrined in current policy. The selection of social workers for the task may or may not say a great deal about what social enquiry is intended to provide. Under the Criminal Procedure (Scotland) Act 1995, courts must seek a report in certain circumstances, the more important of which for our purposes are; prior to making a Probation Order, Community Service Order or Supervised Release Order (s. 228, s. 238 and s. 209(2)), prior to imposing a first custodial sentence on persons aged over 21 (s. 205), and prior to imposing any period of detention on persons aged 16–20 (s. 207). Evidently these circumstances begin to provide an intuition of the purposes which policy makers may have in mind for SERs.

3   There are other important influences on the process of social enquiry which cannot be considered here. These would include, for example, the interpersonal processes between the report's subject and its writer, as well as the local team culture, local policies and the local court culture in different areas.

4   The exception being perhaps during Michael Forsyth's brief tenure at the Scottish Office. The retributivist title of his consultation paper, 'Making the Punishment Fit the Crime' (Scottish Office 1996) was, in some respects, misleading, since again the paper's proposals included provision for extended sentences for sexual and violent offenders. Although the public discourse at the time played the 'truth in sentencing' card, the notion of protecting the public through longer periods of incapacitative detention was an equally strong theme. The current Home Secretary's recently announced review of the sentencing framework in England and Wales (Home Office 2000a) perhaps signals the strongest evidence yet of the extent to which the public protection agenda is supplanting proportionality in that jurisdiction as the predominant guiding principle in sentencing.

5   Cavadino and Wiles' (1994) research, reported above, was prompted by the provisions of the 1991 Criminal Justice Act in England and Wales which, to an extent formalised the notion of a 'tariff' of penalties related to the seriousness of crimes. This controversial idea of a 'tariff' of penal sanctions is discussed below. As has been noted, there is no sentencing policy as such in Scotland and judicial independence is prized. There is no tariff of prescribed penalties for particular crimes and there is no explicit hierarchy among penalties. However, in practice, within a criminal career, offenders will experience a range of disposals, tending to escalate in their impact on liberty, towards custody.

References

Ashworth, A. (1997), 'Sentencing', in M. Maguire, R. Morgan, and R. Reiner (eds), *The Oxford Handbook of Criminology*, 2nd edn, Oxford: Clarendon Press, pp. 1095–135.

Bottoms, A. (1983), 'Neglected Features of Contemporary Penal Systems', in D. Garland and P. Young (eds), *The Power to Punish: Contemporary Penality and Social Analysis*, London: Heinemann, pp. 166–202.

Bottoms, A. (1995), 'The Philosophy and Politics of Punishment and Sentencing', in C. Clarkson and R. Morgan (eds), *The Politics of Sentencing Reform*, Oxford: Oxford University Press, pp. 17–49.

Braithwaite, J. (2000), 'The New Regulatory State and the Transformation of Criminology', *British Journal of Criminology*, Vol. 40, pp. 222–38.

Braithwaite, J. and Pettit, P. (1990), *Not Just Deserts*, Oxford: Clarendon Press.

Brown, L. and Levy, L. (1998), *Social Work and Criminal Justice: Vol. 4 – Sentencer Decision Making*, Edinburgh: The Stationery Office.

Cavadino, M. (1997), 'Pre-sentence Reports: The effects of legislation and national standards', *British Journal of Criminology*, Vol. 37, No. 4, pp. 529–48.

Cavadino, M. and Wiles, P. (1994), 'Seriousness of Offences: The perceptions of practitioners', *Criminal Law Review*, pp. 489–98.

Chapman, T. and Hough, M. (1998), *Evidence Based Practice: A guide to effective practice*, on behalf of Her Majesty's Inspectorate of Probation, Home Office Publications Unit, London.

Creamer, A. and Williams, B. (1989), *Social Enquiry Within a Changing Sentencing Context*, Edinburgh: Scottish Office, Central Research Unit.

Cullen, F. and Gilbert, K. (1992), 'Reaffirming Rehabilitation', in A. von Hirsch, and A. Ashworth (eds), *Principled Sentencing*, Edinburgh: Edinburgh University Press, pp. 31–40.

Curran, J. and Chambers, G. (1982), *Social Enquiry Reports in Scotland*, Edinburgh: Scottish Office, Central Research Unit.

Daly, K. (1989), 'Criminal Justice Ideologies and Practices in Different Voices: Some feminist questions about justice', *International Journal of the Sociology of Law*, Vol. 17, No. 1, pp. 1–18.

Downing, K. and Lynch, R. (1997), 'Pre-Sentence Reports: Does Quality Matter', in *Social Policy and Administration*, vol. 31, no. 2, pp. 173–90.

Drakeford, M. and Vanstone, M. (eds) (1996), *Beyond Offending Behaviour*, Aldershot: Arena.

Duff, A. and Garland, D. (eds) (1994), *A Reader on Punishment*, Oxford Readings in Socio-Legal Studies, Oxford: Oxford University Press.

Feeley, M. and Simon, J. (1994), 'Actuarial Justice: The emerging new criminal law', in D. Nelken (ed.), *The Futures of Criminology*, London: Sage, pp. 173–201.

Fitzmaurice, C. and Pease, K. (1986), *The Psychology of Judicial Sentencing*, Manchester: Manchester University Press.

Garland, D. (1989), 'Critical Reflections on Punishment, Custody and the Community', in H. Rees and E. Hall Williams (eds), *Punishment, Custody and the Community*, London: London School of Economics and Political Science.

Garland, D. (1996), 'The Limits of the Sovereign State: Strategies of crime control in contemporary society', *British Journal of Criminology*, Vol. 36, pp. 445–71.

Garland, D. (2000), 'The Culture of High Crime Societies: Some preconditions of recent law and order policies', *British Journal of Criminology*, Vol. 40, pp. 347–75.

Gelsthorpe, L. and Raynor, P. (1995), 'Quality and Effectiveness in Probation Officers' Reports to Sentencers', *British Journal of Criminology*, Vol. 35, No. 2, pp. 188–200.

Gelsthorpe, L., Raynor, P. and Tisi, A. (1992), *Quality Assurance in Pre-sentence Reports*, report to the Home Office Research and Planning Unit.

Hagan, J., Hewit, J. and Alwin, D. (1979), 'Ceremonial Justice: Crime and punishment in a loosely coupled system', *Social Forces*, Vol. 58, pp. 506ff.

Harris, R. (1992), *Crime, Criminal Justice and the Probation Service*, London: Routledge.

Home Office (2000), *A Review of the Sentencing Framework*, London: Home Office Communications Directorate.

Hudson, B. (1996), *Understanding Justice*, Buckingham: Open University Press.

Hutton, N. (1999), 'Sentencing in Scotland', in P. Duff and N. Hutton (eds), *Criminal Justice in Scotland*, Aldershot: Ashgate, pp. 166–81.

Kingsnorth, R., Cummings, D., Lopez, J. and Wentworth, J. (1999), 'Criminal Sentencing and the Court Probation Office: The myth of individualized justice revisited', *Justice System Journal*, Vol. 20, No. 3, pp. 255–73.

McGuire, J. (ed.) (1995), *What Works: Reducing reoffending – guidelines from research and practice*, Chichester: John Wiley and Sons.

McGuire, J. and Priestley, P. (1995), 'Reviewing "What Works": Past, present and future', in J. McGuire (ed.), *What Works: Reducing reoffending – guidelines from research and practice*, Chichester: John Wiley and Sons, pp. 4–34.

McIvor, G. (1992), 'Intensive Probation Supervision: Does more mean better?', *Probation Journal*, Vol. 39, pp. 2–6.

McNeill, F. (1993), *Coincidence, Collusion or Compromise? A Research Project Examining Social Enquiry Report Recommendations and Disposals at Three Sheriff Courts*, unpublished MSW dissertation, University of Glasgow.

McNeill, F. (1999), *An Aid to Sentencing? Five Years of Social Enquiry*, a paper presented at 'Sentencing and Society: an International Conference, 24–26 June, Centre for Sentencing Research, University of Strathclyde.

McNeill, F. (2000a), 'North and South: Changing ideologies of probation in mainland Britain', a paper presented at 'Crimes of the Future: The Future(s) of Criminology', British Society of Criminology Conference, University of Leicester, 5–7 July.

McNeill, F. (2000b), 'Making Criminology Work: Theory and practice in local context', *Probation Journal*, Vol. 47, No. 2, pp. 108–18.

Moore, G. and Wood, C. (1992), *Social Work and Criminal Law in Scotland*, 2nd edn, Edinburgh: Mercat Press.

Nellis, M. (1995), 'Probation Values for the 1990s', *Howard Journal of Criminal Justice*, Vol. 34, No. 1, pp. 19–34.

Nicholson, C.G.B. (1992), *Sentencing: Law and practice in Scotland*, 2nd edn, Green's Practice Library, Edinburgh: W. Green/Sweet and Maxwell.

Paterson, F. and Tombs, J. (1998), *Social Work and Criminal Justice: Vol. 1 – The Impact of Policy*, Edinburgh: The Stationery Office.

Pease, K. (1999), 'The Probation Career of Al Truism', *The Howard Journal of Criminal Justice*, Vol. 38, No. 1, pp. 2–16.

Raynor, P. (1980), 'Is There any Sense in Social Inquiry Reports?', *Probation Journal*, Vol. 27, pp. 78–84.

Raynor, P. (1985), *Social Work, Justice and Control*, Oxford: Blackwell.

Raynor, P., Smith, D. and Vanstone, M. (1994), *Effective Probation Practice*, Basingstoke: Macmillan.

Rifkind, M. (1989), 'Penal Policy: The way ahead', *The Howard Journal*, Vol. 28, No. 2, pp. 81–90.

Rose, N. (2000), 'Government and Control', *British Journal of Criminology*, Vol. 40, pp. 321–39.

Rosencranz, J. (1988), 'Maintaining the Myth of Individualized Justice: Probation pre-sentence reports', *Justice Quarterly*, Vol. 5, pp. 235ff.

Scottish Office (1996), *Making the Punishment Fit the Crime – a Consultation Paper on the Government's Proposals to Change the Law in Scotland Governing the Early Release of Prisoners*, Edinburgh: Scottish Office.

Shapland, J. (1987), 'Who Controls Sentencing? Influences on the Sentencer', in D.C. Pennington and S. Lloyd-Bostock (eds), *The Psychology of Sentencing: Approaches to consistency and disparity*, Oxford: Oxford Centre for Socio-Legal Studies.

Social Work Services Group (SWSG) (1991), *National Objectives and Standards for Social Work Services in the Criminal Justice System*, Edinburgh: The Scottish Office Social Work Services Group.

Social Work Services Group (SWSG) (2000), *National Standards for Social Enquiry and Related Reports and Court Based Social Work Services*, Edinburgh: Scottish Executive Social Work Services Group.

Social Work Services Inspectorate (SWSI) (1996), *Helping the Court Decide – Report of an Inspection of Social Enquiry Reports for the Criminal Courts*, Edinburgh: HMSO.

Tata, C. (1997), 'Conceptions and Representations of the Sentencing Decision Process', *Journal of Law and Society*, Vol. 24, No. 3, pp. 395–420.

Tata, C. and Hutton, N. (1998), 'What "Rules" in Sentencing? Consistency and Disparity in the Absence of "Rules"', *International Journal of the Sociology of Law*, Vol. 26, pp. 339–64.

Walsh, A. (1985), 'The Role of the Probation Officer in the Sentencing Process', *Criminal Justice and Behaviour*, Vol. 12, pp. 289ff.

Whyte, W., Ramsay, J., Clark, C. and Waterhouse, L. (1995), *Social Work in the Criminal Justice System in Scotland: Competencies required by the National Objectives and Standards for Social Work Services in the Criminal Justice System*, a study commissioned by the Social Work Services Group, from the University of Edinburgh, published by the Department of Social Work, University of Edinburgh.

Worrall, A. (1997), *Punishment in the Community: The future of criminal justice*, London: Longman.

Young, J. (1981), 'Thinking Seriously about Crime: Some models of criminology', in M. Fitzgerald, G. McLennan and J. Pawson (eds), *Crime and Society – Readings in History and Theory*, London: Routledge/Open University Press, pp. 248–309.

Chapter Twenty-one

Dangerousness and Risk: from Belgian Positivism to New Penology

Hilde Tubex

Introduction

Belgium, as most west European countries, is faced with an increasing prison population, in which long-term prisoners form an ever-growing proportion. This observation was the starting point for our study on the problem of long-term imprisonment.[1] While we are conscious that the size and characteristics of prison populations result from a complex interaction of different factors (Snacken, Beyens and Tubex 1995), in this study we concentrate on the (changes in) criminal legislation.

Legislation has a major impact on sentencing: it not only determines what has to be considered as criminality, it also set the boundaries in which sentencing operates. In Belgium the judge decides what punishment is to be applied, within the maximum and minimum stipulated by law. Recent legal initiatives have changed the definition of certain crimes (e.g. rape), have increased the penalties and have made it possible to impose additional preventive measures and deprivations. In this way legislation influences the number of prisoners entering prison with long sentences. On the other hand restrictions have been introduced concerning the possibilities for early release, whereby the number of long-termers leaving prison has been limited. In this way the legislation is the first and an important step in the criminal justice system.

Our analysis of the literature revealed that the emerging bifurcation in penal policy, which was already described by Bottoms in 1977, continued to gain ground. This bifurcation consist of a two-track policy where on the one hand, shorter prison sentences or alternative, noncustodial measures are applied for minor offences, while on the other hand long-term prison sentences are reserved for offences which are considered to be very serious. The categories that are considered as deserving a severe approach from the 1970s and 1980s are sexual offences, drug offences, violent offences and recidivism. An overview of these initiatives can be found elsewhere and does not form the subject of this chapter (Tubex and Snacken 1995; Snacken, Beyens and Tubex 1995). These initiatives are often justified by the (perceived) dangerousness represented by the offender and the need to protect society. Dangerousness is not a new concept in sentencing. The concept of dangerousness was introduced to penal theory by the Italian positivists at the end of the nineteenth century. The importance of the concept of dangerousness changed several times throughout the twentieth century, as it was influenced by economic and socio-politic developments (Pratt 1995, 1996a). Thus, even today, dangerousness remains an important concept in sentencing. At the same time, we see the emergence of risk management in criminal policy. The risk of recidivism has become an increasingly important factor in decision-making about punishment and early release. Feeley and Simon describe this development as actuarial justice.

This chapter discusses the origins of the concept of dangerousness and the legal initiatives that have been taken against dangerous criminals. This will be illustrated by a number of examples in Belgium and the Netherlands. Although these countries were important pioneers in the development of modern penology, their role has seldom been described in Anglo-Saxon publications. This is compared with developments in the UK. After an overview of the most important characteristics of actuarial justice, we will consider what the underlying relation is between dangerousness and risk. Is there really a different approach and, if so, what are the consequences for sentencing, and hence the prison population, more especially for long-term prisoners.

Dangerousness

At the end of the ninteenth century a 'doctrinal war' was raging between those of the classical school who believed in the concept of free will, and the positivists who believed that the behaviour of individuals was determined. While the classical school considered the application of a punishment to be proportional to an objective assessment of the seriousness of the crime, the positivist school, in contrast, shifted the attention from the crime itself towards the person of the criminal and the factors that determined him. Positivists tried to discover and demonstrate these factors in a scientific way. Consequently, punishment was to be replaced by preventive measures proportional to the dangerousness of the delinquent. In the classical school danger was also taken into account, but it was more an objective danger linked to the seriousness of the crime, while in positivism it was a subjective danger, dependent upon the person of the perpetrator.

In the application of the concept of dangerousness in Belgium and the Netherlands, the role of the *Internationale Kriminalistische Vereinigung* (International Union of Criminal Law) was of an essential importance. The International Union of Criminal Law was founded in 1889 by von Liszt (Germany, 1851–1919), together with Adolphe Prins (Belgium, 1845–1919) and van Hamel (Netherlands, 1842–1917). In origin, the statutes of the International Union of Criminal Law were very close to the philosophy of positivism.[2] However, after several internal discussions they were modified into a more eclectic vision, as we find also in the doctrine of Prins (Prins, 1910).

Core Ideas of the Social Defence Theory by Prins

Positivism developed in Belgium in a less radical, more pragmatic form that was named the theory of social defence. From his critical position,[3] Adolphe Prins tried to establish a compromise between the principles of the classical school on the one hand and the new ideas of positivism on the other. For Prins, free will is omnipresent in every person, but the strength of this free will is determined by physical and social situations which set the boundaries. People living in bad conditions have limited choice, they are less free. Considering the protection of society is central to social defence theory, the system must act against the criminal who disturbs the social order, irrespective of whether he acted out of free will or not (Prins 1910, pp. 56–7).

Prins tried to reconcile both models by maintaining the punishment of the classical school (as laid down in the penal code) for most of the delinquents. The preventive measures of the positivists were only applied to the really dangerous criminals. What was meant by dangerousness was not clearly defined, but according to Prins dangerousness was mostly present in some categories, particularly vagrants, recidivists and mentally diseased offenders. Vagrants are a symbol of potential danger, as they do not have enough resources to live in obedience of the law. Recidivists have proven not to respect the current norms and not to be deterred by their penalties, while the mentally ill cannot respect them since they are not responsible for their deeds (ibid., pp. 70–98).

Concerning recidivists, a more severe punishment can more or less be reconciled with the principles of the classical school. The Belgian penal code already included optional or compulsory increases of the sentence in case of legal recidivism. This purely repressive approach turned out to be inefficient, as was illustrated by the high recidivism figures appearing in the emerging criminal statistics. How to handle recidivists and habitual criminals was an important debate within the International Union of Criminal Law. The introduction of preventive sentences proved to be the major obstacle. It was Prins who connected these security measures with the concept of dangerousness. According to Prins, the statistics revealed clearly that recidivists show a specific character which calls for the use of special measures when dealing with them (Bulletin de L'UIDP 1909, pp. 958–9; van der Landen 1992, pp. 195–206).

Regarding the category of mentally ill offenders, who are not responsible for their actions, the concept of risk emerged in social defence theory. Because the social defence theory in no way rejected the classical principles, Prins had to find a justification for actions against those that carry no or insufficient responsibility for their deeds. To justify this, Prins cited the concept of risk as it was applied in civil law. As a consequence of the importance placed on the compensation for damage in a civil law, the responsibility was no longer dependent on the fault but on the origin of the damage. Prins argued that this principle could equally be applied to penal law. His aim was to make the punishment dependent upon the risk that the delinquent represented to society. The person who was the origin of the risk, whether he acted out of free will or not, whether he could be accused of being in fault or not, was considered as the one responsible. Through the introduction of responsibility without fault it became possible to protect society against dangerous criminals, even if they were not responsible for their actions (Prins 1910, pp. 56–7; Foucault 1981, pp. 418–22).

Foucault explained this viewpoint in the context of nineteenth century society. Through industrialisation, mechanisation, regular payment for labour and the structure of society, the concept of risk changed. More particularly, a greater risk to inflict damage on another emerged in the way that a small fault can cause a great damage (Foucault 1981, pp. 418–19). One of the foundations of social defence was the fear and the threat of the new industrial society. The more affluent members of that society were confronted by fast-growing towns, with overpopulated areas where the working classes concentrated. In addition, they experienced an increase in the number of different types of crime and became aware of the shortcomings in the existing penal system. There was a wish to be protected against the risks of the industrial society, to be assured of compensation for any damage. The call for protection and repression was urgent. The importance of the notion of dangerousness in the social defence theory should be understood against this background of threat and insecurity. The social defence movement is based upon the struggle against criminality and this requires efficiency, realism, certainty and a reachable goal (Tulkens 1988, pp. 42–3).

Prins' concept of dangerousness had as a consequence that the dangerous delinquent was no longer exempt from the penal law, as was the aim in positivism, but that the application area of the penal interventions widened. The concept of dangerousness was added to the penal responsibility. Many examples of this policy can be found in Belgium and the Netherlands.

The Results of Social Defence Theory

Different levels throughout the criminal process are influenced by the social defence theory. The first development was the introduction of the conditional sentences and conditional release (which is similar to parole in the UK).

In Belgium, the law concerning the conditional sentence and conditional release was introduced in 1888. Conditional sentences were an answer to the criticism of social defence to short prison sentences. Conditional release existed already in some of our neighbouring counties (it was introduced in Great Britain in 1833, in France in 1885, in Germany and several Swiss cantons). Conditional release is an answer to insistence within social defence to individualise the penalties. Although this initiative is often described as humanitarian and progressive, this was not the primary consideration of the minister of justice. In practice, it contributes to maintain discipline in prison. Additionally, it provides a significant expansion of control over the delinquent after release, since the probation period at that moment is double the remainder of the sentence (Jaspar 1911, pp. 259–61; Ugeux 1955, pp. 8–9).

In the Netherlands, the possibility for conditional release existed already in the penal code of 1886. However, this code reflected mainly the ideas of the classical school and therefore, as a consequence, conditional release was seldom applied. In spite of the objections of classically inspired politicians, in 1915 a law was passed introducing conditional sentences and expanding the circumstances under which conditional release could be applied (Franke 1990, pp. 517–31, 615–16; van der Landen 1992, pp. 234–8, 264–65).

A second development was the introduction of preventive detention to restrain (potentially) dangerous offenders. We distinguish two categories.

Vagrants and Beggars

The Belgian law of 1891 to restrain vagrants and beggars is a typical expression of the social defence idea that those who do not conform to the current social order are potentially dangerous and carry a higher risk of criminal behaviour. Here preventive detention was brought in against a dangerous lifestyle. Vagrants were seen as potential delinquents since they lacked the resources to live in respect of the law. Basically, it is a preventive punishment towards criminal acts that have not yet been committed. Professional beggars and vagrants could be incarcerated in an institution for between two and seven years where they were subjected to a repressive regime based upon labour (Depreeuw 1988, pp. 365–6).

In the Netherlands, a similar security measure was approved in 1929 which made it possible to restrain dangerous people. The measure was recommended from a minimum of five years up to 10 years. However, this rule was never actually applied, more because of financial and practical problems than from objections of principle. In 1986 this measure was deleted from the penal code (Franke 1990, pp. 616–20; van der Landen 1992, pp. 266–75).

Mentally Diseased, Recidivists and Habitual Offenders

The Belgian law for 'the protection of society' of 1930 provides security measures against abnormal and habitual offenders: the so-called internment. The law is applicable for those guilty of a felony or a misdemeanour in state of insanity, serious mental illness or disability, which make them unfit to control their acts. For them, the preventive measure takes the form of a treatment, whose length is dependent upon the dangerousness of the individual involved. For recidivists, the penal code already provided optional or compulsory increased sentences.[4] The preventive detention was added to the sentence, also optional or compulsory, whereby the recidivist and the habitual offender were kept 'at the disposal of the government'. The same measure is applicable for habitual offenders.[5] Although having served their prison sentence, the latter can still be held in restriction for 10 and up to 20 years if this is considered to be in the interest of the protection of society (Cornil 1930–31, pp. 837–879, 1019–69).

In the Netherlands one speaks of 'psychopaths'; those suffering from a mental disease without being completely irresponsible for their deeds. Here, the fiercest struggle between the modernists and the classicists took place. Finally, a so-called two-track policy was adopted: psychopaths who are considered irresponsible for their actions receive a measure of preventive detention. Its length is two years and is renewable when thought essential from the point of view of public order and the safety of the society; and, for those who are considered to be partly responsible the preventive measure is combined with a punishment. The length of this sentence is related to the degree of guilt of the involved, while the preventive detention must provide protection for society. When originally, those who were completely irresponsible for their acts, the insane, escaped prosecution, this was later considered insufficient from the social defence point of view. In 1928 the law was modified to make it possible to subject them also to preventive detention (Franke 1990, pp. 533–4, 616; van der Landen 1992, pp. 238–61).

In Belgium, other proposals were made within the framework of social defence theory, such as the introduction of a preventive measure against alcoholics. Nevertheless, these were rejected. Preventive measures against minors do also exist, but are beyond the scope of this contribution.

The Development of Modern Penality in Great Britain

Positivist ideas were initially not very welcome in Great Britain. Their influence was restricted to a few individual supporters (e.g. Ruggles-Brise). The British medics did not agree with the theory of Lombroso that considered the criminal as a special type of person. For them, criminals were mostly normal people. Most widely recognised was Charles Goring (1870–1919) whose book *The English Convict* (1913) is the antithesis of Lombroso's work. Goring did not base his analysis on individual or anthropological research, but instead on the statistical analysis of large population groups.

The resistance to positivism was mostly directed to its more extreme form. As positivism itself evolved towards a more eclectic vision, resistance in Great Britain declined. Garland identified the acceptance of these ideas as between the Gladstone report (1895) and the start of the First World War. He describes this period as an evolution towards modern penality. Following the examples of continental Europe, we see changes arise, such as individualisation in punishment, classification and a specific approach for certain categories of offenders In 1898 the Inebriates Act introduces the possibility to bring alcoholics together in a special institute for a period up to three years after their punishment. After the turn of the century, preventive detention is introduced (Prevention of Crime Act, 1908). It was a security measure directed at habitual offenders, determined at the time of the sentencing and applied after the sentence. Its length would be between five and 10 years. Finally, the Mental Deficiency Act followed in 1913, which added the possibility to place mentally disturbed offenders in a special institution. It is a one-year measure, which is renewable for a period of five years (Garland 1985, pp. 19–32, 216–30; 1994).

The way Garland described these developments, highlights many points of similarity with the evolution on continental Europe. The transition to modern penality originated from dissatisfaction with the existing criminal system. The effectiveness of the prison sentence was questioned, especially concerning short sentences and recidivism. One attempted to improve its functioning through the introduction of classification and differentiation. This implied more extensive knowledge of the offender, especially of those who were considered as special cases because they formed a danger to society. Because of the assumed dangerousness of the offender, possibilities were developed to impose longer or even undetermined sentences. By this means, the individual rights, guaranteed by the classical school were put aside and the protection of society became paramount. The impact and application area of criminal law expanded, which in its turn called upon other disciplines such as psychiatry, psychology and sociology. The further development of social defence/modern penality became characterised by the growing influence of medical thinking. After the Second World War, and partly as a reaction to the horrors therein, humanisation and resocialisation came to the fore. The belief in the effectiveness of prison sentences remained strongly held. Its aim was to treat and thus improve the offender during detention. The attempt to develop treatment during detention failed in Belgium, whereas in the Netherlands more genuine programs can be identified. For both countries efforts were made to increase the normalisation and humanisation of the prison system. Great Britain followed the same course: the Criminal Justice Act of 1948 was here an important milestone. But at the beginning of the 1970s, the belief in the resocialisation-ideal came to an abrupt end. Critical evaluations of the results of treatment, complaints about abuse of treatment and sociological and psychological research on the effects of long-term imprisonment announced the end of the treatment model.[6] The gap that appeared from that moment resulted into the development (especially in the USA) of a number of models that were part of a new era, described by Feeley and Simon as 'new penology'.

Risk and New Penology

Feeley and Simon describe the developments in punishment theory that have occurred since the Second World War, and especially since the rejection of resocialisation theory, as an evolution from old penology to new penology. We assume that their vision is sufficiently well known, and hence restrict ourselves to a few of the main themes of their argument.[7]

Feeley and Simon argue that a characteristic of the old penology is the fact that the individual was the central issue and that his guilt formed the essential element of the punishment. In recent evolution in punishment they see the development of a new paradigm. This new penology is no longer directed towards the criminal as individual but instead is directed towards the system and its efficiency. With this in mind, society tries to develop a form of control based on rationality. Or, in other words, crime policy becomes a problem of risk assessment.

Feeley and Simon emphasise that the new penology is not a new model or a new school, rather they see it as a framework that allows us to interpret these recent developments. In this new penology, they see changes taking place at three levels: at the level of discourse, at the level of objectives and at the level of punishment techniques.

At the discourse level, the individual is no longer central but is replaced by the group or category to which he belongs, according to the level of risk that he represents. The causes of criminality have become less important than the possible consequences. At the level of the objectives of punishment, there is no further discussion required over treatment or sanctions, moreover the objective has become to identify the individuals that are a treat to society and to deal with them. Crime prevention is no longer the justification of punishment, criminality is a calculated risk that society must manage in a rational way. This rational approach requires a new, cost-effective process. It is not so much the techniques that change as the way they are implemented. Penal techniques no longer seek to reintegrate the criminal, they seek to make criminality manageable. We no longer combat criminality, we just try to learn to live with it.

The results of new penology, according to Feeley and Simon, can be found in a number of existing techniques. We can consider this is a symptom of new penology, which infiltrates the old penology almost unnoticed and thereby changes an established concept. The authors call the characteristics of this new development actuarial justice. Actuarial comes from the world of insurance, where the price of an insurance premium is dependent upon the expected risk expressed statistically. Feeley and Simon give a number of examples where, in their opinion, actuarial justice has been applied. We limit ourselves here to the example of detention. In the new penology, prison sentences remain an important instrument and there is even an expansion of the penal boundaries, but imprisonment fulfils a different role. From the population who are liable to end up in prison, a selection is made of those representing a greater risk and these are locked away for a long(er) time. The role of the prison remains limited to that of warehousing. Imprisonment is no longer seen as a period where the prisoner can be treated or can change. Rather it is seen as another possible control mechanism in the spectrum of possibilities going from probation and other alternatives for those considered a low risk, to a long-term detention for those considered a high risk. Feeley and Simon mention in this context the example of the previous categorisation of prisons according to the target group and the regime approach that they promote. In the USA, this is gradually replaced by a categorisation based upon security-levels.

From Dangerousness to Risk

From the above discussion we can conclude that the dangerousness of (certain) offenders began to take an important place in sentencing policy at the end of the nineteenth century. For the offenders deemed dangerous, special preventive detention measures of unlimited duration were provided. Initially, these measures were meant principally to neutralise the offender and to protect society. At that time, there was also a certain consensus that the presence of criminality in society was an ontological fact, dependent upon biological or social factors, which determined the actions of the delinquent. The belief in changeability was limited. Prins accepted that certain groups of the population were more criminal than others. He called this phenomena 'dégénérescence'.

The attention given to the offender as a person, in the sense that attempts are made to change or cure him, is mostly present in the later period of resocialisation theory, which itself is linked to the rise of medical science and the interest in human rights. Treatment was expanded to be available to all criminal offenders. Accordingly, the concept of dangerousness receded. After the decline of the rehabilitative ideal, a number of models emerged where dangerousness was no longer determined on an individual basis. The disappointment in the possibilities of treatment and the prediction of future recidivism on the basis of case study led to a more actuarial evaluation, which was mostly directed at the assessment of risk.

Risk assessment, as Feeley and Simon also state, is not new. Risk has always been an important element in determining punishment. Even at the beginning of the twentieth century, the risk that someone may commit a crime (vagrants and beggars), or the risk of recidivism (habitual offenders) allowed certain categories of *potential* offenders to be considered as dangerous. The notion of risk expanded the application area of criminal law to crimes that were not yet committed. The concept of risk also legitimised a second expansion. Sentencing was no longer based on the guilt of those who were only partially or not at all responsible for their actions, but the presence of a risk was considered sufficient to take penal measures. Those, who in positivism were categorised as born criminals, and who according to Prins were the victims of dégénérescence, were held responsible even through there was no evidence of guilt. This was necessary because they formed a danger to society, they were a risk.

The difference between the approach at the beginning of the twentieth century and the actuarial approach is that in the latter the estimation of dangerousness at an individual level is dropped. In social defence, punishment was directed against the individual. Criminals were also divided into categories, whereby especially vagrants, recidivists and the mentally ill were the object of strong preventive measures, but the individual offender was the subject of penal action, and the attention was directed towards assessing the risk he presented. In the new penology the foremost aim is to identify certain groups according to the potential risk which they represent, and to attempt to control that risk. While dangerousness, as it was encompassed in social defence theory still stood for an individual assessment and a certain belief in the possibility of change, risk in new penology relates only to a statistical estimate and management of criminality. Moreover, dangerousness is disconnected from the person of the offender. Dangerousness is measured using objective attributes. It is sufficient for these attributes to be detected for dangerousness to be confirmed. The offender as a person is no longer the prime concern, priority is given to determining the risk that he poses to others (Castel 1991).

The importance of the individual in social defence was a consequence of the focus on the origin of criminality. The causes of criminality were sought in both internal and external factors, which, when identified, were dealt with. At the end of the nineteenth century, criminality was seen as a moral problem, whereby those that deviate from the established norm had to be cured or placed under surveillance. New penology by contrast, stands for a fatalistic vision of punishment, with little or no expectations of the offender or the punishment. The extreme individualisation as characterised by social defence, which was later reinforced by the introduction of medical aspects, also had its negative points, as it led to the expansion of penal interventions and the addition of preventive measures. Since these were not classical punishments, the offender lost his legal rights of defence and other legal guarantees. In this way the principles of legality and proportionality, which were the basics of the classical school, were no longer respected.

This was also the basis of the criticism by the just deserts movement. Originally they campaigned for a correct and just punishment which no longer had resocialisation as its main aim. They also disapproved of indeterminate punishment and of administrative decision making in the execution of the sentence (e.g. parole). Originally, the justice model stood for a liberal and reductionist approach. They also attached great importance to the respect of human rights. The criterion of dangerousness was rejected and the seriousness of the offence became once again the leading principle of decision-making (von Hirsch 1976, 1981; Morris 1974; Fogel 1979). This reductionist approach was not realised in practice and the justice model evolved into a more repressive way. This repressive development further continued in the theory of general and selective incapacitation.

In general incapacitation the possibility to change the individual is no longer important. Instead, the system attempts to achieve a better distribution of criminals in general. By identifying those that are a danger to society and by setting them apart for a sufficiently long time, the penal system tries to limit the amount of criminality in society. Selective incapacitation goes a step further in this new penology concept. It is aimed at these categories of offenders who represent the greatest risk and who, once identified, are isolated from society for a long period. In this scenario, it is no longer the person of the offender who is important but the risk which he represents. One of these risk categories are the so-called career criminals. The difference between the career criminal and his predecessors, the born criminal and the habitual criminal, is that the system is no longer looking for the origin of his behaviour, his identification is sufficient for a severe punishment. The Three Strikes and You're Out laws in the USA are a perfect example of the new approach of making society safe from those that are supposed to form a great risk to it.

The peril in this approach is that one starts from the assumption of dangerousness without having this explicitly established on an individual basis. The risk of false negatives remains, even with the application of actuarial techniques. Moreover, the person involved no longer has the opportunity to show that he, as an individual, in spite of the fact that he exhibits certain characteristics of a risk-group, is not dangerous. As a consequence, this assumption mostly leads to a long-term imprisonment, with heavy security standards, whereby the prisoner never gets the chance to prove that he is no longer dangerous.

What then are the consequences of this shift in policy? Although not all countries have an increased use of imprisonment (e.g. in Belgium annual admissions decline), most European countries are confronted with a growing prison population. Additionally, the characteristics of this population have changed to include an ever-increasing proportion of long-term prisoners. In particular those who are convicted for sexual, drug or violent offences receive long sentences. They are the dangerous offenders of today. Recidivism as an indicator for dangerousness has remained constant but new categories have been added as the standards and norms that we consider important in our lives have changed (Pratt 1996b, 1997). Finally, the substance of imprisonment changed. It became more a way to neutralise offenders for the interests of society. If we keep evolving in the direction of new penology this then implies that belonging to one of these risk-groups is sufficient justification alone for a long neutralisation through deprivation of liberty.

As we take a reductionist standpoint towards imprisonment as punishment, we are conscious of the damaging consequences of a (long) prison sentence. Furthermore, we do not think that imprisonment reduces the risk to society. The deprivation of liberty in the fight against criminality is based upon a static view on human behaviour which takes no account of the possibilities of personal change. It seems to us that long-term imprisonment is counter-productive to any possible reintegration. So, we argue for a restricted use of imprisonment and believe that the execution of sentences should be oriented towards the preparation for the period after release (e.g. use of a detention planning). In order to make this possible, the length of the imprisonment should be limited in time.

In conclusion we examine recent developments in our own country. Belgium, with its eclectic model, takes a particular course with additional consequences for its penal future.

What does the Belgian Penal Future look like?

In Belgium no specific choice has been made about a particular sentencing model. The sentencing rules are a reflection of successive influences. The penal code is based upon a classical philosophy. In addition we find a number of measures of social defence. Most of these measures are still applicable, although it must be said that they continue to be the subject of discussion and reform.

- The law concerning conditional release was modified in 1998. A number of changes reinforce the classical influence, for example increased attention to the rights of the prisoner. On the other side, preventive detention to keep someone 'at the disposal of the government', whose use in practice had all but disappeared, was reinstated. Disposal of the government (for a period of 10 to 20 years in the case of specific recidivism) is now possible for offenders of certain sexual offences from the first conviction to a 1 year prison sentence.
- Vagrancy and begging were decriminalised in 1993. In our social context these were no longer seen as a threat. On the other hand, attitudes and policies towards drug users and illegal immigrants seem to proceed from the same premise that a 'dangerous lifestyle' raises the risk of criminality.
- Internment of mentally ill offenders, still for a unspecified time, has been under attack for many years because there is no adequate treatment offered within the context of penitentiaries, but is still applied.

Belgian penal policy since the seventies has developed in the direction of selective incapacitation. In 1975 the law with respect to drugs was hardened, whereas through the 1990s sexual offences were the object of stronger laws, especially offences against minors. These new measures provided for longer sentences and restricted the possibilities for early release. Additionally, a compulsory treatment was imposed upon the perpetrators of certain sexual crimes. In this way the treatment ideas of the 1960s and 1970s make a comeback but within the more repressive jacket of the 1980s and 1990s. In fact, we detect a tendency in these discussions and reforms towards an even stronger attention being paid to risk and not to the reintegration of the offender.

The result of this policy is that, at this moment in Belgium, not only offenders who are thought to be dangerous, such as sexual delinquents, can receive a longer prison sentence; moreover, the judge can decide to impose supplementary security measures and the offender's agreement to undergo treatment is a necessary condition for early release. Which punishment philosophy best fits most of these measures? The punishment of the offender in accordance with the seriousness of the committed crime? The improvement of the dangerous criminal? Or the neutralising of those categories of offenders which one assumes to form a significant risk to society? The eclectic approach includes all of these ideas and results in increasing use of long sentences for these criminals.

Considering that recent initiatives create the opportunity to impose longer punishments and/or a longer stay in prison, we are monitoring anxiously the growth of the Belgian prison population with its proportionately increasing number of long-sentence prisoners. A sustained and critical monitoring of the sentencing policy seems to us to be vitally important.

Notes

1 PhD thesis, H. Tubex (1999), 'Dualisering en selectiviteit in de vrijheidsberoving. Toepassing op (levens)lang gestraften' ('Bifurcation and Selectivity in the Deprivation of Liberty. Application on Long-term prisoners and Lifers').
2 In the original statutes it was argued for preventive sentences for habitual criminals. Unable to reach a consensus, the IUCL had to delete these statutes in 1897.
3 At that moment he was Inspector-General of the Belgian prison system, a function he combined with an academic career. Furthermore, he extended an important influence on several highly placed figures in criminal justice.
4 Increase of the sentence is compulsory after the second conviction for a crime, if the second crime is punishable with a sentence of 15 to 20 years (compulsory increase to 17 years), in the other cases (also misdemeanour after crime, misdemeanour after misdemeanour, contravention after contravention) increases are optional.
5 Recidivism of three misdemeanours in 15 years, leading each to a sentence of at least 6 months of imprisonment.
6 Although the belief in the possibilities of treatment never disappeared completely.
7 These main themes are based upon the following publications: Feeley and Simon 1992; 1994; Simon and Feeley 1995.

References

Bottoms, A. (1977), 'Reflections on the Renaissance of Dangerousness', *Howard Journal of Criminal Justice*, Vol. 16, pp. 70–96.
Bulletin de l'Union International de Droit Pénal (1909), 'Le congrès de l'Union en 1910', *Revue de Droit Pénal et de Criminologie*, pp. 957–9.
Castel, R. (1991), 'From Dangerousness to Risk', in G. Burchell, C. Gordon and P. Miller (eds), *The Foucault Effect: Studies in governmentality*, London: Harvester Wheatsheaf, pp. 281–98.
Cornil, L. (1930–31), 'La loi de défense sociale a l'égârd des anormaux et des délinquants d'habitude du 9 avril 1930 (1)', *Revue de Droit Pénal et de Criminologie*, pp. 837–79.
Cornil, L. (1930–31), 'La loi de défense sociale a l'égârd des anormaux et des délinquants d'habitude du 9 avril 1930 (2)', *Revue de Droit Pénal et de Criminologie*, pp. 1019–69.
Depreeuw, W. (1988), *Landloperij, bedelarij en thuisloosheid*, IRCS No. 16, Antwerpen-Arnhem: Kluwer Rechtswetenschappen, Gouda Quint.
Feeley, M.M. and Simon, J. (1992), 'The New Penology: Notes on the emerging strategy of corrections and its implications', *Criminology*, Vol. 30, pp. 449–74.

Feeley, M.M. and Simon, J. (1994), 'Actuarial Justice: The emerging new criminal law', in D. Nelken (ed.), *The Futures of Criminology*, London/Thousand Oaks/New Delhi: Sage Publications, pp. 173–201.

Fogel, D. (1979), *We are the Living Proof. The Justice Model for Corrections*, Ohio: Anderson Publishing Co.

Foucault, M. (1981), 'L'évolution de la notion "d'individu dangereux" dans la psychiatrie légale', *Déviance et Société*, Vol. 4, pp. 403–22.

Franke, H. (1990), *Twee eeuwen gevangen. Misdaad en straf in Nederland*, Het Spectrum bv. Utrecht: Aula-paperback.

Garland, D. (1985), *Punishment and Welfare. A History of Penal Strategies*, Aldershot: Gower.

Garland, D. (1994), 'Of Crimes and Criminals: The development of criminology in Britain', in M. Maguire, R. Morgan and R. Reiener (eds), *The Oxford Handbook of Criminology*, Oxford: Clarendon Press, pp. 17–68.

Jaspar, H. (1991), 'Jules Lejeune et son oeuvre de législation criminelle', *Revue de Droit Pénal et de Criminologie*, pp. 257–69.

Morris, N. (1981), 'Punishment, Desert and Rehabilitation', in H. Gross and A. von Hirsch (eds.), *Sentencing*, Oxford: Oxford University Press, pp. 257–71.

Pratt, J. (1995), 'Dangerousness, Risk and Technologies of Power', *The Australian and New Zealand Journal of Criminology*, Vol. 28, pp. 3–31.

Pratt, J. (1996a), 'Governing the Dangerous: An historical overview of dangerous offender legislation', *Social and Legal Rtudies*, Vol. 5, pp. 21–36.

Pratt, J. (1996b), 'Reflections on Recent Trends towards the Punishment of Persistence', *Crime, Law and Social Change*, Vol. 25, pp. 243–64.

Pratt, J. (1997), 'Dangerous, Inadequate, Invisible, Out', *Theoretical Criminology*, Vol. 1, pp. 363–84.

Prins, A. (1910), *La défense sociale et les transformations du droit pénal*, Bruxelles: Médecine et hygiène.

Simon, J. and Feeley, M. (1995), 'True Crime. The New Penology and Public Discourse on Crime', in T.G. Blomberg and S. Cohen (eds), *Punishment and Social Control. Essays in Honour of Sheldon Messinger*, New York: Aldine De Gruyter, pp. 147–80.

Snacken, S., Beyens, K. and Tubex, H. (1995), 'Changing Prison Populations in the Western Countries: Fate or policy?', *European Journal of Crime, Criminal Law and Criminal Justice*, Vol. 1, pp. 18–53.

Tubex, H. (1999), 'Dualisering en selectiviteit in de vrijheidsberoving. Toepassing op (levens)lang gestraften', PhD thesis, Vrije Universiteit Brussel.

Tubex, H. and Snacken, S. (1995), 'L'évolution des longues peines, aperçu international et analyse des causes', *Déviance et Société*, Vol. 19, pp. 103–26.

Tulkens, F. (1988), 'Un chapitre de l'histoire des réformateurs Adolphe Prins et la défense sociale', in F. Tulkens (ed), *Généalogie de la défense sociale en Belgique (1880–1914)*, Bruxelles: Story-Scientia, pp. 17–46.

Ugeux, G. (1955–56), 'Jules Lejeune. Ministre de la justice (1887–1894)', *Revue de Droit Pénal et de Criminologie*, pp. 3–46.

Van der Landen, D. (1992), *Straf en maatregel. Een onderzoek naar het onderscheid tussen straf en maatregel in het strafrecht*, Anhem: Gouda Quint.

Von Hirsch, A. (1976), 'Giving Criminals their Just Deserts', *Civil Liberties Review*, 3, pp. 23–35, reprinted in *Criminological Perspectives: An introduction*, London/Thousand Oaks/New Delhi: Open University/Sage Publications, pp. 315–24.

Von Hirsch, A. (1981), 'Doing Justice: The principle of commensurate deserts', in H. Gross and A. von Hirsch (eds.), *Sentencing*, Oxford: Oxford University Press, pp. 243–56.

Chapter Twenty-two

Sentencing as Performance: Restoring Drama to the Courtroom[1]

David Tait[2]

Introduction

The 'punitive turn' in criminal justice is one of the more disturbing features of contemporary western societies. Tougher sanctions imposed gleefully on disadvantaged sections of the community seem to provide an ideal social policy for opportunistic politicians, bringing jobs, votes and consumer satisfaction. Yet from a criminological perspective it is all madness: harsher sanctions increase re-offending and decrease public safety (Zimring and Hawkins 1995), while more money spent on prisons means less spent on education, and more family disruption. How can sentencing become a process that restores rather than destroys societies?

Andrew Ashworth (this volume) has laid down the challenge, arguing for the need for 'replacement discourses' of sentencing that are more effective in challenging the assumption that harsher penalties promote greater community safety. Julian Roberts (Hough and Roberts, this volume), by varying the amount of sentencing information given to the public in social surveys, provides solid evidence that a better informed public will be less vengeful. Tata (this volume) focuses on the reasoning process used by the judiciary, arguing for researchers to pay more attention to the social production of 'sentencing accounts' by judges. He argues that judges construct their interpretation of the evidence in terms of 'typical whole case stories' rather than abstract principles. All of these, in different ways, are proposing more sustained attention to the decision-making rationality involved in sentencing, by increasing information, understanding how the information is processed, and packaging the result in an accessible form.

Clearly sentencing is a highly refined science of reasoning, a deployment of language to provide a link between past behaviour and future penalty. The appeal process further refines and explicates this verbal rationality. Some of the most elegant justifications of rational sentencing program is provided by sentencing scholars such as von Hirsch (1976), and Morris and Tonry (1990). How reasoned arguments are developed and elaborated is appropriately a central issue for sentencing research.

Sentencing may also be conceptualised as a public performance invoking state power to exact, or forego, vengeance. Specifically, it can be seen as a symbolic ritual that authorises measured violence against the bodies of citizens. As Cover puts it, criminal justice system operates in the field of "pain, suffering and death". Prisoners 'willingly' walk away towards the cells because they know that if they do not walk they will be dragged (Cover 1992).

This chapter is about this other face of sentencing: the violence-invoking performance, the official ritual of denunciation or forgiveness. This type of approach had a short, but largely abortive, run in the English-speaking world during the 1970s. After an overview of some of this literature, a discussion of the seminal work of Antoine Garapon on judicial rituals will be provided, which (it is argued) provides the basis for a re-examination of the symbolic dimension of sentencing.

The chapter takes three short vignettes from different jurisdictions and styles of justice, all related to sentencing in some form, and raises some questions from these about the relevance of paying attention to the ceremonial aspect of sentencing. It will be argued that the current Anglo-American 'rational' approach to sentencing, even in its most humane and enlightened form, represents only one part of the 'human process' that is sentencing.

Degradation and Reintegration Rituals

The debate about court rituals in the Anglo-American world was seduced by Garfinkel's powerful metaphor of trials as 'degradation rituals' (Garfinkel 1965; Carlen 1976; King 1978, McBarnet 1981). This degradation was found to be standard fare, not just for defendants, but also for victims, most particularly rape victims (Edwards and Heenan 1994; Matoesian, 1993, 1995), or victims of domestic violence (Beaman 1994). It might perhaps be noted that Garfinkel himself considered that a proper understanding of status degradation ceremonies allows one to "render denunciation useless" (Garfinkel 1965, p. 424). So humiliation was not a natural and inevitable part of the process. Apart from Garfinkel's own highly evocative work, Goffman provided an additional set of insights and approaches which allowed the tricks and stratagems of legal professionals to be scrutinised and chuckled over (Goffman 1976; Carney and Tait 1997; Asma 1999). Judges and lawyers formed alliances and boundaries to exclude lay participants (Vittoria 1983). 'Ritual' was given a bad name, as a superfluous and obsolete set of practices designed to confuse and mystify ordinary people.

Countering this gloomy narrative was the optimistic voice of Braithwaite (1976), arguing for the development of 'reintegration' rituals, which provided a context in which offenders could be held accountable, shamed, but welcomed back into society. As a result of Braithwaite's work and a range of other parallel developments in 'restorative justice' (such as circle sentencing in Canada and family group conferences in New Zealand), the hearing process again became the subject of scholarly attention (see Alder and Wundersitz 1996). Proponents of this approach make a strong argument that the quality of the process is highly relevant to both the subsequent behaviour of the offender and the acceptance by victims that the thirst for vengeance has been assuaged (Sherman and Strang 2000). This argument has far wider implications for the judicial process than just the few processes identified as 'restorative'.

One issue posed by this paper (but not answered) is how to interpret the performances. Some might be correctly characterised as 'shaming' or 'reintegrative', but there are many other narratives which may be used by judges, magistrates or the various forms of lay conferences involved in sentencing (such as those discussed by Tata in this volume). Before we can conclude whether 'shaming' and 'reintegration' are the dominant features of a ceremony, we need some more general framework that allows the process to be recorded and analysed. It is argued that Garapon's work provides the basis for beginning such an analysis.

Rethinking Court Performances

Court performances take place in particular historical circumstances, in which memories, hopes, fears religious faith and prejudices may be expressed in the images and practices of justice (Jacob 1993). They occur within specific spaces frequently redolent of power, majesty and hierarchy and resonant with reminders of national history and fictional links to antiquity (Taylor 1993). Courts may be thought of as performance spaces, where judges, lawyers, juries, witnesses and others participate in a set of rituals collectively referred to as 'justice'. These rituals, including the part referred to as 'sentencing' enact, embody and enliven the law. Sentencing may be thought of as a quasi-religious social ritual, designed to restore social harmony, remedy evil and reproduce society (Garapon 1997). For Garapon, the key concept is order, preserving, undermining, proclaiming, and restoring the social order.

The repetitions, juxtapositions and deployment of familiar images and symbols in the ritual provide continuities and connections across time and within societies. Law becomes a living process connecting general principles to specific issues, formal guidelines to historically specific practices. Without the context of the living performance, justice would remain inert.

A methodological note here: 'sentencing' in the Anglophone literature is usually taken to refer to one stage of the traditional common law trial, the part when guilt has been established and judgment is being passed. In two of the three vignettes presented below, this distinction does not make sense, so the analysis will be widened to the criminal trial (or hearing) as a whole, including the part when level of culpability or responsibility is being established.

For Garapon, the trial is a symbolic drama or pageant in which the crime is re-enacted verbally through the production of evidence. The evil is named, penance and absolution provided, and the social order that had been disrupted by the crime is restored. The judge turns back the anger of the lynch mob by providing a ritual process in which their anger may be channelled, expressed and if not satisfied, at least diverted from vigilante justice. The court, acting on behalf of society, exercises its monopoly of legitimate force to authorise measured violence against the body or property of the miscreant. The court may also, again on behalf of society, exercise mercy or forgiveness. The punishment or other outcome symbolically expunges the evil represented by the crime.

One crucial question hinted at by Garapon is how to measure the success of judicial performances, or more generally court processes. How should we weigh up the value and usefulness of rituals? Which type of court performances are 'better', what institutional forms facilitate practices that are more accessible, intelligible and inclusive and more able to collect and evaluate evidence? Can there be democratic justice? Is it possible to provide a user-friendly face to the state's authorisation and apportionment of violence? The ritual drama of the court performance provides a mythical framework within which these questions may be asked.

By focusing on sentencing as a quasi-religious social ritual, Garapon forces one to reflect on the more holistic and moral aspects of sentencing. The religious imagery is useful in reminding us that we are not dealing with summing cells on a spreadsheet or filling cells in a prison. Rather, we are dealing with fundamental questions of human existence, questions of good and evil, sin and guilt, society and the individual, free will, vengeance, human frailty, pain and death.

There is also a strong practical dimension to this understanding of sentencing. If the ritual can symbolically relive the crime, it can also symbolically provide vengeance. The trial is not just a prelude to punishment, it can temper demands for revenge, or restore the social order without needing to inflict further suffering. This is the argument most relevant to understanding and responding to the 'punitive turn' in criminal justice.

This perspective is radically different from the view that sees sentencing as little more than calculation and announcement of the 'tariff'. At a time when the English-speaking word is growing sceptical about the possibilities of the sanctions imposed by sentencers making much difference, it might be thought to be adding another layer of incredulity to the argument to suggest that the process might have an important impact on offender attitudes or behaviour. But this is precisely what is proposed here; that the performance of justice can impact on the public understanding, and support for the fairness of the outcomes.

Some Illustrations of the Approach

Three short vignettes are presented, each based on a single sentence taken from a different type of sentencing hearing. The first is from a French murder trial involving a jury, the second from a diversionary conference in the Australian Capital Territory, and the third from a sentencing hearing in a large local (i.e. magistrate's) court in Sydney. Clearly one phrase cannot adequately summarise a whole case, any more than one case can represent the practices of justice in that jurisdiction. But the juxtaposition of the three phrases in their historical settings provides some useful clues about how to think about sentencing as a performance.

The focus of the brief analyses is on key moments of the process where emotions are running hot, interactions are particularly lively, or the dialogue seems to touch on the important aspects of human nature. There is a sense in which the selection is arbitrary: what is hot, lively or important may vary according to the observer. Consequently a more adequate methodology would require multiple observers, and clearer expectations about what to look for. Nevertheless in this preliminary sketch of the idea of a comparative methodology, it is useful to follow the intuitive and exploratory style of Goffman (and to a lesser extent Garfinkel) in identifying significant features of an interaction and raising questions about them.

Case Study 1: I Beg Your Pardon

The alleged murderer, a man in his 40s, was being interrogated by the presiding judge. She was thumbing through her dossier, confronting him with the evidence amassed by the investigating magistrate. The defendant was finally able to tell the world his story of how he came to have a gun, and how he came to kill an intruder who had entered the warehouse where he had been sleeping. The two associate judges and the nine lay jurors sitting around the presiding judge at the curved judicial table looked on attentively. His defence lawyer kept shaking her head and whispering unheeded advice to him. The *parti civile* (relatives of the deceased) were seated in the well of the court, looking up at the defendant across the evidence table displaying the murder weapon; the presiding judge asked them if they wanted to ask anything. They did; the ten-year old son of the victim asked an insightful question about cigarette butts which got at the question of the number of intruders. This was followed up by the presiding judge. Shortly afterwards the defendant made an insensitive remark about the victim. The presiding judge pulled him up, reminding him that the *parti civile* were present in court and deserved respect. He bowed his head a little, looked across the well of the court at the widow and son, and offered the apology 'je m'excuse' ('I beg your pardon'). The three judges later retired with the lay jurors to consider culpability and sentence.

There are several features of this exchange which deserve attention. One is that it happened at all. The ceremony includes a central place for the victim (or in the case of murder, the relatives of the victim). The courtroom had a reserved section of seating for *parti civile*, and they could actively participate in the process. Given that the defendant had admitted to firing the fatal shot, the question at issue for sentencing was one of culpability, and the *parti civile* were making their contribution to this process. The second feature of the incident was the direct exchange between the boy and the man accused of killing his father. The question was asked in the second person and the judge insisted that the apology be made directly to the family, and not through her. A third feature of the ceremony was that the defendant was able to tell his own story in his own words, without being framed by the narrative of an attorney, but one which was susceptible to challenge by those most affected by the crime.

The trial was scheduled for two days, and two days it took, thanks to careful management by the presiding judge, including selection of relevant witnesses. This was less onerous on victims than a longer trial would have been. The jury stayed in the courtroom the whole time; they were not sent out during legal arguments. The circular arrangement of the courtroom meant that the public attending the drama mostly saw the faces of those who were speaking rather than their backs.

As a public show, it was lively, dramatic and moving. Many ritual elements were in evidence here: shaming, denunciation, contrition (perhaps artificial), inclusion, and public display. The phrase 'I beg your pardon' represented the direct engagement of lay parties within the formal setting of a murder trial, and the way the suspect was being held accountable by the state both for his past deeds and his present manners.

Case Study 2: That's Just Some Free Advice

The defendant, a 15 year old boy who looked much older, had pleaded guilty to drink-driving and the magistrate asked him to stand. The magistrate noted that he himself had sons and was conscious of the temptations to drink. He chastised the boy for drinking spirits (liquor); he looked across the bench at the offender and warned: "Don't drink spirits until you are 25 – that's just some free advice". The magistrate acknowledged the presence of the young man's mother, and continued "I hope you have the manners and grace to apologise to your mother". He then passed sentence – a good behaviour bond without conviction, with required attendance at a traffic offenders program. The offender managed a couple of "Yes, sir"s as his contribution to the exchange. One of these (in reply to "have you learned your lesson?") was met with some disbelief, the magistrate pointing out that "generally kids come back – but prove it wrong in your case".

This was a solo performance. The offender was not asked to think or explain himself but required to listen to a negative evaluation of his behaviour and some 'free advice'. The punishment was effectively this verbal reprimand. The advice was 'free' in the sense that it was not formally related to the sentence, and was offered more in the magistrate's capacity as a concerned father than a judicial officer passing sentence. It was also free in the sense that the statement stood alone, without challenge or interchange. "Yes sir" was the only answer available. But the 'free' advice also provided the foundation for the offender to leave the court free of a criminal record. Effectively the magistrate was exercising his discretion to forgive the offender what in some circumstances might be considered a serious offence, in return for participating appropriately in a rite of official censure ('denunciation' or 'humiliation' do not capture the flavour of the event).

Whether delivering a stern lecture would make any different to the young man's drinking was unclear; apparently the magistrate had serious doubts. But that was what the performance of sentencing was about, the judge as stern parent talking firmly to the miscreant child, warning him of the dangers faced in pursuing a dangerous path. Such moral lectures are sometimes codified as 'cautions' within police procedures, they appear to operate in a similar way in open court.

Case Study 3: We are not Talking about Punishment

The two young offenders were seated in a circle with the 'victims' of their crime, numerous family members, a 'community representative', and two uniformed police officers running the juvenile diversionary conference. The boys had admitted engaging in a 'knock and run' incident; they had knocked on people's doors and run away. One variant on the practice was putting a water sprinkler on the front verandah, knocking on the door, then turning the hose on before the person opened the door. The boys were charged with property damage, and given the opportunity to attend a conference rather than go to a children's court. It was later established from the owner of the property in question (where the sprinkler had been used) that there was no damage. However three neighbours who had seen the boys carrying out their pranks had given chase; two of these had fallen over and hurt themselves (these were the 'victims' in attendance), and the third had caught one boy and pinned him up against a wall.

The boys confessed not just to 'knocking and running' but to causing injury by their activities, and they apologised directly to the injured chasers. The father and girlfriend of one of those who had given chase outlined the suffering caused by the injury. The discussion turned to how the boys could make up for the trouble they had caused, and various options were canvassed including mowing lawns, cleaning up rubbish and giving public talks about their activities. The offenders and their parents gladly volunteered additional tasks, as if bidding up the sanctions. The community representative reminded the gathering as these options were outlined "we are not talking about punishment". Finally everyone agreed that appropriate activities would include some community work plus speaking to six school classes about the dangers of 'knocking and running'.

The most immediately striking feature of this style of performance is its inclusiveness: everyone gets the chance to speak, there is no obvious hierarchy, and the decision is achieved (generally) by consensus. The offenders are fully included: they have a central role in the performance which involves apologising, expressing contrition, and agreeing to whatever sanctions are imposed.

The phrase "we are not talking about punishment" is in one sense obviously false: type and quantum of sanction was precisely what was being negotiated, as in any other sentencing hearing. Community work imposed by consensus is no less a punishment than community work imposed by a judge. And yet the statement is also true in the sense that the activities proposed were not talked about in terms of inflicting pain on the defendants but rather as providing a way to welcome them back into society. The phrase "not talking about punishment" was positioning the diversionary conference as the 'other' to the juvenile court. One provided 'punishment', the other tried to deliver 'restorative justice'.

Conclusions

The above discussion has highlighted the importance of acknowledging the performative aspect of sentencing. In both the murder trial and the conference, the defendants were required to perform, specifically to be articulate and put on a good verbal show. They were expected to explain their behaviour, show remorse, indicate respect for the victims. Whether this form of inclusiveness was to compound their disgrace by exposing them to public scrutiny, or relieve their anxiety by ensuring they understood what was happening, is one of the issues that would need to be explored. Both sentencing hearings provided opportunities for the offenders and the victims to speak. In one case a panel of three professional judges and nine jurors retired to work out a sentence, in the other the victims and offenders participated in the process.

If verbal engagement of lay participants characterised these two types of hearing, polite silence was the expected mode of behaviour during the drink-driving sentencing hearing. The only performance was by the magistrate; but it was this ritual of verbal chastisement that provided the foundation for forgiveness, a good behaviour bond without conviction.

The disparity in sanction between the conference and the court might be noted. In the conference the offenders agreed to put in a substantial amount of time to make up for the 'damage' they had done. In the second, the offender was released without any demands on his time or finances, for a more serious offence. The point of this comparison is not to make a general claim about patterns within either jurisdiction, but to point out the irony of a system which was designed to avoid punitiveness providing the opportunity for relatively harsh sanctions, while a 'traditional' system displays its flexibility, by mixing displays of authority with mercy.

One feature of the criminal trial that Garapon points out is the way violence is an integral part of the process: the crime, the symbolic reliving of the crime, and the prospect of further, state-sanctioned, violence to provide atonement. In the case of the French jury trial, violence permeates the images and practices of the court, including the confinement of the defendant, the presence of family members of the deceased, the control of proceedings by the judge, the threat of prison, even the prominent display of the murder weapon under glass in the centre of the court. It is at least a plausible hypothesis that this display of violent symbolism when combined with a colourful and speedy performance, and a high level of inclusiveness both of defendant and victims, can enhance the intelligibility of the process and the plausibility of any decisions that emerge from it. And perhaps, it can be added, reduce the public clamour for revenge, since symbolic revenge in a powerful and dramatic form has already been achieved. Whether or not a more inclusive, intelligible and well-managed trial process could reduce public punitiveness is an open question, but given the emotional character of public opinion about crime, it makes sense to look at the forum where such emotion could be at its most intense.

Violence is also present in a more modest and limited way in the drink-driving sentencing hearing. The defendant is required to stand and listen to his behaviour being severely criticised without the right of reply. The magistrate exercises his authority by offering unsolicited advice. The threat of serious penalty is offered as a spectre, then the threat is lifted.

But where is the violence in the conference? Perhaps the violence is in the subtle coercion to confess, to 'take responsibility' and to offer to make amends. Or in the sanctions, the 'non-punishments' that are negotiated. The violence of the state is hidden behind the inclusiveness of the rituals; or is it that the full horror of the crime (where there are real crimes) can be expressed openly and the emotions relived by the participants? Shaming may be one of the aspects of the performance, but so too could trust, ambivalence, envy, relief, gratuitous adult advice, and the 'voluntary' confessions characteristic of religions penance or show trials. Precisely how the performances should be understood is open to debate, and cannot be conclusively decided from the short selected extracts presented here. The point is that the performances are complex, varied and may have consequences for public acceptability of justice (as Garapon argues) and possibly even the future behaviour of offenders (as Braithwaite and colleagues argue).

So it can be argued that all three cases (and in particular the three key phrases) represent different ways of incorporating and representing violence. But each allows violence to be symbolically presented in a way that potentially allows penal severity to be curtailed.

Notes

1   The paper forms part of a larger project, carried out with Antoine Garapon and Katherine Fischer Taylor, which compares judicial rituals and practices across a range of jurisdictions. The project is attempting to operationalise Garapon's theoretical arguments about the way correct rituals produce justice. This article touches on two of his claims: the importance of inclusive rituals, and the dangers of 'informal justice'.

2   The author wishes to thank the following colleagues for ideas, discussions and shared empirical ventures into courts: Antoine Garapon, Katherine Fischer Taylor, and Rick Mohr. Funding for the fieldwork was provided by the Institut des Hautes Études sur la Justice, Paris, and the University of Wollongong (with Rick Mohr).

Bibliography

Alder, C. and Wundersitz, J. (eds) (1994), *Family Conferencing and Juvenile Justice: The way forward or misplaced optimism?*, Canberra: Australian Institute of Criminology.

Asma, D. (1999), 'Genuflecting at the Bench: Rituals of power and the power of rituals in American courts', *Red Feather Journal of Postmodern Criminology*, 5, http://www.tryoung.com/journal-pomocrim/pomocrimindex.html (accessed 12 July 2000).

Beaman, H. (1996), 'Abused Women and Legal Discourse: The exclusionary power of legal method', *Canadian Journal of Law and Society*, Vol. 1, No. 1, pp. 125–39.

Braithwaite, J. (1989), *Crime, Shame and Reintegration*, New York: Cambridge University Press.

Carlen, P. (1976), *Magistrates' Justice*, London: Martin Robertson and Co.

Carlen, P. (1978), 'The Staging of Magistrates' Justice', in J. Baldwin and A. Bottomley (eds), *Criminal Justice: Selected readings*, London: Martin Robertson and Co.

Carlen, P. (1979), 'Control in a Magistrates' Court', in C. Campbell and P. Wiles (eds), *Law and Society*, Oxford: Martin Robertson and Co.

Carney, T. and Tait, D. (1997) *An Experiment in Popular Justice: Adult guardianship in Australia*, Sydney: Federation Press.

Cohen, G.D. (1999), 'Comparing the Investigating Grand Jury with the French System of Criminal Investigations: A judge's perspective and commentary', *Temple International and Comparative Law Journal*, Vol. 13 No. 1, pp. 87–105.

Conley, J. and O'Barr, W. (1990), *Rules vs Relationships: The ethnography of legal discourse*, Chicago: University of Chicago Press.

Cover, R. (1992) 'Violence and the Word', in M. Minow, M. Ryan and A. Sarat (eds), *Narrative, Violence and the Law: The collected essays of Robert Cover*, Michigan, Ann Arbor: University of Michigan Press, pp. 203–38.

Edwards, A. and Heenan, M. (1994), 'Rape Trials in Victoria: Gender, socio-cultural factors and justice', *Australian and New Zealand Journal of Criminology*, Vol. 27, pp. 213–35.

Garapon, A. (1997), *Bien Juger: essai sur le ritual judiciaire*, Paris: Editions Odile Jacob.

Garfinkel, H. (1965), 'Conditions of Successful Degradation Ceremonies', *American Journal of Sociology*, Vol. 61, pp. 420–24.

Goffman, E. (1967), *Interaction Ritual*, Harmondsworth: Penguin.

Hogarth, J. (1971), *Sentencing as a Human Process*, Toronto: University of Toronto Press.

Hutton, N. (1987), 'The Sociological Analysis of Courtroom Interaction: A review essay', *Australian and New Zealand Journal Of Criminology*, Vol. 20.

Hutton, Neil (1995), 'Sentencing, Rationality, and Computer Technology', *Journal of Law and Society*, Vol. 22, No. 4 pp. 549–70.

Jacob, R. (1994), *Images de la justice. Essai sur l'iconographie judiciaire du Môyen Âge a l'Âge classique*, Paris: Le Leopard d'Or.

King, M. (1978), 'Mad Dances and Magistrates', *New Society*, Vol. 45, No. 832, pp. 564–6.

Konradi, A. (1996), 'Preparing to Testify: Rape survivors negotiating the criminal justice process', *Gender and Society*, Vol. 10, No. 4, pp. 404–32.

Lees, S. (1996), *Carnal Knowledge: Rape on trial*, London: Hamish Hamilton.

McBarnet, D. (1981) 'Conviction', in D. Brown et al. (eds), *Criminal Laws, 1*, Sydney: Federation Press.

McBarnet, D. (1981) 'Two Tiers of Justice', in D.J. McBarnet (ed.), *Conviction: Law, the State and the Construction of Justice*, London: Macmillan Press.

McBarnet, D. (1983), 'Victim in the Witness Box: Confronting victimology's stereotype', *Contemporary Crises*, Vol. 7.

Morris, N. and Tonry, M. (1990), *Between Prison and Probation: Intermediate punishments in a rational sentencing system*, New York: Oxford University Press.

Nicholson, R.D. (1995) 'The Courts, the Media and the Community', *Journal of Judicial Administration*, Vol. 5.

Roberts, J.V. and Stalans, L.J. (1997), *Public Opinion, Crime and Criminal Justice*, Boulder, CO: Westview Press.

Rock, P. (1991), 'Witnesses and Space in a Crown Court', *British Journal of Criminology*, Vol. 31, No. 3, pp. 266–79.

Sherman, L and Strang, H. (2000), Preliminary Report of the Reintegrative Shaming Experiment, Australian National University.

Taylor, K.F. (1993), *In the Theater of Criminal Justice*, Princeton, NJ: Princeton University Press.

Vittoria, A. (1992), 'The Elderly Guardianship Hearing: A socio-legal encounter', *Journal of Aging Studies*, Vol. 6, No. 2, pp. 165–90.

Von Hirsch, A. (1976), *Doing Justice: The choice of punishments*, New York: Hill and Wang.

Zimring, F. and Hawkins, G. (1995), *Incapacitation: Penal confinement and the restraint of crime*, New York: Oxford University Press.

PART V
DOING JUSTICE:
POWER, EQUALITY AND
EQUITY

Chapter Twenty-three

Sentencing Policy and Racial Justice

Doris Marie Provine

Introduction

The elimination of race as a consideration in arrest, prosecution, and sentencing is an important objective in modern campaigns for criminal justice reform. This commitment rests on basic principles about which there is social consensus. When the government discriminates by race, it undermines fundamental commitments to fairness and equality for all citizens and erodes public confidence in the rule of law. Racism by government officials acting with or without legal authority offends ideas of individual liberty and limited, evenhanded government.

Racial neutrality in criminal justice, however, is proving an elusive goal. Nowhere is this more obvious than in the United States, where recent criminal justice reforms seem to have exacerbated, rather than reduced, racial disadvantage. Both the numbers and the percentage of African-Americans in US prisons have climbed sharply and steadily since the late 1970s, when the states and federal government began to undertake major changes in the manner by which offenders would be sentenced and the standards that would be applied. Prison populations immediately began to grow, more than doubling between 1985 and 1998; the total is currently in excess of 2 million people. African Americans, who account for only about 12 per cent of the population, now constitute 53 per cent of new admissions to prison; their rate of incarceration is 8.2 times higher than that for whites (Human Rights Watch 2000). About one in every 11 black males in his late 20s was serving a sentence of a year or more in state or federal prison in 1999. These are historic highs.

The United States is a particularly interesting case for several reasons. The reduction of racial discrimination in criminal justice has been a central goal in the government's reform efforts, providing a much-touted rationale for drastically overhauling sentencing systems at both the state and federal levels. Legislators have become actively involved in sentencing, creating administrative bodies to determine appropriate penalties and sometimes acting directly to establish specific, minimum sentences for particular crimes. Judges have lost much of the virtually unfettered sentencing discretion they had enjoyed during the first 200 years of the nation's experience. The expectation was that the shift to more standardised approaches would reduce or eliminate the impact of irrelevant personal factors like race in sentencing.

Reforms like these are being enacted in many countries because crime control is popular with voters. Legislatures are looking for ways to sound tough, but fair, on crime. Reforming sentencing laws to establish greater uniformity in punishments is an obvious and politically inexpensive strategy. Proportionality promises equity and transparency in punishment. The old system of individualised justice was not well understood by ordinary citizens and has few defenders, except among judges and defence attorneys, who carry little political clout. The experience of the United States in sentencing reform is thus worth examining because similar reforms have been enacted elsewhere, for similar reasons, and with a similar commitment to equal treatment for all citizens.

Finally, the US experience deserves study because the nation appears to have strong feedback mechanisms in place that should ensure a fit between policy experience and policy goals. Public officials are necessarily aware of the changing racial demographics in US prisons, and this information is freely available to the public. The situation has attracted considerable attention from human-rights organisations and from activists, academics and journalists (e.g. Miller 1996; Cole 1999; Donziger 1996; Kennedy,1997). Judges are involved because constitutional standards give them authority to overturn racially discriminatory practices. The 14th amendment to the US constitution guarantees that no state shall "deny to any person within its jurisdiction the equal protection of the laws".

How could sentencing reforms designed to reduce racism have created a sentencing regime that incarcerates more African-Americans than at any time in the nation's history? The US experience demonstrates that eliminating racial disadvantage in criminal justice requires more than neutral laws and elimination of broad judicial discretion to set sentences. The reduction of judicial sentencing discretion, in fact, seems to have accentuated racial disadvantage. The American experience also reveals a disturbing lack of public, political, and legal reaction to the extraordinary growth of the non-white prison population. Politicians deny the significance of these numbers, implicitly suggesting that African-Americans are simply more prone to crime. Judges have declared the changing racial make-up of prisons constitutionally irrelevant, demanding proof of intent to discriminate. Even public debate among ordinary Americans, unconstrained by legal niceties or political opportunism, reflects uncertainty about what to do. An important question then is why the dramatic rise in black imprisonment has failed to impress the American public and policy makers that something must be done about sentencing. This case appears to be an exception to the usual logic in which negative experience with a policy ultimately encourages its makers to change the rules.

One problem is that there is little public support in the United States for honest dialogue about race in public policy. Public opinion data suggest that while the impulse to discriminate has diminished in the American public, the nation is still divided – by race – over what to do about institutional practices that maintain or exacerbate racial inequality (Schuman et al. 1997). Politicians have no firm footing in this terrain. Any policy maker would be tempted to avoid the morass of conflicting opinion and widespread uncertainty about the racial consequences of legislation. It is easier to treat the numbers of blacks in prison as a regrettable, but unavoidable, fact.

The failure of the political leadership to respond effectively to the alarming growth in black imprisonment reveals, not just division over the existence of racial discrimination in American society and disagreement about how to deal with it, but also a national character trait associated with liberal individualism. The well-known American bias toward individualistic explanations for personal success and failure downplays the role of social, situational, and structural forces, including racism, to explain social patterns. As long as there is formal and individual equality, there is a tendency to turn a blind eye to substantive inequality. It is easy to blame growing racial imbalance in US prisons on the prisoners themselves.

The bias toward individualism also distorts popular understanding of what racism entails. The tendency is to assume that there is a significant intentional component in racism, sexism, and other forms of discrimination. 'Racism', in particular, tends to be understood in historical terms, as white prejudice against other races coupled with a dangerous willingness to tolerate or use violence to enforce the white-dominant racial order. A familiar reference point is white attitudes and behaviours in the deep south of the pre-civil rights era. The assumption that racism cannot occur without intention tends to make discussion of policy impact difficult. Criticising a policy on the basis of its racial impact comes dangerously close, in the American political tradition, to suggesting that racial prejudice was involved in drafting the law. There is little middle ground in this conversation.

The tendency to blame individuals for their problems and to focus on formal, rather than substantive, equality affects other racially charged issues besides sentencing. Public agencies at every level are being criticised for the racially disproportionate burdens they require some groups of citizens to bear and the advantages they bestow on other groups. Invariably, the laws and regulations in question are neutral on their face. And, in contrast to the rules condemned in an earlier generation of civil rights activism, the outcome is never complete separation by race, but rather disproportionate racial impact. Consider, for example, the decisions associated with siting schools, waste dumps, and other forms of public investment. Another relevant context concerns minimum standards of behaviour or performance, including academic or job performance. The racial consequences of the nation's war on drugs, the focus of this chapter, is a particularly difficult case because it involves activities that nearly everyone condemns, and because it is directed toward a stratum of society that is politically inert and socially marginal.

The situation confronting the United States is of tragic proportions. There will be long-term consequences for failure to do something about an increasingly black prison population. The impact on minority communities is significant and confidence in the criminal justice system is dangerously low among non-white Americans. Formal equality and the appearance of racial neutrality in legislation cannot obscure the inequality evidenced by the skewed racial demographics of imprisonment. The growing number of prisoners also creates new constituencies for ever-harsher punishments among prison builders and the communities that look to new prisons for employment. Finally, the failure to engage, politically and legally, with growing black imprisonment marks a fundamental failure of our constitutional system. The political system seems to lack, not just the will to engage in a serious debate about racial justice, but the necessary vocabulary. The missing link, this chapter suggests, is a broad-based appreciation for the way racism works in law.

The lessons that can be drawn from one nation's experience are inevitably limited. Race relations in the United States are the product of a long history. Policy making processes and policy evaluation procedures also grow out of historical commitments and particular institutional arrangements. The issues raised by the aftermath of US sentencing reforms are nevertheless of general significance. The problem of neutral-appearing laws that put disproportionate burdens on already disadvantaged groups is common in all nations and raises fundamental questions about whether racial justice entails more than adherence to a neutral standard in crime and punishment. The United States may be an outlier in the extent to which it has been able to ignore the problem of substantive inequality in sentencing, but the dilemma it faces is widely shared.

Why Sentencing Reform has had a Racial Impact

The drug war, more than anything else, is responsible for the growing proportion of African-Americans in prison. Drug offenders now account for 21 per cent of all state and about 60 per cent of all federal prisoners, an estimated 400,000 people, nearly one quarter of the total incarcerated population in the US (Bureau of Justice Statistics 1999; Human Rights Watch 2000). The annual rate of drug arrests tripled between 1980 and 1997, and the rate of commitment to state prison quintupled in that period (Human Rights Watch 2000). The implementation of the anti-drug initiative has been selective, focusing particularly on crack cocaine, and particularly on African-Americans. Blacks make up 63 per cent of drug offenders sent to state prisons; in two states they make up over 90 per cent of new admissions. At the federal level, over 90 per cent of those convicted for using or selling crack are African Americans, and these cases make up a majority of all drug convictions. Sentences for crack offences are long; possession alone carries a mandatory prison term (five years) under federal law.

The impact of such laws on disadvantaged black communities has been devastating. The particular severity of the crack penalties and the resources provided for arrests has encouraged police to make apprehension of crack dealers and users a top priority. Arrests are easiest in poor urban neighbour-hoods. The result has been increased police surveillance in black neighbourhoods, racially targeted drug-courier profiling on streets and highways, and, with the help of the courts, the easing of rules on searches and stops. There is also evidence of race discrimination in the processing of cases (see Mustard 2000). All have contributed to the pattern of rising levels of black imprisonment (see Cole 1999; Miller 1996). In some communities nearly half of the young males are either in prison or are under some form of supervision from the criminal justice system. There is every sign that the trend toward an increasingly black prison population will continue.

The war on drugs is being fought on both the state and federal level, with the states tending to incarcerate for a broader range of violations, but for shorter periods of time. The total number of people in state prisons, consequently, is much higher than in federal prisons. Nevertheless, the severity of the federal law and the leadership role federal officials have taken in keeping the drug war alive make it the obvious choice for this analysis. The federal approach to drug law reform has been mixed, with both mandatory minimum legislation and the US Sentencing Commission playing important roles. Mandatory minimum laws are simple, blunt, sentencing formulae for punishing offenders based on the quantity of drugs they deal or carry. Mandatory minimums thus are based on the narrowest possible grounds for sentencing; the circumstances of the crime or criminal are irrelevant.

The federal sentencing commission works from a much different approach. As noted earlier, the objective of sentencing commissions is to develop punishments proportionate to the crime and criminal. Congress created the Sentencing Commission with the 1984 Sentencing Reform Act and charged it with creating mandatory guidelines for the whole range of federal crimes. Before the Commission could implement its guideline system, however, Congress passed the 1986 Anti-Drug Abuse Act, a statute mandating minimum penalties for a variety of drug offences, including 10 years of imprisonment for a person convicted of possession with intent to distribute 50 grams or more of crack cocaine. In adopting these mandatory minimums Congress appears to have reacted to the tremendous publicity the media was giving to the menace of crack cocaine (Baum 1996). In 1988, just as the Sentencing Commission's guidelines system was getting underway, Congress added another important mandatory minimum: five years imprisonment for simple possession of 1–5 grams of crack cocaine. These laws give federal prosecutors considerable discretion in selecting cases for prosecution as federal crimes, with higher penalties than are generally available under state law.

Mandatory minimum laws, it might be objected, are not really sentencing-reform legislation. They represent a political response to a real or imagined crisis in public order. It is true that Congress enacted mandatory minimums for various drug offences in a highly political matter, acting quickly and severely, without much consultation with experts. It must also be presumed that Congress meant to let its mandatory minimums override the Sentencing Commission's more deliberate, balancing approach to penalties in crack cases. From the perspective of those who voted to change the law, these actions, however ill-considered, must nevertheless be denominated 'reforms' if the word is to carry its normal meaning.

The mandatory minimums complicated the work of the Sentencing Commission, both because they set forth penalties by legislative fiat, but also because they were formulated without regard for individual culpability and criminal history, critical variables in the highly-nuanced guideline system. Congress gave no guidance on how to reconcile these legislative mandates, so the Commission superimposed the mandatory minimums on its sentencing grid, creating much higher penalties than it would have otherwise employed for all crack-related offences. The upshot was highly differentiated sentencing by drug type, with penalties for crack vastly higher than those for other illegal drugs, including powder cocaine, crack's pharmacological twin. Federal law punishes possession and sale of one gram of crack as harshly as possession and sale of 100 grams of powder. A repeat crack offender can get life imprisonment without the possibility of parole.

What makes this gap significant is the racial make-up of the two offender populations. Powder cocaine attracts a significant middle class white clientele, while crack is a drug of the poor inner cities. Powder is more difficult to transport, tends to be sold in larger, more expensive, quantities, and provides a less immediate and intense high than crack. The upshot is that more whites than blacks are arrested for offences involving powder cocaine, while the opposite is true of crack. Law enforcement practices and priorities almost certainly make the association between African-Americans and crack look even stronger. Nearly everyone prosecuted for crack is African-American. In Los Angles between 1988 and 1994, for example, blacks and Hispanics constituted 100 per cent of the federal drug prosecutions. That disproportion prompted a lawsuit challenging the government's criteria for selecting cases for federal prosecution.

The question examined here, it will be recalled, is not how the federal government arrived at the drug sanctions it employs, but why it has been so resistant to criticism based on the clearly racially-disproportionate impact of drug laws. One thing is clear: the problem is not official lack of awareness about the racial patterns of enforcement or use of illegal drugs. Indeed federal agencies keep close track of the percentage of blacks and whites arrested and sentenced for drug offences. The federal government also estimates the frequency with which various racial and ethnic groups use drugs. The Department of Health and Human Services regularly conducts a national household survey of drug use that analyses drug use by race and ethnic group. The Substance Abuse and Mental Health Services Administration even publishes prevention resource guides targeted to specific racial and ethnic groups, including, not just African-Americans, but also Asians, Pacific Islanders, and Caucasians.

These studies reveal that white and black Americans do not differ significantly in their propensity to ingest illegal drugs. The racial differences are in the drugs people use, and possibly in the propensity to deal drugs. As noted above, African-Americans appear to use more crack cocaine than whites, while whites tend to use more powder cocaine. Racial differences in the propensity to deal drugs can be traced to racial differences in barriers to full economic opportunity, such as poverty, lack of education, and geographical isolation. Drug dealing may be a plausible employment opportunity for the most desperate elements in society, a pattern that exists in all morals crimes, e.g. prostitution. A relevant question then is why selling drugs is more culpable than buying them.

A sentencing regime that punishes black-dominated types of drug offences much more heavily than white-dominated offences suggests racially discriminatory legislation. Nevertheless, not one federal appellate court has supported defence contentions that the drug laws, specifically the vastly different sentences prescribed for crack and power cocaine, infringe equal-protection guarantees, and the Justice Department has strongly defended the conduct of its agents, the US attorneys, in litigation challenging prosecutorial decisions for racial bias (Provine 1998). The President's Office of National Drug Control Policy did not even address the issue in its 10-year plan (1998). Only the federal Sentencing Commission has engaged substantively with the racism critique, and its response has taken some odd turns that will be explored later in this chapter.

The Role of the Courts in Maintaining Inequality

One should perhaps not be surprised that American public opinion is divided on the moral significance of rising black imprisonment, nor that legislators have ignored the situation. The role appellate courts have played in deflecting equal protection challenges to federal drug sentencing rules, however, deserves explanation. Litigation has been a significant battleground in the historic struggle against racism in the United States. Supreme Court decisions have helped to define racism in constitutional terms, thus identifying the nation's obligations as well as the evil that must be stamped out. Herein lies the problem.

Constitutional law has reinforced the tendency to conceptualise racism in terms of bad intentions, rather than racially disproportionate impact. In the early civil rights era, when the objective of most litigation before the Supreme Court was to dismantle racial apartheid, the Court quite naturally focused on the intentions of the legislature and other legal decision-makers. Discriminatory actions provided an obvious and morally compelling basis for judicial intervention to protect the 14th Amendment right of black citizens to equal protection of the law.

The practical problem was to get beyond the official denials of racial animus. This often involved talking about impact, but always in the context of bad intentions. Officials might deny discriminating, but the evidence of racial exclusion spoke louder than their words. The courts would rely on the rule's racially exclusionary impact to establish that it effectively disenfranchised black citizens. The absence of black voters in a district, for example, might be used to undermine the credibility of local officials who claimed their rules were neutral. This stratagem worked because white racism was the only plausible explanation for the absence of blacks from benefits of citizenship like voting, jury service, and public services. It was significant that these cases tended to arise in a region of the nation where whites had held black slaves, and had, since emancipation, used law to preserve white hegemony.

In adjudicating cases arising outside the old south, courts have been more circumspect about the constitutional significance of racially disproportionate impact. A key precedent is *Washington v Davis*, a 1976 case questioning the constitutionality, on equal-protection grounds, of a hiring test that disqualified a greater proportion of black than white applicants. The court found the test constitutional, despite its impact. In articulating a rationale for its decision, the court reviewed prior cases involving school desegregation, legislative apportionment, jury service, and distribution of public benefits, all areas in which racially disproportionate impact has been used to argue that rules and statutes that look neutral are in fact discriminatory. The court claimed that it had been consistent in requiring a persuasive demonstration of discriminatory intent. The impact of a statute or rule might be used to infer that purpose, but it had no independent significance:

> Necessarily, an invidious discriminatory purpose may often be inferred from the totality of the relevant facts, including the fact, if it is true, that the law bears more heavily on one race than another ... Nevertheless, we have not held that a law, neutral on its face and serving ends otherwise within the power of government to pursue, is invalid under the Equal Protection Clause simply because it may affect a greater proportion of one race than another. Disproportionate impact is not irrelevant, but it is not the sole touchstone of an invidious racial discrimination forbidden by the Constitution (p. 242).

The court admitted that this line of demarcation had not always been clear. It summarised its reading of previous cases in guarded, negative terms: "Our cases have not embraced the proposition that a law or other official act, without regard to whether it reflects a racially discriminatory purpose, is unconstitutional solely because it has a racially disproportionate impact" (ibid.).

The court went a significant step further in circumscribing its consideration of both impact and intent when it decided *McCleskey v Kemp*, a death penalty appeal. The issue this time was not racially motivated exclusion from benefits, but the differential imposition of burdens. McCleskey charged that Georgia's standards for determining who would receive the death penalty, which appear neutral, are in fact discriminatory, as evidenced by their impact. Statistical analysis showed that both the race of the murderer and the race of the victim were associated with the imposition of the death penalty. McCleskey provided no evidence of discriminatory decision-making in his own case, nor could he point to discriminatory intent at any particular point in the prosecution and punishment of those accused of murder. The case is famous for accepting the statistical evidence, but rejecting the constitutional claim. Racially disproportionate impact alone, the court reasoned, is not evidence of discriminatory intent. But the court went further in this discussion, suggesting that even if the Georgia legislature had been aware that its rules might disadvantage certain racial groups, it was under no constitutional obligation to avoid this effect. The constitution's equal protection guarantee extends only to intentional discrimination. Quoting in part from an earlier case the court stated:

> 'Discriminatory purpose' implies more than intent as volition or intent as awareness of consequences. It implies that the decisionmaker, in this case a state legislature, selected or reaffirmed a particular course of action at least in part 'because of' not merely 'in spite of' its adverse effects upon an identifiable group.' For this claim to prevail, McCleskey would have to prove that the Georgia Legislature enacted or maintained the death penalty statute because of an anticipated racially discriminatory effect (p. 298).

The reasoning in *McCleskey* forecloses serious consideration of sentencing rules associated with growing black imprisonment. Without evidence of specific intent to discriminate, there is no case. Impact has been rendered almost constitutionally irrelevant. This became clear in a series of lower court challenges to federal sentencing rules associated with crack and powder cocaine. The challengers were able to show that the huge differential in punishments prescribed for similar drug offences had a racially disproportionate impact. They occasionally won at the trial level, but consistently lost on appeal for lack of evidence that Congress intended to discriminate when it created particularly harsh penalties for possession and sale of crack cocaine.

The Supreme Court's unwillingness to factor racially disproportionate impact into its thinking about the equal protection of law is unfortunate, as is its extraordinarily narrow interpretation of its self-imposed intent requirement. Courts not only resolve disputes about public policy; they also help to set the terms of policy debate. Adjudication requires courts to articulate standards that might otherwise remain inchoate in society. The courts thereby help to set the framework for debate, even those that occur without reference to legal standards. The fundamental problem with the response of the judiciary to disproportionate racial impact, however, is further reinforcement of the widespread tendency to see racism only in terms of clearly intended action.

Implicit Limits in the Critique of Current Policy

Even those most critical of the drug war run into problems when they discuss the psychology of discrimination. Drug war critics, unlike the courts, find great significance in the disproportionate imprisonment of African-Americans for drug crimes. How, they ask, can such pernicious consequences be explained? Policy makers must have known exactly what they were doing. Increased black imprisonment must have been deemed an acceptable consequence of the politically popular combination of harsh sentencing reforms aimed particularly at inner-city blacks and increased prison construction that benefited the largely white, rural communities where the new prisons have been constructed (Tonry 1995; NYT). The failure of government to change these policies once their effects became evident reflects a deep racial animus running through American society (see, e.g. Cose 1997; Cole 1999; Christenson 1998). This critique gains persuasive power when cast in broad historical terms. Drug wars in the United States have always had a racial subtext, with Chinese and Mexican immigrants once playing the scapegoat role now foisted upon urban blacks (Musto 1987; Gordon 1994; Chambliss 1995; for a similar interpretation of the Canadian experience see Mosher 1998).

Diana Gordon's book *The Return of the Dangerous Classes: Drug prohibition and policy politics* (1994), exemplifies this almost conspiratorial perspective. Gordon suggests that politicians have undertaken the contemporary war on drugs, not to protect society, but in order to serve a covert racial agenda that stigmatises blacks to gain white support (see also Baggins 1998; Baum 1996; Lusane 1991). Playing upon white fears of black criminality, sexuality, and licentiousness, public officials draw upon evocative, racially-coded symbols of predatory drug dealers and dissipated users, avoiding politically unacceptable explicit racial appeals. Examples of the same phenomenon in other contexts include presidential candidate Bush's use of the image of rapist Willie Horton against his rival in the 1992 campaign, and President Reagan's talk of welfare queens in the early years of the debate over welfare reform. Congress and the executive stand to gain in a similar way from being oblivious to the racial consequences of the war on drugs. They can even justify their inaction as a form of concern for law-abiding African-Americans endangered by drug dealers and addicts. The racial dimensions of the drug war thus become a wedge issue dividing blacks from whites and upwardly-mobile blacks from other members of their communities.

This explanation has significant rhetorical appeal. It is simple and it covers the necessary ground, offering both a rationale for current policy and a clear moral position. This take on the war on drugs is also deeply pessimistic, drawing as it does from America's troubled racial history to suggest that white racism has not faded, but has simply taken new forms. The role of politicians is self serving: they play to, and perhaps accentuate, latent white racism and racial fears. The judicial branch participates by inaction, signalling either complicity or extraordinary weakness in the face of this evil. Whether or not these public officials are themselves racists by personal inclination is unclear and perhaps unimportant.

Anyone distressed about the racial dimensions of the drug war would be quite understandably drawn to an explanation that rests straightforwardly on political exploitation of white racism and white fears. As public policy, the drug war has obviously failed to stop the sale and ingestion of illegal drugs. It is hard to understand how so much money can be spent so ineffectively without public outrage and without deep concern on the part of public officials, especially when the consequences of the policy are so cruel (Ryan 1998). Although there is no way to test the hypothesis, it seems obvious that if middle class white communities were affected by the drug war in the way that poor black communities are, this highly punitive approach to illegal drugs would be changed.

While political opportunism undoubtedly sustains the drug war, theorising about a covert racial agenda raises certain analytical problems. Evidence that the drug war was undertaken in order to repress blacks is indirect. Even the judges who have been most sympathetic to defence contentions that the racially-disproportionate impact of the war is constitutionally significant have found no evidence of racial animus in the debate and deliberation surrounding these laws. Consider, for example, Michael Tonry's analysis, which masterfully draws upon evidence that Congress should have known better. Tonry poses a series of questions:

> The crucial question is whether the architects of the War on Drugs should be held morally accountable for the havoc they have wrought among disadvantaged

members of minority groups. The answer is that they should, and this section explains why. Three sets of issues arise. First, were the disparate impacts on black Americans foreseeable? The only possible answer, as the data presented in the following sections demonstrate beyond peradventure of doubt, is yes, they knew what they were doing. Second, putting aside its disparate impact implications, were there valid grounds for believing that the war's prohibitionistic approach would diminish drug trafficking and drug use? Third, is there any arguable basis for justifying the war's foreseeable effects on black Americans? (1995, pp. 104–5).

Tonry's answer to these latter questions is 'no'. Yet while he finds no excuse for how Congress has acted in creating, financing, and continuing the drug war, he finesses the question of racist intent, labelling it 'malign neglect'.

Others have also struggled with the inadequacy of easily available terms like 'racist' and 'racism' to describe the legislative role in the war on drugs. David Cole, for example, states that his purpose in describing the double-standard that operates in criminal justice generally (and in the drug war in particular) is not just "to shake the confidence of those who believe the system is fair", but also "to demonstrate to those more sceptical of the system that the problems cannot be explained by simple charges of racism, and cannot be solved by banning intentional racism from the system" (1999, p. 10). Lieberman and others distinguish 'institutional' and 'structural' racism from personal animus directed against people of other races in discussing racially disproportionate impacts in public policy (Lieberman 1998; Wineat 1998). In *US v Clary* a federal judge took the unusual approach of describing the motivation animating drug-war politics as 'unconscious racism' (1994, p. 78).

These efforts to distinguish varieties of racism are inevitably imprecise and therefore somewhat unsatisfying (Winant 1998, pp. 757–8). 'Racism' is a term too historically freighted with the potential for action to sit easily next to modifiers like 'structural' or 'institutional' or 'unconscious'. What is needed is a broader understanding of the basic term. 'Racism' should be redefined to mean, not just active, mindful racial hostility, but also unconscious racial stereotyping, self-serving pandering to racial fears without admitting the consequences, and other half-thought-out habits of thought and action that callously disregard the best interests of African Americans and other racial minorities. Racism, in short, can be unconscious and inadvertent as well as conscious and intentional.

Limited Vision in Official Circles: An Illustration

Criticism of the drug war in official circles is infinitely more muted than among activists, academics, and journalists. The significance of this inside-Washington debate lies in its narrowness and ineffectiveness. It is clear that both defenders of the policy and its critics have worked from a conception of racism that includes only intended action. This shared understanding shaped and diminished the debate. Officials critical of the sentencing rules have in general taken care to avoid suggesting that the results could have been foreseen. Defenders of the sentencing rules have nevertheless heard themselves accused of racism, no matter how mild the policy critique. Their vehement denials of racial motivation in pursuing the war on drugs allowed them to finesse the troublesome reality of its racial impact.

The Federal Sentencing Commission has been at the centre of what little serious discussion has occurred concerning the racial consequences of federal drug law penalties. The issue emerged in the early 1990s, as the increasing numbers of African-Americans sentenced for drug offences began to be noted. Defence lawyers helped to bring the issue to the Commission's attention. Many of them were pursuing arguments that the high federal penalties for crack cocaine in comparison to powder violated constitutional guarantees. The Commission quite appropriately took an interest in these claims; it even issued a report discussing the relevant cases and outcomes. A few members of Congress also had a role in bringing the issue to the fore. They had been alerted to the racially skewed pattern of drug prosecutions in the towns and cities in their districts by interested citizens and by some of the families of those prosecuted for drug crimes. The racial disparities these observers reported were striking. In some jurisdictions, reportedly, no whites at all were being prosecuted for drug offences, and in others, federal authorities appeared to be singling out blacks for federal prosecution. Under pressure to respond, Congress directed the Sentencing Commission to study the matter and make recommendations.

The Commission was embarrassed by the racial impact of its drug penalties, but it did not really feel responsible. The Commission blamed Congress for imposing unreasonable mandatory minimum penalties for the possession or sale of tiny quantities of crack cocaine. The Commission had been forced to abandon its effort to achieve fair sentences in cases involving crack cocaine because the mandatory minimums superseded the formulae the Commission had been using in creating the guidelines. The Commission's proposed solution, unsurprisingly, was to propose that Congress reduce, or even better, eliminate, the mandatory minimums. If the mandatory minimums were abandoned, the Commission would be able to develop more rational, proportionate standards that would reflect considerations besides the amount of the drug captured in the arrest and would bring penalties in crack cases into line with other offences.

Congress rejected this approach each time the Commission suggested it. The Commission's struggle to arrive at a policy solution Congress might accept revealed its timidity in discussing race issues and its preoccupation with achieving formal, rather than substantive, equality in sentencing. The Commission did not seriously investigate the possibility that the decision to single out crack cocaine for harsh mandatory minimums was motivated, at least in part, by racism. It accepted, without investigation, the strong denial of racist intent offered by pro-mandatory minimums legislators. That issue was regarded as a nonstarter.

The Commission, according to one member whom I interviewed, believed it had been asked to make an important and controversial decision when Congress first charged it with studying the disparity between sentences prescribed for crack and powder cocaine. "The racial thing", he remembered, had attracted most of the public's interest. The commissioners did look into disparities in prosecution and punishment by race, even going so far as to study journalistic accounts of possible discriminatory treatment. What most impressed the Commission, however, was how arbitrary the mandatory minimums were in comparison to the guidelines. The Commission decided that racial disparity in prescribed sentences and in law enforcement was only part of the problem, though it was a very volatile part: "The racial flag gets you great support in some areas, but strong opposition in others".

The available evidence suggests that, while the Commission found allegations of racism in drug enforcement troubling, it ultimately found them unpersuasive. It investigated – but ultimately took no action on – research and reports suggesting that the sentencing law was being administered in a way that discriminated against African-Americans (Meirhoefer 1992). In its 1995 report to Congress, the Commission ignored studies indicating that some of the variance in sentences could not be explained by legitimate sentencing considerations and focused instead on a study that suggested that if the crack/powder disparity were eliminated, racial differences in drug sentencing would also disappear (p. 162). Only one page of the book-length report was devoted to a discussion of the racial disparity issue.

Although the commissioners agreed on the undesirability of the current mandatory minimums, they ultimately were divided on what to recommend.

One side recommended parity in penalties for crack and powder cocaine. The other side was convinced that crack is somewhat more dangerous than powder; it recommended a five to one ratio in amount of the drugs required for a particular sentence to replace the current hundred to one ratio. The vote, which occurred after much discussion, was four to three in favour of parity.

In presenting the Commission's findings to Congress, Chairman Richard Conaboy stressed the unfairness and irrationality of the mandatory minimums in crack cases, not their racial impact. He brought up race as the last consideration on his list:

> Fifth and finally, because there is such a clear impact of those high penalties on minority defendants, the policy, the 100-to-1 ratio, leads directly to very strong perceptions of unfairness. Crack is cheap, and it is thus distributed and attractive to the poor, many of whom are minorities. With a 100-to-1 ratio we have, we think, unintentionally developed the anomaly of punishing the poor and minorities more severely under the guise of trying to protect them (House of Representatives Hearing 1995, p. 12).

Congress took the opposite approach when it discussed the matter in October. Members of Congress focused on the racial impact of the crack penalties and argued over whether it should be condemned or ignored. Some argued that the hundred to one ratio could be defended as serving the interests of the black community. The Black Congressional caucus, however, had already expressed its support for the Sentencing Commission's recommendation. Anti-parity spokesmen nevertheless claimed to speak for the true interests of black Americans. Rep. Shaw, for example, said that he spoke for all of America, which wanted "to put them in jail and throw the key away. That is the voice of America. That is the voice of the minorities in the areas that are responsible who want to get their areas up out of poverty, get out of the gutter, get the problems out of their neighborhoods ..." (p. 10262, and see McCollum, p. 10264 and Bryant, p. 10266).

The most heated disagreement was over whether a policy that produces such racially disparate results rightfully can be called 'colour blind'. Some members tried to drain the racial dynamic from the issue, but Rep. Rush charged the Republicans who favoured the hundred to one disparity with racism: "Is there a conspiracy among the Republican majority to incarcerate as many African-American males as possible? ... It is dishonesty, if not intellectual heresy, to introduce a bill such as this" (p. 10273). Rep. McCollum rejected this interpretation, asserting that numbers alone can never constitute evidence of racism:

It is not, in my judgment, at all racist. If you think about those words, the idea of racism implies prejudice. It implies that we in Congress or those in law enforcement are out there intentionally attempting to put somebody in jail because of the color of their skin or to make them serve a longer sentence. That is not so (p. 10275).

Congress rejected the parity proposal by an overwhelming vote and sent the matter back to the Commission for further study with the message that "the sentence imposed for trafficking in a quantity of crack cocaine should generally exceed the sentence imposed for trafficking in a like quantity of powder cocaine". The Commission, forced by this mandate to soften its position, responded in April 1997 by recommending a fivefold difference in penalties. The Commission gave many reasons for its recommendation, with the race issue positioned near the end of its report:

> While there is no evidence of racial bias behind the promulgation of this federal sentencing law, nearly 90 percent of the offenders convicted in federal court for crack cocaine distribution are African-American while the majority of crack cocaine users is white. Thus sentences appear to be harsher and more severe for racial minorities than others as a result of this law. The current penalty structure results in a perception of unfairness and inconsistency (1997, p. 8).

Vice-chairman Michael Gelacak joined the rest of the Commissioners on the five to one recommendation, but dissented to express his dissatisfaction with the accommodation the Commission had reached under Congressional pressure. The original recommendation, he argued, should stand: "Political compromise is a function better left to the Legislature" (1997, p. 1). At this point the issue seems to have died. Congress appears to have lost interest in sentencing, and, for a time, even in staffing its Sentencing Commission. Congress appointed no new members as the terms of the current membership expired, waiting until all had left before making any new appointments.

The new Sentencing Commission, carefully balanced to reflect the political balance in Congress, appears disinclined to reopen this controversial issue. The Justice Department stands firm in demanding significantly higher penalties in crack cases, advocating at ten to one ratio. The appellate courts have consistently rejected all equal-protection arguments based on the racial disparity produced by the sentencing rules. Electoral contests at the federal level, including the race for president, have ignored the issue of racial disparity in sentencing and the burgeoning numbers of people in prison. At the state level there are some indications of weariness with the drug war and concern about the racial disparities it produces. A few governors and some local officials have proposed softening penalties in drug cases. So far, however, most of the concern has been directed toward penalties for marijuana, not crack. Even so, federal law enforcement officials have done their utmost to deter state level initiative in this area and to maintain enthusiasm for the drug war.

Conclusion

The large and increasing number of black Americans imprisoned for drug offences rubs an ancient wound, made all the more painful because of the government's failure to deal with it. For African-Americans, it provides further evidence of the long tradition of racial prejudice in criminal justice. Non-African-Americans may find support for their assumptions about criminality in "other races" (Hodriger 1995, p. 168). Abroad, our tolerance for a drug policy with such racially-skewed results is interpreted as one more indication of America's brand of moralistic racism. We are seen as hypocritical, embracing pluralism, multiculturalism, and diversity, condemning racial references in ordinary conversation and public policy, yet unwilling to realistically confront evidence of racism in our public institutions. Our drug war can be interpreted in terms of the purpose of racism at its outset, which was to justify repression of indigenous peoples under colonial rule (Anderson 1983).

Political leaders have not faced up to this failed discriminatory policy. At the federal level, leadership has been lacking, not only in the Congress and executive branch, but also in the judiciary, and even in the Commission charged with ensuring that sentencing is fair. Just as disconcerting is the lack of public outcry for a change in policy. I suggest that the problem is not just failure of nerve among politicians, bureaucrats, and judges, even in combination with crass political opportunism and racist attitudes, although all of these appear to be relevant. Our working conception of racism tends to be too limited. As Howard Winant says: "The understanding we have of racism, an understanding which was forged in the 1960s, is now seriously deficient ... In fact, since the ambiguous triumph of the civil rights movement in the mid-1960s, clarity about what racism means has been slipping away" (1998, pp. 757–8). The realisation that fighting racism means more than overcoming prejudiced attitudes, brotherhood, and the passage of laws prohibiting discrimination in public accommodations, Winant suggests, has been slow in coming.

There is a theory of race and racism, Winant suggests, behind every public policy. What then, is the underlying logic of the drug war at this point, now that the indications of its shortcomings are clear to nearly everyone? One must begin by asking why supporters of the policy reject evidence of its racial impact. Perhaps part of the reason is that the drug war is emblematic of a struggle that is going on in the United States between those who see impending disaster in our social fabric, and therefore seek to reinforce the moral bounds of community through law, and those who are more optimistic about the direction of social development and more cautious about the power of law, particularly criminal law, to do good. If reinforcing and rebuilding the social fabric through criminal sanctions is seen as necessary, it is easy to understand why the focus on racism would be considered a dangerous diversion that could undermine the whole project.

The relevant racism, I suggest, is not so much active racial animus as racialised fear and racially-conditioned willingness to disengage from hardships others face. This is the largely unrecognised and unacknowledged base upon which the war on drugs is waged. The racial impact of drug-war effort is thus no surprise, even though it would not be accurate to say that it was specifically intended or planned. Unfortunately, in the American political context, this type of racial thinking, although pernicious, is not ordinarily called racist.

The power of the drug war to symbolise broader problems of moral degeneracy and community decay, however, may be waning. Drug wars, as some observers suggest, tend to be cyclical phenomena (viz. Ryan 1998; Chambliss 1995). Signs of coming change include growing public dismay with the ever-greater mismatch between spending to end drug use and the results achieved and a growing interest in the medical control of addiction and the scientific study of addiction. Practical approaches to controlling drug abuse, such as drug courts, are getting more attention. The drug war will be easier to abandon when the costs of its pursuit begin to seem both outrageously high and unnecessary. The role of racism in launching and sustaining this war, however, will probably never be fully acknowledged because it teaches a harder lesson about America, and more generally about the tension between liberalism and commitment to a robust equality.

References

Anderson, B. (1983), *Imagined Communities: Reflections on the origins and spread of nationalism*, London: Verso.
Baggins, D.S. (1998), *Drug Hate and the Corruption of American Justice*, Westport, CT: Praeger.

Baum, D. (1996), *Smoke and Mirrors: The war on drugs and the politics of failure*, Boston: Little Brown.

Beckett, K. (1997), *Making Crime Pay: Law and order in contemporary American politics*, New York: Oxford University Press.

Bureau of Justice Statistics (1999), *Sourcebook of Criminal Justice Statistics*, Washington: US Department of Justice.

Chambliss, W.J. (1995), 'Crime Control and Ethnic Minorities: Legitimizing racial oppression by creating moral panics', in D.F. Hawkins (ed.), *Ethnicity, Race and Crime: Perspectives across time and place*, Albany: SUNY Press.

Christianson, S. (1998), *With Liberty for Some: 500 years of imprisonment in America*, Boston: Northeastern University Press.

Cole, D. (1999), *No Equal Justice: Race and class in the American criminal justice system*, New York: New Press.

Cose, E. (1997), *The Darden Dilemma: Twelve black writers on justice, race, and conflicting loyalties*, New York: HarperPerennial.

Donziger, S.R. (ed.) (1996), *The Real War on Crime: The report of the National Criminal Justice Commission*, New York: HarperCollins.

Gordon, D.R. (1994), *The Return of the Dangerous Classes: Drug prohibition and policy politics*, New York: Norton.

Hodriger, D.A (1995), *Postethnic America: Beyond multiculturalism*, New York: Basic Books.

House of Representatives (1995), Disapproval of Certain Sentencing Guideline Amendments. Report together with dissenting views on HR 2259, 29 September, Report 104–272, Washington: USGPO.

Human Rights Watch (2000), *Punishment and Prejudice: Racial disparities in the war on drugs*, New York: Human Rights Watch.

Kennedy, R. (1997), *Race, Crime and the Law*, New York: Pantheon.

Lieberman, R.C. (1998), *Shifting the Color line: Race and the American welfare state*, Cambridge, MA: Harvard University Press.

Meirhoefer, B.S. (1992), *The General Effect of Mandatory Minimum Prison Terms: A longitudinal study*, Washington: Federal Judicial Center.

Miller, J.G. (1996), *Search and Destroy: African-American males in the criminal justice system*, New York: Cambridge University Press.

Mosher, C.J. (1998), *Discrimination and Denial: Systematic racism in Ontario's legal and criminal-justice system, 1897–1961*, Toronto: University of Toronto Press.

Mustard, D. (2000), 'Racial, Ethnic and Gender Disparities in Sentencing: Evidence from the US Federal Courts' (draft version in possession of author), to appear in *Journal of Law and Economics*, Vol. 44, April, 2001.

Musto, D.F. (1987), *The American Disease: Origins of narcotic control* (expanded edn), London: Oxford University Press.

Provine, D.M. (1998), 'Too Many Black Men: The sentencing judge's dilemma', *Law and Social Inquiry*, Vol. 23, pp. 823–56.

Ryan, K.F. (1998), 'Clinging to Failure: The rise and continued life of U.S. drug policy', *Law and Society Review*, Vol. 32, pp. 221–42.

Schuman, H. , Steeh, C., Bobo, L. and Krysan, M. (1997), *Racial Attitudes in America: Trends and interpretations*, Cambridge, MA: Harvard University Press.

Sentencing Project (1999), Briefing Sheet: Crack cocaine sentencing policy, www.stentencingproject.org/pubs/+sppubs/1090bs.html.

Smith, R.C. (1996), *Racism in the Post-Civil Rights Era*, Albany: State University of New York Press.

Subcommittee on Crime of the Committee on the Judiciary (House of Representatives) (1995), Cocaine and Federal Sentencing Policy, Hearing on 25 June, Serial No. 19, Washington: USGPO.

Tonry, M. (1995), *Malign Neglect: Race, crime, and punishment in America*, New York: Oxford University Press.

Tonry, M. and Hatlestad, K. (eds) (1997), *Sentencing Reform in Overcrowded Times: A comparative perspective*, New York: Oxford University Press.

US Sentencing Commission (1991), *Mandatory Minimum Penalties in the Federal Criminal Justice System*, Special Report to the Congress as directed by Sec. 1703 of PL 101–647, August, Washington: US Sentencing Commission.

US Sentencing Commission (1995), *Cocaine and Federal Sentencing Policy*, Special Report to the Congress as directed by Sec. 280006 of PL 103–322, February, Washington: US Sentencing Commission.

US Sentencing Commission (1995), *Update on the Activities of the US Sentencing Commission*, September, Washington: US Sentencing Commission.

US Sentencing Commission (1997), *Cocaine and Federal Sentencing Policy*, Special Report to the Congress as directed by Sec. 2 of PL 104–38, April, Washington: US Sentencing Commission.

Winant, H. (1998), 'Racism Today: Continuity and change in the post-civil rights era', *Ethnic and Racial Studies*, Vol. 21, pp. 755–66.

Cases

McClesky v Kemp 481 US 279 (1987).
US v Clary 846 F. Supp. 768 (SD Mo. 1994); reversed and remanded: 34 F. 3d 709 (8th Cir. 1994).

Chapter Twenty-four

Sentencing Sexual Offenders in the UK and Australia

Kate Warner

Introduction

Criticisms have been directed at sentencing for rape and sexual offences on the grounds that courts treat offenders too leniently and that as in other areas of rape law, the phallocentrism of sentencing principle and practice reinforces a social construction of sexuality which harms women and some men.

In England critics have suggested that courts have failed to adhere to the *Billam* guidelines by continuing to impose noncustodial or very short custodial sentences in a significant minority of cases (Robertshaw 1994; Lacey and Wells 1998, p. 402). Lees (1997, p. 122) has complained that while sentences for rape increased after *Billam*, the effect of the changes has been exaggerated and that since 1987 the length of sentences has decreased.[1] In Australia, sentencing for rape is said to be too lenient. Respondents in a national survey complained of a lack of consistency within states and territories and across states and territories and also of leniency in comparison with sentences for other crimes (Bargen and Fishwick 1995, p. 109). These criticisms have not been confined to the common law world. In Germany, for example, dissatisfaction with the relativities between sentencing levels for rape and other crimes resulted in changes to the penalties for rape after publicity given to a case in which a couple who were camping were attacked. The woman was raped and the man was threatened with a weapon and robbed of his tent. The sentence for the rape was subject to a minimum of two years but for the armed robbery the minimum was five years.

Comparisons with another crime, such as robbery, and interjurisdictional comparisons may be one way of shedding some light on the issue of appropriate sentencing levels for rape. As the chapters in this volume by Freiberg and Davies, Tyrer and Takala demonstrate, there are many difficulties with interjurisdictional comparisons of sentences. First, the definition of crimes varies between jurisdictions. Comparing England, Victoria, Western Australia and Tasmania, the definition of 'rape' is widest in Victoria and Western Australia where sexual intercourse includes penetration of the mouth by the penis (not included in English definition) and penetration of the vagina and anus by a part of the body other than the penis and by an object (not included in England or Tasmania). In Western Australia rape has been replaced by aggravated sexual penetration without consent and sexual penetration without consent. Because it is not particularly informative to consider sentences for 'rape' in isolation, a comparator crime such as robbery should be used. But the problems of definition are then compounded. Robbery in England – theft accompanied by the use of force – covers a wide range of conduct. In Victoria, Western Australia and Tasmania robbery is divided into a number of separate crimes. A second difficulty is that provisions for early release differ. In England conditional release is automatic after half the sentence is served for prisoners sentenced to less than four years. For sentences over four years the normal release time is after two-thirds. In Tasmania, prisoners are normally eligible for parole release after one half of sentences of 12 months and over. In Victoria, for sentences over two years a non-parole period will normally be imposed of 70–80 per cent of the head sentence.

Despite the problems of interjurisdictional comparisons,[2] an attempt is made to compare rape and robbery with respect to the maximum penalty, appellate guidance as to the tariff and sentencing ranges in England and Wales and three Australian jurisdictions: Victoria, Western Australia and Tasmania. This is followed by a discussion of attempts to determine the appropriate sentencing level for rape. It is argued that a useful and necessary contribution to attempts to locate rape in a scale of offence seriousness is to examine the relativities between different kinds of rape. Because this chapter is seeking to explore the assertion that sentencing for rape is too lenient, the analysis concentrates on the kinds of cases and factors which attract leniency or mitigation.

Penalty Comparison for Rape and Robbery

Maximum Penalties

The maximum penalty should at least give some indication of the seriousness with which the legislature views an offence. In England and Wales the maximum penalty for rape is life. In Victoria it is 25 years, in Tasmania it is 21 years and in Western Australia 20 years (aggravated sexual penetration without consent). For robbery it is life in England and Wales, in Victoria and Western Australia it is 25 years for armed robbery and in Tasmania 21 years (for all categories of robbery). So the maxima for robbery or armed robbery and rape are at the same level in all jurisdictions except in Western Australia where there is a higher maximum penalty for armed robbery than for armed rape (aggravated sexual penetration).

Appellate Guidance as to the Tariff

Courts in England and Wales have the benefit of guideline judgments for rape and armed robbery. In *Billam* (1996) 82 Cr.App.R. 347 the Court of Appeal stated that sentences for rape were too short, with 28 per cent receiving sentences of two years or less in 1984, and 69 per cent receiving sentences up to and including four years. The court said the starting point in a contested case of rape without any mitigating or aggravating factors should be five years. The starting point should be eight years if the victim's abode was entered, the offender was in a position of responsibility for the victim or the victim was abducted. A sentence of 15 years was the suggested starting point for a campaign of rape. Seven aggravating factors and two mitigating factors, which ought to take the sentence higher or lower than the starting point, were mentioned.

In *Turner* (1975) 61 Cr.App.R. 6 the Court of Appeal specified a starting point of 15 years for robbery of a bank or a post office van if firearms were carried and no injury caused (the same starting point as a campaign of rape), going up to 18 years for two such robberies. "The 'irreducible minimum' in such cases is said to be 11 years" (Wasik 1998, p. 341). Ashworth's (2000 pp. 106–7) summary of the effect of later Court of Appeal guidance for less serious forms of the offence suggests 7–10 years for armed robberies of post offices and betting shops where there is less planning, smaller gangs and less lucrative gains, and 5–7 years for robberies of small post offices and shops involving firearms and moderate amounts of cash. Wasik (1998) suggests the approved tariff for street robbery or mugging is 2–5 years, although criminal statistics indicate some less serious cases receive shorter or noncustodial sentences.

Neither in Victoria nor Tasmania do courts issue guideline judgments. In Western Australia the Supreme Court has the express statutory authority to do so but, despite invitations from the Director of Public Prosecutions and defence counsel, the court has declined these invitations (Morgan 1999). However, courts in all these jurisdictions have been prepared to give guidance in relation to particular offences without attaching the label guideline judgment and without necessarily acknowledging a particular tariff or going rate. In Tasmania, the Court of Criminal Appeal has acknowledged that four years is a common sentence for rape but the suggestion that this is the tariff has been rejected. The Court has indicated that sentences of six to eight years are the top of the range for armed bank robberies where no physical injuries are caused. In Victoria the Court of Appeal accepts sentencing statistics as a very general guide but has not suggested appropriate ranges for rape or robbery. Fox and Freiberg (1999, pp. 925–9) report that in the case of sentences reviewed by the Court of Appeal, sentences at the top of the range (15 years) are imposed for multiple rapes or similar offences, for rapes accompanied by the use of weapons or violence, or rapes committed in company or accompanied by gross indignities to the victim. Sentences in the mid-range (5–10 years) cover an enormously diverse set of circumstances and sentences in the lower range may reflect the existence of a number of the following features in combination such as: the fact that the offence was one that may have previously been classified as indecent assault rather than rape; there was no ongoing psychological harm; there was a plea of guilty; or the offender was youthful. Sentences at the top of the range for armed robbery (10 years and above) are imposed for multiple offences, or where the offender has prior convictions for the same offence. Sentences at the lowest part of the range (under four years) are awarded to young offenders who have few if any prior convictions (Fox and Freiberg 1999, pp. 955–8).

Statistics on Sentencing Ranges

The table below displays some information on sentencing patterns for rape and robbery in England and Wales, Victoria, Western Australia and Tasmania. The problems of differences in definition and early release need to be borne in mind. Where 'rape' or 'robbery' includes separate categories, these have been combined.

In each jurisdiction rape is usually dealt with more severely than robbery. According to the above data, courts in Western Australia are most likely to impose an immediate custodial sentence for rape and for robbery. But at the same time the average sentences for these crimes is by no means the highest. England has the highest mean sentence for rape and for robbery, and Tasmania the lowest. Western Australia and Victoria are between the two. While Tasmania has shorter sentences for rape and robbery the differential between the average sentences of rape and robbery is greatest in this jurisdiction – the average

Table 24.1 Custodial sentences for rape in the United Kingdom, Victoria, Western Australia and Tasmania

Crime/measure	England (1997)	WA (1998)	Victoria (1996)	Tasmania (1990–98)
% immediate custodial (rape)	91%	98%	87.5%	96%
% immediate custodial (robbery)	82%	85%	66%	75%
Average prison sentence (rape)	77m	54m	59m	40m
Average prison sentence (robbery)	54m	39m	44m	22m
Min. and max. prison (rape)	7–12m over 10y	9m 15y	18m 14y	6m 8y
Min. and max. prison (robbery)	under 4m over 10y	6m 12y	1m3m 10y	8y

rape sentence is nearly twice as long as that of the average robbery. The differential between average immediate custodial sentences is smallest in Victoria where the average robbery, if it receives an immediate custodial penalty, is 74 per cent of the average rape. The relativities between rape and robbery in England and Western Australia are similar.

What can be drawn from the above? In each jurisdiction rape is usually dealt with more severely than robbery. But jurisdictions differ in the severity of sentences imposed for rape; and they also differ in the relativities between rape and robbery. While rape is usually viewed as more serious than robbery, particularly in Tasmania, clearly some kinds of robbery are viewed more seriously than some kinds of rape because some robberies attract sentences which are longer than the sentences imposed in some cases of rape. This is in accordance with Court of Appeal guidelines in England, which suggest firearm armed robberies of banks, post offices and shops should attract sentences higher than sentences for a rape without aggravating or mitigating factors.[3] In Tasmania too, decisions of the Court of Criminal Appeal suggest that armed robberies with guns by adult offenders, particularly if the target is a bank or financial institution, should attract sentences above those imposed for a 'standard rape'. If the offender has prior convictions for armed robbery, the sentence is likely to be considerably higher (about 6–8 years). But if the offender is young (under 22) then even armed bank robberies with a gun are unlikely to attract a sentence above three years. The differences in sentencing patterns raise questions about how far these differences are attributed to definitions of the crime and to early release provisions. A more detailed analysis is needed to clarify this.

What is Rape Worth?

What is an appropriate sentencing level for rape? What should the relativities be between rape and robbery? Rape and other crimes? These questions are not easily answered. The question of how much to punish raises the issue of which aim or aims of punishment are relevant. If general deterrence is thought to be an important sentencing aim, is it equally important in cases of robbery and rape? Does increasing the penalty level for some crimes have an adverse impact on conviction rates? Edwards (1996, p. 362) claims that *Billam* has contributed to an increase in acquittals in England and Wales because, in cases which do not fit the paradigm of a real rape, the jury are loath to convict if they have the view that a sentence of five years is not appropriate. Even if sentencing for rape is too lenient, is it desirable to advocate more severe penalties in the context of high imprisonment rates, a tough talking media and politicians anxious to appeal to populist concerns about lenient sentencing?[4] Even if we just focus on the issue of comparative seriousness of crimes and attempt to get the relativities right between rape and other offences on the basis of the harm dimension of seriousness, the issue remains difficult. It is true that ordinary people, according to surveys, are capable of reaching a degree of agreement on the comparative seriousness of crimes. In one such survey of London residents, rape with 'no other injuries' was ranked over a robbery of £25 with serious injuries but under an attack with a knife causing serious injuries and under sale of marijuana to a person aged 15 (Sparks, Genn and Dodd 1977). Such surveys are an indication of public opinion but they are based on stereotypes of the crimes in question and are unlikely to be considered views based on evidence of the actual effects of certain crimes on victims.[5] Clearly they are inadequate as a touchstone of gravity for sentencing purposes (Ashworth 2000, pp. 94–5). A theoretical approach to measuring offence seriousness is von Hirsch and Jareborg's (1991) living standard analysis. This ranks the gravity of victimising harms according to how much they reduce a person's living standard. It involves first determining the various kinds of interests typically infringed by the crime. The second stage involves a preliminary quantification of the effect of a typical case on a victim's living standard. Effects are banded into four levels from level 1, which is subsistence, to level 4 which is significant enhancement. Later stages involve adjustments for culpability of the offender and remoteness of harm. Examination of the standard cases used for the preliminary quantification of the effect of a typical case on a victim's living standard reveals the kinds of difficulties likely to be encountered in assessing the penal value of rape.[6]

Two standard/typical rape cases are suggested: forcible rape (the classic stranger rape) and date rape. In the case of a stranger rape at gun point or knife point two interest dimensions are involved: bodily safety, assessed as a discounted 1 because a threat to survival is involved, and freedom from humiliation or intrusion of self respect, rated at the highest for this interest at a level 2. The standard or typical date rape example suggested is the case of a female student with her capacity for physical resistance reduced by excessive alcohol consumption who is forced to have sex over her protests. It is assumed in this example that the threat to bodily safety is eliminated because she is not threatened with serious injury. The interest in sexual integrity, however, is intruded upon and so this involves a level 2 for humiliation. So according to this measure, a standard date rape is not as serious as a standard armed robbery which is given a discounted 1.

A rape by a stranger with threats with a weapon such as a knife or gun clearly involves a threat to physical integrity compounded by humiliation and intrusion to sexual integrity. In such cases there is likely to be general agreement about the seriousness of the crime relative to other serious crimes like armed robbery. But where there is no weapon or overt threat and the victim submits through fear, assessment of the gravity of the crime will depend on the seriousness with which forced sexual intercourse is viewed and with the extent to which forced sexual intercourse is taken to imply threats to bodily safety. Von Hirsch and Jareborg's standard date rape case ignores the violence and threat of violence inherent in non-consensual sex. It treats date rape as sex and not violence if there is no overt threat. Contesting the application of the von Hirsch-Jareborg principles in a case of date rape does not necessarily mean that the living standard analysis as a means of determining parameters for ordinal proportionality is fatally flawed. But it does show that the outcome of the analysis, even in standard cases, is likely to be hotly contested.

Assessment of the assertion that rape sentencing is too lenient is a difficult task. The comparison between England and the three Australian jurisdictions demonstrates that increasing the seriousness of rape in relation to a crime like robbery does not necessarily mean that penalty severity will be increased overall. In Tasmania the differential between rape and robbery is greatest but the sentencing level for rape (and robbery) is the lowest. However determining the relativities between rape and other crimes and then anchoring the penalty scale is complex. Attempting to unravel the relativities between rape and other crimes raises questions about what we mean by rape. For while the classic stranger rape is seriously regarded, once cases fall outside this paradigm, the case can be viewed quite differently, if it is regarded as real rape at all. This dichotomy is apparent from von Hirsch and Jareborg's description and analysis of standard cases. It is in fact the cases outside the paradigm of stranger rape that give rise to the most controversy and to accusations that courts do not take sexual assault seriously. So we need to go further than looking at overall penalty ranges for rape and relativities between rape and other crimes and ask about relativities within rape. How do courts deal with particular kinds of rape like relationship rape, date rape, oral rape, same sex rape, rape of prostitutes, rape of a person who is intoxicated by alcohol or drugs and the rape of a person who is said to have contributed to the offence by her conduct. A simple examination of sentencing statistics such as average or median sentences can obscure the fact that a significant proportion of cases is attracting sentences well below the usual sentence on grounds which should not justify leniency. Regional disparities can also be obscured by such statistics. Lacey and Wells (1998, p. 402) and Lees (1997, p. 122) have noted with concern that Robertshaw's research has shown regional disparities in rape sentencing in England with certain courts handing down noncustodial or very short sentences in a significant minority of cases. Lacey and Wells also draw attention to the 18 cases in 1995 (3 per cent of convictions) in which convicted rapists were cautioned. This suggests that before we can determine what the sentencing level for rape should be in relation to other crimes we need to examine the relativities between different kinds of rape. We need to examine the kinds of cases that fall outside the 'real rape' paradigm. In the absence of a detailed statistical study of first instance decisions a beginning can be made by looking at appellate guidance in cases of rape.

Sentencing Guidance in Cases Outside 'Real Rape'

Relationship Rape

Stranger rape is perceived as the paradigm of real rape. In England this was demonstrated by Lloyd and Warmsley (1989) who, in a study of rape sentencing between 1973 and 1985, found stranger rapists received a much larger proportion of sentences of over five years than non-strangers. More recently Rumney (1999) has compared sentences imposed or upheld by the English Court of Appeal in cases of stranger rape, marital rape, relationship and acquaintance rape. He concluded that the average sentence was highest for stranger rape followed by acquaintance rape and then marital and relationship rape. The average sentence for stranger rape was 9.7 years and for marital and relationship rape it was five years. There appears to be no research in Australia which compares sentences for stranger rape with relationship rape and other kinds of rape.

Why should non-stranger rapes, and marital or relationship rapes in particular, be dealt with more leniently than stranger rapes? What have the courts said about the relevance of a prior intimate relationship between the victim and perpetrator? Elsewhere I have analysed English Court of Appeal decisions in cases of relationship rape (Warner, 2000). What follows is a summary. Relationship is not mentioned as a relevant factor in *Billam*, the Court of Appeal's sentencing guideline judgment for rape. However, in *Berry* (1988) 10 Cr.App.R.(S) 13, the first post-*Billam* decision to deal with the issue of relationship rape, there is a clear indication that the existence of a prior or continuing relationship is mitigating. Lord Mustill gave two reasons why. First, the emotional stress on the offender of a disintegrating relationship is mitigating and secondly, the violation and defilement are likely to be less where there has been a previous settled relationship. This second reason has been used to justify the principle that the existence of a prior relationship is mitigating in many subsequent cases; other cases have simply stated that the existence of such a relationship is mitigating without explaining why.[7] *Thornton* (1990) 12 Cr.App.R.(S) 1 suggested a reduction of six months from the *Billam* 5-year starting point for cases of relationship rape, but later cases suggest a greater reduction, especially if the parties are still cohabiting. In *Paul M* (1995) 16 Cr.App.R.(S) 770, the sentence was reduced to one of 18 months, and in *Pearson* (1996) 1 Cr.App.R.(S) 309 to two years.

To allow a discount in cases of relationship rape on the assumption there is less violation and less defilement is wrong. It is an assumption based on a male view of the wrong of rape and it suggests that the autonomy that rape law protects is in part the autonomy of the owning, possessive male. Rather than treating the existence of the relationship as mitigating, it should be treated as an aggravating factor. To rape a person with whom one has had an intimate relationship is surely a violation of a relationship of trust, and the hurt and humiliation experienced by the victim could well be greater in such a case than if the same act were done by a stranger. Nor can it be argued that cases of relationship rape are less serious than cases of stranger rape because there is less danger to the victim. The evidence is that women who have separated from their husbands or who are contemplating doing so are at risk of violence, physical and sexual – not from strangers – but from their partners. Marital rape is most likely to occur during or after break-up (Finkelor and Yllo 1982; Russell 1990; Painter 1991). And at this point women are most vulnerable to being killed by their partner (Jones 1980). There is some evidence too that victims of marital/relationship rape more frequently suffer additional physical injuries than other rape victims (Easteal 1994). Rumney (1999, pp. 254–7) has surveyed the evidence on rape trauma and concluded that rather than being less traumatic than other forms of rape, marital rape is more distressing and has a greater long-term impact.

In Australia, Lord Mustill's views have been cited with approval in a number of cases.[8] But while Australian cases are littered with references to the existence of a prior relationship together with suggestions that this has mitigatory relevance, most cases give no reasons or foundation in sentencing principle why this should be so (Kift 1995). My analysis of sentencing appeals in cases of marital rape discerned a trend for recent decisions to reject the general proposition that a more lenient view should be taken of rapes which are committed within or against a background of a sexual relationship with the victim.[9] A number of such cases have asserted that the type of relationship may be of such a nature to suggest that the offence involved a gross breach of the trust that the victim had placed in the applicant.[10] As Slicer J said in *R v S*: [1991] Tas.R. 273 at 280:

> Indeed a rape victim, who has been involved in a previous sexual relationship, may suffer greater harm because of the betrayal of trust or the humiliation of the abuse of physical power.

The reality probably is that Australian decisions are mixed.

The principle that an intimate relationship with the victim is mitigating is not the end of problematic sentencing issues in cases of relationship rape. There are two other factors which can be relied upon which have the effect of diminishing the seriousness of the offence in ways which support and condone a male view of the wrong of rape: the attitude of the victim and emotional stress of the offender.

Victim's Attitude to the Offence and Forgiveness

The survey of English appellate decisions shows that the attitude of the victim – the victim's attempt to withdraw charges, victim forgiveness and the victim's wishes can have a powerful ameliorating impact on sentence in cases of marital and relationship rape.[11] It is a factor that can operate independently of the mitigation on grounds of the previous relationship. So it can be very significant even in cases where the court determines that no, or minimal weight, should be given to the relationship.

   Hind (1994) 15 Cr.App.R.(S) 114, *Hutchinson* (1995) 16 Cr.App.R.(S) 388, and *Mills* [1998] 2 Cr.App.R.(S) 252, all cases in which sentences were reduced, were the only cases where the Court of Appeal sought to explain why the victim's forgiving or ambivalent attitude was a mitigating factor. In all cases the explanation was that forgiveness or partial forgiveness indicated that the victim had suffered less emotionally. In *Hutchinson* the trial judge recognised that the victim's forgiveness and continuing love for the appellant exacerbated her suffering. The offender had maintained his plea of not guilty and the complainant had indicated to the magistrates that she still loved the defendant and that she had done all she could to withdraw the complaint. After the trial the judge said to her, "I do not wish to cause you any more suffering. I do not think I have seen anybody quite so racked with conflicting emotions and loyalties as you have been these last few days. I am sure you have everybody's sympathy". And yet Owen J felt able to say of the effect of her attempts to withdraw the charges:

> It seems that the fact of forgiveness must mean that the psychological and mental suffering must be very much less in those circumstances than would be the case in respect of a woman who very understandably could not forgive such an offence as that with which we are dealing.

It is wrong to equate forgiveness with less emotional harm. To do so is again to misunderstand the wrong of rape. Moreover to accept forgiveness or withdrawal of charges as mitigating is objectionable for other reasons. It too readily assumes that withdrawal of the charges or continuation of the relationship is motivated by forgiveness. It may be motivated by fear. And even if there appears to be genuine forgiveness, there is a failure to give adequate consideration to the motivation for this, to the need for a woman to put such an experience behind her and to get on with her life. There is inadequate recognition of the feelings of self-blame many victims experience, the psychological and social pressures to return and to forgive, and the very real dangers many of these women face in such relationships even if they have terminated them. Recognition of this is partial at best.

In Australia, courts have expressed differing views about the relevance of the victim's attitude to sentence. Some courts have asserted that the wishes of the victim are irrelevant. Others have given them considerable weight.[12] Maintenance of the family unit and family hardship were the reasons for giving victim's wishes and forgiveness considerable weight in the decision of the Western Australian Court of Criminal Appeal in *H* (1995) 81 A.Crim.R. 88. The applicant, in a drunken and jealous rage, had attacked his wife, dragged her by the hair to the bedroom and orally and anally raped her. In his comments on passing a sentence of two years 11 months on each of three counts of sexual assault, the sentencing judge made it clear that because of the entreaties made by the complainant and her wish that the family unit continue, he had reduced the sentence very considerably from the sentence that he would otherwise have imposed (a sentence in the order of seven to eight years). The applicant appealed on the ground, inter alia, that the sentencing judge failed to have sufficient regard to the victim's wishes. By a majority decision, leave to appeal was granted, the appeal allowed and a probation order substituted. Malcolm CJ considered that the wishes of the victim are significant in cases where maintaining the family unit is an important factor. In his view the case fell within the exceptional circumstances in which a noncustodial sentence was justified. Kennedy J considered that it was an appropriate case to consider the impact on the offender's family and to impose a noncustodial sentence, but Murray J, the dissenting judge, thought that victim's wishes should have no impact on sentencing outcome. He would have dismissed the appeal.

Giving weight to victim's wishes on grounds of the desirability of the maintenance of the family unit is fraught with difficulty. It can put pressure on a woman to forgive and return, exposing her to the risk of further violence. Moreover, allowing a victim's wishes to dictate the outcome of a case transfers the matter from the public realm into the private. One of the purposes of sentencing is to send a message to the community about the seriousness of the crime. This is particularly important in the case of violence to a partner or ex partner, where there has been a traditional ambivalence about whether the matter is truly criminal. The English Court of Appeal, in a recent causing death by dangerous driving case, has accepted that there is a general principle that attitudes of the victim should not influence sentence, subject to a limited exception in cases where there is clear evidence that the sentence was actually aggravating the victim's distress by its length.[13] In such a case there may be some scope for a limited reduction of sentence provided it does not substantially depart from the normal sentence. The second exception, that victim forgiveness in a case of relationship rape is evidence that the impact on the victim is less, should be abandoned. If weight is to be given to victim attitude and forgiveness it should only be done under the first exception. And if the case is one of relationship rape, because of the pressures and dangers identified above, special care should be taken in relation to evidence of forgiveness.

Emotional Stress and the Perpetrator's State of Mind

Although *Berry* is usually cited to support the proposition that relationship rape is mitigating because it involves less violation than stranger rape, Lord Mustill also regarded the emotional stress arising out of the breakdown of a relationship as mitigating:[14]

> Here we have the case of a man ... facing the disintegration of a relationship that had probably reached the level of infatuation, and where his contact with his daughter must at least have been in peril.

In Australia, the emotional state of the offender as a victim of a broken or deteriorating relationship has been used to explain why some mitigatory weight should be allowed.[15] This is rare in the judgements of the Court of Appeal, but *Maskell* (1991) 12 Cr.App.R.(S) 638 is an example. Hardship arising from marital break-up was regarded as mitigating (p. 640) and the court also noted with apparent sympathy that the appellant 'found the deprivations imposed by the separation, both in general terms and in terms of his sexual desires, a considerable hardship' (p. 639). Courts should not seek to justify giving mitigatory weight to the existence of an intimate relationship on the grounds of the emotional stress of a deteriorating relationship. To do so gives cultural endorsement to the behaviour of men who lose control of their emotions and violently assault their wives. Rather the courts should acknowledge the dangers faced by women in the context of the termination of a relationship.

The Relevance of Sexual Experience and Moral Character – the Rape of Prostitutes and Virgins

The rape of a prostitute is another example of a case falling outside the paradigm of a serious 'real rape'. It raises the issue of the relevance of the sexual experience and moral character of the victim. In my view, the sexual experience of the victim is not relevant to sentence. To focus on the sexual experience of the victim diverts attention from the offence to the victim, fostering assessments of moral worth and generalisations to the effect that those more sexually experienced and less morally worthy are less affected. Such generalisations confuse sex with rape. The amount of sexual experience is irrelevant to psychological capacity to deal with the violence inherent in non-consensual sex. The English Court of Appeal in *Billam* listed prior sexual history of the victim as a factor which was not relevant to sentence for rape.[16] This suggests that the fact that the complainant is a prostitute is not of mitigatory relevance. However, subsequent cases indicate that the fact the victim is a prostitute will operate to reduce the seriousness of the rape somewhat because the victim's hurt "is to some extent different from that of another woman who would only be prepared to have sexual intercourse with a man whom she knows and respects".[17] The comment in *Cole and Barik*, that to "some extent the hurt in such cases as this is not simply the act of intercourse but the fact that no payment has been made for it" is a clear example of confusing rape with consensual sex, in fact the court reduces the hurt to little more than theft. *Masood* [1997] 2 Cr.App.R.(S) 137 is the most recent decision of the Court of Appeal on the rape of a prostitute, and it is not entirely clear on the relevance of prior sexual history. The Court considered that because of the 'catalogue' of indecencies, gratuitous violence, false imprisonment, threats and insults, the crime was as painful to the complainant as it would have been to anyone else. While it endorsed its comments in *Cole and Barik* adding, "No doubt the actual act of intercourse is the more traumatic to a young inexperienced virgin than it would be to an older ... prostitute", it also seemed to say that this was counterbalanced by the fact that prostitutes need protection from men who resort to violence.

Australian courts have differed as to the relevance of sexual experience of the complainant and also as to the relevance of the fact that the complainant was a prostitute. In Victoria the Court of Appeal has held that the fact the complainant was a prostitute is a mitigating factor for two reasons. First, a prostitute would probably suffer no psychological harm and secondly, rape is a risk inherent in prostitution.[18] This was followed in a later case,[19] and despite widespread criticism and controversy, the Court has failed to resile from this position.[20] This Court has also asserted the relevance of the victim's virginity, rejecting the submission that such evidence was irrelevant and contravened the section in the *Evidence Act* prohibiting its reception.[21] In contrast, the New South Wales Court of Criminal Appeal has rejected the idea that sexual assault is less serious because the victim is a sex worker.[22] Whether the Court is quite as firm about the irrelevance of general sexual experience is not clear. While a study of 73 sentencing hearings in New South Wales did not find evidence of the victim's general sexual experience being referred to or taken into account (van de Zandt 1998, p. 139), the Court of Criminal Appeal in New South Wales has referred to the fact the victim was a virgin.[23] It is one thing to treat the fact that the victim is very young as a matter adding to offence seriousness on the grounds of the physical and psychological vulnerability of such a victim; it is a different matter to regard the fact of virginity itself as aggravating. The trap of allowing sexual experience to be relevant is that it facilitates stereotyping. The moral worth of the victim will be judged, not the impact of the crime on the particular victim. And stereotyping fails to challenge the dominant conception of real rape as the attack on a female 'of good repute' by a stranger.

Imprudent Behaviour and Raising Expectations

To treat the rape of a prostitute as mitigating on the ground of the risk of rape inherent in prostitution, as the Victorian Court of Criminal Appeal did in *Harris*, is an endorsement of the mitigating effect of imprudent or risky behaviour by the complainant. There are many other instances of Australian courts being prepared to adopt a more lenient attitude to a case of rape where the victim has acted imprudently and 'contributed to her own downfall'. So participating at a party in a game of 'strip-jack-naked',[24] and drinking with a man and offering him marijuana have been held to be in the defendant's favour.[25] Accompanying a man in a car after drinking with him has been treated as raising his expectations and therefore as mitigating.[26] Some decisions now seem to reject the view that behaviour like hitchhiking justifies a reduction of sentence.[27] And some judges have even shown a disinclination to interpret the victim's behaviour as raising the offender's expectations and therefore as mitigating.[28] But the decisions are mixed.[29]

In *Billam* the Court of Appeal drew a distinction between imprudent behaviour and behaviour which can be interpreted as raising the offender's expectations. So the fact that the victim may have exposed herself to danger by acting imprudently was said not to be a mitigating factor.[30] But behaviour calculated to lead the defendant to believe in consent was said to be mitigating. The problem with this approach is that, in determining what is behaviour calculated to lead the defendant to believe in consent, so-called 'imprudent behaviour' is likely to be included. Certainly in Australia accompanying a man in his car has been regarded as raising his expectations. Informed by a

seriousness is difficult as discussion of the von Hirsch-Jareborg living standard scheme shows. It is suggested that a useful beginning is to explore the relativities between different kinds of rape, in particular the kinds of rape that do not fall within the traditional conception of real rape. An analysis of appellate guidance in such cases reveals that a number of sentencing principles demonstrate a failure to understand the real wrong of rape and that they tend to bolster an active and aggressive masculinity and a passive and victimised femininity, a construction of sexuality which is implicated in the seemingly intractable problem of the incidence of rape. It is well accepted that reducing the incidence of rape requires a change in the social construction of sexuality and a change in the dominant traditional understanding of the meaning of real rape. It follows that the law should not bolster a conception of sexuality that sustains rape. It should challenge it and try to change the meaning of 'real rape'. This means the following principles should be changed:

1) the principle that the existence of a prior or current relationship is a factor mitigating rape. There is no less violation or defilement in such cases. Relationship rape is not less serious than other kinds of rape and research on rape trauma suggests it is in fact more serious. Instead, recognition should be given to the fact that relationship rape is about violation of trust, exploitation of power and the infliction of punishment and humiliation;

2) victim forgiveness and the victim's attitude should not be given mitigatory weight on the basis that it indicates the victim's suffering is less, nor on the basis of maintenance of the family unit. Courts should apply the general principle that victims' attitudes and wishes cannot influence sentence. There should be no special exception for cases of marital rape. The only possible exception should be a general one. If there is evidence that the victim's distress would be increased by the sentence then, as in dangerous driving cases in England, this could perhaps moderate sentence to a very limited degree;

3) prior sexual history should not be a relevant factor in sentencing, whether the victim is homosexual or heterosexual, a virgin or a prostitute. To generalise that there will be less psychological harm if the victim is a prostitute confuses sex with rape and fosters stereotyping based on the moral worth of the victim. This fails to challenge the orthodox understanding of what is real rape and encourages the view that some people are more rapeable than others;

4) neither imprudent behaviour nor raising expectation should be a mitigating factor. The apparently conventional image of normal sex, reflected by

allowing behaviour calculated to raise expectations of consent as mitigating, is inimical to a view of sexuality that entails equal and shared enjoyment. Rather it suggests normal sex involves active and aggressive masculine behaviour and passive, albeit tempting, feminine submission. And treating raising the offender's expectation as mitigating reinforces the myth that men cannot control their sexual behaviour and again confuses sex with rape;

5) courts should avoid categorising oral rape as a lesser form of rape, or anal rape as more serious than vaginal rape. To do so can lead to stereotyping and unacceptable outcomes particularly in the context of comparisons between male and female anal rape.

The criticism that courts can be too lenient in sentencing some rape offenders seems valid when appellate decisions are analysed. Courts should review the guidance they give in cases of rape. In England, the Sentencing Advisory Panel should formulate new draft guidance to replace the *Billam* guidelines. In Australia, appeal courts should review their guidance in cases of rape, prompted in Western Australia and New South Wales by requests for guideline judgments from the Directors of Public Prosecutions. It is worth repeating that asserting that sentencing for rape in cases outside the real rape paradigm is too lenient and that a number of mitigating factors should be rejected does not mean that an overall rise in sentencing severity is advocated. Rather what is advocated is a review of the relative seriousness of different kinds of rape and of the factors that aggravate or and mitigate sentence for this crime as the first stage in a review of offence seriousness.

Notes

1   This does not appear to be supported by the data. The Criminal Statistics Supplementary Tables suggest that while the proportion of rape prison sentences up to five years increased from 39 per cent in 1987 to 49 per cent in 1990, it again fell and in 1996 it was 33 per cent and 32 per cent in 1997.
2   See especially the chapters by Freiberg and Davies, Tyrer and Takala.
3   *Billam* (1986) 82 Cr.App.R. 347; *Turner* (1975) 61 Cr.App.R. 6 and see Ashworth (2000) at pp. 105–7; Wasik (1998) at p. 341.
4   On this point see the chapter by Crewe, Lutz and Fahrney.
5   For further discussion of public knowledge, attitude and opinion research see the chapters in this volume by Hough and Roberts; and McCoy and McManimon.
6   For further discussion of von Hirsch's 'New Scales' see the chapter in this book by Julia Davis and von Hirsch's reply.

7   Referred to in Warner (2000); see also Rumney (1999) at pp. 246–55.
8   By the Federal Court in *Lyttle* (1991) 57 A.Crim.R. 398 and the Court of Criminal Appeal of the Northern Territory in *Wiren* unreported 13 November, 1996, BC 9605435.
9   *Stephens* (1994) 76 A.Crim.R. 5; *Brooking* (unreported, CCA NSW, 7 December 1994), Carruthers J at 18; *Harvey* (unreported, CCA NSW, 23 August 1996, BC 9603734); *R v S* [1991] Tas R 273; *Szasz* (unreported, CCA Vic, 22 November, 1994, BC 9401327).
10 E.g. Southwell J in *Szasz* (unreported CCA Vic 22 November 1994, BC 9401327); Cummins J in *Ramage* (unreported, CCA Vic, 15 September 1993, BC 9300951); *R v S* [1991] Tas R 273. For a more detailed discussion of these cases see Warner (1998) at p. 177.
11 *Collier* (1992) 13 Cr.App.R.(S) 33; *Hind* (1994) 15 Cr.App.R.(S) 114; *Hutchinson* (1994) 15 Cr.App.R.(S) 134; *Henshall* (1995) 16 Cr.App.R.(S) 388; *Dredge* [1998] 1 Cr.App.R.(S) 285; *Mills* [1998] 2 Cr.App.R.(S) 252.
12 See cases cited in *Laws of Australia*, Title 12, Criminal Sentencing [56].
13 *Roche* [1999] Crim.LR 339; and seen *Nunn* [1996] Crim.LR 210.
14 (1988) 10 Cr.App.R.(S) 13 at 15.
15 E.g. *Stephens* (1994) 76 A.Crim.R. 5.
16 How rigorously this is adhered to is not clear, the Court of Appeal itself does not always appear to have heeded it, in *Rowe* (1989) 11 Cr.App.R.(S) 342 the fact the victim was not a virgin was given as a reason for reducing the sentence.
17 *Cole and Barik* (1993) 14 Cr.App.R.(S) 764 at 765; cf. *A-Gs Reference (No 12 of 1992 (Khaliq)* (1993) 14 Cr.App.R.(S) 233 where a sentence of just two years was increased to three for the rape of a prostitute at knife point.
18 *Harris* (unreported, CCA Vic, 11 August 1981).
19 *Hakopian* (unreported, SC Vic, Jones J, 8 August 1991).
20 *Hakopian* (unreported, CCA Vic, 11 December 1991); *Myers and Ward* (unreported, CCA Vic, 31 August 1993, BC 9300725); *Smith* (unreported, CCA Vic, 7 December 1995, BC 9502538).
21 *Matthews* (unreported, CCA Vic, 9 October 1996, BC 9604884).
22 *Marteene* (unreported, CCA NSW, 76 of 1982) and *Leary* (unreported CCA NSW, 6 October 1993) in which Kirby J denounced the reasoning in *Hakopian*.
23 In *Many* (1990) 51 A.Crim.R. 54 at 56, the Court said this made it 'more poignant'; see also *Pinder* (1992) 8 WAR 19 at 40.
24 *Ives* [1973] Qd R 128 at 138 and 141.
25 *Huggard* (unreported, CCA Vic, 1/10/1986, BC 8600181) at 4.
26 *Schuhmacher* (1981) 3 A.Crim.R. 441 and *Athanasaiadis* (1990) 51 A.Crim.R. 292; see also Case 44 in the 'Heroines of Fortitude' study (van de Zandt 1998, p. 140).
27 *Hussey* (1980) 23 SASR 178; *Lyne* (unreported, CCA NSW, 7 October 1982) and *Raggett* (1990) 50 A.Crim.R. 41 at 53.
28 *Kelly and ors* (unreported, Fed Ct, 20 December 1989) Pincus and Miles JJ at 31; compare Morling J at 24; *Ridsale* (unreported, CCA Qld), 21 June 1996, BC 9602694).
29 The Australian decisions are discussed in more detail in Warner (1998).
30 This has not always prevented counsel, nor even the Court of Appeal from relying upon it, see *Bowley* [1999] 1 Cr.App.R.(S) 232.
31 E.g. *Dann* (unreported, CCA WA, 13 September 1995, BC 9504136); *Hyland* (unreported, CCA Tas, A82/1996) Cox CJ at 8 and Zeeman J at 7) and cases referred to in Warner (1998).
32 E.g. see *Pinder* (1992) 8 WAR 19.

33 *Jenkins* [1991] Crim.LR 460; *Mendez* (1992) 13 Cr.App.R.(S) 94 followed in *S* (1993) 14 Cr.App.R.(S) 324.

References

Ashworth, A. (2000), *Sentencing and Criminal Justice*, 3rd edn, Butterworths, London.

Bargen, J. and Fishwick, E. (1995), *Sexual Assault Law Reform: A national perspective*, Canberra: Office of the Status of Women.

Barrington, R. (1984), 'The Rape Law Reform Process in New Zealand', *Criminal Law Journal*, Vol. 8, pp. 307–25.

Criminal Law Revision Committee (1984) *Sexual Offences*, 15th Report, Cmnd 9213, London: HMSO.

Easteal, P. (1994), 'Survivors of Sexual Assault: An Australian survey', *International Journal of the Sociology of Law*, Vol. 22, pp. 329–54.

Edwards, S. (1996), *Sex, Gender and the Legal Process*, London: Blackstone Press.

Finkelhor, D. and Yllo, K. (1982) 'Forced Sex in Marriage: A preliminary research report', *Crime and Delinquency*, Vol. 34, pp. 29–39.

Fox, R. and Freiberg, A. (1999), *Sentencing, State and Federal Law in Victoria*, Melbourne: Oxford University Press.

Jones, A. (1980), *Women who Kill*, New York: Holt, Rinehart and Winston.

Kanin, E. (1984) 'Date Rape: Unofficial criminals and victims', *Victimology*, Vol. 9, pp. 95–108.

Kift, S. (1995), 'That all Rape is Rape Even if not by a Stranger', *Griffith Law Review*, Vol. 4, pp. 60–111.

Lacey, N. and Wells, C. (1998), *Reconstructing Criminal Law*, London: Butterworths.

Lees, S. (1997), *Ruling Passions*, Buckingham: Open University Press.

Lloyd, C. and Warmsley, D. (1989), *Changes in Rape Offences and Sentencing*, Home Office Research Study, No. 105, London: HMSO.

McColgan, A. (1996), *Taking the Date out of Rape*, London: Pandora.

Morgan, N. (1999), 'What's in a Name? Guideline Judgments in Australia', *Criminal Law Journal*, Vol. 23, pp. 90–107.

Painter, K. (1991), *Wife Rape, Marriage and the Law*, Manchester: Manchester University Press.

Robertshaw, P. (1994), 'Sentencing Rapists: First Tier Courts in 1991–92', *Criminal Law Review*, pp. 343–5.

Rumney, P. (1999), 'When Rape isn't Rape: Court of Appeal sentencing practice in cases of marital and relationship rape', *Oxford Journal of Legal Studies*, Vol. 19, pp. 243–6.

Rumney, P. and Morgan-Taylor, M. (1998), 'Sentencing in Cases of Male Rape', *Journal of Criminal Law*, Vol. 62, pp. 263–70.

Russell, D.H. (1990), *Rape in Marriage*, Indianapolis: Indiana University Press.

Scully, D. (1990), *Understanding Sexual Violence: A study of convicted rapists*, London: Unwin Hyman.

Sparks, R., Genn, H. and Dodd, D. (1977), *Surveying Victims*, Chichester: Wiley.

Van de Zandt, P. (1998), 'Heroines of Fortitude', in P. Easteal (ed.), *Balancing the Scales: Rape law reform and Australian culture*, Sydney: Federation Press, pp. 124–42.

Von Hirsch, A. and Jareborg, N. (1991), 'Gauging Criminal Harm: A living-standard analysis', *Oxford Journal of Legal Studies*, Vol. 11, pp. 1–38.

Warner, K. (1998), 'Sentencing for Rape', in P. Easteal (ed.), *Balancing the Scales: Rape law reform and Australian culture*, Sydney: Federation Press, pp. 174–90.

Warner, K. (2000), 'Sentencing in Cases of Marital Rape', *Legal Studies*, Vol. 20, pp. 593–611.

Wasik, M. (1998), *Emmins on Sentencing*, London: Blackstone Press.

Chapter Twenty-five

Sentencing the Corporate Offender: Legal and Social Issues

Hazel Croall and Jenifer Ross

The sentences received by corporate offenders have traditionally been seen as an example of injustice in the criminal justice system. The vast majority receive fines which are often characterised as too small, whether in relation to the harm which offences involve or to their limited impact on the resources of the corporation. This can be attributed to a combination of legal and sociological factors. Legally it can be argued that the criminal justice system does not deal adequately with the corporate form, neither in attributing responsibility generally to the company, nor in devising a range of sanctions which effectively deal with the corporation by any measure of the aims of punishment. The reliance of criminal law and punishment on notions of individual responsibility makes it difficult to find the business or corporation 'guilty' of a crime and to see it as 'deserving' of punishment (Wells 1993; Slapper and Tombs 1999; Ross 1999). This is related to how crime is socially constructed with corporate crimes being legally and popularly regarded as 'technical' matters of regulation rather than as 'real crimes' (Croall 2001). Attempts to strengthen the law and sentencing in relation to corporate offenders must therefore take into account both the legal difficulties surrounding corporate liability and the way in which corporate crime is socially and ideologically constructed. Tailoring law and sentences to the corporate form can lead to 'downgrading' corporate offenders, seeing their offences as distinct from and thereby less 'criminal' than those of conventional offenders.

This chapter will start by examining the proceedings following the E-coli outbreak in Scotland in 1997 which illustrates some of the problems associated with prosecuting and sentencing businesses. It will go on to critically examine the legal issues involved in attributing responsibility to corporate bodies and the problems of applying theories of punishment to corporate offenders. Finally, it will explore a range of sentencing options which might address corporate offending more directly than current sanctions and go some way towards dealing with such offences as 'crimes'.

Punishing the Corporate Offender: the E-coli Outbreak

In April 1998 a Fatal Accident Inquiry (FAI) was held in Motherwell into the deaths of 21 people in the course of an outbreak of E-coli poisoning in Central Scotland. The Inquiry was conducted by the Sheriff Principal (Cox) of the Sheriffdom of South Strathclyde, Dumfries and Galloway. His determination (Cox 1998) found that 17 of these deaths had been caused by E-coli poisoning and identified the source of the outbreak as the premises of John Barr & Sons, butchers who supplied raw and cooked meat to the public and to a number of suppliers throughout Central Scotland. It found several deficiencies in the firm's operations, which probably caused the outbreak: deficiencies in cooking methods, work flow and cleaning, and a failure to comply with registration requirements, as well as deficiencies in the quality and frequency of inspections by the local authority inspectors. The butcher was criticised for his approach to inspections:

> he regarded the visits by EHOs as something which all food premises had from time to time to tolerate. He paid lip-service to them and all the time managed to conceal from them the full extent of his business (p. 105).

Following the publication of these findings, victims criticised the butcher's lack of remorse and aggressive, unhelpful attitude, with their legal representative pointing to an "ethos of 'no blame, no responsibility'" from both the butcher and North Lanarkshire Council (*The Herald*, 20 August 1998, p. 5).

The role of the environmental health department was examined in the FAI, particularly its operation in the year preceding the outbreak, when the company premises had been inspected on three occasions. The Sheriff Principal criticised the quality of these inspections, unfavourably comparing their rigour with the approach taken once the premises had fallen under suspicion of being the source of the bacteria. The efforts of individual Inspectors and the system in the department were criticised. The Sheriff Principal and the Pennington Group, set up by the government to look at the outbreak as a whole, called for enforcement of food safety to be given an enhanced priority and adequate resourcing, and strongly supported the implementation of the Hazard Analysis and Critical Control Point system (HACCP) which places the responsibility for ensuring safety and consumer protection on the business itself (Pennington 1997 ch. 9).

Before the Inquiry there had been two prosecutions involving John Barr, the principal partner in the firm, the other two partners and the firm itself. In

Scotland a firm is a corporate body which can sue and be sued, and also prosecuted, independently of its partners. In the first trial, in October 1997, John Barr was prosecuted for the common law offence of culpable and reckless conduct: this related to the supply of contaminated meat to a birthday party. Since no deaths occurred as a result of the consumption of that meat, it was not relevant to charge him with culpable homicide. The meat had been supplied after the outbreak, and its probable source in John Barr's shop, had been identified. As a common law offence involving *mens rea* the prosecution had to prove that he had supplied the meat, either knowing that it might be infected with the bacteria or else indifferent as to whether it was or not. In Scotland corroboration is a requirement of proof in criminal cases. In the event there was insufficient evidence to corroborate the crucial issue of *mens rea* and Mr Barr was acquitted (*The Herald*, 28 October 1997).

A second prosecution was brought in January 1998 against Mr Barr, the other two partners and John Barr & Sons for offences under the Food Safety Act 1990 s. 8 and the Food Safety (General Food Hygiene) Regulations 1995. In Scotland the decision to prosecute, and the conduct of the prosecution, is the responsibility of the generic public prosecution service, the procurator fiscal. In the event the charges against all the individuals were dropped in exchange for the firm pleading guilty to two charges, one of selling meat unfit for human consumption and the other of breach of hygiene regulations. It was fined £1,500 in relation to the former and £750 in relation to the latter. In explaining the level of the fines the Sheriff stated that the outbreak had brought "notoriety and financial loss" following which the company had lost 40 per cent of its business, adding that "however the court has a duty to mark its displeasure at lapses which form this complaint" (*The Herald*, 21 January 1998).

These two prosecutions highlight many of the problems associated with criminal responsibility for business crime. In the second trial the conviction of the firm rather than the partners had two related effects. It enabled the individuals involved to avoid responsibility, which reinforced the tendency to view a breach of strict liability offences as technical rather than blameworthy. In the case of a small firm such as John Barr & Sons, there appears to be little to gain in substituting the firm for the individual. While it may be the practice of the enterprise itself which led to the failures, in a company with a small management base, company failures can be closely identified with individual failures. The stigmatising effect of the conviction on the firm exists, but is seen to be less than on a large company with a more diffuse management structure. In the case of a larger firm or company where individual blame may be difficult to identify, corporate conviction would have a distinct function. Nevertheless the strict liability of the offence removes much of the moral force from conviction.

The firm was not prosecuted in relation to the common law offence which required proof of recklessness. There would almost certainly have been no additional difficulty in prosecuting the firm as well as Mr Barr since the responsible individual was a partner, and thus the 'controlling mind' of the firm (see below). It was thus a policy decision not to prosecute the company for this offence. Although the arguments used already (i.e. that there is little point in prosecuting both the small firm and the partner in the small firm) apply equally here, the failure to prosecute the company for the common law crime involving *mens rea* and the failure to pursue the prosecution of the individual for the statutory crime reinforce further the quasi-criminal status of the latter. In the case of a larger company, where prosecution of the company independently of the director would serve a social aim, is there a convincing argument for not prosecuting the company for the more 'wicked' offence, where the offence can be attributed to corporate failure?

The whole prosecution and sentencing process in both trials was criticised by victims, their families and politicians (*The Herald*, 21 January 1998). Criticisms were directed at the so-called 'plea bargain' which resulted in the dropping of charges, and the size of the fine. A victim's relative was reported as commenting:

> how can anyone talk about a business's financial loss when 20 lives were lost and hundreds of people were made ill? ... like the other families involved, we still don't know who is responsible (*Guardian*, 21 January 1998).

Conviction of the firm rather than the individuals ensured that there was no alternative to the fine as a sentence. The small fines imposed (which may have been appropriately tailored to the circumstances of the firm by the sheriff) were incapable of meeting deterrent or retributive objectives. The statutory scheme for enforcement of the legislation, criticised, as seen above, in two Reports, is completely irrelevant in relation to any criminal trial which might take place, even for breach of the statute. It may be considered that the operation of the environmental health officers could be the key to ensuring that no future outbreaks of E-coli or other bacterial poisoning occurred. Future deterrence, or rehabilitation, might be most effectively ensured by targeted enforcement. However, this regime is completely distinct from the criminal trial. The sheriff had, therefore, no alternative but to impose a fine.

This case illustrates the legal and social factors underlying seemingly unfair sentencing outcomes. Convicting the firm, as opposed to the individual, removes much of the moral stigma from the offence. The decision to take such a course of action arose from a combination of legal factors and prosecutorial decisions. A fine was inevitable and its amount 'fairly' reflected the circumstances of the business and the regulations which had been broken. This appeared derisory however in relation to the perceived blameworthiness of the individual, who in this case could readily be identified with the firm, and to the severity of the outcome. The background to the events in question such as the much criticised (in)actions of the enforcement agency and the butcher's attitude to hygiene which emerged in the subsequent inquiry was not and could not legally be available in the criminal trial, thus omitting inculpating information. In this case therefore the individual could be said to have used the 'cloak' of corporate responsibility to his advantage. A full appreciation of sentencing must therefore take account of the legal issues surrounding corporate liability.

Legal Construction of the Corporate Offender

Corporations, whether firms, companies or public authorities are artificial persons, abstractions incapable of doing or thinking and thus of being responsible for anything themselves. To enable corporations to undertake legal obligations in the marketplace, they have legal personality and rights and duties in contract and tort/delict. There are difficulties associated with attributing criminal liability to them, which could be attributed to the moral dimension in criminal law or, it could be argued, to the powerful position of corporations. In general there has been no difficulty in holding corporations responsible for strict liability offences. There is no formal moral dimension, and companies and other corporations are routinely held to account for the failures of employees and other agents and for the unattributed failures of the corporation itself (Smith 2000). Where a crime involves proof of *mens rea*, however, it is necessary to prove that the company itself had the necessary mental element.

In order to do this, the 'controlling mind' theory is the approach of the UK courts (*Tesco Supermarkets Ltd v Natrass* [1972] AC 153; *Purcell Meats (Scotland) Ltd v McLeod* 1986 SCCR 672). The prosecution must prove that the crime was committed on the corporation's behalf by a 'controlling mind', that is those senior officers of the company who report to no-one and with whom the company can itself be identified. Ignoring the criticisms of this theory from the perspective of clarity alone (e.g. by Lord Maxwell in *Dean v John Menzies (Holdings) Ltd* 1981 JC 23; Law Commission 1996), its major limitation is that it attempts to apply to a corporation, an inherently collectivist notion, the same legal framework which applies to an individual. The major issue becomes the need to identify someone of sufficient seniority who is guilty of the offence and with whom the corporation can be identified. This was unsuccessful in the case which established the test, *Tesco Supermarkets Ltd v Natrass* and also in the prosecution of P&O Ferries for the manslaughter of the passengers drowned when the Herald of Free Enterprise sank (*R v P&O European Ferries (Dover) Ltd* (1991) 93 Cr.App.R. 72). There the judge withdrew the case against the directors (the 'controlling minds') and consequently against the company because the prosecution had not produced sufficient evidence of the necessary gross negligence against any one of them. The notion of 'aggregation' of the combined carelessness of a number of officers had previously been rejected (*R v H M Coroner for East Kent ex parte Spooner* (1989) 88 Cr.App.R. 10), and has been rejected again more recently in the unsuccessful prosecution of Great Western Trains for manslaughter of those killed in the Southall train crash (*Attorney General's Reference No 2 of 1999* [2000] 3 All ER 182). The controlling mind theory is really only suited to the small company which is effectively owned and controlled by one or a very small number of people. This was the case with the firm of John Barr & Son, although the Crown did not prosecute the firm for the *mens rea* offence. It was also the case in *R v OLL Ltd and Kite* (1994) where the company was convicted of the manslaughter of three school children drowned in Lyme Bay.

The prosecution in *Attorney General's Reference No 2 of 1999* attempted to break out of the straitjacket of the theory. The company was charged on the basis of its own gross negligence without seeking to identify it with any individual controlling mind, on the basis that gross negligence relates solely to conduct and not the mind. However this distinction was rejected and the need for identification of the company with an individual or individuals emphasised. The limited expansion of corporate liability in recent cases was viewed as an extension of the controlling mind theory not its replacement (*Seaboard Offshore Ltd v Secretary of State for Transport* [1994] 2 All ER 99; *Meridian Global Funds Management Asia Ltd v Securities Commission* [1995] 3 All ER 918).

The controlling mind approach does not relate to the corporate form. While corporations are fictions and can only act through individuals, they are more than simple abstractions. They have their own systems, policies and culture which can operate independently of the individuals currently comprising them (Wells 1993; Fisse and Braithwaite 1993). Much of the impetus for developing the concept of corporate responsibility has derived from the apparent inability of the law to hold any senior individual or organisation to account for major disasters involving loss of life. As part of a review of unintentional manslaughter the Law Commission in England subjected controlling mind theory to thorough criticism, proposing a new offence of corporate killing involving a requirement of 'management failure' (Law Commission 1996). The Home Office has adopted these proposals and is consulting with a view to legislation (Home Office 2000), further strengthening them by extending the offence to 'undertakings', that is unincorporated bodies, and also by permitting accessorial liability for Directors.

While this reform would enable prosecutions of companies for manslaughter to be brought more readily, there are a number of issues to be considered. The definition of management failure would have to be developed by the courts, and issues might arise about the level of management concerned (raising in another guise the controlling mind). It is also possible that corporate killing might become devalued since it is the third (and least serious?) of a trio of unintentional homicides (Clarkson 1996). The downgrading effect that corporate liability has in strict liability crime might apply with equal force here. Meanwhile, the much criticised controlling mind doctrine would remain for other *mens rea* crimes, including the other forms of manslaughter proposed by the Law Commission (reckless killing and killing by gross carelessness).

Denial of Responsibility: Downgrading Corporate Crime

This 'downgrading' of corporate crime is also evident in court, where the law provides 'space' for business offenders to further reduce their apparent blameworthiness. A major feature of regulatory law is that offences are of strict liability, which, while often portrayed as a strict form of law, can, in court, provide the basis for strategies aiming to portray defendants as responsible businesses undeserving of a criminal conviction (or punishment). While many businesses plead guilty, sometimes as the result, as in the E-coli case, of actual or alleged plea bargains (Mann 1985), such pleas can become the basis for mitigation and for limiting damaging information (Croall 1988). Defendants regularly seek to blame others for the offence – in the case of larger corporations by blaming employees, in the case of employees, by blaming superiors and company policy. Victims may also be blamed for not being sufficiently vigilant. Evidence may be provided that 'systems' within the company seek to secure compliance and breaches are represented as 'unavoidable accidents' which no regulations can completely prevent. In some cases appeals are made to business values and it is stressed that while the basis of regulations are accepted, over regulation would impede profitability. Complying with regulations is therefore presented as a 'technical' as opposed to a moral issue and on occasion, defendants contrast their responsible attitude with the 'rogues' against whom the law is 'really' aimed. Larger companies often provide considerable evidence to back up their claims of responsibility and a long history of compliance. Smaller companies may find it more difficult to establish their responsibility or to 'pass the buck' through the chain of responsibility, but as the E-coli example shows, they too can seek to reduce the moral element in offences by using the corporate 'veil'. Pleading guilty further limits damaging information as few witnesses are called and the often long history preceding prosecution is not relevant to the court. The law, therefore, enables defendants to reduce their apparent culpability, and to play upon the accepted construction of many business crimes as 'not really crimes'. To the extent that these strategies are credible, they serve to reduce sentences which are also affected by the difficulties of applying traditional approaches to punishment to corporate offenders.

Theories of Punishment: Sentencing the Corporate Offender

The corporate form poses difficulties for traditional theories of punishment which more readily apply to individual 'guilty' offenders. In short, corporations have "no soul to damn, no body to kick" (Coffee 1981). It is therefore difficult to apply theories based on 'just deserts' or rehabilitation and there are also practical limitations to sentences. A business cannot be sent to prison and companies are not, in Britain at any rate, considered for probation or community sentences leaving the fine as virtually the only option. It has nonetheless been argued that some theories can be better applied to corporations and that a wider range of approaches could be adopted. A brief summary of these arguments follows.

Deterrence

Deterrence, along with prevention, is often seen as the main rationale for the use of the criminal law in 'business regulation' and companies are often represented as 'amoral calculators' primarily interested in profitability or survival. Prosecution, publicity and heavy fines are therefore a potential deterrent, as they threaten profitability by adversely affecting investment, consumers and public reputation (Braithwaite 1984; Croall 1992; Wells 1993; Pearce and Tombs 1998). They may also provide a general deterrent by providing symbolic examples (Pearce and Tombs 1998). Directors and senior management prosecuted as individuals have much to lose, making the threat of prison a powerful one (Punch 1996). While persuasive, many of these arguments can be contested. Corporate activities do not always reflect 'rational calculations', and many 'dangerous practices' can be encouraged and persist within corporate cultures (Pearce and Tombs 1998). As is the case with conventional offenders the likelihood of being caught and prosecuted may act as a greater deterrent than the eventual sentence, suggesting the potential of more resources for enforcement and a more 'punitive' prosecution policy (Croall 1992; Punch 1996; Slapper and Tombs 1999). While in theory financial penalties provide a deterrent, in practice, fines are often affordable and can be seen as a 'licence' to offend (Croall 1992).

Rehabilitation

Although rehabilitative approaches, often seen as being directed at the 'minds' of individual offenders, have not generally been applied to the corporation, they can be applicable (Braithwaite 1984; Fisse and Braithwaite 1993). As Braithwaite (1984) points out standard procedures and organisation charts are easier to change than individual psyches thus targeting what is arguably the root of the problem. Sentences could be directed at the sloppy organisational procedures and lack of accountability on the part of individuals and corporate cultures so often seen as underlying many offences (Braithwaite 1984; Punch 1996; Slapper and Tombs 1999), and an 'interventionist' approach could render corporate management open to scrutiny, and enhance the power of regulators (Pearce and Tombs 1998). Rehabilitative approaches could also be useful for small companies for whom deterrent sentences may not be appropriate, and where the problem is often seen by enforcers as lying in poor management and a lack of knowledge about the law and compliance matters (Croall 1991). In addition, a rehabilitative approach could limit the adverse fall out to employees and shareholders of larger fines suggested by deterrent approaches. Probation or community service orders could therefore be appropriate for corporate offenders.

Retribution

One of the major rationales for sentencing conventional offenders is that they 'deserve' punishment and that sentences should be in proportion to the harm done, thus stressing the moral basis of punishment. While fines do reflect elements of retribution, criticisms of their 'derisory' amounts reflect a view that 'justice' has not been done in that the sentence does not reflect the harm done or signal public disapproval. The lack of individual blameworthiness and the ability of defendants, illustrated above, to reduce this create difficulties for retributive approaches as does the downgrading of business offences to 'technical' matters of regulation rather than 'criminal' offences. It has also been seen that the attitude of defendants to regulations and their history of compliance is not relevant in court and the individual regulation, rather than the harm done, is the matter at issue – all of which further reduces retributive and moral elements.

Denunciation

Punishment also plays a denunciatory role, expressing abhorrence towards offences and subjecting offenders to shame. Thus the criminalisation of the corporation can be justified not only as a means of protecting the public, but of underlining the unacceptable nature of offences. In order for this to be achieved the public must be aware of both the nature of corporate offences and their punishment. Thus the attraction of 'naming and shaming' and the use, in some jurisdictions, of publicity orders (Fisse and Braithwaite 1983). This also may go some way towards challenging the perception that corporate offences are not really crime and sensitising the public to the widespread nature of corporate offending. Thus criminalisation and publicising sentencing play an important symbolic role. There are a number of problems with this approach, not least that sentences are often inconsistently reported and do not reach a wide enough audience (Fisse and Braithwaite 1983).

While it is difficult, therefore, to apply some theories of punishment to the corporation, some could be more imaginatively applied. Moreover, in practice, sentencing often reflects a combination of aims which, applied to corporations, could provide additional sentencing options. A good example of this is Fisse and Braithwaite's (1993) argument for the use of an enforcement 'pyramid' with a range of sentences with increasing severity, including corporate probation and 'capital punishment'. However, adopting a more flexible and innovative approach to the corporation is at odds with the individualised and unrealistic approach adopted by the criminal law to identifying the corporate offender as can be seen when existing options are considered.

Sentencing the Corporate Offender: Current Options

Fines, the main sentence, may be supplemented by compensation orders, another monetary penalty. These reflect deterrent and retributive aims and, where particularly high fines are given, may be denunciatory, although even record fines can be criticised for failing to meet any of these objectives. While low fines are often seen as reflecting judicial 'sympathy' with corporate offenders, they also reflect a combination of different legal factors – as in the E-coli case, fines may be 'fair' in terms of sentencing principles, however 'unfair' they may be perceived. In addition, the relatively simple option of raising levels of fines creates a number of difficulties as seen in a number of cases which have sought to clarify the law.

Concerns that fines in the health and safety field have been too low to be effective have been accepted by the Court of Appeal in England in *R v Howe & Son (Engineers) Ltd* ([1999] 1 All ER 249). After criticism of the level of fines by the Health and Safety Commission (Health and Safety Commission 1991), when the average fine for a breach of the Health and Safety at Work etc. Act was £732, the maximum fine after summary prosecution was raised to £20,000, and the level of fines has risen to an extent. In 1992–93 the average fine in the magistrates' courts in England Wales (where the limit is £20,000) was £2,100. In 1997–98 this had increased to £6,223: in the Crown Court where the fine may be unlimited the average fine was £17,768 (*R v Howe & Son (Engineers) Ltd*.

In this case the company had appealed against fines totalling £48,000 and an award of £7,500 costs imposed for offences under Health and Safety at Work legislation which had caused the death by electrocution of a worker, in 'an accident waiting to happen'. The appeal was partially successful, the fine being reduced from £40,000 on the main count to £15,000, and the other fines rescinded. While the court refused to lay down any tariff or to say that the level of fine should bear a specific relationship to the turnover or profit of the company, it took the opportunity to look generally at the factors which should be taken into account in determining the appropriate level of fine (pp. 254–5). Certain factors affected the gravity of offences. Firstly, how far the company fell below the 'reasonably practicable' standard in committing the offence;

secondly whether death resulted from the offence. Although it acknowledged that the causing of death or serious injury is "a matter of chance", the court felt that the penalty should reflect "public disquiet at the unnecessary loss of life". This is an interesting move away from the view that it is the breach alone which is relevant and not the consequences (Slapper and Tombs 1999; Wells 1993). Thirdly, whether there had been a deliberate breach as a cost-cutting measure with a view to profit. This is described as 'seriously' aggravating the offence, and is a clear moral position. Fourthly, the degree of risk and extent of danger created by the offence. Fifthly, the extent of the breach, in particular whether it was an isolated incident or continued over a period. Sixthly (and 'importantly' – a key factor in the case itself), the company's resources and the effect of the fine on its business.

Two factors were identified as particularly aggravating: a failure to heed warnings, and the deliberate profiting from failure to take necessary safety steps or from running a risk to save money. Three mitigating factors were identified: prompt admission of responsibility and timely plea of guilty; steps to remedy deficiencies (in this case the company had spent £15,000 on rewiring the premises since the incident), and a good safety record. The court also emphasised that the size of the company is irrelevant: the employee of the small company must be as safe as the employee of the large company. There was evidence that safety standards in small organisations may be lower than those in large ones. Although many of these factors are moral, the overall objective identified was the utilitarian one of "achiev[ing] a safe environment for those who work there and for other members of the public". The fine "needs to be large enough to bring that message home where the defendant is a company not only to those who manage it but also to its shareholders" (p. 255).

In spite of the court's view that it was a "bad case" involving "a flagrant disregard for the safety of the company's employees", the fine was reduced because of the financial resources of the company. Interestingly the court rejected the notion that a fine should always be set at a level which would enable the company to stay in business. Lord Justice Rose observed that "there may be cases where the offences are so serious that the defendant ought not to be in business" (p. 255). Does this envisage a financial form of incapacitation of a company (Braithwaite and Geis 1982)?

As this case shows, the financial resources of the company are a critical element (though not the only one) in determining the appropriate level of fine. In general, in imposing a fine a court is obliged to look at the financial resources of the accused (in England and Wales: Criminal Justice Act 1991 s. 18; in Scotland Criminal Procedure (Scotland) Act 1995 s. 211(7)). Assessing the financial resources of a business may not be easy. Its capital assets as well as its income may not be clearly identified, or valued. The Court of Appeal in *R v Howe & Son (Engineers) Ltd* acknowledged the difficulty of the sentencing judge in obtaining "timely and accurate information about a corporate defendant's means": "such financial information as he had was not supplied until the very last moment" (p. 256). A company is more likely to present financial information of its poor position in mitigation of sentence, than to provide full details of all its assets as a submission to the sentencer.

The precise financial logic for the level of the fine in this case was not given. It ruled out any precise relationship between turnover, or net profit, and fine. However, in a Scottish case, *Topek (Bur) Ltd v H.M.A.* (1998 SCCR 352), the High Court of Justiciary upheld a £20,000 fine against a company which amounted to half their net annual profit. A worker employed by a subcontractor had been killed when the mobile platform he was working on was blown over in 50 mile an hour gales. The sentencing sheriff felt that a substantial fine was necessary "to express society's disapproval" of such failures by companies carrying out dangerous activities, "especially when that failure resulted in a fatality". Because the blame resting on the company was substantial, the sheriff felt that the correct level was half their annual net profits. The High Court agreed without discussing this point. In imposing the fine the sentencing sheriff indicated that the solicitor acting for the company "said he had their latest accounts which were in draft form", that he "was told that the profit for the following year was not likely to be any more" and that "the company's profits had been falling over the last few years", that he "had no note of being told" what the company's net worth was. As with the previous case the mechanisms for assessing the turnover, profit and worth of a company seem to be haphazard. It suggests, particularly given the reliance on fines, that a more sophisticated and accurate method of providing the court with this information should be introduced. Bergman (1992) has suggested the adoption of a form of corporate enquiry report which would provide accurate information on relevant financial and other aspects of the company which the court may wish to take account of: such as for example, its turnover, annual profits, history of relationship with the regulatory agency or its general health and safety record (Slapper and Tombs 1999). This might go some way to combating the strategy of companies to restrict inculpating information.

While, therefore, fines could be increased and more realistically calculated, there remain some difficulties with relying on monetary penalties. Levels of financial penalties are inevitably constrained, particularly for large companies, by the possibility of a 'spillover' effect onto employees, consumers and shareholders. Against this it can be argued that shareholders take a risk by investing (Braithwaite 1984) and indirectly profit from offences (Pearce and Tombs 1998). In addition, higher fines could encourage shareholders to ask more questions about management (Geis 1978). These sentiments were evident in a case where one of the biggest fines in a Scottish Court, £250,000, was imposed on Royal Ordnance, following an explosion which seriously injured a worker. After commenting on the company's "sad history" of neglecting safety, Lord Dawson stated that the fine would fall on "innocent shareholders" and that he trusted they would take action to prevent a similar accident happening again (*The Herald*, 27 February 1998). Nonetheless employment may be adversely affected by punitively high fines. In addition, amounts of financial penalties are limited for public service organisations as illustrated when British Rail was sentenced following the Clapham rail disaster, where it was argued that a higher fine might lead to higher fares or to a reduction of investment in the rail system (Wells 1993).

An additional problem is that to be fully deterrent, fines could be "astronomical" – Etzioni (1993) for example argues that on the assumption that companies and senior executives are rational calculators, the size of fines must take account of the small chance of being prosecuted. This could be politically unacceptable as was the case in the United States, where fines based on these kinds of calculations were suggested by the Sentencing Commission. Following objections on the part of business groups, the high suggested fines had to be withdrawn (Etzioni 1993; Pearce and Tombs 1998; Slapper and Tombs 1999). Implementing higher financial penalties may also exacerbate the differences between larger and smaller companies as large corporations can more easily afford to pay (Croall 1992; Pearce and Tombs 1998). As seen above, they cannot be backed up, as for conventional offenders, with the threat of prison (Wells 1993) and may not prevent further offending, indeed Slapper and Tombs (1999) point out that while fines have recently risen for occupational safety cases there has been no decrease in prosecutions.

Sentencing the Corporate Offender: New Approaches

It is now more widely recognised that there is a clear need to develop a wider range of sanctions for corporations which recognise the uniqueness of the corporate form but which must also take account of the above difficulties. A large number of commentators, from a variety of different perspectives, have advocated that a wider range of sentences be considered (Braithwaite 1984;

Bergman 1992; Wells 1993; Pearce and Tombs 1998; Slapper and Tombs 1999). The most commonly suggested alternative options include the use of rehabilitative sentences such as probation and the application, to companies, of community sentences.

The Law Commission's proposal for a corporate killing offence (Law Commission 1996) and the government's subsequent consultation proposals (Home Office 2000) propose an additional sanction restricted to corporate killing. The Commission's earlier Consultation Paper (Law Commission 1994) rejected "company probation, or the imposition of penalties something like those operating in market regulatory systems" (para. 5.91) in favour of a fine plus the stigma attaching to conviction. However on consultation several respondents, including Disaster Action and Victim Support, criticised the failure to consider other alternatives. As a result the Commission's draft Bill includes a provision enabling a sentencing court to make a 'remedial order', for which both prosecution and the Health and Safety Executive could apply. Such an order would require the corporation to take such steps as the court considers appropriate to remedy whatever 'management failure' had caused the death in question. Failure to comply with the order would itself be an offence for which the punishment would be, of course, a fine. This is an acknowledgement of the paucity of sanction available to the sentencer of a corporation. While it is limited in that it applies only to corporate killing on the one hand and to the narrow limits of the specific offence on the other, it is an interesting proposal to provide an alternative which would have a practical, rehabilitative function. It is related to wider arguments about the potential of corporate probation.

Corporate Probation?

Following the above arguments in relation to rehabilitation, corporate probation has been implemented in some jurisdictions (Box 1983; Braithwaite 1984; Bergman 1992; Croall 1992). Box for example suggested the appointment of probation officers to monitor operating procedures, and Braithwaite discusses a system of probation orders supervised by auditors – in both cases with the costs being borne by companies. The court may impose conditions such as an insistence on safety procedures and the employment of staff responsible for monitoring compliance (Slapper and Tombs 1999). Probation can be, and in the United States is, accompanied by other sentences such as a fine or community service – in some cases companies have been required to lend executives to community programmes for a period of time

(Punch 1996). Regulatory officials may be involved in such schemes (Slapper and Tombs 1999). It can also be argued that such orders direct attention to and intervene in the specific conditions of an organisation and may considerably strengthen the legal foundation of corporate liability (Lofquist 1993; Slapper and Tombs 1999). In addition it may be appropriate for smaller companies, who are often seen as needing advice and education. In the E-coli case discussed above for example, a form of probation order might have been directed towards the shortcomings identified in the subsequent FAI, and might also have mitigated some of the critical public reaction to the fine. It could also signal to the public that efforts are being made to prevent re-occurrences.

While this may be seen as an attractive option it does raise important issues. The appointment of special probation officers could be rejected on the grounds of its cost (Slapper and Tombs 1999), although in many suggested schemes the costs would be borne by companies. This in turn however could provoke strong reactions detailed by Etzioni in relation to punitive fines. Finally, while it may be seen as appropriate for companies, some dispute its effectiveness for individual offenders within corporations who may be less amenable to 'reform' and are not in need of education (Punch 1996). On the other hand Wells, citing policies in the United States, argues that it can be used to rectify the imbalance between corporate and individual sentencing (Wells 1993). In one case she cites, the court required a defendant company to lend an executive to a charitable organisation for one year to develop a programme for ex offenders.

Corporate Community Service?

A combination of rehabilitation and deterrence, along with elements of retribution and denunciation underlie the popularity of community service orders for conventional offenders. This form of sentence is relatively undeveloped in relation to companies for whom it is argued to have considerable potential. In part its appeal is symbolic as it clearly expresses the loss to the community which corporate crime may involve, but it also contains both rehabilitative and deterrent aspects, particularly where it is accompanied by fines and/or probation orders and it may also avoid the 'deterrence trap' – rather than threatening employment and thereby local communities, it may involve the company doing something positive for the community. As seen above some orders require companies to release employees to work for the community. In another case, cited by Braithwaite, a chemicals company was required to fund an environmental protection programme following a major pollution incident (Braithwaite 1984). He also suggests that pharmaceutical companies could be required to produce drugs for sufferers of rare diseases for whom the price of drugs may be prohibitive. Other suggestions have included requiring food companies who have sold adulterated food to use their facilities and resources to provide food for deserving groups, executives in car companies who have deliberately produced unsafe cars to do voluntary work in Emergency Rooms, or the requirement that companies found to have manufactured and sold dangerous toys provide free toys for children's hospitals and homes (Box 1983; Croall 1992; Etzioni 1993; Slapper and Tombs 1999). Using the E-coli case as an example, the butcher concerned could have been required to not only clean his premises but provide some services for community groups which might have mitigated the harsh reaction to the sentence.

While such suggestions do have a number of attractions, some problems must be addressed. It tends to be assumed that these options would arouse public reaction – little evidence however is cited to support such claims (Slapper and Tombs 1999). They could however be combined with publicity orders and for some time their novelty might in itself provide publicity. It could also be asked whether they would work in practice and who might supervise such schemes, and they could also add to the downgrading effect by using what is often seen as a 'soft option' for conventional offenders for corporate offenders. Unlike probation, they do not intervene in operating procedures, and, like fines, may leave underlying practices and culture untouched, and be more affordable on the part of larger corporations. On the other hand, as existing options are seen as overly lenient, these would be no less so.

Other options, hitherto underdeveloped in Britain, could also be combined with the above or used as part of an escalating range of sanctions. These could include publicity orders, and more use of prison where individual responsibility can be established, although this latter could lead to the scapegoating of employees for what are essentially company problems (Wells 1993). Companies can also be ordered to take internal disciplinary measures against directors and strengthening provisions for the licensing of businesses, suggested for food outlets following the E-coli outbreak, can also act as a powerful deterrent and involves elements of public "shame" (Pearce and Tombs 1998).

Conclusion

A combination of legal and social factors therefore underlie the apparent shortcomings of the criminal law and criminal justice process in relation to corporate offenders. The approach of the courts in applying criminal law to companies has been to seek to identify them with individuals, except in cases of strict liability where no moral/legal blame is attributed. The criminal law does not recognise the corporate form in attributing blame in the context of responsibility. A similar approach has also meant that sanctions devised for conventional offences have been inappropriately applied to the company. In fact, so inappropriate is the ultimate sanction, imprisonment, that it cannot apply at all. The unique form of control which has been devised in the business sphere, regulation and enforcement, has no role to play in punishment, even although it may be viewed as potentially more effective than the inevitable fine. Corporate offences have therefore become downgraded, viewed legally and socially as 'not really crime'. The concentration of the criminal law on strict liability offences as most appropriate for corporations enables businesses to evade moral responsibility and heavier sanctions. At the same time the refusal to develop more imaginative corporate punishments than the fine leave the system of justice open to justified charges of inequity, ineffectiveness and irrelevance.

Nonetheless, there are signs of change in legal attitudes to the liability of the corporation which also affect sentencing. A number of alternative strategies have been reviewed and while these undoubtedly have limitations, it can also be argued that, as Wells points out in respect of corporate probation, they are no less efficient than a fine (Wells 1993). Moreover, they can be used in combination, provide greater flexibility to take account of both individual and corporate liability, and could lead to the development of a more cohesive strategy toward corporate offending. On the other hand such changes might do little to change the situation in which corporate crime is not socially constructed as crime, which to many reflects the limiting effect of corporate power on the law. Nonetheless even the most critical of commentators argue that a combination of criminalisation, deterrent and rehabilitative strategies can be positive and provide a significant tool in the armoury of measures to combat corporate offending (Pearce and Tombs 1998). Arguing from a Marxist perspective, Pearce and Tombs contest that constructions of corporate crime as "not really crime" can be "challenged and changed" and that the criminal law and punishment are part of a wider movement to render corporations accountable for the harms which they cause. Moreover, describing offences as "corporate manslaughter" or "corporate killing" reveals, they argue, the power of language in challenging such representations and the same could be said for concepts of "corporate probation" or "corporate community service" as these underline the "criminal" element of offences and move some way towards breaking down the different construction of corporate and conventional crime (Pearce and Tombs 1998). Care however must be taken, as pointed out above, to avoid the situation in which any reforms which create special situations for corporate offenders reinforce rather than break down the distinction between regulatory and real crimes. This may be accompanied by the growing influence of victim movements following so called 'disasters' who, like the victims quoted in the early part of this paper, wish to see those responsible for offences 'named and shamed' and a greater level of 'justice'.

References

Bergman, D. (1992), 'Corporate Sanctions and Corporate Probation', *New Law Journal*, Vol. 144, p. 1312.

Box, S. (1983), *Power, Crime and Mystification*, London: Tavistock.

Braithwaite, J. (1984), *Corporate Crime in the Pharmaceutical Industry*, London: Routledge and Kegan Paul.

Braithwaite, J. and Geis, G. (1982), 'On Theory and Action for Corporate Crime Control', *Crime and Delinquency*, April, pp. 292–314.

Carson, W.G. (1979), 'The Conventionalisation of Early Factory Crime', *International Journal of the Sociology of Law*, Vol. 7(1), pp. 37–60.

Clarkson, C. (1996), 'Kicking Corporate Bodies and Damning their Souls', *Modern Law Review*, p. 557.

Coffee, J.C. Jnr (1981), '"No Soul to Damn No Body to Kick": An unscandalized inquiry into the problem of corporate punishment', 79, *Michigan Law Review*, pp. 386–459.

Cook, D. (1989), *Rich Law, Poor Law: Different responses to tax and supplementary benefit fraud*, Milton Keynes: Open University Press.

Cox, G.L. (1998), *Determination in the E-coli O 157 Fatal Accident Inquiry*, Dumfries and Galloway: Sheriffdom of South Strathclyde.

Croall, H. (1988), 'Mistakes, Accidents and Someone Else's Fault: The trading offender in court', *Journal of Law and Society*, Vol 15/3, pp. 293–315.

Croall, H. (1991), 'Sentencing the Business Offender', *Howard Journal of Criminal Justice*, Vol. 30, No. 4, pp. 280–92.

Croall, H. (1992), *White Collar Crime*, Buckingham: Open University Press.

Croall, H. (2001), *Understanding White Collar Crime*, Buckingham: Open University Press.

Etzioni, A. (1993), 'The US Sentencing Commission on Corporate Crime: A critique', in G. Geis and P. Jesilow (eds), *White Collar Crime*, Newbury Park, California: Sage Periodicals Press, pp. 147–56.

Fisse, B. and Braithwaite, J. (1983), *The Impact of Publicity on Corporate Offenders*, Albany: State University of New York Press.

Fisse, B. and Braithwaite, J. (1993), *Corporations, Crime and Accountability*, Cambridge: Cambridge University Press.

Geis, G. (1978), 'Deterring Corporate Crime', in R. Ermann and R. Lundman (eds), *Corporate and Governmental Deviance*, New York: Oxford University Press.

Health and Safety Commission (1991), *Annual Report 1989–90*, London: HSE.

Home Office (2000), *Reforming the Law on Involuntary Manslaughter: the Government's Response*, London: HMSO.

Law Commission (1994), *Involuntary Manslaughter*, Consultation Paper No. 135, London: HMSO.

Law Commission (1996), *Legislating the Criminal Code: Involuntary Manslaughter*, No. 237, London: HMSO.

Lofquist, W.S. (1993), 'Organisational Probation and the US Sentencing Commission', in G. Geis and P. Jesilow (eds), *White Collar Crime*, pp. 157–69.

Mann, K. (1985), *Defending White Collar Crime*, New Haven and London: Yale University Press.

Pearce, F. and Tombs, S. (1998), *Toxic Capitalism: Corporate crime and the chemical industry*, Aldershot: Ashgate.

Pennington Group (1997), *Report on the circumstances leading to the 1996 outbreak of infection with E-coli O 157 in Central Scotland, the implications for food safety and the lessons to be learned*, London: HMSO.

Ross, J. (1999), 'Corporate Criminal Liability: One form or many forms?', *The Juridical Review*, Part 1, pp. 49–65.

Slapper, G. and Tombs, S. (1999), *Corporate Crime*, London: Longman.

Smith J.C. Commentary on Attorney General's Reference (No. 2 or 1999) [2000], *Criminal Law Review*, pp. 477–9.

Wells, C. (1993), *Corporations and Criminal Responsibility*, Oxford: Clarendon Press.

Wells, C. (1996), 'The Corporate Manslaughter Proposals', *Criminal Law Review*, p. 545.

Chapter Twenty-six

Sentencing, Inequality and Justice

Neil Hutton

Introduction

Barbara Hudson's critique of the just deserts approach to punishment has been one of the most important attempts to construct a 'progressive'[1] approach to punishment, an area of policy which has always been problematic for those on the left. This discussion of her work is in sympathy with Hudson's political stance but critical of her specific proposals to resolve the problem of how to punish justly in an unjust society. The central argument of this essay is that Hudson's proposals for a "social theory of culpability" are unlikely to help the progressive agenda because of a confusion between the proper disciplinary projects of law and politics.

A 'Progressive' Revision of Just Deserts

In her debate with Andrew von Hirsch (1993), Hudson has developed an accommodation with desert theory (Hudson 1987, 1993, 1996). In a 1995 article Hudson sets out her ideas of a "principled parsimony" which adds a more social view of culpability to a limiting retributivism (Morris and Tonry 1990) based on parsimony. For Hudson, desert alone, even under the overall aim of crime reduction, does not provide an adequate justification for punishment. Punishment must pursue constructive instrumental goals which promote a more just and equal society. She accepts that the principle of desert should set limits to punishment for particular offences but argues that within these limits, punishment ought to be allocated on rehabilitative principles. This approach combines reformative efficacy with public protection and deterrence. These are seen as being aims of punishment which would be acceptable to both progressives and conservatives and also to the public.

Hudson's version of a liberal approach to punishment embraces four standard liberal principles and aims: parsimony, protection of the public, deterrence and rehabilitation. Parsimony requires that we should punish as little as possible and would be accepted by most liberals. Hudson also accepts that no penal policy will survive unless it acknowledges the public demand for protection particularly from dangerous violent and sexual offenders. Despite the evidence which shows the limited deterrent effectiveness of punishment, Hudson argues that there is a widely held belief in the deterrent effect of punishment which is unlikely to be disturbed by this research evidence and so deterrence needs to be an aim of punishment. Finally Hudson believes in reformative efficacy which is a restatement of the importance of rehabilitation as a justification for punishment. As with deterrence, the research on rehabilitation shows relatively modest success rates. While it appears that some programmes are better than others at helping offenders to stop offending (McGuire 1995), few have success rates of more than around 40 per cent, although there is a considerable debate which challenges the use of reconviction rates as a measure of the effectiveness of community sanctions (Mair 1997). Hudson argues that even if the success rates are modest, it is morally important for the state to offer offenders the opportunity to change and that resources are better spent on rehabilitative projects with some chance of success than on forms of punishment which make no efforts to assist offenders to change their behaviour.

Thus far, Hudson's view of the proper justification for punishment appears to be a fairly conventional progressive approach. Under an overall principle of parsimony which tries to use a minimum amount of punishment, and subject to limits on maximum punishments set by the principle of desert, punishment should protect society from dangerous violent and sexual offenders but otherwise seek to use carefully selected rehabilitative punishments for those remaining offenders who wish to change their behaviour. This level of punishment will be sufficient to serve the purpose of deterrence in the broad sense that the mere existence of a criminal justice system and a penal system acts to discourage many of us from committing offences. Their existence supports the socialisation processes of family and school which are broadly effective for most of us.

Many liberals and progressives would agree thus far with Hudson's approach which tries to minimise punishment and to punish humanely and constructively within a political climate of populist punitiveness (Bottoms 1995) and political pragmatism (Brownlee 1998). However the final part of Hudson's approach is more controversial. Hudson argues that the levels of punishment imposed on those systematically disadvantaged sections of the population are unjust, and she tries to develop a conception of culpability which could be used to reduce these unfair levels of punishment.

Culpability

From a desert perspective, offence seriousness is comprised of harm and culpability, that is the extent of harm or damage caused to victims added to the extent of the offenders' responsibility for the harm. Hudson argues that in practice, seriousness has been primarily related to harm factors and culpability, a characteristic of the offender, has been under-emphasised.

Hudson wants to focus more attention on culpability and argues that offenders who "through poverty, mental disorder, racism or other obstacles have been denied chances of achieving through lawful means the goods to which we all aspire" may be less blameworthy than those whose choices are less constrained by their circumstances (Hudson 1995, p. 65). Her argument is that the criminal justice system focuses its attentions disproportionately on certain disadvantaged sections of the population. These populations are disproportionately subject to arrest, prosecution and punishment. They make up a disproportionate section of prison populations. Hudson argues that members of these populations should be held to be less culpable for their offences on the grounds that their misfortune in being a member of the disadvantaged population puts them at greater risk of offending. Hudson gives the following examples in the text: women shoplifting groceries, young burglars who have never had the chance of a job and young, unemployed homeless people who are not entitled to benefit and who have to resort to begging and petty theft to survive.

Hudson is proposing that the liberal theory of culpability based on the discourse of individual responsibility ought to be replaced by something different which might be described as a 'social theory of culpability'. Hudson only provides a sketch of this idea and in what follows I try to imagine what a social theory of culpability would look like and also to examine how it might be put into practice. First it may be helpful to provide a brief review of the main points of the liberal theory of individual responsibility.

Individual Responsibility and Liberal Theory

The theory of individual responsibility is instantiated in the criminal law. Alan Norrie (1993) traces the historical development of this idea from the Enlightenment as a vital part of the attempt to establish individual freedoms protected by law as an alternative to the previous political regimes of absolute power with their "punitive reigns of terror" (Norrie 1993, p. 19). The underpinning assumption of liberal theory is that society is composed of free rational individuals all equal before the law. As all individuals are in this sense the same they must be treated in the same way. Law thus provides a discourse of individual liberty which seems to transcend particular social interests. For the American philosopher Stanley Fish, however, this discourse of individual liberty is only half the story, "... law is a discourse continually telling two stories, one of which is denying that the other is being told at all" (Fish 1994, p. 176).

In general, one story is that law is free from all ethical and political judgements. It is rational, formal, neutral and objective. The second story is that this in itself is a value position, promoting the values of a liberal society such as individual freedom, rationality, universality, equality and so on. This second story is not told openly, indeed, the first story denies the possibility of the second story. However, law promotes a particular set of values and helps to secure legitimacy for these values by presenting itself as independent of particular values and therefore as attractive to all.

The first story is of course a fiction and not an accurate empirical description of society. Not only is power and wealth unequally distributed in society, law protects this unequal division. In a divided society, (and all societies are composed of conflicting interests and unequally distributed power), law may serve the interests of the powerful but it also places restraints on the exercise of power by the powerful and by constituting people as legal individuals creates formal opportunities for participation which, at least sometimes, provide power for relatively powerless people. Thus law works by presenting itself plausibly as neutral and disguising its partisan basis. This is what Norrie (1993) describes as the "cunning" of law or what Stanley Fish (1994) quoting Scheiber (1984) also calls law's "amazing trick". Law is able to conceal its social control functions and partisan commitments behind formal procedures which rhetorically promise to deliver equal justice to all. For Fish, this capacity to make claims for universality while in practice protecting particular interests is not conceived as a problem which needs to be resolved, rather it is what makes law a distinctive and useful social practice. To put this argument in another way, the gap between 'law in the books' and 'law in action', is not a hole which needs to be filled, but a distinction which is inevitable and constitutive of the way in which law works to create community in a world of difference (Nelken 1983; Hutton 1986).

This rhetorical trick in the area of sentencing operates in at least two related ways: firstly in the way that the law deals with individual responsibility and secondly in the way that sentencing practice deals with the idea of equal treatment.

Responsibility and Culpability

Individual responsibility is a legal fiction. Responsibility is formally located at the level of the individual. Responsibility is in this sense an absolute. However, law also recognises the idea of culpability which is not an absolute but subject to degrees of variation. Various disciplines which purport to provide 'scientific' knowledge about the extent of culpability have been accepted by law as providing evidence which can either in a strong sense overrule the presumption of individual responsibility or more commonly in a weaker sense allow factors to be held to have diminished the extent of individual responsibility e.g. psychiatry, psychology and social work/probation (Norrie 1993). However, responsibility is always located at the level of the individual. In those rare cases where an individual is held to have no responsibility, this is because they have no capacity for reason. Responsibility disappears with the absence of individual reason, it is not allocated elsewhere.

In sentencing, judges may take account of a very wide range of factors which may be presented to them by defence lawyers as mitigating factors, that is, as factors which reduce the extent of culpability of an offender. Some examples might be domestic circumstances, employment status and previous convictions.[2] This reduction in culpability is held to reduce the seriousness of the offence and thus merit a proportionately reduced penalty. Thus culpability may be reduced on the basis of the particular circumstances of an individual case but the responsibility still lies with the individual. How does a judge assess culpability? This question takes us to the idea of equal treatment.

Equal Treatment

In a recent article (Hutton 1995), I analysed sentencing using Max Weber's ideal typology of legal decision-making. My central argument was that sentencing was best characterised as a substantive irrational type of decision-making which was in contrast to the formal rationality of most other modern legal decision-making. Sentencing, at least in the UK, is not governed by rules and judges exercise considerable discretion. From a judicial point of view, sentencing can be characterised as a tension between two opposing principles. On the one hand, the principle of equality of treatment for each individual requires that like cases should be treated alike. However this is in tension with the equally important idea that each case is a unique combination of facts and circumstances and must be judged on that basis. These two approaches might be seen as contradictory discourses of justice. Even though they are contradictory, judges make sentencing decisions with both discourses in mind. From a judge's point of view, just sentencing is achieved by a balance between treating like cases alike, and taking into account the facts and circumstances of each individual case: a balance between formal and substantive narratives of justice (Hutton 1995). One narrative says that like cases should be treated alike but fails to give any guidance as to how sameness and difference are to be ascribed. The narrative provides a formal account of sentencing but fails to explain the mechanics of this formalism. The other says that sentencing is an art and that the choice of sentence is an 'instinctive synthesis'[3] arising out of all of the facts and circumstances of a particular individual case. This mimics the importance in other areas of law of establishing the detailed facts of a case prior to applying the appropriate legal rules to these facts. However, in sentencing, there are no formal rules which specify which facts and circumstances are relevant nor any calculus which specifies how a sentence can be calculated from these factors. Sentencing is less rational and formal than most areas of modern Western law. Its appeal to a fair and evenhanded notion of justice is based less explicitly on reason than most legal decisions and more on substantive and irrational considerations.

This is further based on the idea that the law applies equally to each individual and universally across all individuals. In order for this balance between substantive and formal versions of justice to work, it is necessary to preserve the idea that the individual is the locus of responsibility in criminal law. The extent to which an individual is to be held culpable for the harm caused by the offence is something which is 'calculated' on a case by case basis. Evidence about the culpability of an individual can be presented and assessed in the light of the facts and circumstances of the case. There is a necessary presumption that all individuals are treated equally, in so far as equal consideration is given in every case to the degree of culpability exercised by the individual offender. Not all offenders are equally culpable, but the locus of responsibility is always found at the level of the individual. As Norrie (1996) argues, "… law respects autonomy and personhood and this is a value in itself" (p. 541).

In this way sentencing achieves the 'cunning trick' by on the one hand rhetorically promising to treat individuals equally by pursuing consistency in sentencing and on the other hand allowing variations in culpability at the level of the individual offender. This is achieved by allowing sentencers very wide discretion and providing few rules specifying how similarity is to be measured.[4] In this liberal model of justice, individuals are addressed by the law as equals, in the sense that responsibility is located at the level of the individual. However variation in degrees of culpability is recognised so long as this does not challenge the location of responsibility as resting at the level of the individual.

A 'Social Theory of Culpability'

Barbara Hudson argues for a different notion of culpability:

> A more socially just grounding for punishment must provide for more complex, nuanced notions of culpability and freedom of choice that take account of circumstantial constraints (Hudson 1995, p. 69).

> … that culpability should be able to be reduced or nullified by economic duress or similar circumstantial constraint, and that in every case, assessment of culpability should be informed by an understanding of freedom of choice as a matter of degree, rather than seeing offenders as either totally freely-choosing, or totally determined (ibid., p. 76).

The idea is straightforward and its moral appeal is clear. Why should systematically disadvantaged people receive the same punishment as offenders who are systematically privileged? However the answer to this rhetorical question is not quite so straightforward. The concept of culpability implicit in the two quotations above is quite compatible with the existing idea of culpability in a liberal approach to sentencing. Sentencers can, and do, already take account of "nuanced notions of culpability" and treat "freedom of choice as a matter of degree".

Hudson's approach requires a further important step. Hudson wants to replace an individual theory of culpability with a social theory of culpability so that certain groups of people are assumed to have less culpability for certain sorts of offending than other groups because of their social disadvantage.

This is different from saying that a particular individual is held to be less culpable for an offence because of certain social circumstances for example extreme poverty. In this case, responsibility is still located at the level of the individual. Not all those suffering from extreme poverty are less culpable, only some and only at the discretion of the judge and there is no requirement on the judge to specify how any mitigation has been taken into account or what effect if any it has had on sentence.

Hudson wants to allocate responsibility at the level of the group rather than the individual. Unequally distributed social factors are held to reduce culpability for all members of a particular disadvantaged group not just some members of this group. In Hudson's scenario, individuals are no longer presumed to be equal, but rather evidence about the unequal social distribution of opportunities is held to demand differential treatment of groups. This view proposes a law which says that group X are to be held less responsible for their conduct than those who are not a member of this group. To take one of Hudson's examples, young unemployed homeless people convicted of theft should be held less responsible for this offence than other social groups:

> ... the young homeless and those with chaotic lifestyles have no incomes at all. Whether one poses the argument in terms of economic duress, or in terms of balance of social rights and social obligations, it is difficult to see how such people should be considered liable to punishment (ibid., p. 71).

The standard criticism of this argument is that since not all members of this group commit offences, reducing the punishment of those who do would be unfair on those who do not. This, however, retains the assumption of individual equality which Hudson's approach wishes to disturb. This privileges the fiction of equality over the empirical facts of social inequality. Hudson's question is how to take account of socially distributed inequality and this requires the setting aside of assumptions of individual equality.

The idea of a 'social theory of culpability' is more accurately described as a social theory of responsibility. Responsibility is shifted from the individual to the group because of certain social circumstances which have disproportionately affected this group. The members of this group either have no culpability as individuals for their criminal conduct or else they have a reduced level of culpability. In either case responsibility, or the lack of it, is located at the level of the group and not the individual. This opens up the possibility of other groups gathering evidence to demonstrate that they too are subject to unequally distributed opportunities. In these circumstances, individuals are no longer treated equally, they are treated according to their group membership. This group membership will have to be formally prescribed. Criteria of sameness and difference will have to be devised and applied so that individuals can be allocated to a group. Group membership will result in reduced culpability regardless of other facts and circumstances of the case. In the next section, I want to examine how a social theory of culpability might be put into practice. My argument is that it is difficult to see how Hudson's suggestion could operate within the existing framework of liberal law without a different set of newly disadvantaged groups being produced and new forms of inequality being created.

Operational Problem

Locating responsibility at the level of a social group rather than at the level of the individual simply does not fit into a liberal conception of law. Although in practice law may treat rich and poor quite differently, in theory it treats everyone the same. Hudson accepts that "in order to be able to apply general rules, legal theory has to specify criteria for sameness and difference" (Hudson 1993, p. 194). Thus a social theory of culpability requires criteria for allocating individuals in or out of particular categories. Hudson's approach would require some means of specifying which socially distributed constraints diminish culpability, to what extent they do so and how these factors should affect the allocation of punishment. This would have to be done in some formal way, similar to the US numerical sentencing guidelines (although designed to achieve quite different ends). There are many difficulties involved. First how are the constraints to be identified, how are they to be measured, what disciplines will be accepted by the court as providing expert evidence on which the court can base a decision? What sort of calculus will be required to properly reflect the relative effect of these factors on culpability? How do we deal with the almost limitless possibility of combinations of factors?

An example might help to demonstrate the range of difficulties involved and the likely consequences.

Hudson argues that young unemployed homeless offenders who are not entitled to benefit should be held to be less culpable for petty theft on the grounds that they have no means of support and therefore have to resort to crime to survive. How could this policy be put into practice within the existing legal framework? Hudson's proposal is that all offenders who fall into this group should be held to have less culpability. This would not be decided on a case by case basis at the level of the individual, rather the individual would have to prove that he or she was a member of the defined group in order to benefit from the reduction in culpability. How would membership of the group be established? A number of facts would have to be verified: the offender would have to fall within a specified age range, prove ineligibility for benefit, prove homelessness presumably by showing that this status had been granted by the relevant authority, similarly with unemployment, and the boundaries of 'petty' theft would have to be established.

A consequence of this process would be the creation of groups of offenders who fall outside this category, who would be held to be fully culpable for their actions and who may legitimately ask why they are being disadvantaged on the grounds that they fall outside the age range, or because they have been unable to have themselves officially recorded as homeless. This is an unavoidable product of the way in which law operates. In defining similarity, that is, in describing a set of characteristics, possession of which will entitle the holder to be ascribed to a group, law inevitably defines another group of those who do not possess these characteristics. The definition of similarity always involves the definition of difference and therefore exclusion.

This is why there has to be a balance between formal and substantive definitions of justice. Substantive justice is always partial. It is always based on a particular value position and always favours one group over those who are not members of the group. Formal justice promises equal justice for all but this rhetorical promise cannot be produced in practice because formal justice is itself partisan. Formal justice promises to treat like cases alike but leaves the definition of similarity so open that sentencers can take into account all the circumstances of the case to produce a decision which they feel is substantively just by some process of instinctive synthesis.

It is a mistake to try to provide substantive definitions of justice where only formal definitions will work. In the attempt to provide substantive justice for a particular population, Hudson's approach will produce another population of people who feel that they have not been treated justly. They will accuse Hudson's law of discriminating against them and not treating them equally. Other groups are likely to claim that they are entitled to a reduction in responsibility because of different unequally distributed circumstantial factors. In other words, law has become politics in that it has revealed itself as political and thus failed to perform the 'cunning trick' of appearing to produce neutral and impartial decisions while in fact reproducing a particular value position. Law has become a site where social groups openly contest inequalities instead of a site which treats all equally and produces neutral and impartial decisions.

Law and Politics

> The dichotomy of the individual and the social which we find in legal theory is not just some unfortunate misconception, but it is the very foundation of jurisprudence in constitutional society (Hudson 1993, p. 196).

It is not clear whether Hudson appreciates the full implications of this point. Law cannot replace the category of the individual with a social category because this disturbs the logic of law. As Fish (1994) argues, the beauty of law is its ability to operate in a discriminatory, partisan way while at the same time presenting itself plausibly as universal, neutral and fair. As soon as law begins to explicitly declare its allegiance, it loses its ability to claim neutrality and thus one of its most fundamental claims to distinctiveness. It would in fact simply become politics. The important point of law is that it is theoretically and rhetorically distinguished from politics. Fish argues that everything is political. The discipline of law allows us to forget this momentarily and to pretend that the world is not simply about the struggle for power, but that human societies have more lofty humanitarian aspirations.

The great strength of law is that it covers its traces. It provides the illusion, and also quite frequently the reality, of equal treatment and universal application. It manages the gap between formal and substantive justice to make it look to most casual observers that most of the time there is no gap. It allows a liberal society to make partial decisions appear to be impartial. Hudson mistakes law for politics. She wants to make law explicitly political, but then it ceases to be law because law can only ever be implicitly political. Of course law does political work all the time, but it does not do so explicitly and openly.

Conclusion

My argument is that Hudson's proposed legal intervention is inappropriate to secure her political aim of fairer punishment for the poor and that there are more appropriate political interventions which are more likely to be effective in securing these aims, providing of course, there is sufficient political support to make these aims real. The operation of the criminal justice system is not neutral. For a variety of reasons, most of the resources are focused on the crimes of the disadvantaged. An institution which is intended to deal with the disadvantaged is hardly likely to systematically reduce the responsibility of its main client group on the grounds of their disadvantage.

Punishment and social welfare are different enterprises. We need to think about punishment in its own terms albeit against a background of a systematic overemphasis on crimes of the disadvantaged. We might not like this situation, for example we might want to put more resources into policing the crimes of the powerful. But we will still have to decide how to punish the disadvantaged and we cannot ask the criminal justice system to operate an approach to punishment which seeks to redistribute social advantages to disadvantaged groups. If the criminal justice system in practice targets the disadvantaged, then an appropriate penal response might be to ensure that the penalties are modest and that repeat offending does not necessarily lead to a custodial sentence because of the increased harm and social costs which a prison sentence might entail (childcare, psychological damage to offender, breakdown of existing community support, stigma and loss of employment prospects etc.) without any significant social benefits.[5] From a progressive perspective, it would be desirable if this was accompanied by social welfare policies to alleviate poverty and expand opportunities for the socially disadvantaged, but these are social policies targeted at distinct populations rather than penal policies addressed to particular individual offenders.

Law cannot be explicitly partial to a particular social group without losing its function of symbolising social solidarity and standing as an utopian model for a society that we would like to live in even though our efforts to achieve it are flawed. If law openly declares itself in favour of a sectional interest, it risks losing the legitimacy of other interests who may say if law is no longer treating everyone equally then why should we pay any attention to it? Politics is the appropriate forum for debating social justice where sectional interests can struggle with each other through democratic procedures. Legal justice is meant to provide a neutral justice above sectional interests. The fact that it does not achieve this in practice is less important for the operation of liberal democracy than the fact that it claims that it tries to do so rhetorically.

Hudson wants to remove the distinction between legal justice and social justice. I want to argue that in a liberal society the distinction is vitally important. Law rhetorically promises to provide justice and this serves as one source of unity in a divided society. It also has complex institutions, procedures, professions, rules, codes etc. which try to operationalise justice. In the field of sentencing this works by devising categories of sameness and difference, in other words by discrimination. The concepts of law are themselves social and political constructs which favour some groups as against others. The operation of the institutions of law systematically discriminate against some social groups in favour of others. However, this is an inevitable part of any attempt to pursue universal goals in a divided society. Any attempt to achieve social justice would develop similar mechanisms although the discriminatory processes might advantage and disadvantage different social groups. Equality is something we aim for but can never achieve. The pursuit of equality will always produce inequality.

Hudson has a political project which she wishes to promote namely, to reduce the levels of punishment imposed on the socially disadvantaged. The strategy which she proposes involves relocating responsibility from the site of the individual to the site of the group. My argument is that this is an inappropriate strategy. First, it tries to make law explicitly political and thus deprives law of its capacity to symbolise solidarity and community. Second, in practice, her strategy will not remove inequality but only substitute one form of inequality for another.

Most progressives want a reduction in the level of punishment. The difficult problem is how to achieve less punishment in the existing climate of public punitiveness (Bottoms 1995). There is no space here to develop policy suggestions. However, the implications of the argument in this essay are that any reform of law needs to respect what Norrie has described as the Janus-like character of law (Norrie 1996, p. 544).

Acknowledgements

This paper was presented at the Sentencing and Society Conference Glasgow 1999 and is reprinted by permission of Sage Publications Ltd from *1999 Social and Legal Studies* Vol. 8:4 © SAGE Publications.

Notes

1   I use the term 'progressive' in a very broad sense to include those who wish to see the use of punishment minimised or abolished, who are sceptical about the effectiveness of punishment as a means of crime control and who are concerned with humanitarian and human rights issues in punishment (see for example Bianchi and van Swaaningen, 1986; Sim, 1994; Christie, 1982; De Hann, 1990). These arguments may also appeal to those who are concerned about the escalating costs of larger prison populations and who seek alternative penal discourses which would authorise a reduction in the use of imprisonment for fiscal rather than humanitarian reasons.

2   An example of the way in which such factors may be taken into account by sentencers occurred in a Scottish case of indecent assault. It was held by the Court of Appeal that a stable background, a permanent job and the absence of previous convictions were mitigating factors which justified a reduction in the penalty imposed by the first instance court. *Mitchell v Carmichael* 1988 SCCR 222.

3   This idea of sentencing as 'instinctive synthesis' comes from the judgement in the Victoria Court of Criminal Appeal case of Williscroft [1975] VR292, 300 quoted in Freiberg (1995).

4   Sentencing Guidelines have gone some way to prescribing what counts as similarity, however, research evidence shows that judges sometimes manipulate guidelines where they feel the guideline sentence is manifestly unjust (Nagel and Johnston 1994; Tonry 1996). This suggests that judges have a strong substantive sense of justice which is not easily accommodated in formalistic attempts to define just sentencing.

5   This is no more than the principle of parsimony which Hudson and Tonry amongst others propose as a basis for any system of punishment. Punishment should be the minimum required. This of course begs the question of what punishment is for.

References

Bianchi, H. and van Swaaningen, R. (eds) (1986), *Abolitionism: Towards a non-repressive approach to crime*, Amsterdam: Free University Press.

Bottoms, A. (1995), 'The Philosophy and Politics of Punishment and Sentencing', in C. Clarkson and R. Morgan (eds), *The Politics of Sentencing Reform*, Oxford: Clarendon Press.

Christie, N. (1982), *Limits to Pain*, Oxford: Martin Robertson.

De Hann, W. (1990), *The Politics of Redress: Crime punishment and penal abolition*, London: Unwin Hyman.

Fish, S. (1994), *There's No Such Thing as Free Speech: And it's a good thing too*, Oxford: Oxford University Press.

Hudson, B.A. (1987), *Justice through punishment: A critique of the justice model of corrections*, Basingstoke: Macmillan.

Hudson, B.A. (1993), *Penal Policy and Social Justice*, Basingstoke: Macmillan.

Hudson, B.A. (1995), 'Beyond Proportionate Punishment: Difficult cases and the 1991 Criminal Justice Act', *Crime, Law and Social Change*, 22, pp. 59–78.

Hudson, B.A. (1996), 'Doing Justice to Difference', in A. Ashworth and M. Wasik (eds), *Fundamentals of Sentencing Theory*, Oxford: Oxford University Press.

Hutton, N. (1986), *Lay Participation in a Public Local Inquiry*, Aldershot: Gower.

Hutton, N. (1995), 'Sentencing, Rationality and Computer Technology', *Journal of Law and Society*, Vol. 22, No. 4, pp. 549–70.

Mair, G. (ed.) (1997), *Evaluating the Effectiveness of Community Penalties*, Aldershot: Avebury.

McGuire, J. (ed.) (1995), *What Works: Reducing Reoffending – Guidelines from Research and Practice*, Chichester: Wiley.

Morris, N. and Tonry, M. (1990), *Between Prison and Probation*, Oxford: Oxford University Press.

Nagel, I. and Johnson, B. (1994), 'The Role of Gender in a Structured Sentencing System: Equal treatment, policy choices and the sentencing of female offenders under the United States Sentencing Guidelines', *Journal of Criminal Law and Criminology*, Vol. 85, No. 1.

Nelken, D. (1983), *The Limits of the Legal Process: A study of landlords, law and crime*, London: Academic Press.

Norrie, A. (1993), *Crime, Reason and History. A Critical Introduction to Criminal Law*, London: Weidenfeld and Nicholson.

Norrie, A. (1996), 'The Limits of Justice: Finding Fault in the Criminal Law', *Modern Law Review*, 59:4, pp. 540–56.

Scheiber, H. (1984), 'Public Rights and the Rule of Law in American Legal History', *California Law Review*, 72, pp. 236–7.

Sim, J. (1994), 'The Abolitionist Approach: A British perspective', in A. Duff, S. Marshall, E.R. Dobash and P.R. Dobash (eds), *Penal Theory and Practice: Tradition and innovation in criminal justice*, Manchester: Manchester University Press.

Tonry, M. (1996), *Sentencing Matters*, Oxford: Oxford University Press.

Von Hirsch, A. (1993), *Censure and Sanction*, Oxford: Clarendon.

Chapter Twenty-seven

Punishment, Poverty and Responsibility: the Case for a Hardship Defence

Barbara Hudson

Introduction

I very much appreciate Neil Hutton's attention to my 1995 article, which put forward the idea of "principled parsimony" (Hudson 1995). In the article, I suggest that sentencing ought to be able to accommodate differences in economic situations of offenders, and argue further that such accommodation should be through the development and application of principled criteria for economic hardship, rather than being on the basis of individual representations for particularly sympathetic cases. In this present article, I clarify and develop my position on the possibility of a hardship defence.[1]

I comment on three points of disagreement between Hutton's article and my own position: two points concern what I think are misrepresentations of my position, and the third concerns an empirical disagreement about the role of the sentencer. The two points of misrepresentation or misunderstanding involve ideas of *responsibility* and of the *social*; the empirical point is the balance of *formal* and *substantive* justice concerns in sentencing.

Responsibility and Culpability

I find some confusion in Hutton's article in the way in which he uses the terms 'culpability', 'responsibility' and 'blameworthiness'. Despite having a subheading 'Responsibility and Culpability', in many places he seems to treat the two words as synonymous. For example:

From a desert perspective, offence seriousness is comprised of harm and culpability, that is the extent of harm or damage caused to victims added to the extent of the offenders' responsibility for the harm (pp. 572–3).

Here, Hutton appears to use the words culpability and responsibility as equivalent. He quotes me accurately as saying that indigent offenders may be less *blameworthy* (emphasis added) than those whose choices are less constrained by economic circumstances, but appears not to allow that I do not use blameworthy as a simple equivalent of responsibility. For me, blameworthiness has two elements, one of which is whether or not someone actually did something (actively and knowingly), and the other is whether the act was something that the actor made a positive choice to do. Legal theorists generally recognise that there is an element to culpability beyond having carried out an act; otherwise, the sentence "And we do not want it [the criminal law] to convict people who are not culpable for doing the *actus reus*" (Simester and Smith 1996, p. 6) would be nonsense.

Although it recognises that there is more to culpability than merely doing the act in question, legal theory has difficulty in moving consideration of culpability beyond a fairly narrow discussion of responsibility, with current debate mainly centred on categories such as recklessness, negligence and omission, rather than on choice. Nonetheless, acceptance of situations such as self-defence and various forms of physical coercion, shows that for law culpability involves an act not only having been done, but having been done from choice. But whereas legal theory has paid much attention to responsibility, it has paid scant attention to choice.

Law's failure to elaborate theories of choice, leaves it with an absolutist, either/or notion of choice, such that action is seen as (freely) chosen if it is not carried out under conditions of physical coercion or mental incapacity. David Garland has also commented on this absolutist notion of choice in law, arguing that it conflates the ideas of *agency* and *freedom*:

> The idea of agency refers to the capacity of an agent for action, its possession of the 'power to act', which is the capacity to originate such actions on the basis of calculations and decisions. Agency is a universal attribute of (socialized) human beings ... Freedom, on the other hand, generally refers to a capacity to choose one's actions without external constraint. Freedom (unlike agency) is necessarily a matter of degree – it is the configured range of unconstrained choice in which agency can operate (Garland 1997, pp. 196–7).

My argument rests on this separation of agency and freedom, even though the dichotomy might not be quite so precise as Garland's formulation indicates. The term 'power to act' conveys to me a certain degree of freedom as well as a Kantian capacity of reason and will. Law's conception of responsibility seems to fit this formula of reason, will and at least a minimum freedom from external constraint very well. What is lacking, though, is acknowledgement of the fact that though agents may possess – in general, and in the abstract –

the power to act and therefore be responsible for any crimes they may commit, in actual concrete crime situations they are operating in a society where possibilities of socially meaningful choices are unequally distributed. Since freedom of choice in an unequal society is necessarily a matter of degree and is unequal between agents, the extent to which they are to be blamed – and therefore punished – should reflect these differences and inequalities.

The Social and the Group

At this point I want to refer to the second of Hutton's misrepresentations of my work, and this concerns the meaning, in this context, of the word 'social'. As Hutton says, I advocate a 'social' theory of culpability. This is *not* the same, however, as advocating a 'group' theory, either of culpability or responsibility. Hutton claims that I want to "allocate responsibility at the level of the group rather than the individual" (p. 577); in this sentence he makes the double error of shifting from culpability to responsibility and from social to group.

My intended meaning of the word 'social' is that of taking into account the social circumstances in which offenders live their lives. This seems the same sense as that conveyed by Simester and Smith:

> The law exists in society, not in the abstract. Correspondingly, the law's labelling of a defendant as 'criminal' should be done with an eye to the social meaning of that term (Simester and Smith 1996, p. 6).

'Social' refers to an environment of economic, political, spatial and personal factors and relationships; 'group' designates a particular cluster of persons who form a specific and distinctive sub-segment of a society or community.

There are writers who suggest group exemptions from liability to state punishment, and whilst I sympathise with their arguments, I think they pose considerable difficulties. US judge David Bazelon (1976), and theorist Martha Klein (1990) conclude that the impoverished offender has "paid in advance" because s/he has already in effect foregone the social rights and privileges supposedly derived from membership in society. The deprivations and burdens of poverty, it is argued, are similar to those of punishment, and so society does not have the right to punish further. Although there is much moral force to these arguments, they pose questions concerning whether they exempt in advance *all* the impoverished from *all* categories of offences, and how the norm-affirming, expressive functions of criminal law are to be served in cases involving impoverished offenders.

I am not, therefore, suggesting group, in-advance exemptions; what I am suggesting is that law should be cognizant of the social circumstances in which crimes occur, as well as physical, mental dimensions of actual crime situations.

Fair Opportunity to Resist

My proposals for 'principled parsimony' take as their starting point the concept of "fair opportunity to resist" mentioned by Hart (1968, pp. 190–91). Hart allows that responsibility might be less for people whose circumstances are such that conformity with the law would be more difficult than for most people. This concept of fair opportunity to resist is unproblematic in the case of physical duress or mental incapacity, but although Hart raises the possibility of its extension to economic incapacity, most desert theorists have rejected the idea. For example, von Hirsch (1976, p. 178) acknowledges that the impoverished defendant

> ... poses a dilemma for our [retributive] theory. In principle a case could be made that he is less culpable because his deprived status has left him with fewer opportunities for an adequate livelihood within the law.

Most desert theorists, including von Hirsch, decide against a hardship defence, however. Their reasoning is partly the difficulty of operating a hardship defence consistently, and partly that allowing for reductions in culpability might lower penalties below a level at which they would be properly reflective of the harm done by the offence. They are also mindful of the experience of rehabilitative sentencing systems where 'needs' have resulted in more punishment for the disadvantaged, on the grounds that they need more penal input than the more fortunate to equip them to resist the pressures to commit future crimes. Returning to the question of poverty and punishment in subsequent works (1992, 1993), von Hirsch however confirms that the key difficulty is the ideas of choice and voluntarism. He says that proportionality cannot be based on the idea of fair opportunity to resist because it concerns

> ... the quantum of punishment levied on persons who, in choosing to violate the law, have voluntarily exposed themselves to the consequences of criminal liability (von Hirsch 1992, p. 62).

The features of desert theory which are attractive to penal progressives[2] hinge to a large extent on desert's insistence that the offender is like the non-offender in remaining a member of the moral community and remains owed a duty of justice, rather than being the vehicle for unlimited crime-control objectives as in some utilitarian approaches. The corollary of this equality of rights to justice, is that offenders must accept responsibility for their actions as rational, autonomous moral agents. Quite apart from the general arguments about the ascription of responsibility in law made by Hutton, there is undoubtedly a profound specific difficulty in reconciling desert theory's insistence on the offender as autonomous moral agent, with the 'soft determinism' implied in the idea of a hardship defence.

This difficulty of reconciling desert with any notion of lack of voluntarism is alluded to by Sandel when he discusses the "puzzle" of why Rawls admits desert as a basis for retributive justice where he does not admit it for distributive justice (Sandel 1998, p. 90). Sandel asks, if it can be held that possession of qualities and attributes which may affect their possessors' chances of material success are 'owned' by the community in general and therefore do not attach to their possessors in any way that ascribes virtue, why should attributes and qualities that are linked with the propensity to commit crime, be thought to reflect on the moral worth of their possessors? The lack of individual ownership and ascribed virtue of qualities such as intelligence, energy and fortunate family circumstances are essential to Rawls' defence of his 'difference' principle in his theory of justice as fairness (Rawls 1972); similar logic with regard to criminogenic characteristics and social situation would, suggests Sandel, lead to a social response to crime based on pooling of risks through insurance and compensation rather than individual liability to punishment. It is thus fundamental to the institution of punishment that crimes are perceived as the outcome of bad moral choices rather than as the outcome of arbitrarily distributed attributes and circumstances. A hardship defence is therefore bound to be problematic for desert theorists.

The Sentencing Framework

Some of the misunderstandings between myself and Hutton stem, I think, from a difference in empirical understandings of sentencing. Hutton argues that the sort of consideration of social circumstances, degrees of freedom of choice and therefore of culpability, with which I am concerned, are dealt with by substantive aspects of law. Since, according to Hutton, the substantive part of criminal justice proceedings – sentencing – operates exactly as I would wish, taking account of nuanced notions of culpability and treating freedom of choice as a matter of degree, he naturally presumes that I must be aiming at the fundamentals of the formal aspects of law: equality of agency and individual responsibility.

Hutton's description of sentencing, however, no longer fits present-day England and Wales, the USA, and many other western jurisdictions. The 1980s and 1990s have seen considerable reductions in sentencers' discretion. Although England and Wales has not introduced the sort of sentencing guidelines and rigid sentencing laws seen elsewhere, concern with sentence disparities and the promotion of consistency in sentencing were the main themes of criminal justice developments from the 1982 Criminal Justice Act onwards. As well as legislation, during the 1980s a series of guideline judgments; the establishment and activities of the Judicial Studies Board; Home Office and Lord Chancellor's Department circulars and booklets directed both judges and magistrates firmly towards selecting the 'going rate' for the offence category concerned rather than choosing the sentence appropriate to the circumstances of the offender as a socially-situated individual. The Probation Service also moved from welfare-oriented 'social inquiry' reports to 'justice model' pre-sentence reports, making recommendations to sentencers on the basis of gravity-of-offence scores rather than personal circumstance concerns.

This clear linking of sentence to offence seriousness, with consistency valued over individual appropriateness, was codified in the 1991 Criminal Justice Act. Even noncustodial sentences were offence- rather than offender-oriented. The Act provided for noncustodial penalties to be graduated along a continuum of restriction of liberty, with the amount of restriction in each community sentence reflective of the seriousness of the offence. In the 1990s this trend has continued. The unit fine, which was the sentence most clearly designed to reflect the economic circumstances of the offender, was quickly abandoned; the 1997 Crime (Sentences) Act brought in new mandatory and presumptive minimum sentences. Although mandatory sentencing is nowhere near as advanced as in the USA, and in Scotland not so much as in England and Wales, the principle of sentencing as the part of the process which dispenses substantive justice to the individual, has been breached.

Even for the group of people for whom individualised justice was formerly commonplace – female offenders – sentencing in the 1980s and 1990s has become less reflective of personal circumstances, with consequent rising imprisonment rates (Daly 1994; Hudson 1998a). There is no doubt that the last 15 or so years have seen a marked and general shift to downgrade substantive justice concerns in criminal justice processes.

In these circumstances of reduced scope for the individualised, person-centred substantive elements in criminal proceedings, attention needs to be given to how these important requirements of justice may be met. Whilst I fully sympathise with those who call for a wholesale change of criminal justice towards a more discursive mode,[3] in my work on punishment and poverty I engage in a less utopian project of making the present juridical mode more sensitive to inequalities between defendants. I am concerned to find ways of building consideration of social factors into legal proceedings which can meet the requirements of formal law, and which could provide some guidance for the principled exercise of judicial discretion should the balance shift again towards giving more scope for substantive elements of justice.

As well as reductions in judicial discretion and the sphere of substantive justice, the other important context of my argument is reduction of the welfare safety-net. Contemporary desert theory has been developed in the context of Rawlsian welfare liberalism, which carries the assumption that the basic needs of food, healthcare and shelter will be guaranteed by the state. In such a situation, the assumption that all offenders who are free from physical coercion or mental incapacity are acting out of at least some degree of positive choice, is reasonable. The shrinking of the welfare safety-net in England and Wales and the USA in two decades of free-market neo-liberalism, though, has produced categories of people who do not have access to any legitimate income, and it is this fact that prompts reconsideration of a defence of economic duress. If an offender does not have the opportunity to afford the means of survival by legitimate means, s/he cannot be said to have *chosen* illegitimate means. It is in this case that I would suggest a defence of economic coercion might be admitted which would be analogous to the defence of physical coercion, and depending on circumstances would – rarely – negate, or – more often – diminish responsibility.

For greater numbers of people, widening social inequalities, with poverty-level wages and progressive reductions in the levels of benefits relative to average incomes and prices, have increased pressures towards crime (Currie 1997). For such people, economic circumstances might not undermine responsibility, but they should significantly mitigate culpability.

I am not suggesting that criminal justice proceedings should be engaging in redistributive politics; what I am saying is that criminal justice must take account of changing contexts of action and narrowing ranges of choice. The argument is in some ways analogous to that for widening behavioural criteria for provocation as defence or mitigation as understanding becomes shared of the effects of domestic abuse on women's perceptions of themselves as active, autonomous agents: they are in the sense of agency free to leave; but they can only leave if they have somewhere else to go, and their self-esteem may be so damaged that they cannot imagine improving their situation. The point is that law does not exist in a vacuum, and must reflect the realities of the society in which it operates.

Structuring Parsimony

My 1995 article raises concerns about Tonry's suggestion of leniency for someone who, faced with adverse social circumstances, has struggled to "overcome the odds" (Tonry 1994). This selective leniency has, in the past, been disproportionately granted to women, and has been the focus of much of the feminist critique of pre-proportionality sentencing (Eaton 1986; Edwards 1984 *inter alia*). Such leniency, critics point out, comes at a high price, and this sort of leniency does indeed involve its recipients being seen as less than fully rational, responsible agents. As Daly (1994) demonstrates, individualised parsimony is only available to women who can be represented as victims as much as offenders – victims of poverty, of addictions, of emotions, and most of all, of men. Such parsimony is both demeaning and discriminatory. This is because what is being accepted as restricted is women's capacity to make choices; what I am proposing, on the other hand, is that indigent offenders be seen as acting rationally within a restricted range of choices.[4]

The question then, is to specify criteria for hardship as defence or mitigation. Groves and Frank (1986) propose that freedom of choice be seen as a continuum with four main divisions: compulsion; coercion; causation, and freedom. The category 'freedom' would apply to offences where things that the offender wants can be obtained just as easily legally as illegally, so that there is a positive choice to use criminal means. Economic compulsion would be a defence where the only alternative is imminent starvation of oneself or one's dependents. This would, presumably be relatively rare, but it is a comment on the present state of our society that it is not inconceivable. Lack of means amounting to coercion is more common. Young people, the homeless and others who do not fit the requirements of the job-seekers' allowance; people on poverty wages; women whose menfolk withhold money; people leaving penal, psychiatric or residential care institutions who receive benefit in arrears but need to pay for food and accommodation immediately, are candidates for a mitigation of economic coercion.[5] Causation (I prefer the less determinist term motivation) would be the standard rational choice case where economic gain provides a motive but not an excuse or justification. These categories recognise the difference between stealing because one wants the latest fashion in footwear or the newest model video and cannot afford it legitimately, and stealing or failing to declare meagre earnings because one cannot otherwise feed oneself or one's children.

It is for politics rather than law to remedy social inequalities, but in the meantime law should reflect the structuring of opportunities which influences patterns of crime. Where crime results from economic compulsion or coercion, justice demands that society acknowledges responsibility by assisting the offender, and reflecting the harm done to the victim by adequate compensation.

Acknowledgements

This paper was presented at the Sentencing and Society Conference in Glasgow 1999 and is reprinted by permission of Sage Publications Ltd from *1999 Social and Legal Studies*, Vol. 8:4, © SAGE Publications.

Notes

The ideas with which this article is concerned are discussed more fully in Hudson (1998a) and Hudson (2000).

1   Development of my thinking on the problems and possibilities of a hardship defence has been assisted by discussions with Neil Hutton himself, with Andrew von Hirsch, by Andrew Ashworth in his comments on my 1998a chapter, and by John Kleinig, Bill Haffernan and other participants in the Conference on Indigence and Criminal Justice, John Jay College, City University of New York, May 1998.
2   I use the term 'progressive' in the same sense here as Hutton, that is, those who hope for reductions in the overall severity of punishment, not the sense that punishment should be more severe for each successive conviction. Unfortunately, this second sense of 'penal progression' is more influential in current penal policy in England, the USA and many other western countries.
3   This is common to proponents of restorative justice and some versions of feminist jurisprudence. See, for example, de Haan 1990; van Ness 1993; Smart 1995; Masters and Smith 1998; Hudson 1998b.
4   These personal circumstances which have, as deserts theorists rightly pointed out, been associated with more intense punishment of the most disadvantaged have not, in any case, disappeared from criminal justice. They are being reintroduced not as 'needs', but as 'risk

factors', and whilst they may not influence sentencing in the same way as in the rehabilitative era, they are influencing decisions about discretionary release, early termination of community supervision, and levels of intensity of community supervision.

5   Asylum seekers may soon be candidates for either economic compulsion or coercion defence or mitigation, depending on the levels and ease of access of 'benefits in kind' to which they are soon to become entitled instead of cash.

References

Bazelon, D. (1976), 'The Morality of Criminal Law', *Southern California Law Review*, 49, pp. 385–403.

Currie, E. (1997), 'Market, Crime and Community: Toward a mid-range theory of post-industrial violence', *Theoretical Criminology*, 1:2, pp. 147–72.

Daly, K. (1994), *Gender, Crime and Punishment*, New Haven, CT: Yale University Press.

De Haan, W. (1990), *The Politics of Redress: Crime, punishment and penal abolition*, London: Unwin Hyman.

Eaton, M. (1986), *Justice for Women? Family, Court and Social Control*, Milton Keynes: Open University Press.

Edwards, S. (1984), *Women on Trial*, Manchester: Manchester University Press.

Garland, D. (1997), '"Governmentality" and the Problem of Crime: Foucault, criminology, sociology', *Theoretical Criminology*, 1:2, pp. 173–214.

Groves, W.B. and Frank, N. (1986), 'Punishment, Privilege and Structured Choice', in W.B. Groves and G. Newman (eds), *Punishment and Privilege*, Albany, NY: Harrow and Heston.

Hart, H.L.A (1968), *Punishment and Responsibility: Essays in the philosophy of law*, Oxford: Oxford University Press.

Hudson, B. (1995), 'Beyond Proportionate Punishment: Difficult cases and the 1991 Criminal Justice Act', *Crime, Law and Social Change*, 22, pp. 59–78.

Hudson, B. (1998a), 'Doing Justice to Difference', in A. Ashworth and M. Wasik (eds), *Fundamentals of Sentencing Theory*, Oxford: Clarendon Press.

Hudson, B. (1998b), 'Restorative Justice: The challenge of sexual and racial violence', *Journal of Law and Society*, 25:2, pp. 237–56.

Hudson, B. (2000), 'Punishing the Poor: Dilemmas of justice and difference', in W.C. Heffernan and J. Kleinig (eds), *From Social Justice to Criminal Justice*, New York: Oxford University Press.

Klein, M. (1990), *Determinism, Blameworthiness and Deprivation*, New York: Oxford University Press.

Masters, G. and Smith, D. (1998), 'Portia and Persephone Revisited: Thinking about feeling in criminal justice', *Theoretical Criminology*, 2:1, pp. 5–27.

Rawls, J. (1972), *A Theory of Justice*, Oxford: Oxford University Press.

Sandel, M.J. (1998), *Liberalism and the Limits to Justice*, 2nd edn, Cambridge: Cambridge University Press.

Simester, A.P. and Smith, A.T.H. (1996), 'Introduction: Criminalization and the role of theory', in A.P. Simester and A.T.H. Smith (eds), *Harm and Culpability*, Oxford: Clarendon Press.

Smart, C. (1995), 'Feminist Jurisprudence', in C. Smart (ed.), *Law, Crime and Sexuality*, London: Sage.

Tonry, M. (1994), 'Proportionality, Parsimony and Interchangeability of Punishments', in A. Duff, S. Marshall, R.E. Dobash and R.P. Dobash (eds), *Penal Theory and Practice: Tradition and innovation in criminal justice*, Manchester: Manchester University Press.

Van Ness, D.W. (1993), 'New Wine and Old Wineskins: Four challenges of restorative justice', *Criminal Law Forum*, 4:21, pp. 251–76.

Von Hirsch, A. (1976), *Doing Justice: The choice of punishments*, New York: Hill and Wang.

Von Hirsch, A. (1992), 'Proportionality in the Philosophy of Punishment', in M. Tonry (ed.), *Crime and Justice: An annual review of research*, Vol. 16, Chicago: University of Chicago Press.

CONCLUSION

Chapter Twenty-eight

Reflections

Neil Hutton

Introduction

This chapter offers a personal reflection on the contributions to this collection. I make no attempt to cover all of the issues raised in the book nor to acknowledge the contribution of each author. Rather, I aim to reflect on the main challenges for sentencing scholarship and research which have emerged from this collection. Almost all of the essays address and indeed form part of, what von Hirsch has described as "the sentencing reform project" (von Hirsch 2001). There is a strong focus on how to transform sentencing and on the forms which sentencing ought to adopt. My argument in this chapter is that sentencing scholarship needs to be informed by a more sophisticated understanding of the social conditions of sentencing, by a better understanding of sentencing as a social practice and by a sharper appreciation of the political context within which sentencing reform takes place.

The philosophical approach to the study of sentencing, which has dominated sentencing scholarship, offers relatively little assistance in understanding sentencing practice. In a sense this criticism is misdirected because the analysis of the normative philosophical principles underpinning sentencing is quite a different enterprise from the sociological study of how sentencing decisions are produced as social constructions. However, if we hope to have an impact on changing sentencing, it is important to improve our understanding of how sentencing works as a social practice. There has been limited empirical research on sentencing because judges have been reluctant to allow access to researchers (Tata).[1] There is clearly a need for more research and new methodological approaches are being proposed.

It has become very difficult to conduct scholarly sentencing research without being forced to confront the political conditions which underpin sentencing. Abstract philosophical debate about sentencing has its place but these abstract debates have little impact on sentencing policy and practice. Sentencing reform is politically motivated and often pays no more than lip service to research and scholarship. Of course, sentencing (and criminal justice) has always been political but, as Garland (2001) has pointed out, the consensus which existed between politicians, policy makers and scholars in the highpoint of penal welfarism in the 1950s and 1960s no longer exists. The challenge for sentencing scholars is how to work in this highly politicised environment.

There have been important challenges to the conventional way in which sentencing has been conceived over the last 30 years. To caricature the conventional wisdom, sentencing had a range of aims broadly acceptable to the public, all concerned with combating crime. Judges, as state representatives, were entrusted with the discretion in many jurisdictions to select an appropriate sentence with very limited interference or guidance from other authorities, and with the broad support of the public. Punishment was not a party-political issue, but rather a matter for professionals applying expert knowledge. Now, evidence suggests that sentencing has very little impact on crime, although the public and politicians still retain (at least in part) this belief. We are now becoming accustomed to living in high crime societies and concerned with how to manage the attendant risks rather than with fighting crime or with transforming offenders (Garland 2001; Tubex). 'Law and order' has become a very important party political issue and the phenomenon of populist punitiveness has emerged. (Bottoms 1995). The state has successfully shifted much of the responsibility for dealing with crime to non-state agencies and there is evidence that public confidence in state agencies and public institutions of criminal justice is rapidly diminishing. The public have diminishing faith in judges and other criminal justice professionals, and diminishing faith in the expert knowledge provided by academic research and scholarship on criminal justice. Many of these changes in the way in which crime and punishment are conceived have their corollaries in other areas of social life such as health care and social welfare and are representations of broader social, economic, cultural and political changes (Garland 2001). However as many of the contributions to this volume suggest, these changes present sentencing research and scholarship with very considerable challenges.

The Social Conditions of Sentencing

One aim of this collection is to promote a social scientific approach to understanding sentencing as a social practice. In his chapter, Ashworth suggests that sentencing practices are explained more effectively by social and political factors than by legal factors. How can we develop a sociological approach to understanding sentencing? It might be argued that there have only been modest advances in this endeavour since John Hogarth's work published 30 years ago (Hogarth 1971). One major reason for the lack of work has been the reluctance of judges to allow access to researchers (see for example the experiences of Ashworth et al. 1984). It may be that the diminishing public confidence in judges (Hough and Roberts) along with demands for greater transparency and accountability (Morgan) may make it more difficult for judges to resist pressure for research access in the future.

A central question for a sociology of sentencing is how to explain the patterns of sentencing which are produced by the exercise of judicial discretion. In the absence of detailed rules specifying how an evaluation of the 'seriousness' of the case is translated into a penalty, how can we explain the patterns of sentencing which emerge from these decisions? Judges themselves describe sentencing as an individualised practice, where each case is decided according to its own unique combination of facts and circumstances. How do these individual decisions produce patterns which can be at least partially predicted?

The dominant approach in the attempts to understand the patterns produced by sentencing decision-making has used statistical techniques to analyse aggregate sentencing data. The most thorough and comprehensive work has been conducted by Austin Lovegrove (see for example Lovegrove 1997, 2000). This tradition is represented in this volume by the work of Ostrom and Ostrom on the measurement of sentencing severity. Within this tradition, cases are broken down into lists of factors which are thought to have some impact on the seriousness of the case and thus on the severity of the sentence passed. The sophisticated statistical analyses attempt to measure the independent effects of different factors with the eventual aim (in Lovegrove's case at least) of constructing a model of sentencing which could predict with an acceptable degree of accuracy, the sentence for a case with a given set of factors. There is no space here for a detailed methodological critique of this approach. The work in this tradition has clearly demonstrated aggregate patterns of sentencing and thus has shown that sentencing is a social practice which requires explanation. However this tradition has been less successful in producing plausible explanations of sentencing patterns. The research has shown that previous convictions and seriousness of the offence are the best predictors of sentence severity, but the predictive accuracy and explanatory power of this research is relatively modest. To a judge or any regular court actor, it would be self-evident that case seriousness and criminal record would have a substantial impact on sentence. This tradition of research provides little assistance in addressing the question of how these patterns are produced. How do judges assess seriousness? How do judges make sentencing decisions?

Sentencing decisions are the conscious actions of social actors. The consciousness of judges, that is the values they hold, the ways in which they think and the categories they employ in this thinking, is a vital element in the production of both routine patterns of sentencing, divergence from these patterns and change in these patterns over time. In this collection Tata argues that sentencing scholarship needs to pay more attention to judicial accounts of sentencing and elsewhere has argued that we should think of sentencing decisions as typical whole case stories (Tata 1997). Davis argues that sentencers do not analyse the factors which comprise a crime and transpose these into a type and quantity of hard treatment. In her view, sentencers evaluate the seriousness of the case in terms of the appropriate punishment. Punishment is not something which derives from the assessment of seriousness, it informs the process through which seriousness is assessed. Punishment is an expression of seriousness, not something which is applied after the assessment of seriousness has taken place.

To express this in a more theoretical idiom using Giddens' structuration metaphor, sentencers are social actors, whose social actions (sentencing decisions) reproduce existing social structures and in so doing may produce changes in these structures which in turn produce changes in the future pattern of actions (Giddens 1984).

> Structures, and above all structural changes, are emergent properties that result
> from the recurring iterative actions of the actors who occupy the social space in
> question (Garland 2001, p. 24).

Sentencers are not making ad hoc individual decisions in a vacuum. The exercise of discretion should not be seen as a hermetic personal act of decision making. The exercise of discretion is a social practice. What structures do sentencers draw upon and reproduce in the exercise of their discretion? This is an under-researched area which requires more empirical work. Clearly, legal rules form part of the social structure of sentencing. Their importance depends on the range of discretion available in any given jurisdiction. As Tata points out in the introduction to this volume, "'rules' always permit discretion and discretion is in fact far more (socially) rule-bound than would otherwise be supposed". Social and organisational norms form another part of the structure of sentencing. Judges are aware that they are members of a profession and co-workers in a local criminal justice community. Court practitioners, including judges, have a shared tacit understanding of the tariff. While they would find it very difficult to describe this tariff explicitly, they would have little difficulty in reporting from their own experience cases which they felt departed from the tariff. They know that one of the demands of justice is consistency. Part of their job as sentencers is to try to treat like cases alike both in terms of their own personal sentencing practice and in terms of the practice of other judges. In other words, the notional 'tariff' which is produced through the negotiations of court actors forms a structure underpinning the sentencing decision making of sentencers.

It has proved difficult to obtain access to conduct the kind of qualitative research which would allow us to investigate sentencers understandings, perceptions and accounts of what they do, in other words to understand how sentencers exercise their discretion.[2] However this kind of work is vitally important. Judges are the human subjects through whom change will come about. We are unlikely to be able to make effective changes without a fuller and more plausible understanding of how sentencing decisions are made.

A Note on Discretion

A common theme of sentencing scholarship has been the contrast between the relatively unstructured exercise of discretion, sometimes referred to as 'individualised' sentencing with the more structured regimes of sentencing guidelines in the United States or penal codes in continental European jurisdictions which are often supposed to have eliminated the exercise of discretion. This is an oversimplification which does not help to understand sentencing. In practice there is considerable variation in the US guidelines systems (Reitz 2001). The US Sentencing Commission Federal Guidelines leave very little room for discretion, but this is not the case in all state jurisdictions. In many jurisdictions judges may depart from the guideline sentence for a range of reasons, some jurisdictions have very broad bands of penalty in each guideline range which leaves judges with discretion to choose within the range. As Mannozi's contribution reminds us, even in codified jurisdictions such as Italy, judges and other criminal justice practitioners have considerable space to make discretionary decisions. In practice jurisdictions are not divided between those which allow discretion and those which impose guidelines. A more accurate characterisation would be that there exists a continuum with a strong rule based system such as the Federal Guidelines at one end and very open discretionary systems with few rules such as in Scotland, at the other. Sentencing in all jurisdictions is a blend of rules and discretion.

The task for researchers is to examine the relationship between rules and discretion in the production of sentencing decisions in particular jurisdictions, i.e. not only to study how legal rules are interpreted and applied by sentencers, but how informal social and organisational norms are drawn upon by sentencers in their decision making. The question for sentencing reformers is how to structure the exercise of judgement in a way which balances the demand for consistency (promised by rules) with the demand for attention to justice in each case (promised by discretion). The answer to this last question requires greater knowledge and understanding of how sentencing decisions are made derived from ethnographic study of sentencing and sentencers. Ethnographic research can explore the ways in which sentencers conceive of sentencing, their values, and their attitudes. It can also explore the social and organisational culture of the court and the ways in which these affect sentencing. With this kind of knowledge, those who seek to influence the future shape of sentencing will be better equipped to anticipate the ways in which reform initiatives are likely to be interpreted and operated in the courts.

The Politics and Culture of Sentencing

If it is important to understand more about how sentencing decisions are produced as social practices, it is also important to become more aware of the political and cultural conditions which underpin sentencing and punishment in contemporary society.

The Politics of Sentencing

Many of the contributions to the collection focus on the political conditions which shaped sentencing policy and reform in a range of jurisdictions. Many also describe the particular local characteristics of populist punitiveness (Bottoms 1995) and its apparent effect on sentencing. For example, van Zyl Smit argues that judges in South Africa were unable to resist the demands for mandatory minimum sentences. These sentences were antithetical to the legal traditions of South Africa and sat uneasily with elements of the new constitution. However there was sufficient demand from vociferous community activists, media campaigns and political opponents of the government from within parliament, that the government was able to impose their will on the judiciary and introduce mandatory minimum sentences as a law and order measure with very broad support.

Judith Greene's essay chronicles the impact of conservative pressure groups on criminal justice policies in general and sentencing policies in particular in the United States over the last 30 years or so. She contrasts this to the lack of impact of broadly liberal scholarly researchers. Conservative pressure groups have been able to connect with 'public opinion' and politicians have taken the line of least resistance. Even Democratic governments have not been able to avoid the populist punitiveness that has driven penal policy in western jurisidictions over the last few decades. Campbell argues that the same populist punitiveness and political opportunism seen in other western democracies has operated in Canada in the 1990s. She cites as evidence private members bills attempting to introduce heavier and more rigid penalities for sex offenders and violent offenders and boot camps introduced despite a lack of supporting evidence for their effectiveness. Ashworth and Hough and Roberts comment on similar trends in England and Wales.

Morgan argues that the new Sentencing Matrix in Western Australia has also been driven by a political law and order agenda which defeated judicial opposition. In this case, the government is concerned to ensure that sentencing was more consistent but also that sentencers were more effective in communicating with the public. The Matrix is intended to improve the accountability, transparency and responsiveness of sentencing. The Matrix requires sentencers to adopt "prescribed sentencing methods" although the legislation is very vague about what these methods are. Morgan points out that there is an almost complete absence of any detail on what the prescribed methods are, what factors will be taken into account, how judges are to explain the effect of factors on sentencing. This rejection of the 'instinctive synthesis' or individualised approach to sentencing may be no bad thing. It might be desirable for the sentencing decision to become more rational, systematic and consistent. However the Western Australian government has made no attempt to describe the procedures which will replace instinctive synthesis and produce justice in sentencing. The devil here is in the detail. The US Federal Sentencing Guidelines have come under considerable criticism because the much more detailed rules and procedures introduced to improve consistency in sentencing themselves produce what appear to many judges and commentators to be substantively unjust sentences (Stith and Cabranes 1998). While it is easy in principle to say that sentencing ought to be more accountable, transparent and responsive, working out how to produce this in practice is a very difficult task. Who could object to sentencing being consistent, rational and systematic? The terms have been used rhetorically by Australian politicians but there appears to be little political attention to research and scholarship which shows the difficulties of operationalising these concepts.

There is plenty of evidence that sentencing is now highly politicised. Sentencing legislation is often introduced to achieve short term political gains. The measures introduced whether they are mandatory sentences, sentencing guidelines, matrices or particular measures against contemporary folk devils such as sex offenders, rarely pay any attention to sentencing research or scholarship. Evidence of the limited impact of sentencing on crime rates, the intricate debates about how to produce justice in sentencing or the literature on the complexities of guideline design appear to have little impact on sentencing policy. As Campbell argues, there is no longer any guarantee that expert knowledge will drive policy. In Canada liberal policy makers playing their traditional independent role of providing advice based on research evidence, risk finding themselves perceived as operating with a left of centre political agenda. It is not that law and order has suddenly become political. It is rather that the consensus which existed between politicians, policy makers and scholars in many jurisdictions in the 1950s and 1960s no longer persists. For many years, politicians were content to leave sentencing to the judiciary, much as penal policy was left to administrators and experts. It was not that sentencing was non-political but rather that in those days it was politically convenient to do so and the aims of sentencers, scholars and politicians coincided (Garland 2001). Increasingly, politicians feel under pressure from their constituents and from the media, to be seen to be doing something about sentencing. Issues of political urgency dominate abstract arguments about the nature of justice in a liberal democratic society and research evidence which shows the very limited impact of sentencing on crime rates.

This poses a considerable challenge for sentencing scholarship and research. Sentencing scholarship currently operates against a background of populist punitiveness and not in a world where the results of academic research are rationally assessed and debated on their merits by policy makers. Most scholars continue to value academic neutrality and the rational collection of evidence, and share a commitment to Weber's idea of science as a vocation. However, many scholars want their work to contribute to 'rational' policy making.[3] Knowledge is valued not just for its own sake but for what it can do to help produce a more rationally ordered society. Sentencing scholarship cannot stand outside the political conditions which shape contemporary sentencing practice. Scholars need to be aware that their work can be used by other actors to achieve ends which may be far removed from their own. (A striking example of this is the way in which the just deserts movement which was orginally conceived by liberals as a progressive force towards a less punitive society was captured by conservative political forces to achieve their aims of increasing the levels of punishment.)

One response might be to choose to conduct research projects where the anticipated results could help to promote a more rational or progressive agenda for sentencing reform.[4] The research would not be explicitly political in so far as the methodology would fully satisfy the criteria for social scientific objectivity, nor would the topic for research be drawn from any party political manifesto. The aim would be to produce data which would help to promote a rational approach. One good example might be the research by Hough and Roberts on public knowledge and attitudes to sentencing. The data which they produce demonstrates that the public are not as punitive as they have been portrayed in other research and in the media. This provides an evidential base for challenging the populist punitiveness that has been identified as promoting 'tougher' sentencing in many jurisdictions. I am not suggesting that Hough and Roberts have an explicit political agenda in their work, but if one wanted to promote a more rational approach to sentencing and penal policy, this sort of research would be very helpful. Of course, there remains the difficulty of persuading politicians and policy makers to pay attention to this evidence. These results may not be what they want to hear but at least they are in an area of great public and political concern and it is harder to ignore them.

There is nothing very new in these arguments, nor is there any straightforward resolution for scholars. Sentencing is unavoidably political and researchers need to take this into account in more subtle ways when pursuing their work. The issue cannot be ignored.

The Culture of Sentencing

In his contribution, Andrew Ashworth poses the question, "What should be the basis of a sentencing system?". This would routinely be understood as a normative question to be answered by philosophical arguments about how we conceive of justice in a liberal society. However, this normative debate takes place in a definite social and political context rather than in an idealised world of the imagination. A sociological perspective suggests a different understanding of what is meant by the 'basis' of a sentencing system. The question might be reformulated as, "What are the social and political conditions which sustain the existing sentencing system?". What kinds of constraints and opportunities do these conditions offer for transforming the sentencing system? Some perspectives on political and social conditions have been sketched above. One important further set of conditions consists of the ways in which we think and feel about sentencing and punishment. I use 'we' here as a shorthand way to refer to a wide variety of social groups with divergent attitudes, sensibilities and modes of thinking. However the values which we want or expect sentencing to promote, the expectations we have about what sentencing and punishment can and should achieve, and our use of particular moral registers to talk about sentencing and punishment, constitute a set of cultural conditions which underpin debate about sentencing. The comparative contributions to this collection demonstrate that there are significant cultural variations in the levels and types of penalty considered appropriate for similar types of offence in different jurisdictions. There are also considerable variations in the organisational procedures of sentencing in different jurisdictions (Freiberg, Davies, Tyrer and Takala, Ashworth). However there may be a broader sense in which sentencing is out of step with contemporary cultural change across jurisdictional boundaries.[5]

Public Sentiment

Perhaps the most significant element shaping sentencing over the last thirty years has been the response by politicians and to a lesser extent by judges to what has been perceived as a demand for tougher punishment from the community, described by Bottoms as the spiral of populist punitiveness. Contributions to this collection suggest that this is a widespread phenomenon. The great danger of this cultural phenomenon is that there appears to be no end to the escalation of punishment. Even when crime rates fall, the public response to media representations of serious cases or apparent leniency by the judiciary (as for example the reaction to Lord Woolf's recent decision in the Thomson and Venables case in England and Wales) is to call for tougher punishment. Research based evidence about the ineffectiveness of punishment as a means of crime control carries little weight with significant sections of the public; the media and thus with politicians.

Public Confidence in Sentencing

As Hough and Roberts show, successive British crime surveys show a diminishing level of public confidence in the judiciary. This may not simply reflect public dissatisfaction with judges. It may well be rooted in a broader cultural phenomenon, which might be described as a diminishing public faith in state institutions. Garland (2001) locates this in a broader lack of commitment to the ideas and values of the solidarity project which emerged in the post war years. In very general terms this can be characterised as a public commitment to the use of state institutions and public funds to ensure a basic level of social security and welfare. There was a belief that social solidarity could be enhanced and even constructed through public works. This world view has gradually given way to a more market based and individualised conception of social order. One important factor for sentencing arising from these cultural changes is that what Garland calls "mutuality", (which I take to refer to the ways in which individuals identify with each other and gain a sense of belonging to the same society), is now much more likely to arise through response to other individuals (typically victims) rather than through the mediation of public institutions (courts). I take this to mean that the public no longer get sufficient emotional satisfaction from the response to offending made by sentencers in courts. They are more likely to empathise with media representations of individual victimhood and less likely to be satisfied with the response which emanates from the courts.

Why does this matter? It suggests that conceiving of sentencing in a purely rational or instrumental register may no longer be adequate. Recent evidence reviewed here by Hough and Roberts, suggests that the public may not be as punitive as some research has suggested. When presented with more information about a case, their sentencing moves closer to the decisions made by judges. This offers one opportunity to try to reverse the upward spiral of punishment, through the presentation of more accurate information about sentencing. But as Mary Campbell asks, is a barrage of information enough? Garland's arguments about the decline in confidence in public institutions suggests that it may not be. More accurate information about sentencing may have little impact on the public demand for tougher sentencing. This public demand is based in a deeper cultural change. Faith and trust in state institutions has waned and people now seek emotional catharsis in different ways, through a greater identification with the suffering of individual victims, and with demands for vengeance (Freiberg 2001; Pratt 2000). To put this another way, the public may no longer be convinced by the discourse of justice used by courts. A number of contributions to the collection raise the issue of the need for a 'replacement discourse' for sentencing (Ashworth, Crew, Lutz and Fahrney).

Replacement Discourse

What is a replacement discourse replacing? For some, the end of the rehabilitative ideal in the 1970s has left a gap which has yet to be filled. Rehabilitation provided a positive and humanitarian justification for sentencing and punishment. Its successor, desert, provided a rational calculus for the distribution of punishment but arguably failed to provide an appropriate justification. Underpinning both of these was Hart's notion that crime control was the fundamental aim and justification for punishment and sentencing. All of these discourses are still used by different agencies and institutions to justify their work, but no single discourse now provides a universal justification for sentencing and punishment. Many of those who seek a replacement discourse seem to be looking for a new grand theory which provides a single elegant justification for punishment and a set of principles for its allocation and distribution.

Restorative justice is proposed by many as such a discourse, but others are sceptical (Ashworth; Daly 2002). Although restorative justice has many virtues, including the inclusion of the victim, the emphasis on constructive and reparative responses to offending, and the attempt to de-centre punishment as the inevitable response to offending, it has one major limitation. Restorative justice promises instrumental results. It promises to repair damage and to restore relationships. One lesson that should have been learnt from the last thirty years of research, is that there have been very few programmes of any kind which have been able to sustain consistently high success rates. The failure to achieve instrumental success may consign the discourse of restorative justice to the same fate as its predecessors. This is not because restorative justice is not effective but because the instrumental expectations of restorative justice are unrealistic. Research has shown that punishment has at best a very small impact on crime control and that even the best organised and funded offender programmes can only offer relatively modest rates of success in terms of crime reduction.

On the one hand, there is a need to 'de-couple' in the public mind, punishment from the instrumental achievement of crime control (Ashworth); on the other hand, there is the political perception of the need to use punishment, even if only rhetorically, as at least one part of an overall criminal justice programme to promote public safety (Smith 2001). Garland has argued that the government response to high crime rates and the limited power of state institutions to reduce crime, has been contradictory. At one level, there has been a shift of responsibility away from government and towards the community and the individual, alongside a recognition of the results of research evidence and a realistic appraisal of what can be achieved. At another level, there has been more frequent resort to a heightened punitive rhetoric which ignores the research evidence and reaffirms the central power of the state as a guarantor of security.

This suggests that the conditions which supported a universal discourse for sentencing and punishment no longer exist. Maybe the problem is that the idea of a single grand organising discourse is no longer tenable or believable? The social, political and cultural conditions which supported the solidarity/ welfare project of the 1960s and 1970s are no longer present. This does not mean that we can no longer have ideals and goals for sentencing and punishment. However, we may have to juggle a range of mutually contradictory discourses simultaneously and we may need to learn to accept much more modest expectations of the capacity of sentencing and punishment to control crime and provide public safety.

Emile Durkheim argued that punishment has an important expressive and symbolic component which allows fears, anxieties, risks and dangers to be projected and resolved. Punishment can be an expression of solidarity and an affirmation of the boundaries of tolerance. Some recent writing in this tradition has argued that sentencing needs to pay greater attention to this expressive and communicative function and in particular to the apparent public demand for the expression of emotional responses to offending rather than purely rational responses (Tait; Bauman 2000; Frieberg 2001; Daly 2002). The study of sentencing needs to pay more attention to communication: to the messages it communicates (about pain, about justice and fairness, about retribution, about the victim); to the audiences it addresses (offenders, communities, victims, politicians, criminal justice practitioners etc.); and perhaps most of all, to the media through which it communicates.

Conclusion

In this brief reflection on the collection, I have tried to bring together some of the themes of a sociological approach to sentencing and to explain why such an approach is valuable. It is not that a rational and principled approach to sentencing reform is wrong. I see myself as involved in what von Hirsch has called "the sentencing reform project" (von Hirsch 2001). This project needs to be based on sound rational principles. However, the project has to operate in particular social, political and cultural conditions. Many of the assumptions of the reform project (the value of research evidence to policy making, the rhetorical power of reasoned argument, the neutrality of law, the independence and objectivity of the academy, etc.) remain important values to be defended, but they are not shared by other powerful actors and institutions which operate in the social field of sentencing and punishment. To be more effective, the reform project needs to develop a more sophisticated understanding of this social field and feed this into the debate about how sentencing might be reformed to achieve the goals of the project.

Notes

1   Where references are undated, they refer to chapters in this collection. Other references are cited fully in the normal fashion.
2   A rare exception (Ulmer 1997).
3   There is of course a critical tradition in research which would resist the production of 'government savoirs'. Stenson (2001, pp. 26–7) argues that a healthy democracy requires resistance to ways of thinking and doing.
4   Of course, results cannot always be anticipated accurately and I am not suggesting that research should not be conducted to collect 'new' knowledge, but in practice, most researchers usually have a reasonable idea of what at least the broad results of their research will be.
5   I refer here predominantly to what Tonry and Frase (2001) refer to as "Western jurisdictions".

References

Ashworth, A., Genders, E., Mansfield, J. and Player, E. (1984), 'Sentencing in the Crown Court: Report of an Exploratory Study', Centre for Criminological Research, Occasional Paper No. 10, University of Oxford.

Bauman, Z. (2000), 'The Social use of Law and Order', in D. Garland and J.R. Sparks (eds), *Criminology and Social Theory*, Oxford: Oxford University Press.

Bottoms, A. (1995), 'The Philosophy and Politics of Punishment and Sentencing', in C. Clarkson, and R. Morgan (eds), *The Politics of Sentencing Reform*, Oxford: Clarendon Press.

Daly, K. (forthcoming 2002), 'Restorative Justice: The real story', *Punishment and Society*, Vol. 4, No. 1, January.

Freiberg, A. (2001), 'Affective versus Effective Justice: Instrumentalism and emotionalism in criminal justice', *Punishment and Society*, Vol. 3, No. 2, pp. 265–78.

Garland, D. (2001), *The Culture of Control: Crime and social order in contemporary society*, Oxford: Oxford University Press.

Giddens, A. (1984), *The Constitution of Society*, Oxford: Polity Press.

Hogarth, J. (1971), *Sentencing as a Human Process*, Toronto: University of Toronto Press.

Lovegrove, A. (1997), *The Framework of Judicial Sentencing: A study in legal decision making*, Cambridge: Cambridge University Press.

Lovegrove, A. (2000), 'Proportionality, Sentencing and the Multiple Offender: Towards a numerical framework', *Punishment and Society*, Vol. 2, No. 4.

Pratt, J. (2000), 'Emotive and Ostentatious Punishments', *Punishment and Society*, Vol. 2, No. 4, pp. 416–38.

Reitz, K. (2001), 'The Disassembly and Reassembly of US Sentencing Practices', in M. Tonry and R. Frase (eds), *Sentencing and Sanctions in Western Countries*, New York: Oxford University Press.

Smith, M. (2001), 'What Future for "Public Safety" and "Restorative Justice" in a System of Community Penalties?', in A. Bottoms, L. Gelsthorpe and S. Rex (eds), *Community Penalties: Change and Challenges*, Devon: Willan Publishing.

Stenson, K. (2001), 'The New Politics of Crime Control', in K. Stenson and R.R. Sullivan (eds), *Crime, Risk and Justice: The politics of crime control in liberal democracies*, Devon: Willan Publishing.

Stith, K. and Cabranes, J.A. (1998), *Fear of Judging: Sentencing guidelines in the Federal Courts*, Chicago: University of Chicago Press.

Tata, C. (1997), 'Conceptions and Representations of the Sentencing Decision Process', *Journal of Law and Society*, Vol. 24 (3), pp. 395–420.

Tonry, M. and Frase. R. (eds) (2001), *Sentencing and Sanctions in Western Countries*, New York: Oxford University Press.

Ulmer. J.T. (1997), *Social Worlds of Sentencing: Court Communities under Sentencing Guidelines*, Albany: State University of New York Press.

Von Hirsch (2001), 'The Project of Sentencing Reform', in M. Tonry and R. Frase (eds), *Sentencing and Sanctions in Western Countries*, New York: Oxford University Press.

Subject Index

Author Index